New Challenges for Documentary

Second Edition

edited by

Alan Rosenthal and John Corner

Manchester University Press

Manchester and New York

distributed exclusively in the USA by Palgrave

Published by Manchester University Press
Oxford Road. Manchester M13 9NR, UK
and Room 400, 175 Fifth Avenue, New York, NY 10010, USA
www.manchesteruniversitypress.co.uk

Distributed exclusively in the USA by
Palgrave, 175 Fifth Avenue, New York NY 10010, USA

Distributed exclusively in Canada by
UBC Press, University of British Columbia, 2029 West Mall,
Vancouver, BC, Canada V6T 1Z2

British Library Cataloguing-in-Publication Data
A catalogue record for this book is available from the British Library

Library of Congress Cataloging-in-Publication Data
A catalog record for this book is available from the Library of Congress

ISBN 13: 978 0 7190 6899 7

First published in 2005 by University of California Press
This edition first published 2005

Printed by Lightning Source

Contents

List of Illustrations

Acknowledgements

First, our thanks to all the authors who appear in this book and who allowed us to reprint their articles.

Thanks and tremendous gratitude also to John Katz, Jerry Kuehl, Henry Breitrose, Jay Ruby, Brian Winston and Ernest Callenbach who all helped enormously in preparing the first edition of this book and to Gary Crowdus, Matthew Frost and Kate Fox who provided similar wonderful help on the current edition. We would like to note the excellent work of the staff at MUP and the invaluable contribution made by Susan Milligan at proof stage.

Grateful acknowledgement is also made to the following sources for their permission to print the articles in this anthology:

"The Voice of Documentary," from *Film Quarterly* 36, no. 3 (Spring 1983), copyright 1983 by the Regents of the University of California. Reprinted by permission of the Regents and Bill Nichols.

"The Image Mirrored: Reflexivity and the Documentary Film," from the *Journal of the University Film Association* 29, no. 1 (Fall 1977), by permission of Jay Ruby and the *Journal of the University Film and Video Association*.

"Television, Documentary and the Category of the Aesthetic," from *Screen* 44, no. 1 (2003), by kind permission of the editors and Oxford University Press.

"Mirrors Without Memories: Truth, History, and the New Documentary," from *Film Quarterly* 46 (Spring 1993), copyright 1993 by the Regents of the University of California. Reprinted by permission of the Regents.

"The Canadian Film Board Unit B," from *Movies and Memoranda*, copyright Canadian Film Institute, 1981. Reprinted by permission of D. B. Jones and the Canadian Film Institute.

"'History Is the Theme of All My Films': An Interview with Emile de Antonio," from *Cineaste* 12, no. 2 (Spring 1982), by permission of *Cineaste*.

"*The War Game*: An Interview with Peter Watkins," from *The New Documentary in Action* (Berkeley and Los Angeles: University of California Press,

1971), copyright 1971 by the Regents of the University of California. Used by permission of the Regents and Alan Rosenthal.

"New Agendas in Black Filmmaking: An Interview with Marlon Riggs," from *Cineaste* 19, nos 2–3 (December 1992), by permission of *Cineaste*.

"Jumping Off the Cliff: A Conversation with Dennis O'Rourke," copyright Dennis O'Rourke 2004. Used by permission of Dennis O'Rourke and Tracey Spring.

"The Politics of Documentary: A Symposium," from *Cineaste* 11, no. 3 (Summer 1981), by permission of *Cineaste*.

"Staying Alive," copyright 2003 by Alan Rosenthal. Used by permission of the author.

"Ethics," by Brian Winston, from Chapter 6 of *Lies, Damn Lies and Documentaries* (British Film Institute, 2000), by permission of author and publisher.

"Ultimately We Are All Outsiders: The Ethics of Documentary Filming," from the *Journal of the University Film Association* 28, no. 1 (Winter 1976), by permission of Calvin Pryluck and the *Journal of the University Film and Video Association*.

"The Ethics of Image Making," copyright 1979 Jay Ruby. Used by permission of the author.

"*Word Is Out* and *Gay U.S.A.*," from *Film Quarterly* 32, no. 2 (Winter 1978), copyright 1978 by the Regents of the University of California. Reprinted by permission of the Regents and Lee Atwell.

"Building a Mock-Documentary Schema," by Jane Roscoe and Craig Hight, from *Faking It* (Manchester University Press, 2001), by permission of authors and publisher.

"Sounds Real: Music and Documentary," by John Corner, from *Popular Music* 21, no. 3. (Cambridge University Press, 2002) by permission of author, editors and publisher.

Review of *Bowling for Columbine* by Christopher Sharrett and William Luhr, from *Cineaste* 28, no. 2 (2003), with permission of *Cineaste*.

"The McCarthy 'See It Now' Broadcast," from *Due to Circumstances Beyond Our Control* (Vintage Books, 1968). Reprinted by permission of Fred Friendly.

"An Independent with the Networks," from *Studies in Visual Communication* 8, no. 1 (Winter 1982), copyright 1981 by the Annenberg School of Communications. All rights reserved. Used by permission of *Studies in Visual Communication*.

"New Boy: An Independent with Israel TV," from *Journal of the University Film Association* 33, no. 4 (Fall 1981), copyright 1981 by Alan Rosenthal. Used by permission of the author.

"Reflections on *An American Family*," from *Studies in Visual Communication* 8, no. 1 (Winter 1982), copyright 1981 by the Annenberg School of Communications. All rights reserved. Used by permission of *Studies in Visual Communication*.

"*American High*: Documentary as Episodic Television," written for this book and copyright by Ben Levin.

"Documentary and Truth on Television: The Crisis of 1999", written for this book and copyright by John Ellis.

"History on the Public Screen, I," by Donald Watt, and "History on the Public Screen, II," by Jerry Kuehl, reprinted from *The Historian and Film*, ed. Paul Smith (Cambridge University Press, 1976), by permission of Cambridge University Press and the authors.

"Historical Analysis, Stage One: Gathering Information on the Content, Production and Reception of a Moving Image Document," from *Image as Artifact*, reprinted by permission of the Robert E. Krieger Publishing Co., Inc.

"Narration, Invention, and History," from *Cineaste* 12, no. 2 (Spring 1982), by permission of *Cineaste*.

"Against the Ivory Tower: An Apologia for 'Popular' Historical Documentaries," from *Film-Historia* 5, no. 1 (1995). Reprinted by permission of Dirk Eitzen and *Film-Historia*.

"The Event: Archive and Imagination," by Stella Bruzzi, from Chapter 1 of *New Documentary: A Critical Introduction* (Routledge, 2000), by permission of author and publisher.

"Dramadoc/Docudrama: The Law and Regulation," by Derek Paget, from *No Other Way to Tell It* (Manchester University Press, 1998), by permission of author and publisher.

"US Docudrama and 'Movie of the Week'," written for this book and copyright by Steve Lipkin.

"*Death of a Princess*: The Politics of Passion, an interview with Antony Thomas," used by permission of Alan Rosenthal.

"Dramatised Documentary," copyright 1981 by Leslie Woodhead. Used by permission of the author.

"Where Are We Going, and How and Why?," copyright 1996 by Ian McBride. Used by permission of the author.

For illustrations we would like to acknowledge our debt to the National Film Board of Canada, *Cineaste* magazine, Dennis O'Rourke, Robert Drew Associates, Lisa Maizlish and Antony Thomas. All photos remain copyright of the original owners. All photos taken by Dennis O'Rourke remain the copyright of Camera Pty Ltd.

Introduction

John Corner and Alan Rosenthal

Documentary, however imprecise a category, continues to indicate a body of media work with a rich, distinguished history and a wide range of current practice and creative commitments. In 1988, the first edition of this book set out to raise some questions about the 'health' of documentary, the directions and tendencies that were then current or imminent and some of the fundamental issues about contexts, forms and purposes which either needed to be raised again or, in some cases, put on the agenda for the first time. It sought to stimulate discussion (to 'revive the debate on ideas') within documentary-making itself, including work in film-schools, and also within the academy, where the fascination and importance of documentary were insufficiently recognised in existing Arts and Social Science perspectives on film and television.

Within the changed circumstances both for documentary work and documentary studies some eighteen years later, these broad aims can still be seen as guiding the selection of writing that follows. They bring with them another crop of 'new challenges' too. However, in addition to the clear political and social importance of documentary, we want to point to its cultural qualities too—its capacity to excite and delight as well as to shock and disturb. In addition to providing material for those already involved in documentary production or study, we hope that this book will extend and deepen the awareness of documentary among both students and general readers who might not have yet considered it in such a focused way. If this leads, however indirectly, to a larger, critical audience for documentary films and programmes, that will indeed be a splendid outcome.

The Introduction to the first edition set out its agenda partly in relation to a sense of problems affecting the field. It noted a feeling that documentary was 'in the doldrums', going through a period where there was a drop in innovative energy and funding opportunity, perhaps also in audience interest. Possibilities for revitalization were sought.

This second edition has also been put together in a period where questions about the future of documentary, and even the possible 'death of documentary' are being mooted. The climate of anxiety about aims and means is further reinforced when we consider the situation internationally. This in turn has induced us to widen the scope of the book in order to deal more fully with these matters. There have been some important changes to documentary culture since 1988. These changes are reflected in many of the new pieces that follow, and it is one task of this introduction to sketch out briefly the character and significance of the shifts.

Perhaps some broad-brush indications can be made before we identify the main factors in a little more detail. Although it is dangerous to assess the health of documentary without regard for specific national circumstances, there is no doubt that the squeeze on funding for serious work requiring extensive research and shooting has been a continuing problem for many documentarists. This has partly followed from narrowing strategies of commissioning, scheduling and/or distribution, which are themselves the consequence of the increased use of the 'market' rather than the 'public' frame for thinking about audio-visual production. In Britain and many other European countries, there have been quite rapid changes in the documentary economy since the 1980s, while in the USA the 'narrowing' has largely been the continuation of already pronounced features. Both in America and Europe, however, there are examples of work that appear to buck this trend. One recent example would be Michael Moore's *Bowling for Columbine* (2002), a feature length film that did well with audiences on both sides of the Atlantic in addition to collecting the Cannes Palme D'Or and an Oscar. The ability for a documentary film to break into popular theatrical cinema is still there, given the right combination of story-telling, directing ability and the presentation of a theme already felt as important in the public imagination.[1]

Alongside this, and causing some disarray and disagreement within the business of television documentary-making, has been the rise of 'reality television' during the late 1980s and 1990s. Such programming, varying in its style from emergency-service *vérité*, through dramatized formats (including those of Soap) and into different kinds of location gameshow, mundane or exotic in setting, has given documentary work a new popular audience at the same time as it has caused questions to be raised about purposes, ethics and the appropriate discourses for 'showing the real'. We return to the phenomenon of 'popular factual entertainment' a little later, attempting to assess its consequences now that its novelty is no longer as marked or shocking.

When we turn to the academic study of documentary, it is possible to see real development since the 1980s. A new space has been created for discussion both within film studies, where there has been a move outwards from the primary concern with the aesthetics of fictional cinema, and also within media studies, where documentary television has become the subject of sociological as well as critical analysis. This is evident in books, journals and conferencing activity, with perhaps the activities of the 'Visible Evidence' group being the most notable regular attempt to bring together an international community of documentary scholarship. New critical attention has been wide-ranging and the first edition of this volume has clearly played a part in stimulating and guiding it.[2] Nevertheless, it is interesting that a few areas identified as neglected in 1987, such as the documentary audience, are still awaiting proper exploration, despite some promising studies.

These changes in the level of academic activity surrounding documentary past and present have had the general effect of opening up even further the opportunities for serious study and debate. The second edition goes out into a livelier and, with some qualifications, in many ways more promising context than the first one.

Perhaps it would be useful here to highlight some of the key areas where we identify factors of change to be at work, underneath the broad tendencies noted above.

Five Aspects of Change

Aware of the risks attached to classification of this kind, including that of undue separation of interconnected processes, we want to suggest that there are five broad aspects or areas in relation to which shifts in documentary culture can usefully be plotted. Obvious enough in themselves, these are: documentary funding, markets and distribution; technology and applications; aims, subjects and addressees; ethics, and what we might call documentary language, which includes aesthetics. All these areas received comment in the introduction to the first edition and they all connect with each other in different ways across the pieces to follow.

Funding, Markets and Distribution

The range of funding and distribution options for documentary has, of course, always been a key factor in the different national histories of the genre. Choices here nearly always carry consequences for what is selected as a subject, how it is approached and what kinds of audience are assembled. The 'public profile' of documentary is profoundly affected by these elements of the documentary economy, as was clearly shown in John Grierson's sometimes awkward play-off between social exploration and sponsored, civic propaganda in the formative period of 1930s British documentary cinema.

In some countries, 'public service' television has offered a framework for documentary work relatively free of direct market pressures, although this has changed quite radically even since the publication of the first edition. Multichannel broadcasting challenges the idea of the 'general audience' as well as reconfiguring scheduling policy and the commissioning that follows from this. Adaptability to the terms of the television 'package' (channel, slot and target audience, often within the context of a series) has become an imperative of survival, setting up factors against which a careful costing of research and production budgets in relation to likely audience 'pull' is made. We have already remarked on how the drive to entertainment in factual output has impacted upon the terms of television documentary ambition. In some cases, it has influenced the departmental and funding structures within which documentary is produced inside the organisations of broadcasting. The generation of dedicated factual channels, and the possibility of increased international distribution, have to some extent offset these new risks with entrepreneurial opportunity, but only at the cost of a reduced degree of editorial freedom and a loss of communicative confidence in the address to a specific audience.

The 'independent' cinema documentary has continued to survive, albeit with a struggle, both in the USA and parts of Europe, finding its distribution and exhibition possibilities, including domestic video and DVD playback, within established educational, political and cultural networks. It continues to offer a range of work both thematically and formally more adventurous than television, and it is interesting to note how imaginative television productions have often drawn on, and adapted, some of its strategies of shock and provocation.

Many of the chapters collected here reflect, sometimes directly, on documentary's economic and institutional settings. However, there is certainly room for more sustained audit and analysis, both at national and internationally comparative levels, of how this particular challenge looks at the moment and is likely to shape up in the next few years.

Technology and Applications

Documentary has always been an imaginative and keen exploiter of technological development, with the shift to 16 mm cameras in the early 1960s representing a key stage in the increased mobility of shooting and the greater accessibility of social and private spaces to filming. Shifts in the quality and technology of sound, including the use of smaller equipment for synchronised recordings, have opened up new applications too. The move towards videotape and the later availability of the camcorder for non-professional, leisure use placed some documentary work in a different audio-visual context from that which prevailed just a few years earlier. All this helped break the rigid demand of the prescripted sequence, encouraged the creation of the documentary in the editing room itself, and brought a more colloquial, personal voice to the form. The professional use of digital kit made the 'one person crew' option even more available for a range of often formally ambitious projects, while investigative work involving hidden cameras was made easier with the new range of micro-equipment.

Electronic and now digital editing are having their effect upon the 'grammar' of documentary and the flexibility of image use. Arguments about digital image manipulation, partly 'new technology' versions of the old anxieties about faking, have been raised by several commentators. However, many agree that the area of underlying ethical criteria and ethical commitments informing professional practice continues to remain the primary issue, still under-addressed and less altered by the amazing new possibilities for fraud than initially might seem to be the case.

It is no surprise that it is the possible applications of the web that are currently getting attention as the most arresting new technological opportunity. There are applications that support the reach, and sustain the impact, of conventional documentary projects (here, again, the example of Moore's *Bowling for Columbine* is instructive—see hyperlink www.bowlingforcolumbine.com) and also, more radically, those in which the primary platform is a website. The non-linear, interactive properties of the web create possibilities for documentary work at the same time as they are an obstacle to the kind of public 'confrontation' of viewer with topic that many documentarists have sought. In this confrontation, it is often quite important that viewers do not have too many options immediately available for negotiating their route through the material, that they just have to 'look and listen', so to speak. However, there is no doubt that web variants of the documentary experience—combining writing, photographs, speech and film sequences—will soon be more common, although it seems to us that much writing on this topic so far has tended to overstate its likely scale and significance.

Aims, Subjects and Addressees

Interrelated questions about these issues have followed from the increasing diversity of documentary work, particularly in television, and its points of fusion with other kinds of audio-visual production. Here, the continuing overlap with modes of fictional portrayal has been joined by the influences of new kinds of factual television, including the talk-show and the varieties of reality TV, noted earlier. The 'cooler' stylings of the image found in advertising and promotional work have also had an impact. A new, more relaxed, colloquial register has emerged in some work. While this can be seen as a welcome informality, extending the range and inclusiveness of documentary address, it has sometimes gone along with a primary intention of diverting rather than informing or challenging the audience. Here the selection of topics has inclined towards the pleasingly exotic, amusing or bizarre, while the viewing position is often established as one of wry detachment and the 'shock of the real' brought reductively close to a form of commodity consumption. Bill

Nichols' much-cited typification of documentary as a 'discourse of sobriety' would now need revision as a general statement.

The shift in the 'terms of engagement' of many documentaries has partly followed from the intensified market for entertainment as described earlier, and it has affected both television commissioning and scheduling and cinema distribution. However, one can also see that in many countries there is a continued interest in serious and committed projects, albeit in revised formats and stylings. So there is some cause for pessimism, but signs of a basis for hope too (the precise balance perceived here will continue to be a focus of debate both within the industry and the academy).

Ethics

As the first edition noted, the ethical dimension of documentary work raises fundamental concerns about practices of representation which go beyond those matters of 'staging' and 'faking' which are the most frequently raised points of anxiety and dispute. The kinds and levels of intervention and contrivance used to get specific sights and sounds on the screen, particularly in a context where narrative continuity and impact often figure as premium values, still remain a very important focus for inquiry and debate. But there are broader questions that require examination, such as the relationship of producers to subjects and the relationships offered to audiences via the camera and the microphone. What are the implications of the different degrees of proximity and distance we enjoy with what we see and hear? How do notions of frankness (of behaviour or of speech) relate to the self-consciously performative and even 'dramatic' dimension of documentary portrayal? What are the guidelines (inevitably normative, not simply technical) that best help us in assessing the relationship of a documentary's emotional pull to its rational, propositional structure? This last question is of course pitched very differently for observational work than for, say, presenter/interview formats. Not surprisingly, given its more adventurously creative approach to story-telling, docudrama has raised it in a distinctive and often controversial way. There has been a tendency in postmodern writing to undercut any idea of the 'authentic' or indeed 'the real'. Nevertheless, concern about the authenticity and reality of documentaries, and about the transformations that documentary-making introduces, continues to be central. Equally strong is a concern about how our *sense of the real* in documentary affects the knowledge and the emotions that our viewing generates. Many of our contributions explore this in more detail.

Documentary Language

Nearly all of the factors mentioned above have made a profound impact upon the development of documentary language. The visual and audio elements of documentary have enjoyed a degree of continuity, for sure, but there have also been exciting experiments in the use of the image itself and further explorations of the uses of voice and of voice/image combinations. Many of these have followed from the continuing adventurousness of documentary 'at the boundaries', as it were—at those points where if pushed further it would seem to merge with, say, the Hollywood thriller, the television drama series, the talk show, surveillance footage or (very differently) the video art loop.

At one level, television work has shown further attention to immediacy and to the modes of portrayal of the 'raw', particularly in programmes where intense and dramatic physical events are being depicted (e.g. accidents, car chases, fights, police raids). Following earlier explorations, it has played around with the possibilities of 'first person' portrayal, with the subjective voice and with the way in which the acknowledgement of the camera's presence by those filmed need not undercut the perceived integrity of the filmed events. In a number of different ways, it has tried to accommodate the active, performative aspect of being in a documentary rather than sticking too closely to naturalistic ambition. At a very different level, both in cinema and television, a concern with the symbolic properties of the image (a concern that can seek to enhance both the referential and the formal appeal of portrayal) has been apparent. Writing suggestively of American work, John Thornton Caldwell (Caldwell 1995: 230–45) notes that the 'videographic' embellishment of the image in some documentaries of the 1990s has reached a point where engagement with the world seen 'through' the image begins to be displaced by a fascination with the pictorial properties themselves. However, tensions between documentary's artistic ambitions and its imperative to 'show the world' have been present since its origins. New recipes for getting this dynamic combination to work should not be dismissed too quickly, even if they can often be employed in ways that appear to evade rather than confront the documentary challenge.

Sensitively placed as it is near the centre of audio-visual culture (although not always recognised to be so) we can expect documentary work to continue to be innovative in its aesthetic design and modes of portrayal. We can also hope that such innovation will continue to be subject to an assessment and debate that is always about a lot more than 'language', even though it takes the details of the documentary text as its starting point.

The Organisation of the Book

In selecting items for the book, we have drawn on material from the first edition that seemed to us to continue to illuminate and provoke and we have combined it with more recent writing. We have taken the work both of film and of television critics and scholars and, as in the first edition, we have also placed some emphasis on the critical reflections of those who make documentaries. The social history of developments, particularly those in television, has also been given its due in a way that is sometimes missing from programmes of study. Comprehensiveness is impossible to obtain, and, as always, space requires exclusions that are only made regretfully. We have worked with a number of criteria, of which clarity and the capacity to highlight through evidence or argument a specific facet of documentary's complexity and significance, are two. The book has six parts, which follow the broad analytical ideas outlined above but allow us to make separations that we thought would be useful in teaching, including a part specifically on history and one which focuses on the forms of docudrama.

Our first part, *Theories and forms: Documentary as Genre*, explores some of the key general issues surrounding the classification, intentions and strategies of work in this area. In what is now regarded as a classic essay, Bill Nichols examines the question of 'voice' in documentary, using this term to indicate what a documentary is saying, what kind of comment about the world is being made. Lucidly reviewing the history of the main documentary formats, Nichols poses questions about the strengths and weaknesses of different uses of image and sound. Jay Ruby tightens the focus down to the issue of reflexivity and self-consciousness, including the impact of the filmmaking process on what and who is filmed. In various ways, this has always been a problem for documentary work, sometimes suppressed in favour of a supposed naturalism but increasingly admitted as a challenge and brought into the design of films and programmes. John Corner looks at how aesthetics as a category has variously figured in discussion of documentary, particularly within the context of studies of television. He highlights the interplay between 'looking through' and 'looking at' which the creative commitment produces, an interplay that deserves a scholarship capable of responding to documentary as art as well as knowledge. Finally, Linda Williams, in a wide-ranging and provocative commentary that picks up on earlier themes in the section, returns to reflexivity and to arguments about the 'limits' of representation. What are these limits? How should they be recognised? How negotiated by the filmmaker? Drawing on a number of films that seem to put interesting new pressure on (and at times subvert) the range of conventional practice, she connects outwards to changing ideas about discourse and history.

The next part, *The Inside View*, shifts the emphasis from text to creator, in particular to some of those filmmakers who have been particularly influential in pioneering forms or changing objectives. The first six essays collected here deal with the filmmaker's purposes, beliefs, styles and methods—in short what to say and how to say it, while the seventh confronts the question, how does the filmmaker survive financially? In regard to the influence of group creation on documentary, the work of the National Film Board of Canada (NFB) is outstanding. It set the professional standards in the 1940s and its pioneering work continued at an even greater pace in the late 1950s and early 1960s. In 1981 D. B. Jones published *Movies and Memoranda*, an in-depth study of the Board, and the two extracts used in this chapter remind us again of the work of some of the pioneers of *vérité* like Wolk Koenig, Roman Kroitor and Tom Daly.

Documentary has always embraced the passionate filmmaker who wants to change the world and whose work centres on political and social action. The next essays deal with three of these individuals. Emile de Antonio was the intellectual revolutionary who cut an immensely influential swathe through American documentary filmmaking for twenty years. In the interview with Gary Crowdus and Dan Georgakas we see a funny, provocative and deliberately outrageous de Antonio commenting reflectively on his work, his chosen topics and his inspirations. This is followed by Peter Watkins, one of England's most radical filmmakers, discussing the making of his celebrated 'history of the future' *The War Game*, and the problem of the BBC's refusal in the 1960s to broadcast such a controversial portrayal of a nuclear attack and its aftermath. Roy Grundmann reminds us of the short but provocative career of Marlon Riggs, whose self-reflexive films, such as *Tongues Untied*, dealt with issues of Black identity and representation and, as Grundmann puts it, fuelled so many debates on issues of authenticity, impartiality and truth. A conversation with Dennis O'Rourke, one of Australia's finest filmmakers, then provides us with the portrait of the maverick unwilling to accept rules, boundaries and conventions—a documentary-maker always in search of a further, deeper truth.

The section concludes with two wider accounts. First, a piece based on a *Cineaste* magazine symposium organised by Barbara Zheutlin, allows a number of filmmakers to express their broad concerns on the methods and purposes of documentary, in a sense summing up many of the concerns of this book. Finally, with a more strongly practical emphasis, Rosenthal discusses the problems and possibilities for a filmmaker's survival in an economic and institutional climate that offers few financial rewards for creativity and effort.

In *Issues of Ethics and Aesthetics*, we collect together a number of pieces that discuss ethical questions concerning aims, practices and modes of portrayal. Brian Winston, Calvin Pryluck and Jay Ruby all offer illuminating commentaries on the ethical dilemmas that documentary work faces. Winston looks at the history of 'reconstruction', going back suggestively to moments in photographic history, and at questions of consent. Consent and the grounding of a sense of documentary responsibility are also taken up by Pryluck, while Ruby, among other things, usefully poses the question of whether documentarists regard themselves as closer to journalists or to artists in relation to their ethical obligations. Lee Atwell examines how two films attempted to change the terms of portrayal of the gay community, exploring their different approaches to positive representation in the context of prejudice. Jane Roscoe and Craig Hight chart the developing range of spoof documentaries and examine how they variously use documentary devices to enlist an initial trust, only to undercut this in order to amuse the audience and also often to bring a critical pressure to bear on the topic and on the documentary form itself. Some rather neglected questions about how music figures in the organisation of the documentary experience, both in terms of knowledge and pleasure, form the focus for John Corner's chapter. He examines why much television documentary has allocated only a marginal, and often cliché, function for music and provides examples of how it might develop more imaginative approaches. Michael Moore's hugely successful feature documentary, *Bowling for Columbine*, is the subject of review by Christopher Sharrett and William Luhr. While appreciative of the film, they raise questions about some of the strategies by which it informs and amuses audiences in the course of making its critical case.

Television as a dominant medium for documentary work internationally is referred to throughout the collection. However, in our section on *Changing Contexts in Television*, we look at how the institutional structures of TV, and its specific market character and relationship to audiences, have shaped developments. Fred Friendly tells the story behind the March 1954 edition of CBS's *See it Now*, a programme that brilliantly explored Senator McCarthy's background and political project in the context of his vigorous 'witchhunt' against those suspected of being communist sympathisers. This is a detailed 'behind the scenes' account. The distinguished observational filmmaker Robert Drew reflects on his time with the networks, providing a working biography of the opportunities and constraints which followed for a filmmaker in this new professional setting. A similar approach is taken by Alan Rosenthal, who examines the minefields of working for Israeli television after years as an independent in the United States. Rosenthal points up the politics of television documentary at the practical levels of access and institutional assumptions about perspective and judgement. Craig Gilbert then offers a reflective case-study of his own celebrated series *An American Family*, showing us how documentary developed in the use of *cinéma vérité* and direct cinema techniques. He looks at the way in which a production based on the observational approach was able to provide a focus on family life and on individual problems, creating a subgenre that has become widely popular.

Ben Levin connects documentary history to the discussion of a recent production in his account of the background to the making of *American High* (Fox/PBS, 2000), a series which was devised in the context of the new 'reality television' and which changed significantly in concept and programme design in the course of being made. This question of the documentary project in the context of emerging forms of popular factual entertainment is also pursued by John Ellis. He looks at British developments in the 1990s, when the new formats became a running story in many newspapers, prompting broader public questioning about television and truth. Ellis assesses how this remarkable upsurge of interest in the way television was put together altered audience perceptions and levels of trust.

The idea of History, as much as that of Society, has been a key category in motivating the making of documentaries and many disputes about documentary have turned on historiographic issues. In *Versions of History* the contributors examine the particular ways in which documentaries relate to the historical world, to the evidence available about past events and circumstances. Donald Watt and Jerry Kuehl explore the relationship between written and audio-visual history and the differences between academics' and filmmakers' ways of doing historical work, engaging different audiences for different purposes. John O'Connor looks closely at the moving image as an historical document, raising questions about motives, construction and reception as phases in the generation of a specific historical meaning around a film, sequence or even just a shot. In the process, he connects with broader themes in media inquiry. There is in many countries a strong tradition of the 'independent' documentary-maker. Jeffrey Youdelman explores what independence can mean when it comes to challenging dominant historical frameworks with narratives that question and confront, giving new voices a platform. What strategies can be put to work here? Dirk Eitzen is concerned both with the function and value of historical documentaries. Taking a number of well-known examples, he stresses the need for recognition of the complex, mediated nature of historical accounts and the requirement not to try to convince the audience with too simple or direct a sense of historical truth whatever immediate appeal this approach may have. Finally, Stella Bruzzi takes a remarkable sequence of filmed history, the Zapruder footage of President Kennedy's assassination in 1963. In a way that connects back to points raised in the earlier pieces, she enquires into the precise organisation of this moment of historical record, and into how it works as an experience of viewing and of evidential knowing.

The last part of the book, *Docudrama: Border Disputes*, brings into focus a few of the many vexed questions surrounding docudrama. The genre is not new, it is studded with some of the most famous names in the documentary pantheon, from Harry Watt and Humphrey Jennings to Peter Watkins and Ken Loach. Although it has always been a problematic form, it has only received sustained critical attention in the last few years, with scholars asking questions more intensively (what is this strange combination? How is it defined? What are its boundaries and why is it so popular?).

Derek Paget opens the discussion by examining the legal framework surrounding docudrama broadcasts, and the pitfalls that await writers and producers who deal in the realm of dramatic reconstruction. Steve Lipkin then asks if there are so many apparent dangers why, nevertheless, is the form so popular among the US commercial networks. His answer is that what television executives term the 'rootable, relatable, and promotable qualities' of docudrama have made it among the most popular genres for attracting big audiences.

But docudrama is a form that always exists on the edge of controversy. The broadcast film *Death of a Princess*, for example, was so explosive that it almost led to a rupture of diplomatic relations between Britain and Saudi Arabia. The whys and wherefores of the film, and the reasons for the choice of docudrama over straight documentary, are discussed at length in Alan Rosenthal's interview with the filmmaker Antony Thomas.

Leslie Woodhead, former head of Granada TV's drama-documentary department, also discusses *Death of a Princess* but he goes on to ask about the appeal of the dramatic form to the serious documentarist. His answer is that it is a form of last resort, a way of telling a story that would be impossible by conventional documentary methods. Woodhead pioneered the modern, probing political docudrama in Britain and his mantle at Granada was later taken over by Ian McBride. In the final essay, McBride points out both what a positive and creative force docudrama can be when used to explore such issues as police and political cover-ups, and what a hornet's nest it can be for the unwary producer. McBride would agree with Woodhead that the good docudrama is the one that rocks the boat but this also has a negative side and, as writer Rob Ritchie put it, 'You know when your docudrama succeeds because they never rebroadcast it.'

Finally, we return to the hopes expressed earlier in this introduction, that the book will aid the development of academic interest in documentary and provide teachers and students with an increased depth of understanding and a wealth of points for further debate and enquiry. Beyond that, to give some support to further documentary initiatives and to the continuation of appreciative but critical audiences, would be a real bonus.

Note

1 As we work on the proofs of this book, Michael Moore's *Fahrenheit 9/11* has become the biggest grossing documentary of all time, regenerating arguments about what a 'documentary' is and what coventions should govern its making. Whatever the critical verdict on *Fahrenheit*, its success underlines the renewed strength of social and political documentaries and their growing acceptance among popular audiences. In addition to the Moore phenomenon, other recent films bear ample witness to this, including for instance Errol Morris's *The Fog of War* (2004), Andrew Jarecki's *Capturing the Friedmans* (2003), Robert Greenwald's *Outfoxed* (2004) and Jehane Noujaim's *Control Room* (2004).

2 The publication of a comprehensive critical account by Bill Nichols (1991) has been followed by major studies such as those of Renov (ed. 1993), Winston (1995), Corner (1996) and Plantinga (1997). Studies with a more specific focus, historical or subgeneric, have appeared, with Nichols (1994), Rabinowitz (1994), Rosenthal

(1995), Bullert (1997), Paget (1998), Grant and Sloniowski (1998), Bruzzi (2000), Roscoe and Hight (2001), Lipkin (2002) and Ruoff (2002) just some of the publications here, reflecting often very different approaches.

References

Bruzzi, Stella (2000) *New Documentary: A Critical Introduction*. London: Routledge.

Bullert, B. J. (1997) *Public Television: Politics and the Battle over Documentary*. New Brunswick, NJ: Rutgers University Press.

Caldwell, John Thornton (1995) *Televisuality: Style, Crisis and Authority in American Television*. New Brunswick, NJ: Rutgers University Press.

Corner, John (1996) *The Art of Record*. Manchester: Manchester University Press.

Grant, Barry Keith and Sloniowski, Jeanette (1998) *Documenting the Documentary*. Detroit, Michigan: Wayne State University Press.

Lipkin, Steve (2002) *Real Emotional Logic: Film and Television Docudrama as Persuasive Practice*. Carbondale: Southern Illinois University Press.

Nichols, Bill (1991) *Representing Reality*. Bloomington and Indianapolis: Indiana University Press.

Nichols, Bill (1994) *Blurred Boundaries: Questions of Meaning in Contemporary Culture*. Bloomington and Indianapolis: Indiana University Press.

Paget, Derek (1998) *No Other Way to Tell It: Dramadoc/Docudrama on Television*. Manchester: Manchester University Press.

Plantinga, Carl (1997) *Rhetoric and Representation in Nonfiction Film*. New York and Cambridge: Cambridge University Press.

Rabinowitz, Paula (1994) *They Must be Represented: The Politics of Documentary*. New York and London: Verso.

Renov, Michael (ed. 1993) *Theorizing Documentary*. New York and London: Routledge/AFI.

Roscoe, Jane and Hight, Craig (2001) *Faking It: Mock-Documentary and the Subversion of Reality*. Manchester: Manchester University Press.

Rosenthal, Alan (1995) *Writing Docudrama: Dramatizing Reality for Film and TV*. Boston and Oxford: Focal Press.

Ruoff, Jeffrey (2002) *An American Family: A Televised Life*. Minneapolis MN: Minnesota University Press.

Winston, Brian (1995) *Claiming the Real*. London: British Film Institute.

Part I

Theories and Forms:
Documentary as Genre

1

The Voice of Documentary

Bill Nichols

It is worth insisting that the strategies and styles deployed in documentary, like those of narrative film, change; they have a history. And they have changed for much the same reasons: the dominant modes of expository discourse change; the arena of ideological contestation shifts. The comfortably accepted realism of one generation seems like artifice to the next. New strategies must constantly be fabricated to re-present "things as they are" and still others to contest this very representation.

In the history of documentary we can identify at least four major styles, each with distinctive formal and ideological qualities.[1] In this article I propose to examine the limitations and strengths of these strategies, with particular attention to one that is both the newest and in some ways the oldest of them all.[2]

The direct-address style of the Griersonian tradition (or, in its most excessive form, the March of Time's "voice of God") was the first thoroughly worked out mode of documentary. As befitted a school whose purposes were overwhelmingly didactic, it employed a supposedly authoritative yet often presumptuous off-screen narration. In many cases this narration effectively dominated the visuals, though it could be, in films like *Night Mail* or *Listen to Britain*, poetic and evocative. After World War II, the Griersonian mode fell into disfavor (for reasons I will come back to later), and it has little contemporary currency—except for television news, game and talk shows, ads, and documentary specials.

Its successor, *cinéma vérité*, promised an increase in the "reality effect" with its directness, immediacy, and impression of capturing untampered events in the everyday lives of particular people. Films like *Chronicle of a Summer, Le joli mai, Lonely Boy, Back-Breaking Leaf, Primary,* and *The Chair* built on the new technical possibilities offered by portable cameras and sound recorders, which could produce synchronous dialogue under location conditions. In pure *cinéma vérité* films, the style seeks to become "transparent" in the same mode as the classical Hollywood style—capturing people in action, and letting the viewer come to conclusions about them unaided by any implicit or explicit commentary.

Sometimes mesmerizing, frequently perplexing, such films seldom offered the sense of history, context, or perspective that viewers seek. And so in the past decade we have seen a third style that incorporates direct address (characters or narrator speaking directly to the viewer), usually in the form of the interview. In a host of political and feminist films, witness-participants step before the camera to tell their story. Sometimes profoundly revealing, sometimes fragmented and incomplete, such films have provided the central model for contemporary documentary. But as a strategy and a form, the interview-oriented film has problems of its own.

More recently, a fourth phase seems to have begun, with films moving toward more complex forms where epistemological and aesthetic assumptions become more visible. These new self-reflexive documentaries mix observational passages with interviews, the voice-over of the filmmaker with intertitles, making patently clear what has been implicit all along: documentaries always were forms of re-presentation, never clear windows onto "reality"; the filmmaker was always a participant-witness and an active fabricator of meaning, a producer of cinematic discourse rather than a neutral or all-knowing reporter of the way things truly are.

Ironically, film theory has been of little help in this recent evolution, despite the enormous contribution of recent theory to questions of the production of meaning in narrative forms. In documentary the most advanced, modernist work draws its inspiration less from poststructuralist models of discourse than from the working procedures of documentation and validation practiced by ethnographic filmmakers. And as far as the influence of film history goes, the figure of Dziga Vertov now looms much larger than that of either Flaherty or Grierson.

I do not intend to argue that self-reflexive documentary represents a pinnacle or solution in any ultimate sense. It is, however, in the process of evolving alternatives that seem, in our present historical context, less obviously problematic than the strategies of commentary, *vérité*, or the interview. These new forms may, like their predecessors, come to seem more "natural" or even "realistic" for a time. But the success of every form breeds its own overthrow: it limits, omits, disavows, represses (as well as represents). In time, new necessities bring new formal inventions.

As suggested above, in the evolution of documentary the contestation among forms has centered on the question of "voice." By voice I mean something narrower than style: that which conveys to us a sense of a text's social point of view, of how it is speaking to us and how it is organizing the materi-

als it is presenting to us. In this sense, voice is not restricted to any one code or feature, such as dialogue or spoken commentary. Voice is perhaps akin to that intangible, moirélike pattern formed by the unique interaction of all a film's codes, and it applies to all modes of documentary.

Far too many contemporary filmmakers appear to have lost their voice. Politically, they forfeit their own voice for that of others (usually characters recruited to the film and interviewed). Formally, they disavow the complexities of voice, and discourse, for the apparent simplicities of faithful observation or respectful representation, the treacherous simplicities of an unquestioned empiricism (the world and its truths exist; they need only be dusted off and reported). Many documentarists would appear to believe what fiction-filmmakers only feign to believe, or openly question: that filmmaking creates an objective representation of the way things really are. Such documentaries use the magical template of verisimilitude without the storyteller's open resort to artifice. Very few seem prepared to admit through the very tissue and texture of their work that all filmmaking is a form of discourse fabricating its effects, impressions, and point of view.

Yet it especially behooves the documentary filmmaker to acknowledge what she or he is actually doing. Not in order to be accepted as modernist for the sake of being modernist, but to fashion documentaries that may more closely correspond to a contemporary understanding of our position within the world so that effective political/formal strategies for describing and challenging that position can emerge. Strategies and techniques for doing so already exist. In documentary they seem to derive most directly from *The Man with a Movie Camera* and *Chronique d'un été* and are vividly exemplified in David and Judith MacDougall's Turkana trilogy (*Lorang's Way*, *Wedding Camels*, *A Wife Among Wives*). But before discussing this tendency further, we should first examine the strengths and limitations of *cinéma vérité* and the interview-based film. They are well represented by two recent and highly successful films: *Soldier Girls* and *Rosie the Riveter*.

Soldier Girls presents a contemporary situation: basic army training as experienced by women volunteers. Purely indirect or observational, *Soldier Girls* provides no spoken commentary, no interviews or titles, and like Fred Wiseman's films, it arouses considerable controversy about its point of view. One viewer at Filmex interjected, "How on earth did they get the army to let them make such an incredibly anti-army film?" What struck that viewer as powerful criticism, though, may strike another as an honest portrayal of the tough-minded discipline necessary to learn to defend oneself, to survive in harsh environments, to kill. As in Wiseman's films, organizational strategies establish a preferred reading—in this case, one that favors the personal over the political, that seeks out and celebrates the irruptions of individual feeling and conscience in the face of institutional constraint, that rewrites historical process as the expression of an indomitable human essence whatever the circumstance. But these strategies, complex and subtle like those of realist fiction, tend to ascribe to the historical material itself meanings that in fact are an effect of the film's style or voice, just as fiction's strategies invite us to believe that "life" is like the imaginary world inhabited by its characters.

A precredit sequence of training exercises that follows three women volunteers ends with a freeze-frame and iris-in to isolate the face of each woman. Similar to classic Hollywood-style vignettes used to identify key actors, this sequence inaugurates a set of strategies that links *Soldier Girls* with a large part of American *cinéma vérité* (*Primary*, *Salesman*, *An American Family*, the "Middletown" series). It is characterized by a romantic individualism and a dramatic, fictionlike structure, but employing "found" stories rather than the wholly invented ones of Hollywood. Scenes in which Private Hall oversees punishment for Private Alvarez and in which the women recruits are awakened and prepare their beds for Drill Sergeant Abing's inspection prompt an impression of looking in on a world unmarked by our, or the camera's, act of gazing. And those rare moments in which the camera or person behind it is acknowledged certify more forcefully that other moments of "pure observation" capture the social presentation of self we too would have witnessed had we actually been there to see for ourselves. When *Soldier Girls'* narrativelike tale culminates in a shattering moment of character revelation, it seems to be a happy coincidence of dramatic structure and historical events unfolding. In as extraordinary an epiphany as any in all of *vérité*, tough-minded Drill Sergeant Abing breaks down and confesses to Private Hall how much of his own humanity and soul has been destroyed by his experience in Vietnam. By such means, the film transcends the social and political categories that it shows but refuses to name. Instead of the personal becoming political, the political becomes personal.

We never hear the voice of the filmmaker or a narrator trying to persuade us of this romantic humanism. Instead, the film's structure relies heavily on classical narrative procedures, among them: (1) a chronology of apparent causality that reveals how each of the three women recruits resolves the conflict between her own sense of individuality and army discipline; (2) shots organized into dramatically revelatory scenes that only acknowledge the camera as participant-observer near the film's end, when one of the recruits embraces the filmmakers as she leaves the training base, discharged for her "failure" to fit in; and (3) excellent performances from characters who "play themselves" without any inhibiting self-consciousness. (The phenomenon of filming individuals who play themselves in a manner strongly reminiscent of the performances of professional actors in fiction could be the subject of an extended study in its own right.) These procedures allow purely observational documentaries to asymptotically narrow the gap between a fabricated realism and the apparent capture of reality itself that so fascinated André Bazin.

This gap may also be looked at as a gap between evidence and argument.[3] One of the peculiar fascinations of film is precisely that it so easily conflates the two. Documentary displays a tension arising from the attempt to make statements about life that are quite general, while necessarily using sounds and images that bear the inescapable trace of their particular historical origins. These sounds and images come to function as signs; they bear meaning, though the meaning is not really inherent in them but rather conferred upon them by their function within the text as a whole. We may think we hear history or reality speaking to us through a film, but what we actually hear is the voice of the text, even when that voice tries to efface itself.

This is not only a matter of semiotics but of historical process. Those who confer meaning (individuals, social classes, the media, and other institutions) exist within history itself rather than at the periphery, looking in like gods. Hence, paradoxically, self-referentiality is an inevitable communicational category. A class cannot be a member of itself, the law of logical typing tells us, and yet in human communication this law is necessarily violated. Those who confer meaning are themselves members of the class of conferred meanings (history). For a film to fail to acknowledge this and pretend to omniscience— whether by voice-of-God commentary or by claims of "objective knowledge"— is to deny its own complicity with a production of knowledge that rests on no firmer bedrock than the very act of production. (What then become vital are the assumptions, values, and purposes motivating this production, the underpinnings that some modernist strategies attempt to make more clear.)[4]

Observational documentary appears to leave the driving to us. No one tells us about the sights we pass or what they mean. Even those obvious marks of documentary textuality—muddy sound, blurred or racked focus, the grainy, poorly lit figures of social actors caught on the run—function paradoxically. Their presence testifies to an apparently more basic absence: such films sacrifice conventional, polished artistic expression in order to bring back, as best they can, the actual texture of history in the making. If the camera gyrates wildly or ceases functioning, this is not an expression of personal style. It is a signifier of personal danger, as in *Harlan County, U.S.A.*, or even death, as in the street scene from *The Battle of Chile* when the cameraman records the moment of his own death.

This shift from artistic expressiveness to historical revelation contributes mightily to the phenomenological effect of the observational film. *Soldier Girls, They Call Us Misfits*, its sequel, *A Respectable Life*, and Fred Wiseman's most recent film, *Models*, propose revelations about the real not as a result of direct argument, but on the basis of inferences we draw from historical evidence itself. For example, Stefan Jarl's remarkable film *They Call Us Misfits* contains a purely observational scene of its two seventeen-year-old misfits—who have left home for a life of booze, drugs, and a good time in Stockholm—getting up in the morning. Kenta washes his long hair, dries it, and then meticulously combs every hair into place. Stoffe doesn't bother with his hair at all. Instead, he boils water and then makes tea by pouring it over a tea bag that is still inside its paper wrapper! We rejoin the boys in *A Respectable Life*, shot ten years later, and learn that Stoffe has nearly died on three occasions from heroin overdoses whereas Kenta has sworn off hard drugs and begun a career of sorts as a singer. At this point we may retroactively grant a denser tissue of meaning to those little morning rituals recorded a decade earlier. If so, we take them as evidence of historical determinations rather than artistic vision—even though they are only available to us as a result of textual strategies. More generally, the aural and visual evidence of what ten years of hard living do to the alert, mischievous appearance of two boys—the ruddy skin, the dark, extinguished eyes, the slurred and garbled speech, especially of Stoffe—bear meaning precisely because the films invite retroactive comparison. The films produce the structure in which "facts" themselves take on meaning precisely because they belong to a coherent series of differences. Yet, though powerful, this construction of differences remains insufficient. A simplistic line of historical progression prevails, centered as it is in *Soldier Girls* on the trope of romantic individualism. (Instead of the Great Man theory we have the Unfortunate Victim theory of history—inadequate, but compellingly presented.)

And where observational cinema shifts from an individual to an institutional focus, and from a metonymic narrative model to a metaphoric one, as in the highly innovative work of Fred Wiseman, there may still be only a weak sense of constructed meaning, of a textual voice addressing us. A vigorous, active, and retroactive reading is necessary before we can hear the voice of the textual system as a level distinct from the sounds and images of the evidence it adduces, while questions of adequacy remain. Wiseman's sense of context and of meaning as a function of the text itself remains weak, too easily engulfed by the fascination that allows us to mistake film for reality, the impression of the real for the experience of it. The risk of reading *Soldier Girls* or Wiseman's *Models* like a Rorschach test may require stronger countermeasures than the subtleties their complex editing and mise-en-scène provide.

Prompted, it would seem, by these limitations to *cinéma vérité* or observational cinema, many filmmakers during the past decade have reinstituted direct address. For the most part this has meant social actors addressing us in interviews rather than a return to the voice-of-authority evidenced by a narrator. *Rosie the Riveter*, for example, tells us about the blatant hypocrisy with which women were recruited to the factories and assembly lines during World War II. A series of five women witnesses tell us how they were denied the respect granted men, told to put up with hazardous conditions "like a man," paid less, and pitted against one another racially. *Rosie* makes short shrift of the noble icon of the woman worker as seen in forties newsreels. Those films celebrated her heroic contribution to the great effort to preserve the free world from fascist dictatorship. *Rosie* destroys this myth of deeply appreciated, fully rewarded contribution without in any way undercutting the genuine fortitude, courage, and political awareness of women who experienced continual frustration in their struggles for dignified working conditions and a permanent place in the American labor force.

Using interviews, but no commentator, together with a weave of compilation footage as images of illustration, director Connie Field tells a story many of us think we've heard, only to realize we've never heard the whole of it before.

The organization of the film depends heavily on its set of extensive interviews with former "Rosies." Their selection follows the direct-cinema tradition of filming ordinary people. But *Rosie the Riveter* broadens that tradition, as *Union Maids, The Wobblies,* and *With Babies and Banners* have also done, to retrieve the memory of an "invisible" (suppressed more than forgotten) history of labor struggle. The five interviewees remember a past the film's inserted historical images reconstruct, but in counterpoint: their recollection of adversity and struggle contrasts with old newsreels of women "doing their part" cheerfully.

This strategy complicates the voice of the film in an interesting way. It adds a contemporary, personal resonance to the historical, compilation footage without challenging the assumptions of that footage explicitly, as a voice-over commentary might do. We ourselves become engaged in determining how the women witnesses counterpoint these historical "documents" as well as how they articulate their own present and past consciousness in political, ethical, and feminist dimensions.

We are encouraged to believe that these voices carry less the authority of historical judgment than that of personal testimony—they are, after all, the words of apparently "ordinary women" remembering the past. As in many films that advance issues raised by the women's movement, there is an emphasis on individual but politically significant experience. *Rosie* demonstrates the power of the act of naming—the ability to find the words that render the personal political. This reliance on oral history to reconstruct the past places *Rosie the Riveter* within what is probably the predominant mode of documentary filmmaking today—films built around a string of interviews—where we also find *A Wife's Tale, With Babies and Banners, Controlling Interest, The Day After Trinity, The Trials of Alger Hiss, Rape, Word Is Out, Prison for Women, This Is Not a Love Story, Nuove frontieras (Looking for Better Dreams),* and *The Wobblies.*

This reinstitution of direct address through the interview has successfully avoided some of the central problems of voice-over narration, namely, authoritative omniscience or didactic reductionism. There is no longer the dubious claim that things are as the film presents them, organized by the commentary of an all-knowing subject. Such attempts to stand above history and explain it create a paradox. Any attempt by a speaker to vouch for his or her own validity reminds us of the Cretan paradox: "Epimenides was a Cretan who said, 'Cretans always lie.' Was Epimenides telling the truth?" The nagging sense of a self-referential claim that can't be proven reaches greatest intensity with the most forceful assertions, which may be why viewers are often most suspicious of what an apparently omniscient Voice of Authority asserts most fervently. The emergence of so many recent documentaries built around strings of interviews strikes me as a strategic response to the recognition that neither can events speak for themselves nor can a single voice speak with ultimate authority. Interviews diffuse authority. A gap remains between the voice of a social actor recruited to the film and the voice of the film.

Not compelled to vouch for their own validity, the voices of interviewees may well arouse less suspicion. Yet a larger, constraining voice may remain to provide, or withhold, validation. In *The Sad Song of Yellow Skin*, *The Wilmar 8*, *Harlan County, U.S.A.*, *This Is Not a Love Story*, or *Who Killed the Fourth Ward*, among others, the literal voice of the filmmaker enters into dialogue but without the self-validating, authoritative tone of a previous tradition. (These are also voices without the self-reflexive quality found in Vertov's, Rouch's, or the MacDougalls' work.) Diarylike and uncertain in *Yellow Skin*; often directed toward the women strikers as though by a fellow participant and observer in *Wilmar 8* and *Harlan County, U.S.A.*; sharing personal reactions to pornography with a companion in *Not a Love Story*; and adopting a mock-ironic tone reminiscent of Peter Falk's Columbo in *Fourth* Ward—these voices of potentially imaginary assurance instead share doubts and emotional reactions with other characters and us. As a result, they seem to refuse a privileged position in relation to other characters. Of course, these less assertive authorial voices remain complicit with the controlling voice of the textual system itself, but the effect on a viewer is distinctly different.

Still, interviews pose problems. Their occurrence is remarkably widespread— from *The Hour of the Wolf* to "The MacNeil/Lehrer Report" and from *Housing Problems* (1935) to *Harlan County, U.S.A.* The greatest problem, at least in recent documentary, has been to retain that sense of a gap between the voice of interviewees and the voice of the text as a whole. It is most obviously a problem when the interviewees display conceptual inadequacy on the issue but remain unchallenged by the film. *The Day After Trinity*, for example, traces Robert Oppenheimer's career but restricts itself to a Great Man theory of history. The string of interviews clearly identifies Oppenheimer's role in the race to build the nuclear bomb, and his equivocations, but it never places the bomb or Oppenheimer within that larger constellation of government policies and political calculations that determined its specific use or continuing threat—even though the interviews took place in the last few years. The text not only appears to lack a voice or perspective of its own, the perspective of its character-witnesses is patently inadequate.

In documentary, when the voice of the text disappears behind characters who speak to us, we confront a specific strategy of no less ideological importance than its equivalent in fiction films. When we no longer sense that a governing voice actively provides or withholds the imprimatur of veracity according to its own purposes and assumptions, its own canons of validation, we may also sense the return of the paradox and suspicion that interviews should help us escape: the word of witnesses, uncritically accepted, must provide its own validation. Meanwhile, the film becomes a rubber stamp. To varying degrees this diminution of a governing voice occurs through parts of *Word Is Out, The Wobblies, With Babies and Banners,* and *Prison for Women.* The sense of a hierarchy of voices becomes lost.[5] Ideally this hierarchy would uphold correct logical typing at one level (the voice of the text remains of a higher, controlling type than the voices of interviewees) without denying the inevitable collapse of logical types at another (the voice of the text is not above history but part of the very historical process on which it confers meaning). But at present a less complex and less adequate sidetracking of paradox prevails. The film says, in effect, "Interviewees never lie." Interviewees say, "What I am telling you is the truth." We then ask, "Is the interviewee telling the truth?" but find no acknowledgment in the film of the possibility, let alone the necessity, of entertaining this question as one inescapable in all communication and signification.

As much as anyone, Emile de Antonio, who pioneered the use of interviews and compilation footage to organize complex historical arguments without a narrator, has also provided clear signposts for avoiding the inherent dangers of interviews. Unfortunately, most of the filmmakers adopting his basic approach have failed to heed them.

De Antonio demonstrates a sophisticated understanding of the category of the personal. He does not invariably accept the word of witnesses, nor does he adopt rhetorical strategies (Great Man theories, for example) that limit historical understanding to the personal. Something exceeds this category, and in *Point of Order, In the Year of the Pig, Millhouse: A White Comedy,* and *Weather Underground,* among others, this excess is carried by a distinct textual voice that clearly judges the validity of what witnesses say. Just as the voice of John Huston in *The Battle of San Pietro* contests one line of argument with another (that of General Mark Clark, who claims the costs of battle were not excessive, with that of Huston, who suggests they were), so the textual voice of de

Antonio contests and places the statements made by its embedded interviews, but without speaking to us directly. (In de Antonio and in his followers, there is no narrator, only the direct address of witnesses.)

This contestation is not simply the express support of some witnesses over others, for left against right. It is a systematic effect of placement that retains the gaps between levels of different logical type. De Antonio's overall expository strategy in *In the Year of the Pig*, for example, makes it clear that no one witness tells the whole truth. De Antonio's voice (unspoken but controlling) makes witnesses contend with one another to yield a point of view more distinctive to the film than to any of its witnesses (since it includes this very strategy of contention). (Similarly, the unspoken voice of *The Atomic Cafe*—evident in the extraordinarily skillful editing of government nuclear weapons propaganda films from the fifties—governs a preferred reading of the footage it compiles.) But particularly in de Antonio's work, different points of view appear. History is not a monolith, its density and outline given from the outset. On the contrary, *In the Year of the Pig*, for example, constructs perspective and historical understanding, and does so right before our eyes.

We see and hear, for example, U.S. government spokesmen explaining their strategy and conception of the "Communist menace," whereas we do not see and hear Ho Chi Minh explain his strategy and vision. Instead, an interviewee, Paul Mus, introduces us to Ho Chi Minh descriptively while de Antonio's cutaways to Vietnamese countryside evoke an affiliation between Ho and his land and people that is absent from the words and images of American spokesmen. Ho remains an uncontained figure whose full meaning must be conferred, and inferred, from available materials as they are brought together by de Antonio. Such construction is a textual, and cinematic, act evident in the choice of supporting or ironic images to accompany interviews, in the actual juxtaposition of interviews, and even in the still images that form a precredit sequence inasmuch as they unmistakably refer to the American Civil War (an analogy sharply at odds with U.S. government accounts of Communist invasion). By juxtaposing silhouettes of civil war soldiers with GIs in Vietnam, the precredit sequence obliquely but clearly offers an interpretation for the events we are about to see. De Antonio does not subordinate his own voice to the way things are, to the sounds and images that are evidence of war. He acknowledges that the meaning of these images must be conferred on them and goes about doing so in a readily understood though indirect manner.

De Antonio's hierarchy of levels and reservation of ultimate validation to the highest level (the textual system or film as a whole) differs radically from other approaches. John Lowenthal's *The Trials of Alger Hiss*, for example, is a totally subservient endorsement of Hiss's legalistic strategies. Similarly, *Hollywood on Trial* shows no independence from the perhaps politically expedient but disingenuous line adopted by the Hollywood 10 over thirty years ago—that

HUAC's pattern of subpoenas to friendly and unfriendly witnesses primarily threatened the civil liberties of ordinary citizens (though it certainly did so) rather than posing a more specific threat to the CPUSA and American left (where it clearly did the greatest damage). By contrast, even in *Painters Painting* and *Weather Underground*, where de Antonio seems unusually close to validating uncritically what interviewees say, the subtle voice of his mise-en-scène preserves the gap, conveying a strong sense of the distance between the sensibilities or politics of those interviewed and those of the larger public to whom they speak.

De Antonio's films produce a world of dense complexity: they embody a sense of constraint and overdetermination. Not everyone can be believed. Not everything is true. Characters do not emerge as the autonomous shapers of a personal destiny. De Antonio proposes ways and means by which to reconstruct the past dialectically, as Fred Wiseman reconstructs the present dialectically.[6] Rather than appearing to collapse itself into the consciousness of character witnesses, the film retains an independent consciousness, a voice of its own. The film's own consciousness (surrogate for ours) probes, remembers, substantiates, doubts. It questions and believes, including itself. It assumes the voice of personal consciousness at the same time as it examines the very category of the personal. Neither omniscient deity nor obedient mouthpiece, de Antonio's rhetorical voice seduces us by embodying those qualities of insight, skepticism, judgment, and independence we would like to appropriate for our own. Nonetheless, though he is closer to a modernist, self-reflexive strategy than any other documentary filmmaker in America—with the possible exception of the more experimental feminist filmmaker JoAnn Elam—de Antonio remains clearly apart from this tendency. He is more a Newtonian than an Einsteinian observer of events; he insists on the activity of fixing meaning, but it is meaning that does, finally, appear to reside "out there" rather than insisting on the activity of producing that "fix" from which meaning itself derives.

There are lessons here we would think de Antonio's successors would be quick to learn. But, most frequently, they have not. The interview remains a problem. Subjectivity, consciousness, argumentative form, and voice remain unquestioned in documentary theory and practice. Often, filmmakers simply choose to interview characters with whom they agree. A weaker sense of skepticism, a diminished self-awareness of the filmmaker as producer of meaning or history prevails, yielding a flatter, less dialectical sense of history and a simpler, more idealized sense of character. Characters threaten to emerge as stars—flashpoints of inspiring, and imaginary, coherence contradictory to their ostensible status as ordinary people.[7]

These problems emerge in three of the best history films we have (and in the pioneering gay film *Word Is Out*), undermining their great importance on other levels. *Union Maids, With Babies and Banners,* and *The Wobblies* flounder on the axis of personal respect and historical recall. The films simply suppose that things were as the participant-witnesses recall them, and lest we doubt, the filmmakers respectfully find images of illustration to substantiate the claim. (The resonance set up in *Rosie the Riveter* between interviews and compilation footage establishes a perceptible sense of a textual voice that makes this film a more sophisticated, though not self-reflexive, version of the interview-based documentary.) What characters omit to say, so do these films, most noticeably regarding the role of the CPUSA in *Union Maids* and *With Babies and Banners*. *Banners*, for example, contains one instance when a witness mentions the helpful knowledge she gained from Communist party members. Immediately, though, the film cuts to unrelated footage of a violent attack on workers by a goon squad. It is as if the textual voice, rather than provide independent assessment, must go so far as to find diversionary material to offset presumably harmful comments by witnesses themselves!

These films naively endorse limited, selective recall. The tactic flattens witnesses into a series of imaginary puppets conforming to a line. Their recall becomes distinguishable more by differences in force of personality than by differences in perspective. Backgrounds loaded with iconographic meanings transform witnesses further into stereotypes (shipyards, farms, union halls abound, or for the gays and lesbians in *Word Is Out*, bedrooms and the bucolic out-of-doors). We sense a great relief when characters step out of these closed, iconographic frames and into more open-ended ones, but such "release" usually occurs only at the end of the films where it also signals the achievement of expository closure—another kind of frame. We return to the simple claim, "Things were as these witnesses describe them, why contest them?"—a claim that is a dissimulation and a disservice to both film theory and political praxis. On the contrary, as de Antonio and Wiseman demonstrate quite differently, Things signify, but only if we make them comprehensible.[8]

Documentaries with a more sophisticated grasp of the historical realm establish a preferred reading by a textual system that asserts its own voice in contrast to the voices it recruits or observes. Such films confront us with an alternative to our own hypotheses about what kinds of things populate the world, what relations they sustain, and what meanings they bear for us. The film operates as an autonomous whole, as we do. It is greater than its parts, and it orchestrates them: (1) the recruited voices, the recruited sounds and images; (2) the textual "voice" spoken by the style of the film as a whole (how its multiplicity of codes, including those pertaining to recruited voices, are orchestrated into a singular, controlling pattern); and (3) the surrounding historical context, including the viewing event itself, which the textual voice cannot successfully rise above or fully control. The film is thus a simulacrum or external trace of the production of meaning we undertake ourselves every day, every moment. We see not an image of imaginary unchanging coherence, magically represented on a screen, but the evidence of a historically rooted act of making things meaningful comparable to our own historically situated acts of comprehension.

With de Antonio's films, *The Atomic Cafe, Rape,* or *Rosie the Riveter* the active counterpointing of the text reminds us that its meaning is produced. This foregrounding of an active production of meaning by a textual system may also heighten our conscious sense of self as something also produced by codes that extend beyond ourselves. An exaggerated claim, perhaps, but still suggestive of the difference in effect of different documentary strategies and an indication of the importance of the self-reflexive strategy itself.

Self-reflexiveness can easily lead to an endless regression. It can prove highly appealing to an intelligentsia more interested in "good form" than in social change. Yet interest in self-reflexive forms is not purely an academic question. *Cinéma vérité* and its variants sought to address certain limitations of the voice-of-God tradition. The interview-oriented film sought to address limitations apparent in the bulk of *cinéma vérité,* and the self-reflexive documentary addresses the limitations of assuming that subjectivity and both the social and textual positioning of the self (as filmmaker or viewer) are ultimately not problematic.

Modernist thought in general challenges this assumption. A few documentary filmmakers, going as far back as Dziga Vertov and certainly including Jean Rouch and the hard-to-categorize Jean-Luc Godard, adopt in their work the basic epistemological assumption that knowledge and the position of the self in relation to the mediator of knowledge, a given text, are socially and formally constructed and should be shown to be so. Rather than inviting paralysis before a centerless labyrinth, however, such a perspective restores the dialectic between self and other: neither the "out there" nor the "in here" contains its own inherent meaning. The *process* of constructing meaning overshadows constructed meanings. And at a time when modernist experimentation is old hat within the avant-garde and a fair amount of fiction filmmaking, it remains almost totally unheard of among documentary filmmakers, especially in North America. It is not political documentarists who have been the leading innovators. Instead it is a handful of ethnographic filmmakers like Timothy Asch (*The Ax Fight*), John Marshall (*Nai!*), and David and Judith MacDougall who, in their meditations on scientific method and visual communication, have done the most provocative experimentation.

Take the MacDougalls' *Wedding Camels* (part of the Turkana trilogy), for example. The film, set in northern Kenya, explores the preparations for a Turkana wedding in day-to-day detail. It mixes direct and indirect address to form a complex whole made up of two levels of historical reference—evidence and argument—and two levels of textual structure—observation and exposition.

Though *Wedding Camels* is frequently observational and very strongly rooted in the texture of everyday life, the filmmakers' presence receives far more frequent acknowledgment than it does in *Soldier Girls* or Wiseman's films, or most other observational work. Lorang, the bride's father and central figure in the dowry negotiations, says at one point, with clear acknowledgment of the filmmakers' presence, "They [Europeans] never marry our daughters. They always hold back their animals." At other moments we hear David MacDougall ask questions of Lorang or others off-camera, much as we do in *The Wilmar 8* or *In the Year of the Pig*. (This contrasts with *The Wobblies*, *Union Maids*, and *With Babies and Banners*, where the questions to which participant-witnesses respond are not heard.) Sometimes these queries invite characters to reflect on events we observe in detail, like the dowry arrangements themselves. On these occasions they introduce a vivid level of self-reflexiveness into the characters' performance as well as into the film's structure, something that is impossible in interview-based films that give us no sense of a character's present but only use his or her words as testimony about the past.

Wedding Camels also makes frequent use of intertitles, which mark off one scene from another, to develop a mosaic structure that necessarily admits to its own lack of completeness even as individual facets appear to exhaust a given encounter. This sense of both incompleteness and exhaustion, as well as the radical shift of perceptual space involved in going from apparently three-dimensional images to two-dimensional graphics that comment on or frame the image, generates a strong sense of a hierarchical and self-referential ordering.

For example, in one scene Naingoro, sister to the bride's mother, says, "Our daughters are not our own. They are born to be given out." The implicit lack of completeness to individual identity apart from social exchange then receives elaboration through an interview sequence with Akai, the bride. The film poses questions by means of intertitles and sandwiches Akai's responses, briefly, between them. One intertitle, for example, phrases its question more or less as follows: "We asked Akai whether a Turkana woman chooses her husband or if her parents choose for her." Such phrasing brings the filmmaker's intervention strongly into the foreground.

The structure of this passage suggests some of the virtues of a hybrid style: the titles serve as another indicator of a textual voice apart from that of the characters represented. They also differ from most documentary titles, which since the silent days of *Nanook* have worked like a graphic "voice" of authority. In *Wedding Camels* the titles, in their mock-interactive structure, remain closely aligned with the particulars of person and place rather than appearing to issue from an omniscient consciousness. They show clear awareness of how a particular meaning is being produced by a particular act of intervention.

This is not presented as a grand revelation but as a simple truth that is only remarkable for its rarity in documentary film. These particular titles also display both a wry sense of humor and a clear perception of the meaning an individual's marriage has for him or her as well as for others (a vital means of countering, among other things, the temptation of an ethnocentric reading or judgment). By "violating" the coherence of a social actor's diegetic space, intertitles also lessen the tendency for the interviewee to inflate to the proportions of a star witness. By acting self-reflexively, such strategies call the status of the interview itself into question and diminish its tacit claim to tell the whole truth. Other signifying choices, which function like Brechtian distancing devices, would include the separate "spaces" of image and intertitle for question/response; the highly structured and abbreviated question/answer format; the close-up, portraitlike framing of a social actor that pries her away from a matrix of ongoing activities or a stereotypical background, and the clear acknowledgment that such fabrications exist to serve the purposes of the film rather than to capture an unaffected reality.

Though modest in tone, *Wedding Camels* demonstrates a structural sophistication well beyond that of almost any other documentary film work today. Whether its modernist strategies can be yoked to a more explicitly political perspective (without restricting itself to the small avant-garde audience that exists for the Godards and Chantal Akermans) is less a question than a challenge still haunting us, considering the limitations of most interview-based films.

Changes in documentary strategy bear a complex relation to history. Self-reflexive strategies seem to have a particularly complex historical relation to documentary form, since they are far less peculiar to it than the voice-of-God, *cinéma vérité*, or interview-based strategies. Although they have been available to documentary (as to narrative) since the 1910s, they have never been as popular in North America as in Europe or in other regions (save among an avant-garde). Why they have recently made an effective appearance within the documentary domain is a matter requiring further exploration. I suspect we are dealing with more than a reaction to the limitations of the currently dominant interview-based form. Large cultural preferences concerning the voicing of dramatic as well as documentary material seem to be changing. In any event, the most recent appearances of self-reflexive strategies correspond very clearly to deficiencies in attempts to translate highly ideological, written anthropological practices into a proscriptive agenda for a visual anthropology (neutrality, descriptiveness, objectivity, "just the facts," and so on). It is very heartening to see that the realm of the possible for documentary film has now expanded to include strategies of reflexivity that may eventually serve political as well as scientific ends.

Notes

1 Many of the distinctive characteristics of documentary are examined broadly in Nichols, *Ideology and the Image: Social Representation in the Cinema and Other Media* (Bloomington: Indiana University Press, 1981), pp. 170–284. Here I shall concentrate on more recent films and some of the particular problems they pose.

2 Films referred to in this article or instrumental in formulating the issues of self-reflexive documentary form include: *The Atomic Cafe* (USA, Kevin Rafferty, Jayne Loader, Pierce Rafferty, 1982), *Controlling Interest* (USA, SF Newsreel, 1978), *The Day After Trinity* ((USA, Jon Else, 1980), *Harlan County, U.S.A.* (USA, Barbara Kopple, 1976), *Hollywood on Trial* (USA, David Halpern, Jr., 1976), *Models* (USA, Fred Wiseman, 1981), *Nuove frontieras* (*Looking for Better Dreams*) (Switzerland, Remo Legnazzi, 1981), *On Company Business* (USA, Allan Francovich, 1981), *Prison for Women* (Canada, Janice Cole, Holly Dale, 1981), *Rape* (USA, JoAnn Elam, 1977), *A Respectable Life* (Sweden, Stefan Jarl, 1980), *Rosie the Riveter* (USA, Connie Field, 1980), *The Sad Song of Yellow Skin* (Canada, NFB—Michael Rubbo, 1970), *Soldier Girls* (USA, Nick Broomfield, Joan Churchill, 1981), *They Call Us Misfits* (Sweden, Jan Lindquist, Stefan Jarl, c. 1969), *Not a Love Story!* (Canada, NFB—Bonnie Klein, 1981), *The Trials of Alger Hiss* (USA, John Lowenthal, 1980), *Union Maids* (USA, Jim Klein, Julia Reichert, Miles Mogulescu, 1976), *Who Killed the Fourth Ward?* (USA, James Blue, 1978), *The Wilmar 8* (USA, Lee Grant, 1980), *With Babies and Banners* (USA, Women's Labor History Film Project, 1978), *A Wife's Tale* (Canada, Sophie Bissonnette, Martin Duckworth, Joyce Rock, 1980), *The Wobblies* (USA, Stuart Bird, Deborah Shaffer, 1979), *Word Is Out* (USA, Mariposa Collective, 1977).

3 Perhaps the farthest extremes of evidence and argument occur with pornography and propaganda: what would pornography be without its evidence, what would propaganda be without its arguments?

4 Without models of documentary strategy that invite us to reflect on the construction of social reality, we have only a corrective act of negation ("this is not reality, it is neither omniscient nor objective") rather than an affirmative act of comprehension ("this is a text, these are its assumptions, this is the meaning it produces"). The lack of an invitation to assume a positive stance handicaps us in our efforts to understand the position we occupy; refusing a position proffered to us is far from affirming a position we actively construct. It is similar to the difference between refusing to "buy" the messages conveyed by advertising, at least entirely, while still lacking any alternative nonfetishistic presentation of commodities that can help us gain a different "purchase" on their relative use- and exchange-value. In many ways, this problem of moving from refusal to affirmation, from protest at the way things are to the construction of durable alternatives, is precisely the problem of the American left. Modernist strategies have something to contribute to the resolution of this problem.

5 After completing this article, I read Jeffrey Youdelman's "Narration, Invention, and History" (*Cineaste* 12 [Spring 1982]: 8–15 [reprinted as Chapter 29 of this collection]), which makes a similar point with a somewhat different set of examples. His discussion of imaginative, lyrical uses of commentary in the 1930s and 1940s is particularly instructive.

6 Details of de Antonio's approach are explored in Tom Waugh's "Emile de Antonio and the New Documentary of the Seventies," *Jump Cut*, no. 10/11 (1976): 33–9, and of Wiseman's in Nichols, *Ideology and the Image*, pp. 208–36.

7 An informative discussion of the contradiction between character witnesses with unusual abilities and the rhetorical attempt to make them signifiers of ordinary workers, particularly in *Union Maids*, occurs in Noel King's "Recent 'Political' Documentary—Notes on *Union Maids* and *Harlan County, U.S.A.*," *Screen* 22, no. 2 (1981): 7–18.

8 In this vein, Noel King comments, "So in the case of these documentaries [*Union Maids, With Babies and Banners, Harlan County, U.S.A.*] we might notice the way a discourse of morals or ethics suppresses one of politics and the way a discourse of a subject's individual responsibility suppresses any notion of a discourse on the social and linguistic formation of subjects" (ibid., p. 11). But we might also say, as the filmmakers seem to, "This is how the participants saw their struggle and it is well worth preserving," even though we may wish they did not do so slavishly. There is a difference between criticizing films because they fail to demonstrate the theoretical sophistication of certain analytic methodologies and criticizing them because their textual organization is inadequate to the phenomena they describe.

2

The Image Mirrored: Reflexivity and the Documentary Film

Jay Ruby

Anyone who recognizes that self-reflection, as mediated linguistically, is integral to the characterization of human social conduct, must acknowledge that such holds also for his own activities as a social "analyst," "researcher," etc. (Anthony Giddens, *New Rules of Sociological Method*)

My topic is the concept of reflexivity as it applies to the documentary film. Before I can approach this subject, I must first briefly examine the parameters of reflexivity, situate it in a historical-cultural context, and discuss my own relationship to the concept.

To be ideologically consistent, I should and will now situate my thoughts within my own history, in other words, be reflexive about my ideas of reflexivity. In the process of organizing the 1974 Conference on Visual Anthropology, I organized a series of screenings and discussions entitled "Exposing Yourself." The panelists—Sol Worth, Gerry O'Grady, Bob Scholte, Richard Chalfen, and myself—discussed a group of autobiographical, self-referential, and self-consciously made films in terms of a variety of concerns within visual communication and anthropology. Some of those films and ideas have formed the basis for my discussion here.

While I do not intend to proselytize, I should point out that I am partisan. I am convinced that filmmakers along with anthropologists have the ethical, political, aesthetic, and scientific obligations to be reflexive and self-critical about their work. Indeed, I would expand that mandate to include everyone who manipulates a symbolic system for any reason. You will find little direct empirical support for such sweeping statements in this paper. Instead, my focus is more modest. I intend to concentrate on a discussion of the manifestations of reflexivity in documentary films.

As a means of delineating the concept, let us examine the following diagram borrowed from Johannes Fabian's article, "Language, History, and Anthropology":[1] PRODUCER–PROCESS–PRODUCT. I am deliberately using general terms because they serve to remind us that the issues raised are not confined to the cinema even though this paper is.

While one can find exceptions, I think that it is reasonable to say that most filmmakers present us with the product and exclude the other two components. According to popular rhetoric as used in our culture by some people to explain the documentary, these films are produced by people striving to be unbiased, neutral, and objective. They employ fair and accurate means to obtain the true facts about reality. Given that point of view, and I realize that I am oversimplifying, not only is it unnecessary to reveal the producer and the process, such revelation is counterproductive. To reveal the producer is thought to be narcissistic, overly personal, and subjective. The revelation of process is deemed to be untidy, ugly, and confusing to the audience. To borrow a concept from the sociologist Erving Goffman,[2] audiences are not supposed to see backstage. It destroys illusions and causes them to break their suspension of disbelief.

On the other hand, assuming a reflexive stance would be to reveal all three components—to see things this way: PRODUCER–PROCESS–PRODUCT and to suggest that unless audiences have knowledge of all three, a sophisticated and critical understanding of the product is virtually impossible.

To be reflexive is to structure a product in such a way that the audience assumes that the producer, the process of making, and the product are a coherent whole. Not only is an audience made aware of these relationships, but it is made to realize the necessity of that knowledge. To be more formal about it, I would argue that being reflexive means that the producer deliberately and intentionally reveals to his audience the underlying epistemological assumptions that caused him to formulate a set of questions in a particular way, to seek answers to those questions in a particular way, and finally to present his findings in a particular way.

There may be some confusion between *reflexivity* and terms which are sometimes used as synonyms: *autobiography*, *self-reference*, and *self-consciousness*. In an *autobiographical* work, while the producer—the self—is the center of the work, he can be unself-conscious in his presentation. The author clearly has had to be self-aware in the process of making the product (i.e., the autobiography), but it is possible for him to keep that knowledge private and simply follow the established conventions of that genre. To be *reflexive* is not only to be self-aware, but to be sufficiently self-aware to know what aspects of self are necessary to reveal so that an audience is able to understand both the process employed and the resultant product and to know that the revelation itself is purposive, intentional, and not merely narcissistic or accidentally revealing.[3]

Self-reference, on the other hand, is not autobiographical or reflexive. It is the allegorical or metaphorical use of self—for example, Truffaut's films *400 Blows* and *Day for Night*. The maker's life in this work becomes symbolic of some sort of collective—*all* filmmakers, and perhaps *everyman*. It is popularly assumed that *self-reference* occurs in all art forms: as the cliché goes, an artist uses his personal experience as the basis of his art. The devotees of an art form try to ferret out biographical tidbits so that they can discover the "hidden meaning" behind the artist's work. Again, there is the cultural fact that we believe it is quite common for producers to be self-referential. What I wish to stress is that this self-reference is distinct from reflexivity—one does not necessarily lead to the other.

To be *self-conscious* in the turgid pseudo-Freudian sense of a Fellini, for example, has become a full-time preoccupation particularly among the upper-middle class. However, it is possible and indeed common for this kind of awareness to remain private knowledge for the producer, or at least to be so detached from the product that all but the most devoted are discouraged from exploring the relationship between the maker and his work; and furthermore, the producer does nothing to encourage that exploration. In other words, one can be *reflective* without being *reflexive*. That is, one can become self-conscious without being conscious of that self-consciousness.[4] Only if a producer decides to make his awareness of self a public matter and conveys that knowledge to his audience is it possible to regard the product as reflexive.

I have just suggested that it is possible to produce autobiographical, self-referential, or self-conscious works without being reflexive. Let me clarify. I am simply saying that if the work does not contain sufficient indications that the producer intends his product to be regarded as reflexive, the audience will be uncertain as to whether they are reading into the product more or other than what was meant.[5]

While I am primarily concerned with reflexivity in the documentary film, it is necessary to mention at least some of the general cultural manifestations of reflexiveness. I believe they are to be found in the growing popular realization that the world, and in particular the symbolic world—things, events, and people, as well as news, television, books, and stories—are not what they appear to be. People want to know exactly what the ingredients are before they buy anything—aspirin, cars, television news, or education. We no longer trust the producers: Ralph Nader, the consumer protection movement, truth in lending and advertising laws are the results of this felt need.

On a more profound level, we are moving away from the positivist notion that meaning resides in the world and human beings should strive to discover the inherent, objectively true reality of things.[6] This philosophy of positivism has caused many social scientists as well as documentary filmmakers and journalists to hide themselves and their methods under the guise of objectivity. This point of view is challenged by both Marxists and structuralists.

We are beginning to recognize that human beings construct and impose meaning on the world. We create order. We don't discover it. We organize a reality that is meaningful for us. It is around these organizations of reality that filmmakers construct films. Some filmmakers, like other symbol producers in our culture, are beginning to feel the need to inform their audiences about who they are and how their identities may affect their films. They also wish to instruct their audiences about the process of articulation from the economic, political, and cultural structures and ideologies surrounding the documentary to the mechanics of production.

Reflexive elements in documentaries are undoubtedly a reflection of a general cultural concern with self-awareness. They are also the continuation of a tradition in visual forms of communication. It has been suggested that reflexivity in the visual arts begins with the cave paintings where people drew the outline of their hands on the wall. It is the first sign of authorship. It reminds us of the process and even tells us something about the maker—most of the hands reveal missing finger joints.

In painting we have early examples of reflexivity in Jan van Eyck's *Giovanni Arnolfini and His Bride* (1434), where we find a mirror in the center of what appears to be merely a portrait. In the mirror are the reflections of two people, one of them assumed to be van Eyck. So that the viewer will know for certain, the painter has written around the top of the mirror, "van Eyck was here." I could trace the development of such genres as the self-portrait and other evidences of this kind of sensibility, but it would take us too far astray. It is sufficient to say that by the time movies were invented there was already established a minor tradition of reflexiveness within most pictorial communicative forms.

Turning to the cinema, we discover that reflexivity is to be found more frequently in fiction film than in the documentary. From their beginnings films have been an imperfect illusion. That is, the suspension of disbelief has been broken through either accident or design. Audiences have been reminded that they are spectators having technologically generated vicarious and illusionary experiences. In one sense, every time the camera moves one is reminded of its presence and the construct of the image. Also, there is an early tradition in film of actors making direct contact with the audience. These "theatrical asides" (undoubtedly having a theatrical origin) of Groucho Marx and other comedians, like Woody Allen in *Annie Hall*, momentarily alienate the audience.[7] However, the overall effect of both camera movements and asides is probably not significant and is hardly constructed in a manner that could be called reflexive.

There are three places where one finds sustained reflexive elements in fiction films: (1) comedies in the form of satires and parodies about movies and moviemakers; (2) dramatic films in which the subject matter is movies and moviemakers; and (3) some modernist films which are concerned with exploring the parameters of form, and in that exploration disturb conventions such as the distinction between fiction and nonfiction.[8]

From Edison to Mel Brooks, fiction-filmmakers have been able to mock themselves and their work more easily than have documentarians. Documentary parodies are uncommon and recent in origin. For example, Jim McBride's *David Holzman's Diary*, Mitchell Block's *No Lies*, and Jim Cox's *Eat the Sun*.

In fact, documentary parody is so rare and out of keeping with the sensibilities of people who make these films that when a parody may exist it is regarded as confusing. In Basil Wright's review of Buñuel's *Land Without Bread*, Wright assumed that the narration and music score were errors and not a deliberate attempt on Buñuel's part to be ironic. "Unfortunately, someone (presumably not Buñuel) has added to the film a wearisome American commentary, plus the better part of a Brahms symphony. As a result, picture and sound never coalesce, and it is only the starkness of the presented facts which counts."[9]

Whether Buñuel is, in fact, responsible for the text of the narration and the music score is unclear.[10] It is sufficient for our purposes to realize that it apparently never occurred to Wright that some audiences might regard the juxtaposition of music, narration, and images as ironic, perhaps even as a parody of travelogues and information films.

It is not difficult to see why the possibility of parody did not occur to Wright. Because parody mocks or ridicules communicative forms, conventions, and codes, it can be said that parody has reflexive qualities. Both reflexivity and parody draw attention to the formal qualities of film as film. Most documentarians wish to make their films transparent, that is, to appear to be merely records. Calling attention to the film *as* film frustrates that purpose.[11]

It is interesting to note that the tradition of parody in fiction films commences at the beginning of cinema and continues to the present. The ironic messages in Mel Brooks's *Blazing Saddles* and in *Uncle Josh Jumps*, a silent one-reeler produced in Edison's studio, are amazingly similar. In *Uncle Josh Jumps* we see a man sitting in a theater balcony watching a movie. He ducks and cringes when a train appears on the screen. As each new scene appears he behaves as if the action were live and not on the screen. When a fight appears he jumps onstage and punches the screen fighters, thereby knocking down the screen, exposing the projector and projectionist. The film ends with the movie-goer and projectionist fighting.

Both *Blazing Saddles* and *Uncle Josh Jumps* are comedies. Because they are parodies they serve an additional function. They cause audiences to become alienated from the suspension of disbelief and to become self-conscious about their assumptions concerning film conventions. As stated earlier, parody can have a reflexive function.

Hollywood has produced many films that deal with movies and the lives of the moviemakers: *A Star Is Born* and *Sunset Boulevard* are two examples.

However, these films serve not to reveal but to perpetuate popular cultural myths about the glamor of the stars and the industry. As William Siska suggests, "Traditional cinema does not expose the process of production to alienate us from the story that's being told; rather, the camera, lights, and technicians are used as icons to authenticate the notion that we are enjoying a behind the scenes look at how the industry 'really works.'"[12]

Some modernist films, such as Godard's *La Chinoise*, Haskell Wexler's *Medium Cool*, and Agnes Varda's *Lion's Love*, tend to blur conventional distinctions between fiction and nonfiction. For example, in *La Chinoise*, Godard (from behind the camera) interrupts Jean Léaud's monologue on the role of the theater in the revolution and asks him if he is an actor. Léaud responds, "Yes, but I believe this anyway," and returns to his speech. The audience is unable to decide whether they are hearing the sentiments of the director spoken by a character, or the actor spontaneously expressing his personal feelings, or an actor who shares certain ideas with the director and is speaking written lines.

Documentary parodies that purport to be actual footage but are staged, scripted, and acted are similar to those films that mix fictional and nonfictional elements. Both cause audiences to question or at least become confused about their assumptions concerning fiction and documentary and ultimately, I suppose, their assumptions about reality. In that sense, they produce audience self-consciousness and have reflexive qualities. Examining the history of the documentary, we discover that it is to the Russians in the twenties and thirties and the French in the fifties and sixties that we must look for the true origins of documentary reflexivity.[13] Taken together, Jean Rouch's film *Chronicle of a Summer* (*Chronique d'un été*) and Dziga Vertov's *The Man with a Movie Camera* raise most of the significant issues.

In the 1920s Vertov, an artist and founder of the Russian documentary, developed a theory of film in opposition to that of Eisenstein. Vertov argued that the role of film in a revolutionary society should be to raise the consciousness of the audience by creating a film form which caused them to see the world in terms of a dialectical materialism. The Kino Eye (the camera eye) would produce Kino Pravda—Cine Truth.

For Vertov the artifices of fiction produced entertainment—escape and fantasies. Revolutionary filmmakers should take pictures of actuality—the everyday events of ordinary people. This raw stuff of life could then be transformed into meaningful statements. In his film *The Man with a Movie Camera*, Vertov attempted to explicate his theory.[14]

He was more concerned with revealing process than with revealing self. Vertov wished the audience to understand how film works, in mechanical, technical, and methodological as well as conceptual ways, thereby demystifying the creative process. He also wanted audiences to know that filmmaking is work and the filmmaker a worker, a very important justification for art in Leninist Russia. We see the filmmaker, but he is more a part of the process than anything else. One of Vertov's major goals was to aid the audience in their understanding of the process of construction in film so that they could develop a sophisticated and critical attitude. Vertov saw this raising of the visual consciousness of audiences as the way to bring Marxist truth to the masses. Like Godard (who at one point founded a Dziga Vertov film collective), Vertov wished to make revolutionary films which intentionally taught audiences how to see the world in a different way. To locate it in modern terminology,[15] Vertov is suggesting that in order to be able to make the assumption of intention and then to make inferences, viewers must have structural competence; that is, they must have knowledge of the sociocultural conventions related to making inferences of meaning in filmic sign-events.

Rouch, a French anthropologist engaged in field work in West Africa since World War II, is one of the few anthropologists concerned with creating a cinematic form which is peculiarly appropriate for anthropological expression.[16] His film *Chronicle of a Summer* represents an experiment to find that form. Rouch is primarily concerned with the personal: the philosophical problems of doing research and the possible effects of filming research. He is also interested in form. But questions about the formal aspects of structure come from his concern with the self more than from Vertov's concern with the process.

Both films were ahead of their time. Vertov's pioneering work had to wait almost a quarter of a century for Rouch to come along before someone would pursue the questions raised with *A Man with a Movie Camera*. Rouch has said that he sees his own films as being an attempt to combine the personal and participatory concerns of Robert Flaherty with an interest in process derived from Vertov. As we know, Morin described *Chronicle of a Summer* as being *cinéma vérité* in emulation of Vertov's Kino Pravda. Rouch's influence in France has been extensive. In the United States, however, his films are seldom seen, and his work is confused with that of such American direct-cinema people as Leacock, Pennebaker, and the Maysles brothers.

Rouch's films signaled the beginning of a technological revolution that caused some documentarians to face several fundamental issues. Prior to the mid-1960s, film technology was obtrusive, and it limited the type of filming possible. The advent of lightweight, portable sync sound equipment made it feasible for filmmakers to follow people around and film virtually anywhere, to intrude on people's lives—observe them and participate in their activities. Documentarians found themselves confronted with problems similar to those of ethnographers and other fieldworkers.[17] For some it became necessary to rethink the epistemological, moral, and political structures that made the documentary possible. They began to grapple with such questions as:

1. If documentarians claimed that they were trying to film people as they would have behaved if they were not being filmed, how could they account for the presence of the camera and crew and the modifications it caused?
2. On what basis can filmmakers justify their intrusion into the lives of the people they film?
3. Given the mandate of objectivity, how could the filmmaker convey his feelings as well as his understanding of the people he filmed and about the subject of the film?
4. What are the ideological implications of documentary film?
5. What obligations does the filmmaker have to his audience?[18]

While these questions are obviously not new—the social documentarians of the 1930s grappled with many of them—they have been raised again in the last ten years with a new urgency because of several factors: (1) the potential created by the new technology; (2) a general shift in our society toward self-awareness; (3) the influence of university education on young filmmakers (i.e., more documentarians received social science training); and (4) the effect of television news and documentary.

The desire to explore the capacities of this equipment and the self-awareness it produced created a need for new methods and forms of expression. Feeling equally uncomfortable with self-referentiality (where the self becomes submerged into metaphor) and with the apparent impersonality of traditional documentary (where the expression of self is deemed improper), some filmmakers found new ways to explore themselves, their world, and in a very real sense, cinema itself. They have confronted these questions by exposing themselves in the same way they expose others. One particular manifestation—the development of nonfiction films dealing with the filmmaker's own family and their immediate world—seems to represent a nonfiction genre which fits neither the traditional definition of the documentary nor the personal art film. In fact, these films violate canons of both genres.

The documentary film was founded on the Western middle-class need to explore, document, explain, understand, and hence symbolically control the world. It has been what "we" do to "them." "They" in this case are usually the poor, the powerless, the disadvantaged, and the politically suppressed and oppressed. Documentary films dealing with the rich and powerful or even the middle class are as sparse as are social science studies of these people. The documentary film has not been a place where people explored themselves or their own culture.

To find this subject matter one must look at the experimental, avant-garde filmmakers or at the home movie. In fact, film artists like Jonas Mekas in the treatment of his life entitled *Notes, Diaries, and Sketches* and Stan Brakhage in

Window Water Baby Moving have developed a deliberate aesthetic from the conventions of the home movie in much the same way as Lee Friedlander and Diane Arbus created a snapshot aesthetic in art photography.

Until recently the division was relatively clear. If you wanted to make films about people exotic to your own experience you made documentaries, and if you wished to explore yourself, your feelings, and the known world around you, you made personal art films. Recently a number of films have appeared which confuse this taxonomy. They are films that deal with the filmmaker's family and culture. In subject matter they violate the norms of traditional documentary in that they overtly deal in an involved way with a personal interest of the filmmaker. Because many of these filmmakers come from a documentary tradition, they do not employ the conventions of the personal art film; rather, they use a documentary style. In other words, they have the look of a documentary even though the subject matter is exotic to the genre. Examples of these films would include Jerome Hill's autobiography *Portrait*, Miriam Weinstein's *Living with Peter*, Amalie Rothschild's *Nana, Mom, and Me*, and Jeff Kreines's *The Plaint of Steve Kreines as Told by His Younger Brother Jeff*.

These filmmakers have created an autobiographical and family genre which cannot be comfortably fit into either the art film or the documentary. This creation, which employs elements from both genres, has the effect of making us self-conscious about our expectations. In addition, these films are clearly self-consciously produced and often quite overtly reflexive.

While it is obviously impossible to reveal the producer and not the process, it is possible to concentrate on one and only incidentally deal with the other. Most of these filmmakers share with Rouch a primary concern with self as maker and person and make that quest dominate their films.

It is in other types of films that we see a concern with the revelation of process emerge. This interest seems to come from two main sources: (1) politically committed filmmakers who, like Vertov and Godard, are interested in the ideological implications of film form—for example, David Rothberg's *My Friend Vince*; and (2) filmmakers who seek validation for their work within social science and who, consequently, feel the need to articulate and justify their methodologies—for example, Tim Asch's *Ax Fight*.

Finally, there are a number of documentaries which contain reflexive elements which appear to be present through accident rather than design. Direct-cinema films, such as Pennebaker's *Don't Look Back* and the Canadian Film Board's *Lonely Boy*, are filled with what were considered at the time to be "accidents"—that is, shots which were out of focus, shots where the mike and/or sound person appeared in the frame, etc. Very soon these "accidents" became signs of direct-cinema style, an indication that the director did not control the event he was recording. Audiences appeared to believe in them so much as a validating device that fiction-filmmakers who wished to increase verisimilitude in their films began to employ such direct-cinema signs as camera jiggle, graininess, and bad focus—for example, John Cassavetes's *Faces* or the battle scenes in Kubrick's *Dr. Strangelove*. In addition to verifying the "uncontrolled" aesthetic of direct cinema as a recorder of actuality these elements served to remind audiences of the process of filmmaking and, of course, the presence of the film crew.[19]

Other films such as Mike Rubbo's *Sad Song of Yellow Skin* and *Waiting for Fidel* and the Maysles brothers' *Grey Gardens* contain interactions between the subject and crew and other "backstage" behaviors which provide audiences with information about the producers and process.

It would appear that these apparently reflexive elements are again an accident of the moment: an unexpected turn of events during the shooting rather than the result of deliberate pre-production planning. What is interesting and does represent a departure from documentary conventions is that these "accidents" are allowed to remain in the final version of the film. It seems that these filmmakers acquired footage which had a particular "look" and which could not be cut in traditional ways. I would argue that it was primarily a professional need for a finished product rather than an interest in the question of reflexivity that motivated them to include those elements which cause these films to appear reflexive. For example, "big" Edie and "little" Edie Beale would not ignore the presence of the camera and crew, that is, learn to behave as "proper" subjects of a documentary film. In spite of this situation (or possibly because of it), the Maysles brothers decided to continue and make *Grey Gardens* even though it has a "look" which is different from their other films. In one sense, the filmmakers were allowing the circumstances of the shooting to dictate the form of the film, which consequently revealed the process and producer.

In contrast to these films of "accidental" reflexivity, there does exist a project which was designed at the outset to explore the consequences of documentary and ethnographic reflexivity. To my knowledge it is the first American film to continue the explorations of Rouch and Vertov. Hubert Smith, a filmmaker, and Malcolm Shuman, an anthropologist, are presently in the field filming an ethnography of some Mexican Indians. According to their proposal, "The principal strategy to be undertaken by this project is to invest ethnographic material in film with additional self-conscious components—the field investigators, their actions, personalities, methods, and their dealings with an advisory panel of colleagues."[20] They intend to accomplish this task by: (1) filming the Indians in a context that includes the observers; (2) filming the field team and the Indians in mutual socialization; and (3) filming the field team as they interact with each other and with the advisory panel.[21]

In addition to the films they produce, they will provide "a written body of field-related methods for investing nonfiction films with internal self-conscious statements of procedure."[22] I mention Smith's project now, even though it is incomplete and its significance is difficult to assess, because it represents a step toward a truly reflexive documentary cinema. Whatever else these films may be, they will have been intentionally reflexive from their inception. They will provide us with a chance to compare "accidental" and "deliberate" documentary reflexivity.

One could argue that the idea of "accidental" reflexiveness is a contradiction in terms and that reflexivity depends on intentionality and deliberateness. In fact, a number of the arguments presented here appear contradictory.

On the one hand, I have generated a definition of reflexiveness which situates some recent documentary films within a tradition in the visual arts, a tradition in which the producer is publicly concerned with the relationship among self, process, and product. In addition, I have tried to show how these concerns have been transformed by a general increase in public self-awareness and by the technological changes that occurred in filmmaking in the 1960s.

At the same time I have said that most documentary reflexiveness has been more accidental than deliberate. In effect, I have been arguing that some documentary filmmakers have used reflexive elements in their films (or at least have been regarded by some audiences as being reflexive) without really intending to do so, or at least without examining the implications. Further, I would argue that based on my examination of these films, on published interviews with the filmmakers, and on personal conversations and correspondence, these filmmakers appear to lack a sufficiently sophisticated philosophical, moral, aesthetic, or scientific motivation for a rigorous exploration of the consequences of reflexivity for documentary cinema. They seem oblivious to the fact that reflexivity has been explored by social scientists and other scholars for some time and that there is an extensive literature.[23] As a consequence, some of the films mentioned above which contain these "accidentally" reflexive elements are regarded as narcissistic, superficial, self-indulgent, or appealing to an elite in-group.

The contradiction can be phrased in the form of a question: Why haven't more documentary filmmakers explored the implications of reflexivity, when reflexive elements crop up in their films? To adequately explore this question would require a lengthy discussion of complicated issues such as the cultural role of the documentary or the adequacy of the concepts of objectivity and subjectivity for the documentary, and so forth. However, I would like to present what I believe to be the kernel of the issue.

To be reflexive is to reveal that films—all films, whether they are labeled fiction, documentary, or art—are created, structured articulations of the filmmaker and not authentic, truthful, objective records. Sooner or later the documentarian is going to have to face the possibility of assuming the socially diminished role of interpreter of the world, of no longer being regarded as an objective recorder of reality. If this is the case, then it is not too difficult to see why these filmmakers are reluctant to explore the idea.

My intention here was to restrain my obvious partisanship. Clearly, I have failed to do so. I should now like to conclude by suggesting that documentary filmmakers have a social obligation to *not* be objective. The concept of objectivity, inappropriately borrowed from the natural sciences, has little support from the social sciences: both social scientists and documentary filmmakers are interpreters of the world. As Sue Ellen Jacobs has put it, "Perhaps the best thing we can learn from anthropological writings [and I would add films and photographs] is how people who call themselves 'anthropologists' see the world of others."[24] To present ourselves and our products as anything else is to foster a dangerous false consciousness on the part of our audiences.

Reflexivity offers us a means whereby we can instruct our audiences to understand the process of producing statements about the world. "We study man, that is, we reflect on ourselves studying others, because we must, because man in civilization is the problem."[25]

Notes

1   Johannes Fabian, "Language, History, and Anthropology," *Journal of the Philosophy of the Social Sciences* 1 (1971): 1947.

2   Erving Goffman, *The Presentation of Self in Everyday Life* (Garden City, N.Y.: Doubleday, 1959).

3   In commenting on the manuscript of this paper, Gaye Tuchman made the following observation, which I believe to be both relevant and important to the distinction that I am trying to make between autobiography and reflexivity: "Autobiography may also be naively self-conscious. That is, autobiography is one's purposive ordering of one's life to create coherence. It assumes coherence and so necessarily eliminates that which cannot be ordered and of which the autobiographer might not even be aware. For, perhaps, we can only perceive those amorphous phenomena which we are ultimately capable of classifying and ordering. Perhaps, then, reflexive self-consciousness is not merely autobiography, but the ability to see ourselves as others see us—as co-present subject and object, as perceiving subject and the simultaneous object of others' perceptions. Such self-consciousness necessarily entails a simultaneous self-involvedness and self-estrangement; a standing outside of oneself in a way that is foreign to the non-reflexive everyday self."

4   See Barbara Babcock, "Reflexivity: Definitions and Discriminations," unpublished paper delivered at the annual meeting of the American Anthropological Association, Washington, D.C., 1977.

5   Sol Worth and Larry Gross, "Symbolic Strategies," *Journal of Communication* 24 (Winter 1974): 27–39.

6   Gunther Stent, "Limits to the Scientific Understanding of Man," *Science* 187 (1975): 1052–7.

7   I am using the term *alienate* here in the sense that Brecht used it—that is, as the breaking of the suspension of disbelief during a performance. See *Brecht on Theatre*, trans. John Willet (New York: Hill and Wang, 1964).

8   It is curious that the concern with form and structure which has dominated the works of some modernist writers, painters, musicians, and filmmakers, and of scientists from physicists to anthropologists, has not interested many documentarians. For example, I know of no documentary filmmakers who deliberately choose uninteresting and trivial subject matter in order to be able to concentrate on the significance of formal and structural elements in the documentary.

9   Basil Wright, "Land Without Bread and Spanish Earth," in *The Documentary Tradition*, ed. Lewis Jacobs (New York: Hopkinson and Blake, 1971), p. 146.

10 Roy Armes thinks that it was Buñuel (see Armes, *Film and Reality* [New York: Pelican, 1974], p. 189): "*Land Without Bread* is also remarkable in the way it anticipates later modernist cinema by its triple impact. It combines devastating images of poverty, starvation and idiocy with a dry matter of fact commentary and a musical score filled with romantic idealism." Barsam, however, seems to disagree (see his *Non-Fiction Film* [New York: Dutton, 1973], p. 83): "As an information film, even a travel film (but hardly one designed to promote tourism), *Las hurdes* is an effective and disturbing record of poverty and neglect; but as a social document it is awkward and as mute as a faded poster despite its tragic theme."

11 Jeanne Allen, "Self-Reflexivity and the Documentary Film," *Ciné-Tracts* 1 (Summer 1977): 37–43.

12 William Siska, "Metacinema: A Modern Necessity," unpublished paper delivered at the annual meeting of the Society for Cinema Studies, Evanston, Illinois, 1977. The quote is from p. 3.

13 I am excluding from consideration illustrated-lecture and adventurer/travelogue films. These cinematic forms predate the documentary. In fact, the illustrated-lecture film finds its origins in the lantern-slide lecture of the early nineteenth century. They constitute an unstudied form of the cinema and have been overlooked by most historians of documentary film. However, they do contain the earliest evidence of reflexive elements in nonfiction film. The makers frequently employ first-person narration to describe themselves as authors and the process they used to make the film. In many cases, these films are primarily about the making of the film and thereby cause the films themselves to become the object of the audience's attention. However, like the traditional fiction films about movies and moviemakers, the apparent reflexiveness of these films is partially based on the assumed difficulties of production and the heroic acts performed by the makers in the process of getting the footage. These films do not lead viewers to a sophisticated understanding of film as communication; rather, they cause them to continue to marvel at the mysterious wonders of the intrepid adventurer-filmmakers.

14 See "The Vertov Papers," *Film Comment* 8 (Spring 1972): 46–51.

15 See Worth and Gross, "Symbolic Strategies."

16 See Jean Rouch, "The Camera and the Man," *Studies in the Anthropology of Visual Communication* 1 (1974): 37–44.

17 "With the development of lightweight equipment and the growth of an aesthetic of direct cinema, the ethical problem of the relationship of filmmakers to the people in their films became more amorphous. . . . Regardless of whether consent is flawed on such grounds as intimidation or deceit, a fundamental ethical difficulty in direct cinema is that when we use people in a sequence we put them at risk without sufficiently informing them of potential hazards" (Calvin Pryluck, "Ultimately We Are All Outsiders: The Ethics of Documentary Filming," *Journal of the University Film Association* 28 [Winter 1976]: 21–9; the quotations are from pp. 21 and 29).

18 James M. Linton, "The Moral Dimension in Documentary," *Journal of the University Film Association* 28 (Spring 1976): 17–22.

19 See Stephen Mamber, *Cinéma Vérité in America: Studies in Uncontrolled Documentary* (Cambridge, Mass.: MIT Press, 1974).

20 Hubert Smith, "Contemporary Yucatec Maya Allegory Through a Self-conscious Approach to Ethnography and Ethnographic Film," a proposal submitted to the National Endowment for the Humanities.

21 The advising panel consists of four specialists in Indian anthropology (one member is Indian by birth and an anthropologist by profession), three visual anthropologists, and a philosopher of social science.

22 Smith proposal, cited n. 20.

23 For example, see Bob Scholte, "Toward a Reflexive and Critical Anthropology," in Dell Hymes, ed., *Reinventing Anthropology* (New York: Random House, 1972), pp. 430–58.

24 Quoted in Simeon W. Chilungi, "Issues in the Ethics of Research Method: An Interpretation of the Anglo-American Perspective," *Current Anthropology* 17 (1976): 469.

25 Stanley Diamond, "Anthropology in Question," in Hymes, ed., *Reinventing Anthropology*, pp. 401–29; the quotation is from p. 408.

3

Television, Documentary and the Category of the Aesthetic

John Corner

The idea of the aesthetic has had a troubled and contradictory history in media inquiry, in ways that have impacted upon the study of television. It has been seen both as a blocking category and a category blocked.[1] The literature has variously placed it as a source of theoretical displacement and mystification yet also as an area of neglect and foreclosure. To put it more expansively, detailed attention to the 'art properties' of television has been seen to waste investigative time that might more valuably be spent on questions of institution, practice, thematic content and consumption, on the framing political and cultural economies and processes within which programmes are produced and circulated. On the other hand, some have clearly thought that emphasis on precisely such matters has produced accounts too inert to register properly the imaginative densities and energies of the programmes themselves, those little power-houses of meaning and value arguably holding a degree of creative mystery even in their most banal modes.[2]

This is more than just the old debate about where to position 'the text' in any given piece of study. For textual analysis can take a number of forms, one of which is a tight mix of cognitive and linguistic concerns in which 'art properties' either do not get a look in at all or appear principally as devices of concealment and manipulation.

The category of aesthetics points us towards the organisation of creative works, the experiences they produce (or, to signal a key crux, that audiences derive from them) and the modes of analysis and theory that can be used in investigation. All three interests interconnect, clearly, but usage of the term sometimes masks priorities and even exclusions. In this short commentary, I want to explore some arguments concerning the relation of aesthetic issues to television's documentary programming bearing in mind all three points of reference. Quite what counts as 'documentary' nowadays, given the hectic generic mutations that have occurred in television's factual output, has been an issue of recent dispute, raising interesting ques-

tions of programme claim and programme value as well of production practice and form.[3]

To talk of the aesthetic in relation to television documentary opens the
much broader question of how ideas of the aesthetic might bear on the
medium itself. There has been a tendency to regard television as an aesthetically rather impoverished medium, too extensively dispersed into industrial
routine on the one side and into everyday life and casual 'distraction' from it
on the other to offer a great deal by way of richness and depth in its own
'works'. The suggestion is that the medium has compensated for this symbolic
deficit by exploiting its realist/relay functions and its potential for real or simulated 'liveness', although exceptions to this easy mutuality with the mundane
are acknowledged.

Of course, a good deal of non-fictional television is not particularly interested in *offering* itself as an aesthetic experience anyway. That is to say it is not
concerned to promote an appreciative sense of its creative crafting in the audience. Strength of content, including that of on-screen activity, is seen to be
enough. Clearly, we would not want to make questions of intentions a firm criterion here—programmes can be judged to have aesthetic organisation and
aesthetic effects without their producers acknowledging this and even when
they explicitly deny it and when audiences seem not aware of it. But it is helpful
to make a differentiation between work that has an overt aesthetic and that in
which it is largely implicit, if sometimes this can only be done with difficulty.

Here, documentary occupies an interesting position in the television spectrum, some of it being extremely self-conscious and aesthetically ambitious
(convergent in this respect with 'high-end drama'), some of it committed to
reportorial or observational naturalisms that make it very close to news in discursive character. Across its history both in film and television, work within
documentary has displayed varied and sometimes rather contradictory attitudes towards what degree of freedom and prominence its aesthetic dimension
should enjoy. At times working with a foregrounded aesthetics (as in classic
1930s texts such as *Coalface, Song of Ceylon* and *Listen to Britain*) in which the
imaginative appeal of the formal design (visual and aural) is part of the 'offer',
it has worked with a marginalised or even suppressed and denied aesthetics in
an attempt to make its referentiality, its documentation, the more direct. The
classic reportage of *Housing Problems* (1935), with its straight-to-camera testimony by people caught up within the 'problem' and its directness in the pic-
turing of bad conditions and attempts at improvement, is an early example
here. Grierson himself can be seen to veer around a good deal on the balance
and priorities to be struck, being alert both to the excitement and appeal of cinematic art but also to the requirement to perform a 'sociological' task.[4]

A gap opens up here between producers, audiences and critics, reflecting in
part the three points of reference that I suggested configured the very idea of

aesthetics. Those involved in documentary production may routinely watch all documentary material, including that in which the topic itself is found of personal interest, with a framing concern for artefactual qualities—for how imaginative, well-crafted or 'beautiful' the documentary work itself is. Audiences, in a way that contrasts with their response to drama, are likely to find these concerns a secondary matter at best, possibly ones of which they are only conscious when something is going wrong (e.g. an editing rhythm that irritates, problems with the use of music, traits of presenter address). Critics and scholars replicate in part the preoccupations of producers, involving a concern for patterns and conventions, albeit within different frames of reference and for their own professional purposes. In tracing any specific medium or generic aesthetics, however, the kind of experience routinely had by intended audiences must not be neglected or displaced (painting, cinema, theatre, music and literature variously pose this awkward issue, of the 'viewer', 'reader' or 'listener' *as well as* 'the critic', to their respective bodies of criticism).

I think we can broadly distinguish between what could be called 'thick text' and 'thin text' documentaries in terms of the density and transformative scale of their mediations. It is not surprising that film and television studies has found it easier to develop critical accounts of the former broad category. Works here follow more closely the narrative, scopic and aural protocols of fiction and of 'art film'; various stylings of the world are offered for the viewer to experience as kinds of imaginative performance, however much the world is also referenced through them. Moreover, their manifest attractions are often accompanied by the deeper pressures and appeals they apply to the unconscious and to desiring fantasy. They may generate lively critical disagreement, since their values and arguments may often be implicit and perhaps sometimes show inconsistency or tension. They may reward repeat viewings in a way that finally has little to do with the extractable knowledge they convey. The documentary format that gets closest to fiction, drama-documentary (although one might regard it as a fiction format getting close to documentary), generates this aesthetic-critical response in a most obvious manner, as do works whose symbolic emphasis places them, for some critics, in the category of 'poetic documentary'.[5] Among other things, this might be to confirm the general idea that 'art values' will be most pronounced in communications that are able to mark off a degree of separateness from the mundane and directly worldly, that are able both to exercise and to signal their capacities for transformation and for play. In his original and suggestive survey of the broader rhetorics of documentary form, Michael Renov cites Hans Richter on the hardening off of this attitude in post-eighteenth-century western art more generally: 'The accent shifted, for a "beautiful" image could not normally be obtained *except at the expense of its closeness to reality*' [orig. emph.].[6]

We might compare this kind of situation with, say, an edition of a current-affairs series, involving reporter exposition throughout, or a piece organised according to current docu-soap recipes, with observation of routine, institutional action overlaid by commentary and interspersed with interview sequences. While there is no difficulty in identifying features of formal construction in such programmes, matters of visual and linguistic organisation which bear on the way they work, there may be comparatively little by way of imaginative thrill, symbolic impact or thematic dissonance in the representational practice itself to excite critical engagement. What *can* be said by way of critical comment is much more likely to take the form of the exposure of implicit textual strategies rather than the appreciation of overt textual display and performance. Such texts will not usually reward repeat viewings unless these are done within the frame either of a 'content' value not exhausted by initial viewing or of professional or academic analysis.[7]

It may be noted how much of the above discussion bears on questions of documentary values. The default assumption is that such values inhere largely in the character of the knowledge that a documentary generates (most bluntly, its 'truth' rating), whether this is primarily propositional or observational in mode. The only way that a documentary can acquire value with some independence from its content is, of course, by marking its own aesthetic status and preferably by doing this in a way that is registered in routine viewing, not just in the vocabularies of specialist critical appraisal. However, such marking may be in tension with a certain strand of 'honest-to-goodness' documentary protocol, as Bill Nichols indicates when he cites as being many a director's motto the statement 'A good documentary stimulates discussion about its subject, not itself.'[8]

Recognising, then, the significance of this aesthetic spectrum for documentary work and for documentary studies, I want now to look more closely at the elements out of which it is constituted. What can be said by way of outlining a typology of documentary aesthetics?

Documentary Aesthetics: A Typology

I have already noted that to talk of an aesthetics requires reference to three key planes—that of artefactual organisation (including its nature as a product of *practice*), that of audience experience and that of theoretical and analytical inquiry. It is the interplay of artefactual design and subjectivity that generates the aesthetic experience and it is important to stop this being collapsed simply into 'form' on one side or 'pleasure' on the other. Pleasurable feeling is certainly a part of much aesthetic experience but a more inclusive attention to its character as a kind of imaginative event is necessary.

The aesthetics of documentary can, I think, be regarded under three broad headings—pictorial, aural and narratological.

Pictorial

The pictorialism of documentary is usefully considered in relation to the long-standing debate about the aesthetics of photography. Once again, the creative tension between reference and artefact is apparent. There is however a certain degree of opacity, a denial of the 'look through' at the world, which photography designed for the gallery can press beyond but which documentary cannot without causing problems of self-identity (which it sometimes may want to do, allowing a primary reading as 'video art', for instance). Documentary portrayal is often drawn to a literalism of representation, its compositions, framings, angles, lighting, colourings and movements designed to engage a kind of unselfconscious, realist assent, although its referentiality is always *performed through style*, however quietly. An apparent absence of style (a kind of 'degree zero' television, in Barthes' terms) constitutes at least part of the conventional grounds of trust and credibility. This has posed a problem more acute for contemporary television documentary than it was for documentary in the 1930s, its social claims-making still set accommodatingly within the broader terms of a young and experimental cinema. But what many television documentarists have rediscovered is the impact and attractiveness of the picture not simply to be *looked through* but also *looked at*.[9] The experience of *looking at* documentary images often combines an aesthetic registration of the qualities of the depiction itself with that of certain, visual properties of the things depicted (their shapes, colours, proportions and spatial relations—as in landscapes, buildings, objects). It may also involve indirect engagement with the subject through the use of metaphor, which usually requires itself to be read as a discourse about the world rather than a depiction of it (a difference which, in different ways, is a recurring theme in Nichols' writing).

Looking at can be seen as one kind of what Niklas Luhmann, in his broad and suggestive review of the discourses of art, terms 'second order observations'.[10] These are 'observations of observations' and their effect is to frame parts of the world in such a way as to transform them into 'imaginary space' without necessarily thereby losing an engagement with 'world'. Luhmann's full account is complex and certainly not neatly transferable to the documentary instance, but I use it here suggestively and will return to it below.

In powerful combination with the pictorial qualities of the documentary image, with its organisation of screen space into a plane both of reference and of formal design, are its kinetic properties. These are in many respects in line with those of cinematic fiction, where a considerable body of scholarship has explored how kinetics can derive from the movement of things within the shot, the movement of the camera during the shot or, more broadly, the temporal organisation of continuity and change introduced by editing. In documentary, the first two of these produce different kinds of scopic satisfaction, respectively referential and pictorial in their grounding. The second of them, the shifting perception brought about by camera movement (its glides, its drifts, its swoops, its trackings, its movements across documented space, its shiftings of the relationships of distance and proximity) is one of the most familiar of aesthetic tropes in documentary practice. Its fusing of the reality of world with the motivation of imaginative design is often stimulating in its bringing together of recognition with kinds of 'making strange' or, less radically, what we might just call 're-seeing'. Here, the connections made between our apprehension of the physical realities shown and the subjective (affective, conceptual or propositional) world that also forms the documentary topic are significant. Feeling and ideas become condensed upon objects, bodies and places, modified by the physical at the same time as the physical itself is perceived within the developing thematics. Such a dialectics, at once sensual and intellectual, referentially committed yet often possessed of a dreamlike potential for the indirectly suggestive and associative, is central to documentary as an aesthetic project. It is often a factor in producing what Vivian Sobchack has called 'the charge of the real' as it appears on the screen.[11] Whatever core this has in the naturalistic co-ordinates of documentarism, it can also be extensively theatricalised too (a 'charged real', so to speak). It can work through a pictorial authorship comparable with that which carries the denser, latent and more volatile significances of fiction. (An imagined example: an aerial shot shows a car following a deserted coast road as dawn begins to break; it turns off to enter a silent village. The musical soundtrack is bleak and broody. Is this the start of a thriller? No, it's the opening to a programme on GM agriculture just before the commentary starts.)

The third level of kinetics, the much-discussed practices of editing, introduces through its modes of linkage and disjunction the broad range of possibilities for organising time, theme, space and style in relation to overall documentary design. In doing so, it necessarily enhances and strengthens aesthetic elements at the local level in the management of seeing, knowing and feeling.

I think it is worth noting here how many documentaries attempt to retain referential integrity and yet generate aesthetic value by what we can call an *intermittent aesthetics*. Such a mode engages a viewing subjectivity of 'looking through' for extensive sequences, projecting a relative transparency in the depiction (and bringing about what Luhmann would see as a kind of 'first-order observation'). Interview, commentary voice-over and archive film, for instance, are likely to establish and sustain this. At other points, however, a shift towards a more opaque representation is made, the aesthetic codings becoming thicker and perhaps more obvious, temporarily transferring viewers into a deeper imaginative space (and perhaps also further into *themselves* too) without breaking engagement with theme. More attention to some of the precise techniques and patterns involved, across different kinds of production, would be rewarding. John Caldwell's remarks about the viewing subjectivities appropriate to the newer kinds of 'videographic' ways of working upon screen space are relevant here.[12] Moreover, it is quite likely that viewers will shift between primary orientations towards 'looking through' and 'looking at' independently of the 'intermittent aesthetics' of production design, although one would expect the latter to exert some cueing functions on the basic viewing frames deployed. It is worth remarking again that is in the combination of these frames, within different recipes and proportions, that the most interesting questions are posed. Any pure sense of 'looking through' reproduces the fallacy of transparent access, against which documentary studies has directed most of its critical energy, although a temporary sense of unmediated encounter continues to be a powerful and necessary feature of many documentary sequences. A pure commitment to 'looking at' blocks documentarist engagement, unless it occurs only as one element or moment in a larger referential design.[13]

Aural

The aesthetic (as distinct from cognitive) possibilities of sound in documentary are in most cases secondary to those of images and in some cases they are not significantly mobilised at all. However, what Barthes called the 'grain of the voice' (made distinctive by factors of, for instance, gender, age, class and geographical origin) can be a factor in the satisfaction we obtain from listening to speech, including that of documentary subjects themselves, and questions of speaking *style* are raised too. Different modes of the formal (e.g. commentaries working essentially as read prose, the speech following literary design) and informal (well-turned anecdotes, colloquial rhythms and diction) can all deliver a style-generated pleasure in listening not reducible to the cognitive. Their impact is, of course, quite often only achieved in combination with specific images and can only be adequately analysed as such (*that* phrasing or even word, or pause, across *that* shot). Here, again, is an aesthetic density that requires more attention, in its local achievement, than documentary analysis has often afforded it to date.

Perhaps the richest and most intriguing aural aesthetic in many documentaries, however, is that provided by music. Its regulation of our sense of place, time and mood as well as its use as punctuation within the documentary narrative system (bridgings; little closures and openings across scenes and episodes) is a regular cue to viewing subjectivity. Its effect is often to provide a (light and unobtrusive) aestheticised framing for scenes working strongly within the 'transparent' mode, although it is also used to accompany sequences of 'thicker' pictoralism too. Here, it may be intended to figure more fully in the consciousness of the viewer, the *resonances* of watching deepening with the direct infusion of feelings that music brings. Although scruples about the use of music exist in the broad area of journalistic documentaries (where it is seen to undercut cognitive integrity and fair appraisal) and in some observational formats (where its extra-diegetic character might risk reducing the power of the immediacy-effect), it is another area to which analysis could profitably give more attention.[14]

Narratological

Most documentary scholarship has acknowledged how narrative satisfactions are a property of nearly all formats, connecting with a broader aesthetics of time and of duration (with its vectors of becoming, of process and transition) that underlies, in different ways, the forms of television. They are particularly obvious in the fictional models of drama-documentary and the action-development structures of observational modes, including docu-soap recipes, but they are at work to varying degrees in the more reportorial and expositional programmes too. Alongside the function of voiced-over or presenter commentary (literally, story *telling*), it is clearly in the practices of editing that narrative design is realised. Stephen Heath and Gillian Skirrow usefully pointed to the 'little stories' out of which an ostensibly expositional documentary on truancy was made.[15] The excursions into story values and story pleasures were sometimes awkwardly related to the development of the official argument, suggesting a degree of production tension between the chosen theme for reportage and the imaginative possibilities to emerge from the case-studies selected to illustrate it.[16] Story formats in television documentary have undergone change and intensification in recent years as part of the requirement to increase viewing enjoyment within circumstances of stronger competition. Attention to their varieties and to the particular kinds of viewing experience they offer will need to be another feature in the development of documentary scholarship.

Aesthetics, Criticism and Documentary Studies

The aesthetic dimensions I have outlined above, merely gesturing towards three of the more obvious categories for attention, of course appear in different combinations and strengths, together with other elements of creative, transforming work, across the full range and history of documentary. In Britain, their appearance, say, in Harry Watt and Basil Wright's 1936 classic about the journey of the mail train from London to Scotland (*Night Mail*, GPO Films) will be different from that in Denis Mitchell's Prix Italia winning film about working-class life in Northern towns (*Morning in the Streets*, BBC, 1959), Michael Grigsby's exploration of different communities under the pressure of political and economic change in 1980s Britain (*Living On the Edge*, Central Television, 1987) or Roger Graef's hugely influential observational series on the operation of the police service (*Police*, BBC, 1982). These will then be in various contrasting and comparative relations with current productions. In the United States, one could range, just for an example, across from the resonant evocations of Lorentz's 1937 film about the management of economic and natural forces in the Mississippi region, *The River* (FSA), its Virgil Thomson score organising the emotional impact, to Connie Field's comic as well as critical use of archival material alongside interviews in *The Life and Times of Rosie the Riveter* (Clarity Productions, 1980), across to the direct cinema applications of Craig Gilbert's ground-breaking series, *An American Family* (NET/PBS 1973). One again, the connections, never strictly chronological, can be made to contemporary work, of which Michael Moore's *Bowling for Columbine* (DogEatDog, 2002) is a striking current example.

I have suggested that, in studying documentary aesthetics, we need to keep in mind the way in which what is at issue interconnects across artefactual organisation, the viewing experience and, at some remove from these, the categories that an analysis needs to understand both. The aesthetically generative role of practice requires consistent recognition too, however difficult this might be to document independently. In recent writing, Georgina Born has eloquently made the case for taking the 'production aesthetics' of television seriously, as part of a more general claim for a non-reductive sociology of art.[17]

In posing the question of how to engage further with television's documentary aesthetics, the notion of 'criticism' remains central if not sufficient. Criticism, unlike linguistics, sociology, political economy or psychology, typically takes its initial ground in a declared subjective experiencing. How does the programme work? What engages and satisfies, what does not? Fine Art, theatre, literature, dance and cinema all show different models of critical practice in which this subjective experience is then made the basis for a more technical, more general and perhaps more socially diagnostic assessment. The dangers of over-categoric approaches are clear enough, but television scholarship, including that on documentary, needs to foster the practice of criticism alongside its other analytic tools and its more general theoretical concerns.[18] A vigorous documentary criticism would help to keep aesthetic issues contentiously in view when other perspectives and priorities show their tendency to hide, displace or reduce them. By taking its bearings from 'inside' the documentary experience, with its distinctive mix of objective and subjective dynamics, criticism's value for understanding lies not in contesting the more externalist approaches to explanation but in keeping up a reflexive commentary on some of the most important things to be explained.

Notes

This chapter is lightly revised from its appearance in *Screen* 44, no.1 and I thank Jackie Stacey and Karen Lury for their comments.

1   Influential examples of the former position include the work of Pierre Bourdieu, for instance, *Distinction*, trans. Richard Nice (London: Routledge, 1986) and Terry Eagleton, in *The Ideology of the Aesthetic* (Oxford: Blackwell, 1990). In both cases, the authors are partly opposing themselves to a dominant, inflexible and categorical 'high aesthetic' that they see to have governed discussion of quality in the areas they survey and to have ignored the material conditions of the artistic sphere.

2   Two recent pieces in *Screen* which consider the more general problem in ways that make contact with ideas of the aesthetic are Simon Frith, 'The black box: the value of television and the state of television research', *Screen* 41, no. 1 (2000), pp. 33–50 and Georgina Born, 'Inside television: television studies and the sociology of culture', *Screen* 41, no. 4, (2001), pp. 404–24. See also the useful consideration of the aesthetic offered in Jason Jacobs, 'Issues of judgement and value in television studies', *International Journal of Cultural Studies* 4, no. 4, pp. 427–47.

3   Among the range of accounts, Jon Dovey, *Freakshow: First Person Media and Factual Television* (London: Pluto, 2000) is the most radical and comprehensive.

4   Several of the essays in Forsyth Hardy (ed.), *Grierson on Documentary* (London: Faber, 1979) show the varying emphases, sometimes in the same piece.

5   A number of scholars use this category to indicate documentaries that place a primary emphasis on their artefactual qualities and the appreciation of this by the audience. See, for instance, the discussion in Carl Plantinga, *Rhetoric and Representation in Non-Fiction Film* (Cambridge: Cambridge University Press, 1997), especially chapter 9. In his recent *Introduction to Documentary* (Bloomington and Indianapolis: Indiana University Press) Bill Nichols offers a helpful outline of the 'Poetic Mode' as part of chapter 6. This mode had not previously figured so strongly in Nichols' modal scheme, so its appearance here is interesting.

6   Michael Renov, 'Towards a poetics of documentary', in Michael Renov (ed.), *Theorizing Documentary* (London and New York: Routledge, 1993), p. 25. The reference is to Hans Richter, *The Struggle For The Film*, trans. Ben Brewster (New York: St Martin's Press, 1986).

7   Aesthetics make contact with the ethics and politics of viewing here. Depending on the subject, repeat viewing of a documentary primarily to gain satisfaction from its depictive styling raises questions about the cultural appropriation of portrayal and the evasion of reference.

8   Bill Nichols, *Representing Reality* (Bloomington and Indianapolis: Indiana University Press), p. x. The statement is a usefully provocative one, denying too easy an answer, and I have employed it frequently with students, including as an essay or even an examination question, to good effect.

9   These approximating terms are generally suggestive about the conditions of documentary organisation and viewing. Vivian Sobchack brings them into her thoughtful essay, 'Towards a phenomenology of nonfictional film experience', in

Jane Gaines and Michael Renov (eds.), *Collecting Visible Evidence* (Minneapolis: University of Minnesota Press, 1999), pp. 241–54. Sobchack draws suggestively on the relatively neglected ideas about film experience of the Belgian psychologist Jean-Pierre Meunier, concerning the different kinds of consciousness engaged in acts of viewing.

10   Niklas Luhmann, *Art as a Social System* (Stanford: Stanford University Press, 2000). The relevant discussion is in chapter 2.

11   Sobchack, 'Towards a phenomenology', p. 253.

12   John T. Caldwell, *Televisuality* (New Brunswick, NJ: Rutgers University Press, 1995). The discussion of documentary occurs in chapter 8. In what amounts to a pathology of some current tendencies in America, Caldwell identifies a degree of opaque styling, an intensified mode of 'looking at', whose effect is to render the viewing experience 'a numbed, alienated trance'.

13   Murray Smith offers an illuminating example of one form of the combination in the course of an essay on the aesthetics of narrative. Taking a scene from Patrick Keiller's film *London* (1993), a mix of fictional and factual elements, he discusses how portrayal of damage to City of London buildings following the IRA bombings of 1992 works not only as abstract composition and political reference but principally in the combination of the two, each through the other. Murray Smith, 'Aesthetics and the rhetorical power of narrative', in Ib Bondebjerg (ed.), *Moving Images, Culture and the Mind* (Luton: Luton University Press, 2000), pp. 157–66.

14   I have tried to take this further in John Corner, 'Sounds real: music and documentary', *Popular Music* 21, no. 3 (2002).

15   Stephen Heath and Gillian Skirrow, 'Television: a world in action', *Screen* 18, no. 2 (1977), pp. 7–59.

16   These imaginative possibilities are fully confirmed in a remarkable letter to *Screen* by the person who actually edited the material, Dai Vaughan, himself subsequently a writer on documentary topics. He notes among things that the way in which a particular sequence (showing a boy with an air-rifle) was shot and cut 'has a great deal to do with the conventions within which sequences of hunting, and in particular of ambush, are traditionally presented in fictional cinema'. See Vaughan, 'Correspondence', *Screen* 18, no. 4 (1977), pp. 123–5.

17   A number of her papers and unpublished talks have explored this theme in original ways. Born, 'Inside television', n. 2 above, incorporates it within broader terms.

18   Here, I agree with the arguments about the need for renewal and re-orientation in the critical project put forward by Alan Durant, 'What future for interpretative work in film and media studies?', *Screen* 41, no. 1 (2000), pp. 7–17. Jason Jacobs also makes the case for greater clarity about the distinctive contribution of criticism in his 'Issues of judgement and value', n. 2 above.

4

Mirrors Without Memories: Truth, History, and the New Documentary

Linda Williams

The August 12th, 1990 Arts and Leisure section of the *New York Times* carried a lead article with a rather arresting photograph of Franklin Roosevelt flanked by Winston Churchill and Groucho Marx. Standing behind them was a taut-faced Sylvester Stallone in his Rambo garb. The photo illustrated the major point of the accompanying article by Andy Grundberg: that the photograph—and by implication the moving picture as well—is no longer, as Oliver Wendell Holmes once put it, a "mirror with a memory" illustrating the visual truth of objects, persons and events but a manipulated construction. In an era of electronic and computer-generated images, the camera, the article sensationally claims, "can lie."

In this photo, the anachronistic flattening out of historical referents, the trivialization of history itself, with the popular culture icons of Groucho and Rambo rubbing up against Roosevelt and Churchill, serves almost as a caricature of the state of representation some critics have chosen to call postmodern. In a key statement, Fredric Jameson has described the "cultural logic of postmodernism" as a "new depthlessness, which finds its prolongation both in contemporary 'theory' and in a whole new culture of the image or the simulacrum" (Jameson, 1984, 58). To Jameson, the effect of this image culture is a weakening of historicity. Lamenting the loss of the grand narratives of modernity, which he believes once made possible the political actions of individuals representing the interests of social classes, Jameson argues that it no longer seems possible to represent the "real" interests of a people or a class against the ultimate ground of social and economic determinations.

While not all theorists of postmodernity are as disturbed as Jameson by the apparent loss of the referent, by the undecidabilities of representation accompanied by an apparent paralysis of the will to change, many theorists do share a sense that the enlightenment projects of truth and reason are definitely over. And if representations, whether visual or verbal, no longer refer to a truth or referent "out there" as Trinh T. Minh-ha has put it, for us "in here" (Trinh, 83), then we seem to be plunged into a permanent state of the self-reflexive crisis of representation. What was once a "mirror with a memory" can now only reflect another mirror.

Perhaps because so much faith was once placed in the ability of the camera to reflect objective truths of some fundamental social referent—often construed by the socially relevant documentary film as records of injustice or exploitation of powerless common people—the loss of faith in the objectivity of the image seems to point, nihilistically, like the impossible memory of the meeting of the fictional Rambo and the real Roosevelt, to the brute and cynical disregard of ultimate truths.

Yet at the very same time, as any television viewer and moviegoer knows, we also exist in an era in which there is a remarkable hunger for documentary images of the real. These images proliferate in the *vérité* of the on-the-scene cops programs in which the camera eye merges with the eye of the law to observe what violence citizens do to one another. Violence becomes the very emblem of the real in these programs. Interestingly, violent trauma has become the emblem of the real in the new *vérité* genre of the independent amateur video, which, in the case of George Holliday's tape of the Rodney King beating by L.A. police, functioned to contradict the eye of the law and intervene in the "cops'" official version of King's arrest. This home video might be taken to represent the other side of the postmodern distrust of the image: here the camera tells the truth in a remarkable moment of *cinéma vérité* which then becomes valuable (though not conclusive) evidence in accusations against the L.A. Police Department's discriminatory violence against minority offenders.

The contradictions are rich: on the one hand the postmodern deluge of images seems to suggest that there can be no *a priori* truth of the referent to which the image refers; on the other hand, in this same deluge, it is still the moving image that has the power to move audiences to a new appreciation of previously unknown truth.

In a recent book on postwar West German cinema and its representations of that country's past, Anton Kaes has written that "[T]he sheer mass of historical images transmitted by today's media weakens the link between public memory and personal experience. The past is in danger of becoming a rapidly expanding collection of images, easily retrievable but isolated from time and space, available in an eternal present by pushing a button on the remote control. History thus returns forever—as film" (Kaes, 198). Recently, the example of history that has been most insistently returning "as film" to American viewers is the assassination of John F. Kennedy as simulated by film-maker Oliver Stone.

Stone's *JFK* might seem a good example of Jameson's and Kaes's worst-case scenarios of the ultimate loss of historical truth amid the postmodern hall of mirrors. While laudably obsessed with exposing the manifest contradictions of the Warren Commission's official version of the Kennedy assassination, Stone's film has been severely criticized for constructing a "countermyth" to the Warren Commission's explanation of what happened. Indeed, Stone's images offer a kind of tragic counterpart to the comic mélange of the *New York Times* photo of Groucho and Roosevelt. Integrating his own reconstruction of the assassination with the famous Zapruder film, whose "objective" reflection of the event is offered as the narrative (if not the legal) clincher in Jim Garrison's argument against the lone assassin theory, Stone mixes Zapruder's real *vérité* with his own simulated *vérité* to construct a grandiose paranoid countermyth of a vast conspiracy by Lyndon Johnson, the C.I.A., and the Joint Chiefs of Staff to carry out a coup d'état. With little hard evidence to back him up, Stone would seem to be a perfect symptom of a postmodern negativity and nihilism towards truth, as if to say: "We know the Warren Commission made up a story, well, here's another even more dramatic and entertaining story. Since we can't know the truth, let's make up a grand paranoid fiction."

It is not my purpose here to attack Oliver Stone's remarkably effective deployment of paranoia and megalomania; the press has already done a thorough job of debunking his unlikely fiction of a Kennedy who was about to end the Cold War and withdraw from Vietnam.[1] What interests me however, is the positive side of this megalomania: Stone's belief that it is possible to intervene in the process by which truth is constructed; his very real accomplishment in shaking up public perception of an official truth that closed down, rather than opened up, investigation; his acute awareness of how images enter into the production of knowledge. However much Stone may finally betray the spirit of his own investigation into the multiple, contingent and constructed nature of the representation of history by asking us to believe in too tidy a conspiracy, his *JFK* needs to be taken seriously for its renewal of interest in one of the major traumas of our country's past.

So rather than berate Stone, I would like to contrast this multimillion-dollar historical fiction film borrowing many aspects of the form of documentary to what we might call the low-budget postmodern documentary borrowing many features of the fiction film. My goal in what follows is to get beyond the much remarked self-reflexivity and flamboyant auteurism of these documentaries, which might seem, Rashomon-like, to abandon the pursuit of truth, to what seems to me their remarkable engagement with a newer, more contingent, relative, postmodern truth—a truth which, far from being abandoned, still operates powerfully as the receding horizon of the documentary tradition.

When we survey the field of recent documentary films two things stand out: first, their unprecedented popularity among general audiences, who now line up for documentaries as eagerly as for fiction films; second, their willingness to tackle often grim, historically complex subjects. Errol Morris's *The Thin Blue*

Line (1987), about the murder of a police officer and the near execution of the "wrong man," Michael Moore's *Roger and Me* (1989), about the dire effects of General Motors' plant closings, and Ken Burns' 11-hour *The Civil War* (1990), (watched on PBS by 39 million Americans) were especially popular documentaries about uncommonly serious political and social realities. Even more difficult and challenging, though not quite as popular, were *Our Hitler* (Hans-Jürgen Syberberg, 1980), *Shoah* (Claude Lanzmann, 1985), *Hotel Terminus: The Life and Times of Klaus Barbie* (Marcel Ophuls, 1987) and *Who Killed Vincent Chin?* (Chris Choy and Renee Tajima, 1988). And in 1991 the list of both critically successful and popular documentary features *not* nominated for Academy Awards—*Paris is Burning* (Jennie Livingston), *Hearts of Darkness: A Filmmaker's Apocalypse* (Fax Bahr and George Hickenlooper), *35 Up* (Michael Apted), *Truth or Dare* (Alex Keshishian)—was viewed by many as an embarrassment to the Academy. *Village Voice* critic Amy Taubin notes that 1991 was a year in which four or five documentaries made it onto the *Variety* charts; documentaries now mattered in a new way (Taubin, 62).

Though diverse, all the above works participate in a new hunger for reality on the part of a public seemingly saturated with Hollywood fiction. Jennie Livingston, director of *Paris is Burning*, the remarkably popular documentary about gay drag subcultures in New York, notes that the out-of-touch documentaries honored by the Academy all share an old-fashioned earnestness toward their subjects, while the new, more popular documentaries share a more ironic stance toward theirs. Coincident with the hunger for documentary truth is the clear sense that this truth is subject to manipulation and construction by docu-auteurs who, whether on camera (Lanzmann in *Shoah*, Michael Moore in *Roger and Me*) or behind, are forcefully calling the shots.[2]

It is this paradox of the intrusive manipulation of documentary truth, combined with a serious quest to reveal some ultimate truths, that I would like to isolate within a subset of the above films. What interests me particularly is the way a special few of these documentaries handle the problem of figuring traumatic historical truths inaccessible to representation by any simple or single "mirror with a memory," and how this mirror nevertheless operates in complicated and indirect refractions. For while traumatic events of the past are not available for representation by any simple or single "mirror with a memory"— in the *vérité* sense of capturing events as they happen—they do constitute a multifaceted receding horizon which these films powerfully evoke.

I would like to offer Errol Morris's *The Thin Blue Line* as a prime example of this postmodern documentary approach to the trauma of an inaccessible past because of its spectacular success in intervening in the truths known about this past. Morris's film was instrumental in exonerating a man wrongfully accused of murder. In 1976, Dallas police officer Robert Wood was murdered, apparently by a 28-year-old drifter named Randall Adams. Like Stone's *JFK*,

The Thin Blue Line is a film about a November murder in Dallas. Like *JFK*, the film argues that the wrong man was set up by a state conspiracy with an interest in convicting an easy scapegoat rather than prosecuting the real murderer. The film—the "true" story of Randall Adams, the man convicted of the murder of Officer Wood, and his accuser David Harris, the young hitchhiker whom Adams picked up the night of the murder—ends with Harris's cryptic but dramatic confession to the murder in a phone conversation with Errol Morris.

Stylistically, *The Thin Blue Line* has been most remarked for its film-noirish beauty, its apparent abandonment of *cinéma-vérité* realism for studied, often slow-motion, and highly expressionistic reenactments of different witnesses' versions of the murder to the tune of Philip Glass's hypnotic score. Like a great many recent documentaries obsessed with traumatic events of the past, *The Thin Blue Line* is self-reflexive. Like many of these new documentaries, it is acutely aware that the individuals whose lives are caught up in events are not so much self-coherent and consistent identities as they are actors in competing narratives. As in *Roger and Me*, *Shoah*, and, to a certain extent, *Who Killed Vincent Chin?*, the documentarian's role in constructing and staging these competing narratives thus becomes paramount.[3] In place of the self-obscuring voyeur of *vérité* realism, we encounter, in these and other films, a new presence in the persona of the documentarian.

For example, in one scene, David Harris, the charming young accuser whose testimony placed Randall Adams on death row and who has been giving his side of the story in alternate sections of the film from Adams, scratches his head while recounting an unimportant incident from his past. In this small gesture, Morris dramatically reveals information withheld until this moment: Harris's hands are handcuffed. He, like Adams, is in prison. The interviews with him are now subject to reinterpretation since, as we soon learn, he, too, stands accused of murder. For he has committed a senseless murder not unlike the one he accused Adams of committing. At this climactic moment Morris finally brings in the hard evidence against Harris previously withheld: he is a violent psychopath who invaded a man's house, murdered him, and abducted his girlfriend. On top of this Morris adds the local cop's attempt to explain Harris's personal pathology; in the end we hear Harris's own near-confession—in an audio interview—to the murder for which Adams has been convicted. Thus Morris captures a truth, elicits a confession, in the best *vérité* tradition, but only in the context of a film that is manifestly staged and temporally manipulated by the docu-auteur.

It would seem that in Morris's abandonment of voyeuristic objectivity he achieves something more useful to the production of truth. His interviews get the interested parties talking in a special way. In a key statement in defence of his intrusive, self-reflexive style, Morris has attacked the hallowed tradition of *cinéma vérité*: "There is no reason why documentaries can't be as personal as fiction filmmaking and bear the imprint of those who made them. Truth isn't guaranteed by style or expression. It isn't guaranteed by anything" (Morris, 17).

The "personal" in this statement has been taken to refer to the personal, self-reflexive style of the docu-auteur: Morris's hypnotic pace, Glass's music, the vivid colors and slow-motion of the multiple reenactments. Yet the interviews too bear this personal imprint of the auteur. Each person who speaks to the camera in *The Thin Blue Line* does so in a confessional, "talking-cure" mode. James Shamus has pointed out that this rambling, free-associating discourse ultimately collides with, and is sacrificed to, the juridicial narrative producing the truth of who, finally, is guilty. And Charles Musser also points out that what is sacrificed is the psychological complexity of the man the film finds innocent. Thus the film forgoes investigation into what Adams might have been up to that night taking a 16-year-old hitchhiker to a drive-in movie.[4]

Morris gives us some truths and withholds others. His approach to truth is altogether strategic. Truth exists for Morris because lies exist; if lies are to be exposed, truths must be strategically deployed against them. His strategy in the pursuit of this relative, hierarchized, and contingent truth is thus to find guilty those speakers whom he draws most deeply into the explorations of their past. Harris, the prosecutor Mulder, the false witness Emily Miller, all cozy up to the camera to remember incidents from their past which serve to indict them in the present. In contrast, the man found innocent by the film remains a cipher, we learn almost nothing of his past, and this lack of knowledge appears necessary to the investigation of the official lies. What Morris does, in effect, is partially close down the representation of Adams' own story, the accumulation of narratives from his past, in order to show how convenient a scapegoat he was to the overdetermining pasts of all the other false witnesses. Thus, instead of using fictionalizing techniques to show us the truth of what happened, Morris scrupulously sticks to stylized and silent docudrama reenactments that show only what each witness claims happened.

In contrast, we might consider Oliver Stone's very different use of docudrama reenactments to reveal the "truth" of the existence of several assassins and the plot that orchestrated their activity, in the murder of J.F.K. Stone has Garrison introduce the Zapruder film in the trial of Clay Shaw as hallowed *vérité* evidence that there had to be more than one assassin. Garrison's examination of the magic bullet's trajectory does a fine dramatic job of challenging the official version of the lone assassin. But in his zealous pursuit of the truth of "who dunnit," Stone matches the *vérité* style of the Zapruder film with a *vérité* simulation which, although hypothesis, has none of the stylized, hypothetical visual marking of Morris's simulations and which therefore commands a greater component of belief. Morris, on the other hand, working in a documentary form that now eschews *vérité* as a style, stylizes his hypothetical reenactments and never offers any of them as an image of what actually happened.

In the discussions surrounding the truth claims of many contemporary documentaries, attention has centered upon the self-reflexive challenge to once hallowed techniques of *vérité*. It has become an axiom of the new documentary that films cannot reveal the truth of events, but only the ideologies and consciousness that construct competing truths—the fictional master narratives by which we make sense of events. Yet too often this way of thinking has led to a forgetting of the way in which these films still are, as Stone's film isn't, documentaries—films with a special interest in the relation to the real, the "truths" which matter in people's lives but which cannot be transparently represented.

One reason for this forgetting has been the erection of a too simple dichotomy between, on the one hand, a naïve faith in the truth of what the documentary image reveals—*vérité*'s discredited claim to capturing events while they happen—and on the other, the embrace of fictional manipulation. Of course, even in its heyday no one ever fully believed in an absolute truth of *cinéma vérité*. There are, moreover, many gradations of fictionalized manipulation ranging from the controversial manipulation of temporal sequence in Michael Moore's *Roger and Me* to Errol Morris's scrupulous reconstructions of the subjective truths of events as viewed from many different points of view.

Truth is "not guaranteed" and cannot be transparently reflected by a mirror with a memory, yet some kinds of partial and contingent truths are nevertheless the always receding goal of the documentary tradition. Instead of careening between idealistic faith in documentary truth and cynical recourse to fiction, we do better to define documentary not as an essence of truth but as a set of strategies designed to choose from among a horizon of relative and contingent truths. The advantage, and the difficulty, of the definition is that it holds on to the concept of the real—indeed of a "real" at all—even in the face of tendencies to assimilate documentary entirely into the rules and norms of fiction.

As *The Thin Blue Line* shows, the recognition that documentary access to this real is strategic and contingent does not require a retreat to a Rashomon universe of undecidabilities. This recognition can lead, rather, to a remarkable awareness of the conditions under which it is possible to intervene in the political and cultural construction of truths which, while not guaranteed, nevertheless matter as the narratives by which we live. To better explain this point, I would like to further consider the confessional, talking-cure strategy of *The Thin Blue Line* as it relates to Claude Lanzmann's *Shoah*. While I am aware of the incommensurability of a film about the state of Texas's near-execution of an innocent man with the German state's achieved extermination of six million, I want to pursue the comparison because both films are, in very different ways, striking examples of postmodern documentaries whose passionate desire is to intervene in the construction of truths whose totality is ultimately unfathomable.

In both of these films, the truth of the past is traumatic, violent and unrepresentable in images. It is obscured by official lies masking the responsibility of individual agents in a gross miscarriage of justice. We may recall that Jameson's argument about the postmodern is that it is a loss of a sense of history, of a collective or individual past, and the knowledge of how the past determines the present: "the past as 'referent' finds itself gradually bracketed, and then effaced altogether, leaving us with nothing but texts" (Jameson, 1984, 64). That so many well-known and popular documentary films have taken up the task of remembering the past—indeed that so much popular debate about the "truth" of the past has been engendered by both fiction and documentary films about the past—could therefore be attributed to another of Jameson's points about the postmodern condition: the intensified nostalgia for a past that is already lost.

However, I would argue instead that, certainly in these two films and partially in a range of others, the postmodern suspicion of over-abundant images of an unfolding present "real" (*vérité*'s commitment to film "it" as "it" happens) has contributed not to new fictionalizations but to paradoxically new historicizations. These historicizations are fascinated by an inaccessible, ever receding, yet newly important past which does have depth.[5] History, in Jameson's sense of traces of the past, of an absent cause which "hurts" (Jameson, 1981, 102), would seem, almost by definition, to be inaccessible to the *vérité* documentary form aimed at capturing action in its unfolding. The recourse to talking-heads interviews, to people remembering the past—whether the collective history of a nation or city, the personal history of individuals, or the criminal event which crucially determines the present—is, in these anti-*vérité* documentaries, an attempt to overturn this commitment to realistically record "life as it is" in favor of a deeper investigation of how it became as it is.

Thus, while there is very little running after the action, there is considerable provocation of action. Even though Morris and Lanzmann have certainly done their legwork to pursue actors in the events they are concerned to represent, their preferred technique is to set up a situation in which the action will come to them. In these privileged moments of *vérité* (for there finally are moments of relative *vérité*) the past repeats. We thus see the power of the past not simply by dramatizing it, or reenacting it, or talking about it obsessively (though these films do all this), but finally by finding its traces, in repetitions and resistances, in the present. It is thus the contextualization of the present with the past that is the most effective representational strategy in these two remarkable films.

Each of these documentaries digs toward an impossible archaeology, picking at the scabs of lies which have covered over the inaccessible originary event. The filmmakers ask questions, probe circumstances, draw maps, interview historians, witnesses, jurors, judges, police, bureaucrats, and survivors. These diverse investigatory processes augment the single method of the *vérité* camera. They seek to uncover a past the knowledge of which will produce new truths of guilt and innocence in the present. Randall Adams is now free at least partly because of the evidence of Morris's film; the Holocaust comes alive as not some alien horror foreign to all humanity but as something that is, perhaps for the first time on film, understandable as an absolutely banal incremental logic and logistics of train schedules and human silence. The past events examined in these films are not offered as complete, totalizable, apprehensible. They are fragments, pieces of the past invoked by memory, not unitary representable truths but, as Freud once referred to the psychic mechanism of memory, a palimpsest, described succinctly by Mary Ann Doane as "the sum total of its rewritings through time." The "event" remembered is never whole, never fully represented, never isolated in the past alone but only accessible through a memory which resides, as Doane has put it, "in the reverberations between events" (Doane, 58).

This image of the palimpsest of memory seems a particularly apt evocation of how these two films approach the problem of representing the inaccessible trauma of the past. When Errol Morris fictionally reenacts the murder of Officer Wood as differently remembered by David Harris, Randall Adams, the officer's partner, and the various witnesses who claimed to have seen the murder, he turns his film into a temporally elaborated palimpsest, discrediting some versions more than others but refusing to ever fix one as *the* truth. It is precisely Morris's refusal to fix the final truth, to go on seeking reverberations and repetitions that, I argue, gives this film its exceptional power of truth.

This strategic and relative truth is often a by-product of other investigations into many stories of self-justification and reverberating memories told to the camera. For example, Morris never set out to tell the story of Randall Adams' innocence. He was interested initially in the story of "Dr. Death," the psychiatrist whose testimony about the sanity of numerous accused murderers has resulted in a remarkable number of death sentences. It would seem that the more directly and singlemindedly a film pursues a single truth, the less chance it has of producing the kind of "reverberations between events" that will affect meaning in the present. This is the problem with *Roger and Me* and, to stretch matters, even with *JFK*: both go after a single target too narrowly, opposing a singular (fictionalized) truth to a singular official lie.

The much publicized argument between Harlan Jacobson and Michael Moore regarding the imposition of a false chronology in Moore's documentary about the closing of General Motors' plant in Flint, Michigan, is an example. At stake in this argument is whether Moore's documentation of the decline of the city of Flint in the wake of the plant closing entailed an obligation to represent events in the sequence in which they actually occurred. Jacobson argues that Moore betrays his journalist/documentarian's commitment to the objective portrayal of historical fact when he implies that events that occurred prior to the major layoffs at the plant were the effect of these layoffs. Others have criticized Moore's self-promoting placement of himself at the centre of the film.[6]

In response, Moore argues that as a resident of Flint he has a place in the film and should not attempt to play the role of objective observer but of partisan investigator. This point is quite credible and consistent with the postmodern awareness that there is no objective observation of truth but always an interested participation in its construction. But when he argues that his documentary is "in essence" true to what happened to Flint in the 1980s, only that these events are "told with a narrative style" that omits details and condenses events of a decade into a palatable "movie" (Jacobson, 22), Moore behaves too much like Oliver Stone, abandoning the commitment to multiple contingent truths in favour of a unitary, paranoid view of history.

The argument between Moore and Jacobson seems to be about where documentarians should draw the line in manipulating the historical sequence of their material. But rather than determining appropriate strategies for the representation of the meaning of events, the argument becomes a question of a commitment to objectivity versus a commitment to fiction. Moore says, in effect, that his first commitment is to entertain and that this entertainment is faithful to the essence of the history. But Moore betrays the cause and effect reverberation between events by this reordering. The real lesson of this debate would seem to be that Moore did not trust his audience to learn about the past in any other way than through the *vérité* capture of it. He assumed that if he didn't have footage from the historical period prior to his filming in Flint he couldn't show it. But the choice needn't be, as Moore implies, between boring, laborious fact and entertaining fiction true to the "essence," but not the detail, of historical events. The opposition poses a contrast between a naïve faith in the documentary truth of photographs and filmic images and the cynical awareness of fictional manipulation.

What animates Morris and Lanzmann, by contrast, is not the opposition between absolute truth and absolute fiction but the awareness of the final inaccessibility of a moment of crime, violence, trauma, irretrievably located in the past. Through the curiosity, ingenuity, irony, and obsessiveness of "obtrusive" investigators, Morris and Lanzmann do not so much represent the past as they reactivate it in images of the present. This is their distinctive postmodern feature as documentarians. For in revealing the fabrications, the myths, the frequent moments of scapegoating when easy fictional examinations of trauma, violence, crime were substituted for more difficult ones, these documentaries do not simply play off truth against lie, nor do they play off one fabrication against another; rather, they show how lies function as partial truths to both the agents and witnesses of history's trauma.

For example, in one of the most dicussed moments of *Shoah*, Lanzmann stages a scene of homecoming in Chelmno, Poland, by Simon Srebnik, a Polish Jew who had, as a child, worked in the death camp near that town, running errands for the Nazis and forced to sing while doing so. Now, many years later, in the present tense of Lanzmann's film, the elderly, yet still vigorous Srebnik is surrounded on the steps of the Catholic church by an even older, friendly group of Poles who remembered him as a child in chains who sang by the river. They are happy he has survived and returned to visit. But as Lanzmann asks them how much they knew and understood about the fate of the Jews who were carried away from the church in gas vans, the group engages in a kind of free association to explain the unexplainable.

> [*Lanzmann*]:   Why do they think all this happened to the Jews?
> [*A Pole*]:   Because they were the richest! Many Poles were also exterminated. Even priests.
> [*Another Pole*]:   Mr. Kantorowski will tell us what a friend told him. It happened in Myndjewyce, near Warsaw.
> [*Lanzmann*]:   Go on.
> [*Mr. Kantorowski*]:   The Jews there were gathered in a square. The rabbi asked an SS man: "Can I talk to them?" The SS man said yes. So the rabbi said that around two thousand years ago the Jews condemned the innocent Christ to death. And when they did that, they cried out: "Let his blood fall on our heads and on our sons' heads." The rabbi told them: "Perhaps the time has come for that, so let us do nothing, let us go, let us do as we're asked."
> [*Lanzmann*]:   He thinks the Jews expiated the death of Christ?
> [*The first (?) Pole*]:   He doesn't think so, or even that Christ sought revenge. He didn't say that. The rabbi said it. It was God's will, that's all!
> [*Lanzmann, referring to an untranslated comment*]:   What'd she say?
> [*A Polish woman*]:   So Pilate washed his hands and said: "Christ is innocent," and he sent Barabbas. But the Jews cried out: "Let his blood fall on our heads!"
> [*Another Pole*]:   That's all; now you know!
>
> (*Lanzmann*, 100)[7]

As critic Shoshana Felman has pointed out, this scene on the church steps in Chelmno shows the Poles replacing one memory of their own witness of the persecution of the Jews with another (false) memory, and auto-mystification, produced by Mr. Kantorowski, of the Jews' willing acceptance of their persecution as scapegoats for the death of Christ. This fantasy, meant to assuage the Poles' guilt for their complicity in the extermination of the Jews, actually repeats the Poles' crimes of the past in the present.

Felman argues that the strategy of Lanzmann's film is not to challenge this false testimony but to dramatize its effects: we see Simon Srebnik suddenly silenced among the chatty Poles, whose victim he has become all over again. Thus the film does not so much give us a memory as an action, here and now, of the Poles' silencing and crucifixion of Srebnik, whom they obliterate and forget even as he stands in their midst (Felman, 120–8).

It is this repetition in the present of the crime of the past that is key to the documentary process of Lanzmann's film. Success, in the film's terms, is the ability not only to assign guilt in the past, to reveal and fix a truth of the day-to-day operation of the machinery of extermination, but also to deepen the understanding of the many ways in which the Holocaust continues to live in the present. The truth of the Holocaust thus does not exist in any totalizing narrative, but only, as Felman notes and Lanzmann shows, as a collection of fragments. While the process of scapegoating, of achieving premature narrative closure by assigning guilt to convenient victims is illuminated, the events of the past—in this case the totality of the Holocaust—register not in any fixed moment of past or present but rather, as in Freud's description of the palimpsest, as the sum total of its rewritings through time, not in a single event but in the "reverberations" between.

It is important in the above example to note that while *cinéma vérité* is deployed in this scene on the steps, as well as in the interviews throughout the film, this form of *vérité* no longer has a fetish function of demanding belief as *the whole*. In place of a truth that is "guaranteed," the *vérité* of catching events as they happen is here embedded in a history, placed in relation to the past, given a new power, not of absolute truth but of repetition.

Although it is a very different sort of documentary dealing with a trauma whose horror cannot be compared to the Holocaust, Errol Morris's *The Thin Blue Line* also offers its own rich palimpsest of reverberations between events. At the beginning of the film, convicted murderer Randall Adams mulls over the fateful events of the night of 1976 when he ran out of gas, was picked up by David Harris, went to a drive-in movie, refused to allow Harris to come home with him, and later found himself accused of killing a cop with a gun that Harris had stolen. He muses: "Why did I meet this kid? Why did I run out of gas? But it happened, it happened." The film probes this "Why?" And its discovery "out of the past" is not simply some fate-laden accident but rather, a reverberation between events that reaches much further back into the past than that cold November night in Dallas.

Toward the end, after Morris has amassed a great deal of evidence attesting to the false witness borne by three people who testified to seeing Randall

Adams in the car with David Harris, but before playing the audio tape in which Harris all but confesses to the crime, the film takes a different turn—away from the events of November and into the childhood of David Harris. The film thus moves both forward and back in time: to events following and preceding the night of November, 1976, when the police officer was shot. Moving forward, we learn of a murder, in which David broke into the home of a man who had, he felt, stolen his girlfriend. When the man defended himself, David shot him. This repetition of wanton violence is the clincher in the film's "case" against David. But instead of stopping there, the film goes back in time as well.

A kindly, baby-faced cop from David's home town, who has told us much of David's story already, searches for the cause of his behavior and hits upon a childhood trauma: a four-year-old brother who drowned when David was only three. Morris then cuts to David speaking of this incident: "My Dad was supposed to be watching us . . . I guess that might have been some kind of traumatic experience for me . . . I guess I reminded him . . . it was hard for me to get any acceptance from him after that . . . A lot of the things I did as a young kid was an attempt to get back at him."

In itself, this "getting-back-at-the-father" motive is something of a cliché for explaining violent male behavior. But coupled as it is with the final "confession" scene in which Harris repeats this getting-back-at-father motive in his relation to Adams, the explanation gains resonance, exposing another layer in the palimpsest of the past. As we watch the tape recording of this last unfilmed interview play, we hear Morris ask Harris if he thinks Adams is a "pretty unlucky fellow?" Harris answers, "Definitely," specifying the nature of this bad luck: "Like I told you a while ago about the guy who didn't have no place to stay . . . if he'd had a place to stay, he'd never had no place to go, right?" Morris decodes this question with his own rephrasing, continuing to speak of Harris in the third person: "You mean if he'd stayed at the hotel that night this never would have happened?" (That is, if Adams had invited Harris into his hotel to stay with him as Harris had indicated earlier in the film he expected, then Harris would not have committed the murder he later pinned on Adams.) Harris: "Good possibility, good possibility . . . You ever hear of the proverbial scapegoat? There've probably been thousands of innocent people convicted . . ."

Morris presses: "What do you think about whether he's innocent?" Harris: "I'm sure he is." Morris again: "How can you be sure?" Harris: "I'm the one who knows . . . After all was said and done it was pretty unbelievable. I've always thought if you could say why there's a reason that Randall Adams is in jail it might be because he didn't have a place for somebody to stay that helped him that night. It might be the only reason why he's at where he's at."

What emerges forcefully in this near-confession is much more than the clinching evidence in Morris's portrait of a gross miscarriage of justice. For in not simply probing the "wrong man" story, in probing the reverberations between events of David Harris's personal history, Morris's film discovers an underlying layer in the palimpsest of the past: how the older Randall Adams played an unwitting role in the psychic history of the 16-year-old David Harris, a role which repeated an earlier trauma in Harris's life: of the father who rejected him, whose approval he could not win, and upon whom David then revenged himself.

Harris's revealing comments do more than clinch his guilt. Like the Poles who surround Srebnik on the steps of the church and proclaim pity for the innocent child who suffered so much even as they repeat the crime of scapegoating Jews, so David Harris proclaims the innocence of the man he has personally condemned, patiently explaining the process of scapegoating that the Dallas county legal system has so obligingly helped him accomplish. *Cinéma vérité* in both these films is an important vehicle of documentary truth. We witness in the present an event of simultaneous confession and condemnation on the part of historical actors who repeat their crimes from the past. Individual guilt is both palpably manifest and viewed in a larger context of personal and social history. For even as we catch David Harris and the Poles of Chelmno in the act of scapegoating innocent victims for crimes they have not committed, these acts are revealed as part of larger processes, reverberating with the past.

I think it is important to hold on to the idea of truth as a fragmentary shard, perhaps especially at the moment we as a culture have begun to realize, along with Morris, and along with the supposed depthlessness of our postmodern condition, that it is not guaranteed. For some form of truth is the always receding goal of documentary film. But the truth figured by documentary cannot be a simple unmasking or reflection. It is a careful construction, an intervention in the politics and the semiotics of representation.

An overly simplified dichotomy between truth and fiction is at the root of our difficulty in thinking about the truth in documentary. The choice is not between two entirely separate regimes of truth and fiction. The choice, rather, is in strategies of fiction for the approach to relative truths. Documentary is not fiction and should not be conflated with it. But documentary can and should use all the strategies of fictional construction to get at truths. What we see in *The Thin Blue Line* and *Shoah*, and to some degree in the other documentaries I have mentioned, is an interest in constructing truths to dispel pernicious fictions, even though these truths are only relative and contingent. While never absolute and never fixed, this under-construction, fragmented horizon of truth is one important means of combating the pernicious scapegoating fictions that can put the wrong man on death row and enable the extermination of a whole people.

The lesson that I would like to draw from these two exemplary postmodern documentaries is thus not at all that postmodern representation inevitably succumbs to a depthlessness of the simulacrum, or that it gives up on truth to wallow in the undecidabilities of representation. The lesson, rather, is that there can be historical depth to the notion of truth—not the depth of unearthing a coherent and unitary past, but the depth of the past's reverberation with the present. If the authoritative means to the truth of the past does not exist, if photographs and moving images are not mirrors with memories, if they are more, as Baudrillard has suggested, like a hall of mirrors, then our best response to this crisis of representation might be to do what Lanzmann and Morris do: to deploy the many facets of these mirrors to reveal the seduction of lies.

Notes

I owe thanks to Anne Friedberg, Mark Poster, Nancy Salzer, Marita Sturken, Charles Musser, James Shamus, B. Ruby Rich and Marianne Hirsch for helping me, one way or another, to formulate the ideas in this article. I also thank my colleagues on *Film Quarterly* editorial board, whose friendly criticisms I have not entirely answered.
1   See, for example: Janet Maslin, "Oliver Stone Manipulates His Puppet," *New York Times* (Sunday, January 5, 1992), p. 13; "Twisted History," *Newsweek* (December 23, 1991), pp. 46–54; Alexander Cockburn, "J.F.K. and *J.F.K.*," *The Nation* (January 6–13, 1992), pp. 6–8.
2   Livingston's own film is an excellent example of the irony she cites, not so much in her directorial attitude toward her subject—drag-queen ball competitions—but in her subjects' attitudes toward the construction of the illusion of gender.
3   In this article I will not discuss *Who Killed Vincent Chin?* or *Roger and Me* at much length. Although both of these films resemble *The Thin Blue Line* and *Shoah* in their urge to reveal truths about crimes, I do not believe these films succeeded as spectacularly as Lanzmann's and Morris's in respecting the complexity of these truths. In *Vincent Chin*, the truth pursued is the racial motives animating Roger Ebans, a disgruntled, unemployed auto worker who killed Vincent Chin in a fight following a brawl in a strip joint. Ebans was convicted of manslaughter but only paid a small fine. He was then acquitted of a subsequent civil rights charge that failed to convince a jury of his racial motives. The film, however, convincingly pursues evidence that Ebans' animosity towards Chin was motivated by his anger at the Japanese for stealing jobs from Americans (Ebans assumed Chin was Japanese). In recounting the two trials, the story of the "Justice for Vincent" Committee, and the suffering of Vincent's mother, the film attempts to retry the case showing evidence of Ebans' racial motives.
    Filmmakers Choy and Tajima gamble that their camera will capture, in interviews with Ebans, what the civil rights case did not capture for the jury: the racist attitudes that motivated the crime. They seek, in a way, what all of these docu-

mentaries seek: evidence of the truth of past events through their repetition in the present. This is also, in a more satirical vein, what Michael Moore seeks when he repeatedly attempts to interview the elusive Roger Smith, head of General Motors, about the layoffs in Flint, Michigan: Smith's avoidance of Moore repeats this avoidance of responsibility toward the town of Flint. This is also what Claude Lanzmann seeks when he interviews the ex-Nazis and witnesses of the Holocaust, and it is what Errol Morris seeks when he interviews David Harris, the boy who put Randall Adams on death row. Each of these films succeeds in its goal to a certain extent. But the singlemindedness of *Vincent Chin's* pursuit of the singular truth of Ebans' guilt, and his culture's resentment of Asians, limits the film. Since Ebans never does show himself in the present to be a blatant racist, but only an insensitive working-class guy, the film interestingly fails on its own terms, though it is eloquent testimony to the pain and suffering of the scapegoated Chin's mother.

4   Shamus, Musser and I delivered papers on *The Thin Blue Line* at a panel devoted to the film at a conference sponsored by New York University, "The State of Representation: Representation and the State," October 26–28, 1990. B. Ruby Rich was a respondent. Musser's paper argued the point, seconded by Rich's comments, that the prosecution and the police saw Adams as a homosexual. Their eagerness to prosecute Adams, rather than the underage Harris, seems to have much to do with this perception, entirely suppressed by the film.

5   Consider, for example, the way Ross McElwee's *Sherman's March*, on one level a narcissistic self-portrait of an eccentric Southerner's rambling attempts to discover his identity while travelling through the South, also plays off against the historical General Sherman's devastating march. Or consider the way Ken Burns' *The Civil War* is as much about what the Civil War is to us today as it is about the objective truth of the past.

6   Laurence Jarvik, for example, argued that Moore's self-portrayal of himself as a "naïve, quixotic 'rebel with a mike'" is not an authentic image but one Moore has promoted as a fiction (quoted in Tajima, 30).

7   I have quoted this dialogue from the published version of the *Shoah* script but I have added the attribution of who is speaking in brackets. It is important to note, however, that the script is a condensation of a prolonged scene that appears to be constructed out of two different interviews with Lanzmann, the Poles, and Simon Srebnik before the church. In the first segment, Mr. Kantorowski is not present; in the second he is. When the old woman says "So Pilate washed his hands . . ." Mr. Kantorowski makes the gesture of washing his hands.

References

Baudrillard, Jean. 1988. "Simulacra And Simulations." In Mark Poster, ed., *Jean Baudrillard: Selected Writings*. Stanford, CA: Stanford University Press.

Doane, Mary Ann. 1990. "Remembering Women: Physical and Historical Constructions in Film Theory." In E. Ann Kaplan, ed., *Psychoanalysis and Cinema*. New York: Routledge.

Felman, Shoshana. 1990. "A L'Age du témoignage: *Shoah* de Claude Lanzmann." In *Au sujet de Shah: le film de Claude Lanzmann*. Paris: Editions Belin.

Grundberg, Andy. 1990. "Ask It No Questions: The Camera Can Lie." *New York Times*, Arts and Leisure (Sunday, August 12), pp. 1, 29.

Jacobson, Harlan. 1989. "Michael and Me." *Film Comment* 25, no. 6 (November–December), pp. 16–26.

Jameson, Frederick. 1984. "Postmodernism or the Cultural Logic of Late Capitalism." *New Left Review* 146 (July–August).

———. 1981. *The Political Unconscious: Narrative as a Socially Symbolic Act*. Ithaca, N.Y.: Cornell University Press.

Kaes, Anton. 1989. *From Hitler to Heimat: The Return of History as Film*. Cambridge: Harvard University Press.

Lanzmann, Claude. 1985. Shoah: *An Oral History of the Holocaust*. New York: Pantheon.

Lyotard, Jean-François. 1984. *The Postmodern Condition: A Report on Knowledge*. Minneapolis: University of Minnesota Press.

Morris, Errol. 1989. "Truth not Guaranteed: An Interview with Errol Morris." *Cineaste* 17, pp. 16–17.

Musser, Charles. 1990. Unpublished paper. "Film Truth: From 'Kino Pravda' to *Who Killed Vincent Chin?* and *The Thin Blue Line*."

Shamus, James. 1990. Unpublished paper. "Optioning Time: *Writing The Thin Blue Line*."

Tajima, Renee. 1990. "The Perils of Popularity." *The Independent* (June).

Taubin, Amy. 1992. "Oscar's Docudrama." *The Village Voice* (March 31), p. 62.

Trinh T., Minh-ha. 1990. "Documentary Is/Not a Game." *October* 52 (Spring), pp. 77–98.

Part II

The Inside View:
Producers and Directors

5

The Canadian Film Board Unit B

D. B. Jones

David Jones studied communications at Stanford University, teaches at Drexel University, and is a director-producer of documentaries. He also writes a great deal, and in 1981 published Movies and Memoranda, *a fine and long overdue interpretative history of the National Film Board of Canada.*

We have selected two extracts from chapter 5 of Jones's work, which deal with the Film Board's Unit B. By 1950 the board was eleven years old and consisted of four units, A, B, C, and D, each with its own staff of writers, producers, directors, and editors. The aim of the board at that time, as characterized by Jones, was to produce good solid films on specific problems, usually identified by sponsoring government departments. What emerged were rather dull films, lacking in quality, variety, and any distinguishing character.

At that point, Unit A was mainly responsible for agricultural films; Unit C produced theatrical films and the "Canada Carries On" series; and Unit D dealt with international affairs and special projects. Unit B's franchise included sponsored, scientific, cultural, and animated films. According to Jones, however, the most important distinction among the units was a difference in values. Unit B was more willing to take risks, and in the first extract included here he describes the growing individuality and experimentation of Unit B after the making of their first two distinctive films, Corral *(1954) and* Paul Tomkowicz *(1954).*

Another prototype that emerged from Unit B was *City of Gold* (1957). Colin Low had discovered in the Dominion Archives a collection of old photographs of Dawson City, the Klondike gold rush town of 1898. With Roman Kroitor and Wolf Koenig, Low planned a film about Dawson City using these still photographs. The team then came up with the idea of using actuality footage of present-day Dawson City to bracket the still-photograph content. In Dawson City—where they discovered even more photographs—they filmed quiet scenes of old men sitting in front of dilapidated stores and young boys playing baseball. For filming the still photographs, Kroitor invented a camera-plotting device that enhanced the filming by alleviating the appearance of "flatness" normally associated with filmed still photographs.

Two years after the filming of the live-action footage in Dawson City, the editing of *City of Gold* was almost complete. The music was being composed. All that remained was to write and record a commentary. Unlike *Corral*, this was a film which absolutely needed commentary. But it needed an *outstanding* commentary, one that would work together with the pictures and the music to evoke the nostalgic mood that the filmmakers were after. Wolf Koenig came up with the idea of using the Canadian author Pierre Berton, who had grown up in the Yukon. Low and Kroitor agreed to try out Berton, but they feared that he would want to change everything around. To their surprise, Berton loved the film. Berton set to work on a commentary, with Stanley Jackson helping him adapt it to the needs of film time and pacing. Berton also spoke the commentary. Despite one or two lapses into forced spontaneity, the commentary as a whole was unpretentious, informative, personal, and elegant. It enhanced the film's nostalgic effect immensely. *City of Gold* won seventeen international awards and remains today the best film of its kind, and much imitated.

As the ability of Unit B—particularly the informal group composed of Kroitor, Koenig, Low, Jackson, and the unit's executive producer, Tom Daly— became recognized by the management of the Film Board, the unit achieved a status that would allow them, occasionally, to break the rules beforehand, i.e., with permission, instead of having to quietly exceed the budget or projected completion date and then justify the transgression with an outstanding film. An example is another prototype, *Universe* (1960), one of the Film Board's most famous and successful films.

Low and Kroitor had had a long-time fascination with cosmology. The project began as a proposed classroom film about five years before Sputnik. Discussions about the project drew in several other interested persons, and the scope of the film grew. The aim of the film, they agreed, would be not so much to convey facts about the universe as to invoke a sense of wonder about it. The film would be an adventuresome project, because there was insufficient knowledge of the techniques that would be required in order to create the images that were desired. As one member of the team remembers, "We couldn't say, 'To shoot these solar prominences we'll have to do this and this and this'; we just didn't know yet how to achieve the images we wanted." Because so much technical experimentation would be required, the team knew that they would need a lot of money to make the film they had in mind.

The team prepared an outline, a rough storyboard, and a budget estimate of about $60,000, which in the 1950s was an enormous sum for a single Film Board film. Tom Daly remembers that Donald Mulholland, the director of production, suggested that the film be divided into three parts, three classroom films. That would make it easier for him to defend the cost of the project. The team argued persuasively that the film should remain a single film, a unity, for among other reasons "unity" was in a large part the very theme that they wanted the film to suggest. Jackson recalls that Mulholland said something like:

> As a responsible director of production, I absolutely cannot authorize putting that much money into a single production. It would knock out other worthy projects. However, I am not the ultimate authority. The commissioner is the ultimate authority. Go see him and tell him your story, and ask him to phone me.

The commissioner, Albert Trueman, responded enthusiastically. He called Mulholland and told him that some way should be found to proceed with the project. Mulholland was, Jackson remembers, delighted, but still concerned about the costs.

> "But," he said, "there's no deadline, no hurry. If I give you $60,000 and say 'go ahead,' that isn't fair [to you or to other filmmakers]. So we'll do it this way: I'll give you $20,000 this year. Get going. When you've spent it, put the film on the shelf until the next fiscal year." This meant that the next time Low and Kroitor could get at the money, they'd be more sure of where they were going.

After the end of the third fiscal year, the film was still not done. More money was required. The money was provided, but with the stipulation that the film must be finished by the end of that—the fourth—fiscal year. The team finished the film on March 31, the last day of the fiscal year.

The film had taken four years, but not four whole years, because after the first few months of each fiscal year the $20,000 allocated for the year had been spent and the film had to be placed on the shelf. This on-again-off-again process may have worked to the film's advantage. William James once remarked that "we learn to swim in the winter and skate in the summer." With *Universe*, this principle was incorporated, intentionally or not, into the Film Board's battery of production strategies.

A filmmaker from outside Unit B remembers that when *Universe* was finished, and test screened, its general reception was summed up in the reaction of one filmmaker, who exclaimed, "You spent $60,000 for . . . *that!?*" But *Universe* became one of the most widely distributed educational films ever made, earning much more than its total production costs in revenues. NASA ordered at least 300 prints of the film, which they used for training and for public information. By 1976, the Film Board had sold over 3,100 prints of *Universe*. Stanley Kubrick, when he started work on his *2001: A Space Odyssey*, discussed the project with Colin Low and hired Wally Gentleman, the wizard who had achieved the optical effects for *Universe*, to do the same for Kubrick's film. And Kubrick used the voice of Douglas Rain, who spoke the commentary (which Stanley Jackson had written) for *Universe*, as the voice of Hal, the computer.

The culmination of the documentary work of Unit B was a series called *Candid Eye*, half-hour documentaries made for television. The series began in 1958 and ran for about three years. Koenig and Kroitor, the series's main instigators, believed that television, with its voracious appetite for material, offered far greater opportunities for experimentation than had been recognized. Most of the documentaries on television—many of them, in Canada, Film Board documentaries—were boring, shallow, and unimaginative. Kroitor and Koenig had seen *Thursday's Children*, a documentary by Lindsay Anderson and the British "Free Cinema" group of the mid-1950s, and believed that the scriptless approach of films like *Thursday's Children* could be adapted favorably to a series of Canadian documentaries. The two filmmakers were equally enchanted by the work of the photographer Henri Cartier-Bresson, who seemed capable of combining the spontaneity of candid photography with an acute sensitivity to form.

When the Unit B team proposed a series of films for which there would be no script at all, the Board's management, and many filmmakers within the Board, were puzzled. They didn't think films could be made without a script and without rehearsals of the action. Management was hesitant to approve the project, because it had no way of knowing what the results might be. Daly has summarized both the problem of getting the project approved and the solution:

> The most you could give for each film in the series was a subject, and perhaps a list of sequences you were likely to cover. It was known that the shaping and structuring would occur in the editing room. In order to get the proposal accepted—and to be able to drop a subject that later proved unsatisfactory—we gave the program committee [about] thirty-two subjects, and asked them to agree on a priority fifteen, from which we would do seven. So they had an input.

The cost of the films would not be any more than the cost of the typical Film Board documentary. Although the lack of scripts meant that more footage would have to be shot, and that editing would take a lot longer, money would be saved by skipping the script stage and by using small crews, with new lightweight equipment.

Terence Macartney-Filgate joined Koenig and Kroitor for *Candid Eye*, Stanley Jackson wrote the commentaries, and Tom Daly served as executive producer. Several French-Canadians also worked on the series. They included Georges Dufaux, Gilles Gascon, Michel Brault, Claude Pelletier, and Marcel Carrière. Roles interchanged considerably. Stanley Jackson directed one of the films. Tom Daly edited sequences of at least one film. Several of the French-Canadians did some directing.

Among the more remembered titles in the *Candid Eye* series are *The Days Before Christmas* (1958), *The Back-Breaking Leaf* (1959), and *Blood and Fire*

(1958). *The Days Before Christmas*, a survey of the rush of activities that precede the holiday, was the pilot film for the series, and at least six filmmakers directed sequences of it: Roman Kroitor, Wolf Koenig, Stanley Jackson, Terence Macartney-Filgate, John Feeney, and Michel Brault. Macartney-Filgate directed *The Back-Breaking Leaf*, a film about the grueling work of tobacco pickers in the annual southern Ontario harvest, and *Blood and Fire*, a film about the Salvation Army.

These films did not solve fully the formal problem presented by the scriptless, high-ratio approach to reality: how to fashion this wider and less contrived range of actuality into some meaningful, aesthetically satisfying whole. But *Lonely Boy* (1962), filmed after the end of the regular *Candid Eye* series as a kind of grand finale, did. More money was spent on *Lonely Boy*, and more editing time, than on any of the regular *Candid Eye* films. More effort, too. Koenig and Kroitor shot and codirected the film; John Spotton and Guy Coté worked on it as editors.

A totally engrossing portrait of Paul Anka, the popular Canadian entertainer who excited tears and screams in worshiping North American teenage girls in the early 1960s, *Lonely Boy* was, for the Film Board and for documentary in general, an advance in "the creative treatment of actuality." The film is a fascinating mixture of the formal and the formless. Raw, vigorous, often spontaneous content is organized into a rigorous structure.

On the one hand, much of the material in the film seems to consist of random shots—snaps, almost—of the Atlantic City environment in which much of the film is set. In one tracking shot, the camera and crew follow Anka hurriedly as he moves down a street. In another scene, the crew surprises Anka by waiting in his dressing room. In some ways, the film is almost arrogantly— for its time—sloppy-*looking*. The microphone appears in the tacking shot of Anka walking down the street. As Anka bursts into the dressing room, he stares at the camera in a brief moment of surprise. Jumpcuts abound in the interview sequences. A question from the filmmaker is heard in one scene. In one of the film's most engrossing scenes, in which Anka presents a gift to the owner of the Copacabana nightclub in New York, the filmmaking team becomes involved in the action. The owner rather insincerely kisses Anka to thank him for the gift. We hear a voice asking him to do the kiss again. Anka and the manager break into laughter. "The camera moved," the filmmaker, off-camera, explains. They kiss again, and then Anka, still laughing, asks if the film crew wants them to do it *again*. The filmmaker tells them no, just keep talking. The entire uncut sequence appears in the film.

On the other hand, *Lonely Boy* is tightly structured. The film opens with Anka singing the song of that title. "I'm just a lonely boy," he intones, as we see billboards (with Anka's name on them in huge letters), the center of the highway, etc., from the point of view of the car in which Anka is riding. The loneliness of an entertainer who has become an idol, worshiped by hordes of silly young girls, is the theme, and this theme is relentlessly held to. At a concert, a human barrier of policemen and security guards protects Anka from the screaming mob. When Anka presents his gift—a huge portrait of himself—to the nightclub owner, the gift is received with no real warmth. Rehearsing a new composition on the piano, Anka looks scared and insecure. He is surrounded by sycophants. At one point near the end, the film becomes highly stylized for a documentary. The shrieking audience, which in an earlier scene had drowned out the words of the singer, is now faded out *in the editing*, so that we hear the song, and only the song, over a series of silent shots of agonized, idolatrous fans. The film ends with more shots down the highway. Anka, inside the car, appears bored with, and alienated from, his crew of managers and agents. A woman in a passing car stares at him. On the soundtrack, we hear, again, "I'm just a lonely boy. . . ."

Paul Tomkowicz, Corral, City of Gold, Universe, and the "Candid Eye" series, each a prototype in its own right, could be taken as benchmarks in the evolution of a distinct Unit B style of *working* that was to affect the Film Board deeply, if not universally or unambiguously. With *Paul Tomkowicz* and *Corral*, perfection became regarded as a criterion far more important than the budget, the schedule, or the norm, i.e., professionalism. Grierson had urged that films must "achieve distinction or they're not worth doing at all," and, for their time, the wartime films were distinctive, or at least technically well made. But there had always been the urgencies of the war, the theatrical release date, and Grierson's Calvinistic strain to keep rein on any one project's pursuit of its full potential. It took several years of peace, and the introduction of a measure of routine, before the board began to free itself from wartime constraints. The beginning does not seem to have been a planned or conscious one. The concept of what *Paul Tomkowicz* should be, and the means to make it that, were both discovered largely by trial and error. The discovery that *Corral* did not need a commentary, and that it would be a far better film without one, occurred while struggling with the material itself, and did not follow from some theory.

With *City of Gold*, the notion of using Pierre Berton as the narrator arose from difficulty with the commentary, but in the filming of the still photos there had been an image of what the film ought to look like and then a problem-solving effort—Kroitor's camera-plotting device—to achieve the image. With *Universe*, there was the imagination and the planned-for exploration and experimentation, and even the budget and scheduling problems were anticipated, so that if the manner of the production departed radically from the professional norm, it did so purposely, with management's prior approval. In the case of *Candid Eye*, the right to experiment on a grand documentary scale was negotiated beforehand, with a minimum of compromise, with management.

The Film Board professional norm was no longer the rule—if you belonged to Unit B, and if you could convince management by the merit of your proposal and your track record.

This striving for perfection, which invariably involved the odious (to Grierson) "cuddling to sweet smotheroo," was nevertheless associated with characteristics Grierson had promoted. The team approach to filmmaking was one such characteristic. The names Kroitor, Koenig, Low, Daly, and Jackson occur again and again in the best Unit B films, although others were involved, too—especially Eldon Rathburn, who did the music for *Corral*, *Universe*, and other Unit B films, and Terence Macartney-Filgate in *Candid Eye*. In several ways, the group's style of working recalled the old Empire Marketing Board in England, and aspects of the early, wartime Film Board. There was in this team and in Unit B as a whole a degree of "role freedom." A filmmaker might produce one film, direct the next, and edit a third. John Spotton, trained as a cameraman, took a pay cut to work as an editor on *The Back-Breaking Leaf* and *Lonely Boy*. Tom Daly, the unit's executive producer, would sometimes edit a film. And in any one production, the roles of producer, director, cameraman, and editor would often overlap. As a film critic wrote in the mid-1960s, the Unit B films "are so thoroughly the product of a group that their names do not matter."[1] Unlike the early EMB and early Film Board films, the Unit B films, like all contemporary NFB films, did carry credits, but the credits did not reflect clearly defined roles. Credits, Tom Daly recalls, were "apportioned at the end of the filming according to where we felt the center of gravity lay." Pay raises—another kind of reward—were also somewhat communally awarded. When there were pay raises, everyone in the unit deserving one got one, whether he had asked for it or not.

The cooperative approach of the Unit B team of Kroitor, Koenig, Low, Jackson, and Daly did not involve simple self-effacement, but something quite different. Tom Daly remembers Unit B as a group which, at its best, combined aspects of communality and individuality:

> There was a desire not to be separate. Each person, confident of his ability in one or two areas, would recognize his lacks in other areas, and other persons' abilities in those areas. Each person had a sense that his own fulfillment could not be fully achieved on his own, but only in connection with a project to which he and others contributed where they could . . . to achieve something greater than the sum of the various contributions. . . . To achieve this harmony, filmmakers don't have to be geniuses, but they do have to be first-rate in *something*. And if they are, they will also be aware of not being first-rate in other things, and will therefore *enjoy* cooperating with people who *are* first-rate in those things.

But the day-to-day process by which such creative collaboration was achieved was anything but harmonious. Wolf Koenig remembers that for all the rosy light cast on old Unit B by the haze of memory and nostalgia, it should be remembered that it had a very tough strand running through it. It's this strand, in my opinion, which made it functional (like the wires inside Michelins). And what it consisted of was opposition and conflict! What made the unit function under such apparently self-destructive impulses was that Tom Daly, our executive producer, accepted this conflict and, intuitively, used it as a source of energy for the group.

The polarities within Unit B were best expressed by the two major personalities within it: Tom Daly and Roman Kroitor. The personalities of these two men were almost diametrically opposed to each other. Tom, the conservative, pragmatic, technically and artistically accomplished, apparently unemotional administrator; raised in the traditions of Upper Canada College; apprenticed to film aristocrats like Grierson and Legg; always conscious of his obligations to pass on tradition and to serve the public's needs. In other words, truly Anglo and the nearest thing we have in Canada to an aristocrat.

Roman, on the other hand, was a rebel (in his way); an accurate but devastating critic; a Saskatchewan Ukrainian—therefore highly emotional; a brilliant student at university (a gold medal winner); a highly creative filmmaker without (at that time) a full technical knowledge, but learning fast; very nervy and, at times, disrespectful of the opinions of "older and wiser" heads; with long hair when it was unfashionable and a life style which bordered on the "bohemian." He was the object of envious ridicule by some, but, like Tom Daly, he was dedicated to the public good (although he saw it from another angle).

Well, these two personalities clashed, mostly in discreet ways, sometimes not so discreetly. Tom certainly could have gotten rid of this Kroitor guy in about five minutes and he would have been applauded for doing so. But he didn't. Instead he helped to train him and supported him in films which were, to many, very far out. At times he fought against management even though this went entirely against his own traditional upbringing. . . . So . . . it was between the polarities of these two men that the strand I mentioned earlier was stretched, and to such fine tautness that all the rest of us could balance on it.

The group dynamics of this team resembled that of the smaller two-person and thus simpler team that discovered the structure of DNA. Both James Watson and Francis Crick were expert in something—Watson in biology, Crick in crystallography—but, as in Unit B, there was a "role freedom" in the relationship that encouraged each to probe the other's area of expertise. Watson and Crick had a similar generosity toward credits; they decided senior authorship by the toss of a coin. And finally, they could criticize each other, bluntly.[2]

The work of the Unit B team and the work of the DNA scientists resembled each other in one more respect. A sociologist has noted that the motivation of scientists cannot be explained solely by desire for fame or reward, and has argued that there is a "charisma" in science which must be adduced as a complementary motivation. Among scientists, "charismatic things are those which bring order out of chaos and which guide, direct, and make meaning-ful human action."[3] Although there were the usual egoistic motivations in the race for the structure of the double helix, awe of the elusive structure itself was a motivation, as is evident, if not explicit, in Watson's account of the discovery.[4]

But to colleagues of Watson and Crick their pursuit of the structure seemed at times zealous or obsessive. Similarly, to many NFB employees outside of Unit B, there seemed to be a touch of messianic zeal in the team's pursuit of aes-thetic perfection. Sometimes it seemed to others that Unit B filmmakers lived only to make brilliant films, subjugating all other aspects of life and living to that single purpose. For Unit B, the pursuit of perfection had apparently become "the sacred commitment" that the theatrical release date had been during the war. It was as if it were holy to seek perfection and sinful to compromise.

On this point, Stanley Jackson comments that

> it did *look* like, at times, a kind of crazy dedication . . . but it was an attitude toward the craft. There was a filmmaker who had produced a number of mediocre films, and if you asked him how the film was, he would say, and I quote, "We got away with it." For *us*, though, it had to be as good as you could make it. You had to get as much out of the material, through structuring, through the use of sound, the orchestration of all the materials, so that it would be as good as possible. It wasn't a holy crusade. It was an attitude toward the craft.

If it wasn't a holy crusade, the "attitude toward the craft" certainly had charis-matic aspects. But there was now no war, and no Grierson, to inspire this charismatic devotion. Its sole source was an ideal of aesthetic fulfillment.

Unit B's aesthetic ideal involved an idea of *wholeness*. A similar idea had pervaded the wartime NFB work. But Grierson's idea of wholeness was such that each film, insignificant in itself, contributed to the "whole" picture of Canada that the Film Board was attempting to produce. An individual film might contain a *thematic* wholeness, in the sense that a *World in Action* or a *Canada Carries On* film would show single events or local situations in relation to world events. Wholeness also referred, for Grierson, to the overall *system* of production and distribution which established a dynamic relationship between production and constituency.

Unit B modified this "wholeness" in a significant way. Unit B emphasized wholeness in the *individual* films, but in none of the Unit B prototypes is the subject related, in an explicit or thematic way, to the rest of the world. The "wholeness" of *Paul Tomkowicz, Corral, City of Gold, Universe,* and *Lonely Boy* lies in the coherent fullness with which the subject is presented. The films contain an organic wholeness, a certain aesthetic integrity that avoids the imposition of forced connections to some larger issue, some greater relevance.

But the avoidance of explicit relevance does not mean that these films were esoteric or trivial. Their popularity was enormous, and still is. These films did not *refer* to a wider world, but *spoke to* the wider world through their integrity of structure and material, or style and content. Perhaps their aim and effect were to find the universal in the particular—the lyricism of ranchhands rounding up horses, the occasionally tremulous inflection in Berton's nostalgic commentary, the moment at the piano when Paul Anka looks so tentative and alone—and to communicate with their audience not intellectually but emotionally. With reference to the *Candid Eye* films, Wolf Koenig wrote that the aim was to "show them on television to millions of people and make them see that life is true, fine, and full of meaning."[5]

Although in part a modification of Grierson's sense of the whole, the aesthetic "wholeness" in the Unit B films was rooted in the work of the Grierson-led wartime Film Board. Two members of the team, Jackson and Daly, had joined the board very early. Daly had developed the stock-shot library. Partly because he was the one "who knew where everything was," he became the editor of the *World in Action* series. This meant that Legg and Daly, between them, had to edit a film a month. Jackson directed and edited films, but increasingly he was called on to write commentaries.

From working in these capacities and under Grierson, Daly and Jackson developed a keen sense of structure. In the 1950s, Daly would often edit a film, but his structural sense was expressed mainly in a kind of informal teaching that was part of his approach to producing. Jackson's structural sense was brought into the work of the unit mainly through writing commentaries, an art which in documentary requires a sense of structure as much as a facility with words. Once, however, it was brought in by *not* writing a commentary, for it was precisely this structural capacity that allowed Jackson to recognize, finally, that *Corral* did not *need* a commentary. A less confident talent might have tried to force a commentary onto the film.

[Again, because of space pressures, I had to omit a section from the middle of the chapter in which Jones deals with Unit B's tendency to report *success* and the achievement of unity in its films. Thus, many of Unit B's films deliberately avoided themes that included the sick, the horrible, and the ugly. A few people, including Norman McLaren, struggled against that tendency and tried not to ignore the more difficult aspects of contemporary life. The second extract I have chosen picks up a discussion of the work of the unit's more socially critical filmmakers.—A.R.]

One such filmmaker was Terence Macartney-Filgate. His *Candid Eye* films were concerned more with the unsuccessful than with the celebrated. And just as the *Candid Eye* films made primarily by the Inner Circle team tended to select individuals as subjects, Macartney-Filgate, an individualist, tended to make films about groups. In *The Back-Breaking Leaf* (1960), Macartney-Filgate, working with several French-Canadians, explored the harsh life of tobacco pickers in southern Ontario. In his *Blood and Fire*, which examined the work of the Salvation Army, there is one scene in which a weeping, deeply troubled person, a genuine down-and-out, responds to the Call to the Mercy Seat. This scene was, during the editing, the subject of heated debates. Some believed that because the scene showed a recognizable man in a state of emotional naked-ness, it should be cut out. It seemed raw and—worse—unethical. *Cinéma vérité* was in its early stages, and some filmmakers had qualms about using such material. But because there had been no attempt to hide the camera, and because the scene was so dramatic, it was kept.

Neither of these films had the coherent richness or energy of *Lonely Boy*. They were aesthetically flat. But neither of them was made under the special conditions and with the grand-finale purpose and license of *Lonely Boy*. And if they failed to achieve a tone of "praise," i.e., a life-enhancing structure or perspective, they dealt in an area that the Inner Circle team generally avoided—unsuccess.

Arthur Lipsett was another member of Unit B who tried to deal in his work with the less cheery side of life. In 1962, he made *Very Nice, Very Nice*, an eight-minute film containing perhaps as many individual shots as an average hour-long documentary. Many of the shots were stills. The sound track was composed from pieces of sound tape discarded from other films. This was several years before Jean-Luc Godard made *Weekend*, a film introduced by the title, "A Film Found on the Scrap Heap." The vision in *Very Nice, Very Nice* was as dour as that of *Weekend* and a lot more succinctly (if far less richly) expressed. The bomb, international politics, materialism, pollution, noise, and alienation are among the pathologies covered in the film.

If the Unit B classics leaned toward an easy praise, in *Very Nice, Very Nice* there was no praise at all. It was a completely sour list of complaints against society as it existed at the time. *Very Nice, Very Nice* was to the Unit B aesthetic as Dostoyevski's underground man was to the optimistic, rational positivism of Dostoyevski's time. Even the title could be taken as a sarcastic comment on the Unit B aesthetic, a sardonic response to the easy optimism that saw life as "true, fine, and full of meaning" by seeing only half of life.

Unfortunately, Lipsett saw only that other half. *Very Nice, Very Nice* was like the underground man, but it was not like *Notes from the Underground*. It was the phenomenon without the form. It stands as a rather gross example of what in literary criticism is sometimes called "the expressive fallacy," the notion that the effect of an artwork should reproduce its subject—e.g., that a novel about boredom should itself be boring. *Very Nice, Very Nice* was a disordered film about disorder, a confused film on confusion. Its effect was accomplished by chopping up random pieces of actuality footage and sound tape found in the Film Board's waste baskets. Almost any pieces would do. With *Very Nice, Very Nice*, the filmmaker was like a poet who attempts to show the decline of language and culture by writing an incomprehensible poem out of bifurcated, misspelled cusswords randomly strung together.

Very Nice, Very Nice was, however, something of a *tour de force*, and was very popular among underground film persons and members of the counterculture in North America. The film achieved an influential niche in the history of experimental film. It became a prototype. The film was influential at the Film Board, too. Several filmmakers regarded Lipsett as the board's first resident genius since McLaren. The extreme positive response to Lipsett's extreme negativism suggests that there was, within the Film Board and outside it, a severe hunger for recognition of the negative side of contemporary life. If the film fails to survive aesthetically, perhaps it was at the time a refreshing challenge to the easy optimism that dominated the screens of the early sixties. *Very Nice, Very Nice* was a filmic restatement of McLaren's milder suggestion that perhaps creative artists shouldn't be frittering their talent away on pretty things when the world was menaced with the possibility of total destruction.

Lipsett, Macartney-Filgate, Bairstow, and McLaren were at various degrees removed from the Inner Circle, the Unit B team responsible for the Board's first classic documentaries. Bairstow belonged to another unit and had little to do with Unit B. McLaren was part of Unit B for a while, but only technically. In Daly's words, McLaren was always "an original, special person, available to all, and ready to help all." Macartney-Filgate joined the Unit B team for *Candid Eye*, but he did not get along well with them. The Inner Circle encouraged Lipsett at first, and actually supported and defended his work on *Very Nice, Very Nice*. Only later, as Lipsett continued to dwell on the same theme, was there a falling out.

It was as if Unit B had a group personality which could not absorb the negative into its aesthetic vision, even though it tried. Unit B's best films were made by the Inner Circle and avoided the negative: the unit's socially critical films were made by others and weren't so good. Unit B did, however, make one outstanding documentary that did not ignore the unsettling aspects of its subject. This film was *Circle of the Sun* (1961), directed by Colin Low. The film's specific subject is the Blood Indian Sun Dance, performed at a gathering in Alberta (Low's home province). This was the first time that the Indians had allowed the Sun Dance to be filmed; the reason for allowing it was that the Indians feared that the tradition might be dying. This possibility suggested the film's larger theme—the possible demise of the whole Blood Indian culture. The Sun Dance and its larger subject are explored through a portrait (and voice-over) of a young Blood Indian, who moves between two worlds, modern industrial civilization (he works as an oil rigger) and what's left of the Blood culture. This theme was not a new one, and the film did not develop new techniques, but it is a reasonably sensitive, honest, and beautiful film, its "praise" consisting in the aesthetic intensity with which the theme is rendered.

But *Circle of the Sun* does not necessarily belie the characterization of the Unit B aesthetic as overly positive. For one thing, as good as the film was, it was not a prototype. For another, it was perhaps aesthetically *too* intense. The film tends to aestheti*cize* its subject. As if the Sun Dance weren't itself sufficiently engrossing, a heavy-handed, overbearing musical score dominates the film in its most dramatic moments.

Additionally, *Circle of the Sun* was less of a team effort than the prototypal documentaries, and more the work of an individual. And its director, Colin Low, would eventually, when the team disbanded, pursue socially relevant film-making with a vengeance.

In sum, it does appear that the aesthetic ideal's difficulty with the negative was in some important way related to the personality of the group, a personality not reducible to those of the individual members of the group. The team had an aversion to rawness. It liked its reality precooked. It preferred to make films about subjects already somewhat coherent, somewhat whole, rather than to create that wholeness entirely itself.

The team's inability to absorb the raw into its aesthetic triumphs was a limitation to its "attitude toward the craft," but perhaps it was also an indication of aesthetic integrity. To expand the range of the aesthetic may have meant destroying it. For the Film Board of the time, the aesthetic was an indisputable advance in the art of documentary. Unit B represented the apex of the development of certain Film Board values and characteristics. It was the height of combining one's living with one's calling. It was the epitome of group filmmaking. And it was the strongest expression of a consciously considered, home-grown film aesthetic.

The unit system came to an end less than two years after *Very Nice, Very Nice*. Therefore, it is hazardous to speculate upon the possibility that the Unit B aesthetic eventually might have widened its scope. But after *Lonely Boy*, the Unit B Inner Circle (and Unit B as a whole) produced no further existent documentaries of note. Possibly the Unit B aesthetic had spent itself with *Lonely Boy*.

But possibly it hadn't. In 1963, the group's attention turned toward planning a multiscreen extravaganza, *Labyrinth*, for Expo '67, Canada's centennial celebration. One of the requirements of Expo '67 was that whatever was shown had to be something that could not be seen anywhere else. It is impossible to see the original *Labyrinth* now[6]—which is unfortunate, because in Daly's view, *Labyrinth* "was perhaps the most complete embodiment of the Unit B philosophy." Daly recalls that

the theme was the whole development of life, dark and light sides, through innocent childhood, confident youth, disillusion and depression, the search for something more, the meeting with the Minotaur (the dark side of oneself), new
directions of life, the facing of death, and the mysteries beyond. This theme was
embodied in architecture, in personal movement of the audience through a
"structure" of events and experiences including films as *part* of it.

If the Unit B aesthetic hadn't exhausted itself with *Lonely Boy*, it surely had
with *Labyrinth*. This single project held most of the team together after the unit
system's demise, but by the time *Labyrinth* was over, Koenig had returned
to animation, Kroitor had left the Film Board, and Low had begun to pursue
a different kind of filmmaking in Challenge for Change. And some of their
younger disciples had tired of documentary and become interested in dramatic
features.

But the contribution of Unit B to the Film Board documentary did not lie
solely in the classics that it put into the Board's catalogue. That Unit B *had* an
aesthetic ideal, that they made films which did not compromise the ideal, and
that their commitment to achieving it was unswerving influenced filmmakers
of various sensibilities. In addition, the success of Unit B earned for all Film
Board filmmakers a greater authority over the purpose and process of filmmaking; the unusual freedoms that Unit B won for itself were transmitted to
all the filmmakers in the form of structural changes that would occur in 1964.
And three members of the Inner Circle—Tom Daly, Colin Low, and Stanley
Jackson—would, as individuals, give generously to the Film Board documentary even into the eighties. Most of the board's later achievements in documentary owed much to the work of Unit B.

Even now, Unit B is remembered vividly. Some of its severest critics remember it with nostalgia or at least respect. One who had been an unhappy fringe
member of the unit laments that

> the *discipline* of the unit system—and in its own informal way Unit B was the
> most disciplined—was a good thing. Everything I know now is because of the dis-
> cipline I learned in Unit B. I'm trying to develop discipline in these new guys, but
> it's not possible. Young filmmakers nowadays want to do just what they want.
> They don't listen.

A filmmaker who had belonged to a different unit remarks:

> They were snobs . . . I couldn't stand them . . . And yet, you've got to be a bit of
> a snob to do something of quality. If you're not a snob, you might be sloppy.

And a sound mixer remembers:

> It was . . . *trying* to work with them. Quite often they'd work by committee, in
> endless sessions, in the mixing studio. They were very meticulous. But they were
> always after a *good film*. It was a challenge and a joy to mix their films.

Notes

1 Peter Harcourt, "The Innocent Eye," *Sight and Sound*, 34 (Winter 1964/65): 19–23.
2 Public Broadcasting Service, "Nova: The Race for the Double Helix," documentary aired Feb. 24, 1976.
3 Bernard H. Gustin, "Charisma, Recognition, and the Motivation of Scientists," *American Journal of Sociology* 78 (March 1973): 1123–4.
4 James Watson, *The Double Helix: A Personal Account of the Discovery of the Structure of DNA* (New York: New American Library, 1969).
5 Louis Marcorelles, *Living Cinema: New Directions in Contemporary Filmmaking* (New York: Praeger, 1968), p. 7.
6 The Film Board has prepared a single screen version of *Labyrinth*.

'History is the Theme of All My Films': An Interview with Emile de Antonio

Gary Crowdus and Dan Georgakas

Cineaste: *How do you go about making a compilation documentary such as* In the Year of the Pig? *Do you start from a predetermined political thesis that you want to illustrate, or do you do film research first and work out a narrative line from the material available?*

Emile de Antonio: I approach all my work from a consciously left viewpoint. It's very hard to articulate what it means to be a Marxist today, but it was a little bit clearer in 1967 when I began *Pig*. The film originally grew out of anger, outrage, and passion, but I knew that all of these, estimable as they are as motivations, are wrong if unchecked in a film, because you end up with only a screed, a poster that shouts, "Out of Vietnam!" It seemed to me that the most passionate statement that could be made was to make a film that would treat the history of Vietnam as far back as the footage would take it, to cover the whole history of the war, from its earliest days to the Tet Offensive in 1968, which was the year I completed the film. Compilation filmmaking lends itself best to history, which is, frankly, the theme of all my films.

The first thing I did was read about two hundred books in French and English on Vietnam, because I figured that was one way I could find the images. Many who do compilation documentaries today come from an anti-intellectual generation, or have no historical sense, and they're motivated primarily by flashy images or simple prejudices, when what they should be looking for are historical resonances which are filmic.

In other words, you're really interested in finding images for a general schema that you've gotten after all your reading, whereas some filmmakers feel that they can just rummage through a lot of archival footage and find a film there.

Yes, that's right. I think you've got to do a hell of a lot of homework. I then proceed to assemble a chaotic draft of the subject. I knew that I was going to pursue a historical line, although not necessarily a chronological line. I had a friend who owned a box factory, and he used to give me corrugated paper in rolls nine feet high, and I'd tack them up on my office walls. I'd start out by writing, "Han dynasty"—even though I knew I'd never put anything about the Han dynasty in the film—because the Chinese experience begins there. I would obviously write down, "Dien Bien Phu, 1954, May 8th," and abstract concepts like "torture," "inhumanity," and other things that interested me. Sometimes I would also paste a picture into it, so I would have visual images as well as words on the walls.

Once this huge outline was done, I started to do extensive film research. I went to Prague, for instance, where the NLF had a main office, and they gave me tremendous footage. I went to East Germany and there I met the Soviets who gave me Roman Karmen's restaging of the battle of Dien Bien Phu. Sometimes it's very sad, by the way, when good research pays off, because most of the people who saw *In the Year of the Pig* thought that really *was* the battle of Dien Bien Phu. When I lecture with the film today, I tell audiences, "You should look more carefully, because if you look at those Vietminh troops, you know they're not actually in combat. They're all so neatly dressed and running at port arms, as if some major were in the back giving orders." Still, it was beautiful footage, and I think I used it well, because I cut from that to the real footage of all those white faces surrendering to yellow faces, which is one of the symbols of that war.

I met with the Hanoi people in Paris, and I was the first Westerner to get an extraordinary film called *The Life of Ho Chi Minh*, which is their view of Ho, with early stills of Ho and his family and great material of Ho joining the French Communist party in 1922. I love that kind of material. I also got access to the French army's film library, the greatest collection of Vietnam footage that exists—it goes back to 1902. While there, I saw Pierre Schoendoerffer's great footage that nobody's ever seen. He was a sergeant in Vietnam, the head of a camera crew, and got some of the greatest shots of tanks in battle in the jungle that I've ever seen. He later made several documentaries, including *La 317ème section* and *The Anderson Platoon*. I had acquired a whole bunch of this stuff when one of the two young French sergeants assigned to me said, "Listen, they're going to pull it out from under you, because now they know who you are, and you're not going to get one frame of this stuff." There's this beautiful shot in *Pig* of something you can't get in this country. It's Ho Chi Minh with Admiral d'Argenlieu, the French commissioner of Vietnam, aboard the battlecruiser *Richelieu*. It's the end of talking, a really symbolic scene, because the war's really going to go now, and as Ho leaves the ship, with the French saluting, he takes a cigarette out of his mouth and, in that casual way of his, flips it over the side. I had to have that shot, so I said to the kid, "Listen, I'm going to steal this. Would you mind going out, because I don't want you to be implicated in all this." So I just cut that shot out of the roll of 35 mm negative and stuck it in the pocket of my raincoat. I realized that since they knew who I was now, there was a good chance that the guys with the guns at the gate would stop me, and I could have gotten five years for that in France, but I thought it was worth it. Making films is risk taking.

The thing that staggered me was that even though the TV networks were going on and on about Vietnam, and other people were making films about Vietnam, no one found the footage I did for *Pig*. I located several great scenes no one ever picked up, including one of the film's best scenes from the 1930s, which is of these absolutely arrogant Frenchmen in their colonial hats and white suits being pulled in rickshaws by Vietnamese. They arrive in front of a cafe where there is a tall Moroccan with a fez—the scene encapsulates the whole French colonial empire—and when the Vietnamese put their hands out for payment, the Moroccan sends them away like trash. To me, that said everything you could say about colonialism without ever saying the word. If anything shows the primacy of the image over the word, what the image can reveal, it's the image of those rickshaws. It's the equivalent of a couple of chapters of dense writing about the meaning of colonialism.

Of course, *Pig* is only partly compilation; it includes a tremendous amount of interview material. I sought out the major left French historians, for instance. Not Communists, because the problem with most French Communists is that they talk like *L'Humanité*, it's a dead language. I filmed people such as Jean Lacouture, who had written a biography of Ho Chi Minh, and Phillippe Devillers, the editor of a French intellectual journal about Southeast Asia who had served in Vietnam. I used them as voice-overs for that early Vietnamese footage of the rickshaws—not talking about colonialism, because the image explained colonialism—but explaining what was behind colonialism, what the *corvée* meant, what the French were trying to do, the white face/yellow face thing, and all the rest of it. At the same time I was weaving the life of Ho Chi Minh in and out of the whole film right down to the end where I film Dan Berrigan, who had just come back from Hanoi where he saw Pham Van Dong at the end of 1967.

The old footage I found went back to the thirties, so the film covers some thirty to thirty-five years of history, from the early colonial experience through the thirties into the imperial experience under us, down to the Tet Offensive, including World War II, the French cooperation with the Japanese, the rise of Ho Chi Minh and the Vietminh, the American intervention in 1949 and 1954, and so on.

How do you respond to those who dismiss the film as propaganda?

There is out-and-out propaganda in the film, obviously, although sometimes I don't know what the distinction is between propaganda and passion, and propaganda and politics. I wanted to make Ho look as good as he could be made to look. It wasn't very hard. Ho was a patriot and a Marxist. There's a lovely sequence of Ho surrounded by a bunch of children, and Dan Berrigan says in a voice-over, "The Vietnamese know what it is to have a leader who leads a simple life." I used another shot they gave me of where Ho lived, which was a small space with a tiny typewriter and one extra Vietnamese suit hanging there, and you knew it wasn't bullshit.

An interesting thing happened when I spoke with the film on May Day in 1969 at Columbia University. It was still tumultuous there, even though it was after the '68 riots. In the film I have scenes of Sam 3 missiles shooting down American planes, and when the first American plane flew over, with its insignia clearly visible, and it was shot down, the whole audience clapped. I thought, "Jesus, that's weird, isn't it? What have I done?" I mean, I was in the Air Force, I flew, and, looking at that scene on the editing table, I wouldn't have clapped. They were right, of course, except that my reaction was a little more complex.

What is your approach to editing?

I'm very slow. I mean, I could cut my new film in two weeks, and it would be OK, but it wouldn't be my film. I work very hard at editing. I'm never satisfied. I always edit with the whole picture in mind. When I finish a sequence, I run the entire film from the beginning to see how it plays. I'll continue working on a scene until I'm satisfied. Finding a suitable ending to *Pig*, for example, proved a real problem. Originally, the ending I was going to use was some footage that the Hanoi people had given me. I had been playing with it for weeks. It was a very quiet scene of a road in North Vietnam, and suddenly the brush around the road gets up, it's the Vietminh, and they come charging out. But I thought, "Shit, I'm an American, I mean, I hope the Vietnamese win this war, I think our position is immoral, and I'm a Marxist, but I'm not Vietnamese. That would be a suitable ending for a Vietnamese film, but I'm an American." I decided to show that, even though we're Americans, the Vietnamese can punish us, so I got all this footage of dead and wounded Americans with bandages around their eyes, blinded, being evacuated. Then I took a shot of a Civil War statue— a young man who died at Gettysburg—and reversed it, put it into negative, to show, in my mind anyway, that our cause in Vietnam was not the one that boy had died for in 1863, and then added a kind of scratchy version of *The Battle Hymn of the Republic*. For me that was a suitable ending, a politically coherent ending.

The temptation of the compilation film, though, is the high, jazzy moment, that plateau moment that you want in there even though maybe it doesn't belong.

In other words, you try to avoid the easy things that would play well for an audience.

The dream, of course, is to find something that's good, that plays to the audience and that's absolutely supportive of what you're trying to do. For example, I had completed *Pig*, the mix date was a day and a half away, when I received a phone call from a young woman at the Sherman Grinberg Film Library. She said, "Mr. de Antonio, I've noticed you here looking for film. I know and support what you're doing, and we've just had come into the shop this extraordinary piece of film featuring Colonel Patton." It's that sequence, of course, in which Patton gives a little speech after some American troops have been killed, and, at the end, he gives that maniacal smile and talks about his men being "a bloody good bunch of killers." Well, no matter what, that just had to go in, and I made room for that at once. Sure, it was one of those plateau moments, the kind of thing you dream about, but it was so quintessentially the position of so much of our brass, that butch, phony-Hemingway sentimentality of the tough guy who's practically in tears about the men in his own company who were killed, but for whom, on the other hand, killing gooks didn't make any difference.

Those plateaus are the temptations. Nixon gives you a lot of those. Making a film such as *Millhouse* or *Point of Order*, where you have so much good material, it takes a lot of discipline to throw some stuff out that's absolutely brilliant, that you know people will laugh and clap about, but that has no meaning.

Speaking about Point of Order, *you took a big artistic chance in making what at that time was a form that hadn't been seen before.*

You're right, but it was the only way it could have been done. There were many mistakes in *Point of Order*—it was the first film I ever did, and it was done over and over. It took almost three years; that's a long time to do a compilation film. It was all there, though, there was no research at all. I had 188 hours of material. It took a month to look at it all, and the first cut I made reduced it to 20 hours. The trick with that film was structural.

I was fascinated with the idea of making a film about a historical event with a theme that would never be mentioned. The theme is the fall of a demagogue—the greatest demagogue of our time—and the idea was to begin somewhere near the beginning and not tell what the issues are, but to let them evolve, to let the struggle evolve between the issues as well as among the different personalities, and conclude with the ending—an artificial ending which I imposed—of the empty, silent committee room.

I had no idea how an audience would respond to it, and when the film was completed and the Museum of Modern Art asked to screen it, it was my virgin experience with an audience. I had a seat in the back row, but I was very fidgety so I finally stood up in the back of the auditorium. Then, the first time I hoped someone would laugh or respond, the whole house did, and it was just amazing. I think it was one of the high points of my life, and then, when people clapped at the end, it surely was. It later opened at the Beekman and ran for a long time. It was during the winter, and cold as hell, but I used to drive by at night just to see people standing in line to see a movie that was hard to look at. I mean, it's a dry, intellectual film—no sex—and yet I still find it exciting. A lot of people have imitated it since, but, as it turns out, I was unknowingly imitating somebody long since dead whose work I had then never seen—Esther Schub.

You've said that you were disappointed with the critical reaction to Point of Order *and the way that audiences tend to see Welch as the hero of the film.*

I saw how effective Welch was, but I thought that people, particularly the critics, would see through it. My point was that there were no heroes in the film, but the press and many people tried to make a hero out of Welch. For instance, a lot of people I know who are gay are disturbed by that sequence in *Point of Order* with the word "fairy." The point I was making, of course, was that Welch was perhaps not as unscrupulous as McCarthy, but nevertheless unscrupulous. Welch was badgering this McCarthy aide, just the way McCarthy badgered people, saying, "Now, where did that picture come from that hung on Schine's wall?" And the guy said, "I don't know where that picture came from," and Welch said, "Well, sir, did you think it came from a pixie?" And McCarthy—then at the end of his career, with that absolutely unerring instinct to destroy himself—interrupts and says, "Let Mr. Welch define pixie for us. I think he might be an expert on that." It was as if Welch had baited a trap. Nobody could have done it better. Welch, who was so quick, looked at him and said, "Sir, a pixie is a close relative of a fairy. Have I enlightened you, sir?" And the camera turns on Schine and Cohn and McCarthy, and the whole audience burst into laughter. There was that rather meaningless rumor that two or three of McCarthy's people were gay, and Welch knew it. But when the film was released, a lot of people asked, "What did you bring up that fag thing for?" My feeling was that it belonged, not because of the allegations against them, but because that was Welch's technique.

What bothered me most about the critics was the political judgment that made them dwell on how funny the film was. All those critics, however, almost without exception, were silent during the McCarthy days, so what they were doing was enjoying a kind of vicarious solidarity with history. Those people had all been intimidated by that monster and demagogue Joseph R. McCarthy, the junior senator from Wisconsin, and some ten years after the events they all had a chance to dump on McCarthy. Critics such as Brendan Gill at the *New Yorker*, Bosley Crowther at the *New York Times*, and Archer Winsten and Jimmy

Wechsler at the *New York Post* all wrote things that made me puke, particularly Wechsler who called the film "a love letter to Miss Liberty."

How did your film Charge and Countercharge *come about?*

In attempting to reach a larger audience with *Point of Order*, a major publishing company came to me and said, "We love your film, but it could never be used in a classroom." I asked, "Why not?" They said, "A classroom hour is like a Freudian hour, it's about fifty minutes. Your film is ninety-seven minutes. That's two entire classes, and it almost makes the teacher an unnecessary appendage. We'd like something about forty-three minutes. That will allow the teacher time to talk." So, in putting together *Charge and Countercharge*, the subtlety had to go, because subtlety depends on time; but all the great moments are kept.

Your "negative" films which attack the establishment, such as In the Year of the Pig *or* Millhouse, *tend to be better, more accomplished works than what might be categorized as your "positive" films about the left, such as* Underground *or* America Is Hard to See. *How do you account for the surprising lack of critical edge in those latter films? Is it a fear of criticizing or undermining the left?*

I don't share that perception entirely. I think *America Is Hard to See* is a film which was not understood. Basically, the subject of that film is the failure of the liberal left. Liberalism came down the pike with its most articulate spokesman, Eugene McCarthy, a genuinely intellectual man, and there was a brief moment when something of a normal democratic process might have worked here if McCarthy had had a little bit more courage, if he had played hard in the convention and attacked Humphrey instead of rolling over like some obscure monk who didn't want to get into a brawl.

As for *Underground*, its weaknesses are many, and among them—speaking only for myself now, since more than one person was involved in that film— was a generation gap. I've never shared all the Weather Underground's politics, although I supported large assumptions they made. They were the last gasp of a movement I had been following, from the early days of SDS on, of an entire generation younger than me. It's a film about endings, not about where life is going, it's the end of that generation's most important political organization.

Do you think that's the way audiences perceived that film?

No, maybe not. It's not downbeat, because I did admire those people personally. It's a very confused film, and, since the truth has to come out on this sometime, collectives of two are impossible. This was basically a collective between Mary [Lampson] and myself. Mary had always worked for me, had been my employee, and then suddenly we were equals. It was a very hard thing, and we struggled over it. I think Mary was much more deeply moved by them than I was. I had to give way a good many places in that film where I would not have given way previously. I was working very hard to be collective and self-effacing, which is something I'm not by temperament. I was trying very hard to be a superfeminist. I mean, I don't have a hard time being profeminist, but being a superfeminist is very hard because it's a false position. The Weather people had that same problem, and it shows in the film.

In fact, I thought the Weather people were incredibly arrogant. I can't remember if we left this in the film or not, but at one point I said, "Look, if you don't want to talk about who you are, why don't we just get a fucking copy of *Prairie Fire* and you can read it?" And they said, "OK, that would be good, that might be better." I said, "No, that wouldn't be better. It's not well written, it's a boring magazine in many places."

I wanted them—and they had originally agreed to do this—to tell how they got to where they were. In other words, how did essentially middle-class people—and some of them came from the upper class—become revolutionaries carrying on an underground war against the government. That was the story I always thought we were going to do, and it was only when we got underground that they pulled their own gig. We argued, and I wanted to put that argument into the film. Mary and I had a lot of problems about that, and I think the reason Mary didn't want it in the film is because I'm the one who did the arguing and it would have made it much more my film. Mary didn't argue with them, Haskell did somewhat, and I argued a lot.

My feeling was that nobody gives a shit about all this abstract political terminology. American political people, especially SDS types, have almost no theoretical formulation to fall back on. Every time I heard them talk about Lenin or Mao, my heart skipped a beat, because it was never anything different from what they wrote in *Prairie Fire*, whereas I thought the human stuff would have been fascinating.

Afterwards, I realized we didn't have enough to make a film, because much of what we shot didn't work, they didn't want to say very much, and the jargon didn't appeal to me. So I thought, "Well, I'll make an anthology of the left. I'll talk to people I know and get excerpts from their films to put in." So there's a great sequence of Malcolm X, there's something from Saul Landau's *Fidel*, something from Chris Marker's film about the Pentagon, and so on. Those are the roots that the Weather people came from. They're the roots, for that matter, of anybody who was in SDS or for most young people in the American left, and I wanted to confer on them a kind of historical authenticity by tying them up to all that. I mean, I found Malcolm X more interesting than they were.

Now, I don't want it to seem as if I'm running down the Weather people. It was my idea to make the film. I was the one who approached them: I was the one who got Mary and Haskell into it. I did it because I found what they were doing exciting. That does not necessarily mean that I shared their politics, but there was something in their desperation that I felt myself. Ford was in office, it was all going to be the same thing over and over again, the whole left seemed shattered, all those great demonstrations, all those forces that seemed to be alive were dying, and these people were the last spark that was left of all that. There was something that appealed to me, almost in an avant-garde sense, about what they were doing. I mean, to put a bomb in the lavatory of the Capitol, to put a bomb in a police station, in Gulf Oil, in Rockefeller Center, and to get away with it every time. There was a Robin Hood quality about that.

Someone at the time said that the Weather Underground's strategy was to destroy capitalism, bathroom by bathroom. It's ironic, but perhaps the most significant aspect about Underground *was how the Hollywood filmmaking community came to your defense when the FBI subpoenaed you to turn over your film and tapes.*

We were supported because our stand was so aggressive and so rational. We kept saying, "Our crime is that we made a film, not that we belong to any organization." Even Peter Bogdanovich, who is a fairly apolitical person, signed the petition in support of us, and Robert Wise, then the head of the Directors Guild of America, spoke out officially in our favor.

You've had a long history of harassment by the FBI, the CIA, and the government in general. You're perhaps the only filmmaker who was on Nixon's Enemies List. Has any of that ever seriously hindered your work?

Sure, I've had a lot of fucking over. Many times I would set up an interview to be filmed and then, at the last minute, it would be short-circuited. I think the government also goes out of its way, directly and indirectly—and the indirect way is the more potent way—to prevent certain films from getting the kind of exposure they might get. *In the Year of the Pig*, for instance, was booked to open in a good house in Los Angeles, and someone broke into the theater in the middle of the night and painted on the screen a hammer and sickle and the words "Communist traitor." News of this spread to other theaters, and that was the end of the film theatrically.

Something strange also happened with *Millhouse.* The film grossed $36,000 in its first week at the New Yorker, which was a house record. It was in the *Variety* charts, so all the other theaters wanted it. Louis Sher of the Art Theater Guild, who owns seventy theaters out West in cities such as Denver and Albuquerque, booked *Millhouse* in his theaters. Then, just like that, they were all canceled. But who knows the real reason why? I got a letter from a theater manager in Denver who said, "My company canceled your film, which I was looking forward to, here at the Bluebird Theater in Denver, and to this day I don't know why it was canceled." I know the kind of muscle the White House exerted, because I have copies of all these memoranda on White House letterhead about the film. I don't moan or complain about it, because if you attack the reigning president of the U.S., if you attack the government, you can't expect them to treat you with a light hand. It comes with the territory. *Millhouse* did show theatrically in twenty cities, but it could have been shown in seventy other cities where documentaries ordinarily don't play.

When *Millhouse* opened in Washington, D.C., Larry O'Brien's assistant at the National Democratic Committee called me at my hotel and invited me to come by for a drink. He asked me, "Mr. de Antonio, how can we use your film?" I told him, "You can't. You'd be tarred with my reputation. But I'll tell you how you could use it. Buy a hundred prints, let me give a week-long course on Nixon to about three hundred young people. Then let them take the prints to all the territories you're sure to lose—the South, the Midwest—and have people look at that life." He said, "Gee, that's a good idea, but you're right, there's no way we could do that."

Millhouse did have a wide distribution for a documentary. Of course, audiences were laughing at Nixon, which I wasn't doing. Basically, I use him as a comic figure, but I wasn't laughing at him. There's a difference. I'm not unsympathetic to that poor, wretched, clumsy, mixed-up man. I wouldn't want him for a friend, but I understand the drive that must have made him from the first moment of his life. What I wanted people to understand in that film is that the souring of the Horatio Alger myth is almost a necessity in our kind of culture. Nixon, the glib opportunist who trampled over Helen Gahagan Douglas and Alger Hiss and everyone else, that is the way you became a Horatio Algerish mythic hero—you know, pluck and luck turned out to be something quite different. He paid the price right along the line, although more of us paid the price in a bigger way than he did.

How do you account for your fascination with history and politics?

I come from a long line of intellectuals, there's no other word for it. My grandfather was a philosophy professor who translated Lucretius, and my father was also an intellectual. I was raised in a home with five thousand books in it. The stories I heard as a little boy were Homer, Dickens, or my father's versions of European history. I knew the French Revolution fairly well, as well as the Italian movement to create a unified Italy.

Was your father a teacher?

No, he was a sort of upper-class gentleman, a doctor who owned a hospital and who had money and time.

How were you politically radicalized?

I was very early confronted with the reality of class. We lived in a big house in Scranton, Pennsylvania, with a chauffeur, cook, and maid. When I was five or six years old, I can remember, every Thanksgiving we collected money for the poor children in Scranton who lived only a mile or so from us. I used to ask why that was. I entered Harvard when I was sixteen and immediately joined the Young Communist League, the John Reed Society, and the American Student Union. I knew that's where I wanted to be. I've never deviated from those ideas, although I left all formal groups long ago.

When did you become interested in film?

I disliked most films. I had very strange, perverse tastes. I thought Louis Jouvet, the thirties French actor, was absolutely fantastic. I loved Renoir's films, and Chaplin and Keaton. I didn't care for John Ford's films at all. I mean, I saw that the images were beautiful, but I quickly got tired of Monument Valley and those tacky songs.

The one movie that turned me on—because I knew all the people in it and the guy who wrote it—was *Pull My Daisy*. It's a movie that doesn't hold up today, by the way, but it was so much of that time, and it made me want to make a movie, that's another reason why it's important to me. I saw that an interesting film could be made for very little money.

We understand that Andy Warhol made a film about you. What was that like?

Andy and I have been friends for a long time, since long before he was a painter. One day he said to me, "De, I think we should make a film together." I said, "Come on, Andy, we're friends, but I like to make political films and you make these frou-frou films." Then one night I saw him at a bar, when I was drunk, and I said, "OK, Andy, let's do it!" He said, "What shall we film?" and I said, "I'll drink a quart of whiskey in twenty minutes." I knew that twenty-two-year-old Marines had died doing it, but I knew what I was doing. I'm a very good drinker.

I showed up at his studio with my wife and a drinking companion. They turned the lights on, and I sat there cross-legged against a wall and drank a quart of J&B whiskey in twenty minutes. It was boring, nothing happened. I didn't want the glass, so I broke it. I had some ice and I threw that away. Andy was filming with a twelve-hundred-foot 16 mm magazine which runs for thirty-five minutes. When it came time to change the magazine, he was so untrained in the use of the camera that it took him about fifteen minutes to change it. So by the time the second roll went on, I was on the floor. I mean, I couldn't even get up. My hand goes up the wall, trying to pull myself up, I'm singing Spanish civil war songs and shouting, "Fuck you!" It was unspeakably degrading. I finally walked out with the help of my wife and friend and went home and slept it off. The next day I was sharp enough to call my lawyer and have him call Andy and tell him, "De never signed a release, so if the film is ever shown, we'll sue." It appears in Andy's published filmography—it's called *Drink*—but it's never been shown.

How does Painters Painting *fit in with your political films?*

I think *Painters Painting* is a political film, too, except it's political in another, more complex sense. In my lifetime, the most significant cultural event, which took place in an absolutely closed circle, was called New York painting. It addresses itself to a few thousand people. I mean, maybe a few million people go to museums, but only two or three thousand people—the painters, the collectors, the owners, and the dealers—actually comprise the scene. That was a scene I knew intimately. Nobody was as well qualified by experience as I was with those people. They would say things to me that nobody else could even ask them. I knew the answers to the questions in advance. I was fascinated by these people. They were amazingly articulate, I loved their work, they were my friends, so I made a film about them.

Their work was the highest commodity we produced. It became something that every sophisticated millionaire had to have. I mean, any asshole could buy a Rolls Royce or a $2 million house, but it took exquisite taste to have a painting by Frank Stella or Robert Rauschenberg. *Painters Painting* is a film largely enthusiastic about American art, and I'm aware of all the political contradictions. The history of the West is replete with similar examples. The great art of the nineteenth century was the art of imperial France when they had African colonies. But for a moment after World War II, all this stuff exploded and New York became the art capital of the world. One of the reasons it happened, of course, is that many European artists fled Hitler, and many of them—particularly Hans Hofmann, Marcel Duchamp, and Max Ernst—came here to New York where their work was immediately shown by Peggy Guggenheim. Jackson Pollock was painting like an American romantic realist when, suddenly, he became acquainted with the unconscious through these people and, boom, developed a genuinely native American art nonetheless. Nothing has happened since then like that explosion between 1945 and 1970.

Would you tell us a bit about your new film? We understand that for the first time you will be utilizing actors and fictional sequences.

The heart of the film is the trial of the Plowshares Eight. Originally I went down to Pennsylvania, hired a very good lawyer, and petitioned the court to film the trial. I was denied the right to film, even after an appeal to the Supreme Court of Pennsylvania. At first I tried to film all around the trial—meetings between the defendants and their lawyers, demonstrations, prayer vigils—but I knew I didn't have a film, so I said, "Fuck 'em, I'll write my own screenplay." I got all the trial transcripts and from thirteen hundred pages of transcript I made a seventy-page screenplay.

Did you elaborate on the trial transcripts?

Well, I changed things. This is not a documentary. For example, all through-out the trial the defendants kept asking to produce expert witnesses, and the judge said, "The only thing that's pertinent here is your crime, not nuclear war." The defendants were going to call witnesses like Robert Aldridge, who'd designed five generations of nuclear warheads for Lockheed then one day realized that what he was doing was wrong, and he became a leader in the antinuclear movement. Daniel Ellsberg, Dave Dellinger, and others were going to be called. The judge refused to allow any of them to testify, but since I'm making my own trial, I've put the witnesses in.

So you're filming the trial they were not allowed to have.

Yes, I've reconstructed the whole trial, with the Berrigans and the other defendants playing themselves, and everyone else is an actor, including Martin Sheen, who plays the judge. I had met Martin in the days of the *Underground* fracas, and he impressed me as being not only a very fine actor, but also a fantastic human being, a person of commitment. I asked him if he'd be in the film, and he said, "Absolutely. I'll give you a week's shooting time for free." Then he asked, "Don't you need some money?" I said, "Yes," and he gave it.

I videotaped every actor who tried out, and ended up with as many as forty actors trying out for one role. So I had very good actors working for scale. The film has a real interaction between real people and actors. The tension began to build during the shooting, you could see it in the defendants. I mean, there was Martin Sheen, acting the way the judge was supposed to act, and George Crowley plays the prosecuting attorney who knows that this is his last chance, that if he's ever going to be anything other than an assistant prosecuting attorney in this small, right-wing town, he *has* to win. So all those other forces and struggles are in there. The actors were wonderful, and the Plowshares Eight really got angry. In fact, Dan Berrigan gave the greatest performance I've ever seen in a courtroom. He did it better than Welch, better even than he did it in the real courtroom. Dan Berrigan is a brilliant guy, a Jesuit priest who also happens to be a great actor, among other things. One of the things I learned on this film is that the Catholic left is a very real left. I was raised in an anti-clerical household and was never very sympathetic to the Catholic church, but they are really a committed left, their bodies are out there.

I'll be integrating documentary material with the fictional sequences. I've already filmed two members of the jury, and in two weeks I'll be filming the real judge, Judge Salus, and the district attorney. They're going to talk about the trial.

Do you know how all of this is going to cut together?

Nope. I've never done this before. But isn't that part of the fun of art? You take those chances, and you can come out looking like a fool or you can come out feeling that you've done something good. Both possibilities are there.

We understand that you used tape instead of film.

Yes, we shot on videotape. I knew that I didn't want to have a tape person shoot it for me, though, so instead I chose Judy Irola, a woman whose work I liked and who had never, ever done anything on videotape. It was the most intelligent thing I did in making the film. We shot on one inch, which is professional gauge, and the technicians in the video truck said, "Wow, we've never seen stuff like this," because Judy shot it like a film.

Why was it shot on tape?

Because I started out shooting the documentary stuff on tape. When you shoot three-quarter inch for documentary, it's incredibly cheap. Later we'll take it up to one inch, and it'll look not quite as good as film, but I don't want it to. The real part will look slightly tacky and the trial part will look highly professional, but that difference between the documentary and fictional scenes is quite intentional.

Where do you find money to finance your films?

Rich liberals. I don't use foundations. I ask people I know who have money and who have been supportive of left projects in the past. It was always easy, I never had any trouble raising money. But I've noticed an enormous difference in my fundraising ability today as opposed to eight or nine years ago. You become unclean after a while, and the times have changed. A friend of mine told me about a fundraising party last night where they screened Diego de la Texera's new film on El Salvador. A lot of theater and film people were there, and ten years ago, during the Vietnam war, the checkbooks would have flashed out at the end of that film, but last night nobody gave, they were all afraid. Some people said, "Here's a hundred dollars in cash," but nobody would put their name on anything. They were afraid that something might happen to their careers. That's reflected in raising money right now to complete my new film: I mean, I never thought that I'd have trouble raising money for Catholic activists, but I'm having a harder time with that than anything I've ever done.

When you receive money, is it an outright gift?

No, rarely. I've a moderately good record of making my own high-handed rules, which is that I pay people back but they get no profit, because I figure they have more money than they need anyway. But they're entitled to be paid back, and they get a tax benefit.

Some of your readers may be interested in a ploy that I think more left-wing filmmakers—particularly compilation filmmakers, and particularly if you're as thorough as I am—should use. When I was done with *In the Year of the Pig*, for example, I had the most complete film library on Vietnam in existence in this country, tens of thousands of feet that I couldn't use. The law says that the artist can't take a tax write-off on such material, so what I would do was to find the person I was going to ask to put money into my next film—*Millhouse*, say—and explain, "Look, this footage is worth $100,000. If you put X amount of money into *Millhouse*, (a) I'll guarantee to repay you, (b) you can claim a loss this year because the film is being made and you obviously can't make a profit on it, and (c) two years hence, as an inducement for getting you to invest in the film, I will sell you these Vietnam outtakes for the money that you're putting into the film, and you can donate them to the University of Wisconsin and claim a tax write-off on their declared value." The film then becomes part of the university's archive—and I'm lucky, of course, because there's an archive about me at the University of Wisconsin—and they make it available for study by scholars, film historians, and the like. If you're in a high tax bracket, you make a fairly good profit just getting your money back, plus that later tax write-off. It's a very good inducement and should be used by young filmmakers who know rich people.

How do you perceive your audience? Who are you making films for, and what sort of political impact can your films have?

A great American, Walt Whitman, said that to have great poetry, you must have great audiences. Since I'm interested in history, I'm obviously interested in what happens to my films over the long haul. Anyone who makes films wants them to be seen, and I would do anything except change my films to reach a larger audience. But in America and most Western capitalist countries, film—from its earliest, nickelodeon days up to the most sophisticated mind control today through television—has been seen as an opiate, as entertainment. As the old Hollywood saw has it, "If you have a message, use Western Union." Well, all my films have messages, but I don't want to send them by Western Union.

I have never looked upon documentary as an apprenticeship for the making of Hollywood films. That's bullshit. I've always chosen to make documentaries. I love documentary film, I love the political tradition of documentary film, and I love the subjects that documentary film can treat. I never saw making documentaries as preparing me to do a *Gidget* film or even a fake serious film like *Coming Home*.

My bet's with history. I'm an American who believes in history. That's a very rare thing, because most Americans live by seconds, they try to live outside of history. But I live in history, and I think that people will be looking at *Pig* and *Point of Order* long after I'm dead. I don't think it will be millions, but there will be audiences who will know that *Pig* is a history of the war in Vietnam as good as any book on the subject. Those images that you have to struggle to find and to make effective will endure, because history endures. That's an optimistic

view of the human race, and I realize it's almost kind of silly to be optimistic
about the human race today at the rate we're going.

But, to answer your question more directly, I get the audience I know I'm
going to get. I suffer from small audiences, I know that. It's too bad that those
gorgeous color spectaculars are the things that reach masses of people, and
that films like mine are customarily seen by college graduates, intellectuals,
East Side audiences, or public television audiences. What kind of audience,
theoretically, would I have wanted for *In the Year of the Pig*? I would have liked
police and working class, blue-collar guys who were for the war to have seen
it. I would have liked them to have seen that the Vietnamese were fighting for
their country, even though they might have hated the film.

*Does it always have to be a question of reaching massive numbers of people? Is it
possible to be politically effective reaching a smaller audience?*

I lecture at universities a lot, and I can't tell you how many times I've been
absolutely *bouleversé* by having some young woman come up to me and say,
"You know, I was radicalized by seeing your film *In the Year of the Pig*. I was
going to the University of Kansas when I saw it, and it made me see the war
in a different way and I joined SDS." Or a young person will come up to me
and say, "I just saw *Point of Order*, and I think I understand something about
McCarthy now." That has happened many times.

Your films are also very popular overseas.

They do well in countries such as Sweden, England, West Germany, and
France—the French in particular like our mad president, our mad demagogue,
and our unsuccessful war, which was just as unsuccessful as their war, because
they think I'm anti-American, which I'm not. I like this country, and if I didn't,
I'd go somewhere else. I'm an American. This is my space, and that's why I
want to change it.

7

The War Game: An Interview with Peter Watkins

Alan Rosenthal

It may be the most important film ever made. (Kenneth Tynan, *The Observer*)

The War Game *was produced and directed by Peter Watkins in 1965 and was denied a television screening by the BBC in 1966 as a result of a directive by the then director general of the BBC, Sir Hugh Greene. But in spite of Sir Hugh Greene's restrictive policy, the BBC finally bowed to pressure and released the film for theatrical but not television screening.*

The War Game *starts with a series of maps showing the vulnerability of England to nuclear attack. It then suggests an international crisis that culminates in a Berlin confrontation between the Russians and the Americans. As a result of the crisis the allies use tactical nuclear weapons in Europe, which in turn provokes the Russians to drop atom bombs on England.*

What follows is a hellish evocation of disaster. Carefully prepared civil defense plans prove futile and useless; children are blinded, firestorms rage, and the dead lie in the streets. After a while there are hunger riots; police are assaulted, and food thievers are shot by execution squads. It seems, in fact, as if civilization is disintegrating.

The style of the film is highly composite. Live interviews are mixed with carefully staged vignettes; the beginning of a storyline is broken by comments quoted from religious and scientific personalities; grainy newsreel camerawork suddenly gives way to the smoothest of Hollywood set lighting. In theory, it shouldn't work; in practice, it all blends together as a unified piece of art.

Although defenders of the film saw it as an authentic vision of catastrophe, it was damned by many British dailies and written off as a grossly distorted message by the British right wing. Watkins was charged with failing to show hope and the resilience of the human spirit. He was also accused of being too harshly realistic and (worst of all) of propagandizing for nuclear disarmament in the crudest possible way.

All art, however, is propaganda in one form or another, and to seek "objectivity" in a film about the atom bomb seems to me to be a red herring. Watkins was presenting a personal vision based on well-researched facts which few critics bothered to challenge. Moreover, a great deal of the criticism very definitely exhibited an ostrich-like approach to life, which Bertrand Russell commented on as follows in his autobiography: "Those who try to make you uneasy by talk about atom bombs are regarded as troublemakers, . . . as people who spoil the pleasure of a fine day by foolish prospects of improbable rain."

In reviewing the whole situation, it seems a pity that The War Game *led to Watkins's resignation from the BBC. It was unfortunate because the BBC in the past has been relatively open to the dissenting voice and the individual opinion (certainly far more so than the commercial networks in the United States) and would have seemed to be the ideal place for Watkins to work out his own personal and committed brand of filmmaking.*

Since 1966 Watkins has trodden a varyingly successful path in feature films, with the direction of Privilege *and* The Gladiators *to his credit. At the time of writing (November 1970), he was engaged on a series of films dealing with key events in American history, such as the Civil War, and their relevance today.*

This interview took place on a freezing Sunday morning in Toronto. Time was very limited, and because James Blue had already covered a lot of the shooting details of the film in an excellent interview with Watkins published in Film Comment,[1] *I decided to concentrate my questions on the preliminary research rather than on the filmmaking itself.*

Alan Rosenthal: *What was your background prior to entering the BBC?*

Peter Watkins: I wanted to be an actor, but my drama training stopped when I did my national service. I came out of the army in 1956 and, for no reason at all, suddenly decided to become a filmmaker. I saw somebody using an 8 mm camera, and I guess it excited me—I can't remember why. It all happened in about a week, and I stopped trying to become an actor and began the long, dreary, uphill trail of getting into the film business. First I became an assistant producer in an advertising agency, doing commercials. I then became an assistant editor and finally a director about seven years later in a London sponsored documentary unit. That was the professional side of it. However, about once a year I spent all my money and made an antiwar film. A couple of them won amateur film awards and were shown on television.

By that time I was getting a little fed up with England, and as my wife is French I decided to try and get some work in France. I bashed away with nothing happening for five months, then decided to apply to the BBC. Luckily, I was saved from some of the hapless formalities that you have to go through in joining the BBC, as Huw Wheldon had seen an amateur film of mine called *The Forgotten Faces.* This was a reconstruction of the Hungarian uprising of 1956 which had been shown on television, and Wheldon had liked it. So I became one of the first of the new wave of people who were taken into the opening of channel 2. As it happened, I never worked in channel 2; I stayed in channel 1, was a production assistant for a year, and then I said I would like to make a film about the battle of Culloden.

Was much supervision given on what was, after all, your first film for the BBC?

They let me do it completely on trust and on my record of amateur filmmaking. I had read a very interesting book on the battle, thought the scope of the subject tremendous, and Huw Wheldon said, "Well, just do it." I don't think he had time or particularly wanted to read the script; he just let me do it. It was completely subjective, of course, as those were the golden days of documentaries; I am not sure that the freedom I had exists any more. But it was marvelous at that time. Unfortunately, Huw Wheldon went up to his high position, and the situation has changed.

Your history of antiwar films seems to indicate that The War Game *wasn't a sudden inspiration but was the result of development over a number of years.*

Well, way back in 1961 or 1962, like most people in England, I was an observer of the Campaign for Nuclear Disarmament. I felt very strongly about the issue but didn't join the campaign because, although I agreed with their objectives, I disagreed with their strategy. Those were the days before I joined the BBC, and I had an idea for an amateur film about a group of atom-bomb survivors in a cellar. I wanted to do face-to-face interviews of what they had been through and that sort of thing. Anyway, it sort of lay there ticking for a number of years; but as soon as I had done *Culloden* I raised the subject with my boss.

At that time I was a good boy in the eyes of the BBC. *Culloden* had been well received, and I had a certain amount of rope given to me. By that stage I suppose I must have abandoned the cellar idea and broadened the whole to include the wider effects of a nuclear attack on England. Wheldon was a bit worried about it but said, "Okay, I'll have to put this to the higher-up people, and they'll probably want to see a script." So it went through to this upper echelon, but they really didn't approve of the thing until five days after I had started shooting, when their reaction was, "Well, we'll wait and see it, and then evaluate it afterwards, because it may be difficult." It was left on a very vague basis.

One of the striking things about The War Game *is the amount of research it must have involved. Was the information on which you based your script readily obtainable?*

The more films I do, the more I research. It's a growing pattern. I tend to put more and more emphasis onto the solid basis of research. With *The War Game*, I had to do a great deal of original research because nobody had ever collated all the information into an easily accessible published form. Quite a lot of books had been written on the effects of thermonuclear bombs, but very few of these had ever been seen by the public.

You must realize that there are an infinite number of books published, which the public can get at, on a normal historical subject like the American Civil War. In contrast, there is an extreme dearth of literature available to the public about the Third World War. What literature there is, is stacked up on the shelves of the American Institute of Strategic Studies and those sorts of places and is never read by the public. So it was an extremely esoteric subject for a filmmaker to delve into and quite hard to find basic facts.

Did you employ a research team?

No, not really. I did it all myself and mounted the research in several different areas, such as technical and sociological. On the technical side I went to Germany and tried to get the essence of Berlin, the Berlin Wall, and the situation there, because even before I started writing, I had an intuitive sense that I would need a hypothetical "bust-up" place, and in 1965 Berlin was a little warmer than it is now. But as I always say to people, the flash point is really immaterial. The point is what happens when the war comes. After Berlin, I met with professors, biologists, physicians, and radiologists from London University. I also met with people from the London Institute of Strategic Studies, and I did research into the payload of rockets, the effects of fallout on white and red blood corpuscles, the effect of radioactivity, and the like.

It was all immensely complicated—the amount of force required to fling a brick three hundred yards in how many seconds, the amount of thermal heat required to melt an eyeball at this and that distance. I read reports from Hiroshima, Nagasaki, and Dresden and found that, though there is plenty of technical material, the emotional effect of an atom bomb on people has been much less thoroughly investigated.

When the various places supplied you with pamphlets, did they want to know your motives or anything like that?

You have to differentiate here between people in general and governmental bodies. The experts, the professors and so on, were extremely cooperative and very interested. A few were a little skeptical of an amateur blundering into their domain, but they freely supplied what little information they had. The governmental bodies were different. In general they said No.

I made formal approaches, realizing that I was rather putting my head in the lion's mouth; but I thought, what the hell, I've got to try it all ways round. So I went to the Home Office—I think the A.G. 4 branch was the department in charge within the Ministry of Civil Defence—and I said, "I would please like to know . . . ," and I gave them a long, long list of questions about civil defense preparation in Britain. I said, "I want to know your placings and the amounts of your stockpiles; I want to know your withdrawal policies; I want to know who are going to be regional senior government officers." It was a long, long list of questions. A few may have touched on semisecret data, but I am sure that 80 percent of the answers came within the realm of information that should be available to the public.

The BBC sort of gingerly supported the request for this information, but the Home Office was rather taken aback. Then there was silence for three weeks before I was called into a BBC office and told, "We're afraid you are not going to get this information, and we believe it's best for you not to push the point." In other words, something appeared to have happened between the BBC and the Home Office. I can't be sure of this, but I think the BBC was told to cooperate in persuading me not to obtain this information. But then what happened later was worse, because the Home Office withdrew all official help.

At that juncture I was in the process of asking for help from the various branches of the Kent Auxiliary Fire Service, the main fire service, the civil defense, and the police. This went right down to the sort of nitty-gritty of technical help in supplying the radioactive meters, civil defense uniforms, rescue packs, ambulances, police information, and so forth. The Home Office put the clamp down on that immediately and told everyone to have absolutely nothing to do with me and to give me no help whatever, of any shape, size, or form. So, in most of the places I went people said to me, "Sorry, we've been told not to touch you."

The only group that helped me voluntarily after that was the Fire Service, which appeared to me to be the only group or agency in England that had and has a realistic approach to the effects of a nuclear attack. They were the only people willing to talk to me and willing to supply me with the needed bits and pieces of equipment. They said, "We've been told not to, but we realize this is an important subject." They didn't say, "Look, if a nuclear attack comes, we'll mop it up easily in England." They took the reverse approach, because they had had to deal with the small-scale fire storms in Kent during the Second World War. They had seen the ravages of a mass incendiary raid, and they knew that a nuclear attack would be infinitely worse. They knew of the terrible toll in the fire storms in Dresden. These practicing technicians were the weak link in the official "happiness bureau." They knew what it would be like, and they helped me. And they did it unofficially. Officially, there was a complete clampdown.

How much time did you put into research?

I suppose the amount of actual pure research, of bashing around and talking to these radiologists—rushing out to Oxford to meet a man who knew about the "Honest John Rocket" in Germany and meeting people doing strategic studies here and there—probably ranged from November 1964 until January or February 1965. It took about three months. I shot the film in April 1965, but I kept on researching up to the end, so you could say solid research was about two to three months, while there was some polishing during the period I was writing the commentary.

You mentioned doing sociological research as well as technical probing. Would you mind going into that a little more?

The sociological background to a third world war was just as important to me as the technical research, but here the research was more in terms of people than books. I went to see from thirty to fifty people, ranging from poets and sculptors to conductors, composers, writers, producers, and so on. I wanted to hear what they felt about the silence on the whole subject of the effects of nuclear war, and what they felt about their part as intellectuals in contributing to the silence. I just wanted to feel the response, which was quite an experience. In fact, one day I'd like to write a book about it. These meetings were the most interesting and moving part of the research, and the responses I obtained were continually fed back into the film.

At what stage did you begin trying to formulate a script?

Script is something I can't be very exact with you about, as I am not very exact about it myself. I wrote a document which was about half the size of the London telephone directory. It was tremendously detailed; I believe it was quite authoritative and, apart from anything else, presented a complete indictment of British civil defense by showing the futility of their planning and methods.

Did the script go through many versions before you were satisfied with it?

Yes. Originally it was much more padded and there were many more incidents. I wanted to follow many more individuals. I seem to remember I had a man in Kent who was working in a factory, but I can't remember what he did. There were also various other individuals, like the doctor, who are now in the film not really as characters but just as human beings caught up in the holocaust. I hadn't developed their characters much more in the original script, but I had placed them with much more regularity throughout the film. We kept going back to them, characters like the police inspector, and they provided a continuing thread.

How close did you work to your final shooting script? Was it a guide or a bible?

The script was overly long and immensely complicated. It had everything in it, almost too much. It certainly had all the logistics of the attack and why the English civil defense couldn't pick up the pieces. It had all this but was far too long, and it was in the back of my mind rather than in the forefront during the shooting. In this kind of a situation you have three or four weeks to make the film, and you just try to extract the essence of what you're doing while facing the daily problems.

What kind of problems—artistic, logistic . . . ?

You are constantly having to grapple with "Has Mrs. Brown gotten up this morning'?" "Who's going to come and be the warden for this street?" "Has Mr. Baker caught his train for Tunbridge?" "Are the police going to let us use this street?" "That guy over there, knocking down that house, is he going to stop acting half mad?" "Is it going to stop raining?" "Is the hotel going to supply lunch for the cast?" All these things were part of the filmmaking. It was a hard, bloody fight, going on for weeks, with a lot of the niceties of the script just going down the drain. When you've got a long document like I had, even more goes down the drain. What you are continually trying to do is hold on the essence of the whole thing. You are having to deal with a myriad of contingencies while you're filming, while at the same time you're doing a stripped-down précis of the script and praying to God that you're retaining a structure, even if it's changed from your original concept.

How limited were you in your budget?

That's an interesting question. No one ever stated precisely how much I could have. I seem to remember that they sort of drew the line at about £12,000, but you must remember that BBC costing is extremely complicated. They have an above-and-below-the-line system, which means in fact that nobody ever knows what you're spending. Quite a lot of overheads are charged to the BBC. I think that they said that the above-the-line costs would be £12,000. It was said that I spent £20,000, but nobody ever told me whether the extra £8,000 was above-the-line or whether it was an expression of the BBC's overheads.

One is struck and overwhelmed by the sense of factual reality in The War Game, *the veracity and truth of the actors, which makes part of the film look like a newsreel. This realism was also one of the most brilliant things about* Culloden. *How do you achieve these results?*

It doesn't happen by accident. My drama training helped somewhat, but I really think that a large proportion of the realism is due to the fact that I try to make my films provide a common experience for the people in them. Both *Culloden* and *The War Game* are films made in unusually adverse conditions. For me, they are practically pure conditions, as I think this is what filmmaking is about. When you do a film like *Culloden* or *The War Game*, people have literally to stand in the gutters, in the howling wind for hours on end, fed probably on beans and a hamburger.

In *Culloden*, people were standing in fairly good reproduction Highland costume, which meant a plaid, probably a pair of jockey shorts underneath, and something on their feet—and that was it. They then walked for the best part of two weeks in the biting wind, in the rain, over moors more than a foot deep in water. And something built up between them. A similar kind of thing happened in *The War Game*. And all this is done out of enthusiasm. The people aren't paid, or are paid only token amounts.

How do you approach these people? How do you get your participants?

There are various ways. A bad way, which still works, is to advertise in local papers that you're making a film and are going to have a mass meeting for people who are interested. The other way is to approach local cine and dramatic groups, of which we have a lot in England, or to go to the schools and universities.

I usually start the ball rolling by having a mass meeting in town, at which there might be two or three hundred people from different drama groups and the like. I then get up on the platform and talk for two or three hours. I tell them why I'm making the film. I try to get them involved in the subject and to understand its importance. I try to get them to understand its connection with them as human beings and what might be the worth of the collective experiences of making a film on the subject. I then usually terminate the meeting and try to meet every single one of these people individually.

I have an idea of the sort of people I am trying to cast, but it has to be immensely flexible. If I see a guy who I think might be a good policeman, I make a note of that. I talk to each person for about ten minutes or a quarter of an hour—it depends on the number of people there and on the time pressures. Then the thing narrows down a little. People drop out; other people stay with you. In *The War Game*, I built up an aggregate of about four hundred people who stuck with me the whole time. Not one was a professional actor, and fewer than half had ever played in front of a camera before.

How do these people get this realism? How does somebody just simply cry?

You can't just pull a man in from a job and say, "Okay fellow, I want you to suddenly become involved in a nuclear war, and I want you to give me a very stark realism which has to come smacking across as if you were actually caught in those circumstances." That doesn't just happen in five minutes. You have to get to know the chap, you have to pull him into the communal thing of making films.

Filming is the most god-awful boring thing for people who are in it, at least in this sort of film where they have to stand around for hours on end watching you grapple with the problems, waiting to do their little bit as a policeman. Maybe you've told Mr. Brown, "Now you've gotta be here at half past nine on

Monday," but at half past two on Wednesday you still haven't filmed him. You have to pull people through all that; and what holds them might possibly be my personality, but it certainly has to do with what you have impressed on them as the meaning of the subject.

What also comes through is their desire as a person to express themselves; and when you make my sort of film, you find yourself unexpectedly tapping this. It's a collective "thing," plus what you say to them just before you start running the camera, or you talk to them the night before—something like, "You're going to be a nurse and I want you to think about holding a child, and it's dying." And you go through this, and you maybe act it for them, maybe you don't—but I try essentially to let them come out with it themselves, which they usually do on the first or second take.

I must emphasize that there's no pat answer to this; it's part of a collective experience. It may have come from something generated for them over a couple of meetings or the collective thing of two or three weeks of filming. What matters is getting people involved in a human experience or emotion and letting it develop and flower in the particular way you need. I have also found that using nonprofessionals in this sort of film is usually a little better, because professionals often bring in a tremendous art and craft and technique which spoils the naturalism. But it's a difficult problem. There are no rules.

You've got a number of comments in the film about what people think of carbon 14, or whether we should bomb Russia in retaliation for their dropping a bomb on us. Were these comments written into the script, or are they real off-the-street reactions?

That's one of the main questions that's been asked over the past few years, and I can understand why. People know that the film is a reconstruction; therefore, they probably say, "Ah, he's reconstructed this." Yet the carbon 14 sections and the "retaliation against Russia" section are the only ones that *aren't* reconstructed. In other sections I've got people playing churchmen or strategists; what they say is what I heard and learned talking to churchmen and strategists during the research. But the statement of the women in the street talking about carbon 14 and retaliation are completely genuine from members of the cast.

One morning I got the cast together and said, "I want to do something a little bit different for the next couple of hours, but I'm not going to tell you exactly what it is." My cast were housewives from Gravesend, and they looked at each other thinking, "Oh, God, what's he going to do with us now"—this was after they had been thrown out of windows and trapped in fires for the sake of the film in the last two weeks. Then I took them aside, one by one, and said, "Okay, now I'm going to ask you questions, I want you to answer me whatever way you feel. Just say whatever you think." And for a moment they became what they really were—ordinary lay members of the British public. I asked these questions about fifty feet away from the main group; no one could hear what I was saying. And those questions and responses—particularly the responses—are perhaps the biggest single indictment in the entire film of the way we are conducting our society and of the lack of common public knowledge of the things that affect humanity.

Could we move into the technical area and directorial decisions?

Technically, the film was very difficult to make and was shot at a ratio of about twenty to one. I think if we discuss the firestorm sequence, that will sum up for you many of the difficulties of the film and the problem of obtaining a kind of documentary authenticity.

A firestorm is very different from an ordinary fire; it's an all-consuming tornado, and it was very difficult to create that effect.

We were working in an old barracks that was about to be pulled down and that gave us the impression of large buildings which might vaguely be taken for office blocks. We put white magnesium flares in all the windows and then built up the fire behind. For the soundtrack we tried a mixture of fire, volcano, and other things, all treated very coarsely. I then brought down a friend of mind, a stunt man, to help me with the management of the people caught in the firestorm.

We put a mattress down and got the people to sort of run and pick themselves up off the mattress. It's extremely difficult, and it doesn't work completely—but it works. As you are running, you have to suddenly feel yourself caught and turned by an air current. To achieve this we started pulling them with wires, but we finally decided not to do that, as we thought it would hurt them. We also thought it would look false. So everything is actually what they do themselves, plus the cutting of the best sort of positions. We also helped the effect by having flares roaring in the background and putting two fans quite close to them to whip bits of shredded paper and flour across so that you get the visual impression of a sudden whipping across of something. As they ran to a particular spot where their mattress was, the white bits of paper would whip across and catch them, that would be their cue for letting themselves be caught in it and turned. That's just a small example of the solution to a technical problem; it really has nothing to do with filmmaking, but it's what that nutty film is about.

As far as camera techniques are concerned, well, obviously we were letting people shout, letting them distort the microphone, and letting them deliberately butt into the camera. What we were trying to do was create a sort of total emotion, or total involvement, which affected us as well as the actors. I would give the cameraman specific directions, but obviously things would often be happening very suddenly and he'd be on his own.

Did you use any stock shots?

Every single frame in that film is us. We put the film through a particular process to try and get it to look as if it had been grabbed out of archives of twenty years ago. I forget how we did it; it was a case of getting a dupe negative, then getting a particular harsh-grain positive and reprinting from the positive—that accounts for that extreme contrast in look in a lot of the film. That was obviously deliberately sought after and finally achieved by us and by the laboratory, which did very well.

There was one scene where a rocket goes off. Was that your rocket?

Yes. My art director went out and built a bit of a rocket. He was able to wheel the thing up the ramp just about three feet, and at that point I'd bring the camera up so that it was near the top of it. The rocket and every other single inch in that film is us. Some of it, I must admit, is not done as well as I would have liked, but it's all us, with all its faults. It's all us, every foot of it.

Note

1   *Film Comment* 3, no. 4 (1965).

8

New Agendas in Black Filmmaking: An Interview with Marlon Riggs

Roy Grundmann

In his relatively short career, Marlon T. Riggs has already made an indelible mark on the documentary tradition and the state of black filmmaking in general. The self-reflexive aesthetics of his videos have opened critical trenches and fuelled debates on issues of authenticity, impartiality, and truth. Even such relatively straightforward works as Ethnic Notions *(1987) never forgo or hide their partisan perspective, which is precisely Riggs's point. His films are politically significant because they have helped redefine agendas of black filmmaking. Riggs is not only black, he is also gay, and as a cultural observer his vision is fused to diverse aspects of black gay life.* Tongues Untied *(1990) is a passionate exploration of the double oppression black gay men face in our society (see review in* Cineaste *18, no.1), attacking both white racism and a certain machismo conspicuously coextensive with parts of the African-American movement. As much as black gay men's ethnicity makes them subject to racist oppression, their sexuality is used to deny them a share in their African ancestry.*

As one might expect, the right wing's response to Tongues Untied *was not slow in coming, and it bore out its own racism twice over. When Riggs, by addressing issues of homophobia, sought to reformulate notions of ethnic struggle, Senator Jesse Helms, presidential aspirant Pat Buchanan, and their ideological cohorts promptly turned their attacks against the video into an exclusively antigay, pro-censorship invective. Interestingly, even the subsequent media debate around NEA funding of homoerotic art somehow omitted the important fact that the men in* Tongues Untied *were also black. Instead, what ensued were fatuous and highly constructed squabbles over tax dollars and gay imagery, making* Tongues Untied *a harbinger of things to come in the struggle of getting sexually explicit material funded.*

Color Adjustment (1991), one of Riggs's two new videos, is a historical outline of the representation of blacks on American television from Amos 'n' Andy *to* The Cosby Show. *A mix of talking head commentary, clips from such shows as* East-side/Westside, I Spy, *and* Julia, *and such reflexive devices as superimposed rhetorical questions, explore the presentational trappings of blacks on TV—and, for that matter, the pitfalls and problems inherent in constructing an alternative agenda steering clear of the term "political correctness."*

Riggs's other video, Non, Je Ne Regrette Rien (No Regrets, 1992) is about the struggle of confronting AIDS and overcoming shame and self-hatred. Five HIV positive black gay men tell us about their experiences with being seropositive and dealing with their friends, families, workplaces, and the church. No Regrets is Riggs's contribution to the Fear of Disclosure project, an ongoing series of videos addressing communities affected by AIDS and dealing with issues of coming out as HIV positive or having AIDS. The project was initiated in 1989 through the tape Fear of Disclosure by the late Phil Zwickler (Rights and Reactions: Lesbian and Gay Rights on Trial), in which an openly seropositive man is rejected sexually even though he only wants to practice safer sex. Fear of Disclosure reveals how the double standards many impose on safer sex lead to a new sexual apartheid.

The Fear of Disclosure project also includes (In)visible Women, codirected by Marina Alvarez and Ellen Spiro, which depicts the struggle of three women of color in their communities to fight AIDS and its stigmata. Next in the series will be a video by Christine Choy (Who Killed Vincent Chin?) on Asian-Americans and HIV/AIDS. Riggs was interviewed by Cineaste shortly after the premiere of No Regrets at the 4th New York International Festival of Lesbian and Gay Film.

Cineaste: *How did you come to participate in the* Fear of Disclosure *project?*

Marlon Riggs: I met Phil Zwickler at the Berlin Film Festival in 1990. At that time he introduced me to the project of which he had completed the first instalment, *Fear of Disclosure.* He invited me to participate in other productions of *Fear of Disclosure,* addressing the different communities which have been impacted by the epidemic.

I realized that there are many productions coming out of HIV/AIDS activism that really privilege activism, about being in the streets and confronting officials, rather than dealing with issues of shame and self-loathing. For individuals who haven't even made that first step of simply saying "I am positive"—even to themselves, let alone to others in their circle of friends and family—that kind of activism is very remote. So I thought it was necessary to address many of the core issues that many black gay men in this country dealing with HIV confront and try to avoid. There's not simply the externalized conflict with homophobic institutions and family and so forth, but accepting and confronting the virus oneself.

How did you find the participants in your project?

Donald Woods and Reggie [Reginald Williams], who is the director of the National AIDS Task Force, are friends. This is central in some ways, because I knew I would not have a lot of time to achieve that level of intimacy, to bring about intimate disclosure and not simply the usual storytelling that you find in so many documentaries. That required a personal relationship pre-existing before the taping began. I also felt that I needed to broaden the demographics. Because I knew that this documentary would in some ways involve a reclaiming of spiritual conditions, I wanted someone who was involved with the church and had not simply discarded it when they came to terms with and accepted their sexual identity, someone who had transformed their church as well as their understanding of the church in order to be embraced for the totality of who they are.

Doesn't this film and, specifically, the discourse around Joseph Long, who you were just talking about, heavily privilege Christianity at the expense of other religious practices among black people?

There are all kinds of religions and spiritual paths that black people in America take, but I couldn't bear the burden of representation and trying to address all of them. In many ways this is a documentary that focuses on the prevailing tradition that many black Americans understand or have shared in. For me it was not doctrinaire Judeo-Christianity. I hope that's not what people read from this, even if hearing the spirituals, because those spirituals come from slavery. The use of those songs and the references to the church ground a whole history of struggle behind which our connections to something more transcendent were a driving force: fighting Jim Crow, slavery, and straight discrimination; fighting the internalised self-hatred that comes from being a second-class citizen and being considered inferior; fighting the shame and silence that attends the desire to cope and to get by without punishment in a society that discourages you.

For me, that's what those songs signified. When I hear "Freedom, oh freedom over me, I will never be a slave," I'm not hearing simply black Baptist Southern upbringing. I'm hearing a whole history resonating struggle, and a refusal to abide by prescribed roles. It's in that way that the church can be and is, in fact, a component in that struggle for life and nobility. No doubt, there's a great degree of homophobia in all kinds of churches, not just in black churches. There's been a tremendous denial and silence pervasive throughout Afro-American society. I didn't feel the need to belabour that point.

The Fear of Disclosure project aims to bring these films and videos to their respective target audiences, in this case black gay men. Do you hope this tape can also reach other organizations, social workers, and public institutions like high schools?

That's the ambition for all the work that we do as people of color, as gay men and lesbians, and as people who are dealing in one way or another with HIV— that what we do will not be confined within one particular context and small community. Because of the nature of the issues and this epidemic, we hope that the work will transcend those particular boundaries so that we can see our connection with each other and the true kind of groundwork of struggle that is premised upon shared interest and shared identities of degree. Unfortunately, if you limit this video simply to black gay men, and then limit another one to Asian-American gay men or women, and then another one to young people, you miss the opportunity to make these communities see how much their struggles interconnect.

But that's a different project isn't it?

That is a different project in many ways. To some degree the documentary *Absolutely Positive* tried to show the connections among all of us within the HIV community. But I think that work did not deal with this as effectively as it might have. If it had been specifically targeted, at African-Americans, for instance, certain issues would have been raised that were not dealt with in that film. For example, the Asian-American participants in that film were treated just as any other group of gay men, so there was no acknowledgement of their specific cultural background, and how the differences that come with it shape the struggle around HIV within that community. I see too often within our own gay and lesbian community how works that are supposed to be multicultural show a range of diverse identities, a certain kind of difference, but in which the difference doesn't really seem to matter. The difference is simply surface, it's color, it's not a source of identity, or division, strife, and inequity. It's in response to that that I would like to show, by bringing together a whole slew of different people affected by HIV, how difference actually *does* make a difference. There's the assumption that, perhaps because we're all threatened by this one particular adversary, no other threats really matter, and that the ways we threaten and oppress each other don't measure up in significance to this common adversary. That's what gets erased in history, in our understanding of political and social struggle and, in turn, it perpetuates our inability to rise up to "defeat the master," to use old terminology. As much as the majority resists us, we resist dealing with each other.

Let's talk a bit about the troubled exhibition history and right wing abuse of Tongues Untied. *Pat Buchanan used footage from the film in one of his election campaign spots to denounce the Bush Administration's arts funding policy. What was your reaction to that?*

I was surprised but not shocked because that kind of misappropriation and abuse of works dealing with homosexuality had been occurring quite frequently, whether Mapplethorpe's or Todd Haynes's work was at issue, or even Jennie Livingston's, which I find politically fairly untrangressive. I'm not saying I didn't like it, but it's not as if it really challenges the majority's hegemony in any real way. I found out by calls from the National Gay and Lesbian Task Force as well as from people who alerted me about this ad circulating in the Georgia primary that used excerpts from *Tongues Untied* as examples of blasphemous, pornographic art, and was blaming Bush as a supporter of this. It was absurd to the point of being ludicrous. In order to win office and influence, the Buchanan campaign was trying to exploit homophobia, racism, and the attempted repression of all kinds of communities who, particularly since the civil rights movement, have been asserting their voices. I wanted to show how Bush is complicit in that, not to let this president get off the hook, so that Buchanan was the bad guy and Bush was by comparison benevolent, but to show how he was as much a part of that dynamic and as destructive of the fabric of this society as the Buchanans and David Dukes and all the other people to the right. This politics of enmity treats others as enemies, which then creates fear and consolidates the majority, which is as fractured as any other group of people, into believing that they share a common adversary and therefore need to bind.

Was your article in The New York Times *op-ed page your only response?*

In addition to *The New York Times* piece, I also appeared on talk shows, was interviewed any number of times by the media, and also alerted other constituencies who were being hurt by this ad. It was important to critique not only Buchanan's ad but also the reporting about Buchanan's ad. Both amounted to the erasure of black gay men from a work designed to empower and affirm us. The media often simply mentioned the footage of the white men with buttocks showing but hardly mentioned my name or, even more importantly, the cultural and social context of this work or its original intentions.

Did you approach The New York Times *or did they approach you?*

The National Gay and Lesbian Task Force, particularly in the person of Robert Bray, approached the *Times* who were quite enthusiastic, to my shock. Then I had a conversation with a *Times* editor, a member of the editorial board, who was extremely delighted and welcomed the editorial and was, quite frankly, a delight to work with. I was shocked that they were so supportive.

What struck me, reading the editorial, was that apart from emphasizing how the ad breeds and exploits homophobia, you also stressed that Tongues Untied *had only been indirectly funded by the NEA. Did you have certain editorial restraints?*

They asked me to include that, because I hadn't originally thought about it. But the point to register was that, apart from a number of fabrications going on in the Buchanan ad itself—one, the grant was given during the time of the Reagan and not the Bush Administration; two, this was not an NEA grant but given by an NEA-sponsored organization—it was a wholesale disregard for facts, not simply the blatant misappropriation of the work but just a general lie. It was this indifference to any fact-finding, which was part and parcel of this campaign, that needed to be illuminated. I needed to show that not simply the politics of enmity but the politics of dissembling had become a common-place feature of American electoral politics. No one really seemed to be bothered by it.

Tongues Untied was also involved in the debate around public television. Although your film had been accepted by P.O.V., some PBS stations refused to show it for fear of alienating their audiences. What was your reaction?

It was extremely clear to me from the beginning that there would be a very bitter fight, and that not only would the right wing nuts come out again and lead an attack on *P.O.V.* and *Tongues Untied,* but also that many of the stations would collude in that attempt of censorship and repression. That's because many of those who run public television are in many ways no different ideologically—except perhaps in their politics of addressing such issues—from those on the right. And I knew that would be thrown into stark relief by *Tongues Untied.* I began writing letters alerting agencies and community groups to the fact that this work will drop by the wayside if we allow it, and that we should force the stations, if not to broadcast *Tongues Untied,* at least to own up to their racism and homophobia.

The Senate recently passed the budget for PBS, so that's a good sign . . .

It's a good sign because at least public television continues to exist as a site through which we can contend the various representations of us—or their absence. At the same time, though, I think most publicly funded institutions these days are chilled by the right's largely successful attacks against them. Therefore the address of sexuality in any way, not simply homosexuality, and the attempt to include feminist perspectives, will be a long time in coming. You see this kind of chill already happening at the NEA in an explicit fashion. The acting director of the NEA, Ann Radice, could have simply carried out her desire not to deal with "sexually explicit" works without telling anybody. The NEA today has become equated with Ken Burns and his Civil War series. I mean, how safe can you get? I'm not saying I didn't like that series, but to move everything back another century and deal with the struggle for national identity where it's reduced to a very clear-cut, manichean world, is too easy. It doesn't address any of the pressing issues that divide us today.

Your new video, Color Adjustment, *seems to be a much more straightforward documentary.*

Even though people have been saying that it's straightforward, one should always ask "straightforward in relation to what?" I think, it uses a form that seems conventional on the surface to deliver a very strong critique, not simply of television, which is easy to do, but also of our investment in the American Dream, particularly for those of us who have been locked out of that dream.

This is something that can be extremely discomforting to us, especially since we've never really questioned it. We've questioned the barriers to our entrance into the mainstream of America, but not what the mainstream is, and what costs there are in trying to live up to that aspiration. I think it is, in some ways, a classic form of African-American signifying in that what seems on the surface to be very familiar and almost corroborative of the majority's aesthetics is, in fact, in disguise undermining us.

Many of the things that aren't explicit in the documentary are really passing by people. The use of James Baldwin's quotations, for example, the use of still images, or even the use of statistics on the increasing number of TV spectators over the years. The viewer is thereby made aware of not only one's own individual responses to the work, but also those of a community and of a larger political and social context in which television is watched, and through which we come to define and understand ourselves as a nation. This project was always wholly different from *Tongues Untied*. *Tongues Untied* offers a certain kind of emotional empathy and cathartic release that I knew *Color Adjustment* would never achieve because it wasn't designed to. *Color Adjustment* is deliberately cool.

Color Adjustment *focuses on the theoretical and historical implications of assimilation. How do you see commercial black filmmaking functioning in this context in the U.S. today?*

Like anyone who is African-American today, I'm heartened by the appearance of so many black filmmakers who are doing work that speaks to some degree to the issues and experiences in our community. That said, I'm disheartened by the fact that, too often, what seems to be privileged is a very old-fashioned patriarchy in which misogyny, sexism and homophobia are simply taken for granted in the empowerment of young black men. Over and over again, we are confronted with the glorification of violence and phallocentrism as the means by which we redeem ourselves, in which black male empowerment is assumed to be equivalent to black liberation.

So I really question whether we can call this tremendous progress, as some are lauding it, simply because we now have a number of black filmmakers who are doing work. For me, I think, as Isaac Julien has said, that it's not sufficient to just have a black face or a black director, but we have also to ask what the work or that face signify in terms of blackness. Are we treated to a fairly standardized notion of what it means to be a man, or a woman, a family, a nation? Are our visions really expanded beyond these fairly pernicious boundaries in which we police difference, even within our own communities? Unfortunately, I see us doing much of the latter, and, to that degree, I can't join in the celebration, the kind of enthusiasm, that I see so many of us now engaging in.

9

Jumping Off the Cliff:
A Conversation with Dennis O'Rourke

Tracey Spring

I believe in a cinema which enlightens, reveals and celebrates the condition of the human spirit. (Dennis O'Rourke)

I met Dennis at a film seminar in the States around 1990. He seemed a typical Aussie. Blond, cheerful, relaxed, rumpled Hawaiian shirt, and a smile on the face. A good guy to have a beer with. It took me just half an hour to realize that under that happy-go-lucky façade lay one of the sharpest and most creative minds in film-making. At the end of two days of looking at his films I was blown out of my mind. Let's not mince words. In my opinion O'Rourke is one of the three or four greatest documentary filmmakers working today.

The facts are simple. Born in Brisbane to a Catholic family. A few years of university and a developing interest in photography. From 1975 to 1979 O'Rourke lived in Papua, New Guinea, where he taught documentary and made his first film, Yumi Yet, *about the area's struggle for independence. Staying around the Pacific area, he made* The Shark Callers of Kontu (1982), Half Life (1985) *and 'Cannibal Tours'* (1987). *Though the early films met with rave reviews, both* The Good Woman of Bangkok (1990) *and* Cunnamulla (2000) *became the subjects of immense controversy, particularly enraging feminists and politically correct dogooders. I suspect that his as yet unreleased film* Landmines—A Love Story *will stir up similar controversy. In spite of the criticism, the awards have piled up, from Best Film at the Berlin Film Festival to a Gold at Sundance.*

I tried for over a year to get Dennis to do the following interview with Tracey Spring. Meeting Dennis had inspired me and changed my own method of filmmaking and I didn't think this book would be complete without him talking about his acts of provocation, heresy and risk taking. It wasn't easy, but in the end he came through just a week before the book went to the publisher. I am eternally grateful.

A.R.

Tracey Spring: *Is there a thread that runs through all your films?*

Dennis O'Rourke: Well I always say I just make the same film over and over again, but the trick is to make them so that nobody seems to notice *(laughs).*

What ties them together? Well these days I call myself an atheist but I really do have this crypto-Catholic sensibility I acquired during my growing up period and I guess what holds them together, in the end, is a sense of redemption. They're often about dark subjects, difficult things, difficult ideas, but I like to think that they're full of love. In that sense I'm no different to anyone else— that is, we're all frightened, we're all searching for meaning and we all want to be loved. That's how I think of all the people who are in my films. And that's how I think of myself too.

What ties my films together is the knowledge that in life there's always this thing which we know to be the public life—what we know is happening—the image of ourselves that we present to others—but there's always this other thing going on. Well I'm interested in the other thing that's going on. And it's often dark in nature. My films are far away from journalism—the codes of journalism are almost constructed so as to avoid having to confront the real truths that are messy and uncomfortable— it's what I call 'official story telling'. Okay, so what is truth? It's a movable feast. There is my truth and your truth. The Irish have this expression, 'it be the truth, to him'. We all understand that. There are multiple truths.

So what draws you to make a film? For example 'Cannibal Tours'.

I can, with hindsight, look at all the films and say how they relate to moments in my life. But you're making films with someone else's money and so with a film like *'Cannibal Tours'* I'm both seeing it from the outside looking in, seeing it as a subject that would work for the people who pay for the films—television executives, television stations. And also it has a germ of an idea of something that I'm interested in. And I'm kind of only interested in the one big idea. What that is, is really the mystery. I don't even really want to know the answer to that idea because to know the answer might . . . kill it.

Is it a feeling?

It's an idea, it's a concept and it's a feeling. At some point though, the light bulb kind of goes off and I kind of see the whole film, even though I have no idea where I'm going to make it or who the characters are going to be—I see the whole film in terms of what its effect will be—on me when I see it, and I hope, what the audience will see. The light bulb goes on and that happened with *'Cannibal Tours'* even before I commenced to shoot anything.

I was working on another film and I encountered these tourists in a Papua New Guinean village called Angoram—doing this buying of artefacts, and I saw a film. I thought here is a situation where—if I make a film about this—I can say something about that part of the human condition that interests me, which is notions of identity and who we are in a 'post-religious' world. And that idea just sat there in the back of my mind for four years while I made other films.

How long do the ideas percolate?

The ideas are bubbling away—fermenting. It's like an itch—you have this itch and you want to scratch it—an itch about something that you're uncomfortable with. So they all start with a kind of itch. With *Half Life*, I was out in the Pacific making some official conventional documentaries for the Australian government, and I was in a bar in a little godforsaken town called Majuro in the Marshall Islands and I was there to make this film which was about the issue of nuclear contamination on Bikini Atoll and the fact that the people who had been there had been removed. Then one night in this seedy little town I met a man called Jeton Anjain and he happened to be the grandly named Senator for Rongelap population, 200 people approximately. And this was the hidden story—the unknown story—about these people who were on the island adjacent to Bikini and were not evacuated for the hydrogen bomb tests of 1954 and subsequently were exposed to fall-out and from then on, I can't put it in any lighter way, they were used as guinea pigs to test the effect of radiation on people who had been subjected to fall-out.

This was in 1954 and the years after, at the height of the Cold War. So there was no research as such . . . I met a man in a bar and we just started talking. He introduced himself as the political representative of the people of Rongelap—'The Senator' as he was called—and he said, 'Look I'm going out there in a couple of days and if you want to come with me you can come.' He said, 'Just come out for a day and a night and have a look and see what's happening on my island.' So I said sure, why not—let's do that. So I took the camera and some film stock with me—thirty rolls—and we got there after a day of flying across the ocean. The next day we heard that the plane had broken down—it was the only plane they had in the Marshall Islands and we were stranded there for ten days.

So you could do nothing but make a film . . .

Well that didn't occur to me straight away. I was with a colleague and each day we're thinking, 'When are we leaving? When are we leaving?', and there was no food to eat except canned food provided by the US government and radiated coconuts and lots of fish. And I started talking to the people there and the story they were telling was amazing. And the story was the story that became *Half Life*.

I filmed and after about three or four days I thought, well—looks like I've got to make this film—fate says that this is a story that's got to be told and it's my job to make it. It was a different kind of story to the government films. And all I did there while we waited for the plane—ten days—was film the Marshallese people talking to me—talking to the camera in their language which I didn't understand.

You have that amazing piece with the woman talking to the camera—you really didn't know what she was talking about, did you?

Well, many of my films are in a language which I don't understand, a language which is only spoken by a few people and I've never really thought it to be a big problem. Because we're dealing in cinema here and that's the great thing about filmmaking and cinema—the camera and the tape recorder are recording it and you just trust in the sense of feeling of what's between you and the subject, and if you just record it, well—why do you have to know what people are saying when they say it? You trust. They're trusting me—they're telling me their story. For them I was probably their first foreigner apart from US government officials and doctors who were examining them that they'd ever met. And there I was and through their political representative I was basically saying—I've made a contract with you to tell your story. Now I had no budget, no funding. In fact I was right in the middle of finishing off this other series. But I said, 'As soon as I finish what I'm doing I will make your story and in the meantime while I'm here let's keep talking.'

And I used up the thirty rolls I had. Not taking pretty pictures of lagoons or palm trees—but on what are sometimes called disparagingly 'talking heads'. But I don't think of talking heads as being disparaging—I think there's nothing more expressive or beautiful in cinema than the landscape of the human face when what's being said is powerful. Quentin Crisp said, 'No-one is boring who will tell the truth about himself', and I think that's a great maxim for documentary.

So here we were. I was sitting with a woman who had lost her son to leukaemia caused by exposure to the fall-out from the first hydrogen bomb test and in the very first of roll I filmed, she spoke to me with huge intensity and while I didn't know what she said, I did know in an intuitive sense. It was sort of translated for me on the spot and our understanding was that she was going to tell me her story, tell the truth about herself and her family. That first roll of film, two years later became a crucial scene in the film that was called *Half Life*.

How much of that first ten days' shooting ended up in the film?

I shot 100 rolls of film (twenty hours) for *Half Life* and there's a scene at the very end of the film where she speaks after Ronald Reagan has talked in an inane way about how lucky they are to have had America looking after them when in fact they'd been used as guinea pigs. And then she comes on the screen, speaking in the Marshallese language, and says, 'The Americans think they're smart. But really they are crazy.'—Then there is a long pause where she stares into the camera and says, 'Smart at doing stupid things.' It's a great moment in the film but in fact it was the very first roll I'd shot. When the film was finished it looks like how clever was I as a director to be able to do that but it didn't happen that way. That's why I always say that you don't make the film—the film makes you.

So *Half Life* was an accident, as it were.

'*Cannibal Tours*' was different. I was shooting a film in Papua New Guinea and we happened to turn up in Angoram, which is on a big river there, and there was this tourist boat there with all these wealthy tourists swarming all over the place bargaining for artefacts, and I thought 'This is some phenomenal scene'—this is some surreal moment that represents something about the clash between the East and the West and the way that we fail to understand each other—which has been essentially the underlying theme of all my films. Anyway I just filed that away and thought—maybe one day I could make a film about it.

After I'd finished *Half Life* the investors were very happy and said, well what would you like to make next, and I really hadn't planned anything so I said I'd make this film about tourists in the Sepik River.

Did you have a title in your head?

The title then was *Society Expeditions*. It became '*Cannibal Tours*' later. I think titles are really important. Not just as a way of having the film stay with the audiences when it's finished but the title in fact—even the working title—defines the film and its thrust, because I don't have scripts—I hardly even have treatments—generally maybe just one page. The notion of having to write, or having to know in advance what I'm going to film, kills it stone dead. I don't know. I just work always off my intuition.

Can you say a word about funding?

All the films were funded in different ways. *Half Life* was funded on one pre-sale to the BBC, plus private investors who obtained a tax break. At that stage the Australian Broadcasting Corporation was not interested. '*Cannibal Tours*' was a bit different—the Australian Broadcasting Corporation by that stage had turned around and decided that they were finally going to show my films, so they invested in '*Cannibal Tours*'. *The Good Woman of Bangkok* was funded through a Documentary Fellowship which was like a grant based on past work and the deal was that the money was enough to make a modest documentary about any subject you wanted. It was a competitive thing—you didn't even have to tell the panel what you were going to make. So when I went to have my interview with my panel of exalted members of the 'culturati', I said, 'Well since you give me the option of not to tell you I'm not going to tell you because I don't even know.' But I already I had in my mind that whatever I was going to do was going to be a film that under normal circumstances would never be made. But I still didn't know what it would be.

But bit by bit—it came around to prostitution in Thailand, and a relation-ship between me and a prostitute in Thailand, and by extension about wider things. All I knew at the beginning was that I was going to make the kind of film that was transgressive—you could never write a proposal to the govern-ment saying, 'I'd like you to give me enough money to go and live with a pros-titute in the red light district of Bangkok and be her customer and then make a film about that'—I mean can you imagine it getting funded by the Australian Broadcasting Corporation? I don't think so—at least not then.

And definitely not now.

I'd decided that I was going to make a film that under normal circumstances would never be approved for official funding, and I was proven right when the film came out and I had all these outraged people baying for my blood saying that it was a scandal that I had used government money to make this film—no mention about what the film might have revealed or said or its usefulness. There was just this simplistic denunciation.

And that's the problem with documentary—it's described as being a holier form or a more moral form of filmmaking than fiction or something—that it has a higher claim to truth—I never felt that. But one of the reasons for making *Good Woman* was that I'd sort of become celebrated, I suppose, as being somebody who was almost unimpeachable as a character because I'd made *Half Life* and 'Cannibal Tours', which were unimpeachable in terms of their Morality—capital M. They were films that made people who watched them in the cinema or on television, it made those people feel that I was *their* filmmaker. I was just reinforcing their beliefs—preaching to the converted—they were *my* people and I was almost revered for that, you know, and that made me feel uncomfortable at the time. And in many ways *The Good Woman of Bangkok* was a reaction to this idea of me being placed in the role of authority figure. While I feel very strongly about my views and want to get them across, I don't want to be like the professor or the politician who can just hand down the edict or more particularly, the priest who hands down the word from on high. I'm always sceptical and I'm always against authority and I always believe that somehow truth is elsewhere, it's not where you think it is.

You wanted to humanize yourself?

Well not so much humanize myself because if I were trying to do that I would have been a massive failure! Because everyone thought that I was less than human for the way that I approached *The Good Woman of Bangkok* and for that matter the way that I approached the film *Cunnamulla*. It was more about refus-ing a sanctimonious morality—and collapsing the distance between the viewer and the filmmaker as the Culture Hero—because he or she is the filmmaker, dealing with the big subject. You have to collapse that moral distance which insulates the audience from the difficult subject matter—because within this subject matter, I think we are all guilty, we are all implicated in some way, particularly any film that deals with sexuality.

I'm jumping around a bit, but with regard to *The Good Woman Of Bangkok*, I said right, what film will I make? Seeing that I can make anything—what subject matter will I take on which normally is not tackled in other documentary films? So I thought it's pretty clear isn't it—even though sexuality, love and romance is the fundamental subject in fiction, in poetry, in music, in novels, in Hollywood movies—documentary totally avoids the subject. Strange, because documentary claims to be about the human condition. It discusses sexual politics, yes, but sexuality *and sex*, that's different.

OK, I was thinking where would I go, where would I do this? Then suddenly, it just got me that the way to do it (and of course it was to do with me making the same film over and over again) was to deal with the third world / first world culture thing—that I would make the film in this collision point between cultures. And then I suddenly found myself in Bangkok and thought, wow I can do it here. It can be about sexuality and some aspects of sexual love, but in this place where it's so separated out. Hell, it's not an original idea—artists have been doing it for hundreds of years—in fact there's a pen and ink etching by Van Gogh of the prostitute that he fell in love with and when I saw it during the making of *Good Woman* I thought, 'This woman looks exactly like Aoi, in her look of desperation.'

Can you talk about Cunnamulla?

Cunnamulla is a town in the 'outback' of Western Queensland. It's in many ways a typical Australian country town. Hot in summer, cold in winter—and it's on the edge of the desert. There are Aboriginal people living there. It's cattle and sheep country. Its politics are generally conservative. It's divided between the few people who have some money because of the land holdings and the people in the town who generally have a low level of education. People whom the big cities sometimes think of as different from us—marginal, caricature people. I know these people because I grew up in parts of Australia that were like that and I always understood what richness there was with people who lived in isolated places—where everybody knew everybody else—everybody knew everybody's business.

I wanted to make a film in my own country—in Australia. I'd done very little of that over the years. And I got this idea about a film I could make in an isolated country town in Australia where issues about race and identity would come to the fore. I thought—well if I could find a country town and I could just go there and live there. And the term I used when I was raising the money for the film was that I would 'anatomize' this town. That is, I would examine it from the inside out.

I didn't have a particular town in mind, but I did have some requirements. It couldn't be a really small town. It had to have what I call a 'critical mass'—there had to be a sufficient number of people there for me to find a cast of characters, because I was trying to create this sort of symphonic effect where there was no plot as such—it was just life. Yet while each of the little parts by themselves—words spoken, action happening—were not momentous, in the whole mix of things they would add up to a way of saying 'that's life'. And that becomes a political statement. So I thought I should make it in Queensland as I have some sort of race memories of growing up in these places.

There was also the political climate at the time and the rise of Pauline Hanson and her populist right-wing party.

That's right—this was a time in Australia when there was a lot of division and comment in the mainstream society about the division between Aboriginal people and white Australians and the division between people in the city and people in the bush. Was very interested in the notion that we look down on fellow citizens in the bush. That somehow because they lived in an isolated place they are somehow less human than us. They are referred to as the 'marginal' people in the bush. It's code for talking about people whose lives are less fulfilled than our own in the city. People who don't even have an erotic life—and from growing up in these places I know that not to be true.

As I've said, these people are not marginal in their own minds or to their own loved ones or in their own community. The trick was how to show it—because people in these towns are very suspicious of city slickers—especially those with cameras like myself. I think *Cunnamulla* was in many ways the most difficult film I've made. Even though it's made in my own country. It was more difficult because I was much more directly implicated in whatever I was seeing. What I was seeing was also me, my society, my country. I figured if I went to such a place and stayed there then through this process I could say something that was about all of us.

You get asked to talk about this a lot—the level of intimacy you develop with the characters . . .

The paradoxical thing about the intimacy with those performances—and I do call them performances—is that it's a totally mediated situation. They're real people acting out their own lives but it's completely mediated by my process of filmmaking/recording—and more particularly my way of relating to the people I'm filming. But the mediation is to make it more truthful—that you are seeing real life. Truth is loaded. People ask me all the time—how do I get people to be so intimate in my films? I truly don't know the answer. If there's any clue I think that I make myself vulnerable to the people who are my subjects. Whatever intimacy is there is a reflected intimacy—that is—I don't think you can process this completely as a technique—but I think my own unconsciously expressed sense of being vulnerable myself and feeling that all is not right with the world and at the same time wishing it to be right—and the way that is communicated to the people that I'm with for extended periods of time when I'm filming them—even though they come from vastly different life experiences than me—as I said—it's reflected intimacy. How it actually happens is truly a mystery to me.

It is a mystery—BUT—there are certain factors involved—like huge amounts of time, trust, working by yourself . . .

Yes, working by myself has been important because all of my energies are devoted to communicating with other people. I do all the technical functions myself, such as photographing, lighting, recording sound, making arrangements—I do all that as second nature. You have to understand and love the camera and all the other equipment—what I call my recording angels. They are an extension of yourself really. I don't think about technology too much.

It's all about engagement. It can be love at first sight—it can be detestation at first sight, or something in between. But whatever it is, it's always engaged. And I don't try to be in any way anything else than totally responsive to the people I'm filming in terms of letting them know who I am. In *Half Life* I'd go out to the boat with the scientists and doctors to have a cold beer with them and sit out on the deck with them and tell them that I thought that the Americans had deliberately exposed these people to radiation. Same in *Cunnamulla*. I refused to fall into the role of the classic Liberal view of relationships between black people and white people. Perhaps before I went there I was a little bit romantic about these relations—although I shouldn't have been. What I like to say about Cunnamulla is that it's a town of about 1500 people— where half the town say they're black and half the other half say they're white—that's really what it's like. It's all mixed up. And that's offended a lot of people. The notion that I didn't express the conventional conflict that exists between Aboriginal people and white Australians. I didn't express those conflicts in the way people wanted them expressed.

But then when Paul talked it put it all in a nutshell really.

I think without the camera—it wouldn't happen. The very idea that it's being recorded sort of heightens everything. I see so many documentaries made today where it's so clear that the process itself has dominated—where two or three people are hanging round—too much talk about 'Will we set up here, and put the boom there?' And then you get a level of performance which is supposed to be non-performance as if there's no camera. I do the complete opposite. The camera and my presence affect every frame of the finished film. The camera is my alter ego. And I'm involved in some intimate conversations—

I don't call them interviews, I call them conversations. And they're very free-ranging things. I'm never thinking 'I must do this or I must do that.' It's the trance again. I could do that especially in *Cunnamulla* because I didn't have any problems with translation. It was all in English—of a kind anyway (*laughs*).

So, the process is very intuitive, it doesn't even look all that 'professional'. I don't even like the term. It's casual. But it's not casual inside my head. It's a bit like driving, you know—you do it automatically. I know the settings—I know the equipment because it's all my own equipment—everything becomes personalized—it becomes an extension of me for that process. You're different people for different stages of each film.

It's difficult sometimes in that it takes me one or two years to make a film at least and so for nine months I have to be the camera person, sound recordist, 'director'. All the time I'm in a sort of trance and when I finally end up in the cutting room it's like it's something that's just fallen off the back of a truck almost. Yes I know I filmed it but it's like a revelation to me. And then I stop all that and I have to start being the producer again, in order to promote the film I've just made and try and raise the money for the next.

Can we talk more about Paul?

Paul was, is a very troubled young man with a very troubled family life. He was about to go to jail for the first time when I met him. I made no attempt to film Paul—for a long time—it seemed to me that he and his friends were very . . . they were ostracized by everyone in the town. And he identified me as one of the opposition—I had a fancy four-wheel drive car, I had money, I was a white man. In Aboriginal slang, I was a 'gubba'. He probably didn't see me as being much different to the police who hounded him every night. It would have been several months since I'd arrived in Cunnamulla—I went to his Mum's for a barbeque and he was pretty shy and retiring. Afterwards we would occasionally say hello. Some of the other people in the film whenever I mentioned Paul to them would say, 'Oh that vermin', that was the word used. When I told them that I had become friendly with Paul and that we'd started to do some filming, they were horrified. And of course they had reason to be because it was the same Paul and his gang who were breaking into their houses all the time.

However, after several months Paul came up to me and said 'Dennis—can you lend me ten dollars?' In Cunnamulla you know that you're giving them ten dollars—it's called 'the bite'. So I said, 'Sure, Paul'. And that was that. Some other time he might have asked me and I would say, 'Well not today' because I might not have had it with me. I didn't feel exploited by him. He'd see me filming in the street and he and his mates would hang around and they'd want to look through the view-finder of the camera. I was interested in his story—

but at the same time I didn't say, 'I need for you to tell me about your whole life', that applied to pretty much everyone in the film, except for Neradah and Arthur, who were necessary to create this symphonic structure I imagined.

How did you end up filming him on that step?

Paul just said 'Come round'. When moments like that happen—I don't think I have that much to do with it. What happens is that there's this crying need that that person has to express themselves—who want to say something. Paul was the most marginal of the marginal in Cunnamulla and yet he speaks in those few words in the film with as much eloquence as a great orator. I love Paul. And Cara and Kellie-Anne also in the film. They don't come across as 'sluts'. They're little heroes. They're fighting against a system that totally oppresses them. Now they've been told that they come across in the film as looking bad but they don't at all.

We've talked about the processes of making 'Cannibal Tours', Half Life *and* Cunnamulla. *Can you talk about how each film has its own journey?*

I've said before, that how I make my films IS a mystery to me. The process seems like a whole series of accidents. Yes I am a filmmaker and I have these films that my name's attached to but most of the time I don't really feel like I'm Dennis O'Rourke, documentary filmmaker, I feel that I photograph films. It all comes from the act of photography first. That is, the film is what comes about from me, turning up in a place, alone with my recording angels, and with enough money and tape and time just to throw myself into whatever situation's there. The whole thing's experiential. I never write a script. For the current film, *Landmines—A Love Story*, I didn't even have a treatment. All I had was a title. When I raised the money to make the Landmines film I didn't know it was going to be set in Afghanistan or that it would be about Habiba and Shah. I knew I was going to make a film about the issues of landmines and it was going to be a love story—hence the title. That's all I knew.

*Landmines—*A Love Story—*what was going on in your head on the plane when you thought of that one?*

I was thinking what delicious champagne I was drinking (*laughs*). No, I was thinking in an abstract way. I guess the title is also meant to be a provocation because documentary takes itself far too seriously. It's the idea that love stories are for fiction made in Hollywood and a film about landmines are for earnest documentary filmmakers dealing with big social issues.

I like to think my work has a feeling similar to fiction although it's firmly rooted in the documentary tradition. But the way the film is structured uses all the techniques of the fictional cinema—the tone of the film, the feel of the film to work at the same level as a narrative fiction film would—that it's a story you fall into it. But with this extra other thing that this sort of film can have—the irreducible fact that it actually happened. The audience is aware that it's manipulated—it's aware of the techniques—the use of the music, the reliance less on words and more on imagery—the whole notion of montage. But it has a power that no fiction film can ever have.

In *Landmines* I wanted to make a film about an international issue but not about the issue. Because all the films I make are really metaphors of one kind or another. If your film doesn't cross over into being something that's universal then it probably hasn't worked.

Back to *Landmine—A Love Story*. It was a conjunction of terms. It's provocative. It's intriguing and it's intriguing to me and it's a challenge.

What was the original concept you sold to Channel 4, the ABC and the investors?

I just said I was going to make a feature-length documentary. I totally relied on their ability to trust me based on past work and, fortunately, they did. All I had was a title, no treatment. We knew in some ways it was going to be about landmines and we knew in some way it was going to be a love story.

Can you talk about filming in Afghanistan?

Sometimes I'm forced to watch my old films. When I do, I always think, 'I couldn't have made that. That's impossible.' If someone said to me you could go back to Bangkok or Cunnamulla and have those experiences again, I'd say I can't do that. What sets you on the journey, each time, is a kind of qualified madness.

Landmines hasn't been completed and released, but when I'm sitting in the editing room and putting it together I can't believe that it was just me there. Whatever it was that was there, whatever rushes were there on that tape, on that soundtrack, whatever people are doing is something that I had a mediating role in, if not an interventionist role. But I can't imagine that person who was me then, doing what I did then. Now I'm another person, I'm the person in the editing room, looking at it all, almost like it's found material.

I have these really bad habits that younger filmmakers probably shouldn't listen to, but, for instance, I never use headphones when I'm recording. I could never use a boom—I think the boom is the most distracting thing you could possibly have in a documentary recording situation. And this is the real heresy—I never look at any of my rushes when I'm filming. Except for maybe the very first tape. I just do a quick check to make sure the equipment's working. Otherwise, I'll just film—it's like a trance. In this sort of state you become obsessed with the little world you're in. Obviously it's me making the film, that is, the film is ostensibly about them but it's no clinical or dispassionate recording process. It's one of total engagement with the people and the ideas. It's like a love affair actually.

Like the love bubble.

It is. Each time you're transported into a new world—in some ways a place like Cunnamulla is more strange to me than a place like Kabul or Bangkok or the Pacific Islands. I sort of just find myself there. And what holds everything together is the idea that I'm there and I have a job to do. Somebody's given me money and I have a job to do—to make a film.

In each film, I've deliberately placed myself in a situation where I'm at risk, as it were—at risk of failing. I always like to go into situations which I'm scared to go into. There's this expression 'fear is the arrow—and it points to the direction you're supposed to go'—whatever you're afraid of. That doesn't mean I'm not afraid, I'm always afraid. It's a combination of arrogance and insecurity, I suppose.

So here I am, starting *Landmines*. I get off the plane—I've never been to the place before—I know that I have the expectations of the broadcasters and investors on my shoulders because they've given me the money to make a film and all I have is a title. A few words have been written—words about the scourge of landmines to convince others that this is a respectable idea for a documentary . . .

I deliberately don't have anyone to meet me in Kabul—I want to metaphorically throw myself off the cliff. Like going to Bangkok and walking into the red light district—you don't know what you're going to find, but in another way you DO know what you're going to find. It's arrogant but you have this absolute belief that just by taking the first step—the big step, that something magical will probably happen. It had better, because if it doesn't, then I'm in trouble.

So I arrive in Kabul just a few months after the Taliban has been routed, alone and with all my equipment. I didn't even do any real research into Afghanistan. I only chose to go to Afghanistan because I was able to—because of the events of September 11th—even though it's one of the most heavily mined countries—one of the three most heavily mined countries in the world, along with Angola and Cambodia—and Bosnia of course. Afghanistan was not on my list of places where I thought I could find a love story because of the restrictions that would have previously been placed on me. No way the Taliban would have allowed me to make my kind of film. Especially a film about where a woman is the central character. If I say I'm going to make a film that has love story in the title, then you can expect that to happen.

Did you think that the central character was going to be the woman?

No, I didn't—this is all bubbling away underneath in the subconscious. You've seen the film in your mind and you haven't seen the film. All you have is this idea. And I've learned over the years that the stories that are most interesting to me are not the obvious ones. They're the ones that you find accidentally. They're the things that you don't expect. They seem to resonate with me—to evolve into the really important story—starting from very unprepossessing beginnings. So my unprepossessing beginning, as in beginning in Afghanistan, was making the decision to go there because it had opened up to the West and the Western media, and I could ignore the umbrella of the UN people and traditional media people. I didn't do any serious research. I just went there—with two cameras, two tripods, monitors, film stock—booked into a crummy hotel (it was supposed to be five star but was about half a star) and I'm planning to make the film.

How long did you plan to stay?

I was prepared to be there up to four months or so. In the end it was only two because things worked out well I think. So I arrive at Kabul, it's 45 degrees, the whole place is looking like a war zone—there's all these wrecked, bombed out planes strewn all over the runway. There are people de-mining in the middle of Kabul airport, because the airport is mined. And I was scared, but excited. I payed my first baksheesh to get my equipment through the customs and walked out into the light and suddenly there's this little Tajik man holding a handwritten sign saying 'Mr Dennis'. He was the cousin of the guy who worked at the hotel and he's rustled up a car and thought that this was an opportunity to get money out of a foreigner. He said two hundred US dollars a day—I said what about one hundred, he said okay—that was the deal. So he was going to be my guide. I said I didn't want anybody—I was going to do this by myself—but he said to me, correctly, 'No foreigner can survive in Kabul without a car and a guide.' In the bubble economy of Kabul all of the media have these quite elaborate fixers and everything is done like back home. I don't think I ever saw filmmakers out in the streets filming life as it was happening. Everything was a set-up and in many ways the translators were controlling what was being reported—though there were some exceptions.

How did you meet Habiba?

I've arrived and all I've got is a title and on the second day I'm there I'm driving into the city with my new translator whom I've agreed to hire for a day or two. I've got my camera with me and it's my first full day in Kabul. I've gone and checked into my hotel and realised that it's a long way from five stars and there's no electricity, the elevator's not working. I have to walk up four flights of stairs with all my bags, the balcony's all shot up with big chunks of concrete missing—the beautiful pool that featured on the website—I look down and it's empty with a dead dog in it. And I'm thinking 'What am I doing here?'

And this is the whole challenge of making a film—and not just a parachute report—'Oh look at wrecked Kabul' and get out—an intimate documentary film, with characters and development and insight and you don't know where to start really. The start is just to turn up. And you're essentially alone.

So the next day, with all that swirling in my head we're driving in this clapped out old second-hand Japanese bus that I've hired—into the central bazaar. I'm hunting for a phone card and the traffic is chaotic and I've got a driver with no English and a translator with no experience. And on this very first morning, suddenly I look out the window, and I'm just sort of gobsmacked by the whole Kabul experience.

It's the wildest place I've ever been really. Everybody's running around with Kalashnikovs on their shoulders and beggars everywhere and ruined buildings and it's crazier and wilder than anything I've seen in the past. Then suddenly I just spy out of the corner of my eye what I thought at the time was a blue puddle. It was a woman in a burka with a plastic leg poking out—the scene's in the film. It was a woman in a burka and she was begging. But my first impression was just this blue puddle. And I had a brain explosion. And I said, 'Stop the car—I'm going to go and speak to that person.' I had no idea of course who was under that blue veil. No idea. But I had this intuition. And my translator said—as I knew he would, 'You can't do that—foreigners can't just approach women in the street and talk to them here in Afghanistan—you can't do that.' Of course I knew that but something said 'you must do it'. So I said to him, 'Come on, one hundred US dollars a day—you get out of the car—come with me', and he reluctantly followed and I approached this person under the burka and I just set up my camera on the tripod to film my first scene in Afghanistan—my first scene in what would become *Landmines—A Love Story*—and I said to the young man, 'Please go and ask her.' She didn't get up and move straight away—and a crowd was starting to gather.

Then I said to the translator, 'Please just go over.' He's protesting, saying, 'We can't do this.' And I'm saying, 'It won't take a minute, please just go and ask her if she could just please look at me through her veil and say what her name is, how old she is, where she's from, how she lost her leg and what she's doing here.' And he went over and approached her and spoke.

From then on everything started to work in my favour. Under that burka was a Tajik woman. If she'd been Pashtun and he Tajik, it wouldn't have happened. But I didn't know. So this person with this young girl's voice said to me through her veil, 'My name is Habiba, I'm eighteen years old, I come from Shomali', which is a farming area one hour north of Kabul, near Bagram where the US forces were based. 'I lost my leg to a landmine when I was a little girl and now I have to beg to support my family.' Just like that.

And my translator came back and said that's what she said and I realised that I hadn't recorded the sound very well. So I went and put the camera right next to her veil and asked him to ask her to repeat what she'd said. By then the crowd had really gathered around and suddenly this crazy ex-Taliban type person came up brandishing his AK-47 and said 'How dare you let foreigners film this horrible image of Afghanistan and show it around the world.' It was more dangerous than even that—he was ignoring me and just haranguing her—this little blue puddle, and the translator was panicking now. I wasn't panicking but I realized it was dangerous because half the crowd were on his side and half the crowd were on my side saying, 'No it's okay, everything's changed' etc. And the translator said, 'Come on, we've got to go'—and I said, 'No I'm not going, she's begging, I'm not going until I give her some money, so you wait here with the camera.' So I went over to this man and got his attention by waving and reached into my pocket, pulled out whatever I had—it was a twenty dollar US bill I think, and I just waved it in front of his eyes and I didn't take my eyes off him and I just bent down and a little brown hand came out from underneath the burka, took the money and I left. This is my first day in Afghanistan—then the translator and the driver were so angry with me and they said, 'That is it—you just did a really dangerous thing—we're not working with you anymore—you're crazy.'

So they sacked you.

They kind of did and they didn't. But by then I was really worried about what had happened to this young woman. I now knew her name, I knew how old she was, I knew a little bit of her story. I was now a little but worried about what was happening to her so after we went back to the same spot and spoke to the policeman who looked after that little corner where she was begging and asked if she was okay and he said yes, 'She took the money and she left.' I was worried that the money was going to be taken from her. And I went back to the hotel and played back my material—it wasn't a lot—one tape. And there it was—an image of an Afghan woman—and the words came out and I looked at the screen and it had meaning and beauty and transcendence and I said to myself, 'That's it, not only do I have a title, I have the central character.'

I still haven't seen her though. So I become obsessed with this idea and I re-negotiate with the people who are taking me around. I say, 'Look, I'll never do that again, it was irresponsible. I promise, I'll do it the proper way, please come with me tomorrow and you can ask her if we can ask her father and her brothers for their permission for her to tell her story.' Which is what one's supposed to do in Afghanistan. So they agreed to that and we went back looking for the person I knew to be Habiba—which by the way, means 'the loved one' in Persian. But she wasn't there.

So for the next two-and-a-half days we went frantically looking all around the bazaars of Kabul. They're promising me they can find her. Our friendship's developing, we're beginning to like each other and eventually they work with me all the way through the two months. Now I'm thinking—well, I've found my character but she's gone and I still have no idea what she looks like. And on the third day we go to the same spot and there she is again. And I do set up the camera from a distance because I suspect that once she sees the camera, given what had happened, that she'll just give up and go away. She saw me but she didn't move. And the young man went over and said if she could take me to her father and she said yes. I was really trembling about it all. We discreetly went around the corner—I couldn't even look at her, even through the veil. She sat in the back of the van, I couldn't even turn around. By talking to the translator in Dari she directed us further out past the city, past the notorious football stadium where the Taliban executed women who were found on the street and into this area called Kalocha. We pass rows and rows of little mud houses, and finally enter a small courtyard. So here I am, following behind this Afghan woman in a burka, hobbling—about to meet her father and brothers in this traditional society and I'm filming it all. She opens the door and her three young children race out to greet her. She's got three children. She takes off her veil and I see her face for the very first time—she's very beautiful, transcendentally beautiful. So I'm in sort of shock really and my translator is sort of saying to me as an aside, 'I don't understand what's happening here—people don't do this—they won't let us come into their houses.' So I asked where her husband was, there had to be a husband, and she explained that her husband was out working—that he was a cobbler, he fixed shoes in the street. So then we left and I agreed to come back the next day and meet her husband. I'd assumed when she had told me that she was eighteen that she was so young that she would be single but in fact she was married with three children. Her eldest daughter Gita would have been seven or eight—so in fact she had had her first child when she was about twelve.

The next day we go back to meet her husband and I'm just beginning to think that their story could be part of *Landmines—A Love Story*. And *he* arrives home and he's also lost a leg. Also to a landmine. Habiba's lost her left leg, at the top of her thigh, he's lost his right leg below the knee when he was a Mujahedin soldier and stepped on a landmine. And we're sitting down drinking tea in this place where they're just squatting—they own nothing and they're saying, 'You're welcome here—we can tell you about landmines, we can tell you about our life.'

I still don't really know them. Obviously they can see I have money and it's clear I am going to pay them. But we didn't talk about specific amounts. And so Habiba agreed that I could film her. They all agreed that I could just film their lives as they went about their lives every day. They didn't have any real knowledge about how the media worked and that was a process that we talked through. I explained that the film would be widely seen around the world.

Normally when I make a film (with the exception of *Half Life*) the first month of rushes are rubbish—thrown away mostly. In this case, from the very first day something magical happened and every day for those five weeks on the first trip that I was there, the story just sort of unfolded. And I was right in their lives, the trance was happening—and I said to Habiba, 'Why are you letting me do this?' It wasn't just about money—every day I'd give her a little bit of money. She said, 'Because God sent you to me, when I saw you the first day I realised that God had sent you to me.' And I said, 'No Habiba, God sent *you* to me.' So it went, and I'm filming her in the bazaar and him doing his thing and after about ten days or so, she was complaining about having a headache. I offered her some of my paracetamol—she said no I won't take those—why—because I'm having another baby—so she's pregnant again.

I'm interested in the dynamics between Habiba and her husband Shah—that it really was a love story as well.

That's what I failed to say—that is, here I am in this household with their three children and they all deeply love each other and it is truly a love story. He's a loving man, she's a loving wife—she loves her God and adores her children. She's called Habiba . . . The Loved One. And it's a depiction of family life under Islam which is something you don't get—I've never seen it in other representations on film.

*I suppose in the journey that we started off talking about—*Landmines *has been very different to your other films.*

Well it's truly miraculous, think how I found these people. Imagine—put it back the other way round, that I'm sitting back in my office in Australia planning a film, writing a detailed treatment. I get a good title and then I want to think 'Well what would be the best film I could make?' If I even had the imagination that it would be a family like the family of Habiba and Shah her husband. If I'd imagined the story of the film and then set out to find that—it would never have happened. It would be impossible to find such a story. And yet I wasn't even there twenty-four hours when I had the brain explosion and I started filming. So I say that when any film of mine turns out well, then it *is* a miracle. It's got to be. This is not a logical process. Of course there has to be some logic to how I do some things myself—like throwing myself into the extreme position. Going to the extreme place. I like to be in places where there is the shifting terminus between cultures and societies, where the fault lines are clear. Where things are happening. Certainly Kabul was, and still is, one of those places.

It seems it was a different process this time—with Good Woman *and* Cunnamulla, *you went there with a clear starting point, but with* Landmines *it seems that all you had when you arrived in Afghanistan was a title.*

Yes, it was a little different. For instance with *Cunnamulla* I was able to write a treatment of a few pages, based on my research, which was like a statement of intent about the kind of film I wanted to make—with Cunnamulla standing as an icon of something about Australian culture. But even so, when I went to Cunnamulla, the only two characters I saw clearly as being in the film were Neradah, the taxi driver's wife, and her husband the taxi driver.

Look it sounds a little bit sort of airy fairy, but when I make films I both don't know what the film's going to be but in another way I know exactly what it's going to be. In terms of its impact. If there's a miracle and if I don't fail. I know that what I want to capture is the essence of what it is to be alive at a certain place, at a certain time. That's it. And as there is no logic, there is absolute clear fundamental logic there.

But you can't force it. My films are not just sort of found on the street corner—they're not just achieved by standing back and observing dispassionately. I detest these people who make these claims for *vérité* filmmaking and the rest of it. They have these rules about not doing what they call interviews, but at the same time forcing people to talk to each other and things like this.

My way of telling stories is very much bound up in the act of photography itself. I think I'd find it very difficult to achieve the kind of powerful effects of my films if I wasn't the person who was creating the images and sound at the same time as I was relating to the people. If I think of my films and what I hope that they do, maybe it's that they just reek verisimilitude—a kind of truth. That is you really feel like you're there, even though the films are very mediated and are not observational documentaries in the sense that the filmmakers pretend that they're not there. I don't do that—quite the opposite. I fully immerse myself and my personality through my relationship with my subjects and through the photographic act—through the whole way of telling the story. The notion of objective reality is ridiculous.

It's hard for young filmmakers to take those risks.

It is difficult. It's supposed to be difficult. It's very fashionable to pick up a little video camera and be a documentary filmmaker. Rock stars do it. Members of royalty do it. Everyone's making their own films these days. And it can be a good thing. But with regard to young filmmakers, all the rules have changed—because the means of production are so accessible and so affordable. First of all you have to take risks. We're talking about art here—if art isn't a risky business, what is? Of course it's risky—have you ever seen a good film where risks weren't taken at all levels? The notion of art involves risks. As for young filmmakers I'd say that it's much easier for them to take risks than me. For me the bar is continually being raised. Each time I make a film the expectations of people increase, as do the budgets and I'm still prepared to take the risk, touch wood you know. No-one wants to fail, but it's always possible that you'll fail.

To me, it's all about intuition with you.

Look, you cannot be taught these things—you cannot be taught the notion of intuition, the notion of the sympathetic engagement of your subject. There are many people making films now who are very highly trained in filmmaking but they probably shouldn't be making films because for starters, they're not risk takers. If you're not a risk taker, you're probably better off being an advertising executive or something. There is really no excuse anymore. Because of the equipment—this is for documentary film, we're getting closer and closer to this notion of the *camera stylo*, that the camera is no different to the pen and that everyone can become a filmmaker. Well of course everyone can, the technology is so accessible. But remember, though we all learn how to read and write we don't all produce the great novel. It's not about technology—the technology's just a means to an end. That's why I call it technological determinism, because it's become like the technology *is* the end. It's become very fashionable to be a documentary filmmaker these days but I think a lot of people are doing it for the wrong reasons. There has to be that epiphany. That thrill of creating something that has meaning. The thrill that I had that night when I sat in the hotel in Kabul and watched the images I had filmed of Habiba begging in the bazaar.

Let's talk about all those areas that always come up in discussing your work, like truth and ethical dilemmas.

I'm always aware of the process of representation, of the relationship between myself the filmmaker and the people who are the subject of the film—the characters. This is a part of the secret contract. That is—I am filming—I'm recording their lives to create my own little artefact—they know I'm doing that—this is not a secret camera hidden in a bag or a security camera on the wall of a bank. But, in this kind of film, it's not as if the people who are in the film are not colluding in that process—that's part of the secret contract. We're constantly dancing around each other—but we're agreeing to dance around each other—and there's a trust there.

I'm always suspicious of people when they talk about their 'code of ethics'. I've said before, I'm sure that they had a code of ethics at Enron—I'm sure there's a code of ethics at the White House. I prefer the word moral because the word ethics is almost a corporatized word now. I tell myself, '*I must always not lie about what I know.*' And if that means that I give offence to somebody— or many—then so be it. I try to be moral. Now I believe in both truth and justice but I don't believe you can have any justice without truth. So if I have to choose between the two, I will try to tell the truth. I could be wrong, but to me the bigger lie is when filmmakers gloss over the more difficult truths so as not to offend. It happens constantly in other films that I see. It happens all the time in advertising, in our public media and in journalism—official story-telling by men and women in suits. I think current affairs journalism is the crudest form of story-telling that exists. Compare that to the subtleties of the little stories that children tell each other—I prefer that kind of story. I try to tell my kind of story in a way through illusion and allusion and understatement. I love the quote from *Don Quixote*, 'Always hold the hand of the child you once were.'

Immanuel Kant, the German philosopher, says 'A lie must always be wrong, because it takes away the autonomy of the other.' Now I've told lies, we all have, that's the nature of the beast. I try not to take away the autonomy of my characters. That is, whether it be somebody I love or somebody I detest, I try in the way I make my films to not take away their autonomy. You can find in my films that I have on the rare occasion—like the way I set up Ronald Reagan in *Half Life* or some of the sex tourists in *The Good Woman of Bangkok*. But in terms of the people who are central to my films—I try to never take away their autonomy—even if I might be accused of unnecessarily exposing them or something. There are these incredibly simplistic notions out there about what happens in the process of making this kind of film. As if it happens in some sort of formulated, mechanical way—that there is not true interaction going on.

It's not as if you've got this totally skewed power relationship where me—as director of the film—is controlling everything that's happening. I'm controlling very little of what's happening in terms of the ideas and emotions being expressed. That's all happening in an extraordinary, magical process of interaction between myself and the people who agreed to be filmed—no matter what it's about. I'm constantly amazed when people think that I've let my guard down in a film where I'll include some reference to the process which is not necessarily very flattering to me. The question is, not how could I have done it but why did I include that particular moment in the film for people to reflect on that process?

Given the nature of all my work, there is always going to be an ethical dilemma involved in the kind of filmmaking that I do, because I'm seeking to dig deep, to uncover those paradoxes and secret truths about people and lives and situations and depict that and describe it. First of all you recognize that there is the ethical dilemma. You try, as it were, to so vividly portray it as to effectively resolve it within the context of the work itself. You don't always succeed—you certainly don't succeed with everybody.

These days I'm quite comfortable with the idea that my films will have mixed reactions. People who will really appreciate them and people who will really detest them. I'd be very worried if I made a film that achieved universal acclaim. I'd think I'd gone soft. I've said it so many times but I am convinced that people only want their truths as fantasy. Escaping from the truth we really know. Maybe I have masochistic tendencies . . . It probably requires a psychiatrist, but I'm fascinated by the flaws in the character. I probably have, overall, a fairly dark vision of what it is to be a human. However, I am a man who has loved a lot, who has five children, who is a romantic, and is really quite optimistic in so many other ways.

10

The Politics of Documentary: A Symposium

Barbara Zheutlin

Several of America's leading social documentarians discuss esthetic and political issues involved in producing documentary films, including the effectiveness of narration, ways of creating drama, the ethics of interviewing, scripting, and preplanning, the use or avoidance of "buzzwords," and the influence of cinéma vérité. *Although this symposium was put together in 1981, most of its points of debate continue to be relevant for documentary politics. While contexts have changed in the intervening years, this itself is instructive.*

The documentary film in America has still not been granted the serious attention it deserves. It's not surprising, therefore, that documentary filmmakers—especially those whose work reflects a social and political commitment—are not often asked to describe their creative process. As a whole, these documentarians prefer to talk about the subjects they've filmed rather than about their craft. They are interested in reality, truth, showing life as it is actually lived, or exposing hidden aspects of our society. It has seemed almost a luxury to them to have time to think and talk about how they do what they do. Questions of art, esthetics, and the craft of communicating have too often been ignored or belittled by politically motivated filmmakers. The results, too frequently, are impassioned and politically well-intentioned but unimaginative and poorly crafted films that are incapable of communicating successfully with the audiences for which they are intended.

In an attempt to initiate a discussion of some of these esthetic and political issues, Cineaste *associate Barbara Zheutlin sent a questionnaire to a number of independent filmmakers whose films have played an important role in educating and inspiring people. Those groups and individuals who responded include Emile de Antonio (director of* Point of Order, In the Year of the Pig, Millhouse: A White Comedy, *and* Underground, *among other films), Pacific Street Films (*Free Voice of Labor: The Jewish Anarchists, Frame-Up!: The Imprisonment of Martin Sostre, Red Squad, The Grand Jury: An Institution Under Fire, *and others), Josh Hanig (codirector of* Men's Lives *and* Song of the Canary), *Dave Davis (codirector of* Song of the Canary, Year of the Tiger, DC III), *Jon Else (*The Day After Trinity, Stepping*

Out: The De Bolts Grow Up, You Don't Live Here, *and* Arthur & Lillie*), Connie Field (*Rosie the Riveter*), and the Kartemquin Collective (*The Chicago Maternity Center Story, Taylor Chain, All of Us Stronger, Trick Bag, Now We Live on Clifton, *and* Winnie Wright, Age 11*).

Many other filmmakers invited were unable to respond due to the pressure of busy production schedules, but we hope the responses published below will encourage other filmmakers—as well as everyone concerned with the development of socially committed documentaries—to a greater appreciation of what is involved in creating better films.

Barbara Zheutlin: *How conscious are you when you are shooting and editing your films about the problem of creating drama and involving the audience? Do you think about casting your documentary? Have you made choices to edit parts of your films to make them more entertaining?*

Josh Hanig: Too many leftist films are too long, too intellectual, and don't have enough music. Most of these films are full of interviews, and because people like to talk when being interviewed and like to make points, they often repeat themselves in subtle ways. I always listen carefully and cut, cut, cut. Better to have cutaways than to be repetitive, thereby throwing off your focus, as well as your flow and pacing.

We Americans like to have fun, to be entertained. We also respect humor. I frequently hear expressions like, "Why go pay to see problems when you've got enough of your own for free?" Somehow, the moviegoing public will pay to be horrified by blood-and-gore movies, but they shy away from being horrified by daily reality shown in documentaries. However, they don't seem to have so much trouble laughing at those same horrors. We need more of a *Strangelove* mentality in our films—more irreverence toward authority.

Dave Davis: You think about all these things, but you really succeed or fail in the editing room. You try to prepare for editing by providing yourself with the right raw material—good interviews, beautiful images for montage cutting, dramatic sound and images, cutaways for every scene where dialogue will have to be condensed, personal and emotionally rich expressions of people's experiences, good camera work and sound recording. You plan to film people to some extent based on how they will come across in front of the camera. Some people freeze up in front of a camera, some don't. This is very important and can often be determined by doing preliminary interviews during preproduction.

I think a storyline, a dramatic unfolding of events, helps a film tremendously. Sometimes this can't be done, and the unfolding is the development of certain themes or ideas or information. The more entertaining films, though, have some suspense, conflict, storyline, and drama to them that holds our interest. I'm personally trying to develop more in this direction—I think I've been prone to a thematic, linear, informative style, rather than in telling a story or building into a film some conflict and tension that holds suspense for the audience.

Jon Else: The most important thing about *Trinity* is that we tried to make it work like a feature film and in that sense tried, I suppose, to invent a weird new genre. The key, the nut, the *sine qua non*, the very heart of what we are about is storytelling. Half the battle in making documentaries is finding subjects which embody an emotionally charged drama, lived by people worth caring about. The other half is finding the money.

Connie Field: One thing I learned from the makers of *Word Is Out* is to videotape before selecting people for the film. I wanted to find people who could express themselves emotionally as well as intellectually, and videotaping was an excellent tool to use in making an accurate judgment toward this end.

Through the influence of Lorraine Kahn, who was an associate producer on the project and who felt strongly about the importance of locations, and the influence of Veronica Selver from *Word Is Out*, who explained how they "dressed the set," I was very careful about locations. I don't believe you should shoot an interview with a white wall behind it—the background has to say something. Remember, people are looking at an image, and you don't want the interview to be visually boring. So all of our interviews were shot in different locations that revealed something about each woman.

Two of the women were filmed where they used to work, Lynn on an old victory ship that was built in the Second World War, and Lola in front of a factory where she used to work, with the New York skyline in the background. I flew Margaret from Los Angeles to my offices in the Bay Area because I couldn't afford to fly my crew down. I then created a clinic-type atmosphere for her in one of our offices because she then worked in a clinic, and I wanted her surroundings to say something about her life now. With Juanita, I rented a Winnebago and drove her out to the Ford River Rouge plant so we could see the factory in the background with the smoke rising out the window, because, in my mind, that image says Detroit. And Gladys was filmed inside her house because it rained. We were going to shoot it outside her house, but it still works well for her because the house is decorated in a way that is characteristic of homes in the southern mountains, which is where she grew up.

Another thing that I consciously went for was a dramatic curve to the film, and I used that concept to structure the film. I was very conscious of wanting the audience to feel the experience, for it to have an emotional impact. First there is the initial excitement of entering new jobs. Then the emotion dips down as we get into the issues of the double day and of occupational health and safety; then it builds up with Lynn's torch story and the thrill of seeing the ship launched, and with Lola's "Work makes life sweet" to the excitement of the war ending. Then, bam!—the disappointment of losing your job and having to go back to lower-paying work.

We also wanted the audience to gain a greater understanding of the propagandistic nature of the newsreels and to learn how to read them *as* the film progresses. In other words, the contradiction between the propaganda and the women's experiences gets more and more obvious as the film goes on.

The simplest way to get your viewpoint across to an audience is to use narration. But there's been a generally shared assumption among political filmmakers that narration is boring, can't be trusted, is not filmic. What has influenced your decision to use or not use a narrator? How did you select the person to narrate?

Emile de Antonio: Among the angelic orders, films are made by purple butterflies with cameras screwed into their gossamer wings, catching every iridescent jagger and flicker. For me, film is tug, pull, conflict, process. Will there be narration? Who will write it? Who will speak it? Dan Talbot and I produced *Point of Order*. I raised the money. In the beginning, all was one. We agreed there would be no narration, only the material itself speaking for itself. Time produced tugs. Our experienced editor did not believe people could understand without explanation. Dan finally agreed with him. I had never made a film. I caved in. I hired Richard Rovere, who was author of the *New Yorker's* weekly "Washington Letter" and of a book on Joe McCarthy, to write the narration. Mike Wallace lived near me in the country; I knew him; I hired him to read Rovere's narration. I was unhappy. We all met in a sound studio, and Mike read. I knew it was wrong. *New Yorker* prose is cadenced harmoniously enough, but not for film; Mike was too blustery.

I listened and listened to that tape of narration. I killed it. I fired the experienced editor. I said to Dan (paraphrase), "Okay, now we'll do it your way or my way. I'll match you." Dan: "Come on, De, be realistic. I've got the theater to run, family responsibility, neither one of us has ever done this before." Me: "Okay, I'll do it. No one else will see except those working with me until we have an answer print." A year later we screened it in the Movielab building. It was 1963. There was no narration. It was my film.

Pacific Street Films: Well, the question of narration is a good one; it's something we've struggled with. The problem with any narration is that if it's a disembodied voice, it always comes out seeming like the disembodied voice of authority. We've tried to stay away from that, although there are times, like in *Frame-Up!*, where information has to be conveyed and there's no way to do it other than with narration. It was the same thing with the grand jury film; we tried to use a male voice and a female voice. However, we basically don't like the use of narration if the characters themselves or the people who are interviewed can get across that information. Somewhere in the middle there is a compromise: to establish the voice in the beginning as belonging to some person, and then continuing it throughout as a voice-over. In *Red Squad*, for instance, we used an interview with ourselves which we had on-screen, and then selected sections as voice-overs. In our current film, *Anarchism in the United States*, we're doing the same thing. We've conducted an interview with ourselves which we'll use on-screen and then, we hope, as voice-over to tie together the rest of the sections.

Josh Hanig: Our documentary ancestors used narration as an integral part of their films. It was considered an art; people such as Archibald MacLeish utilized it with great effectiveness. Our generation seems to shy away from it. It is more mysterious and artful not to use it. Certainly the mass audience is used to it and accepts it all the time on TV documentaries. They, in fact, feel comfortable with it, to be guided along through the film, so to speak. If you have a strong storyline, and don't need it, why use it? But if you want to get across information and be analytical, it can be both effective and unobtrusive in the feel of the film—it can, in fact, enhance it.

   On both films we tried to avoid it, but in the cutting realized it was too complicated to tell the story without it. I like to think it was because the films were so complex. What we got on film was not in the design, but had to be added with meticulous writing and rewriting at the rough-cut stage. My preference, even in a political film, is first-person narration. It can be involving.

   I like to think my films are for a mass audience, and I don't think a mass audience gives a damn about whether or not there's a narrator. If it works for that particular film, it works. The only people who look down on narration are effete film theoreticians and people who think their film is not art if it's narrated.

Dave Davis: Necessity. Sometimes there is just no other way to get certain information into the film. Subtitles are very expensive, so often verbal identification of the subject is most economical. I also like it better. Narration can also work extremely well if it's well written and dramatic, as in Jon Else's film *Day After Trinity*.

Jon Else: A word on narration: I get terribly frustrated by the feeling among filmmakers, particularly on the left, that narration is, per se, a bad thing. Bad narration is a bad thing, and we grew up, for the most part, on bad narration. There are, however, as many kinds of narration as there are kinds of films, and a well-written, evocative ten seconds of narration can often do a better job than two minutes of tortured film. In dealing with the overwhelmingly complex subjects which so often attract us, narration should be thought of as a friend and ally, not as a necessary evil. Every documentarian should sit down and really listen to *Night and Fog* or *Day After Day* or *Volcano* or *Night Mail* or *The River*. Narration might also be the key to accessibility for a mass audience. If an audience can't trust the narration, why should it trust anything else in the film? Is there any less potential for manipulation in editing, music, composition?

Connie Field: It obviously depends on the type of film one is making, but I lean toward the nonnarrated documentary. In *Rosie*, I thought the vitality would come across better without narration. Because I was dealing with a controversial issue, I thought it would be better to let the material speak for itself, and I think the choice was correct because it's hard to argue with people's experiences combined with historical documents, and this gives the film a lot of credibility.

I think the disembodied voice of a narrator distances people from the material. And I don't mean Brechtian distance, which is a whole other thing. I mean the kind of distancing that can minimize the impact of the material. I believe that audiences are intelligent enough to get the point, even subtle points. I believe in presenting the material in an analytical structure that's accomplished in the editing room, if possible, and in letting people deduce for themselves—aided by an analysis you give in the way you structure the material.

Kartemquin: Questions of style are also affected by considerations of use. *Taylor Chain*, for example, has no narration. When information was needed that wasn't present in the scenes, we wrote a title card. This was extremely difficult. We must have gone through $50 of Pilot Fine Points rewriting those title cards to achieve the correct tone—conveying the necessary information, but also indicating what was important about that information. We had decided that narration would be wrong because we had no authentic voice from within the story that could say all that needed saying. An anonymous narrator would have been distracting and might have diluted the film's reality and credibility. Possibly another reason for the decision, in hindsight, is that a story about democracy can be "acted out" much more persuasively than it can be "narrated." In any case, it's obvious that often the questions of effectiveness, or usefulness, and questions of stylistic coherence are closely related.

The Chicago Maternity Center Story had to have narration. There was no other way to guide the viewer through such complex historical and analytical material. In this film we were lucky enough to have an acceptable voice close at hand, one that could speak with authority and feeling and had no need of objective pretense. For us, a narrative voice that comes from the subject is the most honest and persuasive. We also feel that letting the narrative bias show, instead of hiding it, lets the audience know that we respect them, that we are not trying to manipulate them with subtle narrative tricks. We like to state our case openly, whether by narration or by the way we structure the scene in the editing room.

To what extent have you scripted your films before shooting? To what extent have you filmed first and shaped your film later in the editing? What are the advantages and disadvantages of the two approaches?

Pacific Street Films: We try to get our point of view across in the editing. Our films have usually not been scripted before we've begun them, but lately we have tried to give them a little more form. In the past, we've filmed first and shaped the film later in the editing, and that's created quite a few problems— being faced with a massive editing job is like trying to piece together a huge jigsaw puzzle. The advantage to a scripted film, of course, is that the editing becomes a way to piece things together simply, according to the paper-cut.

Josh Hanig: With *Men's Lives*, we produced a twenty-five minute prototype slide show which we showed for fund-raising. Surprisingly, we followed the style and format of the slide show fairly closely in the film. With *Song of the Canary*, I wrote a treatment for PBS (again, in order to raise the money), and upon recently rereading it I was surprised to see how closely the finished film resembles the treatment, not in specifics, but in style, pacing, and effect. The problem, of course, is that in documentary, what you film is what you get, not necessarily what you want or intend to get. So the cutting becomes the process of carving out the original intentions from actuality.

In shaping both *Men's Lives* and *Canary*, we had the problem of writing narration toward the end of the process in order to tie together loose ends, clarify hazy points, and make transitions. In both of those films, that kind of thinking could have been done a little bit more beforehand. In both cases, I'd hoped we wouldn't have to use narration, and in both cases it became clearly necessary only after months of cutting.

Dave Davis: I don't script films. I outline the content I want to cover—the issues, the themes, the types of sequences I want to include in the film and what they will hopefully convey in terms of the issues. The rest is done in the editing room and in writing narration. Often things emerge in the editing that you hadn't anticipated and couldn't have scripted.

Jon Else: *Trinity* was not scripted. We did several years of research, an extensive story outline (not of the film, but of the history involved), and, most importantly, a "toy movie," which David W. Peoples wrote and which was a hypothetical full-blown screenplay for a finished film. We never intended to actually produce the toy movie, but it was the foundation for getting at the meat of our story. In the end, the film was shaped about 50 percent before shooting and 50 percent during editing, and it would have been shaped 85 percent before shooting had we not cut it down from four hours to forty minutes during the last month of postproduction. Here again, the overriding reason for truncating *Trinity* was that American television does not acknowledge four-hour programs.

Connie Field: In *Rosie*, the point of view was grounded in historical reality and based on extensive research. I let the government films and the women express themselves.

Although *Rosie* was not scripted, it was carefully planned before shooting. I outlined the history, all the issues. The women I had chosen for the film—five of them—I had interviewed quite extensively before filming, and then, in filming, I asked specific questions which would elicit certain stories I knew they could talk about.

What was set in the editing was the pacing and, of course, final content selection. I went very broad in terms of the stock footage I collected and in the scope of the interviews. Obviously, in the editing certain of the stories fit and others didn't. When a woman would use abstractions, it would never work. If she spoke of *the* "black experience," it didn't work as well as when she gave a specific experience from her life. Some stories I particularly wanted—for example, Juanita actually broke down the color bar at Murray Bodies; she was the only black woman courageous enough to do that. But the story was not told clearly enough to communicate its dramatic impact to an audience. We must have worked on that story for a month, trying it over and over again in the editing. It was a very hard story to lose, because it was so important.

What this shows is that the form that I chose to use also limited the content, even though I would never have chosen any other way for this particular film. I feel very strongly that interview documentaries can be extremely powerful if people are revealed in such a way that you can care and feel for them and can receive their stories as drama. If I was using people *just* for information, I could have used some of these stories which, for whatever reason, didn't carry the emotional weight that matched up to the events they were describing.

How familiar are you with the history of documentary films? Have you been influenced by them? What role do you think cinéma vérité *has played in shaping the political documentary?*

Emile de Antonio: I was familiar—when I began making documentaries—with Flaherty, Lorentz, and a few Europeans. I did not see the work of Esther

Schub until 1972, when Anna-Lena Wibom of the Swedish Film Institute gave me a retrospective. I was overwhelmed.

I realize now, after years of work, how uncomfortable I am with the myth of Flaherty and why. The charm and power of his camera are marred by distortions, lies, and inaccuracies which pander to a fake romantic, fake nature-boy view of society. The struggles of modern man are not between man and economic and social models inimical to life and growth. *Louisiana Story* was financed by Humble Oil. The oil riggers, their rigs, the crocodiles, the boy, the bayou are romanticized to the point where one understands very clearly why Humble Oil gave away prints to any theater in the country which would play them. *Nanook* is a masterpiece of cinematography, and grossly wrong. The Eskimo did not live apart from Western influence. Nanook was not self-indulgent and romantic; he was an actor in a film by a self-indulgent romantic.

I have not been influenced by the work of any documentary filmmaker. *Cinéma vérité* is two halves of an apple, half rotten and half rather decent eating. The decent part is the technical improvement of light sync-sound camera equipment that came from Leacock, the Maysles, Pennebaker. The rotten half is most of the work, the pretentiousness behind it. There lies behind *cinéma vérité* the implication of a truth arrived at by a scientific instrument, called the camera, which faithfully records the world. Nothing could be more false. The assumption of objectivity is false. Filmmakers edit what they see, edit as they film what they see, weight people, moments, and scenes by giving them different looks and values. As soon as one points a camera, objectivity is romantic hype. With any cut at all, objectivity fades away. It is why so many *soi-disant vérité* filmers made rock-docs. The least appetizing of all *cinéma vérité* is Wiseman's watery stew, made up of his debt to light cameras and my use of nonnarration structure. Suitable pap for PBS. Bland, floury stuff offensive to no one, only to the art of films.

Pacific Street Films: We're very familiar with the history of documentary film, and we've seen quite a number of historical documentary productions. We all grew up on those kinds of films and were influenced by them, particularly by the compilation films that were produced by the networks in the fifties and sixties, like "The 20th Century" and "Victory at Sea."

Cinéma vérité has, of course, been an extremely crucial part of political documentary, but not so much in our films; we've done some *vérité*, but we haven't structured our films totally around the use of *vérité* footage. We don't think that works. You have to have some kind of historical context or dramatic style that supersedes the use of a totally *vérité* approach.

Josh Hanig: I wish we Americans were seeing more European and Japanese documentaries. I really have very little idea what they're up to, but I know there's some interesting work being done. I love looking at other documentaries, especially when they break the mold. I was very influenced by the Murrow documentaries of the fifties, and, of course, the early *vérité* work. Lately, I find myself very influenced by filmmakers who take some personal risks, like Mike Rubbo's Canadian Film Board films. He puts himself in the middle of a social milieu and tries to tell the story from the point of view of the outsider who's been thrown inside trying to figure it out. He can be your guide, and if it doesn't all make sense, well, we people on the left have a hard time accepting that everything doesn't make sense. A hard thing to accept with a materialist training. But I think it's much more human and accessible to an audience to perhaps once in a while admit this or acknowledge it.

Jon Else: I am very familiar with the documentary tradition and feel influenced by it, although certainly not by political *cinéma vérité*. When I think of political documentaries which have made some difference to me and, perhaps, to audiences, I think of *Night and Fog, The Sorrow and the Pity, Memorandum, Hearts and Minds*, and only secondarily of *Harlan County*, which I loved, or the Maysles and Wiseman films. Joris Ivens falls somewhere in between, I guess. It is ironic, I suppose, that nearly all of my own filmmaking prior to *Trinity* has been hybrid *cinéma vérité*, and that is what I most love doing.

How consciously have you sought out interviewees to express your view? Do you interview people before selecting them to appear in your film? To what extent do you try to make your arguments by providing facts and logic, and to what extent do you try to appeal more to the audience's emotions—to arouse their sympathy or anger, rather than to convince them through information? How do you balance the two?

Pacific Street Films: Before we start a film we try to do as many preinterviews as possible, both with people who express our viewpoint and with people who are antagonistic to it. Usually, one of the ways we try to give form to our films is by finding people who are not necessarily sympathetic to our position and then utilize them to draw attention to some of the key themes. In *Frame-Up!* we gave a lot of play to the county sheriff who was instrumental in framing Martin Sostre; he came off so ridiculously that there was no question in anybody's mind that he had been part of that frame-up. So it often pays to give that kind of antagonist a fair amount of publicity.

Josh Hanig: I usually like to interview people first, unless I know there will be an urgency to them spilling out a particular story. Then you want it fresh. I, myself, like to look for "the common wisdom" in normal nonanalytical people—the simple truth. If that can't be found and there are gaps, or things are misleading, then it's often necessary to find that person with a point of view you want represented. Of course, now that our point of view is less and less visible, maybe I'll stack my next film with gadflies.

Dave Davis: I often do preinterviews in order to select people for a film. Usually one character or speaker in the film will not represent the filmmaker exactly, but partially. A part of the truth, as I see it, when combined with many other parts, creates the whole of the film which does represent my perception of what was going on at the time, as I saw it at the time—all of this is very subjective, of course.

Jon Else: We sought out people, not for their views but for their credibility as characters, their storytelling charm, and their depth of knowledge. I preinterviewed about seventy-five people and filmed sixteen, of whom fourteen ended up in the film. I was always forthright (and I feel that a filmmaker must always be forthright) about the film we were making, and about our point of view—which was not, in fact, a point of view, but a genuine curiosity about where the atomic bomb came from.

I always tell subjects that I am filming: it is dirty pool not to tell them. As Bertolt Brecht put it, "Alas, we who would teach others kindness could not ourselves be kind."

Connie Field: I chose women whose stories and job histories were typical of the times and who could also reveal important historical events such as the black struggle for employment and union organizing drives. We did extensive preinterviews—seven hundred women were interviewed over the phone, two hundred in person on audio tape; thirty-five were videotaped; and we filmed five. We interviewed so many for two reasons. First, the response to our press releases was overwhelming. Second, the oral histories were a crucial part of the original research necessary for the film.

Many of the women do express our point of view, but some of that came as a surprise when filming. For instance, Lola Weixel, who makes that incredible statement at the end of *Rosie* about how society prepares women psychologically for whatever role it wants women to play—after losing so many men, America wanted babies and we wanted babies, but we gave up everything for that—had never expressed that thought to me until the day I filmed her. I had no idea she felt that. And someone asked me if I wrote that for her.

None of my questions was ever that direct. Sometimes they were like, "Tell me what happened when you went to Murray Bodies . . ."; or if it was a specific story, I'd say, "Oh, tell me that story again," or, "What happened with your union?" They were broad questions, but not leading questions. One thing that I did seek out consciously was a couple of women who were conscious of what happened to them in the larger historical framework. To that end I chose someone like Margaret, who talked about the propaganda and the media after the war.

Another interesting thing that happened with the film is that I didn't consciously set out to have two white women and three black women. It was a matter of just having certain issues and certain stories covered, and these five women were the ones to do it, and three of them happened to be black. Though I'm immensely pleased with the effect because all too many times blacks are used in films just to elicit the black experience, and therefore become tokens, and I think that the effect of this film is the opposite. The black women aren't tokens, they are integral to the whole concept of the entire film.

How do you decide whether or not to use the words socialism *or* communism *or* capitalism *in your interviews? In your narration? Do you think these words should be avoided because of their impact on an audience?*

Pacific Street Films: Words like *socialist* or *communist* or *capitalist* are not necessarily evil in themselves, only in terms of their context. With certain people, who are going to react in certain way to those buzzwords, perhaps it's better to substitute something else. It depends on what kind of a reaction you want and what the situation is. They shouldn't be avoided in general just because they might have a negative effect on the audience. If the situation is appropriate and the best description is in terms of communism or capitalism, then that's the way to phrase it.

Dave Davis: In most cases, I avoid them, although I think in certain key spots it's good to use words like *capitalism* or *socialism*. That has to be done very carefully, so that the use of these words seems very natural, nonrhetorical, and is fully justified and explained by the development of the film. The audience must be convinced, by what they've seen and experienced in the film, that these terms are totally appropriate and nonrhetorical. And here I mean audiences that are not already sympathetic or oriented toward the left.

Connie Field: This is a very difficult question. We live in a very oppressive society. Ideas that oppose the status quo are not looked upon very favorably. And most Americans do not understand what socialism and communism mean. What people do understand—some of which I feel is true—is that some of the realities of communism as it is lived out in the Soviet Union today are bad. It's true that there isn't freedom of the press there. It is true that there isn't the same production of consumer goods in socialist societies as we have in the U.S. But people in socialist societies take for granted things that we do not have, such as full employment, day care, and virtually free medical care. But because the meaning of socialism and communism is not understood by Americans, we need to be careful about our use of these terms.

I think when a person's experience of belonging to the CP or the Socialist Workers' Party is integral to the experience that you're filming, then it definitely should be said. It's doing an injustice to the true history of America by not saying it. I think it's obviously much better to let the people in the film say this, and to avoid it in the narration. But I don't think *capitalism* is a dirty word in this country. It's our system.

The word *communism* is used in *Rosie*. I didn't avoid it or delete the story that Lynn tells. I also feel that her story puts the issue in the most uncannily accurate perspective when she talks about being accused of being a communist. This is something labor audiences all over the country have had a hearty laugh over, because anyone who has organized or been involved in standing up knows that they are going to be called "communist," whether they are or not.

At the time, Lynn did not know what it meant. Her response to it at that point was to say, "Well, if communists object to the kind of treatment that officer was giving the Filipinos, then I'm the biggest communist you ever saw in your life." At that point the colonel wants her to shut up, which is also typical of a certain American who thinks it's too dangerous to go around saying those words.

How do you decide what subject to make a film about? In picking your subjects, do you think about what kinds of films the left should be making today?

Jon Else: On the matter of esthetics and choosing subjects, I do try very consciously to choose subjects that "the left should be making," but I do not try to make them for the left. The left doesn't need them. With *Trinity*, we very deliberately tried to make a film that would be accessible to and even enjoyed by people who would not ordinarily choose to sit down for ninety minutes and hear about "some left-wing pinhead who got himself involved with Faust."

We tried to make *Trinity* as simple as possible on one level (story, drama, humor, suspense, narration) so that it would have as wide an audience as possible. I feel very strongly that if one is going to make these films, they have to be made and distributed in such a way that millions of people will see them and be moved by them. For better or worse, this means prime-time television, and I take great pleasure in the fact that *Trinity* was scheduled for nationwide broadcast in prime time.

The thorn in all of this, of course, is the potential betrayal of your own politics and esthetics. The only solution I've been able to come up with is one that involves using fairly conventional stylistic devices on the surface level and avoiding the exposition of specific ideology or doctrine. Hand in hand with this is the notion that documentaries are best at evoking feeling and raising questions, and worst at listing facts and answering questions.

If I did not care about a mass audience, *Trinity* probably would have been a different film, and probably would not have had structural elements such as an extensive expository narration and a linear chronological structure. On the other hand, the feeling that *Trinity* generates is exactly what I sought, regardless of form.

Emile de Antonio: The documentary film artist lives in opposition. He or she is nurtured best on revolutionary soil: Ivens, Grierson, Rotha, Schub. My films come from the life and times of my country. Our government provides us with subjects daily: General Plague; thermonuclear war; El Salvador; declaration of war on the poor at home, and on the Third World everywhere. Let PBS and the networks sell news. Let the documentarians' world be full of surprises. Let the form, the film, grow organically, so that the maker doesn't know its look until it's finished.

Pacific Street Films: There are many different reasons why we pick a particular subject. Sometimes it's circumstances, like when we were involved with an anarchist group that became subject to governmental surveillance (*Red Squad*). Or it could be because someone has called us up and told us that there are certain things that ought to be investigated, like in *Frame-Up!* Or, currently, we've always had an interest in anarchism, and we've wanted to make a film that would really bring to light what we think is an overlooked movement.

Josh Hanig: I have three criteria. The subject has to be one that I care about deeply; there has to be a need for the film—in other words, there cannot be a glut of films on the same subject; and it has to be an issue of strong concern to a broad group of people. In the mid-seventies there were several films on Chile. Now, I felt a burning desire to do something on Chile, but there were so many films being done on the subject it seemed absurd for me to do a film on Chile, even though I very much wanted to. I look for subjects that I know need some exposition but have little exposure, even though large numbers of people are affected by the issue. After I became interested in the issue of occupational health and safety, I made a review of the films made on the subject and couldn't believe how little had been done, considering the scope of the issue and the tremendous potential for showing some of the more raw and brutal effects of capitalist economics. That's when *Canary* started to become a reality.

If you pick a subject which hasn't been covered extensively, and one for which there is a need, your film will be seen by many more people. On the other hand, there are some subjects that translate well into film and others that don't. I have asked myself the question, "Could this issue be better served by using the thousands of dollars of film budget to print up a flier and hire a lawyer to pressure government or file a lawsuit?" For me, the subject has to have some strong emotion to it.

Dave Davis: A number of factors come into play: my own interests, my own political judgment, the judgment of others I work with and trust, my perception of where there is an audience that can use the film, where there is a political movement that would benefit from having a film, whether or not money can be raised for the film, and whether or not the film has a broad enough or politically important enough audience to merit the tremendous expense.

Connie Field: I do think about what films the left should be making, and political relevance is therefore my first criterion. I also ask myself, Is the subject something that will help people understand the social conditions under which they live in a way that can help them change those conditions? Also, will the subject lend itself to film so that the impact of the information can be both emotional and dramatic? I also consider how the film can be used as an organizing tool and whether there are active groups which will actually use it.

Kartemquin: We always attempt, whenever possible, to base our ideas for films in the use the films will have. What is it for? How will they use it? Beginning with these questions can do a lot to answer broader political questions, such as, "What kinds of films should the left be making today?"—not to mention eliminating exercises in self-indulgence. But certainly, if politics are in command, the use of a film will control most of your basic decisions, no matter how many surprises the subject might have in store for you along the way.

In *Trick Bag*, an interview film about the changing attitudes toward racism among white working-class youths in Chicago neighborhoods, we worked directly with a community organization, Rising Up Angry, which, in effect, gave us the idea for the film, gave us assurance of its use, and also provided a lot of the people we interviewed. This was close to being a "sponsored" political film, except for the fact that no money changed hands between us and the community group.

In contrast, two films about younger city kids, *Now We Live on Clifton* and *Winnie Wright, Age 11*, were at first just ideas we had that grew out of our dissatisfaction with existing images of kids that age on film. When grant money came along, we got more disciplined and went back to the problems of "audience" and how we could present positive but provocative images of working-class city kids, their neighborhoods, their everyday lives—and make films that would be used in the public schools. When the films were finished, we were so involved in those questions that we took the films to dozens of schools, ourselves, to test the results.

Sometimes the outcome of a project is impossible to foresee. *Taylor Chain* started out to be a film that would teach workers how to bargain for health and safety language in their contracts, but it ended up telling a story about the dynamics of democracy in a union local during a strike. As the situation in which we were filming changed, so did our ideas of what it was most important and useful to make the movie about.

The Chicago Maternity Center Story was supposed to be a short descriptive film about the struggle to save a model institution. It ended as an hour-long film which provides an analysis of the politics of health care in America, and at the same time documents a year-long struggle to save the center. Through all the changes in these latter two projects, we continued to be guided by the use the two films would have. We saw how the story at Taylor Chain would be important to unions and labor educators, and how the expanded Maternity Center material would cut across many layers of economics and history for a number of audiences.

Do you see your role as calling attention to a problem or issue, or as suggesting solutions and/or plans of action?

Pacific Street Films: Our films can be seen in two ways—they call attention to a problem, as in *Frame-Up!*, and they also suggest a solution or plan of action, as in *The Grand Jury: An Institution Under Fire*, where we had a number of different people at the end provide the alternatives to the current grand jury system.

Josh Hanig: In *Canary* we clearly are trying to show and warn against a widespread problem. We are also trying to dissect the reasons for the problem, and therefore are attempting to point toward broad-reaching solutions. On that film, several union officials said they couldn't use our film much because it didn't show workers how to file a health-and-safety grievance or to file a complaint with OSHA. So it doesn't try to solve problems in a nuts-and-bolts way, as many sponsored or educational films do.

Why do you make documentaries instead of fiction films?

Pacific Street Films: We make documentaries primarily because our background has been in that genre, and we consider ourselves political filmmakers. Documentaries currently provide the only real framework to make a political statement.

Dave Davis: Because, personally, I have always been more interested in looking at real people as they are affected by the social or political process than in constructing a fiction treatment of the same. Also, the process of making documentaries is to me much more satisfying—less cumbersome, there's more control, more direct contact with people and issues and institutions, less film technology, and less expense. The frustrations are that documentaries have a much smaller audience and are taken less seriously in most cases.

Connie Field: *Rosie* was made as a documentary because the story could not have been told as a fiction film. One of the main concepts was myth versus reality. The film is as much a statement about the effect of media propaganda on our lives as it is a history of women workers. Therefore, the documentary form, which allows for the juxtaposition of real experiences as told by the women themselves with the actual newsreels of the day, creates a stronger impact.

Emile de Antonio: Because I choose to. The documentary is not a step to fiction film but a step to freedom. Commercial fiction film is only real estate. When real *auteurs*, the Harvard Business School graduates, produce films, their concern is neither art nor ideas, but money. Maximize rents for a space called a seat. In documentaries, I confront our history on my own terms. Brecht said that only boots can be made to measure. He was right.

11

Staying Alive

Alan Rosenthal

Documentaries don't just appear out of the blue. They are a media product and often take years to produce, and even then only come to birth because of the dreams, energy, sweat, doggedness and perseverance of the filmmaker. I think this is too often forgotten by critics and academics.

Documentary filmmakers are madmen. They work against the odds and more often than not have little to show financially for all their efforts at the end of the day.

Though this book is mainly about the documentary theory, genres, approaches and practices I thought it would be amiss if we didn't pay attention for a few pages to how documentaries actually get off the ground and get funded.

To do this I've used a short extract from my book Writing, Directing and Producing Documentary Films and Videos. *The chapter it comes from is called 'Staying Alive' and besides discussing funding addresses the filmmaker's task of keeping his or her head above the water in an increasingly competitive world.*

It's no use being the world's greatest filmmaker if you can't get your film funded. In an expensive medium you have to be a business person as well as an artist. You have to find a sponsor or you're dead. By sponsor, I mean anyone with money who will support your film. This can be a university department, a television station, an industrial corporation, a government agency, a church, a film distributor, or even friends.

You can interest people by telling them your idea, sending letters, proposals, and so on, but one thing is vital: showing them your previous work. Sponsors want to see your track record. They want to assess what you promise in the future by seeing what you have done in the past. This means you must have some work to show them, which is very hard if you are a student. Film diplomas are fine if you want to teach; otherwise, the more films you can finish or participate in while you are at university, the better your chances of landing a sponsor.

As a filmmaker you have various possibilities for jobs. The television station and the industrial corporation with its own film unit offer the safest bet. They need films, they have the money to make them, and they can sometimes offer a degree of permanence in the notoriously unstable film world. In reality, though, most of us end up as independent filmmakers. How do we raise the money for our films that will change the world?

Abe Osheroff got his $50,000 for *Dreams and Nightmares* through the backing of enthusiastic political supporters. Emile de Antonio picked up the $100,000 for *Point of Order* while having a drink with a wealthy liberal friend. *Antonia*, by Jill Codmilow and Judy Collins, was backed by the latter's concert earnings.

The Television Market

One way into filmmaking is to submit your idea to television. Knowing where to turn and to whom to submit your proposal then becomes crucial. In the United States this entry route is not an easy path, but it can be done, particularly in public television. Occasionally PBS decides to sponsor a documentary series with a marvellous-sounding name like *Great Americans* or *The Living World* or *The Spirit of the Future*. This means three thousand people apply for grants to make ten films. The odds aren't great, but occasionally a newcomer slips in. Proposals can also be made to independent PBS stations. In theory, each station has a planning department that evaluates proposals. They are supposed to see whether the proposal fits the station, whether it is unusual or innovative, and whether funds can be raised on the proposal. But little of this touches reality, and I know of hardly anyone who has made a film this way. And there is a further catch. Even if the station accepts your proposal all this may mean is that they will screen the film after *you* have raised all the money. And if they do raise the money they will often put in for 21 percent of the budget as overheads.

The greatest problem for independent filmmakers in the USA till recently was that the main TV market was dominated by the commercial networks. Using various arcane arguments the networks, on the whole, refused to show any documentaries except those made by themselves. That left PBS as the only available national showcase. Cable has now drastically altered the situation. Since the mid-eighties, new cable stations such as the Discovery Channel, Arts and Entertainment (A&E), Turner Broadcasting (TBS), Bravo, and Home Box Office (HBO) have started offering new possibilities both as documentary sponsors and as outlets for finished films.

In Europe things are also improving. First, the European networks, particularly in Germany, are more open to accepting outside suggestions for productions and coproductions. Second, the English broadcast system is opening up to greater participation from independent filmmakers. Channel 4 has, of course, been available to the independent since its inception and has either totally or partially funded a great number of documentaries.

Finding a Home

For TV you can, of course, merely write to the station and propose your idea or try to sell them your film. It is much better, however, to pinpoint a specific programme or a specific department that will really be receptive to the project you are involved in. At PBS, for example, four long-running programmes come immediately to mind, which are open to independent filmmakers' work but managed through individual stations.

For starters there is *Nova*, a science series, usually done on film, that places great emphasis on look and stunning visuals. On average the shows are budgeted between $400,000 and $600,000 and can vary from an investigation of in-vitro fertilisation to an update on the Dead Sea Scrolls. However to get a sense of the competition one needs to realise that *Nova* only produces twenty shows out of at least 600 submissions each year.

Nova comes out of WGBH, Boston, which is also the originating station for *Frontline* and *The American Experience*. The address of the station is 125 Western Avenue, Boston, MA, 02134. The main subjects for *Frontline* are politics and world events. This means that one week you may be looking at the Middle East, and the next week you may he watching a documentary on Clarence Thomas and Anita Hill. The third series, *The American Experience*, deals with US history, from the American Revolution to the fairly recent past. While the series provided a home for Ric Burns's study of the Donner party, it also found space for Michael Orlov's controversial look at American reaction to the Holocaust. The fourth series, *Point of View*, is a showcase for highly opinionated documentaries such as Ellen Bruno's *Satya* or Marlon Riggs's *Tongues Untied*. It's worth noting that PBS issues an Independent Producer's Kit that can be obtained by writing to the PBS Development Office, 609 Fifth Avenue, New York, N.Y., 10017.

HBO also claims to have an open submissions policy but in practice few make it through the front door. Of the 3000 or so pitches and entries per year HBO only accepts twelve *America Under Cover* ideas and two or three miscellaneous projects. *Cinéma vérité* is especially favoured, and pitches should be limited to three to five pages.

While A&E offers some interesting openings and continues to blossom with *Biography*, *American Justice*, *America's Castles*, and *Mysteries of the Bible*, the real phenomenon of the last two decades has been the expansion of the Discovery network. Under its banner it now includes Discovery, the Learning Channel, Animal Planet, and the Travel Channel. There is also a Discovery Kids, Discovery Wings, and Discovery People. The range of the network, which goes in for series as well as individual films, is clearly very broad and makes one feel sometimes that no subject is sacred. For example, while glancing through *TV Guide* for one week I found the following Discovery presentations: *Supernature*, about the supernatural behaviour of animals and plants, *The Rise and Fall of the Mafia*, *The Secret World of Toys*, *The Secret World of Speed Demons*, and *Robots Rising*.

The Discovery Channel is very specific about the information it requires from you when making a submission. First, before doing anything, you must sign a release letter for the network, absolving it from any future claim that it stole or copied your ideas. Having signed your life away you then submit a one- or two-page treatment which, besides outlining your idea, will include:

- the film format
- the production team and the job performed by each person
- résumé with credits for each member
- demo tape
- budget summary, showing how much you expect from the network
- list of coproduction partners
- production timeline.

The necessity of pinpointing your efforts continues when you go overseas and are trying for help from the BBC. Like the US commercial networks, the BBC was closed to the outside for years. Owing to the intervention and pressure of Margaret Thatcher's government, both the BBC and the English commercial stations have now opened their doors to independents. The present rule is that the companies must take at least 25 percent of their output from external sources. Since the BBC produces more than two hundred hours of documentary features per year, there is much time to fill.

The BBC is actually divided into two main sections, BBC1 and BBC2, but both produce documentaries. BBC 3 and 4, both new digital stations, also carry documentary. Although BBC television is based at the BBC TV Centre, Wood Lane, London W12, the main headquarters for documentaries is BBC, Kensington House, Richmond Way, London W9. When in doubt you should send your proposals to the latter rather than the former address.

BBC series have varied over the years, but the main ones at the moment are:

- *Reputations*: This, as the name suggests, is the biography strand;
- *Inside Story*, *Panorama*, and *Correspondent* all deal with investigative stories and current affairs;
- *Omnibus* and *Arena* for their part deal with music and the arts;
- *Bookends*: Here the subject is literature and literary profiles, such as portraits of Robert Cheever or Elmore Leonard;

- *Everyman*: This focuses on religion and interesting personalities, but in a trendy, non-preaching style;
- *Horizon*: This, together with *Tomorrow's World*, is the British equivalent of *Nova*;
- *Timewatch* and *Ancient Voices* cover history, the one modern, the second ancient.

For its part the main strands on Channel 4 are:

- *Witness* (religion)
- *Secret History* (history)
- *To The Ends Of The Earth* (travel and adventure)
- *The Real* (biography).

In order to get your film idea considered, you should send your proposal to the executive producer of each series. Competition is stiff, but it's worth a try. If your idea passes the commissioning editor's scrutiny, it will go before a further selection committee that meets twice a year, usually April and October. If you get the green light at that stage you go into production.

Sometimes the BBC is willing to take the initiative in reaching out to independents. In its *Fine Cut* series, the BBC deliberately went out of its way to help various world documentarists realise their most current and passionate projects. The results, according to series supervisor André Singer, varied. Four dealt with the horrors of war, while two others centred on the filmmakers themselves. Altogether it was a very worthwhile experiment, ultimately responsible for Robert Gardner's *Forest of Bliss*, Les Blank's *Innocents Abroad*, John T. Davis's *Hobo*, and Peter Adair's *Absolutely Positive*, among others. In short, the BBC is well worth investigating. What makes things a trifle easier is that the BBC actually issues something called "The Foreign Producer's Guide."

This invaluable pamphlet gives you all the ins and outs of working for the BBC, and the lowdown on current series. It can be obtained by writing to the BBC's Wood Lane office. I would also advise you to look at *Video Age International* which, from time to time, publishes details of TV programming, not just in England but around the world.

Marketing Overview

It is difficult to assess trends when you are living through them, but looking back, it is clear that the nineties marked a clear revolution in the marketing of documentaries. Documentaries became *hot*. Film festivals started paying attention to them. New specialised documentary channels were created. And new terms like "factual programming" and "factual entertainment" started hitting the headlines.

In practice the market is now split into what writer Jan Rofekamp calls "the first market" and "the second market." The first market includes the principal public and private networks in each country. In the US this means PBS and all the major cable stations I mentioned earlier, plus Court TV. In the UK we are talking about the BBC, Channel 4, and Channel 5, while in Germany we are referring to ZDF, Spiegel, and ARD. For France the major players are Canal Plus, Arte, FR2, and FR3. The second market includes players like Globo Sat in Brazil, Rai-Sat and CNI in Italy, Bravo and HBO in Latin America, and Canal Plus in northern Europe.

On the surface, all this looks great. In practice competition among film-makers for cable slots has created a buyers' market. This has meant that fees in the first market have been considerably reduced. Whereas a few years ago a filmmaker could get a deal for $50,000 of financing, allowing the station four runs in five years for that amount, the current deal is more likely to be $20,000 for two runs in two years. While this means that the rights are available more quickly for the second market, the fees paid for exhibition in this market are considerably lower than in the first. A $2000 contract for unlimited runs is not likely to make you throw your hat in the air.

Markets and Festivals

One recent trend which can be helpful to you in selling your programme is the expansion of documentary markets and festivals. Markets like MIPCOM (in Cannes), NATPE, and MIP-TV have now become essential venues for sales, and the exchange of ideas regarding single films and series, financing and coproduction.

Another development has been the rise of festivals, which besides showing films also devote a considerable amount of time to seminars on idea-pitching, financing, and the establishment of coproductions. For a novice these festivals can be highly instructive and well worth the registration fee. Though these festivals are spread out over Europe and the US I would say the most useful ones are the Co-financing Forum in Amsterdam (IDFA), the bi-annual seminar/festival of the International Documentary Association (IDA) in Los Angeles, and the Toronto Documentary Forum, affectionately known as HOTDOCS. You might want to note that the AIVF (Association of Independent Video and Film-makers) puts out a very useful guide to international film and video festivals. The organisation's web address is www.aivf.org.

Documentary Magazines and the Web

The two documentary magazines most concerned with marketing are *RealScreen* (realscreen.com), which comes out of Toronto, and *International Documentary* (documentary.org), which is published in Los Angeles. Both contain the occasional interesting article but are essentially geared to selling. With *RealScreen* the emphasis is on what is happening with all the cable shows being done for Discovery and the like. *RealScreen* also publishes an International Factual Broadcast Guide which contains information on broadcasters around the world. The information is very down to earth, and tells you about factual strands, themes, and length of favoured programs. The guide also gives you station bios, the names of commissioning editors, and their contact addresses and e-mails.

Standard features of *International Documentary* include a listing of upcoming film festivals and a monthly guide to cable programming. Its most useful section, however, may be its listing of current funding opportunities telling you what's on offer, where to apply, and the deadlines for grant submissions. It's also worth noting that the magazine's publisher, The International Documentary Association (e-mail: idf@netcom.com) also puts out a useful Membership Directory and Documentary Survival Guide.

A third magazine I very much like is *DOX*, (dox.dk) published in Denmark. *DOX* has been coming out bi-monthly since 1993 and has since become essential reading for documentary filmmakers in Europe. However its European bias shouldn't put off Americans and in fact the magazine provides essential information for anyone interested in the European scene. While paying attention to distribution and production possibilities it also publishes some excellent general documentary articles, probably slightly more academic than those appearing in *RealScreen* or *International Documentary*. It also publishes a useful European Producers Guide somewhat similar to that put out by *RealScreen*.

A few web sites dealing with documentary have also put in a recent appearance, but the best of them, head and shoulders above the rest, is Docos.com, available as www.docos.com. Although it's based in England the reach is truly global. Put simply, Docos.com is the broadest provider of documentary information I have come across. Its range is truly staggering and in its free daily news bulletin it covers everything from industry directories, production companies and new books, to markets, festivals and a free showcase for new titles. It is extremely good on coproduction information and advice, and also runs a unique and remarkable "commissioning engine," which tells producers and distributors who, world wide, could be interested in producing or financing a given film. (www.commissioningengine.com). Finally, Docos publishes a fortnightly print newsletter, *DOCtv* (subscription based), which provides a very good analysis of industry trends and is very useful for fast decision making. If I've gone on at length about Docos it is because I find it less advert-cluttered than the magazines, very down to earth, and that it gives me the information I need very speedily and extremely efficiently.

Genres and Fads

What is it that makes you want to make a particular film? Are you perhaps obsessed by an idea? Do you find yourself pushed towards a certain subject?

Do you feel you have no choice? Yet many people work the other way around. They find what sells, and then make a film to fit into that category. We may smile at such an approach, at all the history-mysteries and Bible secrets series, yet realistically we have to be aware of what's going on.

As I write, *Survival* and *Big Brother* are all the rage and reality programming the magic words that bring a ray of light to a TV programmer's eye. So do you rush out to film a group of fifteen-year-old boys surviving without McDonalds or Starbucks? Or do you turn your lens perpetually on yet another group of crazies eating, sleeping, fornicating, and pontificating in sealed rooms? I doubt it. By the time this book comes out those fads will probably have bitten the dust.

But what about docusoaps? Here I am not so sure. This essentially English creation, light years away from Griersonian tradition, has become almost the mainstay of UK broadcasting. In the five years between 1999 and 2001 over sixty-five docusoaps appeared on the major British TV channels—no small achievement.

The basic ingredients for the successful docusoap, or documentary soap opera, are stunningly simple. First you take an industry, preferably a service one, or a minor business, and find a group of people who are slightly charismatic or quirky, and who enjoy being in the limelight. You then follow them for a few months with a crew straight from film school and centre in on their disputes, their love affairs, their foibles, and their pranks. With luck, and high shooting ratios, some interesting stories inevitably emerge.

Starting with driving school teachers and life at a London airport, British viewers were subsequently given the lives of marriage counsellors, trainee journalists, nurses, emergency wards, and investment brokers. A Channel 4 series called *Love in Leeds* followed single women in pursuit of the perfect man.

Not given to missing a trick, the Americans have also embraced the formula, with *American High*, which follows the lives of various kids at a high school in Los Angeles. There has also been a series following women in Las Vegas. I sense, however, the formula won't go down quite as well in the US as in Britain. It seems to me that American reality drama tends towards action and cops stories rather than daily stories of ordinary human beings. But I may be wrong.

In the end I think the TV enthusiasm for docusoaps is based on financial considerations rather than any philosophic interest in the human condition. Docusoaps offer more returns for fewer bucks. Even allowing for diverse crews and high shooting ratios, docusoaps still come out far cheaper to produce than an hour's drama or a movie of the week. And as long as the viewing figures aren't that different docusoaps will continue to get support. They are easy to make, being just an extension of observational documentary, so you might want to consider them. But don't make them with your own money because by the time you finish your series they may just be out of fashion.

Foundations and Corporations

So how do you stay alive if you don't want to do another search for sunken submarines, if you don't want to hunt for Nazi war criminals, and if you don't want to do a docusoap on circus performers or ships' stewards? In other words where do you go for the money if your subject is not sensational, does not make Discovery's heart beat faster, but makes a quiet appeal to the human mind and intelligence, and assumes that most people have an IQ higher than 50? The answer for you is to beat a path to the doors of the foundations and corporations. Most independent American filmmakers I know who work seriously in documentaries raise their funds through applications to local arts councils and foundations.

These foundations have, in fact, become the chief sources of independent film financing in the last few years. Broadly speaking, these agencies are divided into federal, state, and private funding bodies. Generally, government agencies tend to fund research and preproduction, while private organisations are more inclined to give completion monies. Sometimes you will go back to the same source more than once, the first time to cover research and development, the second time for production.

The big hitters among the granting bodies are the Rockefeller, Ford, MacArthur, and Guggenheim foundations, the American Film Institute, the New York Council for the Arts, the National Endowment for the Arts, and the National Endowment for the Humanities. Funding is intensely competitive and dozens of applicants are turned down for every grant awarded. For example, Barbara Kopple was turned down again and again while trying to fund *Harlan County*, which eventually went on to win an Oscar.

You should note that most state humanities commissions work hand in hand with the National Endowment for the Humanities. Similarly, most state or city arts councils work closely with the National Endowment for the Arts. In addition to all the above you should be aware of the existence of the Independent Documentary Fund, which is run by the Corporation for Public Broadcasting (CPB).

The Funding Proposal

Foundation funding has certain inherent difficulties. Many of these relate to the writing of the proposal, a document that can sometimes reach the length of *War and Peace*. Most foundations require a proposal that clearly states the nature of the film, its objectives and limits, and a well-defined distribution and use programme relating to the film itself. Foundations also like to play it safe by requiring the participation of "experts" to provide academic respectability to a project. Such requirements make sense sometimes, but they are obstructions to the filmmaker operating in a field that the scholarly mind has not yet penetrated. What you have to do is acknowledge the basically conservative nature of foundation activities. The art film, the science film, and the educational history film pose few challenges to them. By contrast, the political, investigative, or critical film rarely finds a place in foundation funding without a great deal of trouble.

The peculiar thing is that this setup may favour those who can write good grants over those who are poor grant-writers but better filmmakers. This has been acknowledged, so many of the major arts foundations will go out of their way to offer you assistance in writing and framing your grant. Various periodicals can also help you considerably in this grant-writing business, such as the *AFI Education Newsletter, The Independent, Foundation News*, and the journal of the Independent Documentary Association. There are also a number of good books that have come out recently that guide you through the grant-writing maze. Among the best of these are *Shaking the Money Tree* by Morrie Warshawski (Michael Wiese Books), *Money for Film and Video Artists* (American Council of the Arts), and *Get the Money and Shoot* (Documentary Research, Inc., Buffalo, N.Y.).

Most good libraries have a copy of the foundation list put out by the Council of Foundations. This gives you the names and addresses of the major foundations in the United States, together with a list of projects that they support. A few days perusing that list (it is immense) can be worth more than a few dollars in your pocket.

Although you may be familiar with writing proposals, it is worthwhile to look at the subject as it specifically relates to foundation grants. Unlike the NEA or the NEH, many small foundations will simply ask you to send them a short letter describing your project. Later, they may ask for additional details, but in many cases that short letter of about two pages *is the application*. Five things go into it. You need to tell them what you want to do, why there is a need for your project, who you are, the amount of money you are seeking, and why they should support you.

Your letter to business corporations should include:

- a list of established corporate sponsors
- the background of the requesting organisation
- a request for an appointment.

Don't be surprised if your letters to small corporations fail to elicit a reply. That's because you and your project simply don't interest the would-be sponsor, so why should he waste time and money in replying. However, even if you get the slightest nibble, it should be pursued.

It is imperative that your proposal be well organised. If the funding agency has no specific format, then try including these sections in this/order:

- abstract and/or summary
- rationale for making the film
- description of the film
- personnel and grant-overseeing agencies
- distribution ideas
- budget
- appendices with letter of support, etc.

A.R.: I then went on to give some examples of how the proposal worked in practice but due to pressures of space it was decided not to include that here.

Part III

Issues of Ethics and Aesthetics

12

Ethics

Brian Winston

Documentary is not fiction, but neither is journalism exactly, for all that it was widely perceived as being so at the end of the millennium. Although its claim on 'actuality' requires that it behave ethically, its unjournalistic parallel desire to be allowed to be 'creative' permits a measure of artistic 'amorality'. In short, the application of even journalistic ethics (themselves complex) to documentary is not straightforward.

The ethical sensitivities of the documentarist have been much eroded because of this constant implicit claim on artistic licence. However, this does not sanction the passing-off of material as, in some way, a privileged image of reality when it is knowingly a fiction. The issue of such 'actual' or 'pure' (as it were) fakery is morally uninteresting. It cannot be made interesting by erecting a need for truth-telling, strictly construing what that is and protecting the audience when lying has no consequences. It is an open and shut case and it is also, even today, quite rare. What are common and increasingly vexed are the everyday subterfuges inevitably used because in the very nature of the case the camera cannot simply deliver an unmediated reproduction of the truth. Production means mediation.

The central question for documentary ethics is how much mediation is ethical? Our ability to answer this question is currently much hampered. First, in effect losing a distinct idea of how documentary differs from other factual programming in general and news in particular destroys the basis upon which a distinct documentary ethic can be made to rest. Second, we have a heightened sense of audience protection—the very fact of content regulation assumes *caveat emptor* is not enough. At the same time we have confused media responsibilities to the audience with the ethical duties owed participants as if the outcomes of taking part were the same as spectating. Finally, the concept of 'fakery' has been so broadly construed that, in its naïveté, it echoes the old error—'the camera cannot lie'.

Sincere and Justified Reconstruction

Not only the law but also photographers themselves had to 'come to grips with' the ethics of the new technology in the nineteenth century. Little was said at the outset about the dangers of manipulating the camera to distort reality and nothing much about the morality of so doing. The expectation was not only that the camera would not lie but that it *could not*, so the silence was understandable. Scientific enthusiasm fed what was to become a common misconception, one that was endlessly exploited by photographers.

One hundred and fifty-five years after Francis Arago in the Chamber of Deputies and Joseph Louis Gay-Lussac in the French House of Peers successfully argued that the French nation should acquire the Daguerre patents for the world, Labour member Andrew Bennett rose in the House of Commons to request 'that leave be given to bring in a bill to require news media to prepare a code of practice to cover the principles by which pictures may be edited, altered and changed using computer techniques' (Hansard, 1994: 951). Bennett's proposal signals how little more sophisticated we are today than we were at the time of photography's birth: 'Most people are aware of the old adage "the camera never lies". It seems to me that many people still believe it. . . . Most people believe pictures, particularly those accompanied by a well-respected voice on the television.' Bennett, in effect, claimed that we had not made much progress since Arthur Conan Doyle insisted on the veracity of the Cottingley photos of fairies.

The scientific heritage, now bolstered by new levels of technology, continues to swamp any awareness of the potential for manipulation. Anyway, why would we have moved on? For most people, the actual experience of snapshots, home movies and camcorders is that images do indeed accurately reflect the world. The everyday camera does not lie and this is the course of the expectation that the documentary will not lie either. But the truth of the amateur camera depends on the knowledge of how accurately the image reflects a remembered reality or can be so thoroughly contextualised by the viewer that all partialities and distortions are corrected for. Public images can seldom hope to match this but the experience of amateur images masks this difference. The limitations of the relationship that any photographic image has to the reality it reflects are beyond everyday experience. The possibility that that relationship, its faults already disguised, can be further distorted is understood only on an abstract level. Manipulation, distortion and fakery have thus far required professionals (although the home computer is well on its way to changing that).

The professionals have always been at hand. For example, within forty-eight hours of the end of the Battle of Gettysburg, Timothy O'Sullivan and Andrew Gardner were on the field making images of the aftermath for their *Photo-*

graphic Sketch of the War. Plate 41, entitled *Home of a Rebel Sharpshooter*, shows a Confederate corpse sprawled in a trench; Plate 40, again of a dead soldier, is called *A Sharpshooter's Last Sleep* (Collins, 1985: fig. 12). This body is not so obviously a member of the Confederate Army. In fact, it is quite hard to tell which side he was on but Gardner's published caption suggests he was a Union man. Both corpses are in a similar attitude lying in the lower third of the frame but the terrain is different. The 'Rebel' is in a trench while the other lies on more open ground. The 'Rebel's' rifle is propped between his legs against the rocky side of the trench whereas in the other image the rifle lies at the man's head. Experts have identified the spots as being about forty yards apart. Others have identified the corpse as being identical in both shots. The only explanation is that Gardner was lugging a body around with him, re-costuming it as he went and even, some suggest, turning the head despite rigor mortis (Fulton, 1988: 23–8).[1]

In a very rare nineteenth-century public row, Doctor Barnardo's Homes were unsuccessfully sued by an outraged Baptist clergyman for a libel that was, in effect, a public fraud. From 1874 Barnardo used 'before' and 'after' shots of street urchins in advertisements soliciting support for his charity. He sold the images in packs of twenty for 5 shillings or single cards for 6d. The uproar occurred in 1877 when the minister discovered that the shots were taken on the same day. Although it was accepted that this was a misrepresentation, there was clearly no damage to anybody. Any hint of public fraud collapsed in the face of Barnardo's good intentions (Collins, 1985: 24–5). By the time Barnardo died in 1905, the orphanages had made over 55,000 images.

The perfect composition of the image of four marines raising the Stars and Stripes on Mt Suribachi, Iwo Jima, in 1945 caused the editors of *Life* to pause. The photographer, Joe Rosenthal, always claimed that it was an authentic picture of an unmediated event, but it is generally agreed that the flag in the shot was a replacement for the one initially raised. The issue is: Who arranged for the replacement? The suggestion is that the larger flag was prepared for hoisting at Rosenthal's instigation and the implication is that this vitiates the authenticity of the image—despite the fact that the photograph, without question, shows four 'real' marines (three of whom were to die in the battle then raging) with a 'real' flag on the actual island of Iwo Jima. These doubts did not prevent the photographer winning a Pulitzer Prize in 1945 or the photograph from being used for a war bond poster, appearing on a 3c stamp and becoming the basis of a statue placed outside the Arlington National Cemetery in Washington. Manipulated or not, the image has been described as a record of 'the soul of a nation' (Fulton, 1988: 160–1).

In 1950, *Life* published a rather different 'soul of a nation' image. The magazine commissioned Robert Doisneau to photograph the romantic French specifically engaging in such activities as kissing in the street. *The Kiss* is the perfect image of young Parisians in love. A debonair man, tieless, tousled hair, scarf casually tucked into his jacket, has his arm round a lithe young woman. She leans back into the embrace as he kisses her oblivious of the people around. One of these, a gaunt-faced 'Frenchman' with beret, coat, tie and pullover, appears to be staring past the couple in studied disapproval. In fact, Doisneau treated the assignment as a photo/love story shot and cast an actor, Jacques Carteaud, and his girlfriend, Françoise Bournet, as the couple. The stereotypical Frenchman in the beret behind them has been identified as the late Jack Costello, a Dublin auctioneer, on a motorbike pilgrimage to Rome, a bit lost in Paris and looking for his travelling companion (Lennon, 1993).

There has never been a public scandal about the lead photograph of a famous W. Eugene Smith *Life* photo-essay on Albert Schweitzer but, again, it can be questioned. Smith had complained about the quality of the photo labs' prints that *Life* photographers usually put up with. He had demonstrated his prints were superior and the editors therefore allowed him the privilege of avoiding the labs. We can note that he routinely adjusted his images at this stage, always in line with accepted professional practice (Willumson, 1992: 248–50). Manipulations included correcting underexposure in portions of the negative and bleaching to achieve high-contrast prints that would reproduce well on the press. This did not offend against *Life*'s policy at this time, the 1950s, although further manipulations other than cropping were not permitted.

'Toilers', captioned 'Schweitzer and a carpenter watch hospital building', shows the doctor, in white shirt and pith helmet, standing before an unfinished structure. Behind him, on the structure, sits an African. Both are looking out of the frame towards something that seems to be causing them concern. They both looked worried. Silhouetted against Schweitzer's shirt is the handle of a saw and a gesturing hand (Anon., 1954: 161). This is actually a composite, a real superimposition. The arm and saw-handle are from another shot. The editors of *Life*, who had forbidden such practices, never knew. The deception (if it can be so called) was discovered, over thirty years later, by Glenn Willumson going through Eugene Smith's negatives (Willumson, 1992: 211–13).

Eugene Smith was working in a tradition of extensive manipulation. For nearly half a century to 1900, newspaper and magazines had used photographs as reference material for engraving because they could not be directly reproduced. Even after half-tone and photogravure first enabled direct reproduction, the low status of photographs as accurate evidence of the news persisted. For example, in 1926, the *New York Daily Graphic* circumvented a judge's ban on courtroom photography by superimposing head shots of the jurors on a specially-taken shot of its own reporters. Circulation jumped 100,000 and the paper composited so often that 'composographers' became a term of art (Anon., 1950: 95).

Despite all this, it would be as foolish now to doubt every image in the archive as it was, previously, naïve to believe them. For instance, it has also been suggested that Robert Capa staged his *Death in Spain* (aka *Death of Loyalist Soldier*), the famous photograph of a Spanish loyalist militiaman at the moment of death as he runs down a slope, his rifle hung wide in his right hand. The lack of uniform and the curiously ornate leather cartridge belt have been questioned. And how come, if this is the moment of death, the rifle is still being gripped? It was finally established in 1996, however, that this is indeed the last moment of loyalist militiaman and member of the anarchist trade union's youth movement, Frederico Borell Garcia from Alcoy at the Battle of Cerro Muriano in defence of Cordoba seven weeks into the war, on 5 September 1936 (*Observer*, 1 September 1996).

There was a significant difference between the popular view of photography ('the camera cannot lie') and professional journalistic use of photographs as, initially, merely a guide for engravers and subsequently a basis for darkroom manipulations of all kinds. It is not surprising that this willingness of the professional to intervene in the reality before the lens was transferred from photography to cinematography wholesale. In the first years of the cinema, 'reconstructions' of major events from battles in the Spanish American War and the Boxer Rebellion to whole prize fights were commonplace. They were almost completely without the legitimacy of prior witness. That is to say, they were not reconstructions of what the film-maker had witnessed during the research phase. Instead the attempt to secure their authenticity was grounded only in the journalistic accounts used as the basis for their scenarios. The earliest film-makers were also not above simply relabelling films. The same single-shot film, *The Sea at Brighton*, in a British film catalogue of the day, becomes *The Sea at Zeebrugge* in a Belgian one.

Two decades later, Allakariallak ('Nanook') was building Flaherty an open-sided, enlarged half-igloo to facilitate filming the pioneering documentary *Nanook* and Grierson had a trawler cabin constructed on the dock-side to obtain interior shots for *Drifters*. Dogfish filmed at a biological station stood in for the unfilmable shoals of herring. The subterfuge of the dogfish, like the naked fictions of many early newsfilms, was deemed not to be acceptable in the long run; but reconstructions of prior witnessed events were. The use of the shot/counter-shot and continuity norms of the Hollywood fiction films had always been a mark of documentary's 'creative treatment of actuality'. These and the limitations of film sensitivity, lighting instruments and, especially synch equipment, all designed for studio use, made reconstruction so inevitably a part of documentary that it had to be built into any new working definition. By 1948 we have seen, this meant 'sincere and justified reconstruction' was as good as 'factual shooting'.

The interior Royal Mail sorting carriage built on the sound stage at

Beaconsfield Studios for *Night Mail* (1936) is a typical example of 'sincere and justifiable reconstruction' in the documentary as is Joris Iven's use of two miners in *Misère au Borinage* (1934) dressed in hired police costumes acting out an incident that had occurred during the strike (Winston, 1999b: 160–2). According to Albert Speer, Riefenstahl necessarily and sincerely got Rudolph Hess in close-up to repeat without an audience his emotional Nuremberg oration in Berlin for *Triumph des Willens* (1934) when the original footage turned out to be unusable (Winston, 1995: 120–1). British film director Humphrey Jennings, not the Luftwaffe, burned St Katherine's Dock in 1942 for *Fires Were Started* providing the archive with some of its best 'actual' images of the London Blitz (Winston, 1999a: 32). As Allakariallak told Flaherty: 'The *aggie* [film] will come first' (Ruby, 1980: 66). It always did—and does.

The Consent Defence

It is in this soil that the documentary tradition grew. Ethics were never a fertiliser:

> Being film people we'd take advantage. We used to go round to sweet vicars living in a twenty-room house and with a congregation of ten, mostly old women. And I'd say, 'What a beautiful house and beautiful church. May I photograph?' Of course I was showing that he was living in this enormous house and having ten parishioners. (Sussex, 1975: 89)

Harry Watt's techniques in the 1930s are by no means unknown today; and only the foolhardy would claim vicars, and everybody else, are now so media-savvy as to no longer fall for such casual subterfuge. If nothing else, much of the 'fakery' scandal suggests—screams—an overall undiminished public ignorance of documentary film's everyday processes. There is still abundant opportunity for unethical behaviour.

This is not to deny that there is also, without question, rising media aware-ness in our societies but, rather, to suggest that it has obvious common-sense limitations. People do not necessarily know how to behave in unfamiliar situa-tions and making documentaries remains outside common experience. As the Broadcasting Standards Commission (BSC) code, somewhat less clichéd then usual and surely this time right, puts it: 'Many potential contributors will be unfamiliar with broadcasting and therefore may not share assumptions about programme making which broadcasters regard as obvious' (BSC (Fairness and Privacy), June 1998: 3). After all, dealing with the media can vex even the most sophisticated; which is why there is a proliferation of busi-ness executive media-savvy courses whose existence speaks to a problem of understanding and presupposes a need for special skills not widely available elsewhere.

There is no question that the *aggie* too often comes first with little reckoning of ethical costs. Fast-talking one's way to winning co-operation or permission from participants is still a factor in professional competence and success. The facility to do this is now exacerbated by the need for programme-makers to deliver what they promised to increasingly sensationalised services, with ever more limited resources. Today's Harry Watt has to con the vicar successfully or see his future film-making prospects threatened—and he has to do it quickly before his meagre budget runs out. Any measure of dubious or even unethical behaviour is justified after the event by the existence of the contract signed by the participant, the release form. These agreements create, in defiance of those who take the BSC Code's view, what might be called a professional 'consent defence'—that people (except minors or the mentally incapacitated) do know what they are doing. In the 1970s, Direct Cinema editor Ellen Hovde was already claiming: 'I don't think people are aware in our society of what a camera is and very aware of what they ought to be doing in front of it' (Rosenthal, 1980: 352). Joanna Biley, director of *Swingers, Faithful to You in My Fashion*, surely better represented the situation (even in America) when she mused in 1999: 'It's odd how many people don't appreciate that being in a documentary does actually involve the possibility that Auntie Maud might see it' (Bailey, 1999: 4).

Either way, this 'consent defence' retrospectively justifies the everyday little white lies and omissions that often characterise the 'bargaining' between film-maker and participant—downplaying the levels of disruption involved in having a film-crew about, being wonderfully optimistic about how long the filming will take, not being fully forthcoming about who else is involved, forgetting to mention possible fall-out when the documentary is transmitted or released and so on.

The consent defence applies whether or not the participants benefit and never have second thoughts on their role; whether or not they benefit a little but also suffer so that they come to regret co-operation; or whether or not they just suffer and rue the day their involvement started them on a disastrous path.

Some of those 'discovered' by documentarists do well out of the experience. In recent years Russian-speaking Jeremy, the 'star' of *Airport*, turned up fronting a live transmission from Moscow on Millennium Eve. Jane McDonald was filmed working as an on-board singer in *The Cruise* (Chris Terrill, 1998) and released her first album as a result. Wannabe singer Emily Boundy was seen working in a shopping mall while taking singing lessons and looking for a show-biz career. Before the series *Lakesiders* (David Hart, 1998) had concluded she had signed with EMI.

Positive experiences have always been possible. We would have to put Maggie Dirran, who played the young 'mother' in *Man of Aran*, on the plus side of the ledger. Forty and more years after Flaherty's film crew quit the island, when she was filmed again by George Stoney in 1978, she could vividly recall with obvious pleasure every last move Flaherty had asked her to make. She was not alone in finding *Man of Aran* had a beneficial effect on her life. Barbara, the daughter of Pat Mullen, Flaherty's local 'fixer' and interpreter, married John Taylor, Grierson's brother-in-law and crew member, and became a famous character actress in Britain. Two other islanders worked in the Irish theatre. The money some earned from the film company was the deposit for a house or the stake for a business. The original *Man of Aran* is the 'historic benchmark by which most older islanders measure their existence' (Stoney, 1978: 2).

Other participants, even some who featured in less than flattering domestic observational films, have also unambiguously benefited by public exposure. Pat Loud, the mother in the pioneering Direct Cinema TV series on family life, *An American Family* (Craig Gilbert, 1973), wrote a book about her experience as a television 'star' and started a New York literary agency on the back of her notoriety.

Oumarou Ganda, one of the main participants in Jean Rouch's ethnographic feature *Moi, un noir* (1957), was a casual labourer in Abidjan, Côte D'Ivoire. After his participation in the film, he became an important West African film director. Market researcher Marceline Loridan became a sound recordist after *Chronique d'un été*, in which she was a central figure, and eventually married the great documentarist Joris Ivens.

Often the 'consent defence' would be notionally strengthened because the participants were uncomplaining or even enthusiastic collaborators. On *Nanook*, for example, Allakariallak had supported Flaherty and made many suggestions about the *aggie*; but such agreement between participant and film-maker (as was the case with this first documentary of all) can be nothing but a conspiracy to misrepresent. The ethical shortfall of so doing must then belong more to the film-maker than to the participant, however much they help. Allakariallak connived at his own representation as a technical naïf (which he wasn't), living in an igloo (which he didn't) and re-enacting his father's generation's experience (when he had a contemporary Inuit lifestyle)—but his agreement to all,this allowed Flaherty to take advantage of him.

Contemporary sensitivities about reconstruction and misrepresentation are seemingly blind to a form of documentary where no pretence is made that the situation being documented existed separately from the filming. Ricky Leacock used to insist that, for the Direct Cinema documentary, the event always had to be more important than the filming. Rouch, for *cinéma vérité*, made filming the event central and put himself on the screen to reveal that he was doing this. The current gambit for setting up situations involves, for example, getting right-winger and hippie, or homophobe and gay to confront each other; or ex-partners to meet up with each other. These events are arranged and filmed by unseen film-makers, in distinction to Rouch's practice. Such films' value as reflections of the world (classically, documentaries' justification and purpose) is, at its best, extremely limited. All moral fall-out firmly falls onto the film-maker, despite the clear consent and collaboration of the participants who, after all, are engaged in situations not remotely of their making.

The strategy has also been deployed to create voyeuristic 'documentary' series where students are given accommodation in return for being filmed constantly. With the development of the Net and minicams, 'voyeur.com' (as it is might be termed) has become a new pornographic extension of this documentary technique. (We usefully learn from this advance that nubile young women living together have an unexpected propensity to play strip poker.)[2] More respectable, if only barely, was the BBC's attempt to start a community, hand picked by producer Jeremy Mills, in the year 2000 on an uninhabited Hebridean island, billed as a 'landmark observational documentary'. I am reminded of *Hook* (Steven Spielberg, 1991), a feature whose central premise was 'What would happen if Peter Pan grew up?' A US National Public Radio cinema critic at the time dismissed this as being about as interesting as asking 'What would happen if Moby Dick was a trout?' Judging by the early returns from the Isle of Taransay, transmitted in January 2000, *Castaways 2000* also promised to be as interesting as a trout-quest. (A real documentary could perhaps be devoted to the tabloid Press corps sitting on the mainland waiting for disasters.) Much was made of the involvement of various academics in setting the series up but this ploy was as convincing an earnest of seriousness as was the presence of ponderous 'experts' in German soft-porn films of the 1970s. The ethical responsibilities will come home to roost if any of the 'castaways' should be seriously damaged by their experience, however much and however obviously they consented.

Although quite rare, such transparent fundamental interventionism was not unknown in the past. *Altar of Fire*, Fritz Staal and Robert Gardner's 1975 ethnographic film of an ancient Vedic ceremony, was created with the willing co-operation of the Brahmins of Panjal, Kerala State but directly at the behest of the film-makers. The *agnicayana* fire ceremony had quite simply fallen into desuetude either in the 1950s or perhaps even in antiquity. The film gives no hint of this nor that, in effect, the Nambudiri Brahmins were working for American anthropologists who are seen on camera merely as interviewees validating the antiquity of the event (Schechner, 1981: 8).

These films all involve relationships between the film-maker and the participants that add a dimension to the normal contractual bargain. The participant does not agree to allow the film-maker to document his or her life but rather joins the film-maker to document situations of the film-maker's creation. In my view, this surely has to be more fictional than the reconstruction by film-makers of prior witnessed events created by the participants, although the former is currently accepted as 'documentary' while the latter, increasingly, is not.

The vogue for documentary autobiography further illuminated the flimsiness of the 'consent defence'. In Ira Wohl's *Best Boy*, for instance, his cousin Philly's parents consented on his behalf, so we can leave aside his own limited capacity to consent (Katz and Katz, 1988: 123–4; 129–30). Maxi Cohen's *Joe and Maxi* (1978) helped her, she claimed, to 'see' her father, Joe, but the difficulty of the 'consent defence' does not go away since Joe, for example, objected on camera to Maxi's public exercise in family therapy, not unreasonably insisting: 'I am not a document. I am a person' (Katz and Katz, 1988: 47). Even in the most benign circumstances, say in Ross McElwee's gently ironic personal account of his less than perfect relationship with the Southern women of his native region (*Sherman's March*, 1986), there is a sense that the family would just as soon the film-maker put the camera down but could not quite say so since they had a vested interest in their relative maintaining his or her curious livelihood. (Joe thought that Maxi was a film-maker instead of having a proper job like being a secretary, but at least he thought it was a job, however improper or improbable.)

Sometimes it is the participants who seek out, and even exploit, the film-maker. Andrew Bethell, whose searingly candid multi-part study of the Royal Opera House, Covent Garden (*The House*, 1996) contributed to the downfall of its management, was approached by Blackpool's PRO, a woman described by Bethell as coming 'from the "there's no such thing as bad publicity" school of PR' to make the series that became *Pleasure Beach* (1998).

There are other situations where the participant consents in dangerous circumstances while fully aware of the consequences—as when a dissident speaks out to the camera about a repressive regime in whose power the speaker will remain after the film crew departs. If the participant is fully aware of possible consequences and sees co-operation as a coherent political strategy, then the burden of the ethical dilemma has been lifted from the film-maker by the participant for his or her own ideological reasons.

As an extension of this, it is possible for a participant to be more exploitative of the film-maker than he or she is of them, and not only in political contexts. In this case the consent defence is beside the point, whatever the outcome for the participant. Apart from business and politics there can also be sex, as when a participant has an agenda that is served by sexual exhibitionism, for example. Given the current vogue for prurience, film-makers can be not only voyeurs but also aiders and abettors of all sorts of varieties of documentary 'flashing' (as it is were). The phoney as participant, where the participant's agenda is to con the broadcaster into allowing an appearance, is the most extreme example of this reversal of the normal balance of power. Even when there is no presumption of misrepresentation, repeated performances by 'members of the public' can be suspect. Research at the University of Stirling noted: 'Surprisingly, 47.5 per cent of out participant interviewees had appeared in two or more television programmes. Some of the forty participants had appeared in as many as seven or eight programmes'—or so they claimed (Stirling Media Research Institute, 2000: 23).[3]

Of all these participatory modes, only in those where the film-maker genuinely seeks to redefine the relationship is the ethical imbalance corrected, potentially at least, whatever the outcome for the participants. The National Film Board of Canada pioneered the exploration of this with, first, variants in the production of a number of fairly conventional observational films. One, *The Things I Cannot Change* (Tanya Ballantyne Tree, 1966), rang warning bells at the Board since the family concerned was unexpectedly ostracised by the community after the film was screened for revealing the poverty of its circumstances. Many at the Board felt that a better way had to be found for giving the disadvantaged a voice.

With this problem in mind, Colin Low attempted to redefine the documentarist's role in a series of films about the island of Fogo, off Newfoundland. The community was being threatened with the loss of its fisheries, its one industry, and enforced depopulation by the provincial government in St John's. The films were exceptional in that they were designed as a means of communication for the islanders specifically to reach their government, which was otherwise deaf to their arguments, rather than as documentaries for a general audience.

The National Film Board then lent its resources to train Native American film-makers, producing, for instance, *You Are on Indian Land* (1969), in its day a rare documentation of the tribal viewpoint. This found ready emulators among those ethnographic film-makers around the world who were increasingly sensitive to the charge that their discipline is, in Rouch's phrase, 'the eldest daughter of colonialism' (Eaton, 1979: 33). The movement among Aboriginal Australians, for example, to use the media to underwrite their land claims, has produced films where the ethnographer has acted as enabler rather than artist—combining Low's approach on Fogo with the logic of the Mohawk/Iroquois unit. Caroline Strachan and Alessandro Cavadini worked for and with the Borroloola people to make *Two Laws* (1981) in which the community not only documented their history, but were filmed discussing how best to do it.

The next stage in Canada began when the Film Board decided to give the community the then new portapak reel-to-reel video tape-recorders and let them get on with it themselves. George Stoney, then at the Board, created a structured programme of work to explore this issue right across Canada, *Chal-*

lenge for Change/Pour un société nouvelle. VTR St.-Jacques (1969), a conventional 16 mm film by Dorothy Todd Henaut and Bonnie Klein, documents a pioneering example of community access video. Although the film-makers were responsible for training the videographers/editors, they otherwise wrote themselves out of the video work as professional documentarists—just as Strachan and Cavadini were to do as professional ethnographers. With the coming of the camcorder, the model of *VTR St.-Jacques* has been followed most assiduously at the BBC's Community Programmes Unit, initially under the leadership of Michael Fentiman, producing the *Video Nation* output. The BBC lent camcorders and trained participants who were then free to offer insights into the minutiae of their lives, normally by a piece to camera.

Notes

The original text from which this is an extract moves on to consider further issues and examples.

1   The Weaver Brothers were also at work on the Gettysburg battlefield moving corpses around a boulder for two views called 'Dead soldiers in Devil's Den' (Collins, 1985: fig. 13).

2   Although those appearing on the minicams must be classed as actors, Bill Nichols has drawn attention to the documentary element generally to be found in the porn film (Nichols, 1994: 74–5). Ejaculation becomes an earnest of documentary veracity. European broadcasters have been ploughing the same furrow of arranged encounters. The most elaborate has been an RTL German language series, *Big Brother*, shot in a specially built house. The output is permanently on the Net but footage is also shown on prime-time television. Every two weeks, the audience can vote to drop one of the ten denizens until only one survives to 'win'. The Federal Interior Minister Otto Schilly has been quoted as saying, 'Those who still cherish feeling for human dignity should boycott the show' (Anon., 2000). *Big Brother* is based on a Dutch original and now has copies in the pipeline in Scandinavia, Portugal and the US. In Britain, 45,000 people applied to be in the show, which became a summer ratings sensation in 2000. In Spain, the participants made a pact not to vote each other out of the house and to donate the prize money to help the handicapped daughter of one of their number (Karacs, Nash and Jury, 2000: 25).

3   This repetitiveness is perhaps less surprising when the realities of the production process are considered. No production office is without some record of the contacts it has made and the participants it has used over time. This database constitutes the first port of call for programme researchers and if, as is too often the case, there is little or no time for further research, the established names become the next invitees. This is probably truer of continuous series such as talk shows than of one-off documentaries but, although the Stirling research divided the forty participants interviewed by age, sex, class and region, it failed, not insignificantly, to acknowledge any difference in the programming types involved. The finding was not analysed along these lines.

References

Anon., 'A man of mercy', *Life*, 5 November 1954.

Anon., 'Composographs', *Life*, 2 January 1950.

Anon., *Medianews*, European Media Centre, 2 March 2000.

Bailey, Joanna, 'Faking it for the cameras', *Guardian*, Media section, 1 February 1999.

BSC, *Codes of Guidance* (June 1998).

Collins, Kathleen, *The Camera as an Instrument of Persuasion: Studies of Nineteenth-Century Propaganda Photography* (Pennsylvania State University PhD, Ann Arbor: University Microfilms International, 1985).

Eaton, Mike (ed.), *Anthropology-Reality-Cinema: The Films of Jean Rouch* (London: BFI, 1979).

Fulton, Marianne, *Eyes of Time: Photojournalism in America* (New York: New York Graphical Society, 1988).

Hansard , 30 March 1994.

Karacs, Imre, Elizabeth Nash and Louise Jury, 'Broadcaster's sensation is captivating audiences across Europe', *Independent on Sunday*, 7 May 2000.

Katz, John (ed.), *Autobiography: Film/Video/Photography* (Toronto: Art Gallery of Ontario, 1978).

Katz, John and Judith Milstein Katz, 'Ethics in the autobiographical documentary', in Gross, Larry, John Katz and Jay Ruby (eds), *Image Ethics: The Moral Rights of Subjects in Photographs, Films, and Television* (Oxford: Oxford University Press, 1988).

Lennon, Peter, 'It started with a kiss', *Guardian*, 26 January 1993.

Nichols, John, *Blurred Boundaries: Questions of Meaning in Contemporary Culture* (Bloomington: Indiana University Press, 1994).

Rosenthal, Alan, *The Documentary Conscience*, (Berkeley: University of California Press, 1980).

Ruby, Jay, 'The aggie will come first', *Studies in Visual Communication* 6, no. 2, Summer 1980.

Schechner, Richard, 'Restoration of behaviour', *Studies in Visual Communication* 7, no. 3, Summer 1981.

Stirling Media Research Institute, *Consenting Adults* (London: Broadcasting Standards Commission, 2000).

Stoney, George, 'Must the film-maker leave his mark?' (unpublished paper, 1978).

Sussex, Elizabeth, *The Rise and Fall of British Documentary* (Berkeley: University of California Press, 1975).

Willumson, Glenn, *W. Eugene Smith and the Photographic Essay* (Cambridge, Mass.: Cambridge University Press, 1992).

Winston, Brian, *Claiming the Real* (London: BFI, 1995).

Winston, Brain, *Fires Were Started* (London: BFI, 1999a).

Winston, Brian, ' "Honest, straightforward re-enactment": the staging of reality', in Kees Bakker (ed.), *Joris Ivens and the Documentary Context* (Amsterdam: University of Amsterdam Press, 1999b).

13

Ultimately We Are All Outsiders: The Ethics of Documentary Filming

Calvin Pryluck

In one of the Ten Commandments, God enjoins us against making graven images. Some contemporary sects, like the Amish, take this injunction literally and consider it sinful to be photographed. There are primitive peoples who have never heard of our God and who feel the same way: the taking of a picture is the taking of a soul. On the other hand, it is less than a hundred years since George Eastman told us: "You push the button, we do the rest." A photograph—perhaps the ultimate graven image—is imbued with a kind of magic that leads children in the street to accost anyone with a camera and raucously cry: "Take my picture!" Perhaps more revealing is the latter-day greeting: "Smile! You're on Candid Camera."

So long as motion picture equipment remained cumbersome and created logistical problems, photographing and being photographed were calculated acts. Immortality lost and immortality gained were matters for theological and aesthetic speculation; the legal, ethical, and moral problems surrounding the two kinds of magic remained manageable. The problems remained almost containable when somebody figured out how to make money from actuality photographs of people making fools of themselves. It was easy to condemn *Candid Camera*, with its cheap comedy based on the humiliation of ordinary human beings going about their private business.

With the development of lightweight equipment and the growth of an aesthetic of direct cinema, the ethical problem of the relationship of filmmakers to the people in their films became more amorphous. It is not quite so easy to condemn the work of men like Leacock, the Maysles brothers, and Wiseman. They have shown us aspects of our world that in other times would have been obscured from view; in this there is a gain. In the gain there is perhaps a loss.

Leacock summed up one goal of direct cinema: "To me, it's to find out some important aspect of our society by watching our society, by watching how things really happen as opposed to the social image that people hold about the way things are supposed to happen." While one can argue about whether we can ever know what *really* happens, inevitably in filming actuality, moments are recorded that the people being photographed might not wish to make widely public: adult citizens riding in a public bus are provoked into making hostile responses to high school students; a long unemployed worker gets rowdy drunk and has an altercation with the local police; a teacher who happens to wear thick corrective lenses is shown in an extreme close-up that emphasizes her heavy eyeglasses.

Many of the best-known people dealing with contemporary documentary film recognize the ethical problem as a perplexing one. These expressions of concern appear occasionally in film reviews and published interviews; rarely are remarks extended beyond the topic immediately at hand—a particular film or a particular filmmaker. Only occasionally is it pointed out that the apparent ethical lapses are recurrent, not isolated. More than morality is involved; ethical assumptions have aesthetic consequences, and aesthetic assumptions have ethical consequences.

These appear to be simple matters. So simple that to Mamber, in *Cinéma Vérité in America*, the whole issue of privacy in *cinéma vérité* "seems like a manufactured problem"; the solution is easy: "Provided that those being filmed give their consent, where is the immorality?" It may be that there is none. But it cannot be settled by fiat. Or by possibly inappropriate assumptions. Consent and privacy are too complex to be dismissed in a dozen words.

Consider the following: You are an old man, a clinic patient in a municipal hospital, terrifed that you may have cancer. While you are being examined there are strangers in the room with strange-looking equipment. Another stranger—a woman, a physician—is questioning you about the sores on your genitals and the condition of your urine. How valid would your consent be, even if one of the strangers tells you, as Wiseman does, "We just took your picture and it's going to be for a movie, it's going to be shown on television and maybe in theaters. . . . Do you have any objections?" Wiseman finds—as did Allen Funt of *Candid Camera*—that few people do object.

This is not surprising. The method of obtaining consent is stacked in the filmmaker's favor. The ethical problem raised by such approaches is that they give the potential subject no real choice: the initiative and momentum of the situation favor the filmmaker. The presence of the film crew with official sanction is subtly coercive. So is the form of the question, "Do you have any objections?"

The filming and the question are like the numerous rituals that are a prelude to receiving treatment in a clinic. There is duress in placing the onus of affirmative refusal on those who do not wish to participate in an activity that has nothing to do with medical treatment. So the picture gets taken, and damn the consequences.

Coercion takes many forms. For *Salesman*, the Maysles brothers followed salesmen on their rounds. All three of the visitors—the salesman carrying his sample case, Albert Maysles with his camera gear, David Maysles with microphone and recorder—would approach a door. A brief explanation would be offered. "That took me maybe thirty seconds," Albert said. "Most people at that point would then say they understood, even though perhaps they didn't. . . . Then when the filming was over . . . they would say, 'Tell me once more what this is all about,' and then we would explain and give them a release form which they would sign." In exchange, the subject would be given a dollar, "to make it legal."

In such situations, the film gear serves to intimidate the wary. Even government officials can be intimidated by something so simple as portable video equipment. A community organizer explained why she takes video equipment into meetings with officials: "The head of the welfare office is not going to be so quick to tell ten ladies to fuck off if they have all that shiny hardware along." If a bureaucrat is reluctant to make an ill-mannered response to ladies with all that shiny hardware, how likely is it that a householder will tell Al Maysles with his gear to get lost?

In actuality filming, the emphasis is on getting a legal release consenting to filming. Even Allen Funt can boast, "We get 997 out of every thousand releases without pressure." Other filmmakers recognize an ethical problem but are candidly cynical about an adversary relationship between themselves and their subjects. Some deny that there is a problem.

Al Maysles reported a conversation where Arthur Barron said, "Jesus, don't you sometimes get awfully disturbed that you might hurt somebody when you film, and don't you sometimes question the morality of what you're doing?" Maysles's response reveals his own stance: "I almost never feel that fear myself. . . . Arthur was saying, 'Aren't you afraid that you're exploiting people when you film them?' and that has never occurred to me as something to be afraid of."[1]

Despite his private fears, Barron has been outspokenly hostile to subjects; he has referred repeatedly to several cities that he "can forget about going back to." Barron described his approach in making arrangements for the production of *Sixteen in Webster Groves:* "I must say I wasn't totally honest in persuading the school board to let me do the film. There was, as in many films, a certain amount of conning and manipulation involved."

Marcel Ophuls is aware of the ethical problem: "As a filmmaker, you're always . . . exploiting. It's part of modern life." Ophuls finds personal "problems and depressions" in the professional exploitation of people's "great urge to communicate because of loneliness, because of insecurity, because of bottled-up complexes." Nevertheless, he explained, "my biggest problem was convincing people to be interviewed. . . . If you have moderate gifts as a fast talker or diplomat, or if you appear moderately sincere, you should be able to get cooperation. . . . It's a con game to a certain extent."

The con during the shooting of *Marjoe* sounds like an excerpt from the life of Yellow Kid Weil or other confidence men. "There was no problem getting permission from the local ministers to shoot. Marjoe convinced them of the filmmakers' integrity. When questioned of their intent, the filmmakers replied that they were making a film about Marjoe and his experiences in the Pentecostal revival movement." This is the pattern of the classic con game. A confederate ingratiates himself with the mark, introduces other operators, and both use partial truths. At no time was it said that the film would show "Pentecostalist crowds who are exploited, demeaned, and manipulated." From the producer's viewpoint, "it was essential that Marjoe not blow his cover before the shooting was completed."

Regardless of whether consent is flawed on such grounds as intimidation or deceit, a fundamental ethical difficulty in direct cinema is that when we use people in a sequence we put them at risk without sufficiently informing them of potential hazards. We may not even know the hazards ourselves. Filmmakers cannot know which of their actions are apt to hurt other people; it is presumptuous of them to act as if they did.

With the best intentions in the world, filmmakers can only guess how the scenes they use will affect the lives of the people they have photographed; even a seemingly innocuous image may have meaning for the people involved that is obscure to the filmmaker.

In the sixties, the National Film Board of Canada made films that were intended as sympathetic portrayals of what it was like to be poor. *The Things I Cannot Change* and *September 5 at Saint-Henri* were both direct-cinema documentaries, and both turned out badly for the people depicted. They felt debased and humiliated; they were mocked by their neighbors; one family felt forced to remove its children from the local schools.

Cultures other than our own are not the only ones that pose problems for filmmakers and their subjects. Even renditions of cultures and life-styles we think we know something about are filled with pitfalls for the people involved.

Ultimately, we are all outsiders in the lives of others. We can take our gear and go home; they have to continue their lives where they are. The criticism—deserved or not—directed toward the Loud family following their appearance as *An American Family* is too well known to bear repeating. Earlier, CBS featured one particular family in a study of an upper-middle-class suburb of Detroit. Whatever the family's faults and virtues, they were used—exploited, if you will—for purposes not their own. As a result of their participation they became the center of a community controversy that included letters to the editor describing the family as "shallow, materialistic social climbers." I don't know how long this kind of thing continued, but can their lives be the same as before they allowed CBS to use them in a film?

These kinds of family misfortunes are notorious examples of the consequences of appearing in a documentary. The results of sequences in other documentaries are less widely publicized, yet one can speculate about them. One can wonder how the teacher in *High School* feels about herself since seeing her bottle-thick eyeglass lenses larger than life on the screen.

The climax of Leacock's film *Happy Mother's Day* is a community celebration in honor of quintuplets born in Aberdeen, South Dakota. In the film there is a scene of the mayor making a speech that one critic has described as "incredibly ludicrous" and another termed "an extraordinarily inflated speech." One can wonder how the mayor felt when he saw himself saying, "Never in the history of the United States has a city official had such a great responsibility." How did his friends and neighbors feel? We already know how some critics felt. Is the good opinion of strangers to be less valued?

The mayor's speech was a public event; in direct cinema, the private scenes are perhaps more problematic. Mamber has described as the more revealing moments in Drew Associates films those where "the subject is stripped of his defenses as a result of failing in some way." He cites as "truly a fulfilling moment" the scene in *On the Pole* when, after losing the Indianapolis 500, Eddie Sachs "shows himself being afraid to show disappointment, trying to act 'natural' but not being sure what natural means in terms of the image he wants to present of himself."

The Maysles brothers' film *Salesman* follows the experiences of Paul Brennan and three colleagues as they travel around selling Bibles. In the last scene, according to Mamber, "the presence of the camera appears to make Paul even more acutely aware of his failure, threatening to expose feelings he might prefer to keep hidden."

Mamber's judgment on these two sequences highlights a central ethical problem in direct cinema as currently practiced. In both scenes we are dealing not with the relationship of men with others, but with themselves. They may have agreed to serve as subjects for the films, but a waiver of privacy is not absolute.

The right to privacy is the right to decide how much, to whom, and when disclosures about one's self are to be made. There are some topics that one discusses with confidants; other thoughts are not disclosed to anyone; finally, there are those private things that one is unwilling to consider even in the most private moments. When we break down the defenses of a Paul Brennan or an Eddie Sachs and force them to disclose feelings they might prefer to keep hidden, we are tampering with a fundamental human right. And making the disclosures widely public only compounds the difficulty. The coerced public revelations of private moments is one of the things that make "Candid Camera" so clearly objectionable.

If this week, or next week, or the week after were all there was, the privacy problem might be balanced by the greater good done by the increase in society's understanding. But actuality footage harbors dormant potential for mischief. Pat Loud, speaking of the effect on the children, speculated: "Twenty years from now, somebody will be knocking on their door saying, 'How [sic] was it like to be a member of *An American Family?*' They may never be able to live it down, or get away from it."

A homey example that has touched just about everyone past a certain age is the pictures of naked babies on bearskin rugs that parents used to have taken. To others the snapshot might be cute, charming, and delightful; to the now grown-up subject the picture might be something else. Does the adult who grew from the infant child have no rights, simply because the image exists?

Thanks to *Marjoe*, the ticking-bomb effect can be seen as more than just speculation. In the film there is a newsreel sequence of four-year-old Marjoe performing a marriage ceremony for a couple, described by one critic as "a nervous red-faced sailor and his heartbreakingly ugly bride." This was a questionable sequence twenty-five years ago; something other than the right to know is involved today. What Marjoe does to himself is his business. But do he and his associates have a right to implicate others in their affairs by resurrecting for selfish purposes tasteless footage? How far into the future may an individual waiver of privacy reach? What are the ethics of once again exposing to public scrutiny the now middle-aged "heartbreakingly ugly bride" in a perhaps aberrant moment?

The known and unknown hazards posed by direct cinema suggest the necessity for extreme caution on the part of filmmakers in dealing with potential infringements on the rights of subjects. While assenting to the serious intention of an aesthetic of direct cinema, one can wonder about the dignity, respect, and pride of the people in the films. Even a partial list of films that have been criticized on ethical grounds reads like a list of the important documentaries of the recent past. Are we asking sacrifices on one side for a positive good on the other? What is the boundary between society's right to know and the individual's right to be free of humiliation, shame, and indignity?

This is not completely uncharted ground; while the problems may be unique to our era, they are not unique to documentary filming or sound recording. The ethical problems of the conjunction of the search for knowledge, new technology, and individual integrity have been extensively considered in the fields of medicine and the social sciences. In many ways, scientists are distinct from filmmakers, yet in their own way they all search for their version of truth. In one important respect the ethical problems of actuality-filmmakers are identical to those faced by research physicians, sociologists, psychologists, and so on: scientific experiments and direct cinema depend for their success on subjects who have little or nothing to gain from participation.

The use of people for our advantage is an ethically questionable undertaking; in its extreme it is exploitation in the literal sense. In documentary filming as in scientific research such exploitation is justified through claims of society's interest in advancing knowledge. This is Wiseman's explicit rationale. Because the films he has made "are about public, tax-supported institutions," Wiseman said, "they are protected under the First Amendment, and the right of the public to know supersedes any right to privacy in a legal sense."

This kind of argument is based on ethical assumptions of an earlier era. If the aesthetic assumptions of documentary have changed, can it be merely stipulated that the ethical relationships remain unchanged? Is there no difference in ethical relationships when the camera is free to peer into every obscure corner in contrast to an earlier time when events had to be consciously performed in front of the camera? Or when the only means of reporting was through word pictures?

Privacy is only part of the counterclaim to society's right to knowledge. In our society there is a profound social respect for the right to decide for oneself how to live one's life.

The right of privacy is part of this broader right of personality, which includes the right to be free of harassment, humiliation, shame, and indignity. For reasons that reach to its core, actuality filming poses a threat of more serious infringement on the rights of personality, than does either traditional documentary production or verbal reports. Staged performances are no threat at all, since the right of self-expression is one of the personality rights. However, lightweight equipment makes endemic the kind of hidden camera and grabshots that were questionable even in traditional documentary.

When using words, private matters can be kept private unless there is an overriding social interest in making the information public. Private information is typically disguised to the largest extent possible to preclude identification of individuals. The confidentiality that can be maintained when using words obviously contradicts the whole idea of direct cinema. And the impossibility of anonymity renders questionable any print-based assumption about the balance between privacy and the right to know.

Society's dual interest in further knowledge and in protection of personality can be seen as complementary; neither means much without the other. An attempt needs to be made to balance these two equally important claims; one mechanism through which balance is maintained is the requirement for consent.

Consent is far from a simple matter; consent, privacy, and related issues have generated extensive discussions in medicine and social science. There is no reason to think that consent is any less complex in film than in science, since both depend on the collaboration of individuals who are not otherwise involved in the enterprise.

In the scientific literature, there is wide consensus that consent is not valid unless it was made (1) under conditions that were free of coercion and deception, (2) with full knowledge of the procedure and anticipated effects, (3) by someone competent to consent. The requirement that consent be truly voluntary is a recognition of the fact that there is typically an unequal power relationship between investigators and subjects; the disproportion of status and sophistication is subtly coercive. It is probably not by accident that large numbers of participants in medical experiments are prisoners and otherwise indigent. In the first place, they are available in prisons and charity wards. As dependents of the state they are (or think they are—which amounts to the same thing) in a weak position to refuse to cooperate. Margaret Mead stated the case bluntly: "The more powerless the subject is, per se, the more the question of ethics—and power—is raised."

The act of volunteering presumes that one knows what is being volunteered for; subjects must be informed about the procedures and possible effects. Considerable argument has developed over what constitutes "informed consent," but one point is clear. *Consent is flawed when obtained by the omission of any fact that might influence the giving or withholding of permission.* The decision to participate is the subject's absolute right; no one may take it away by the manner in which the question is asked or the circumstances explained or not explained.

A third component of voluntary informed consent—competency to consent—is also shrouded in complexity. By law, a child is not competent to consent; approval must be given by a parent or guardian. Where the child has an interest in the contemplated procedure, this is a reasonable requirement. Presumably, the adult will consider the child's best interest in making important decisions. There are, however, sometimes conflicts between the interests of parents and those of minor children; in these cases an impartial decision may be sought from the courts.

The ethical status of responsible consent becomes obscure where what is being agreed to is only marginally for the benefit of the minor child—as is the case in nontherapeutic research. It can be argued that a child's integrity is infringed when a parent or guardian makes these decisions without considering the child's wishes. A minor has rights, the argument goes, and these rights cannot be waived by anyone else.

A similar kind of argument in an ethically even more murky area involves the question of who is competent to give consent for institutionalized subjects such as prisoners or mental retardates. The officials of the institutions are in many cases the legal guardians of their charges. Yet it is clear that in some situations there could be a conflict between the interests of the guardians and the interests of the individuals they are responsible for. This ethical dilemma underlies the difficulties of *Titicut Follies* in the courts of Massachusetts.

The officials of the hospital where the film was made may have had selfish reasons to prevent their practices from becoming public knowledge. At the same time, Wiseman was not exactly a disinterested party when he sought to make the film. Caught between these two interests, the legitimate interests of the patients were lost.

The basic point of the restrictions around voluntary informed consent in medical and social research is the protection of the physical and psychic well-being of the subjects. Extending the general ideas around consent, there are specific propositions and practices that are particularly germane to actuality filming. A basic postulate in social research is that subjects should not be humiliated by the experience; they should not leave the experiment with lowered self-esteem and social respect. The ethical sense of this postulate is violated with regularity in actuality filming, sometimes consciously, sometimes innocently.

A Vietnamese peasant understood this when he said, "First they bomb as much as they please, then they film it." Peter Davis, director of *Hearts and Minds*, understood when he commented, "The second confrontation of Vietnamese with American technology is only slightly less humiliating than the first."

On the assumption that no one can know a culture as well as its members, it is a practice in the social sciences for investigators to state their understanding in their own words and check these formulations with members of the culture. The information-gathering process thus becomes a collaborative seeking after knowledge on the part of scientists and their subjects. It is not unusual for this process to continue through to the final draft to permit subjects second thoughts about the propriety of disclosing certain private information.

If all of this sounds familiar, it should. It stretches back to Flaherty and the Eskimos: "My work," Flaherty said later, "had been built up along with them. I couldn't have done anything without them. In the end it is all a question of human relationships."

The idea of the subject participating in the creative process past the actual shooting stage is not completely unknown in direct cinema. Often, however, this follows from a simple dictum: Respect flows to power. Levine had veto right over *Showman*, as did John Lennon over *Sweet Toronto*, as did Queen Elizabeth over *Royal Family*.

On the evidence, I am forced to wonder whether less-powerful personages than Joe Levine, John Lennon, and Queen Elizabeth would have been given the same assurances. The more common stance seems to be an extension of the adversary approach that emphasizes the filmmaker's exclusive control over the film.

Barron is on record that he would never show rushes to subjects "unless I wanted to incorporate them into the film." The production group of *An American Family* was willing to eliminate some objectionable material, yet Pat Loud has a long list of alleged distortions. "The thrust of the film was their decision, and they were adamant about that."

In his defense, Craig Gilbert, producer of *An American Family*, made the point that "eight reasonably intelligent, compassionate, caring people reviewed the footage to make the film an accurate, compassionate, and un-biased portrayal of the family." Maybe. A skeptic can ask, though, what happened to the seven reasonably intelligent, compassionate, caring people who were the most important collaborators—the subjects of the film.

Marcel Ophuls mocks the whole idea of collaboration. "During these dis-cussions [of ethics], the idea seems to come up that in documentary films there's some sort of participatory democracy—that the fair thing to do, the only really decent thing to do, is to have the people you have used look at the rushes and then decide collectively what should be used."

It is a charming vision—all those people seated around a Steenbeck trying to decide what shot comes next. But that's not the way it works. Typically, the filmmaker starts the cut and carries it through. In the traditional approach, the people in the film are presented with a completed film.

In a collaborative approach to editing, the participants have an opportunity to offer their interpretations of the material before the form of the film is irrevocably set. George Stoney has done this for yeas. At various stages in his editing, Stoney shows a copy of his workprint to the people in the film and anyone else who might be able to contribute some insight. All of this feeds back into subsequent editing.

Perhaps because he is a social scientist, Jean Rouch follows the social science practice of showing his material to the people he is working with. Sometimes, as in *Chronique d'un été*, these showings serve as impetus for further filming, but unlike Barron, this is not why Rouch shows his films. Rouch is emphatic on this point: "The great lesson of Flaherty and *Nanook* is to always show your films to the people who were in it. That's the exact opposite of the ideas of Maysles and Leacock."

Other filmmakers have used variations of the collaborative approach. In the making of *Asylum*, a film about an R. D. Laing therapeutic community, provi-sional consent was obtained before filming. The original twenty hours of rushes were cut to a four-hour version. Final consent was obtained on the basis of this version of what would be included in the final ninety-minute film. It was perhaps Laing's influence, but the schizophrenics in his care were accorded the dignity of deciding for themselves how they wanted to be presented on the screen.

Canadian critic Patrick Watson summed up the filmmaker's antipathy to collaboration in editing: "Ceding authority over the edit is revolutionary; it requires a curious submission of the director's ego." Yet, established filmmakers like Colin Low and Fernand Dansereau do not feel threatened by the collaboration of their subjects in the editing process.

Dansereau has described how the process worked in the National Film Board of Canada production of one of "his" films. *Saint-Jerome* is a study of the way in which people and institutions in the small town of that name behave in periods of rapid change. At the outset, in contrast to current practice for many filmmakers, Dansereau made a pledge to the less powerful that was not extended to the more powerful. Ordinary citizens—but not politicians— received assurance that they would have control over the final product.

In the process of successive screenings of rushes and workprint, there was an interplay between filmmaker and participants—each trying to put meaning to the experience. After "considerable stirring up of ideas and emotions . . . the two approaches coincided and grew together, and the film was accepted without difficulty." When the local Chamber of Commerce tried to restrict showings of *Saint-Jerome*, the major community organizations defended the film.

Dansereau was not degraded by the collaboration; quite the opposite: "I can feel within me, infinitely stronger and more durable than that from either critics or any anonymous public, the recognition of the people with whom we lived. It is they, finally, who assure me of my functions as an artist."

Filmmakers who insist on sole control of a film overlook a crucial point about the nature of actuality filming. They are using assumptions that are only questionably appropriate to the situation. Although actuality may be used as inspiration in other art forms, such as painting and writing, these creations are solely the result of the artist's activity. No one mistakes *Moby Dick* for anything but an interpretation by Melville. No one criticizes the behavior of the people in a painting by Hieronymous Bosch. The words of Tom Wolfe (either one) are inevitably and uniquely his, regardless of the source of inspiration.

The situation in fiction film and old-style documentaries is not exactly the same as in other art forms, but the characters are instrumentalities of the creators. They would not exist except for the lines written for them, the actions prescribed for them by the writer and the director. The romantic assumptions about artistic control and self-expression are appropriate to these conditions.

None of this is true for direct cinema. It would not exist without the uniquely personal speech and lines made available by the people being depicted. A direct-cinema film is irreducibly the product of the personalities of the subjects as refracted through the personality of the filmmaker; this strength of direct cinema is vitiated when filmmakers insist instead on imposing their own personalities. Since filmmaker and subject are embarked on a collaboration from the moment of conception, romantic aesthetic assumptions are inappropriate.

The logic of complete collaboration is the logic of direct cinema. If one is serious about using direct cinema to make valid statements about people, then collaboration should be welcome. The subjects know more than any outsider can about what is on the screen. Without the insider's understanding, the material could be distorted in the editing process by the outsider.

It makes a difference, for instance, in the scene with Eddie Sachs whether he is struggling to maintain his self-image or whether, as Leacock claims, "Eddie is just damn well pleased to be alive." If Leacock is right, but the audience is led by the editing to believe otherwise, then the audience is being deceived just as if the scene were staged altogether.

It turns out that the ethical problem is also an aesthetic one. The tension between filmmaker and subject can be creative or destructive. It is likely to be destructive when filmmakers try to make new ethical facts conform to inappropriate aesthetic assumptions. We are then all demeaned: filmmakers, subject, and the audience. The new assumptions that have begun to be sketched, notably by Marcorelles in *Living Cinema*, recognize that both filmmaker and subject have unique contributions to make to the creative process of direct cinema.

Collaboration obviously discharges one ethical responsibility. When others supply themselves as characters telling their own story, filmmakers incur an obligation not to deform the subject's persona for selfish motives. Collaboration fulfills the basic ethical requirement for control of one's own personality. If the mayor has no objection to showing his speech, I can have none.

Things get complicated if the mayor changes his mind after the film is in release. Obviously, a filmmaker's commitment to a subject cannot be openended. It need not be. There is less basis for grievance if subjects actually collaborate in the editing while the film is still being worked on than if they had merely been offered a final print for approval. However, some subjects do not realize that they make easy targets, or during the editorial screenings they become so entranced with their images that they are unable to consider the implications of the persona on the screen.

The filmmaker's best guess on the potential effects of the film and particular scenes must be part of truly informed consent. A simple human principle can be invoked here: Those least able to protect themselves require the greatest protection. In the extreme, utter helplessness demands utter protection.

When Dansereau yielded control over the final print to ordinary citizens but not to politicians, he was following a general policy at the National Film Board of Canada. The tendency there in recent years has been to give more power over a film to those who were vulnerable and could suffer as a result of being filmed. Those who can defend themselves—whether politicians or celebrities—are offered little or no control over the final product.

Such a practice, of course, makes it more difficult to obtain permission to film celebrities, but it might result in more revealing portrayals. Otherwise the agreement of celebrities to appear in a film becomes one more business enterprise like any other personal appearance; when such a venture suffers a reverse, filmmakers have no special claim to attention.

If subjects by their own actions have abrogated a claim to humane consideration, then filmmakers have little ethical responsibility toward them. It is not always easy to know when deceit is ethically acceptable. "Candid Camera" is probably indefensible even if permission is subsequently sought and granted; World War II resistance cameramen had no ethical obligations toward those who had placed themselves outside of the filmmaker's moral community. Between the extremes we must each make our own judgments.

Caution is required. Unless the judgment is clearly motivated and justifiable, it is easy to slip into narrow prejudice against Pentecostalists, homosexuals, or upper-middle-class families. Perhaps as an emotional guide, filming should be considered like any other human relationship; is the filming practice something that would be done in a private social context?

Collaboration does not solve all of the ethical problems raised by the new possibilities of actuality filming. Still to be detailed on some other occasion are the implications stemming from the critical fact that different people make different interpretations of the things they see in films. What is the ethical situation where only a few people perceive an ethical violation? Does the situation change when a basically honest interpretation is possible despite a blatant ethical violation? An obvious part of the answer is that people start from different ethical premises. Beyond this the questions are even trickier than questions of ethical conduct.

My own incompletely worked out feelings tell me that once standards of conduct are accepted, their application is more or less objective; yet it is not always easy to know from a film when standards have been properly applied. Even though what appears on the screen must be the central evidence, an infringement is not mitigated because it is overlooked by some part of an audience. Any other position trivializes an ethical discussion. Where audience acceptance is the only criterion, the end justifies the means—ethical considerations are irrelevant.

We are not quite at a standoff between the subjective component of interpretation and the objective nature of violations of accepted standards. As we make explicit our ethical standards there will be a greater sensitivity to ethical violations, and determination of deviations will become more objective. We will then be able to discuss more rationally whether the social gain outweighs the individual loss.

Where there is still a split judgment on ethical violations we may have to go outside of the internal evidence of the film; suspicion of a violation might have to be resolved on the basis of external evidence. A related possibility is that scrupulously ethical productions will begin to recognize—in the filming and the film—that the production crew is in social interaction with its subjects. Wiseman, for instance, claims to record on film his request for consent. If the audience had these available, we would be better able to judge the degree to which unequal power influenced the agreement to appear in the film.

Discussion of ethical issues will not by itself solve the problems; it may remind us of their existence and perhaps lead to a more fruitful relationship between filmmaker, subject, and audience. Application of these ideas in actuality filming would not always be easy, but some guidelines are needed if we are to avoid cynical exploitation.

The acrimony surrounding a controversial film may be good for the box office; it is sometimes of questionable value for art. The hustlers among us will make increasingly bizarre films for the sake of controversy. In the whirlwind, the more thoughtful and profound films will be lost.

In the end, since the dignity of others is best protected by a well-informed conscience, sober consideration of our ethical obligations may serve to impress all of us—beginner and old pro—with the power we carry around when we pick up a camera.

Note

1   In a subsequent interview, Al explained what he meant: "It's so hard for me to imagine that what I'm doing might hurt people in any way because I'm not imposing any kind of thing on what they're doing" (Calvin Pryluck, "Seeking to Take the Longest Journey: A Conversation with Albert Maysles," *Journal of the University Film Association* 28 [Spring 1976]: 14).

Notes on Sources

The basic sources for the material on documentary practices were G. Roy Levin, *Documentary Explorations* (Garden City, N.Y.: Doubleday, 1971), and Alan Rosenthal, *The New Documentary in Action* (Berkeley and Los Angeles: University of California Press, 1971). The basic sources for the discussion of scientific practices were Paul A. Freund, ed., *Experimentation with Human Subjects* (New York: Braziller, 1970), and Freund, ed., *Experiments and Research with Humans: Values in Conflict*, Academy Forum no. 3 (Washington, D.C.: National Academy of Sciences, 1975). Material on right of personality is from O. M. Reubhausen and O. G. Brim, Jr., "Privacy and Behavioral Research," *Columbia Law Review* 65 (1965): 1184–211; a classic, and still valuable, discussion is Roscoe Pound, "Interests of Personality," *Harvard Law Review* 28 (1915): 343–65 and 445–56.

Additional material on direct cinema and *cinéma vérité* includes: Stephen Mamber, *Cinéma Vérité in America* (Cambridge, Mass.: MIT Press, 1974); Stephen Mamber, "*Cinéma Vérité* in America," *Screen* 13 (Fall 1972); and Louis Marcorelles, *Living Cinéma* (New York: Praeger, 1973).

The material on the National Film Board of Canada and community organization is from *Challenge for Change Newsletter*, no. 7 (Winter 1971/72) and no. 1 (Winter 1968/69), and Patrick Watson, "Challenge for Change," *Artscanada*, April 1970. The second Wiseman quote is from Janet Handelman, "An Interview with Frederick Wiseman," *Film Library Quarterly* 3 (Summer 1970). The Flaherty quote is from "Robert Flaherty Talking," in *The Cinema 1950*, ed. Roger Manvell (Harmondsworth, Eng.: Penguin, 1950).

Further material about specific filmmakers came from individual interviews. Those from *Film Comment* include: Maxine Haleff, "The Maysles Brothers and 'Direct Cinema'" 2 (Spring 1964); James Blue, "One Man's Truth: An Interview with Richard Leacock" 3 (Spring 1965); Arthur Barron, "The Intensification of Reality" 6 (Spring 1970); Harrison Engle, "Hidden Cameras and Human Behavior: An Interview with Allen Funt" 3 (Fall 1965); and Melinda Ward, "Interview with Pat Loud" 9 (Nov.–Dec. 1973). See also Pat Loud, *A Woman's Story* (New York: Bantam, 1974). Interviews in *Filmmaker's Newsletter* include: Bruce Berman, "The Making of *Hearts and Minds*: An Interview with Peter Davis" 8 (April 1975); Betty Jeffries Demby, "A Discussion with Marcel Ophuls" 6 (Dec. 1972); and Steven T. Glanz, "Marjoe" 6 (Nov. 1972). See also "Hollow Holiness," *Time*, Aug. 14, 1972, p. 45, and Thomas Meehan, "Portrait of the Con Artist as a Young Man," *Saturday Review*, Aug. 26, 1972, p. 67.

14

The Ethics of Image Making; or, "They're Going to Put Me in the Movies. They're Going to Make a Big Star Out of Me..."

Jay Ruby

In this paper I will discuss the moral questions that arise when one person produces and uses a recognizable image of another. I am interested in an exploration of the ethical problems that stem from the justification of the use of human beings in the pursuit of art, science, news, or entertainment when those uses involve the production of realistic and recognizable images of people. The questions that can be raised are seemingly infinite, and many important issues will merely be touched on here. Let me cite a few of the more obvious. What does "informed consent" mean when a family is asked by a television crew to have their lives recorded and packaged into a series for national television? How does one balance the public's right to be informed with the individual's right to privacy? Are objectivity and "balance" the primary obligations of the photojournalist? Do visual artists have a moral license to use people in ways different from the ways scientists or reporters use them?

I am not a lawyer, philosopher, or theologian. I will not attempt to deal with the legal controversies or with the larger moral issues these questions imply. I am an anthropologist involved in the study of visual communication as a cultural system. For the past twenty years I have been a participant/observer in the production and consumption of documentary and ethnographic photographs and films. I speak as both native and researcher.

I am concerned about society's shifting moral expectations of the image maker and the consequent ambivalence some professionals feel about their own ethical base. This uneasiness bespeaks a deep-seated and widespread concern with the nature of images. At times we seem to be more confused than informed by them. The traditional arguments used to justify the behavior of artists, journalists, and scientists who make images are becoming increasingly inadequate, convincing neither the professionals involved nor the public as thoroughly as they once did.

As we enter an era of telecommunications where image-producing, -distributing, and -consuming technologies are becoming ever more decentralized and Andy Warhol's idea that eventually everyone will be a star for fifteen minutes is no longer futurist thinking, the urgency of these questions increases. The moral base on which image producers have relied is shaky, if not crumbling. Before every city block has its own news service and resident visual artist, we should have a better understanding of how one reaches the decision to use someone else's image and where our responsibilities lie.

Ethnic minorities, women, gays, third- and fourth-world peoples, the very rich and the very poor are telling us—the middle-class, middle-aged white males who dominate the industry—that our pictures of them are false. Some wish to produce their own representation of themselves and control or at least monitor the ways we now image them. The New World Information Order cannot be ignored any more than can the organized protests against the Metropolitan Museum's photographic exhibition *Harlem on My Mind* or the gays' rage against the film *Cruising* or, most recently, the Puerto Rican community's displeasure over *Fort Apache, The Bronx*. The list is long and grows daily.

The time when an artist could take photographs of strangers, usually poor or in some other way removed from the mainstream of America, and justify the action as the inherent right of the artist is, I believe, ending.

The time when one could reconstruct a historical event by creating composite, and therefore fictional, characters for the sake of plot and not be held legally and ethically responsible ended with the popularity of the television docudrama.

The time when a reporter could rely on the principle that the public's right to know is more important than the individual's right to privacy, when people believed that a journalist's primary ethical responsibility was to be objective, fair, and honest, is over.

The time when a scientist could depend on the public's belief in the material benefits of scientific knowledge to justify the use of double blind studies, often employing hidden cameras, ceased with Stanley Milgram's frightening explorations of people's willingness to obey authority.

Examples are endless, and they signal the demise of our naive trust that since the camera never lies, a photographer has no option but to tell the truth. We are beginning to understand the technologically produced image as a construction—as the interpretive act of someone who has a culture, an ideology, and often a conscious point of view, all of which cause the image to convey a certain kind of knowledge in a particular way. Image makers show us their view of the world whether they mean to or not. No matter how much we may feel the need for an objective witness of reality, our image-producing technologies will not provide it for us.

I believe that the maker of images has the moral obligation to reveal the covert—to never appear to produce an objective mirror by which the world can see its "true" image. For in doing so we strengthen the status quo, support the repressive forces of this world, and continue to alienate those people we claim to be concerned about. So long as our images of the world continue to be sold to others as *the* image of the world, we are being unethical.

To pursue this argument efficiently I must be specific, and so I confine myself to one variety of imaging. I will not try to separate assertion from supportable theses; I will simply state that the argument presented here is based on a combination of personal experience, research, and passionately held belief. I make no claim that all aspects of the argument are verifiable, only that all other points of view are much less convincing to me.

I use case studies from the documentary tradition—still and motion pictures—simply because I know the tradition well. A similar case could, of course, be made using fiction films or paintings, but since the documentary is such a marvelously confused genre of motion pictures, it allows me to deal with art, science, reportage, etc., in a rather inclusive way. In addition, the production of documentary images and the production of anthropological knowledge are in fundamental ways parallel pursuits. The moral and ethical concerns of one can be applied to the other. Most documentarians would agree that the following quotation from Dell Hymes could just as well apply to the documentary tradition:

> The fundamental fact that shapes the future of anthropology is that it deals in knowledge of others. Such knowledge has always implied ethical and political responsibilities, and today the "others" whom anthropologists have studied make those responsibilities explicit and unavoidable. One must consider the consequences of those among whom one works of simply being there, of learning about them, and what becomes of what is learned.[1]

For a variety of reasons, anthropologists have been conducting public discussions about their ethical responsibilities longer than documentarians have. I believe that the experience social scientists have had in grappling with these questions provides documentarians with usable insights into their own problems. I have consequently incorporated some of those findings into this paper.

The production and use of images involves three separable yet related moral issues which when combined into a professional activity becomes an ethical position. These three issues are: (1) the image maker's personal moral contract to produce an image that is somehow a true reflection of the intention in making the image in the first place—to use the cliché, it is being true to one's self; (2) the moral obligation of the producer to his or her subjects; and (3) the moral obligation of the producer to the potential audience. The solution to these questions will vary with the producer's intention, his or her sociocultural role and that of the image's subjects, and the contexts in which the image appears.

I have argued elsewhere that images are polysemic, that is, a photograph or film has a variety of potential socially generated meanings.[2] The cultural expectations producers, subjects, and audiences have about the various communication events that transpire in the production and consumption of images predispose people to employ different interpretive strategies to derive signification and meaning from images.[3] These interpretive strategies are embedded within a larger body of cultural knowledge and competencies which encompass or are supported by a moral system. That is, systems of knowledge and epistemologies are attached to moral systems. As an anthropologist I would argue that morals and ethics are only comprehensible in relation to other facets of a culture.

The particular signification or meaning that is appended to an image emerges as a consequence of a variety of factors: (1) the label attached to the image—for example, photographs that are considered to be news photos are regarded differently from art photos; (2) the context in which the image appears—for example, news photos which are made into high-quality enlargements and placed in an art museum tend to be regarded primarily as art; and (3) the socially acquired expectations of the audience toward certain types of images produced by certain types of image makers which tend to appear in certain types of settings.

An illustration will help make these abstractions less abstruse. At the beginning of the century, Lewis Hine, a sociologist turned social reformer, took a series of photographs, commissioned by the National Committee to Reform Child Labor Laws, of children working in factories. The archetypical Hine image is that of a prepubescent child, quite small, often frail, and always dirty, standing in front of an enormous piece of machinery. The child is staring into the lens of the camera, and consequently into the eyes of the viewer. The machines are black and dirty, and the factory so dark that the edges of the machine disappear into nothingness. These images were designed to appear in tracts that detailed the social and psychological abuses of child labor. They were often printed on inexpensive, porous newsprint with a cheap half-tone process. All of the subtlety of tone and detail present in the negatives disappears. These tracts were sent to legislators, the clergy, and prominent citizens and handed out at meetings. The intended message of these images in this context is a pragmatic one—they are a call to arms. One is to feel pity for the child and anger at the exploitation by the factory owner implied in the large and ominous machine. If the photographer is thought of at all, he is assumed to be on the side of truth and justice, providing irrefutable evidence of wrongdoing.

If we were to prepare a set of Hine's photographs for exhibition at the Museum of Modern Art in New York, enlargements of fine quality would be matted, framed, and hung with a brief but articulate and insightful explanatory text in a stark white room with subdued lighting. The audience in this context becomes people whose primary interest lies in art and photography, not in reforming labor laws. The photographs are now regarded chiefly for their syntactic elements, that is, formal and aesthetic qualities. The waifs are no longer pitiable examples of capitalistic exploitation, but aesthetic objects with interesting, if not haunting, faces. The machines are now examined for their texture and lines—as industrial art objects, not as symbols of oppression. A little girl's stare is now simply a sign of her willingness to be photographed, not an indictment of our economic system. It is unlikely that anyone seeing the exhibit would be motivated to do anything except admire and applaud the artistic accomplishments of Lewis Hine. I am virtually certain that no one would rush to West Virginia to see whether similar conditions might still exist.

The photographs in these two scenarios are the same, but the cultural expectations created by the two contexts cause us to regard the photographer and his works in different ways. I am not suggesting that Hine was never regarded as a photographic artist when his images were used in political tracts or that no one would ponder the political or economic implications of the photographs in the museum. I am suggesting that one interpretive strategy seems more appropriate to most people given a particular setting. It's hard to imagine people concerned with the plight of children in factories arguing about Hine's compositional style, or tuxedoed gentlemen and bejeweled ladies rushing out into the streets to picket a corporation thought to be exploiting children.

In fact, our readings of most images vacillate between these two extremes.[4] It is a case of the confusion I alluded to earlier with regard to documentary images. We are often uncertain whether the image maker is an artist who is to be critiqued for his mastery of the form or a technician who holds the mirror to the world.

This lack of clarity confronts producers with a moral dilemma that can be traced back to the beginnings of the tradition. Robert Flaherty, the American father figure of documentary film, was immediately accused by his critics of "faking" *Nanook of the North*. The film confused many film commentators— some failed to see any coherent story, since the narrative line was not obvious; others accused him of using actors and staging the entire movie. Criticism of the documentary form has not progressed far since the 1923 reviews of *Nanook*, and as a consequence, theory, criticism, and even review flounder on the question: Is the documentary art or reportage?

This cultural confusion has so limited the semantic and syntactic possibilities that some leave the documentary tradition for the apparent freedom of fiction. The moral obligations of the producers of fiction—written and visual— are certainly not clear, and some recent court decisions (particularly the 1978 decision against Gwen Davis Mitchell for apparently basing one of the characters in her novel *Touching* on a California psychologist, Paul Bindrim) appear to greatly limit the artistic license of even fiction makers—but seldom do its producers get accused of faking or criticized for staging or for misrepresenting their subject.

If documentarians choose to regard themselves as artists and are so received by the public, conventional wisdom argues that their primary ethical obligation is to be true to their personal visions of the world—to make artistically competent statements. In this way artists are thought to fulfill their moral responsibilities to the subjects of their work and to their audiences.

The artist is often regarded as being somewhat outside the moral constraints that confine other people—as having license to transform people into aesthetic objects without their knowledge and sometimes against their will. Until recently, few critics except Marxists argued that art contains and espouses the ideology of the artist, that even photography is in no way a universal language transcending cultural boundaries. Now, even Susan Sontag acknowledges that a Nazi film like *Triumph of the Will* was produced by a fascist filmmaker who must bear the moral responsibility of her art no matter how competent it might be. Some people argue that ethics should have priority over aesthetics, or perhaps more correctly, that a morally acceptable ethical position produces the foundation for a good aesthetic.

If one takes the everyday lives of people—a favorite subject matter of the documentary—and transforms them into an artistic statement, where does one draw the line between the actuality of their lives and the aesthetic needs of the artist? How much fiction or interpretation is possible before the subjects not only disagree but begin to be offended, or even fail to recognize themselves at all? These questions have recently been raised with great passion with reference to videotapes produced by video artists, people not from the documentary tradition but in the field of nonrepresentational video art. When a Juan Downey or an Edin Velez produces tapes that include images of native people such as the Yanomano Indians of Venezuela, some audiences become quite upset about the "exploitation" of the subjects for the sake of art. It would appear that documentarians who employ more subtle and less obvious techniques of construction are less likely to be criticized for being exploitive than are the video artists who employ overt techniques of aesthetic manipulation. Where does the documentary artist seek verification and justification for his or her work? Must the subject agree with the artist's interpretation? Or is it sufficient that the artist remains true to a personal vision regardless of how offensive it might be to others? I believe that we are now less certain of an easy answer to this question than we once were.

Where does the documentary artist's responsibility to the audience lie? Most audiences believe documentary images to be accurate representations of reality, unless they are overtly altered as in the case of the videotapes just mentioned. Given our belief in the image, should the documentary artist remind the audience of the interpretive and constructed nature of the documentary form—that is, demystify the construction? For example, is it important for people to know that Flaherty cast his films by looking for ideal types? "Family members" in *Nanook of the North*, *Man of Aran*, and *Louisiana Story* are not related to each other; they were selected because they suited Flaherty's conception of what makes a good Eskimo, Irish, or Cajun family. Is the documentary artist being more ethical if methods and techniques are revealed? Does that knowledge, cause us, the audience, to regard the film differently?

Traditionally, documentarians have not revealed these things within their films, and some have never discussed the mechanics of their construction anywhere. (Obviously Flaherty has, or we would not be able to contemplate the consequences of his revelation and actions.) To remind an audience of the constructive and interpretive nature of images is regarded by some as counterproductive, if not actually destructive, to the nature of the film experience, that is, to the creation of an illusion of reality. Moreover, some people regard such revelation as self-indulgent, in that it turns the audience's attention away from the film and toward the filmmaker. For many, effective art requires a suspension of disbelief; being reminded that the images have an author disrupts the fantasy.

It is commonly assumed that art should be a little mysterious to be successful. A reflexive art has never been very popular and, at least in film, has become confused with a kind of self-indulgent autobiographical film that has recently become popular, in which young filmmakers expose themselves, exploit their families, and use the camera as therapist. Reflexivity has gotten a bad name because of its mistaken association with narcissism, self-consciousness, and other forms of self-contemplation.[5] I believe, however, that an intelligently used reflexivity is an essential part of all ethically produced documentaries. I will return to this idea later.

The confusion about which moral guidelines should be used to judge a documentary is compounded by the fact that some documentarians respond to aesthetic and moral criticism of their art by suggesting that their works are mere reflections of the reality observed and that their role as producer was to faithfully record and transmit what they experienced. They are not really the "authors" of their works, nor are they responsible for any conclusions audiences might draw. If one sees someone in a documentary image who appears stupid or disgusting, the implication is that the person so imaged is in reality stupid or disgusting, since the camera merely recorded what was in front of it without any modification. This aesthetic and moral "neutrality" is to be found in films like Frederick Wiseman's *High School*.

When the American direct-cinema movement, founded by people like Robert Drew and Richard Leacock, used television as their primary outlet, they associated the documentary with the ethical canons of broadcast journalism. Fairness, balance, and objectivity became paramount. In doing so they brought the tradition full circle. As Dan Schiller has argued, objectivity became an ideal for journalism partly as a consequence of the photograph's being introduced into newspapers.[6] As newspapers capitalized on the public's belief in the objectivity of the photograph, print journalists sought to emulate this objectivity in their writing. Fifty years later, documentary film became concerned with being objective because of its association with broadcast journalism.

Documentarians as journalists logically assume the ethical codes of the latter profession. In doing so they become virtually unassailable, for, unlike their printed-word brethren, photo and film journalists are thought to be employing a medium that when used properly is inherently objective. Thus, apart from the occasional accusation of the outright faking of a picture or the staging of a scene in a television program, documentary broadcast-journalism has not been subjected to much critical examination.

The recent arguments raised by Marxists, structuralists, and others about the relation between ideology on the one hand and the producer of images on the other have, however, caused some people to begin to critique broadcast journalism in a fashion similar to that discussed earlier for art. Stuart Hall and other British scholars of mass communication are among these analysts. Criticism of objectivity as the primary ethical responsibility of journalists is on the increase. As James Carey pointed out:

> What are lamely called the conventions of objective reporting were developed to report another century and another society. They were designed to report a secure world . . . about which there was a rather broad consensus, . . . a settled mode of life: . . . which could be rendered in the straightforward "who says what to whom" manner. . . . Today no accepted system of interpretation exists and political values and purposes are very much in contention . . . and cannot be encased within traditional forms of understanding. Consequently, "objective reporting" does little more than convey this disorder in isolated, fragmented news stories.[7]

Print journalists have responded to this criticism by acknowledging the active role of the reporter in creating, not finding, news. The so-called new journalism of Tom Wolfe and Hunter Thompson is written in the first person and employs narrative techniques of fiction. With Truman Capote and Norman Mailer writing fiction in the same style, it is often impossible to know from the text whether you are reading fiction or not, and often even then there is no easy answer. Is *The Right Stuff* by Wolfe or *The Executioner's Song* by Mailer fiction or not? Does it really matter? It is a fascinating legal and ethical question but too great a detour for now. However, I would like to point out that there has yet to be invented a visual equivalent to new journalism. When Truman Capote's nonfiction novel *In Cold Blood* was made into a movie it became straightforward fiction.

Most documentarians who consider themselves more journalist than artist are people interested in investigating rather than merely reporting. They are committed people motivated to make images of social or political concerns. Since Jacob Riis and John Grierson, many documentarians have been social reformers, and some, even radical revolutionaries who shared Lenin's belief in the power of the cinema. They produce images to inform audiences of injustices, corruption, and other societal ills, often to persuade people to act against these evils.

The ethical considerations of these image makers differ somewhat from those of the documentary artist. Since politically committed image makers have definite points of view, often prior to the production of any images, they approach the content of the images, the people imaged, and their audiences with a fairly clear agenda. Unlike the documentary as art, here the pragmatic features of the image must dominate—they must have their desired effect to be successful, and that effect is known in advance. People in these images are no longer aesthetic objects, but rather symbols of some collective force. A poor person is often used to stand for poverty, or a factory owner for all of capitalism. The question has to arise: Is it acceptable to use someone's life to illustrate a thesis? Are the considerations different when you are seeking to aid someone you regard as a victim by using that person in your film, as opposed to using a subject in order to expose him as a villain?

Let me use an example from one of the favorite themes of documentary images—housing conditions for the poor. Let us say you are making a documentary on slums for local television and you select a family who appears to have suffered directly because of an irresponsible landlord. How do you weigh the possible harm that might come to the family as a consequence of their public exposure in the film versus the possibility that the film may cause city officials to crack down on slum owners and consequently improve the living conditions for a large number of people?

Is it justifiable to try to avoid explaining your motivation and point of view to the landlord in order to be able to interview him on film? To be blunt about it, is it ethical to lie to an assumed evil person in order to perform what you regard as a positive act? For example, a film like Rogert Mugee's *Saturday Night in City Hall*, an exposé of then mayor of Philadelphia, Frank Rizzo, could not have been made if many of the people in it had known the maker's intention.

Because of the economic realities of distribution, documentary images with a political intent are usually viewed by the already committed, people who immediately comprehend the film's thesis. However, some find their way into theatrical release or public television and hence to a more diverse audience. Should the makers reveal themselves, their methods, and their goals to their audiences, or are they justified in employing the techniques of advertising and other forms of propaganda and persuasion? A recent example is to be found in Julia Reichert and Jim Klein's film *Union Maids*, a skillfully edited set of inter-views of three women active in union organizing in the thirties. The makers failed to mention that the women were members of the Communist party, because they felt that some audiences would be alienated from the primary message of the film—the unsung role of women as union organizers. Does this sort of selection taint a film to such an extent that all of it becomes suspect? Are political-documentary makers caught in the dilemma of having a respon-sibility to reveal methods and motives, which might lessen the impact of their message? Can political-image makers justify their sins of omission on the basis of the service they provide in helping to bring public attention to our social problems? I think not. I am skeptical of the motives and sophistication of many political-image makers. Even though thousands of films and millions of photographs have been employed in political causes in the past fifty years, there is little or no empirical evidence to suggest that they are a significant means of influencing people.

If all the money expended on all the images of the plight of migrant labor-ers since Edward R. Murrow and Fred Friendly's *Harvest of Shame* program had been used for day-care centers and the improvement of these workers' living conditions, their plight would be significantly improved. I doubt that the "pro-fessional sympathizers" who produced all these images can defend their work with much tangible evidence. Power comes more directly from the end of a gun than it does from the lens of a camera. Few revolutions were won in a movie house or on the six o'clock news.

I have barely touched on a large number of important questions concern-ing the ethical obligations of the professional image maker. Whether artist, journalist, or social documentarian, image makers need to confront their responsibilities in a more reflective and reflexive way than they have so far. I have argued elsewhere for the necessity of a reflexive documentary and anthropological cinema.[8] I would extend the argument to all image makers.

I believe that the filmic illusion of reality is an extremely dangerous one, for it gives the people who control the image industry too much power. The major-ity of Americans, and soon the majority of the world's population, receive information about the outside world from the images produced by film, tele-vision, and photography. If we perpetuate the lie that pictures always tell the truth, that they are objective witnesses to reality, we are supporting an indus-try that has the potential to symbolically recreate the world in its own image. Technology grows out of a particular ideology. The Western world created image-producing technologies out of a profound need to have an irrefutable witness—to control reality by capturing it on film.

We stand on the threshold of the telecommunications revolution—a revolution potentially as profound and far-reaching as the agricultural and industrial revolutions. The one significant difference between the present changes and past changes is that the telecommunications revolution is happening so fast, we can actually be aware of it. It took five thousand years of gradual change from the first experiments in plant domestication until people were fully sedentary farmers. Today, there are people still active in television who contributed their talents at the very beginnings of the industry. We have the opportunity to make the revolution anything we want it to be. As privileged members of that segment of the world who manage, if not control, the image empires, we have an obligation to pause and reflect on the past and to contemplate the future. We should not let the rush of the marketplace destroy our responsibility to act intelligently. We need to demystify these technologies so that we can cultivate a more critical and sophisticated audience. We need to make it possible to include a greater variety of human experience via these media—to give the many voices available access to this revolution. The human condition is too complex to be filtered through the eyes of a small group of people. We need to see the world from as many perspectives as possible. We have the means to do so now.

Notes

1 Dell Hymes, ed., *Reinventing Anthropology* (New York: Random House, 1972), p. 48.
2 Jay Ruby, "In a Pic's Eye: Interpretive Strategies for Deriving Significance and Meaning from Photographs," *Afterimage* 3, no. 9 (1976): 5–7.
3 Sol Worth and Larry Gross, "Symbolic Strategies," *Journal of Communication* 24, no. 4 (1974): 27–39.
4 Alan Sekula, "On the Invention of Meaning in Photographs," *Artforum* 13, no. 5 (1975): 36–45.
5 Barbara Myerhoff and Jay Ruby, Introduction to *A Crack in the Mirror: Reflexive Perspectives in Anthropology*, ed. Jay Ruby, pp. 1–38 (Philadelphia: University of Pennsylvania Press, 1982).
6 Dan Schiller, "Realism, Photography, and Journalistic Objectivity in Nineteenth-Century America," *Studies in the Anthropology of Visual Communication* 4, no. 2 (1977): 86–98.
7 James Carey, "The Communications Revolution and the Professional Communicator," *Sociological Review Monographs* (Jan. 1969): 35.
8 Jay Ruby, "Exposing Yourself: Reflexivity, Anthropology, and Film," *Semiotica* 3, no. 1–2 (1980): 153–590.

15

Word Is Out and Gay U.S.A.

Lee Atwell

Historically, the cinematic image of the homosexual, which has only come into focus within the last decade, has consistently suffered from stereotypical distortion, derision, and condescension. As minority members who have never been in control of their public image, gays have witnessed in narrative fiction film an almost systematic attempt to devalue, while giving token recognition to, their lives and feelings. If television responds on occasion with a sympathetic episode, movies are largely content with liberal notions of obvious "fairies" for humorous relief or, worse, unhappy psychopathic villains, reinforcing ignorance and prejudice among what Christopher Isherwood terms "the heterosexual dictatorship."

In the field of documentary, or *cinéma vérité*, where the index of reality is somewhat more reliable and where we at least have the advantage of experiencing not actors impersonating gay types but the real thing, isolated examples have failed to have any significant impact. In *The Queen*, Frank Simon penetrates behind the facade of male drags participating in a beauty contest, while at another extreme, Rosa van Praunheim's *The Homosexual Is Not Perverse but the Society Which Produces Him* offers a cynical, candid glimpse into the S&M/motorcycle/leather faction of the macho gay world, and Shirley Clarke's feature-length interview with a black male prostitute, *A Portrait of Jason*, conveys an unsparing, unpleasant confessional vision.

Diverse and positive images of gay persons were not forthcoming for two basic reasons. First, in spite of the clarion call "Out of the Closets" by liberationists, large segments of the gay populace feared any sort of public exposure that might mean loss of jobs, friends, or family support. Simply getting an openly gay woman or man to appear before a camera was a primary difficulty. And second, the difficulties in financing a nonsensational (noncommercial) treatment of the subject were virtually insurmountable.

The first work reflecting the otherwise extremely vocal politics of Gay Liberation was a highly professional student production, *Some of Your Best Friends* by Ken Robinson of the University of Southern California. Employing a *cinéma vérité* format, Robinson captured the spirited genesis of the movement in New York and Los Angeles, interviewing up-front participants about feelings and experiences of oppression and freedom. Especially memorable is a Los Angeles man walking through Griffith Park, relating his entrapment by a local vice officer and his plans to defend himself in a court trial (which he subsequently won). A gay contingent is seen confronting a psychiatric convention, challenging its oppressive advocacy of aversion therapy with a rousing debate. Representatives of a New York homophile organization are shrouded in shadow to protect their identity while the bright shining faces of the street folk project pride, prominently including women as well as men.

Six years were to pass, however, before other gay filmmakers were to significantly take up the direct-cinema approach begun by Robinson. Though financial support was still virtually nonexistent for pro-gay films, the rising tide of anti-gay propaganda, spearheaded by Anita Bryant's Bible-thumping crusade, provoked social consciousness and a revitalization of the movement throughout the land. A highly sophisticated quality gay news medium began to unite divergent forces into political cohesiveness, and at the same time the awareness of a need to communicate prompted socially conscious filmmakers to action. Their efforts resulted in two unique and exceptional human documents, *Gay U.S.A.* and *Word Is Out: Stories of Some of Our Lives*. Both films employ the interview as a fundamental technique, but their production circumstances and organization of material differ distinctly in spite of occasional parallels.

In 1975, Peter Adair, then a producer for San Francisco's KQED, had become dissatisfied with the quality of his work there. "I felt that I needed to make films that were of value to me . . . I wanted to get into some sort of social filmmaking. I started with the issue that concerned me most—that was rights for gay people." He envisioned a short film to be used as a teaching aid for college and professional groups, made of interviews with diverse individuals. But after two years of perseverence, Adair discovered foundations were unresponsive to such a project, and he finally resorted, like the makers of *Gay U.S.A.*, to private and individual investors. He joined forces with his sister, Nancy, assistant cameraman Andrew Brown, sound editor Veronica Selver, New York filmmaker Lucy•Massie Phenix, and Rob Epstein—and the Mariposa Film Group came into existence. With the expansion of the group came the decision to enlarge the scope of the work. What had begun as a modest presentation of positive role models for gay people became a much larger sampling of the vast range of America's gay population.

Every attempt was made to engage filmmakers and participants in a collective expression, decentralizing all procedures from shooting to editing. In preparation, the members "preinterviewed" on videotape two hundred persons from various sections of the country. The team then collectively viewed this material and selected twenty-six women and men whom they returned to film. As Teresa Kennett notes in *The Reel Thing*, certain ground rules were agreed on by the Mariposa Group. "The setting for every interview was worked out very carefully between subject and filmmaker. Choice of location and 'props'— photographs, pets, clothing, etc.—was made on the basis not only of what looked good visually, but of what was meaningful to the interviewee. Making the subject feel at ease was of utmost importance; to this end a stationary camera setup was decided upon, thus eliminating any extra distraction. And since whoever operated the camera also conducted the interview (usually with only one other person on sound) it was possible to develop real unbroken communication between interviewer and interviewee." In addition to the interview material, several hours of *vérité* footage were filmed, depicting working and living situations of the subjects and songs performed by Trish Nugent and the gay rock band Buena Vista.

Four of the Mariposa Group spent over a year editing various cuts down from approximately fifty hours of material, From time to time cuts were screened for predominantly gay audiences, with responses solicited in questionnaire form. Thus, the larger community was able to participate in determining the actual final content of the film. In this process it soon became evident that the large amount of cutaway material detracted from rather than amplified the succession of interviews, and in the final 135-minute version, its presence is minimal. This undoubtedly accounts for the strength of the film's emotional and psychological impact, as well as for its structural and conceptual weaknesses.

Word Is Out is divided into three broad sections: "The Early Years," "Growing Up," and "From Now On." The rather vague nature of these arbitrary categories becomes evident as each section unravels, prefaced by an introductory montage of the personalities included in each segment. Although the interviewees have been carefully chosen to display a richly diverse and contrasting series of views and life-styles, no apparent structural pattern emerges in the editing scheme. Individual interviews are broken up and reappear from time to time, often being used in more than one section, as remarks seem generally relevant to the broad category.

The static stationary camera angle is consistently a frontal medium-close to close shot, giving the impression of a talking portrait in which the subject directly addresses the camera/audience, creating an intimate, engrossing and often emotionally charged rapport between subject and viewer. However, in a film of two-hours-plus duration, variety and contrast are essential to retain the viewer's interest, regardless of how riveting the interview material is assumed to be. In the final analysis, though each individual shot has its own mood, composition, and dynamic center, it is an isolated unit that only marginally relates to the other units that make up the framework.

In addition to the gay musicians, who are seen at random intervals in studio and in concert performances, three sequences deviate significantly from the armchair interview format, giving a much-needed variation in the cinematic space. Elsa Gidlow, 79, the oldest member of the cast, is seen in her Northern California home talking with three young women about lesbian politics and her feelings about appearing in the film. Suddenly, for the first time we see the faces of interviewer(s) and interviewee in the same space, engaged in a conversational exchange, while the handheld camera freely moves from face to face. Similarly, after we have become familiar with a blond lesbian named Whitey who lives in a Northern California cabin, we see an early-morning excursion in which she and her friends saw off a section of a giant tree that is threatening her domicile. The operation, shot from a variety of angles, is successful, and audiences invariably cheer and applaud this rustic interlude. Following interviews separately and together with lesbian mothers Pam Jackson and Rusty Millington, we see a beautifully filmed sequence in which the two women play touch football with Rusty's children on a beach and serve a picnic supper, during which one of the children is interviewed. Other cutaway material, such as the film's self-proclaimed drag queen, Tede Mathews, frolicking with children at a playground or the middle-aged couple Harry Hay and John Burnside picking berries together in the countryside, displays a charm that is more poignant than their speech.

In spite of its diversity of ethnic and sexual types, it would be a mistake to draw anything other than superficial sociological arguments from *Word Is Out*, which is only a bare suggestion of the variety of gay life-styles. Brooklyn professor Betty Powell, one of the film's most articulate speakers, emphasizes, for instance, that she should not be taken as in any sense representative of black lesbian feminists (though she is in fact the only one to appear in the film).

Nevertheless, certain patterns begin to emerge in the selection of material that assert a strongly middle-class value structure. The large number of stable couples suggests an ideal of traditional matrimonial bliss. Only one person speaks up for the single, casual-sex status that characterizes vast numbers of gay people. Although only one speaker, a vice-president of a New York corporation, defines himself as a conservative ("I feel that radicals are necessary and I feel that we are necessary"), the majority of persons interviewed can be categorized as politically conservative, especially those whose formative years preceded the sixties and Gay Liberation. Comedienne Pat Bond, a middle-aged ex-WAC who talks of communal, role-defined lesbian life in postwar years and recounts the terrors of the army's inquisition during the McCarthy period (which resulted in five hundred dishonorable discharges), is nevertheless nos-

talgic about the past. Although she sees the necessity of gays coming out publicly now and finding a new sense of identity, she misses the butch/femme role
dichotomy and the secrecy of "the Little Orphan Annie decoding society" of
her early years.

The film's final section, "From Now On," tends to focus on the more radical
dimension of gay politics, and its most eloquent and persuasive arguments are
presented by lesbian feminists Betty Powell and Sally Gearhart. Powell, who is
a member of the National Gay Task Force, tells of coming out of a heterosexual marriage and realizing her love for a woman through the women's movement. Her assertion that "lesbians and gay men have a great deal to offer in
terms of restructuring the world culture" is more fully articulated by Sally
Gearhart, who asserts that all humans are born with a bisexual potential, but
from the moment they are born they are made half-persons by society's strict
programming of appropriate gender behavior and attitudes. Gays tend, on the
other hand, more toward a natural balance of male and female in one person.
This is, of course, an ideal, and the film's inclusion of stereotypical dykes like
Pat Bond (who quaintly classifies herself as "femme") and effeminate men like
Roger Harkenrider (who honestly admits to archetypal "faggoty" behavior)
suggests the infinite complexity of sexual role-playing in the gay world. On the
other hand, there is a typically male model present in Donald Hackett, a black
truck driver, and a female model in Linda Marco, an attractive former "American dream daughter," both of whom came out from heterosexual marriages
(another significant pattern in the cast). It is also interesting to note that while
the film's most cogent intellectual arguments come from women, its strongest
emotional moments emerge from men. Probably the most memorable is George
Mendenhall's tearful reminiscence of a male opera singer named José encouraging men in the gay bar to sing "God Save Us Nellie Queens" in the fifties,
when San Francisco police mercilessly harassed gays. More deeply touching is
the confession of young David Gillon: "In high school I thought I was just one
of those people who could never love anybody. When I fell in love with Henry,
it meant I had incredibly deep emotions—it meant I was human."

Like *Word Is Out*, *Gay U.S.A.* is also a collective production, made by a large
number of persons under the banner of Artists United for Gay Rights, and a
considerable part of the work is made up of interview footage. But the point
of view and structure are radically different.

Rather than being assembled by democratic communal decisions over a five-
year period, *Gay U.S.A.* was filmed largely on one day: June 26, 1977; and,
apart from actual materials, it was created with donated talent and labor from
a vast number of individuals, all coordinated by one filmmaker who conceived
the project and gave it its final creative form: Arthur Bressan, Jr.

In the angry wake of the defeat for gay rights in Miami on June 7, Bressan, who had begun to establish his gift as a director in the gay porno circuits, joined in the San Francisco evening demonstration that grew spontaneously. "My movie camera jammed in front of City Hall. I stood there and felt the energy swirl around me. If this was 'defeat,' what would Gay Freedom Day be like?" Bressan began to "cinematize" the approaching spectacle in his mind, and gradually the idea emerged of forming units of six cities (ultimately, San Francisco, San Diego, New York, Chicago, Houston, and Los Angeles) and using the parades as metaphors for an emerging gay consciousness in America.

The material Bressan eventually received, though varying in quality, was largely overwhelming. The San Francisco parade, made up of almost 250,000 participants from many parts of California and the United States, was captured in its diverse splendor by eight camera crews at varying distances from the swirling tide of humanity, with sync interviews filmed against the constant flow of marchers and observers. However, by cutting from San Francisco to New York to Los Angeles to Chicago and back, the film gives the impression of a united, growing struggle against conformity, bigotry, and oppression from coast to coast. Before discussing the structure of *Gay U.S.A.*, however, it is important to assess the nature of the materials of which it is constructed.

In *Word Is Out*, one has the impression of distinct, unrelated, reflective, private experiences being expressed; in *Gay U.S.A.*, one is confronted with persons caught up in the communal excitement of the "politics of celebration," in which spontaneous feelings and attitudes are highly charged. Certainly, *Gay U.S.A.* is the first film ever to fully capture the intense anger, joy, and love embodied in these very public expressions of freedom. In addition to the sync interviews, Bressan amplifies the 1977 material with historical footage of the first Christopher Street Parade in New York in 1970 and of subsequent parades in Los Angeles and San Francisco leading up to the present; slides, still blow-ups, and "found" footage of civil rights marches and Nazi parades are also interpolated in the film's elaborately edited finale.

Before making a total commitment to film, Bressan lectured on history, philosophy, and American civilization in New York, and his avowed primary cinematic models, Frank Capra and Sergei Eisenstein, reveal his strong personal political stance. His admiration of Capra's social criticism, the individual confronting the political establishment, is tempered by a collective spectrum of values. "Politics is a dangerous game for a filmmaker," says Bressan. "It's double jeopardy when it's a low-budget film. You can't afford second thoughts. And political winds are always changing. I was lucky. I got solid political advice from people in the Bay Area—and long distance help from Houston, Chicago, New York, and Boston. The rest I trusted to good intent and the margin for error audiences allow when they're feeling kind." In *Gay U.S.A.*, Bressan orchestrates a richly diverse spectrum of faces, opinions, and lifestyles: lesbian lovers, sympathetic straight families, drag queens, gay professionals, children and youths, gay women, ex-prisoners, dykes on bikes, blacks, school teachers, Asiatics, anti-gay dissenters, and critics of every social, economic, political, and religious persuasion.

From Eisenstein Bressan has evolved a system of montage that is composed of dialectical oppositions in both sound and image. The lengthy pretitle sequence begins with a series of black-and-white stills of the San Francisco March underscored by a series of voice-overs. A New Yorker: "I think it's at least double what it's been in the past. As we expected, there's new militancy in the gay movement and it's here today." A black male: "I'm not prejudiced or anything like that, but when they come in the street and mess with normal people . . ." An elderly Jewish male: "I'm surprised to see so many women in the parade . . . there must be an awful lot we don't know about." A Puerto Rican male: "I have two beautiful children, both boys—seven and nine years old. If they grow up to be gay I'll love them as much as I love them now." A deep-voiced Southern male: "I think they're *nuts*," followed by what sounds like a shrewish Brooklyn housewife, "We understand they have a problem. We want them to be cured, we don't want them to go on living in sin." A proponent for repealing laws against gays is juxtaposed with an anti-abortionist who supports Anita Bryant and flatly admits, "I'm not for gay rights." A young male gay Catholic: "The reason we're staying in the church is to protest its policies against gay people," followed by a fundamentalist who claims, "Homosexuality is condemned by Christ in the Bible as an unnatural way of living." This negative pseudoreligious/pseudoscientific diatribe, which introduces the film's first actual synchronized interview, is counterbalanced visually with individual and collective images of happy, smiling faces united in a common struggle that belies the thrust of the opposition. Positive gestures and statements from gays and friendly nongays give the work a spirited tone of debate that reveals much spontaneity and healthy thinking in this tribal gathering.

Image and sound continue to combine moments of frivolity and seriousness, one of the features of these large demonstrations which Bressan uses to great effect. A quip by a Florida gay about California orange juice is, for instance, set against a unisex figure covered in funeral black holding a prominent cardboard sign: "I am the homosexual you are afraid to see." One is constantly aware of the mixture of humor, sometimes of a bizarre, extravagant nature, with a truly painful, sometimes tearful struggle in the face of a hostile environment, which gives us a unique insight into the dimensions of human courage combating ignorance and superstition. The pretitle sequence ends with a brief statement by two tiny boys, about nine or ten. The older places his arm around the other and says, "I can probably speak for all the kids in the United States—and my brother even. We all believe in equal rights for kids . . . I think that should be made into a law too."

With the brightly punctuated titles we realize that we have been witnessing a preparatory overture and that the parades are beginning. The "Dykes on Bikes" lead off the procession down San Francisco's Market Street, followed by thousands of women sporting banners: "We are your teachers," "Gay, Alive and Healthy," and "Remember the Witch Hunts," against a strong ballad, "Reflections" by Marjie Orten, on the track. Breaking into the procession is the second long sync interview, with two lesbians from northwest Kansas, one of whom was married for $15\frac{1}{2}$ years before coming out in the army reserves in Alabama. She tells of losing jobs because of being gay and finally, out of desperation, leaving for the coast with her lover.

The pace picks up its rhythmic momentum, however, with a three-part "Are You Gay?" sequence, beginning with an aerial view that yields to a handheld tracking camera cutting from response to response, from yeas to nays, from "I don't think I can classify myself" to "That's none of your business." The flow of responses is an introduction to the next sustained interview, shot against the constant movement and sound of the parade. Its subject is a handsome businessman, dressed in a three-piece suit, sixty years old but looking easily twenty years younger, who talks about coming to San Francisco after World War II. He speaks positively about the parade as a "show of individualism and people power that we saw in other minority movements back in the fifties and sixties." His interview continues as a voice-over, a springboard for a visual recap of the history of Gay Liberation and its public manifestations. As he remarks that "parades have changed over the years as gay consciousness has changed," we see black-and-white footage of the boarded-up Stonewall Bar and demonstrators preparing for the first Gay Pride March in June 1970, intercut with views of the first march on Hollywood Boulevard—indicating the celebratory quality of "coming out" that such events began to signify. As the sequence gains momentum, verses of James O'Connor's upbeat ballad "Great Expectations" are interwoven with further interviews, climaxing in the intercutting of a 1972 view of the San Francisco march—thirty stories above the City Hall plaza—with an identical composition from 1977; a movement grows from about two thousand people to approximately one hundred thousand.

As the crowds pass by, one observer says, "This parade is bigger than any one reaction," a statement that accurately describes the kaleidoscopic vision imparted by *Gay U.S.A.* Following positive and moving images of men and women affectionately gathering in Central Park, a debate is heard between a constitutionalist and several Fundamentalist Christians. The former argues that churches have always backed repression: war, witch burning, the Crusades, and the Spanish Inquisition, while the Fundamentalist blandly asserts that the Bible says sex, aside from procreation, is "degrading, decadent, weakening, childish" and, astonishingly enough, that "man was not intended to enjoy his senses"! But his opponent argues for a separation of church and state.

"It's right there in the Constitution—freedom of religion. And you can't have freedom of religion if you have religion in the law."

Although the tone of Bressan's film is primarily positive, the inclusion of dissenting opinions offers the viewer a climate of dialectic in which prejudices may be questioned. Even in a city that traditionally is "open" for gays to pursue a free and equal life in diverse ways, there still are elements of intimidation and violence. Just days prior to the 1977 San Francisco march, Robert Hillsborough, a handsome young man, was brutally stabbed on the streets by a trio of youths. Bressan has dedicated *Gay U.S.A.* to him and closes the film with a spontaneous floral remembrance on the steps of City Hall seen from an aerial view. Several young men recount experiences of being called "fag" by black men on the streets. But the anger that emerges is channeled back into creative impulses in Pat Parker's unforgettable recitation of her poem "For the straight folks who don't mind gays but wish they weren't so blatant," which should give many self-righteous heterosexuals plenty of food for thought.

Bressan's feeling for ideological and aesthetic contrast extends to differences within the gay community itself. The notion of drag is viewed with disfavor by a woman who sees it as degrading to women, "I don't pretend to understand what motivates the men to do that but I know that the whole society mocks women at the same time that it pushes them into that role"—meaning the stereotype of femininity. Her interview is intercut with the positive view of an intelligent, bearded youth in a sequined drag costume. He contends that "drag is just the tool that you use to express who you are in terms of clothes." He personally finds a political sentiment in wearing women's clothing, which makes him feel like a whole rather than a half-person. Again the interview becomes a voice-over that leads to the film's most complex constellation of ideas and imagery. A parade float featuring blow-ups of the faces of Stalin, Hitler, Anita Bryant, a Ku Klux Klan member, and Idi Amin is intercut with Nuremberg rally footage from Leni Riefenstahl's *Triumph of the Will*, as the young man notes that "in fascist societies, people are taught to dress alike, to act alike, to perform alike, as opposed to following their inner needs. When you look at mass demonstrations in totalitarian societies, I mean where you see as many people as there are here, you don't get a sense that these are real people . . . I mean you see herds of sheep." Bressan's brilliant juxtapositions clearly demonstrate the lack of individuality that his subject sees as the basis of stereotyping in racism and sexism, and precisely how this is refuted by the diversity of the gay marchers. Suddenly another voice informs us of the history of "The Pink Triangle," a mark used by the Nazis to designate homosexuals, who died by the thousands in the concentration camps—with a visual evocation of the past, dissolving into the present and back to a historical truth.

This chilling reminder of past persecution shifts quite naturally into a positive, major key with the "Gays in History" sequence, in which an interviewer asks various persons, "If you could invite one gay person from any period in history, who would you like to see here today?" The answers are interesting: Alexander the Great, Sappho, and Diana the Huntress, Jesus Christ, Herman Melville, André Gide, and Bessie Smith. Countless other names are cited as the parade floats by with pride and dignity.

Word Is Out and *Gay U.S.A.* are unique documents in the history of cinema because they represent, for the first time, a truly open response to the world of a vast and extremely divergent human minority that is now on the move to secure its human rights and full participation on an equal basis with the heterosexual majority. Each film speaks with a voice long denied the access to the media which has been granted other minorities, and one which will no longer remain silent in the face of bigotry and oppression.

Ironically, although these films are largely intended to educate nongays about the realities of gay existence, they have so far been seen chiefly by predominantly gay audiences in metropolitan areas. While *Word Is Out* is greeted with a calm, reflective response, *Gay U.S.A.* tends to generate a spirited air of celebration and an emotional "high" that can be felt by any viewer sensitive and open to feelings. There is no question that these films, if seen by large numbers of people, could prove to be highly effective tools for social change, for a revolutionary transformation of consciousness and an acceptance of sexual, as well as religious and political, differences that might lead to a true "liberty and justice for all." Meanwhile, the struggle to be heard continues; those of us who refuse to listen may be seen as part of the problem, and those who elect to listen with patience and openness may prove to be part of the solution.

16

Building a Mock-Documentary Schema

Jane Roscoe and Craig Hight

Here we will outline the framework which we use to differentiate mock-documentary texts from each other. Our approach essentially involves identifying three main 'degrees' of 'mock-docness' within the texts we have analysed, degrees which are derived especially from the type of relationship which a text constructs with factual discourse. Before outlining our mock-documentary schema, we need to mention a number of qualifications for the interpretative framework which we propose.

Firstly, it needs to be stressed that the model outlined below is not intended to provide comprehensive or fixed categories. The degrees which we propose cannot be considered ideal or 'pure' forms, but are instead suggestive of groupings of textual tendencies. The mock-documentary form is a complex one, incorporating as it does a variety of filmmakers' intentions and range of appropriations of documentary aesthetics, and encouraging layered interpretations from audiences. Our aim here is especially to promote discussion on mock-documentaries which acknowledges the evident complexity of the form, and especially the degree of *reflexivity* which these texts construct towards the documentary genre.

Secondly, our approach draws upon the range of audience research traditions which have emerged particularly from the post-structuralist developments within sociological theory.[1] The essential common insight within post-structuralist approaches is that the meanings associated with any text are assumed to be generated through interaction with an audience (Philo, 1990; Ang, 1991, 1996; Fiske, 1992; Jancovich, 1992; Morley, 1992).

This is an insight which is also increasingly accepted within the established audience research traditions which have tended to dominate this form of qualitative research. Jensen and Rosengren (1990) provide a summary of five such traditions and they conclude that there is an increasingly complex theoretical basis to each of these traditions, and within audience research in general. In particular, audience members are increasingly assumed to play an active and selective role in the use and interpretation of mass-media messages. What has developed within these various audience research paradigms to date is a continuum of models of reception operating between two poles; those that assume viewers' readings from textual analysis, and those that dissolve the text itself into a potentially infinite number of audience re-constructions.

Post-structuralist approaches to audience research typically construct a comprehensive understanding of the significance of a variety of social, political and historical contexts for audience readings of a text. The reading which any viewer makes of a programme or film is 'unstable' in the sense that meaning is never fixed but is constantly being reconstructed (Dahlgren, 1992). Any text still has a degree of determination in the 'fixing' of its meaning, to the extent that the effect of its construction is to work to constrain, or at least shape, the range of possible interpretations which an audience can make. The specific objective of audience research, then, is to explore the variety and nature of such interpretations.

Individuals who make up the audience are understood to be first of all social beings, able to draw upon a number of different social and political knowledges in order to make sense of a text. The social locations (such as those associated with class, ethnicity or gender) of each individual audience member determines the social and cultural contexts within which she/he is immersed. These contexts shape such aspects of social experience as subjectivity, individuality and an individual's membership in social groups, all of which are 'constructed, defined and articulated' through discourse (Wetherell and Potter, 1992: 59). In other words, each of us inevitably (and often largely subconsciously) draws upon a discursive field which serves to shape our interpretations of media texts.

Within this theoretical framework the viewing experience itself is seen primarily as a discursive encounter, one which involves a complex interaction between the narrative constructs of the text, the field of discourses accessed by members of the audience, and the constraints on discourse generated by the immediate viewing context (Philo, 1990; Ang, 1991, 1996; Fiske, 1992; Jancovich, 1992; Morley, 1992). It is important to note that these are not one-way relationships; each individual is involved in fluid, complex, dynamic and dialectical relationships with both immediate and wider social-political contexts (Fiske, 1989; Ang, 1989, 1991; Hoijer, 1990; Dahlgren, 1992; Roscoe et al., 1995). In this sense, audience interpretations are inherently fluid and unstable; they are not fixed but are part of a constant process of mediation (Dahlgren, 1992: 206). The ways in which individuals discuss and understand a media text not only change over time, but are shaped by a myriad of factors such as immediate social relationships and physical surroundings. Within any such context, each individual's social experiences (especially those based on differences in such socio-demographic factors as gender, age, class and ethnicity) provide for rich and varied discursive resources which have the potential to shape the nature of social interactions.

A more complex understanding of any viewer's interpretation would need to consider the specific circumstances in which an individual or group response to a text is formed; that is, the specific historical and socio-political contexts which framed that particular audience's encounter with a given text. Ideally, this would incorporate a detailed assessment of the role played by factors such as the medium through which the text is accessed by an audience (whether it is seen as a broadcast, fractured by advertising, on video and so on), and the variety of social factors which come into play in any given viewing environment (such as whether a viewer is alone or part of a group, the level of conversation among viewers, or any other types of distractions).

Within this general understanding of the heavily contextualised and discursive nature of spectatorship, Roscoe et al.'s simplified schema of ways of conceiving of viewers' interpretations of media messages becomes a useful interpretative tool (Roscoe et al., 1995). These writers suggest that within audience research there are three common constructions of viewers' responses to media texts: 'social', 'active' and 'critical'. The term 'social' draws upon the ideas regarding the place of the individual within various discursive systems discussed above,[2] while the term 'active' refers to the ways a viewer's reading of a text involves him/her drawing upon, and actively engaging with, pre-existing frames of reference in order to produce 'meaningful inter-pretations'. Viewers, then, are assumed to be involved in a continual process of negotiation with the text, either accepting, contesting or critiquing the information it offers. Viewers may also be 'reflexive', in the sense that they are capable of drawing upon wider social, political and/or economic debates associated with any given event or issue, in making sense of a text.

Within this general theoretical model, audience research itself emerges as a social and discursive practice, one in which the researcher brings his/her own conceptual frameworks to the task of re-constructing audience inter-pretations of media texts (Ang, 1996). As Ang has correctly observed, there is no objective, scientific knowledge which can be gained from the study of the reception of cultural texts (Ang, 1989: 105)—the 'social world of actual audi-ences' is too complex and fluid a field of practices and experiences to be incor-porated into any discourse on reception (Ang, 1991: 155). At the same time, as Fiske has noted, such analysis should not incorporate the assumption that notions of 'text' and 'audience' have no practical relevance, that only the process of viewing itself is worthy of study (Fiske, 1989: 57).

These broad assumptions concerning the nature of the engagement which audiences make with any text shape the nature of the schema used here to dif-ferentiate between various mock-documentary texts. We argue that an inte-gral part of the 'mock-docness' of a text is the extent to which it encourages audiences to acknowledge the reflexivity inherent to any appropriation of the documentary form. Much depends on the ability of viewers to recognise, acknowledge and appreciate the *fictional* nature of mock-documentary texts, and the typically parodic nature of the appropriation of factual codes and conventions. A text may be explicitly reflexive for a particular audience, but not engage other viewers in this manner. Consequently, it needs to be emphasised that our degrees are fluid groupings. They are not mutually exclusive; individual texts may activate different degrees of reflexivity with different audiences, and individual viewers may engage in a variety of interpretations while viewing mock-documentaries. *Forgotten Silver* (1955) is an obvious example known to the authors which seemed to encourage a number of readings amongst New Zealand audiences during its initial broadcast on New Zealand television.

The framework of analysis which we develop here is not intended to suggest the full extent of interpretations which any audience may make of mock-documentaries. Our analysis is indicative of the variety of relationships which the appropriation of documentary aesthetics entails, and particularly those strategies of appropriation pursued by mock-documentary filmmakers. In other words, we are dealing, both here and in the following chapters, with the writers' assessment of the *preferred reading* of such texts. As stated previously, our intention with this study is to provide an overview of the mock-documentary form, one which could ideally be subsequently explored by audience researchers.

We suggest an initial schema of three degrees, a model which approaches mock-documentaries according to the intersection between the intention of the filmmakers, the nature and degree of the text's appropriation of documentary codes and conventions, and the degree of reflexivity consequently encouraged for their audience.

Degree 1: Parody

This degree includes those fictional texts which involve what could be termed the 'benevolent' (or not deliberately reflexive) use of documentary codes and conventions. Generally, these texts feature the consistent and sustained appropriation of documentary codes and conventions in the creation of a fictional milieu. The intention of these texts is generally to parody some aspect of popular culture. These are fictional texts which both make obvious their functionality (the audience is expected to appreciate the text's comic elements) and are comparatively muted in their challenge to the nature of the documentary project itself. While the appropriation of documentary codes and conventions by these fictional texts is *inherently* reflexive, this is not an issue which the filmmakers themselves explicitly explore.

Here documentary aesthetics are appropriated largely for stylistic reasons. These tend to be texts where humour is emphasised by having a rational or deadpan approach to examining and investigating openly fictional figures and events. The Classic Objective Argument—that is, the generic form which collectively relies upon expositional, interactive and observational modes of documentary representation[3]—is constructed largely as a prop, a cultural reference point of sobriety and rationality. The humour in these texts, then, comes in part from the contrast between the rational and irrational, between a sober form and an absurd or comic subject.

It is a significant tendency within this degree for texts to offer a conservative perspective on aspects of culture, in the sense that the ultimate intention and effect of these 'documentary' examinations of a subject are often their ultimate reinforcement as cultural reference points. One key aspect of parody is that it often comments upon cultural forms which are 'easy targets'; their cultural currency is typically exhausted and they are ripe for mocking. The mock-documentary texts which we group in degree 1, however, tend not to carry their parodic intent through to a detailed and explicit critique of their subject. Instead, many of this group of mock-documentaries adopt a strong frame of nostalgia in their presentation of fictional representatives of an era or cultural idiom—such as the love of Beatles mythology which underlies *The Rutles* (1978), the sense of loss of the 'innocent' America of the 1920s which frames *Zelig* (1983) and the appeal to cultural myths which made *Forgotten Silver* popular with its New Zealand audience.

Perhaps unsurprisingly, it is the fictional subjects of texts within this degree which are most often celebrated by audiences. Some viewers of key mock-documentaries such as *The Rutles* and *This Is Spinal Tap* (1984) have adopted their musical subjects in virtually the same way they would an actual musical group—both of these 'bands' have released albums, both have their own official internet websites and Spinal Tap have even conducted an (unconventional) rock tour in America. And the actor who played the political candidate who is the subject of *Man with a Plan* (1996) has developed a political career, of sorts, based on his character's appeal. These are aspects of the extra-textual impact of these texts which open up the interesting issue of the deliberate confusion of their ontological status by audiences.

While documentary proper typically involves a 'call to action'—an implicit demand for some form of social or political response to the knowledges which the form reveals—these mock-documentaries construct a more varied and complex relationship with their audience. In some sense, these fictional constructs have developed a 'real' existence—not because they are convincing as simulations of reality, but precisely because viewers appreciate the commentary they carry on actual cultural figures. Here audiences are able to actively aid in the obscuring of the fictional nature of their subjects, although not to the extent that they explicitly engage with mock-documentary's inherent reflexivity towards factual discourse.

The Return of Spinal Tap (1993), for example, is a sequel which features the concert revival of a fictional band. The film portrays the real performance of a fictional band, a contradiction which perfectly illustrates the complexities of interpretation typically demanded of the mock-documentary form. The audience, both within and outside the text, are encouraged to enjoy this contradiction, as part of a parodic stance toward cultural practices of which both they and the band are part. The result is that these audiences participate in a commentary on their own status as consumers of popular culture. As suggested above, however, this and other examples of degree 1 mock-documentary do not look to extend this reflexive interpretation into an open deconstruction of factual discourse itself.

Degree 2: Critique

Like degree 1 texts, degree 2 mock-documentaries feature some degree of acceptance of the assumptions and expectations of factual discourse—or at the very least a recognition of the cultural status of the codes and conventions associated with factual discourse. However, this group of texts also includes those instances of mock-documentaries where the appropriation of documentary aesthetics could be termed 'ambivalent'. Here the Classic Objective Argument provides a familiar legalistic or investigative stance that the text adopts in order to offer a parodic critique of those aspects of popular culture which a character and/or event is seen to represent . . .

These texts' appropriation of the documentary form is termed 'ambivalent' because they generally also incorporate a partial or muted critique of media practices themselves (and especially documentary as a mode of inquiry, investigation and examination). In other words, the manner in which media representations are themselves constructed also typically forms part of the subject matter of degree 2 mock-documentaries. A consequent intention of these mock-documentaries is to open more space for an audience to recognise the problematic nature of any appropriation of documentary codes and conventions. In this sense, these are mock-documentaries distinguished from degree 1 texts in that, to varying degrees, they begin to engage more explicitly with the mock-documentary form's latent reflexivity towards factual codes and conventions. While the intention is not to engage the audience in a thorough critique of the documentary form, to some extent the practices of the factual media become the subject of the text even if this is often only implicitly expressed.

For example, the 1997 series premiere episode of *ER* contains a critique of what could be termed one of the 'bastardised' form of the genre: reality TV shows, and their assumed failure to adhere to the ethical standards of documentary texts. However, the series as a whole also characteristically makes extensive use of, and perhaps relies upon, a *cinéma vérité* type of representation, in effect reinforcing these aspects of the observational documentary form.

Another key text we position within this degree is *Bad News Tour* (1983), a half-hour television parody of rockumentaries in a similar vein to *Spinal Tap*. Unlike its predecessor, however, *Bad News Tour* more directly explores the tensions and contradictions inherent to any collaboration between a documentary filmmaker and his/her subject. Much of the humour in this mock-documentary stems from the repeated failures of the heavy metal band ('Bad News') to collaborate with their documentary crew in the construction of an appropriate rock myth. Here the tension between the band and crew effectively undermines the pretence that a documentary filmmaker necessarily adopts a neutral and non-interventionist stance toward his/her subject.

A second textual concern we have identified within degree 2 are mock-documentary texts which deal explicitly with a *political subject*. Here we assume that there is a political aspect to documentary aesthetics; that the rational, objective ideology articulated by factual discourse itself is associated with the social-political status quo. In other words, the effort to remain 'balanced', 'objective' and 'fair' inevitably involves an acceptance of a particular vision of society, one which implicitly tends to support existing institutions and political interests. This is an adopted political stance which underpins the supposedly 'apolitical' nature of journalistic practice (Ericson et al., 1987, 1991). It is also a stance which forms a significant part of the ideology which links documentary to notions of citizenship and public service objectives.

One potential effect of the appropriation of the codes and conventions of factual discourse is an (even if partial) subversion of this political agenda. The mock-documentaries which we group within this tendency of degree 2 are those which begin to engage with this underlying documentary agenda; these are mock-documentaries which develop the *satiric* possibilities of the form in order to critique an aspect of popular culture.

A key text within degree 2 mock-documentaries is *Bob Roberts* (1992), where both an ambivalence toward factual discourse and a rare satiric intent are combined. This film uses the documentary form to comment specifically upon modern political processes, especially the selection of political candidates, within the American system. It is a coherently argued political satire which (like documentary) encourages political action from its audience, rather than operating simply as a self-contained piece of humour. Although this is an example of sustained political commentary in the form of entertainment, it also includes pointed suggestions that any form of representation contains an inherent political agenda. *Bob Roberts* incorporates a satiric commentary on the factual media as an integral part of its critique of a wider political system. As with *ER*, there is a real complexity in the way the text operates towards the documentary genre. A critique of the media and of media personnel is constructed within a text which nonetheless offers an implicit acceptance of fundamental aspects of factual discourse. In *Bob Roberts* the revelation that an assassination can be successfully faked is revealed by a British (BBC-styled) journalist who is able to present convincingly evidence of this deception. However, this demonstration of the investigative possibilities of the documentary approach is directly contrasted with the film's overall pessimism toward the trivial, sensationalist form of journalism provided by the American news media.

Hoaxes

Included within this section on degree 2 texts are those mock-documentaries which deliberately look to create confusion within audiences over their factual status, and especially those which effectively perpetrate a *hoax*. These mock-documentaries, while not necessarily containing messages which are deliberately intended to be reflexive towards factual discourse, still trigger reflexive interpretations among viewers because of the subsequent uncovering of their fictional status. Audiences are initially encouraged, by the text itself and extra-textual events to adopt a factual mode of reading toward the text—the final question of the ontological status of the text is left to the deliberation of viewers.

The key texts discussed here are *Alien Abduction* (1998) and *Forgotten Silver*. Both are television 'documentaries' and represent instances in which broadcast institutions supported their deceptive guise as factual programmes, an aspect disturbing for a significant proportion of their audiences. These texts' reflexive potential, then, derives from the success of their fakery, and in particular from the context created for their reception, including the extra-textual cues deliberately created by filmmakers and broadcasting institutions.

Degree 3: Deconstruction

This group of mock-documentary texts demonstrates what could be termed the 'hostile' appropriation of documentary aesthetics. Their central distinguishing characteristic is that even if they focus on other subjects their real intention is to engage in a sustained critique of the set of assumptions and expectations which support the classic modes of documentary. The documentary project itself, then, is ultimately their true subject. They critique assumptions such as the notion that filmed images have a direct, unmediated relationship with reality, that a documentary text is based upon a specific ethical relationship between the filmmaker and subject, and that the filmmaker

Table 1 Degrees of mock-documentary

	Intentions of the filmmaker	Construction of the text	Role constructed for the audience
Degree 1 Parody	To parody, and implicitly reinforce, an aspect of popular culture	The 'benevolent' or 'innocent' appropriation of documentary aesthetics The Classic Objective Argument accepted as a signifier of rationality and objectivity	Appreciation of the parody of popular culture, and the reinforcement of popular myth Nostalgia for traditional forms of documentary The more critical viewers are able to explore the form's latent reflexivity
Degree 2 Critique	To use the documentary form to engage in a parody or satire of an aspect of popular culture	The ambivalent appropriation of documentary aesthetics A tension between an explicit critique of documentary practices and practitioners and an implicit acceptance of the generic codes and conventions	Appreciation of parody/satire of popular culture Varying degrees of reflexivity toward aspects of the documentary genre
Degree 3 Deconstruction	To critique an aspect of popular culture To examine, subvert and deconstruct factual discourse and its relationship with documentary codes and conventions	The 'hostile' appropriation of documentary aesthetics Documentary as a representative of a mythical and problematic social-political stance toward the social-historical world	Reflexive appreciation of parody or satire of popular culture An openly reflexive stance towards factual discourse and its associated codes and conventions

is capable of adopting an objective, balanced, non-interventionist stance toward his/her subject. Degree 3 texts, then, bring to fruition the latent reflexivity which is inherent to, and which in large part distinguishes, mock-documentaries as a screen form.

David Holzman's Diary (1967) is an early example of a text which directly critiques documentary modes of inquiry in this way. Its apparent story is of a filmmaker seeking to discover himself, but its real subject is the level of expectations associated with the camera and its perceived ability to record 'truths'. The prime example discussed in relation to degree 3 is *Man Bites Dog* (1992), which looks to deconstruct the political-ethical role performed by documentary filmmakers, the censorship and discursive limitations inherent to documentary texts, and the value system constructed by audience expectations of such texts. This text, in other words, seeks to deconstruct the documentary genre at a variety of levels.

To date, most mock-documentaries can be grouped in degrees 1 and 2—the potential subversion of documentary inherent to all mock-documentaries but most explicit in degree 3 texts seems to be a less commonly engaged concern of filmmakers than an effort to use the form for the purposes of various forms of parody, satire and critique. The open attack on the ethical and political stance adopted by documentarists seen in *Man Bites Dog* is still comparatively rare. However, we would argue that even openly parodic examples of the form are becoming sophisticated enough to generate an increasingly subtle form of subversion of factual discourse.

Our schema outlines a variety of wider trends which characterise the growth of the mock-documentary form (within the texts which we have studied). There is an increasing complexity in the appropriation of documentary codes and conventions within the mock-documentary form. These texts' appropriation of documentary form are, in a sense, becoming more convincing, derived from both an explosion of technical possibilities for the manipulation of images and from an increased range of approaches adopted by mock-documentary filmmakers.

In some sense, our schema of degree 1, 2 and 3 mock-documentary texts also looks to chart the increasing maturity of mock-documentary as a distinctive screen form. Filmmakers are exploring a wider range of subjects and agendas using this form, incorporating various levels of parody, political intent and reflexivity towards the documentary genre itself—often within the same text. In other words, mock-documentary texts can seek to engage all three degrees, to activate a complex range of interpretations from audiences. In part, this has meant a developing tendency to place upon the viewer the task of determining which aspects of the texts are fictional. Some of these texts, despite incorporating clues to their fictionality, apparently confuse and even convince audience of their status as non-fiction documents. The development of the mock-documentary form has arguably been both symptom and cause in the construction of an increasingly reflexive position, for the viewer, in relation to factual discourse.

Notes

1　A useful summary of the origins of the post-structuralist challenge to sociology can be found in Seidman (1994).
2　This involves the assumption that each individual brings a variety of knowledges and experiences to his/her interpretation of a text, which derive from his/her membership in various social groups. The term also implies that the process of interpretation is 'social' in the narrower sense that it is framed by the immediate social context of viewing.
3　See Nichols (1991).

References

Ang, Ien (1989) 'Wanted: Audiences: On the Politics of Empirical Audience Studies', in E. Seiter, H. Borchers, G. Kreutzner and E. Warth (eds), *Remote Control: Television, Audiences, and Cultural Power*, Routledge, London.

Ang, Ien (1991) *Desperately Seeking the Audience*, Routledge, London.

Ang, Ien (1996) *Living Room Wars: Rethinking Media Audiences for a Postmodern World*, Routledge, London.

Dahlgren, P. (1992) 'What's the Meaning of This? Viewers' Plural Sense-Making of TV News', in P. Scannell, P. Schlesinger and C. Sparks (eds), *Culture and Power: A Media, Culture and Society Reader*, Sage Publications, London.

Ericson, R. V., P. M. Baranek and J. B. L. Chan (1987) *Visualising Deviance: A Study of News Organisation*, Open University Press, Milton Keynes.

Ericson, R. V., P. M. Baranek and J. B. L. Chan (1991) *Representing Order: Crime, Law and Justice in the News Media*, Open University Press, Milton Keynes.

Fiske, J. (1989) 'Moments of Television: Neither the Text nor the Audience', in E. Seiter, H. Borchers, G. Kreutzner and E. Warth (eds), *Remote Control: Television, Audiences, and Cultural Power*, Routledge, London.

Fiske, J. (1992) 'British Cultural Studies and Television', in R. C. Allen (ed.), *Channels of Discourse, Reassembled: Television and Contemporary Criticism*, 2nd edition, The University of North Carolina Press, Chapel Hill.

Hoijer, B. (1990) 'Studying Viewers' Reception of Television Programmes: Theoretical and Methodological Considerations', *European Journal of Communication* 5, no. 1.

Jancovich, M. (1992) 'David Morley, The *Nationwide* Studies', in M. Barker and A. Beezer (eds), *Reading into Cultural Studies*, Routledge, London.

Jensen, K. B. and K. E. Rosengren (1990) 'Five Traditions in Search of the Audience', *European Journal of Communication* 5, nos. 2–3.

Morley, D. (1992) *Television, Audiences and Cultural Studies*, Routledge, London.

Nichols, Bill (1991) *Representing Reality: Issues and Concepts in Documentary*, Indiana University Press, Bloomington.

Philo, Greg (1990) *Seeing and Believing: The Influence of Television*, Routledge, London.

Roscoe, J., H. Marshall and K. Gleeson (1995) 'The Television Audience: A Reconsideration of the "Taken-for-granted" Terms "active", "social" and "critical", *European Journal of Communication* 10, no. 1, 87–108.

Seidman, Steven (1994) *Contested Knowledge: Social Theory in the Postmodern Era*, Blackwell, Oxford.

Wetherell, M. and J. Potter (1992) *Mapping the Language of Racism: Discourse and the Legitimation of Exploitation*, Harvester Wheatsheaf, London.

17

Sounds Real: Music and Documentary

John Corner

Within the aural profile of television, music plays varying roles and functions, quite apart from its vital job in signalling programme identity through signature title music. These functions include generating *thematic* support for what is on the screen—indications of historical time, of geographical place and of appropriate mood being prominent—and providing *formal* support for programme organisation, pacing and the shifting 'intensities' of portrayal. In all these modes of application, the way in which rhythm, tempo, harmony, melody etc. feed into contextual, associative patterns of cultural meaning will be a matter for careful production judgement, however 'intuitively' exercised. Clearly, a challenge is posed for analysis in tracing the specific dynamics of this process across its diverse formal and contextual factors (Tagg 1987 poses the terms of this challenge most suggestively from within a semiotic perspective).

In this article, I want to concern myself largely with the varied function of music within documentary programming. How does music figure within television's documentary aesthetic and, as the whole area of factual programming undergoes shifts of form and function, in what ways might the mode of its employment change? Given the lack of writing on this topic to date, an exploratory and provisional approach seems appropriate.

Music and the Documentary Aesthetic

In assessing the use made of music in documentary production we have to recognise from the outset documentary's widely varying profile and emphases. It is a genre of inquiry and argument, of observation and illustration and, particularly in the last few years, of diversion and amusement. Within British television, a strong journalistic dimension to documentary emerged quite rapidly in the early 1950s, as the medium became a primary source of national news and public knowledge. This contrasted sharply with the promotional and propagandistic uses to which cinematic documentary was often put during the 1930s and 1940s.[1] It is perhaps not surprising that the more the representational scheme of a documentary is framed by rationalistic imperatives and concern about 'balance', the more music is likely to seem extraneous if not wholly suspect, an importer of unwelcome emotion and feeling. But the history of documentary's musical relations is not simply a matter of its proximity to the journalistic. For perhaps the biggest broad movement in international documentary since the 1950s has been that influenced by the '*vérité*' and 'direct cinema' traditions of sustained observational film-making. These have often embraced a degree of depictive purism that places question marks alongside anything likely to adulterate a direct relaying of the primary events, circumstances and interactions before the camera.

Taken together, then, what we might call *journalistic rationalism* and *observational minimalism* have acted to keep many producers (and quite possibly sizeable sections of the audience) concerned about the risk of a musical ingredient somehow subverting programme integrity. There has been work outside of these protocols of course, including various kinds of expansive, more freely expressive reportage and dramatised productions. In these productions, music has continued to be important.

It might be worth noting here the basic differences between musical accompaniment to fictional narratives, on the one hand, and to documentary-style programmes on the other. These have to be treated as indicative rather than definitive, and they collapse altogether in the case of drama-documentary productions, but recognition of them is analytically useful. Musical soundtrack in scenes of acted narrative and dramatised setting, perhaps underneath dialogue, guides us in our imaginative response to a fictional world, a world that it is the rhetorical project of the film or programme to encourage us to be drawn within. The music works to position us in terms of this diegetic containment. However, documentary's images, interviews and commentaries work largely within the terms of display and exposition. Our involvement here is different from the way in which we are spectators to a 'visible fiction'. We may be the addressees of direct, spoken address, images may be offered to us as an illustration of explicit propositions, we may be cued to watch sequences as witnesses to the implicit revelation of more general truths. In this context, musical relations are likely to become more self-conscious, and less intimate, than when watching fiction.

Some indication of how the use of music is viewed from within the perspectives of documentary production can be got from the latest edition of what is undoubtedly the most widely-used production manual. This is Michael Rabiger's *Directing the Documentary* (Rabiger 1998). In his bullet point notes on post-production, Rabiger comments as follows:

- Music should not inject false emotion.
- Choice of music should give access to the inner life of a character or the subject.
- Music can signal the emotional level at which the audience should investigate what is being shown.

(Rabiger 1998, p. 310)

What we see here, I think, is clearly both a sense of risk and of possibility. Music is regarded as primarily emotional in its effects, either by way of signalling appropriate levels of emotion or, more indirectly, by providing support for an interiority which cannot itself be visualised or perhaps even spoken ('inner life'). There are some awkward questions raised by this, certainly. How are we to judge the 'falseness' of an emotion and by what independent means will the conditions of 'inner life' be available to producers so that they may be secure in indicating it musically? But questions of documentary integrity are notoriously difficult to resolve cleanly by sole resort to evidence lying outside of individual creative judgement. In the light of what I shall say below, it seems to me particularly appropriate that the third rubric uses 'investigate' rather than simply 'respond to'. An invitation to some kind of participatory dynamic, not a conditioned reflex, appears to be part of the plan, at least in this account.

In pursuing my brief exploration into music and the documentary aesthetic I shall draw on a number of examples, some of them recent. However, I want to start with a consideration of how music figures in one of the classics of the British documentary tradition—Humphrey Jennings' 1941 film *Listen to Britain* (Crown Films). Although it is an example drawn from documentary cinema, it seems to me that some aspects of the way this film works have a very useful bearing both on practice and on potential in television.

Listen to Britain and the Arts of Looking

The film that finally became *Listen to Britain* started out on the drawing-board as a film about music and the military, potentially organised around the idea of marching tunes. The final version, a film offering different sights and sounds of wartime work and life in Britain over a twenty-four-hour cycle, departs radically from this initial plan but preserves the emphasis on music (see Vaughan 1983). Throughout its length, the film 'finds' its music from marching bands, dance bands, canteen concerts, orchestral concerts, small groups of singers (fireman, soldiers and children) and different radio programmes. Since these are almost all sourced within the film's visual presentation, they form part of its invitation to 'Listen to Britain'. They are offered as Britain's own sounds, not an added soundtrack, but they are expanded across scenes other than their source scene. Between the music, a range of other sounds is heard too. These are the overheard sounds of work and play, of aeroplanes, of trains, of factories and of fragments of casual conversation in a variety of settings. Perhaps the most radical element of the film is that it completely eschews commentary. It proceeds entirely through its succession of linked images, music and sounds, organised within a subtle and always implicit sense of relationship and development.

What does this emphasis on the hearing of music and sounds but not words mean for the way in which we watch the film, for our experience as viewers? I think the answer here is that it greatly intensifies our engagement with the images. It helps provide the resources for a viewing disposition allowing us to respond fully to the charge of meanings in each composition and actively to read the screen not only in the detail of the shot but in its relationship within an associative sequence. Music saturates the images, informing them by fusing its meanings with their own, and at the same times it bonds the shots together through its own aesthetic continuity. It frees them from the literalism of commentary and underwrites the possibility of delivering surprise and juxtaposition as well as of expected connections. Through listening to Britain, we are enabled properly to *look* at it. For this to work, what we are offered visually must have sufficient resonance and depth to hold active attention without accompanying speech. This is partly a matter of generating a formal interest (through such factors as framing, composition, lighting and movement within the shot). But it is also, in close combination, very much a matter of *what* is shown and the wartime viewer's social and personal relation to the depicted sights and the connoted themes. In Jennings' film, the contemporary audience's ability to connect directly and powerfully with what they saw, as elements of a common present and of shared hopes and anxieties, could be assumed. Clearly, these conditions cannot be met so easily if at all with other kinds of topic, intended audience or viewing situation.

We can also ask some closer questions about the form. What would be the effect were Jennings' images to be shown with actuality sound but either with no music at all or with music only within those shots depicting its source? First of all, I think screening the images unaccompanied would have critically depleted the contemporary audience's experience, reducing its emotional fullness and pushing it too far towards a communicative uncertainty. The codes for watching silent depictions are relatively undeveloped in Western culture. Watching a real event in silence is one thing, the existential fact of *being there*, closing the potential distance between self and circumstance. Moreover, the silence is a motivated part of the watching itself. Watching a silent representation involves a very different relationship. Even watching on television a minute's silence being observed at the start of a football match carries an awkwardness for the viewer which is distinctive to the secondary status of the experience and to the fact that it is the representation, not us, which initiates the silence. There are other, cognate, experiences we might want to consider, for instance a visit to an art gallery or a photo exhibition. Here, however, the silent contemplation of the exhibits is accompanied by purposive movement through the physical space of the gallery; though it may be silent the experience is partly one of motivated behaviour. Once again, the silence essentially belongs to us, not the depiction, from which no sound can be expected. The post-sound technology screen offering its *deliberately* silent images to a static audience poses a challenge to comfortable viewing relationships. It raises questions about the informational yield, aesthetic satisfaction and directed thoughtfulness that the image track can successfully generate within the viewer on its own. Even the silent cinema used inter-titles and, often, live accompaniment as a partial 'solution' to this. Silence presents the possibility of an embarrassing insufficiency of meaningfulness and a more embarrassing uncertainty about whether this insufficiency is essentially in the work or in the viewer. One very basic function of music, then, is to reduce the risk of the attention frame slipping towards *too much* self-consciousness and loss of focus in this way.

In *Listen to Britain*, restricting the music to source-scenes only would clearly be better than the complete loss of musical accompaniment. However, it would occasion a radical loss of continuity and of cumulative force across the film's design, marking a separation of scenes and settings instead of using form to strengthen thematic interconnection. The duration of many scenes, wonderfully constructed as they are, would be seen to out-run their perceived interest even by an audience for whom they were thick with wartime significance.

Of course, *Listen to Britain* is not the only film of the British Documentary Movement to use music imaginatively. Other classic works such as *Coalface* (GPO Films, 1935) were in many ways more inventive in this respect, using special compositions to work, often dialectically, with the images (see the discussion in Corner 1996). However, they also used a commentary too, thus stabilising their audio-visual aesthetic around the words of an information flow directly addressed to the viewer. In *Coalface*, Benjamin Britten's score is used to suggest machine noises related to the visual portrayal and to fit in with, and further emphasise, the speech rhythms of the commentary. This is in addition to performing the more conventional functions of enhancing the viewing experience—signalling shifts of mood and giving a strengthened continuity and development. Its percussive and dissonant modernism would provide a challenging aural input on its own, but in combination with the mechanistic energy of the film's images it forms an integrated experience. Another example combining music, words and mechanical energy would be Harry Watt and Basil Wright's celebrated *Night Mail* (1936). Here, the words of Auden's poem are spoken in a way that further supports the musical idea, without fully becoming song.

Listen to Britain is unusual in the trust it shows in supporting images through music alone and also, in some scenes, in supporting the music through the images. That is why its visual experience is so distinctive. Key scenes here include shots of a canteen full of workers singing along to Flanagan and Allen on stage, of female lathe operators joining in with the rendition of 'Yes, My Darling Daughter' coming over the Tannoy and of a National Portrait Gallery performance of a Mozart piano concerto performed by an RAF orchestra (with, pointedly, Dame Myra Hess as soloist). The latter is played across shots of the Queen and various members of the concert audience (predominantly armed service personnel) as well as across street scenes and panoramas of wartime London. The example of this film, though distinctive to a period both of cinematic and social history, is one that can help us in thinking more creatively as well as more critically about television practice and its continuing possibilities.

'To Document': Subgeneric Variety and Audio-Visual Codes

In looking at how music has been employed across television's documentary output, two axes of documentary type can be useful guides, however approximate they may be and however much the one needs often to be mapped on to the other. First of all, there is the axis running from 'serious' to 'light', an axis regularly subject to changing criteria and one which has been made newly prominent in the schedules by the last decade's developments in 'reality television'. Secondly, there is the axis from 'Art' to 'Record', to use the terms that I have found more generally helpful in thinking about documentary practice. Along this axis can be plotted a number of issues to do with authorship, self-consciousness, stylistic range and what we can call the particular 'reality claim' of the programme (see Winston 1995).

In relation to the first axis, a strong tendency has been for music to be employed more frequently the 'lighter' the topic and/or treatment. As a documentary topic and approach becomes more serious, a matter of issues and problems, of controversy and argument, then there is likely to be a more strategic kind of attention paid to the 'mood cueing' that music brings. There is also likely to be more uncertainty about the *kind* of music that should be used, should it be considered at all. The possibilities offered by classical works are likely to be found in some cases more appropriate than popular forms. Brief passages, perhaps just a phrase, can reinforce a more sombre and contemplative viewing experience but they still need to be used with care and sparingly. Jazz is interestingly placed here. Within British television, scores in the John Dankworth orchestral idiom are used in the late 1950s and 1960s to connote 'the city' and sometimes 'youth'. A typical scene might have bluesy saxophone-led phrases over a shot of a London night scene, borrowing the American connotations for a wider resonance. Yet problems of class are raised by the use of Jazz, since it has never been a popular working-class form in Britain. For a period, Jazz was a preferred music for mapping the indigenous documentary subject within an essentially cosmopolitan, 'noir-ish' view of urbanism and its new restlessness.

In relation to the second axis, that between art and record, the tendency here has been for music to be used more extensively in those programmes which operate confidently within a sense of themselves as artefacts, as authored 'works'. This need not mean a claim to high aesthetic status, it simply indicates a level of self-consciousness about the crafting and styling of the account, the degree of creative and imaginative freedom exercised in its con-struction. Clearly, *Listen to Britain* worked strongly within a version of this mode of documentation, as did many films from the British Documentary Movement.

As well a developing line of 'audio-visual essays' in this broad vein, continu-ing through to current schedules, there are other strands of documentary that have exercised a creative licence as 'art' more freely than mainstream output. Here, biographical documentaries, with their directly personal focus, have drawn extensively on music to establish both tone and circumstance. Drama-tisations of all kinds (including reconstruction 'emergency' series like the BBC's *999*) have often been keen to use it in order to support their attempt at offering some of the narrative development and emotional intensities associ-ated with fiction. Archive series, committed to a grounding in 'record' but also often involved in kinds of imaginative projection, have needed it not only to sustain and to shift mood but also to help fill out a basic communicative profile otherwise depending extensively on silent footage and commentary. For a rather similar reason, wildlife series and the increasing range of popular science and history series, both using lengthy sequences without significant actuality sound, have resorted to it more frequently over the last decade.

Against such exercises in directorial styling and affective address, we can place the modes of reportage and observation noted earlier, where the audi-tory profile is often organised around a less declamatory and affective address to the viewer.

Within the formats of documentary reportage, the news-based protocols of journalism have tended to regard the use of musical soundtracks as an intru-sion in programmes offered essentially as professional reporting and analysis. This is so both at the level of form (a well-organised report does not need any extra dynamics) and of theme (what to feel should be a matter of individual viewer reaction to what is shown and said). In the latter case, a risk of manipu-lation, and perhaps a breach of impartiality requirements, has also been perceived. This is particularly so in those sequences of a programme where interview testimony and/or visual evidence is being placed within a framework for assessment on a matter of established controversy. At points like these, the journalistic function is at its most accountable, not simply documenting but organising the terms of a conflict of opinion. Both the established professional broadcaster codes as well as institutional protocols and (in some cases) national legislation are at issue here.

An example can be taken from a study I carried out with colleagues on British television and video accounts of the debate about nuclear energy in the late 1980s (Corner et al. 1990). One of the programmes we looked at, the last episode in a series of three BBC programmes entitled *Taming the Dragon* (BBC2, 1987) examined the safety record of the British nuclear industry in the wake of the Chernobyl disaster. In exploring this record through voiced-over film and interview, it made extensive use of an eerie, slow, electronic soundtrack,[2] connecting the account to recent fictional portrayals of nuclear mishap, including the BBC thriller series *Edge of Darkness*, screened to popular success in the previous year. There is little doubt from the viewing analysis we undertook that this music made a significant contribution to the sense of threat carried in parts of the programme. However, the programme's ostensible journalistic purpose, carried in the commentary and interview structure, was precisely to explore the existence and level of this threat. The addition of such a soundtrack can be seen as working to reinforce a conclusion about nuclear risk that the journalistic discourse was still only entertaining as one interpretation among others. Not surprisingly, in the nuclear industry (and amongst a few of our researched respondents) there was some dissatisfaction expressed with this kind of premature 'closure' of judgement, especially when achieved in such an indirect, affective manner. No discussion of audio-visual practices in public information could fail to recognise the real problems posed by cases like this. Whatever the degree of musical inhibition introduced into television documentary practice by journalism across its very wide range of descriptive work, in its core 'forum' functions, as a means of reporting and assessing public dispute, the issue of covert judgement will require continued care.

Within the very different framework of observational filming, there has been a commitment, not to informational impartiality, but to the delivery of a raw viewing experience—the witnessing of ongoing action and overheard speech in the most direct of modes. Here, the apparent spontaneity and naturalism of the approach, the very artlessness of its rhetoric, has worked against the employment of musical soundtrack. The inhibitions here have not been grounded in ideas of propriety or legal requirement, like those of journalism. They have been seen as an essential part of successful recipes for generating and sustaining the effect of 'directness'. It is significant, for instance, that even *Big Brother* (Endemol Entertainment for Channel 4, 2000 and 2001), the most innovative and successful factual entertainment format of the last few years, preserves its naturalistic address by using music only for title sequences and break points.

Re-imagining Documentary: New Spaces for Music?

I have set out a situation in which the use of music in documentary television has been characterised both by its conventional employment as a supplementary, affective stimulant and, often, by a degree of restraint. The twin television emphases on journalistic integrity and on observational directness (the latter reinforced by the 'raw' effect sought by many recipes for reality programming) have, in different ways, positioned music as a potential intrusion. More imaginative forms of reportage (for instance, those based on travel) have introduced it as a device to point up a theme or underscore an irony but they, too, have often been wary of a bolder use. Most frequently, it has been seen as useful in getting the viewer through 'bridging' sequences, including journeys. Again, the advice in Rabiger is instructive:

> Transitional sequences of any kind can benefit from music, especially if it lifts the film out of a prevailing mood. Music can highlight an emotional change when, for instance, an aspiring football player learns he can join the team, or when someone newly homeless lies down for the first night in a doorway. (Rabiger 1998, p. 286)

As the varieties of audio-visual documentation are further dispersed and hybridised, it would be a pity to see music as *merely* offering a more widely used set of cliches for injecting punctuation, pace and intensity into the viewing experience. With game-shows, gardening, holiday and cookery programmes and a whole range of lifestyle output increasingly trading on varieties of the documentary image, this will undoubtedly be one mode of use. Here, the energies of the music sometimes appear to be compensating for the paucity of visual interest and perhaps even the perceived limitations of the speech. Not surprisingly, a number of low-budget and rapidly-shot location programmes, especially holiday and sports series, contrive to keep things bright and 'strong' in this way. Tagg (1987) comments illuminatingly on the diverse categories of 'catalogue' music designed expressly to be used in such kinds of professional application.

Other possibilities, however, still remain under-explored—possibilities that would allow a more considered connection with visual portrayal. As in *Listen to Britain*, this is music providing us with the time to *look* properly, giving us a framework in which to gaze and to *think*. To refer back to my quotation from Rabiger, it is music as part of 'investigation'. Such an approach goes along with the use of more generous shot lengths and with restraint in voiced-over speech, at least for given segments. It encourages a more adventurous approach to the television image at a point where the technology can do full justice to audio-visual creativity. This is after decades of development that have tended towards visualisations cut back to the demands of speech and of narrative pace. As I suggested earlier, this bolder musico-visual approach is not just another mode of musical subservience, since there is a clear sense in which our experience of the music itself (whether 'borrowed' or specially written) benefits from the combination. And although the music's generated meanings will tend to fuse with those of the image sequence, the very directness of the approach means that we are conscious of listening to music as well as of attending to the screen. Moreover, the aesthetic options extend well past their cliché instances (e.g. rural lyricism, the bustle of the city) and await further, committed innovation.

One notable, recent example is *Wisconsin Death Trip*, a film made for the BBC2 *Arena* series (and transmitted in 2000) but also distributed to independent cinemas (see the website at www.wisconsindeathtrip.com). Working imaginatively from local newspaper records and photo archives that document one year in the nineteenth-century history of the township of Black River Falls in northern Wisconsin, this programme offers a potent combination of data and mood (see Corner, 2005 for a detailed account). A key element in its portrayal of past events, an exploration using archive stills and reconstructed action, is the specially written orchestral score (including work by John Cale). Mixing the rhythms and textures of different American musics, including traditional forms, this provides the essential medium in which the evocative power of the images and commentary works. It opens up the space to look properly and thoughtfully at the visual record in its localised times and places and is central to the film's resonance and success.

Such attempted extensions of the visual language of documentary in combination with music, pushes well beyond the experience of the documentary image provided by journalism, by the varieties of tele-*vérité* or even by those transitional moments of music-image combination indicated in Rabiger's account. For many years, the mixing of the creative and the factual on television was viewed with suspicion by those who, unlike the pioneers of documentary cinema, drew on too rigid a sense of demarcation between imagination and knowledge. After this false separation, there has come a kind of false conflation suggested by such terms as 'infotainment'. This is false because it too easily suggests, both for advocates and for critics, that it is only within a limited range of novelty formats that certain aesthetic 'boundaries' can be crossed.

Documentary reportage around controversial issues will clearly continue to want to keep some of its core discourses free of the kinds of prematurely evaluative closure that I discussed earlier. But documentary exposition includes much more than journalism, and even within documentary journalism I believe there is more room for expressive depiction and for the musico-visual exploration of topic than is currently being used.

The real potential that television offers for connecting knowing to feeling, and hearing to viewing, remains larger than we might guess from what is now in the schedules. A more varied, inventive and risk-taking employment of music within television documentary would be a welcome part of the wider and continuing exploration of the role of art in the quest for understanding.

Notes

I am grateful to the editors of the journal *Popular Music*, where a first version of this essay was published.

1   I have drawn here mainly on British examples, well aware however of the tradition of earlier work in the United States and in Europe. Perhaps the finest essay on music in documentary film is on an American example, Virgil Thomson's music for Lorentz's 1937 film *The River* (see Lerner, 1999).

2   Further attention could be paid to the implications of synthesised music for the documentary experience. The wider range of sounds and tones, the increased sense of flow and the enhanced connotational range, at a remove from that of conventional musical instruments, are all significant.

References

Corner, J., Richardson, K. and Fenton, N. 1990. *Nuclear Reactions: Form and Response in Public Issue Television*. London: John Libby.

Corner, J. 1996. *The Art of Record*. Manchester: Manchester University Press.

Corner, J. 2005. '*Wisconsin Death Trip*: Space, Place and the Historical Exotic', in J. Ruoff (ed.) *The Time Machine: Essays on Cinema and Travel*. Durham, N.C.: Duke University Press.

Dovey, Jon. 2000. *Freakshow: First Person Media and Factual Television*. London: Pluto Press.

Lerner, N. 1999. 'Damming Virgil Thomson's Music for *The River*', in Jane. M. Gaines and Michael Renov (eds.) *Collecting Visible Evidence*. Minneapolis: University of Minnesota Press. 103–15.

Rabiger, M. 1998. *Directing the Documentary*. London: Focal Press.

Tagg, P. 1987. 'Musicology and the Semiotics of Popular Music'. *Semiotica* 66, 1/3. 279–98.

Vaughan, D. 1983. *Portrait of an Invisible Man*. London: British Film Institute.

Winston, B. 1995. *Claiming the Real*. London: British Film Institute.

18

Bowling for Columbine: A Review

Christopher Sharrett and William Luhr

Produced by Michael Moore, Kathleen Glynn, Charles Bishop, Jim Czrenecki, and Michael Donovan; written and directed by Michael Moore; cinematography by Brian Danitz and Michael McDonough; edited by Kurt Engfehr; original music by Jeff Gibbs; animation by Harold Moss; with Michael Moore, Charlton Heston, Marilyn Manson, Matt Stone and Denise Ames. An MGM-UA release.

Leftist filmmakers working in nonnarrative formats aren't hard to find, but their films seldom receive mainstream distribution. Except for those by Michael Moore. He stands virtually alone, not as a filmmaker who interrogates social and corporate power, but as one able to place such films into the multiplexes of America.

Why? Two reasons come immediately to mind. The first is that his works—whether *Bowling for Columbine*, his first film, *Roger and Me* (1989), his various television shows (such as *TV Nation* or *The Awful Truth*) or his best-selling book *Stupid White Men*—are commonly classified not as socio-political criticism but as 'comedy.' Moore's comedy, however, serves a subversive agenda—a goofball wrapper encasing social critique. The second, related reason for his success in mainstream venues is his persona—a big, potbellied slob from the American heartland in a baseball cap who looks like he buys his clothes in Kmart and sleeps in them. During the 1960s and 1970s, Tom Smothers was perceived as having been able to push a leftist agenda on network television because, with his short hair, red sports coat, and aging choirboy appearance, he didn't *look* like a counterculture threat. Mainstream America saw him as one of 'us,' rather than one of 'them.' Moore, with his shambling demeanor, looks less like Leon Trotsky than one of the good ol' boys at the auto-body plant in his home-town of Flint, Michigan.

Moore places himself at the center of his work, which is almost as much about his persona as it is about the issues he engages. His films jubilate in the fish-out-of-water effect that his personal appearance radiates when shown shuffling through the corporate offices of General Motors, of Kmart, or Charlton Heston's LA mansion. He initially appears comically out of his element and unthreatening—a yokel without the common sense to suit up and wear a tie in such august surroundings. There is, however, a quick rebound effect. His apparent naiveté when dealing with officious corporate security personnel or the expensively dressed power elite garners him considerable spectator sympathy. Isn't he, after all, just a simple guy looking for answers to a few simple questions? Although he often uses 'ambush' interview tactics, his persona makes him appear less aggressive and manipulative than, say, Geraldo Rivera in similar situations.

But is he? The reception of *Bowling for Columbine* has raised questions about the credibility of his persona and about his integrity as a documentary filmmaker that are not new. This 'good ol' boy,' who purportedly lives in a $1.9 million home in New York City, was accused over a decade ago of manipulating and even falsifying elements of *Roger and Me*. Comparable accusations have circulated about *Bowling for Columbine*. Although Moore attacks the statistical maneuvering of various groups in the film, the reliability of his own statistical assertions has been questioned. He has also been accused of various other distortions, such as doctoring the Willy Horton footage he uses in the film and of reenacting the footage showing a dog that inadvertently shot a man in deer camp when a rifle was placed on its back for a prank photograph.

Such carping also suggests an agenda on the part of certain reviewers, since Moore's humor makes transparent the 'doctorings' or reenactments of which he is accused. One commentator notes that Moore doesn't alert the viewer to reenactments when he tests the laid-back Canadian lifestyle by opening several unlocked residential doors in Windsor, Ontario. Obviously Moore would have been insane *not* to get clearances from the residents, and reviewers yammering about such moments reveal either naiveté or stupidity. An idea implicit in complaints about Moore past and present is that he somehow violates the aspirations of 'objective' documentary filmmaking (as if film history hasn't exposed this delusion decades ago), or that he fails to 'tell both sides of the story,' which would make his work about as compelling as network television. Such complaints reveal a conservative impulsive having nothing to do with addressing Moore's real strengths and limitations.

Bowling for Columbine focuses on American gun violence, using the horrific 1999 shootings at Columbine High School in Littleton, Colorado as its centerpiece and model of exploration. Moore puts numerous issues on the table as he takes the viewer through a first-person tour across the heartland, opting for a steady, at times annoying, ironic humour in his rapid-fire montage approach. This style is often merely suggestive, outlining for the viewer a sense of the illnesses within American society and of what is at stake, but doing so in too allusive a manner to foster substantive understanding. Moore's great talent is for uncovering the grotesque, almost incomprehensible features of American life, such as a bank that gives away guns as premiums to customers opening new accounts, or the fact that Eric Harris and Dylan Klebold, the two shooters who killed or wounded their classmates at Columbine High, went bowling on the morning of the atrocity. Moore visits the home of John Nichols, brother of Terry Nichols, convicted in the Oklahoma City bombing case. When Moore asks Nichols if his own ardent defense of gun rights would extend to allowing citizens to store weapons-grade plutonium, the unnerving Nichols, apparently wishing to appear to add a dollop of cautionary temperance to his agenda, replies, 'There's a lot of nuts out there.' This and other moments— including Moore's interview with camouflage-garbed survivalists—might have been little more than humorous diversions or cheap shots were it not for Moore's sympathetic interest in many of the people he encounters, and his efforts to merge his dramatis personae of the cult of weaponry with broader meditations on the nature of the American fascination with bloodletting.

On a number of occasions, Moore steps back from a simple agenda of indict- ment to open up broader social issues. The indictment aspect at times seems confused and confusing. Although much of the film condemns the actions of the NRA, Moore does not theatrically burn but repeatedly brandishes his own NRA card, describing himself as a product of America's gun culture. In one of the film's central sequences, he mounts a highly theatrical ambush interview by bringing two seriously handicapped victims of the Columbine massacre to Kmart headquarters. Arguing that the bullets used by the Columbine killers were purchased at Kmart, they petition management to stop selling ammuni- tion in their department stores. While the episode reveals the sliminess of the PR-supported corporate world, it takes an unexpected turn when Kmart's PR representative agrees to implement Moore's demands. Moore seems genuinely surprised and openly grateful. The sequence ends not on the expected note of 'Evil Corporation swatting liberal yokel and handicapped victims away like flies,' but with an unsettling progressive moment. Yet the moment actually addresses little of major importance, and one can't help but notice that Moore is too much at center stage throughout.

Part of Moore's complicated, at times disjointed, project is to suggest that violence is not caused by the kooks and weirdos who draw so much media attention. He rejects the concept of Harris and Klebold as 'monsters,' the term commonly used in media descriptions; instead, he presents them as logical products of American life, no different from any kid at a video arcade, or any self-deluded military manufacturer. Moore builds a case for the cynical inter- connectedness of ostensibly disparate elements within the corporate/politi- cal/ideological power structure and the disastrous social effects of those interwoven elements. He points out the presence in Littleton (not far from Columbine High School) of Lockheed Martin, and its role not only as a key defense contractor but also as a major sponsor of 'workfare' alternatives to welfare that endanger the whole fabric of American society.

Attempting to connect the dots, Moore traces the gun murder, by another child, of a six-year-old left unattended by his mother in Flint, Michigan (whose economic destruction by General Motors was the subject of *Roger and Me*). On the day of the shooting, the boy's mother, a parolee, was bused miles into the suburbs, forced to fulfill her workfare obligations by tending a soda fountain at a shopping mall retro diner owned by rock impresario Dick Clark. In a moment rivaling Moore's off-hand exposure of game show host Bob Eubanks as an anti-Semite in *Roger and Me*, Moore tries to interview Dick Clark outside his headquarters in Hollywood. Remaining within the dark confines of his van, the ever-cheerful whitebread promoter of rock and roll, when asked his views on the workfare horrors of which he takes advantage, tells the driver to slam the door in Moore's face.

This makes for dramatic footage but it again raises questions about Moore's tactics. It is, after all, an ambush interview. While it drives home its point about the complex network of corporate/governmental involvement, it also involves grandstanding by Moore. The issue is not discussed and explored as much as it is dramatically asserted. Furthermore, Moore's choice of a media figure such as Dick Clark to discuss workfare presages his choice of Charlton Heston to discuss the NRA. These confrontations seem to say more than they do. The Heston scene, which also contains more accusatory questions than substantive discussion, veils the fact that, in taking on an easy target like Heston, Moore has not interrogated anyone in the NRA lobby, the people with genuine political clout. But would they have been more illuminating than Heston, their ideology any different? Moore has always acknowledged his own nurturance by the mass media, and bringing in celebrities like Clark and Heston gives a more recognizable face to social crises than those of gray-bird corporate or government functionaries. Catching these celebrities off guard tends to render their public charm—and the policies in which they are complicit—suddenly very ugly.

Moore brings smog, corporate crime, racism, and other issues into play before finally associating American gun violence with simple hate and fear. In trying to debunk traditional shibboleths about the causes of violence, Moore tends to leave his own assertions only marginally explored. He raises questions he can't, and hardly tries, to answer. Using Canada's relatively low rate of gun murder as a locus of comparison, he questions traditional presumptions about US violence. He notes that poverty can't be at the root of violence, since Canada has a very high unemployment; neither can a violent pop culture (much of it an import from the US); neither can a large number of gun fanatics; neither can the tensions of a multiracial society.

This proves a provocative opening up of *Bowing for Columbine*'s central issues while, at the same time, marking the point at which the film loses its focus. Moore makes tentative forays into cross-cultural explanation for the national differences in gun violence but his mode of exploration ultimately imperils the film's cohesion. On a trip to Windsor, Ontario, Moore concludes that the *treatment* of poverty and race are at issue. He places Canada's handling of social programs and generous welfare system head and shoulders above the US (not a big discovery really, and a situation rapidly changing with the corporatization of Canada flowing from free-trade agreements). Rather than deal with social problems, the US tries to stigmatize them, scapegoating the poor and minorities in news reports and 'true-crime' shows about cops tracking down the raging underclass. The effect is to raise violence as an issue far beyond its actual reality. In support of this, Moore cites paranoid myths created by the mass media, ranging from poisoned Halloween candy to tweaked or unreported statistics about the actual (rather flat) level of violent crime in the last decade.

But if violence isn't so bad in America, what's the point of the film? From its early images of the realistic toy guns so popular in 1950s male juvenile culture, *Bowling for Columbine* argues that America is not only a nation obsessed with guns, but also one never hesitant to use them, especially against the racial Other. Moore makes great capital from the horrors of Columbine: the widespread gun culture; readily available weapons and ammunition; the insensitivity of the NRA; the links among Lockheed-Martin, the defense establishment, and other structures of social repression, but then seems to reverse direction and undercut all of it.

Moore discounts the notion of America as an endemically violent nation—after going through a checklist of US aggression in the postwar period from the imposition of the Shah of Iran in 1952 to the overthrow of Jacobo Arbenz to the Vietnam War, the 1972 coup in Chile, the Iran-Contra scandals, and the training of Osma Bin Laden by the CIA. Yet Moore still counters notions of American exceptionalism, intercutting fleeting atrocity footage of Nazi Germany and imperialist Britain, France, and Japan to undercut notions that American violence has its foundations in the especially brutal conquest of its Wild West past. But comparing America to Europe may create a false debate.

Considering its very short history as the only major nation founded during the Enlightenment under principles of democratic compromise, US history has been especially violent. Noam Chomsky has noted that the conservative European business press of the twentieth century was shocked at US capitalism's savage assaults on workers. The Civil War, a conflict, as Shelby Foote notes, at the crossroads of our being, showed the murderous failure of democratic compromise, which may exist only as a façade to protect powerful financial interests, suggesting a basic hypocrisy regarding American notions of liberty and prosperity that may in the last several decades be coming home to roost for the white middle class. Acknowledging this demands that we reject a view of the Columbine shootings and other forms of juvenile violence as aberrant, which Moore clearly does. His refusal contains, however, a glaring omission long noted by scholars critical of media representations of Columbine: schoolyard shootings have been commonplace in inner city minority communities for decades. As with the spread of narcotics, such crimes are frightful tragedies, it seems, only when the middle class is threatened.

Associating gun violence chiefly with hatred and paranoid fear of the racial Other tends to ignore the evidence of the political economy of violence that Moore rather haphazardly assembles. Racism isn't about racial paranoia alone. After all, racialist mythologies in America flowed from the need to dehumanize the people serving the stoop-labor economy of the agrarian slavocracy (African Americans), and the people in the way of mining, railroad, and cattle interests (Native Americans). Moore gives impressions of this dynamic, but not an ordered understanding.

At certain times Moore's compare/contrast editing sustains his insistence on humor; at other times it misfires. He deftly juxtaposes a speech by the smarmy, rabble-rousing Senator Joe Lieberman, the quintessential opportunist politician who loves to blame pop culture for the world's problems, with a chat with shock rocker Marilyn Manson, who, not surprisingly, is one of the more intelligent voices in the movie. But a long 'cartoon history of America' is cute for only a bit, and almost stops the movie with its sense that Moore can't make a transition without a joke, and that these issues, which the film poses as overwhelmingly important, are regularly represented with a hip blitheness. The soundtrack for a montage of American atrocities is Louis Armstrong's version of 'What a Wonderful World'—Moore's constant need for forced irony often feels adolescent.

Bowling for Columbine loses any attempt at sustained argument after its raising of the provocative comparison of American with Canadian violence. It builds to its climactic interview with aging film star and National Rifle Association front man Charlton Heston, whom we have earlier seen in file footage proudly uttering his mantra about not giving up his primeval flintlock rifle until it is taken 'from my cold, dead hands.' Some have argued that Moore bears down too brutally on the slightly enfeebled actor, who is, after all, courteous enough to allow the interview. It is a complex moment, filled with awkward tensions. While it provides the film with a dramatic conclusion, it also enables it to sidestep its central issues. Moore shows Heston his NRA card, then raises the question of the differences between the US and Canada; Heston fumbles for a response. Moore then shifts gears and assaults Heston's insensitivity and the NRA's viciousness in staging rallies in towns such as Littleton while they are mourning children lost to gun murder. Heston walks away from the interview in a snit, losing himself in his LA estate. Moore leaves behind a photo of a child killed by a gun in a town where the NRA quickly flexed its considerable organizing muscle.

It is a curious ending. On one level it deflects the major concerns of the film because NRA insensitivity isn't really the issue, at least not the sole one. Moore himself repeatedly proclaims his NRA membership. The ending enables the film to drop its larger issues in favor of an awkward interview with Charlton Heston that implicates him in a social dynamic leading to a little girl's death. On another level, however, the image of the irate actor scurrying away as Moore props up the photo of the dead child of the American underclass against a pillar of Heston's palatial, gated home may be the best coda any recent film has enjoyed, a summary statement on life in a miserably polarized, heartless society.

1 Looking for the yellow streak in *City of Gold* (National Film Board)

2 Marlon Riggs, courtesy *Cineaste* magazine

3 *"Cannibal Tours"* Photograph by Dennis O'Rourke.
Copyright Camerawork Pty Ltd

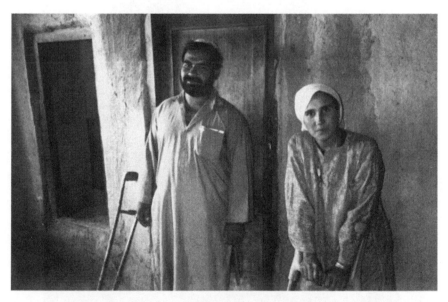

4 Habiba and Shah—a scene from *Landmines—A Love Story*.
Photograph by Dennis O'Rourke. Copyright Camerawork Pty Ltd

5 Dennis O'Rourke during the making of *Landmines—A Love Story*. Photograph by Dennis O'Rourke. Copyright Camerawork Pty Ltd

6 Robert Drew, producer, behind John Kennedy during filming of *Primary*

7 Robert Drew editing *Jane* with colleague

8 Filming in progress on *American High*

9 Director Jonathan Mednick and producer R. J. Cutler viewing rushes from *American High*

10 Director Antony Thomas filming *Death of a Princess*

Part IV

Changing Contexts in Television

19

The McCarthy "See It Now" Broadcast

Fred W. Friendly

Fred Friendly's Due to Circumstances Beyond Our Control *was published in 1968. At the time, it received excellent reviews, but it now seems to be all but forgotten. This is a pity, because Friendly's book contains not only a detailed account of the birth of "CBS Reports," but also a fascinating inside look at the tensions between a documentary unit and a broadcasting organization (CBS). It is, indeed, a seminal work for any serious student of the history of broadcasting.*

"The McCarthy Broadcast" is taken from chapter 2 and deals with the circumstances of the broadcast. Unfortunately, space limitations necessitated our omitting the second half of the chapter, in which Friendly discusses the mixed reactions to the broadcast, the attacks on Murrow's patriotism, the answering broadcast of McCarthy himself, and the comments of media critic Gilbert Seldes.

Seldes, although a longtime friend of Murrow and a foe of McCarthy, nevertheless severely criticized the broadcast. He thought it was unfair for only showing McCarthy at his worst and damned it for pretending to be a report when it was actually an attack. His most biting comment came early in the review, with the words "In the long run, it is more important to use our communications system fairly than to destroy McCarthy."

Interestingly, Broadcasting Magazine, *which generally reflects the sentiments of station owners—many of whom objected to the McCarthy broadcast—went against type and praised the program. Its publisher, Sol Taishoff, called it the "greatest feat of journalistic enterprise in modern times."*

After listing many of the comments both for and against the program, Friendly closes off the chapter by setting out Murrow's own reactions, which were mixed. Murrow told Seldes personally, and the press generally, that he felt uncomfortable about the broadcast and hoped that so drastic a use of the medium would not be required again. However, he also stated that he would never regret having done the program. It is a verdict which time has endorsed.

A.R.

When the record is finally written, as it will be one day, it will answer the question, Who has helped the Communist cause and who has served his country better, Senator McCarthy or I? I would like to be remembered by the answer to that question. (Edward R. Murrow, April 6, 1954)

To say that the Murrow broadcast of March 9, 1954, was the decisive blow against Senator McCarthy's power is as inaccurate as it is to say that Joseph R. McCarthy, Republican, Wisconsin, single-handedly gave birth to McCarthyism. The disease was here long before he exploited it. Elmer Davis compared it to malaria and prescribed courage as the only antidote. What Murrow did was administer a strong dose of that medicine, then in such short supply, and it was fitting that he did it on television, where the disease had reached epidemic proportions long before McCarthy became its chief carrier.

By the early fifties the central nervous system of the vast broadcast industry was so conditioned that it responded to self-appointed policemen and blacklists as though they were part of the constitutional process. For me, one scene, enacted in an office on the fourteenth floor of CBS, still retains all the noxious atmosphere of the period.

Murrow and I never believed in background or mood music for documentaries, but we did want to commission an original composition for the opening and closing titles and credits of our broadcasts. I had gone to see the vice-president in charge of programs, who at that time had administrative control over "Hear It Now," and later "See It Now," to explain the project and request special funds for it. When the vice-president asked me what composer we had in mind, I handed him the names of three well-known modern composers listed in order of our preference. He glanced at the top name and asked, "Is he in the book?"

"I don't know," I said, "but I'm sure Music Clearance has his number."

"I know," said the vice-president, "but is he in the book?"

I started to ask a secretary for a telephone directory when the vice-president pulled open a drawer in his desk and said, "This is the book we live by." It was a pamphlet called *Red Channels*.

Even today I can recall every item in that desk drawer: the *Red Channels* blacklist, a rating book beside it, some paper clips, pencils, an eraser, an extra set of cuff links, a small Civil War memento. Luckily, "the book" did not contain the name of our first choice, though both of the other composers were listed.

Red Channels and its weekly companion piece, *Counterattack*, the bible for broadcast companies, sponsors, advertising agencies, and motion picture studios, among others, was a catalogue of quarter-truths, gossip, and confessions of ex-Communists and other informers of questionable credentials. In the fifties it was the death warrant for the careers of hundreds of talented actors, playwrights, directors, composers, authors, and editors. Some of the most valued and loyal news broadcasters were rendered unemployable by *Red*

Channels. Raymond Swing, one of the innovators of radio journalism in serious interpretation of foreign affairs, chose to fight *Red Channels* publicly by debating its publisher and suffered grievous personal loss because of his stand. His career was never the same again, and for a time his employment with Voice of America was jeopardized. Called before the McCarthy committee, which of course could not prove any of its allegations, Swing stayed with Voice of America until he was reconfirmed, and then resigned in protest at the State Department's failure to defend its own agency. Later Swing joined CBS in a nonbroadcast capacity to assist Murrow with his nightly radio series. Even the great Elmer Davis, who even earlier than Winston Churchill had alerted Americans to the Cold War and warned of Stalin's aggression, was attacked by *Counterattack* as a "smearer of anti-Communists."

Red Channels was not the only blacklister at that time, however. Sponsors, who in those days exerted much more control over program content than they do today, had their own little dark books. When I was at NBC in 1949 producing a news quiz broadcast called *Who Said That?*, the sponsor, an oil company, dictated a blacklist of its own, which NBC accepted. The list of objectionable guests included Norman Thomas, Al Capp, Oscar Levant, Henry Morgan, and several prominent congressmen—not because they were necessarily part of the Communist conspiracy, which they weren't, but because in a live, adlib broadcast "they just might say something." Perhaps the classic example of this kind of dreaded spontaneity occurred at Christmas of 1952 when on a CBS broadcast, *This Is Show Business*, George S. Kaufman said, "Let's make this one program on which no one sings 'Silent Night.' " Though this was a wish shared by others, the advertising agency decided to banish Kaufman from the show even before the program was over.

The case of Jean Muir, the actress barred from playing the mother of Henry Aldrich on an NBC situation comedy because of a *Red Channels* blacklisting which disturbed the sponsor, was to have its echo as late as 1966 when ABC deleted a reference to the incident during an interview with Miss Muir.

The flat Indiana twang of Elmer Davis kept pleading, "Don't let them scare you," but the industry *was* scared, and by winter of 1954 much of Washington was so terrorized by McCarthy that national policy was often made in reaction to his tirades. Dean Acheson, whom the *New York Daily News*, a McCarthy supporter, later called a strong secretary of state, was dubbed the "Red Dean" by the senator, and his last years in office were ineffective partly because of this monstrous slander. General Marshall, whom Harry Truman called the "greatest living American," was denounced in the Senate as virtually a traitor by the junior senator from Wisconsin: "A man steeped in falsehood [and part of] a conspiracy so immense and an infamy so black as to dwarf any previous venture in the history of man." The Eisenhower administration fared little better. By 1953 it was "twenty years of treason," and the guilt included the

Republicans, the State Department, the U.S. High Commissioner for Germany James Conant, the ambassador to the USSR Charles Bohlen, and Mutual Security Administrator Harold Stassen.

On Thursday, March 4, we informed the company that next week's "See It Now" would deal with McCarthy. Whether the news ever reached the twentieth floor I am not certain. We did ask Bill Golden to run an advertisement on the morning of March 9, and when he said that the management had turned down his request, Murrow and I came up with some money of our own—part of it award money we had put aside for just such a purpose. The ad was scheduled to appear in the *Times* on Tuesday, but we still had not made a final decision on whether to run the program. The point of no return, a decision to go or scrub, would be made on Sunday night.

We had made a veiled reference to the McCarthy project on our previous broadcast on March 2, and this was fortunate because of a strange series of events that clouded the weekend. In a Miami speech, Adlai Stevenson made a strong political attack on the Republican party, including several critical references to McCarthy. CBS and NBC televised the speech, and McCarthy demanded equal time to answer, which was denied. McCarthy supporters protested vehemently, and when the Murrow broadcast was officially announced a few days later, the cry was heard that this was CBS's way of getting even with its critics. Nothing could have been further from the truth, and our mention of the program on March 2 was evidence. (The networks finally did provide the Republican party with time, and Vice-President Nixon answered Stevenson.)

At nine o'clock that Sunday evening we viewed the next-to-the-last edit of the film. It was still seven minutes longer than the hour allowed us, and Ed and I had our usual tug of war over the cuts. We had to drop four minutes from the McCarthy–Reed Harris inquisition, but even when cut it still held much of its original impact. No network or newsreel service had had cameras running during McCarthy's castigation of Zwicker because it was a closed session, but by rare good luck Mack and Wershba, two of our personnel, had been present in Philadelphia when the senator restaged the entire episode—including the verbatim reading of the transcript—for a Washington's Birthday celebration. The scene, enacted under a huge mural of the first president, took on additional terror because of McCarthy's obvious delight in reliving it all—the unbridled bravado and rage were interspersed with the famous McCarthy giggle.

We had also extracted from the Philadelphia speech the senator's savage attack on Secretary of the Army Robert T. Stevens, the bland, naive defender of the army's position. Of Secretary Stevens, McCarthy intoned: " 'On what meat does this our Caesar feed . . .' "

We moved the Philadelphia re-enactment up near the beginning of the show in order to establish the senator's violent streaks early, and placed the Reed Harris sequence toward the end as a lead-in to Ed's final comments. In between there was a variety of the McCarthy techniques; after each one, Murrow would point out the misuse of the facts. There was also a glowing tribute to the senator by one of his ardent supporters at a testimonial banquet, and McCarthy's emotion-choked reply. There were some McCarthy quotes on Eisenhower, on the Democratic party's twenty years of treason, and on the Republicans' share of the guilt from another West Virginia speech.

After the cutters had taken the reels back to their editing tables, we sent out for coffee and ran a final critique on our footage. I had sensed a certain uneasiness on the part of some members in the unit. I was not sure whether this was timidity over our confrontation with the senator or whether there was something in their own background which might make us vulnerable. Looking back on it now, I suppose it was my own uncertainty and fear that made me decide that it would not be fair to Ed or CBS to enter into this battle if we had an Achilles heel. Also, I wanted all hands to share in a decision that would obviously involve everyone's future.

Ed agreed, and so a meeting of the unit was called. We asked each member, first, whether he thought our analysis of the senator's technique was effective enough to make the points we were striving for; and second, whether anyone knew of any reason why we should not do the broadcast. Was there, in other words, anything in their own backgrounds that would give the senator a club to beat us with, because if this broadcast was successful, he and his supporters would certainly be looking for one. Although this was a team effort, we all knew from the aftermath of the Radulovich show that Murrow would be the target of all the attacks.[1] But if there was anything in any of our lives that might make us vulnerable, we had to know now. Ed reminded everyone that we were not referring to *Red Channels* or any other such blacklist.

We moved around the room from editor to cameraman to reporter to field producer, and each indicated his position. Two or three of our colleagues were unhappy that we did not have the Wheeling speech and that the material was not as dramatic or cohesive as the Radulovich and Indianapolis programs. Perhaps we should wait another few weeks and assemble more McCarthy material; the senator had some speeches scheduled for the following week, and there would undoubtedly be more hearings in Washington. I said that I disagreed; if we were going to do the program at all, this was the time, and I was convinced that if we could sustain the proper mood for the first twenty-five minutes, Ed's ending would more than justify our stand.

Then each person talked for a few minutes about himself; no one had any personal reservation or indicated any vulnerability. One man told us that his first wife had been a Communist party member but that their marriage had been dissolved years before.

At the end we all turned to Ed. In a characteristic pose, his elbows on his knees, his eyes on the floor, he was silent for about ten seconds. At last he said, "We, like everyone in this business, are going to be judged by what we put on the air; but we also shall be judged by what we don't broadcast. If we pull back on this we'll have it with us always." He snuffed out what was probably his sixtieth cigarette of the day and said he would have his summation on my desk by morning.

When I got up on Monday and went to work, it was the beginning of a grueling but stimulating weekly routine; few of us would see a bed or get home until early Wednesday morning. In the meantime, the life of the broadcast took over. We told Bill Golden to give final confirmation to the advertisement in the *Times.* The copy read simply: "Tonight at 10:30 on 'See It Now,' a report on Senator Joseph R. McCarthy on Channel 2"; there was no CBS eye or any other trademark, and it was signed "Fred W. Friendly and Edward R. Murrow, Co-producers."

We were tempted to tell Alcoa that because of the importance and nature of the broadcast we wanted to run their commercials at the beginning and end, thus eliminating a middle break, but decided that rather than involve them in any of the decision making we would simply exercise our prerogative and do it on our own. We tried to persuade CBS to do some air promotion, but there was little interest. Shortly before noon, Murrow showed me his closing piece, and I asked him to rewrite the opening I had drafted. He changed a few words and inserted the sentence "If the senator believes we have done violence to his words or pictures and desires to speak, to answer himself, an opportunity will be afforded him on this program."

Ed's conclusion, the product of six or seven rewrites, was tight and forceful. There was no doubt in his mind that this ending crossed the line into editorial comment, but we both knew that that line had to be crossed. To do a half-hour on so volatile and important a matter and then end with a balanced "on the other hand" summation would be to dilute and destroy the effect of the broadcast.

We briefly debated sending a copy of the ending to Sig Mickelson [director of news and public affairs], but again decided against it. It would be unfair to him to involve him in the editing process in this isolated instance, when we were not inclined to accept any major changes. Of course, if Mickelson asked to see the script, it was available.

On Tuesday morning [CBS chairman of the board] Paley called Ed, as he occasionally did on the day of an important broadcast, and wished us well. "I'll be with you tonight, Ed, and I'll be with you tomorrow as well." Murrow was moved by the implication and tone of the message.

This was one broadcast we wanted time to rehearse so that there would be no chance of being run over by the stopwatch. We determined to go into triple-pay overtime in the cutting room and Studio 41 in order to start our final run-throughs by 8:30. Ed could have a quick sandwich after his 7:45 radio program and we would still have time for two complete rehearsals. But we ran late in the cutting room with the mix, though we had started early on Tuesday afternoon, and it was almost nine o'clock before Murrow and I and all the film and tape were in the studio.

Because the control room was also our studio, we had standing orders that there were to be no visitors, no company brass or sponsors. But on this night I asked the security department of CBS to furnish uniformed guards at the Grand Central elevator and just outside the studio. By this time Murrow was getting crank telephone calls, and emotions on the senator ran so high that conceivably some fanatic would try to crash the studio while we were on the air.

Fifteen minutes before broadcast time we finished the final run-through. Don Hewitt, our control-room director, told us that it was thirty seconds too long, and we decided to kill the closing credits if we needed the time. The test-pattern easel was pulled away from camera 1 as Ed settled into his chair. At 10:28 the assistant director whispered that we had one minute. Hewitt picked up the private line to Master Control and asked them not to cut us off if we ran long: there might not be time for credits, and we needed every second we could squeeze. "Give us till 10:59:26," he pleaded. One of the outside lines rang and Don smothered it. "No, this is not the eleven o'clock news. Try 44. Operator, I tell you every week to shut off these phones. Now, *please*, no calls until eleven o'clock."

Murrow was usually "unflappable," but as broadcasters go he was a much more tense performer than Walter Cronkite or Robert Trout. When he was emotionally involved in a story it usually showed. At the close of one of our Korean reports about a wounded GI fighting for his life, Ed's voice broke ever so slightly. It was because he always cared so much, and also because he had a trace of camera fright which he never completely lost. But this was one night when he wanted a steady hand, when he did not want to be accused of an emotional attack.

The preceding program ended; it was followed by what is known as "system"—thirty seconds of blackout, when local stations identify themselves and insert their local commercials. During this seemingly endless void, I leaned over to Ed and whispered, "This is going to be a tough one." His answer was, "Yes, and after this one they're all going to be tough."

Suddenly the hands on the clock pointed straight up and the red light came on. Ed leaned into the camera. "Good evening. Tonight 'See It Now' devotes its entire half-hour to a report on Senator Joseph R. McCarthy, told mainly in his own words and pictures." Looking up at the long bank of monitors, I knew that Murrow was in complete control of the air and of himself; in contrast, my right hand was shaking so that when I tried to start my stopwatch I missed the button completely and had to compensate by two seconds all through the half-hour.

For the next thirty minutes that control room was like a submarine during an emergency dive; fourteen technicians and a director were all responding to Murrow's cues, and he to theirs. Murrow into a 1952 film of McCarthy . . . Murrow to radio tape of the senator . . . Murrow to Eisenhower . . . Murrow live in the studio reading from a stack of American newspapers, most of them critical of the senator's attack on the army . . . Murrow introducing film of the senator laughing and scoffing at Eisenhower . . . the Zwicker affair . . . the senator attacking "Alger, I mean Adlai," which was how McCarthy referred to Stevenson.

Finally we came to the Reed Harris hearing. Somebody in the control room started to talk while the mikes were closed during this footage. Murrow shut him up quickly; he wanted to hear every word of the questioning, almost as though he were listening to it for the first time instead of the tenth. I suspect that subconsciously he wanted no one in the entire nation to miss a single word or nuance of the questioning.

Murrow: Now a sample investigation. The witness was Reed Harris, for many years a civil servant in the State Department directing the Information Service. Harris was accused of helping the Communistic cause by curtailing some broadcasts to Israel. Senator McCarthy summoned him and questioned him about a book he had written in 1932.

McCarthy: Mr. Reed Harris, your name is Reed Harris?
Harris: That's right.
McCarthy: You wrote a book in '32, is that correct?
Harris: Yes, I wrote a book, and as I testified in executive session—
McCarthy: At the time you wrote the book—pardon me, go ahead. I'm sorry, proceed.
Harris: —at the time I wrote the book the atmosphere in the universities of the United States was greatly affected by the Great Depression then in existence. The attitudes of students, the attitudes of the general public were considerably different than they are at this moment, and for one thing there certainly was no awareness to the degree that there is today of the way the Communist party works.
McCarthy: You attended Columbia University in the early thirties, is that right?
Harris: I did, Mr. Chairman.
McCarthy: Will you speak a little louder, sir?

Harris: I did, Mr. Chairman.

McCarthy: And you were expelled from Columbia?

Harris: I was suspended from classes on April 1, 1932. I was later reinstated and I resigned from the university.

McCarthy: You resigned from the university. Did the Civil Liberties Union provide you with an attorney at that time?

Harris: I had many offers of attorneys, and one of those was from the American Civil Liberties Union, yes.

McCarthy: The question is, did the Civil Liberties Union supply you with an attorney?

Harris: They did supply an attorney.

McCarthy: The answer is yes?

Harris: The answer is yes.

McCarthy: You know the Civil Liberties Union has been listed as a front for and doing the work of the Communist party?

Harris: Mr. Chairman, this was 1932.

McCarthy: I know it was 1932. Do you know they since have been listed as a front for and doing the work of the Communist party?

Harris: I do not know that they have been listed so, sir.

McCarthy: You don't know they have been listed?

Harris: I have heard that mentioned or read that mentioned.

McCarthy: You wrote a book in 1932. I'm going to ask you again: At the time you wrote this book, did you feel that professors should be given the right to teach sophomores that marriage "should be cast off of our civilization as antiquated and stupid religious phenomena"? Was that your feeling at that time?

Harris: My feeling was that professors should have the right to express their considered opinions on any subject, whatever they were, sir.

McCarthy: I'm going to ask you this question again.

Harris: That includes that quotation, they should have the right to teach anything that came to their mind as being a proper thing to teach.

McCarthy: I'm going to make you answer this.

Harris: I'll answer yes, but you put an implication on it and you feature this particular point out of the book, which of course is quite out of context [and] does not give a proper impression of the book as a whole. The American public doesn't get an honest impression of even that book, bad as it is, from what you are quoting from it.

McCarthy: Then let's continue to read your own writings.

Harris: Twenty-one years ago, again.

McCarthy: Yes, we shall try and bring you down to date if we can.

Harris: Mr. Chairman, two weeks ago Senator Taft took the position that I taught—twenty-one years ago—that Communists and socialists should be allowed to teach in the schools. It so happens, nowadays I don't agree with Senator Taft as far as Communist teachers in the schools is concerned, because I think Communists are in effect a plainclothes auxiliary of the Red

Army, the Soviet Red Army, and I don't want to see them in any of our schools teaching.

McCarthy: I don't recall Senator Taft ever having any of the background that you have got.

Harris: I resent the tone of this inquiry very much, Mr. Chairman. I resent it not only because it is my neck, my public neck that you are, I think, very skillfully trying to wring, but I say it because there are thousands of able and loyal employees in the federal government of the United States who have been properly cleared according to the laws and the security practices of their agencies, as I was, unless the new regime says no. I was before.

Senator McClellan: Do you think this book you wrote then did considerable harm? Its publication might have had adverse influence on the public by an expression of views contained in it.

Harris: The sale of that book was so abysmally small, it was so unsuccessful that a question of its influence . . . Really, you can go back to the publisher, you'll see it was one of the most unsuccessful books he ever put out. He's still sorry about it, just as I am.

McClellan: Well I think that's a compliment to American intelligence, I will say that.

Murrow: Senator McCarthy succeeded only in proving that Reed Harris had once written a bad book, which the American people had proved twenty-two years ago by not buying it, which is what they eventually do with all bad ideas. As for Reed Harris, his resignation was accepted a month later with a letter of commendation. McCarthy claimed it was a victory. The Reed Harris hearing demonstrates one of the senator's techniques. Twice he said the American Civil Liberties Union was listed as a subversive front. The attorney general's list does not and has never listed the ACLU as subversive, nor does the FBI or any other federal government agency. And the American Civil Liberties Union holds in its files letters of commendation from President Eisenhower, President Truman, and General MacArthur.

That was the technique of the entire broadcast. The viewer was seeing a series of typical attacks by the senator, which they had seen many times before, but for the first time on television there was a direct refutation—Murrow's correction of McCarthy's "facts." Each time the senator was his own worst witness; each time the facts countered his distortions.

At 10:54:30 the film portions of the program were over, and Murrow went into his ending right on schedule. I think I knew then for the first time that we were home.

Murrow: Earlier the senator asked, "'Upon what meat does this our Caesar feed.'" Had he looked three lines earlier in Shakespeare's *Caesar* he would have found this line, which is not altogether inappropriate: "The fault, dear Brutus, is not in our stars but in ourselves."

No one familiar with the history of this country can deny that congressional committees are useful. It is necessary to investigate before legislating, but the line between investigation and persecuting is a very fine one, and the junior senator from Wisconsin has stepped over it repeatedly. His primary achievement has been in confusing the public mind as between [the] internal and . . . external threat of Communism. We must not confuse dissent with disloyalty. We must remember always that accusation is not proof, and that conviction depends upon evidence and due process of law. We will not walk in fear, one of another. We will not be driven by fear into an age of unreason if we dig deep in our history and our doctrine, and remember that we are not descended from fearful men, not from men who feared to write, to speak, to associate with, and to defend causes which were for the moment unpopular.

This is no time for men who oppose Senator McCarthy's methods to keep silent, or for those who approve. We can deny our heritage and our history, but we cannot escape responsibility for the result. There is no way for a citizen of a republic to abdicate his responsibilities. As a nation we have come into our full inheritance at a tender age. We proclaim ourselves—as indeed we are—the defenders of freedom, what's left of it, but we cannot defend freedom abroad by deserting it at home. The actions of the junior senator from Wisconsin have caused alarm and dismay amongst our allies abroad and given considerable comfort to our enemies, and whose fault is that? Not really his. He didn't create this situation of fear; he merely exploited it, and rather successfully. Cassius was right: "The fault, dear Brutus, is not in our stars but in ourselves."

Good night, and good luck.

Then it was over. Ed slumped in his chair, head down. I thanked everyone for a perfect show; it had gone off without a hitch and we had not run out of time. A few seconds later Don Hollenbeck was on Channel 2 with the local news. He was our first contact with the outside world, and he was obviously exhilarated: "I don't know whether all of you have seen what I just saw, but I want to associate myself and this program with what Ed Murrow has just said, and I have never been prouder of CBS."

Still, at 11:03 the phones remained quiet, until finally a messenger came in with a note from the operators: "We are swamped. Could we now put through some calls to Studio 41?" We all roared with laughter, and in a moment the greatest flood of calls in television history—at least up until that time—swamped the control room, the switchboard, and the affiliates. CBS Press Information had set up a bank of receptionists, but they could handle only a fraction of the traffic. Some of the messages were vicious and obscene; many were against Murrow and the broadcast; but the majority, by a ratio estimated at ten to one, were favorable.

The scene at the Pentagon bar was much more sober than after the

Radulovich program. We knew that we had dropped a bomb, and now we were all awaiting the resulting shock wave. The reports from Press Information and the switchboard kept pouring in. Most callers were getting a busy signal, but it was obvious that the contagion of courage had been infectious. Many people were calling because, as they said, "I just had to do something."

By 12:30 I had dropped Ed off at his apartment. He told me later that the doorman and the elevator attendant shook hands with him. At two o'clock New York time, the switchboard at KNXT–Los Angeles reported hundreds of calls, all but a handful congratulating Murrow. The Washington switchboard said that it received over five hundred calls, all but forty of them favorable to the broadcast. Milwaukee registered four hundred phone calls and told the *New York Times* that not one was anti-Murrow—a claim difficult to believe from McCarthy's home state. Chicago reported more than twelve hundred calls, with a ratio of two to one for Murrow. San Francisco said they'd had more messages than on any broadcast since Vice-President Nixon's "Checkers" speech and that the balance was favorable to "See It Now."

So it went all night, and by morning there were thousands of telegrams as well. By noon, more than ten thousand phone calls and telegrams had been counted. In the next few days the letters swelled the total to something between seventy-five and one hundred thousand; we never really knew the exact count, and unfortunately we did not have the machinery to acknowledge more than a few of them. At best, the count ran about ten to one in favor of Ed, though there were places where the tally was far less favorable.

The Wednesday morning papers in the East carried little about the broadcast; eleven o'clock was past the deadline for many, and there were only a few news stories. In the Wednesday afternoon *New York World Telegram*, Harriet Van Horne called the program an autopsy: "distilled culture of McCarthyism. . . . Those who regard the senator as the scourge . . . went to bed feeling that Mr. Murrow had permitted . . . McCarthy to hang himself." His supporters, she said, "may feel it was a splendid thing." The *New York Journal American* quoted the CBS figures but reported that the paper itself had been flooded by calls hostile to the broadcast, as had "other papers." The *Journal*'s television critic, Jack O'Brian, had a long piece about Murrow's "hate McCarthy telecast" in which he reported—falsely—that CBS board chairman William S. Paley had "personally ordered the pompous portsider to take a more middle ground," and that Murrow had refused. He also berated Hollenbeck for praising the broadcast, which O'Brian later called part of the Murrow-Machiavellian-leftists propaganda.

As for the management's general reaction, one innocuous conversation that occurred the next afternoon said it all. I had kept a promise made to my wife, Dorothy, to take Wednesdays off. These were particularly important Wednesdays because we had recently bought a house in Riverdale and were planning to move in March. Each Wednesday was spent visiting the house with painters, carpenters, and electricians and ratifying the plans that Dorothy had set in motion. But by noon of March 10, feeling sure that the foundations of broadcasting must be quaking, I could stay in Riverdale no longer. Shortly after two o'clock I entered the CBS building on Madison Avenue; as I did, Jack Van Volkenburg, then president of the television network, got out of a taxi. It was my first encounter with any member of the management since the broadcast.

"'Afternoon, Jack," I said.
"How are you, Fred?" Our elevator door closed. Jack said, "How's your family?"
"Fine, Jack. We're getting ready to move, you know."
"Really? Where to?"
"Riverdale. We found a nice house. How's your family, Jack?"
"Fine. How's Ed?"
"Good. A little tired. Well, here's where I get off, Jack."
"So long, Fred."
"So long, Jack."

Note

1   Before the McCarthy show, Murrow had done an earlier broadcast presenting the case of Lt. Milo Radulovich, who was threatened with dismissal from the Air Force because of anonymous charges that his father and sister had procommunist sympathies.

20

An Independent with the Networks

Robert L. Drew

I have been asked to write about myself and two questions: How do I happen to make documentary films the networks seem willing to broadcast? What role do I play as executive producer of Drew Associates films?

An Independent

About myself, I was a high school student in Fort Thomas, Kentucky, when I ran into a kind of music man. He stomped on the floor to beat time, smoked powerful cigars, and taught music by shouting into your face. His name was McKenna and he had a temper. He drove me to practice the trumpet a lot over a period of years. He also led the band and made good music. What that got me when I left for the Army Air Corps was an appreciation of fresh air and a lot of bugle playing. I graduated from flying school on my nineteenth birthday. On my twentieth I was taking a long walk through occupied Italy after my last mission as a fighter pilot.

Back in California, I flew the first U.S. jet fighters and wrote a story about that for *Life* magazine. I spent the next ten years as a *Life* correspondent and editor in Los Angeles, Detroit, New York, and Chicago.

As for my role as an executive producer, it began in 1954, the year I had an idea about television. Television was reaching more and more people, but its documentary films were not reaching me. However interesting I might find the subject matter, I dozed off in the middle of documentary programs. Why that had to be I could not imagine. My job was covering the real world, and I found it exciting. Every few days I would go out with the likes of Alfred Eisenstaedt, Leonard McCombe, or Eugene Smith to bring back still pictures of reality that captured the excitement, spontaneity, and, sometimes, even emotion.

The idea was no very great leap. It simply occurred to me to go after some of the qualities in motion pictures that we were already getting in still pictures. But it was an idea that could grow on you. For instance, if one made a more interesting documentary, one might interest larger audiences and inform viewers on levels that journalism had not reached before. Such storytelling might pay for itself, develop its own independence, and improve the lot of journalism, television, and the public.

Because the changes I had in mind were so simple and the steps to make them so obvious, I decided to take a few months off and do them myself. *Life* gave me leave. NBC gave me the money to make a magazine of the air. I put *Life* photographer Alan Grant behind the main camera and set off to cover a half-dozen stories.

The crew was not immediately enthusiastic, I think because wrestling with the big, blimped camera, the oak-hewn tripod, a table-sized 16 mm tape recorder, movie lights, and trunks full of cables had diverted their attention from the finer things in filmmaking. Spontaneity didn't wait around for all this stuff to be set up, and the only real surprises that took place in front of the camera were the shock of the clap-sticks and outbursts of the sound man shouting "Cut!"

I found that an operation like this had to be planned and directed, and I directed it. I edited the film, wrote a narration, and delivered to NBC a magazine show under two different titles—*Key Picture* and, naturally, *Magazine X*. NBC professed to like the program and set off to try to sell a series based on it. I retreated to *Life* to try to figure out what had gone wrong.

After a few months I thought I had figured out most of the answers. Yes, we could get more talent into the process. Yes, we could reduce the size and complexity of the equipment, given money and time—maybe a million dollars and three or four years. Add a year or so at the front end to raise the money and a couple of years at the tail to make some breakthrough films and my simple fix had grown from a project of a few months to maybe six or eight years.

That's how you get hooked. I was pretty committed by now, and I had a terrible feeling that one problem remained for which there might not be a solution. Grant and I had done some good things. But the film we turned out was not measurably better than some other documentary films. The things we had done were really not that important to the overall power of the film. Something was wrong that photography and writing did not remedy. As we tracked it down, the problem appeared to be the editing, the way we put the pictures together. On one level they made perfect sense, but on another they didn't build power. Until we got a line on that problem I feared that other improvements might not make the big difference I was after.

For clues I looked to Walter Lippmann, William Allen White, John Grierson, Henry Adams, Robert Flaherty, Josiah Royce, George Bernard Shaw. Josiah Royce? Yes, he was a philosopher, a contemporary of William James, and he wrote one book for laymen, *The Philosophy of Loyalty*. Royce had an inflammatory impact on me, not because he offered an answer, but because he offered an injunction: "Plunge ahead!"

I went off to Harvard on a Neiman Fellowship and spent the year on basic storytelling—the short story, modern stage play, novel. I wish I could tell you just how the answer grew on me over the course of that year, the realization of exactly what was wrong with the editorial thinking behind *Key Picture* and much other documentary filmmaking. The hints came from many sides and built up slowly until the answer seemed to me convincing and, yes, simple. It was so simple that I was embarrassed at the time it had cost me to realize it.

I am sure it is all perfectly clear to you today, but here is what I finally saw. Most documentary films were in fact lectures. They were then, and most remain today, lectures with picture illustrations. It was as clear as the lectures I was attending every day at Harvard and thrown into relief by the novels and plays I was reading every night. In television documentaries the logic was in the words, the narration, the lecture.

I tuned in to watch Murrow's "See It Now." As the program progressed, I turned off the sound and watched the picture. The progression disintegrated. What power had been there turned to confusion. The logic left. When I turned the picture off and listened to the sound, the program tracked perfectly. Later that year, Murrow's television programs were printed in book form. They read very well.

Obvious as all this must seem to you, it was staggering news to me. It made many things clear. A lecture on the living medium of television must be dull. The apparent exception is when the lecture contains news, but then it is the news that sustains, not the lecture. A lecture can promise a great deal. But the level of excitement it can deliver over a television hour cannot build. At best it remains flat. Even in a very good lecture, the curve of interest will generally droop.

The kind of logic that does build interest and feeling on television is the logic of drama. Dramatic logic works because the viewer is seeing for himself and there is suspense. The viewer can become interested in characters. Characters develop. Things happen. Whether the drama is a movie or a football game or a well-made play, the viewer is allowed to use his senses as well as his thoughts, his emotions as well as his mind. Dramatic logic may build power on a curve that has the possibility at least of going right through the roof. When this works, it puts viewers more in touch with the world, in touch with themselves and revelations about events, people, and ideas.

By this time, later in the Neiman year, the storytelling problem was beginning to sort itself out. Candid photography would capture the spontaneous character and drama that make the real world exciting. Editing would use dramatic logic to convey the excitement of the natural drama captured by the camera.

The other Neiman Fellows, all of them newspaper people, were not shy about offering me a challenge now and then, usually an alcoholic challenge as well as an intellectual one. I wondered what would give first, my liver or my brain, as we debated over martinis into the night the question of what, if anything, all this stuff about storytelling had to do with journalism. Whatever the damage, I came out of the experience having considered some questions about knowledge, journalism, and storytelling.

Henry Adams lived through perhaps the most dramatic of the knowledge explosions. When he went off to college in the mid-1800s, it was expected that he would learn all there was to know. By the time he finished *The Education of Henry Adams* in 1904, diversities in knowledge were so great that he believed any sense of unity to be impossible. But, he said, I am old, and it may be that as I die, a baby will be born who will grow up to believe that he can see the unity of it all. Unity, like beauty, may be in the mind of the beholder.

By 1955 Walter Lippmann had applied Henry Adams's pessimism to American politics. Democracy cannot continue to function, said Lippmann, because the electorate can no longer know enough facts to vote rationally. Newspapers are declining. Television is leading us down the path of diversion and escapism. Knowledge is exploding, and nothing can make up for our not being able to keep up with it.

Such pessimism did not impress John Grierson at all. He agreed that no voter could know enough to vote rationally, but, he said, we've never made our decisions that way anyhow. It is "commonly shared experience" that has allowed us to make decisions together in the past.

But Grierson agreed with Lippmann that we do have a problem. Nations have become too large and complex to function as tribes, towns, or courts, or what the founding fathers had in the past. Grierson had a plan to fix all that. All we need to do, he said, is build multitudes of theaters across the landscape, put films about the real world into them, and persuade whole populations to go to those theaters. Thus would Grierson use technology and filmmaking to give the millions the commonly shared experience necessary to the workings of their democracies.

I couldn't help taking Grierson's side because I recognized a certain kindred megalomania there and also because I had seen his improbable theaters actually materialize. I had one in my living room. Television had gone Grierson one better, and now what were we going to do about it?

Journalists have problems deciding what to do with television because most good ones are captives of the medium in which they learned their trade. Thus an Indian smoke signaler might fail to appreciate the possibilities of the telegraph key. A radio reporter might have trouble showing things instead of telling them. A lecturer might have trouble allowing a drama to unfold.

But journalism is not one medium or another. It is a function that combines what is going on (news) with the means to communicate it. Each means of communication survives by doing what it can do uniquely and best. Thus the *New York Times* does not try to print *Life* pictures. Nor does *Life* try to print all the facts. Try to do what some other medium does uniquely better, and you are misusing your medium.

In television the nightly newscast is its own medium. What it does uniquely and best is summarize the news. Thus it calls for talkers to tell you many things quickly—a lecture with picture illustration that works because of its timeliness. The prime-time documentary is a different medium altogether. What it can add to the journalistic spectrum is something absolutely unique—strong experience of what it is like to be somewhere else, seeing for yourself into dramatic developments in the lives of people caught up in stories of importance.

To address the question raised by my fellow Neimans, all this storytelling stuff has to do with creating a new television journalism that will bring the documentary into action doing what it can do uniquely and best. This means leaving to other media what they best can do. So don't look for facts. Do be ready for some illuminating, high-voltage experience. And the print media should also be ready for floods of new and interested readers. The right kind of documentary programming will raise more interest than it can satisfy, more questions than it should try to answer. It should create interests to fuel a multimedia engine for informing, a system for knowing that leads from television to newspapers to books.

That is how the year went. At the end I wrote a piece on some of these things for Neiman Reports called "See It Then."

I went back to *Life* hoping to quickly assemble my teams and engineer the lightweight equipment. But I found myself running in place to try to keep up with writing and editing chores. The managers of Time Inc.—Henry Luce, Roy Larsen—had looked at *Key Picture* and passed. Networks kept offering me jobs. I already had one of those. I was making $13,000 a year, and I needed a million dollars.

I was getting inspiration and sometimes help from a number of talented people: Richard Leacock, cameraman and filmmaker on a remarkable film for "Omnibus," *Toby in the Tall Corn*; Arthur Zegart, a producer of CBS documentaries; Bill McClure, a cameraman for "CBS Reports"; Morris Engel and Fons Ianelli, experimenters with mobile equipment and filmmaking.

It took me five more years before I had the team, the lightweight equipment, and the story for a breakthrough film. In the meantime I had made a number of short films financed by Andrew Heiskell, the publisher of *Life*. Bullfighters in Spain, experiments with weightless men, a balloon flight to look at Mars through a telescope above most of the atmosphere, a college football game—each of these was the subject of a *Life* story and also of a short film by me. The films were picked up and broadcast on network television by the "Today" and "Tonight" shows, between variety acts on the "Ed Sullivan Show," and on network news programs. *Life* got its money back in promotion. I got to exercise my teams and develop techniques. But we did not yet have our lightweight equipment, and the films were only preparation for making the candid dramas.

In 1960 I was invited to move from *Life* to Time's broadcast division. It owned television stations and had a terrific capital equipment budget. Wes Tullen, vice-president in charge of Time Inc.'s real estate and television operations, welcomed me aboard and asked me to teach the people in his stations "to make your kind of film." In return he would provide funds to buy and modify equipment and make my candid films.

To carry out my side of the bargain I commissioned a West Coast equipment maker, Loren Rider, to build a new machine that would allow us to edit complex films while mixing many sound tracks in any hotel room. It would be completely portable, and we could take it to any Time Inc. TV station, set up, and make our kind of films. To engineer our lightweight cameras I asked Leacock to lay out the specifications, and we assigned Don Alan Pennebaker, a filmmaker who once managed an electronics company, to translate these specifications to our equipment modifier, Mitch Bogdanovich. By March 1960 I felt I was ready to make the first really candid film in which the camera-recorder would live intimately with characters involved in a real story.

I settled on a young senator, John F. Kennedy, running for president in a Wisconsin primary against another senator, Hubert Humphrey. I told both senators that for this new form of reporting to work we would have to live with them from morning to night, shooting anything we wanted to shoot, day after day. They could not know or care when we were shooting, and that was the only way we could capture a true picture of the story. When Kennedy raised an eyebrow I said, "Trust us or it cannot be done." Kennedy agreed. Humphrey agreed.

To shoot the film *Primary* I assembled three teams in Minneapolis. Each was composed of a photographer and a correspondent who also took sound. I assigned Leacock with myself as correspondent to Kennedy and photographers Al Maysles and Terrence Macartney-Filgate to swing between coverage of Humphrey and political gatherings. Pennebaker was on his way to set up the new, portable editing machine in a Minneapolis hotel room.

It was six years since *Key Picture*, five years since Leacock and I had met, four years since we had begun preparing, and now we felt the excitement of a beginning about to begin.

On our first day with Kennedy, Leacock and I were riding in the candidate's car when it stopped in a small town. Kennedy bounded out, down a sidewalk, into a doorway, through a hall, and into a photographer's studio. The photographer posed Kennedy and took his picture, and Kennedy walked back out to his car. Leacock had never stopped shooting; I had never stopped recording. Now we looked at each other. It was a thrilling moment—the first time we had ever exercised such mobility in sync sound—maybe the first time anyone had.

We shot for most of a week. I gathered the teams every night to trade notes on what we had shot and make assignments for the next day. Two dramatic lines unfolded—Kennedy fighting to overcome the prejudices against a Catholic candidate, Humphrey warning the farmers against "easterners who laugh at you." We followed those lines down to the night of the election. Kennedy was holed up in his hotel suite, and he had agreed that one of us would be there shooting. But Leacock was down in the coffee shop, reluctant to intrude on Kennedy's privacy. A laudable, decent fellow, this Leacock, I thought, as I walked him to the door and saw him into Kennedy's room. Leacock dropped midgetape recorders in a few ashtrays and shot what happened as Kennedy first appeared to be losing, then came from behind to win.

We arrived in Minneapolis with forty thousand feet of film. The door opened to the hotel room in which Pennebaker and Ryder had set up our new portable editing machine. It was the size of a ballroom and full of machines and cables. "Don't worry," Pennebaker said, "we've wired the fuses." The thing was a monster. We worked around the clock to get it working and to synchronize the sound and tape. There had been an invisible break in the wire Leacock and I had struggled so hard to maintain between the camera and my recorder. There was no sync signal. The film and tape would not match up. But Ryder had included a new gadget in his system. He called it a resolver, and all we had to do was turn the crank at the right rate in the right direction and we could transfer the sound in sync. The rates and directions changed constantly, and each piece took hours to bring into sync. Pretty soon we did not know whether it was day or night.

The people from the Time Inc. station would look in on us as they arrived for work in the morning and again as they left after work in the evening. They never showed the slightest interest in learning to make films our way.

This was the year I decided that photographers and correspondents must also edit. This would give them responsibility for paying off on what they shot and help each one of them develop as a "filmmaker"—a person capable of going beyond his or her specialty to also produce and manage the editing of films.

In this hotel room my theory ran into the first of the considerable problems it was to trigger over the next few years. Al Maysles was a brilliant cameraman, but there was something about sitting at an editing table hour after hour that immobilized him. Filgate, notorious for a corrosive wit, became positively ferocious after a few days and nights staring into a viewer.

The editing soon boiled down to Leacock, Pennebaker, and me. We schemed out sequences together. They cut them long. I cut them down. In the end I called in an editor from New York, Bob Farren, who combined the sequences. I gave the film a final pacing and wrote a spare narration. The film ran fifty-two minutes. Later Leacock reduced this to thirty minutes for air.

Primary seemed at that moment like a culmination. It was only a beginning. One thing it began was a period of furious production by an independent who was about to encounter the networks.

With the Networks

Independent documentary filmmakers have tended to regard the networks as huge, hostile, and indestructible. Yet the networks' actual output of documentaries has been limited in number and style, and many independents will probably survive the networks very nicely.

Not all networks have been hostile all the time. ABC has used or accepted outsiders from time to time—myself, David Wolper, the Raymonds. NBC has accepted some documentary making when it came through the entertainment side (the "Life Line" series), and it has employed or bought from independents for particular jobs (John Alpert's forays into Afghanistan and Cambodia). CBS has been more consistently closed to independents, though the entertainment division has been able to float documentary series such as "National Geographic" and "The Body Human." But some tough reasons for hostility have remained—reasons of pride, style, and overhead.

When *Primary* was ready to be screened in mid-1960, nearly all network documentaries were based strictly on the written word. Narration carpeted almost every film, with spots left open for interview, all edited so that the word flow never ceased. *Primary* contained less than three minutes of narration. It showed characters in action, and it was meant to be looked at as one would look at a theatrical film. The reaction of network executives to *Primary* was summed up by my friend Elmer Lower, then an NBC News VP and later to become president of ABC News. "You've got some nice footage there, Bob."

The program was broadcast by station groups (Time Inc., RKO) and syndicated to local stations. It was never broadcast by a network.

Primary won the Flaherty Award for best documentary and the blue ribbon at the American Film Festival. In Europe, *Primary* was received as a kind of documentary second-coming. It was broadcast on the television networks, won prizes, and made its way into theaters. Film critics in Paris rated it above the top fiction films of the year. My colleagues were lionized by the Europeans, and new wave directors paid us the compliment of sending back our camera style in fiction films such as *Breathless* and *Tom Jones*.

After *Primary* things began to happen on the network front. I made a film on Indianapolis race driver Eddie Sachs, *On the Pole.* The vice-president in charge of programming at ABC, Tom Moore, had been watching the evolution of our films. He showed *On the Pole* to his chairman, Leonard Goldenson, and came back to me with our first network proposition. Edward R. Murrow had just gathered a lot of credit for several documentaries on Africa. Moore wanted me to make a program for ABC on Latin America.

I protested that television journalism should be making films on people. I suggested we let Murrow have the continents and that we do something else.

"What else?" asked Moore.

I took a week to puzzle out what else in regard to Latin America and came up with a story that could be seen through people in conflict who represented the nations, factions, and ideas that were clashing there. Moore commissioned it, I shot and edited it with my team in a hurry, and the program, *Yanki No!*, was broadcast in the fall of 1960. It made a splash with critics and the public. ABC News's vice-president quit because his management had made the film with an independent. The sponsor, Bell and Howell, asked for more.

So the first network deal I made was for a single program on Latin America. It came about on the network's initiative because its chairman had a need his organization could not fulfill. We were selected because we were there at the right time with something promising to show. What we made for the network attracted commercial demand from a sponsor. That cemented a major agreement between this independent and that network with Time Inc. as a profit-taking financial partner.

The arrangement called for me to produce programs in volume. I had never done that, but it fitted my theories. To build audiences big enough to pay for our programs and develop our independence we would have to broadcast the programming in a regular pattern. To do that we would have to produce in volume—perhaps two or three dozen hours a year. My theory called for most of those hours to be multisubject programs (magazine shows). I believed that we were selling "an experience," not "subject matter." But the network, sponsor, and Time Inc. wanted hours devoted to particular subjects, and that is what we were assigned to produce.

So far I had pretty much hand-made the programs one by one. But my theories called for training specialists who showed talent for producing—cameramen, journalists, editors, writers—to conceive the films, manage the shooting, and "make" them in the editing. I called them "filmmakers" and began crediting at least one person as filmmaker on every production.

With Time Inc.'s help, I formed Drew Associates and saw that it was owned by the key, creative "associates." I set up a research staff to find stories. I developed the concept of each program with a filmmaker and sent him or her off to shoot the story.

When the film came back, the whole production team would screen it, the filmmaker would present his "scheme" for editing it, and usually a free-for-all would ensue among the team members. Out of this I would adjudicate or, if necessary, compose a final scheme for editing. The filmmaker would go off with the scheme, the raw film, and a half-dozen or so editors to make the first cut. A month or two later, I would see that cut and either approve it or recut it. Once or twice I was able to approve a cut. Mainly I found myself deep in the editing business. This was hurtful to filmmakers' pride, and I regretted it, but I conceived it to be part of a necessary training process. In later years I have come to believe that the theory was wrong. It is true that a number of fine filmmakers have emerged. The first generation included Richard Leacock, Gregory Shuker, Don Alan Pennebaker, Hope Ryden, and James Lipscomb. Mike Jackson, Nick Proferes, Tom Bywaters, and Anne Drew rose from the ranks of editors. From the correspondents came Tom Johnson and Harry Moses. From the production side came Peter Powell, Phil Burton, and Sidney Reichman. I am now persuaded, however, that a great photographer does not have to be a total filmmaker and that anyone who sets himself up to make himself one may be defying the laws of art and nature.

Thus, in the first season with ABC, Drew Associates produced a half-dozen "Close-Ups" for Bell and Howell, broadcast at irregular intervals by ABC.

But Time Inc. and ABC were giants who competed. They both owned television stations. ABC "stole" a Time Inc. station. A Time Inc. executive insulted ABC's president. Time Inc. lost its access to ABC air time. Against my feverish advice, Time Inc. placed a multimillion-dollar order with Drew Associates for a dozen new programs. I could see disaster for Time Inc.'s pocketbook and my whole editorial idea if I produced a revolution on film that could not find its way to the public via regular scheduling on a network.

Time Inc. ordered the programs. I produced them. They were syndicated at odd times in odd places. The film festivals loved our programs, but they built no television audience. Time Inc. finally had to release Drew Associates from what had been an exclusive contract.

This move set up Drew Associates' first direct network deal. We were shooting on speculation a film on President John Kennedy in the White House, working with his brother, Attorney General Robert Kennedy, to counter the governor of the state of Alabama, who was trying to prevent black students from attending the state university. Tom Moore called to say that ABC would like to buy the program. That was nice because we had just run out of money and I was about to call back our team, call off the film, and, in fact, call off the company.

ABC sold the film, *Crisis: Behind a Presidential Commitment*, to Xerox, and we negotiated a two-year arrangement by which Drew Associates would produce six documentary specials for ABC News. The day after the deal was signed, a new ABC News president arrived to take over his duties—it was Elmer Lower. We had a nice lunch at Tavern-on-the-Green. He made me an offer. "Tear up the contract," he said. "Bring your people aboard as a unit of ABC News and you can make films as long as you like." There was a pause. "If you insist on remaining independent, these will be the last films you make for us."

For two years it was quite clear that we were "independent." We made films on Vietnam and Malaya and the death of President Kennedy, but Elmer and I didn't see too much of each other. The end of that period, 1964, was the end of our production for ABC News.

In 1965, Xerox asked me what subjects were too tough for networks to assign. I gave them a two-page list. They assigned an hour on drug addiction. The film, *Storm Signal*, won a first prize at Venice, but it was rejected by every network. Xerox bought time on stations in the top fifty markets, ran the film several times in each, and got back figures proving that it was the most looked-at documentary of the year and ranked among the top ten specials of any kind.

In 1967, the Bell Telephone Company decided to commission a series of documentaries on the arts. The first year I produced three specials: Gian Carlo Menotti's "Festivals of Two Worlds," the opening of the new Metropolitan Opera House, and a jazz festival in Belgium with Benny Goodman. The programs were broadcast as specials on NBC and won all kinds of prizes, including a Peabody Award.

The next year, Bell Telephone asked me to produce all their specials—an even dozen. For the first time in my life I turned down business. I agreed to produce half of the hours, six, and suggested they stick with their original producer, Henry Jaffee, for the other six. I felt I owed Jaffee something because he had brought me together with Bell, but also I wanted more time for hand-making the films. One of the programs, *Man Who Dances*, on ballet dancer Edward Villella, won an Emmy.

It was now 1969. Looking back, some interesting things had happened that had influenced relations between this independent and the networks. The one network that had known it could use independents now had a news president who felt that he didn't want any. This closed down our access to public-affairs subject matter for network broadcast.

The sponsors who had influenced networks to go after special qualities in documentaries were fading. Bell and Howell and Xerox and other companies had shifted into a less active and more conservative mode of broadcasting. As the costs of network hours increased, fewer sponsors could afford to buy whole programs. The networks gained strength as a buyer's market became a seller's market. They became less responsive to sponsors' wishes. As network competition for audiences increased, culture disappeared as a regular commodity in prime time. The Bell Telephone Company was denied airtime for a continuation of its series. At the same time, a kind of program that appeared to be a documentary but entailed none of the risk of dealing with the current real world was becoming fashionable—the "Cousteau Undersea" series and the "National Geographic" series. Finally, the cost of film increased, making it so costly to shoot real life uncontrolled that for me it became nearly impossible to continue to make really candid films. A lot of imitations appeared that tarnished the name that had been applied to our films in Europe, *cinéma vérité.*

Thus came about, simultaneously, a network freeze and an economic hold on development of the ideas on which we had been making some progress. For me, the 1970s became what the 1980s seem to be becoming for television in general, a move to more specialized audiences. This was a bit hair-raising and exciting, and demanded new combinations of filmmaking and technology. In science, we made a series of films for NASA on planets, Mars, astronauts, and extraterrestrial life. In the arts, we made films on dance, opera, mime, and the struggles of young artists as they tried to make careers. In government, we made a series of films on how a state, Pennsylvania, tried to manage its most pressing problems. For corporations (LTV, IBM, Portec, Westinghouse, Mutual Benefit Life), we made films on corporate mergers, computers, Tall Ships, the Bicentennial, and Einstein. For a number of these corporations, we also made commercials—our major representation on network television being minidocumentaries running thirty seconds to three minutes. We also made political films for Nelson Rockefeller and a feature-length film for theaters on soaring.

Our network relations were at a standstill as the '70s brought on the blossoming of a multisubject hour, in the form of CBS's "60 Minutes" and later magazine shows at NBC and ABC. These shows frustrated me because I was not producing them, because they were still relying mostly on word logic, and because I thought I knew how they could be better done.

In 1979 I proposed a one-hour special to NBC that wound up as an assignment to produce a shorter film for the "NBC Magazine" show. As he was beginning to make the assignment, Paul Friedman, executive producer of the show, said, "Wait a minute, I'm not sure I can do this." He disappeared down the hall and came back; "Yep, I can do it," he said. This magazine show, it appeared, could do what it wanted with independents.

Over the next two years I produced a half-dozen pieces for the "NBC Magazine" show, half of them on videotape. This gave me a view on videotape and on some of the problems and prospects of the current "Magazine" shows.

I believe "Magazine" shows should provide opportunities for independents to work with networks. Those opportunities will entail some frustration because the magazine-show styles that are working with audiences provide an odd pattern for any broad-ranging or deeply felt journalism. "60 Minutes" entrapment journalism is no way to try to look at the world in general. Nor is "20/20"'s talky consorting with show business celebrities. NBC I regard as not frozen into a pattern because it has not yet been successful in attracting an audience.

On the subject of videotape, I expect to see a more powerful, experience-based journalism appear when we marry the journalistic ideas on which we have been working to tape. By removing the cost barrier posed by film, tape is freeing us to shoot candidly in ways that we have never been able to do before. I am determined that we will produce the new material in volume, program it regularly, and engage larger audiences with a true, broad-ranging form of real-life reporting.

I hope the networks, the public television network included, remain intact. We need ways of assembling audiences. The many alternative ways of broadcasting that seem headed our way promise to fragment audiences. I think our purposes could be more allied with than against the networks. But if I am wrong, one thing appears clear: the networks will be outlasted by independents who have learned to flourish in other environments.

21

New Boy:
An Independent with Israel TV

Alan Rosenthal

Outside the graveyard the soundman was looking at me as if I was a cross between Dracula and Frankenstein. "I don't care what you're shooting . . . I can't go in." "Why not?" I asked, puzzled. "Because I'm a *cohen*, a member of the priestly cast. And under Jewish law a cohen can't go into a cemetery." The "priest" was dressed in stained levis and an old denim shirt, and carried the nagra and two gun mikes. Some priest! But because of his hesitations we shot the scene from outside the offending area.

That wasn't the first such incident. There had been one like it a few days earlier. I'd shot an innocuous ten-minute film profile of Yaakov Pins, a Jerusalem artist, and was going over the rushes with the editor. He was one of the best cutters around but had recently returned to very strict Jewish ortho-doxy. So he literally edited with the Bible open next to the Steenbeck. In the middle of viewing, he'd stopped and thrown up his hands in horror. "Graven images! You've shot graven images! I'm not touching any footage that has idols in it." I looked again. In my shot the artist was admiring a head of Buddha he had acquired in Indonesia. This was the idol that had offended my editor. We argued, but the scene came out.

These two incidents were typical of the rather surrealistic, esoteric atmos-phere surrounding my first few months filming in Israel. It was May 1968, and I'd been invited to Jerusalem for a year to help set up Israel TV. For ages there had been talk, now suddenly there was to be action.

Israel was in fact very late coming onto the television scene, deciding to establish a government-controlled television only after the Six Day War.[1] This was after years of dallying with the idea and years of anti-TV sentiment among the conservative and religious elements of the country. The showing of the 1967 war on the neighboring Arab screens had demonstrated the propaganda value of television, and now the government wanted TV as fast as possible.

So after a decade of hesitations, things began to move. Equipment was ordered from America. CBS experts arrived in Brooks Brothers suits carrying wondrous organizational charts. Would-be filmmakers were corralled (mainly from the radio and press). And finally, to cap the whole thing, eighteen foreign advisers, including myself, were invited to spend a year teaching Israelis the splendid art of film and television and to assist in getting the operation off the ground.

Prior to the invitation I had been working as a filmmaker and lawyer in England and the United States and had established a fairly good reputation in documentary. I'd also filmed a few times in Israel: with the Eichmann trial in 1961, and a piece on kibbutzim in 1964. I guess those two facts, added together, had occasioned the invitation—and I was looking forward to the third visit. But this time there was some trepidation. I knew that working in Israel on a long-term basis would present a completely new set of challenges, both on the practical and technical side and in terms of cultural understanding.

Nitty Gritty Practicalities

To come from the United States with its hundreds of stations to Israel with its one fledgling station[2] was to enter a weird and wonderful world—a world where very little of what one knew before counted or even made sense. But it was a stimulating and vibrant world, where talent was high and technique low, where almost anything could be tried (at least once), and where nobody paid the slightest attention to anybody else, least of all to the advisers. It was a world where the students studied directing on Monday and set up their own school for production techniques on Tuesday.

The training of TV crews started in April 1968, and by September the station was already broadcasting a few programs. In less than a year the station was in full swing and broadcasting between two and three hours a day to 80 percent of the country. In its turn, television gave a boost to Israeli film-making in general, so that the early years of the 1970s saw a massive growth in the production of both shorts and features in the country.

For most of 1968 and 1969 I worked full-time on the TV staff. My job consisted in the main of training film crews, trying to build a documentary department, advising on policy, and acting as producer-director on six or seven films. I then left Israel for a couple of years, and in 1971 I came back to try my hand as a freelance filmmaker. As anyone can easily guess, the story then became very different, and the work conditions much more difficult and confining.

The way a freelancer worked was fairly simple. Although Israel TV preferred to make all its films with tenured staff and on its premises, by 1971 it had begun to contract films out to private production companies. These companies in turn then contracted out the writing and directing to freelancers, and it was at this last stage that I entered the game.

Because I had been a founding father, so to speak, the work was fairly easy to come by, but the most appalling restrictions applied. For the staff of Israel TV, neither time nor materials mattered very much. One could take between three and six months making a half-hour film and not too many questions would be asked. Nine months on a film was not unusual, and one friend of mine boasted that quality demanded that he not do more than one film a year. The point is, no matter how long the film took, the TV paid a fairly good salary to the staffer every month.

Working as a freelancer you saw the other side of the coin. Israel was broke, we were told, and the TV could afford only a pittance for our films. Thus—regrettably—time, money, and materials all had to be restricted.

At that time, the total budget for a twenty-minute freelance film would probably be between $4,000 and $6,000. For such a film you were allowed four days for research, three days for filming, and, with luck and a lot of pressure, nine or ten days for editing. The film was always shot in black-and-white (Israel had no color television then) and on a strict five-to-one ratio. As often as not the research was done by the writer-director without any backup, and production help was minimal: you never went out with a production assistant, and a production manager was uncommon.

I should add that unions did not yet exist, and the private production companies took full advantage of this fact. Thus an average shooting day would run some thirteen to fourteen hours. Why didn't we complain? Because it was a classic buyer's market, with everyone dying to get into the industry no matter how lousy the conditions. You didn't want to direct? Fine, there was another director waiting outside the door.

A typical example of the situation is a film I did in 1971 called *Battle Officer*, about two lieutenants in the Israeli army stationed near the Suez Canal. For research I was allowed one day to drive from Jerusalem to the canal, tour the length of the canal, do the interviews, and then drive home the same evening. All together that involved six hundred miles of driving, by myself, mostly through desert and sandstorms.

The shooting merely repeated the story, though this time I was with a crew and didn't drive. We left Tel Aviv at noon on a Tuesday and drove across the northern Sinai desert to get to the canal in the evening, where we started shooting immediately. On Wednesday we arose at 5:00 A.M.; we shot through Wednesday and Thursday until midnight; and we traveled back through the desert early Friday morning. No one said anything—it was simply standard procedure.

Our complications came from the production companies' budget maneuvers and scrimping. Their contracts with the TV often stipulated six or seven days of shooting, budgeted, let us say, at $500 a day. The company, however, would only allow the director three days' shooting, thus quietly pocketing $1,500. Everyone knew about this practice but could do very little.[3]

Although the TV had a documentary department, films could just as well be made for the religious department or the children's department, or as a cultural special. For the most part they were in Hebrew, but occasionally they had to be in Arabic. At that stage my Hebrew was fairly fluent, since I had attended a government language course, but I had practically no Arabic. This didn't matter too much, as I could interview in Hebrew or English or through an interpreter, then write the full commentary in English and have it translated into Arabic. There was only one catch: Arabic comes out about three times as long as English. So when I wrote "I like you," which takes a second and a half in narration, I had to keep in mind that in Arabic the phrase would emerge as "Your eyes are luscious as dappled swans floating over the moonlit sea" and allow ten seconds for the commentary track.

It would be nice to say the rewards were commensurate with the effort, but they weren't. Most of my films took two to three months from start to finish. In almost every case I acted as writer-director, and occasionally I took on the job of working producer as well. In the end these Herculean labors would bring in all of $700, of which a third went to the government in taxes.

Generally speaking, these conditions had a very negative effect on film quality, but not necessarily on the filmmaker. On the downside the conditions meant hasty surface research, inability to let a situation develop over time, the abandonment of anything approaching a true *vérité* style, hesitation in the face of experiment, a hurried news style of shooting, and frantic editing. It also meant ulcers, worries, tension, and gray hair. Yet ironically, because of these very conditions, one often emerged at the end of the process a better filmmaker. Because of the sheer hunger for television in a new country, a tremendous number of films could be made under a fantastic variety of circumstances. So in my first years I found myself doing films on bedouin festivals, road safety, the Israeli Olympic team, scientific research, psychology, urban renewal, and child welfare.

As a freelancer, time was money, and once the film was thrown at you you learned to go like a bomb. First you learned the necessity of shaping your film very clearly and strongly before you began shooting; you learned very quickly what would and would not work; you learned to shoot and direct under immense pressure; you learned to work with minimum footage and against the clock; and finally, you worked the whole time with the thought in your mind, "How will this edit?" In short, you couldn't afford to go wrong.

In its own way it was fun. You could feel yourself changing. You became honed and focused. The final result was that although the films may not have been superb, you emerged from the process (if you weren't killed by it) a competent and technically proficient filmmaker, with skills you hoped to put to better use when the chance arose.

The Minefield

With perseverence and sheer bloody-mindedness, I eventually learned to cope with the practical aspects of the work—even to laugh at them. Coping with the culture and the pressures around Israel TV, however, was infinitely more tricky and complex.

For example, I was, for the first time, making films about Israel for Israelis and not for a foreign audience. That doesn't sound too hard, but it was a situation I felt quite uneasy about. Put simply, the question I had to ask myself was, did I know enough to make meaningful films about the culture and society without appearing a complete idiot in front of the natives? I just wasn't sure!

Experience would suggest that this area is a minefield, having taken the toll of many foreign filmmakers. Antonioni's film on China was blasted by the Chinese. Louis Malle's *Phantom India* series was scorned by the Indians. Both filmmakers were ostensibly condemned not because they criticized the culture (though this is certainly part of the reason for the attacks on Malle) but because they failed to understand the subject—the society—and the mores and beliefs with which they were dealing.[4]

Israel, too, has had its share of itinerant foreign filmmakers, and it has usually viewed them with suspicion. There have been too many digests of Israel based on a week's "expertise" or a three-day briefing. The irony is that many of these efforts, scorned by the Israelis as sheer misreadings of a situation or the culture, have been praised to the skies abroad. Thus Susan Sontag's *Promised Lands* (1973) was hailed by *Commentary* magazine as possibly the best short ever done on Israel.[5]

In contrast, Claude Lanzmann's three-hour *Pourquoi Israel* (1975) was an incredible tour de force for a foreigner. Almost every Israeli I met agreed that for once a stranger had really understood and shown what was going on. But even then there were a few faux pas. For example, in an interview with an Ashdod port worker, the worker complains about his miserably low wage, which Lanzmann obviously accepts as true. When I saw the film at the Hebrew University, the audience burst into hysterics at this juncture. It knew, only too well, that the port workers were the highest-paid workers in Israel, getting an incredible amount per day. Clearly, Lanzmann had taken the image of the Marseilles port laborer and applied it to his Israeli counterpart, where it just didn't fit.

When I came to Israel in 1968, I was seen as a foreigner—my having previously spent six months in the country counted for nothing. Nor did the fact that I knew Hebrew. "You're a bloody Englishman and you don't know our ways. You're a new boy. You haven't been in a youth movement. You haven't been in the army. You haven't got a clue." My students at the TV said this to me. They were pleasant but cocky, arrogant Israelis. They *knew*, because of their birthright—I didn't. And, to my chagrin, they were largely correct. The only thing I could do was look, learn, observe, read, talk, and hope that time would bring insight.

My first problem of filmic acculturation was to understand the audience—to grasp very completely that I was making films for the locals and not for Americans, Australians, or Englishmen. Further, I had to grasp that the difference between making Zionist films and making Israeli films was like the difference between night and day.

This acculturation may sound simple, but it had an immense number of ramifications. I had to understand emotionally, and not just in my head, the sheer diversity of the audience. We were making films for a population of over three million, the majority being Jews, but a large minority were Moslem Arabs. Whereas the Arabs were fairly homogeneous, the Jewish population was divided in every way imaginable. There were the sophisticated Berliners who had arrived in the thirties; the Yemenites from Saana who came in 1949; the North Africans from Morocco and the semi-bedouin Jews from the Atlas Mountains who came in the fifties; and the Russians from Georgia, Moscow, and Leningrad who came flocking in in the seventies.

And Israel's fantastic diversity extended well beyond the population. One stumbled on Christian tour groups going over Crusader castles, Moslems celebrating Ramadan, and blue-shirted Jewish youngsters visiting the site of the Dead Sea Scrolls. Geographically, historically, and religiously it presented a painting of a thousand different colors. And to add to the fantasy, one always saw in the background a Hollywood television team shooting the story of Moses in the Sinai desert or reconstructing the Masada epic. At last I understood the expression "mind-boggling." For that first year my mind well and truly boggled.

This worked very negatively on my filming. Everything was exotic, everything was a wonder. This included the rabbi who looked as if he'd walked out of a medieval Polish village. It included the bedouins who looked to be straight from *Ben Hur*, and their disgruntled camels. And it certainly included the sexy, flamboyant Greek Orthodox priests with their majestic grey beards and hair tied behind in a bun.

But for the Israelis all this was commonplace, not worth a second glance. I was seeing a *New York Times* travel section on Israel, but what had to appear on the screen was a different Israeli reality—more subtle, more somber, more probing—a vision relevant to life as it was lived in Tel Aviv, in the Negev, and in the kibbutzim rather than to life as lived in the great beyond.

My social acculturation took time. I had thought about the problems before I came and was therefore on my guard. What I hadn't considered too seriously, though, were the areas of censorship and security—how careful you had to be, and how the possible impact of your films could never be dropped from your mind for a moment.

From its beginnings, Israel has been surrounded by countries with whom it was in a state of war, and except for Egypt, this is still the case. Yet because of proximity, nearly all Israeli broadcasts can be seen in parts of Lebanon, Syria, and Jordan. The impact of one's broadcasts on the enemy, then, while not central to one's filmmaking, is always in the background. The impact of one's films on Israel's own Arab population also warranted serious thought (more on that shortly).

Official censorship was the easiest to handle. It came up mainly in the context of films dealing with the border situation, terrorism, and the army. In nearly all these cases permission had to be sought for filming and the films had to be cleared before broadcast. Though I didn't deal much with the first two subjects, I did do two films on the army, *Battle Officer* and *Letter from the Front*, and so went through most of the stages of censorship.

The first move was to apply to the army bureaucracy for approval to do the film. The outline idea was submitted, and in 80 percent of cases it was approved. Occasionally the army would get difficult. No one could be spared! The subject was under wraps! The film would undermine army morale! But these were exceptions, as in general the army was slow but helpful. Restrictions usually extended to saying you could only film in X, not Y, or only do a picture about officer A, not officer B.

Once official permission had been given, your director's credentials had to be approved by the army spokesman's office. During the actual filming itself, an officer from the same office accompanied you everywhere. His task was to tell you what you could and couldn't film. The battles consisted of the officer saying no, it couldn't be done, and myself trying to recall where I had just seen a published picture of that tank, that new artillery piece, that new carrier. If I could quote chapter and verse, I could go on filming. Buildings up to eye level could be filmed, but nothing revealing place or situation. Everything was quoted as taking place *esham bamidbar*—"somewhere in the desert." General dialogue was OK, specific battle comment and operating procedures definitely out. No names could be mentioned, no units cited.

Later the rushes were seen in toto by another censor, and the final censorship took place when the married print was ready. *Battle Officer* had featured some fortifications near the canal, tanks on maneuvers, and searches for mines and terrorists. It had good, exciting material that I was loathe to lose, and I was quite fearful that the film would be emasculated. In the end, the censors left all the visuals and merely cut out three passages of dialogue dealing with specific operations, cuts that I recognized as being totally justified.

During the Yom Kippur War, while working on *Letter from the Front*, I saw another aspect of the censorship game. What was unique about the war was the immediacy and involvement of the coverage. This was not a war being filmed a thousand miles away, to be shown to viewers who were for the most part uninvolved: it was a war being filmed a mere fifty or one hundred miles from the TV set. It was also a war that was being shown not weeks and months after the battle, but scarcely half a day later. In a country as small and as intimate as Israel, few of the faces on the screen were anonymous: all were immediately known and recognizable as sons, husbands, friends, and acquaintances.

All this implied both practical and emotional censorship rules that provoked different reactions among foreigners and among Israelis. In the early days of the war, journalists couldn't really get to the front, and when they did their copy was severely restricted. This irked many of the foreign journalists used to relatively free battle coverage from Vietnam. The Israeli attitude, with which I agreed, was that what was merely a news story for some people involved matters of life and death for others, and that security and human feeling came before world information or war as entertainment.

Letter from the Front, shot during the war, was a ragbag of film grabbed on the run everywhere from the Sinai front to the Golan Heights. Seven camerapersons participated, three directors, and a couple of editors. I shot two sequences in Safed military hospital, one at Fayid (the old British Egyptian airfield), one around the tank battles in the north, and another sequence of soldiers at a kibbutz.

The material was heartrending—just too much to bear—and I was happy to leave the film to the two other directors (which word is really a misnomer when applied to war footage) to finish. I hadn't a clue what they would do with the material or what shape they would give it. I merely knew they were up against a bind, as film had to be out within two weeks.

A few days later I got a call from the producer. The film was finished, which is to say totally edited, with picture locked and a music and effects track recorded—but somehow it wasn't working. Could I write a link commentary for it, but . . . er . . . no visuals could be changed and the commentary had to be ready by tomorrow.

I looked at the film on the editing table. It was half an hour long and went all over the place. One moment we were with the fighting, the next moment with a family, the next moment back at war again. It was a mess, but it had some marvelous sequences. And it was a challenge. Because of its confusion, an A to Z script was out (thank God), but I felt some interesting things could be done if the script was internalized and personalized and told how people *felt* rather than how wars were fought.

Everything then became simple. I looked at the film a few times, took a shot list and timing, and went home. In my bedroom I drew out copies of my recent letters to family in England, took out my diary, poured a glass of brandy, and started to work. The script was the easiest I've ever written—to use a cliché, it wrote itself and was finished in about an hour and a half. The following day we recorded the narration and then put the film into the lab. In retrospect I think it's the most personal film I have ever done, and certainly the one which has brought the most satisfaction.

War films and military films were only a small part of my life. My films had much more to do with religion, history, urban politics, and the social scene. And here the informal censorship of the system was much more subtle than that of the military censors.

Now, every TV system has its own unwritten rules. These can vary from dealing with the Irish situation with kid gloves and being polite to the Queen to keeping quiet about Vietnam, not knocking the FBI, and leaving the president's family in peace. So what I am discussing is not new, but just an indication of where Israel's sensibilities lie as opposed to those of England or America.

Because the TV came into existence only in 1968, the ground rules were at first quite fluid. At least that was my sense of the situation at the time. When I came back to Jerusalem in 1971, the ground rules, though never openly stated, had crystallized very clearly. These guidelines were (a) no criticism of religion[6] and (b) no documentaries analyzing the rough house of politics, political parties, or problematic situations, social or otherwise—in short, no rocking the boat.

From the start the religious affairs department produced a lot of documentaries and was a good bread supply to freelance directors. In the main these films were fairly simple pieces, such as the profile of a young rabbi, the scientist as believer, or a righteous convert. Outside of Judaism there was always something to be done on Ramadan or Christmas at Bethlehem.

The films on Judaism, however, suffered from two peculiar problems. First, some of the small ultraorthodox groups objected vehemently to being filmed, any time, any place—the old graven-image taboo. Thus they would take refuge from photographers by covering their faces with their traditional black felt hats. This, of course, was their right, as is anyone's to privacy. However, they would often interrupt filming in accepted public places, which could be a bit much. Sometimes they did this by stoning the photographer; other times they hurled imprecations. Once while filming around a wonder worker's tomb I was told to stop, otherwise the objector would write to the Hassidic rabbi of Bessarabia to excommunicate me. Lunch was ready, so I stopped, otherwise who knows what would have happened to my immortal soul.

The second drawback to filming religious subjects was that because of the strictly interpreted ban in Jewish law regarding Sabbath work, it was forbidden to film on the Sabbath and on certain Jewish holidays. Now, this makes things a little bit tricky when so much of one's filming consists of trying to shoot a Saturday morning bar mitzvah, a New Year celebration, or a Passover seder. The answer—not totally satisfactory—was to stage most of these events and then superimpose a title reassuring the righteous that these events were not shot on the Sabbath or whatever.

All the above was in its own way quite funny and a challenge to the inventiveness of both director and cameraperson. Subject censorship was much more serious. In no way as a documentarist could you get through with a film that might offend orthodox religious susceptibilities or comment critically on the religious state of affairs.[7] You couldn't do a film debating the power of the religious courts: the subject was simply out of bounds. You knew this and wouldn't even waste time writing a proposal on the subject. The same was true if you wanted to do a piece looking at some of the slightly shady goings-on involved in conversion.

My own run-in in this area came in a film I wanted to do on marriage. In Israel there is no civil marriage, only religious. Thus, not only can a Jew not marry a Christian or a Moslem, but the marriage—even for unbelievers—has to be religiously performed. Naturally, this state of affairs has been a battle ground for years, with traditionalists opposing civil reformers. Like others, I thought this would be a good subject for a film if I could find the right approach. The best answer seemed to be to come at the general subject through the particular incident, and I chose three stories that would illustrate the dilemmas.

My first profile was to be a Jewish kibbutz girl who wanted to marry an Arab. Then I found a cohen (a "priest," like my sound man) who wanted to marry a divorced woman, a relationship forbidden by Jewish law. Finally, I wanted to film a director friend who wanted to marry a non-Jewish American girl. He had found this was impossible in Israel and was planning to marry in Cyprus.

I thought the film had tremendous potential for investigating the subject. I also thought I was the right person to do it because, though in favor of reform and not particularly religious, I was fairly sympathetic to religious traditions. So, buoyed with high hopes, I took a ten-page proposal to the head of programming at the TV.

We drank a few beers. He slapped me on the back. "Great subject. Fantastic idea. But of course we can't do it. Maybe in two years time. Just now it's . . . er . . . a bit sensitive." So the idea got dropped. Instead, the TV did a film on three ethnic wedding celebrations—what I would call a lovely moving wallpaper picture.

My film *Battle Officer* also brought up awkward moments for the TV. Here my central character, a tank officer, had made two "offending" statements. The first was that few soldiers in his unit wanted to attend morning prayers. The second, also highly personal, was that his deeply religious parents objected to his serving in the army.

The executive producer argued that these passages be cut. The impression he wanted to create was that the army was gung-ho for religion and that the religious community was right behind the army. I argued that the passages were personal and must stay. In the end we compromised. The expressions stayed in but were "balanced" by commentary supporting the executive producer's views.

Aside from the religious limitations, many of us were also troubled by the unseen political limitations. At the root of the problem was a mistaken belief on the part of the government and politicians concerning the power of television to influence opinion, something professional communicators were and are much more cautious about.

So the unstated messages filtered down through the ranks. Not so much "Don't do that subject," but rather, "If you do it, it is going to create a lot of problems for us, so why don't you try something else. Something safer, less noisy"—all complicated by the fact that you were an independent director. Thus, if your controversial films were made and created a ruckus, your chances of getting another film from the system were diminished. As I've said, I don't think it's much different elsewhere, but it is frustrating when you think your films might be able gradually to create a climate of change.

Nevertheless, and happily, people fought this situation. Early in 1968 a friend of mine, Ram Levy, did a film on two families—one Jewish, one Arab—both of whom had lost sons in the 1967 war. It was a very sensitive and human story showing that grief and tragedy know no political barriers. The film was finished in 1968 and then reviewed by committee after committee. I'd see them meeting in the editing room next door, pontificating on whether this mild, gentle film would spark riots in the Gallil or would cause Arabs in the Old City to rise in revolt. Eventually it was shown, in 1972 or 1973—a mere four years late.

Sitting in the TV cafe with friends in the early seventies I would go through the films we had suggested that had been turned down without consideration. They ranged from the obvious "naughties"—Jewish converts to Christianity and the Zionist dirty linen of the twenties and thirties—to more shaded areas such as drugs, homosexuality, poverty in Israel, and the character of the political parties. This last area really attracted me, especially after seeing a BBC film on the British Labour party called *Yesterday's Men*. But cold water was poured on the idea in the preliminary discussions. According to the pundits, such a film would either propagandize for the party or probe too many grubby secrets. Neither result was acceptable.

I must add at this juncture—in order to be fair—that all this was in the early seventies and that the mid-seventies saw an improvement in the situation. All the controversial sex subjects were discussed, poverty was admitted, and the buried pages of history were uncovered. Nor did Judgment Day follow. In fact, one of the highlights of the last few years was a drama, shot documentary style, which showed some actions of the 1948 war in a distinctly unfavorable light. The film, *Chirbat China*, became a *cause célèbre*, and though there were protests galore the film was screened as scheduled. Unfortunately, at the time of writing—March 1981—the situation has again slightly deteriorated.

Sometimes the constraints of the Israeli political atmosphere made for a double-edged sword. On one cutting edge were all the forbidden subjects. The other edge, equally dangerous, represented the special-interest subjects. Here care was needed to avoid being "used" if you were to maintain some kind of integrity as a filmmaker.

In this area the biggest traps were usually encountered in attempts to show aspects of the Israeli Arab conflict on the screen. Sometimes the problem would be historical, such as dealing with the old Hebron killings by the Arabs or the Deir Yassin killings by the Jews, or it might arise out of contemporary life and problems in the administered territories.

My own turn to be involved arose out of a suggestion from the Arabic department of the TV. Could I write and direct a twenty-minute film about a village called Abu Ghosh? Nothing serious—just a short profile piece depicting its history, its current life, and featuring a few of the village personalities.

The village lies about eight miles from Jerusalem and straddles the old road to the capital. It was founded by the Abu Ghosh brothers a few hundred years ago, and its strategic situation made it a favorite bandit "tax point" for robbing pilgrims and travelers. Today the village shelters hundreds of the descendants of the original brothers. It also talks of a Crusader tradition, claims a few biblical remains, and boasts a few rather lovely churches. All in all, a dead easy film to do.

The catch lay in the motivation behind the film proposal. Abu Ghosh had been taken as a positive example of an Arab village that didn't flee in 1948 and whose inhabitants had lived ever since in prosperity and peace with their Jewish neighbors. In short, a positive, picturesque story of harmony and friendship to counter some of the propaganda about Arab refugees. So the underlying interest of the TV was fairly clear. But if the story were true, I was all in favor of telling it.

My research turned up a rather more complex situation. In the 1948 war, the Arabs had in fact been asked to leave the village so that the Jewish *haganah* forces could better defend the entrance to Jerusalem. The Arabs were reluctant to go but eventually complied with the wishes of the Jewish officers after being reassured that they could return in a few weeks. After the war, however, their return was denied them. In the end it took the forceful intervention of Yitzhak Navon—a future president of Israel, president of Israel, then a young officer—against the authorities to ensure the villagers' return and the fulfillment of the original promise. Even then the Arabs claimed that much of their land had been forcibly requisitioned, with only a small recompense paid.

This was not quite the story the TV had hoped for. Yet any film on Abu Ghosh would be nonsense unless this history was brought out. I discussed this with the head of Arabic programs, who had proposed the film, and he was rather taken aback. To his credit, he decided the story must be told and supported me the whole way through. Given the internal pressures of the TV, this was quite courageous. The only thing he insisted on was that I interview Navon (not in my original script) to get a fuller understanding of the context of promises and counterpromises.

While making that film I also became prey to a few Arabs who wanted to use it for an anti-Israel diatribe. Did I know that conditions in the village stank? That social help was being deliberately withheld? That the youth of the village was being exploited? That village lands had once stretched from Jerusalem to Tel Aviv and had been taken and ruined?

The charges couldn't be ignored, and I spent about a week tracking down welfare grants to the village, statistics on aid it received, compensation it had been paid, and so on. I also interviewed about fifteen people from the village to try to cross-check stories as to what happened between 1948 and 1975. In the end I found most of the charges were unsubstantiated nonsense, and I didn't even refer to them in my program.

Abu Ghosh was almost the last picture I did for the TV. After it came two films on archaeology in the Sinai and a profile of a bedouin musician, but none of the films had problems. That was in 1977. Since then I have worked almost exclusively for American and foreign network television via my own production company. This has meant a better financial reward, but also some emotional loss, as my films are not going to the audience that counts: the Israelis themselves.

Looking back, between 1968 and 1977 I made over twenty films for the TV. They ranged from pieces on soldiers, academics, and workers, through films on the holocaust, politics, and Israeli history to social investigations, child welfare, and profiles of musicians. I learned scuba diving for a film on underwater archaeology, did a three-hour climb up Mount Sinai to get the desert at dawn, traipsed through almost every religious site in the country, shot factories beyond recall, and amused myself making a film about Burt Lancaster playing Moses.

In all this I count myself very privileged. I saw the country from the ground up (and underwater) and learned to understand firsthand its ways, its nuances, its peoples. At the same time I would like to think my work made a small impression on a country in a state of flux, a country in the process of defining itself and its character and institutions. Maybe. One never knows.

Recently I've had a renewed appetite to work for the TV, and I gave them a few proposals. One of them deals with the difference between the Israeli dream and reality. The head of the department liked it but had a few negative comments. "Where are the rabbis? What's happened to the Arabs? No camels. No deserts. Why can't you begin to think like a tourist?" Hearing that, I knew my time as a "new boy" was over. Graduation day had come at last.

Notes

1   Israel TV takes the BBC independent corporation idea as its model but in practice is subject to much more political pressure.

2   In fact, a small educational television station had been set up in Tel Aviv by the Rothschild Foundation in the early 1960s. In 1968 it was still broadcasting, but only to a limited audience of a few thousand pupils.

3   This practice has diminished as the Directors' Guild has grown in strength.

4   What *can* be done and shown by foreigners with a deep knowledge and understanding of an alien culture is seen in the China films of Joris Ivens and Marcelle Loridan. In contrast, Shirley MacLaine and Claudia Weill's film *China: The Other Side of the Sky* is a highly praised but superficial piece in which almost everything is accepted at face value and almost all serious questions are evaded.

5   *Commentary*, Oct. 1976, p. 78.

6   For years the religious parties, though small, have held the balance of power in the government. Their few votes have given the ruling party its majority, whether Likud or Labor. Thus, no one is willing to ruffle the feathers of the religious, particularly not on TV.

7   The news department, because it dealt with immediate events in the public eye, was a much freer department in this respect. Even then, its broadcasts on controversial issues were made only after a struggle.

22

Reflections on *An American Family*

Craig Gilbert

What appears below is the first part of a very long article by Craig Gilbert on the making of An American Family. *The second part of the article which deals primarily with the ethical questions which arose in the filming unfortunately had to be left out of this book because of space considerations. It can, however, be found in the first edition of* New Challenges for Documentary, *pp. 288–307 (Berkeley: University of California Press, 1988). For an appreciative book-length account of the series, its context and its reception, see also* An American Family: A Televised Life *by Jeffrey Ruoff (Minneapolis: University of Minnesota Press, 2002).*

Finding the Louds

On that first night at 35 Woodale Lane, there were drinks and pleasant conversation. I met all the children with the exception of Lance, who had gone to New York to work on a new underground magazine. We talked about television and the series and the practical considerations of how it would all work. After about an hour the family agreed to participate. As a matter of fact, my private feelings were that they had agreed a little too rapidly, that they did not fully realize what they were letting themselves in for. I thought it would be good for them to experience being followed around for a day by a camera crew. On the following day there was to be a runoff election between Kevin Loud and another student for the office of president of the student body at Santa Barbara High School. In anticipation of Kevin's winning the election, a party was planned at the Loud home. This sounded like an ideal situation in which to introduce the family to the conditions of *cinéma vérité* filming. They agreed, and I returned to the motel to make the arrangements.

After several phone calls I contacted a Los Angeles film crew (unknown to me) who were willing to come to Santa Barbara the following day. Once the shooting started it became quickly apparent that the crew was not very skilled at *cinéma vérité* filmmaking, a highly specialized technique which demands a kind of sixth-sense understanding between the person who is doing the shooting and the person who is doing the sound. Much of what was interesting that night was missed, and most of what was shot was badly framed and included not only the microphone but the man holding it. However, I really didn't care. I had no intention of using the footage; I just wanted the family to know what it felt like to be followed by a camera, lights, and a microphone.

My suspicion that the Louds had agreed to the project without really knowing what they were getting into proved to be correct. Around midnight, Pat and Bill asked if we could talk for a while. Their first question was whether they could have final approval of what was included in the series. It was clear what they were concerned about. Liquor was flowing quite freely at the party, and I had noticed the cameraman getting quite a few shots of both Pat and Bill serving drinks to kids who were both underage and already quite obviously drunk. Two years later, when the Louds were claiming publicly, on television talk shows and in newspaper interviews, that we had shown only the bad times in their lives and none of the good times, they always mentioned this party as an example of the happy life that we had excluded from the series. I allayed their fears about the party footage by explaining that none of it was going to be used. But I made clear that in the future, when the shooting got started in earnest, I would have to retain the right to make that decision. However, I agreed that before any of the episodes were "locked up," the family or any member of the family would be allowed to see it and raise objections, which I promised would be listened to seriously and discussed fully, and changes would be made if they were warranted.

There were other problems, but the party was still going on and I wanted the children to be involved in any further discussions. So I dismissed the camera crew and suggested we all get some rest on Saturday and I come back on Sunday to discuss the matter thoroughly. When that was agreed on, I went back to the motel and slept for almost thirty-six hours. It had been a little more than two months since I had started the search for the family, but I still did not feel secure enough to call Curt Davis and tell him the search had been successful. With a day's rest and plenty of time to think over the pressure of Friday night, I had no idea whether the Louds would change their minds.

Setting Ground Rules

The discussion on Sunday centered around three main points. The first had to do with privacy: where would the camera go and where would it not go? In this respect I promised the camera would never go through a closed door. If the family or any member of the family wanted to be alone, all they had to do was go into a room and close the door. In addition to this, I explained that a normal shooting day would begin around eight in the morning and end around ten at night. There might, of course, be exceptions to this, but generally that would be the schedule. If the family wanted to talk over anything they didn't want us to see or hear, it should be before or after those hours.

The second point had to do with what would happen if the family collectively came to the decision that they had made a mistake, that the whole thing was too much for them and they wanted to quit. I said that if this happened I would of course want to talk it over with them to find out what was bothering them. If possible, whatever it was would be eliminated. If that could not be done, I said, the family would have the right to call it quits, and that would be it.

The final point revolved around how much the filming would interfere with their lives. This was a difficult thing to talk about, since there were so many imponderables. Obviously, it is not normal to have a camera crew following you around all day. For a while at least, I explained, it was going to feel strange and awkward. But my hunch was it wouldn't take long for the new circumstances of their life to feel reasonably comfortable. How quickly and how easily this happened would depend on the skill of the camera crew and the ability of the members of the family to get used to their presence and go on about their lives without feeling self-conscious.

My instructions were that they were to live their lives as if there were no camera present. They were to do nothing differently than they would ordinarily. This would be hard at first but would, I promised, become increasingly easier. We would never ask them to do anything just for the camera. In other words, we would never stage anything and we would never ask them to do or say something over again if we happened to miss it. To the best of our ability we would not become involved in the family's problems. By that I meant that as far as was humanly possible we would not intrude our feelings, opinions, or personalities into family disputes, discussions, or relationships. This last restriction became, as the filming progressed, the hardest restriction to live up to.

I wish to make it clear that at no time did I bring up the subject of payment, nor did any of the Louds ever ask for any compensation for participating in the project.

After we had talked about all these problems, the unanimous decision of the family was that they would participate in the project. We now had to set a date for when the filming would get started in earnest. Pat Loud said she would be flying to New York the following Saturday to spend a week or so with Lance in New York. We decided to start the shooting officially then. Pat said she would call Lance at the Chelsea Hotel and tell him what was happening, and I said I would go back to New York and get in touch with him sometime before Saturday.

I spent the rest of the day with the family, eating and talking and just getting acquainted. The next morning, I called Curt Davis at NET and told him I had found the family. He said it was a good thing I had, because he had decided to give me only one more week and then was going to call a halt to the whole undertaking. I told him I was going to fly back to New York on Tuesday and asked if he could set up a meeting with the appropriate production executives for Wednesday morning. He said he would.

Establishing a Budget

Back in New York, the major production problems were the budget and the fact that I wanted to start shooting in two days' time. Most of the production people took the position that this was impossible. They were adamant that there would be no shooting until a firm budget had been established. I was just as adamant in maintaining that Pat Loud's visit to New York to see Lance had to be covered.

As I mentioned earlier, before I left on my search for a family, $600,000 had been found somewhere to fund the project. I now discovered the money had come from cancelling a series called *Priorities for Change*, a public affairs series scheduled for production in the new season.[1] Without my knowing about it, *Priorities for Change* had been dropped from the schedule, its budget had been made available to my project, and its six producers had been given their notice. Needless to say, this did not make me very popular with the Public Affairs Department or with Bill Kobin, the vice-president in charge of programming, whose background was hard news and whose relationship with Cultural Affairs had been strained over the years.

In preliminary conversations with the production people it soon became clear that $600,000 would not be enough to cover the cost of *An American Family*. To find out just how much more would be needed, I was told to sit down with a production manager and figure out a realistic budget. One of the barriers that stood in the way of doing this quickly was the question of the camera crew and what their individual salaries would be. On the last film I had made I had used the camera and sound team of Alan and Susan Raymond. When that film was completed, I had promised the Raymonds that they would work on my next project.

After *The Triumph of Christy Brown*, and to a certain extent on the strength of that film, Alan Raymond and his wife had gotten several assignments from other producers at NET, in the course of which they had dealings (most of them fraught with antagonism and anger) with several of NET's production managers. In fact, on one of those films Alan had managed to antagonize the very man he would now be negotiating with about his salary and the salaries of his crew. It was a very delicate situation, and I told Alan as much when we met in my office prior to our first budget meeting. That meeting proved to be a disaster whose ramifications continued to be felt for the first two months of shooting. Alan's initial request (or, more accurately, demand) caused the meeting to end almost before it started, just short of a fistfight, and generated so much anger that no progress of any kind could be made for almost a week.

What Alan wanted, before the specific question of salaries even came up, was an advance from NET so he could buy his own camera and thus eliminate the expense of renting one. On the face of it this did not seem an unusual request; in fact, it made sense, inasmuch as NET would ultimately have to pay the rental fee anyway. The problem was the way Alan demanded this concession. Something in his voice and attitude touched off a lingering dislike of him, and within minutes the two men were glaring at each other, all pretence at maintaining the ordinary amenities out the window. When Alan called the production manager every obscene name he could think of, the meeting ended abruptly. The result of all this was that Alan Raymond wasn't close to having an agreement with NET, and Pat Loud was scheduled to arrive in New York in two days.

Some NET production people took the position that there would be no filming until an agreement was reached with the Raymonds, no matter how long it took. This, of course, was totally unacceptable to me. It was finally agreed that the Raymonds would be allowed to shoot for the length of time Pat Loud was in New York at a rate that, it was understood, was for that week and that week only and would have no bearing on the long-term agreement if and when it was ever worked out.

With this first problem at least temporarily solved, we turned our attention to the coverage of Pat Loud's visit; this meant contacting Lance at the Chelsea Hotel. Numerous phone calls by Alan Raymond and myself had been unsuccessful—Lance was never in, and he never returned our calls. About three hours before Pat was due to arrive, Alan reached Lance, who said yes, he had been told what was going on by his mother, and sure, the camera crew could come down to the Chelsea to meet him and to see what problems might be encountered in shooting in Lance's room.

At this meeting it became clear for the first time that Lance was a homosexual and was not in the slightest way ashamed of the fact. One of the more idiotic charges leveled against *An American Family* was that, through some strange alchemy, the process of shooting the series induced Lance to reveal his hitherto hidden sexual preference to the American public. This is pure nonsense. Lance was a homosexual before the shooting, during the shooting, and after the shooting. The fact that we didn't find out about it until we did neither excited nor depressed me. In my original talks with Bill and Pat in Santa Barbara it had been agreed that whatever happened would happen, whatever came up in the course of the filming should not be considered a good thing or a bad thing but simply another thing that occurred in their daily lives.

Pat's visit to New York ended up as episode 2 in *An American Family*—an episode I have always considered one of the best in the series. From New York,

Pat went to Baltimore to take care of some business for her husband, and the Raymonds and their assistant were allowed to follow and film her at the same temporary weekly rate which had been agreed to for the shooting at the Chelsea Hotel.

As I write this I have my notes from that period in front of me, and as if it were happening all over again I can feel the incredible frustration of trying to mediate the salary dispute between the Raymonds and the people at NET responsible for agreeing to a final budget. The NET position was that the Raymonds could continue to shoot on a weekly basis but I could not leave New York until the dispute was settled. This meant that when Pat Loud flew back to Santa Barbara on June 9 accompanied by the Raymonds, I was not on the plane. For the first crucial week of shooting with the entire family I was three thousand miles away.

My absence, of course, naturally disturbed the Louds. I had entered their lives out of the blue, asked them to take part in this crazy undertaking, and then disappeared. Why? What had happened? Could they really trust someone who acted this irrationally? The Raymonds did nothing to help the situation. Although they knew perfectly well I was being kept in New York to try to write a budget that could include their salary demands, they never volunteered this information. To questions from the Louds about why I wasn't there, they would shrug their shoulders and claim they had no idea.

After long hours of pleading with NET executives and several quick weekend trips to the coast to reassure the family that I was not a figment of their imaginations, I was finally allowed to conduct the endless budget negotiations from Santa Barbara. I say "endless" advisedly. According to my notes, the first meeting at NET about the Raymonds' salary (the one in which Alan Raymond and the production manager almost came to blows) was held on May 27. A deal was finally made with the Raymonds around the middle of July.

Much has been written about how unnatural it must have been for the Louds to have a camera crew following them for twelve or thirteen or fourteen hours a day and how difficult, if not downright impossible, it must have been under these conditions to lead a normal life.[2] Citing the Heisenberg principle became a favorite gambit for all manner of critics, columnists, and feature writers who felt the need for scientific justification to question the worth of the series.

Shooting

In point of fact, on a normal day the crew (Alan and Susan Raymond and an assistant) would arrive at the Loud home at about eight in the morning and would leave at about ten at night. Sometimes they would get there earlier or leave later, but not often. While they were at the Louds', the Raymonds obviously would not shoot continuously. When, in their view, something interesting was going on, they would shoot; the rest of the time they would put their camera and sound recorder down and, in effect, become two more members of the family, talking, listening to music, or watching television. And some days they did not shoot at all.

When actual shooting was going on, the Raymonds were the only outsiders present in the house. The assistant remained outside loading fresh magazines with film, and I was hardly ever present, having decided at the beginning of the project that the fewer people standing between the camera and the Louds, the better. A director or a producer or anybody else on the production staff, for that matter, would have been merely a distraction to the crew and to the family.

After the crew departed at night I would try to spend an hour or so chatting with the family to keep in touch with what its various members were up to and to try to get some idea of what might be happening in the next few days. I also tried, in this way, to stay in touch with the emotional state of the family, without, as I have said earlier, becoming involved in its affairs. On those days when the crew was filming Bill Loud at his office or at a business meeting, I sometimes spent the whole day at the house.

When the Raymonds were not shooting, I would talk to them in person or on the phone about what was happening in the family, what we felt was going on, and what kinds of things to pay particular attention to. Despite this day-to-day communication with the Raymonds and despite their apparent understanding of my basic premise for the series, Alan's perceptions about the family and its individual members were not always my perceptions, his view of what was important was not always my view.

Since the moment-to-moment decisions as to what to shoot and what not to shoot were up to the crew, the arrangement was not always a happy one. Indeed, from time to time it was the cause for some serious and painful disagreements. But there was no viable alternative, and in the long run I think the Raymonds did a remarkable job. Because life has a tendency to repeat itself—which meant that if Alan missed something I wanted the first time, he could get it the next time it happened—I think that over the seven-month period he and Susan recorded an extraordinarily accurate picture of how the Louds lived.

As for lights, whenever possible the Raymonds relied on natural light and sensitive film. For night shooting, they substituted photo flood bulbs for the regular bulbs in all the lamps and overhead fixtures in rooms where shooting was likely to take place. These photo floods stayed in place for all seven months, so as a matter of course there was enough light for evening shooting in the house without any frantic last-minute preparations. This also meant the Louds soon got used to living in a house that was somewhat more brightly lit than usual. There were no reflectors and no yards of black cable winding sinuously through the living quarters.[3]

I do not want to imply that having their daily lives recorded for seven months was easy or normal for the Louds, or without problems. It wasn't. I am simply trying to point out that it was not as disruptive as many people, including the critics, believed.

For the production staff, the period from the end of May 1971 to January 1, 1972, was hardly problem-free. Almost every day there was a new crisis—personal, emotional, logistical, technical. Some of them—those that shed light on the filmmaking process—are worth mentioning.

Crises During Shooting

One of the early crises was caused by Lance's announcement that he was going to spend the summer in Europe. It was imperative to cover his trip, but the budget, in its final, approved state, did not allow for a second 16 mm crew to wander around Europe for a couple of months. Our problem was finally solved through the good graces of Richard Leacock, a pioneer *cinéma vérité* filmmaker in the fifties and early sixties, who had started an 8 mm film department at MIT. He and his students had spent a good deal of time trying to develop a Super 8 mm recorder and camera rig that could shoot acceptable *cinéma vérité* film with synchronous sound in the field. He agreed that Lance's trip would provide an ideal test for the equipment. I do not remember what the exact financial arrangement was, but I do know it was reasonable enough to pass the careful scrutiny of the zealous guardians of the budget. The result was some marvelous footage (shot by John Terry) which, when blown up to 16 mm, added immensely to the overall interest of the series.

Pat Loud's trip to Taos, New Mexico, with her daughters Michelle and Delilah triggered a whole series of problems. Pat and the girls had not been gone for more than an hour before Bill was quite openly making arrangements to fly to Hawaii with his current girlfriend, the manager of a boutique in Santa Barbara. The fact that he made no attempt to hide these shenanigans put an enormous burden on all of us. As I mentioned earlier, I had tried to impress on the entire production staff the importance of not getting involved in the family's affairs. This was, of course, an extremely difficult ideal to live up to, and none of us was totally successful at it. The very fact of living as close to the Louds as we did for seven months made it humanly impossible to remain completely detached and unaffected by what was happening in their lives.

Like most of us, Bill Loud was a complicated man: he could be devious, irritating, and breathtakingly obtuse; he could also be astonishingly sensitive and quite perceptive. And when he wanted to, he could be irresistibly charming. So when he went out of his way to introduce his girlfriend to me, as if to do so was the most natural thing in the world, it was very difficult to know exactly how to act. I didn't want him to think I approved of what he was doing (which is what he wanted), nor did I feel in a position to lecture him on the subject of infidelity.

Bill's flaunting of his relationship with the boutique manager also created filmmaking problems. Once the shooting of the series got underway, it didn't take long to realize that Bill was a compulsive woman-chaser; from time to time he would allude to the affairs he had been involved in over the past several years. But to be faced with his current girlfriend in the flesh was quite different from hearing about his conquests of the past.

In the days following Pat's departure for Taos and preceding Bill's departure for Hawaii with his girlfriend, the question arose as to whether we would shoot them together having drinks at her house and dining at various restaurants in Santa Barbara. I made the decision not to. God knows, I was tempted. But in the final analysis it seemed to me that doing so would put us in an impossible position with Pat and seriously endanger the completion of the series. From time to time Bill and Pat and the kids would ask to look at various pieces of film, and I didn't want to have to lie about what we had shot while she was away. After Bill and Pat separated, there was no need to continue this self-imposed limitation.

The Raymonds and Susan Lester, the production assistant, flew to Taos to cover what was called Pat's "vacation," but which, in fact, turned out to be an intense period of soul-searching during which she made up her mind to ask Bill for a divorce. This decision was reinforced by a phone call from a well-meaning friend in Santa Barbara informing Pat that Bill had flown to Hawaii with the boutique manager.

One night three or four days after the crew arrived in Taos, I received a phone call from Alan Raymond. He complained that he was getting very little on film. For one thing, Michelle and Delilah hated Taos and sat around all day complaining about what a dull town it was. And for another, Pat seemed very uptight and nervous and spent most of her time talking to Susan Lester, thereby making it impossible for him to do any shooting. Alan ended by asking me to get Lester out of Taos so Pat would not be venting all her emotions in conversations which could not be filmed. I told him to do the best he could and said I would speak to Susan when the crew returned to Santa Barbara. (Incidentally, the best Alan could do, in this instance, was very good indeed. Somehow or other he managed to get on film a portrait of a woman at the end of her rope, trying to divert herself by attending art classes, engaging in aimless chitchat at dinner parties given by people she hardly knew, and wandering, under threatening skies, through Indian ruins with a sullen and alienated Michelle.)

When the crew returned to Santa Barbara I had a long talk with Susan Lester. Susan is a bright, talented, ambitious young woman. *An American Family* was the first major film project she had ever worked on. Her reaction to Alan Raymond's criticism of her conduct was not unexpected. As she reminded me, she was one of the members of the production staff who felt my early admonition not to get involved in the affairs of the Loud family was not only unworkable but inhuman. From the very beginning of shooting, Susan had developed a close relationship with Pat which I attributed to their both having an offbeat sense of humor and a sharp eye for the ironies of life and the pomposities of people. Evidently, Pat had slowly but surely opened up to Susan about the dark side of her life, and Susan had proved a willing and intelligent listener. In Taos, while Pat was wrestling with the painful question of divorce, she depended heavily on Susan for advice, support, and the understanding of a trusted friend.

Susan readily admitted to all this. She also agreed that, very likely, her long conversations with Pat had made it difficult for Alan Raymond to do his job. She added that if there had to be a choice (as there appeared to be in Taos) between maintaining a friendship and the integrity of a film, she would opt for the friendship every time.

We talked for many hours. I sympathized with her point of view; indeed, there were times during our discussion when I felt that her point of view was the only sensible and decent one. But in the end I held to my commitment to make *An American Family*, as far as possible, a series of films about the Louds, and not about how the Louds interrelated with a film crew from NET. I knew damn well that no matter how we conducted ourselves we could not avoid having some effect on the family. But I was adamant about trying to keep that effect to an absolute minimum.

There was no question about firing Susan; she was much too valuable a member of the staff. We worked out a reassignment which was mutually acceptable, and in the final credits for the series Susan Lester's name appears as associate producer. Today Susan is a producer in her own right, and though we are still friends, I have no idea what her position would be now if faced with the same problem.

One evening early in September, while Bill Loud was away on a business trip, the Raymonds returned to the motel and told me that Pat had announced she was going to file for a divorce. They added that the following day she was going to drive to Glendale, a suburb of Los Angeles, to inform her brother and sister-in-law of her decision. I asked the Raymonds if they had made any plans to go along. They had not talked to Pat about it, they said.

I phoned the house and told Pat I had just heard about her decision, and we discussed it for a couple of minutes. I tried to be as noncommittal as possible. After a while I mentioned her planned trip to Glendale and asked if we could film it. She said it was all right with her but it was really up to her brother and his wife, since any shooting would have to take place at their house.

Pat planned to reach Glendale late the next afternoon. I told her that I would get there earlier to talk to her brother and his wife. If they didn't want their talk with Pat filmed, I would be gone by the time she got there. If it was all right with them, I would meet her at the house with the crew. Pat agreed to the arrangement.

Her brother and sister-in-law not only agreed to the filming, they were enthusiastically in favor of it. Although they were against the divorce and planned to tell Pat as much, they felt the series should include Pat's side of the story if the divorce actually took place. When Pat arrived, however, she had a change of heart; she no longer wanted the discussion to be filmed.

This was a moment I had dreaded; it was the first and last time anyone in the family objected to our shooting a sequence which I felt was absolutely necessary for the series. I asked Pat if we could talk privately. She agreed and requested that her sister-in-law be present. Now, almost nine years later, I cannot possibly recreate that conversation. But at the end of half an hour Pat consented to have the film crew present.

In interviews after the series was on the air, Pat sometimes said I had talked her into letting us film her explanation of why she was getting a divorce. And sometimes she said it was her "best scene." Because of these apparently conflicting statements, I could never figure out whether she was condemning me or thanking me, whether she was angry or happy that the scene had been filmed. I'm not sure she knew herself.

When Pat actually confronted Bill with a request for a divorce and asked him to pack his clothes and leave the house, one family became, in effect, two families, and I had serious doubts about whether the Raymonds could cover both of them. It did not take long for my doubts to crystallize into a conviction; I decided to hire another camera crew. First I had to convince NET that this was an absolute necessity and that the expense could be accommodated with a certain amount of budgetary juggling. As hard as this was, it was nothing compared to the problems which arose when I broached the idea to Alan Raymond. He hit the roof and didn't come down for a couple of days. When he did, he threatened to leave the series. (He did in fact disappear for several days, after which I received a phone call from him in which he said if I wanted to talk he would meet me in a Hollywood restaurant. I met him, we talked, and he returned to Santa Barbara.)

I had been through a less intense version of this dispute with Alan during the making of *The Triumph of Christy Brown* in Dublin. Then, I had let him have his way, and I had lived to regret it. He had badly botched the shooting of a key scene simply because he could not be everywhere at once. I had learned my lesson the hard way and was not about to let it happen again. His position, of course, was that he could cover Bill's life and the lives of Pat and the kids perfectly adequately by himself. I was convinced there was no way he could possibly pull this off. I knew what was going on in his mind. He simply didn't want to share his credit with anyone. And there was nothing I could say that would get him to budge one inch. He knew he had me over a barrel; after almost four months of shooting, he was indispensable to the series. There was no way I could fire him (I considered this option through many sleepless nights) without seriously jeopardizing the delicate personal and professional balance that had been established with the Louds.

Finally I had no choice but to ignore his objections and hire another crew and try my best to keep the whole undertaking from falling apart. And it almost did. Faced with another crew on what he considered his territory, Alan submitted an ultimatum that included the following points: (1) under no circumstances was the new crew to be allowed to shoot in the Loud house; (2) he would not consent to communicate with the new crew in any way whatsoever; and (3) he would not attend any screening at which "dailies" shot by the new crew were shown.

Luckily, the cameraperson of the new crew was an understanding, intelligent, easygoing woman named Joan Churchill who, though she thought Alan Raymond was crazy, agreed to go along with the restrictions. In fact, Bill's social activities increased to such an extent once he was on his own that there was more than enough to keep her and her crew busy. And from time to time, when Alan was busy elsewhere, she even shot in the house.

Finally, there was one more production crisis that should be mentioned, not because it is of any earthshaking importance, but because it graphically illustrates how convictions, deeply held in theory, can evaporate in a minute under the pressure of actual shooting conditions.

It occurred on Thanksgiving day. Alan and Susan Raymond were at the house filming, and I was at the motel feeling sorry for myself. It was the first Thanksgiving I had been alone in sixteen years (in my life, as a matter of fact); memory and desire were giving me a hard time. Suddenly the phone rang; it was Alan complaining that Thanksgiving dinner at the house was turning into a disaster. It was the first major holiday without Bill, and although nobody was actually saying as much, it was clear, according to Alan, that he was sorely missed. There was nothing to film; everyone was sitting around looking gloomy. He and Pat had talked and agreed it would be a good idea if I rounded up as many production people as I could find at the motel and brought them up to the house for some turkey. Alan said he would not get the production people on camera, and that it might make Pat and the kids more animated.

This was a total reversal of the position Alan had taken in Taos (I thought this but didn't mention it). For reasons which even now I cannot quite be sure of, I agreed, thereby also completely contradicting the position I had taken in my discussion with Susan Lester.

I rounded up five or six members of the production staff, and we went to the house. It was clear from the minute we got there that it wasn't going to work. Everything was strained and artificial. After a while—if I remember correctly, before the turkey was actually served—I told Alan that it wasn't going to work and that I was going to leave and take the production people with me. He didn't object strenuously.

It was a sad day all around. It was a sad Thanksgiving for us at the motel, and it was a sad Thanksgiving for Pat without her husband and for the kids without their father. But at least it was an honest sadness and not a phony gaiety.

Editing

The filming of *An American Family* ended in the early morning hours of January 1, 1972. On or about February 1, the editing of *An American Family* began, a process that lasted a full twelve months and strained the patience and taxed the talents of almost twenty people.

In the seven months of shooting we had accumulated 300 hours of film. The first thing we had to do was look at every hour of that film in chronological order (i.e., the order in which it had been shot). When I say "we," I mean the two editors, David Hanser and Eleanor Hamerow; their two assistants; Susan Lester; Jacqueline Donnet, the coordinating producer; and myself. Of the seven people in the screening room, only two, Susan Lester and I, had been involved in the shooting and had any day-to-day relationship with the Louds. This was purposeful; I wanted to guard against the possibility of reading anything into the film that wasn't there. The five pairs of fresh eyes were a guarantee that this would not happen. The possessors of those eyes had never met the Louds and knew next to nothing about them. Unlike Susan and me, they could view what was happening on the screen with something approaching reasonable objectivity.

For almost three months—five days a week, six hours a day (more than six hours was intolerable)—we sat in a darkened screening room and watched as the Louds lived their lives from the end of May 1971 to January 1, 1972. To put it mildly, it was a strange and unsettling experience. Slowly but surely, the lives of the people on the screen started becoming more real than our own; without even being aware of it, we found ourselves using words and phrases common to the Louds and talking about family situations as if we had actually participated in them.

Finally that particular purgatory was over, and then for a week, in a bright, sunlit room, we discussed at length what we had seen, our individual reactions to the footage, and the best way of turning that footage into a series people would find interesting. In the discussions that arose I tried to make one point over and over again: what we were dealing with was a record (not complete by a long shot, but certainly representative of the major events) of how the Louds had lived their lives for a period of seven months. Whether we liked or disliked the individual members of the family, or whether we approved or disapproved of how they lived those lives or how they dealt with those events, was irrelevant. Our job was to put this film record together in such a way that it would not violate the characters of the individuals, the lives they led, or the events they participated in.

To put it simply—in practice it turned out to be a very hard thing to do—I was asking the editors to let the material speak for itself rather than, as editors are trained and paid to do, create something out of the material. A couple of examples: if, for reasons of clarity or for some other reason, we decided to use a sequence that was filmically dull, we should not, through tricks of editing, try to make it less so; if a family member had a certain speech habit, we should not, simply because we were tired of hearing it and thought it repetitive, try to minimize it through editing; if we decided to deal with a particular event, we should deal with it (as far as humanly possible) in its entirety and not compress it, through editing, to a more manageable length. During the week, we discussed all these things and much, much more. We also agreed that each episode would be one hour long and that the episodes would run chronologically.

Then I went home and faced the problem of breaking down the 300 hours into episodes. I worked with a log, listing the contents of every roll of film that had been shot—a log, incidentally, as thick as those enormous dictionaries in libraries that have special stands of their own. As I remember, the first breakdown I came up with had about thirty episodes. This was obviously an unworkable number, and I enlisted the aid of Susan Lester to sweat the total down to twenty-four.[4]

The problem of how many episodes there would be in the completed version of *An American Family* continued to plague me and the editors and the management of WNET/13 even after the series had started to appear on the air.[5]

Now, seven years later and under no constraint to be scrupulously fair (at least in interviews) to my employer, I can also say it is a classic illustration of the penny-wise, pound-foolish attitude that continues to prevail in public television. The final budget for *An American Family* was $1.2 million. In other words, each one-hour episode cost $100,000, which was dirt cheap when you remember that, even in those days, it was not unusual for a single one-hour documentary to cost anywhere from $150,000 to $200,000.

The three extra episodes (13, 14, and 15) would have fulfilled the artistic unity implied in the structure of the series.[6] The cost for all three of the extra episodes, the total cost of three more hours, would have been somewhere between $40,000 and $80,000—a small price, it seemed to me then and still seems to me now, to make a logical and aesthetic whole out of something that had already cost $1.2 million. After the final decision was made to spend no more than was necessary to finish episode 12, I asked management if I could try to raise the money outside the station for the last three shows. They gave me permission.

Bob Shanks, who at that time was in charge of the late-night 11:30 to 1:00 A.M. time period at ABC, was very interested. We started to talk after the series had been on the air for two or three weeks, and he was intrigued about the possibility of getting some cheap shows that would cash in on all the publicity being generated by *An American Family*. What he wanted was four shows. The first would be a recap of the highlights of episodes 1 through 12, and the others, of course, would be episodes 13, 14, and 15. He was very excited about the possibilities of this arrangement. I wasn't very happy about the recap idea, but I did want the money to complete the series properly.

Our talks proceeded smoothly—so smoothly, as a matter of fact, that one day Shanks announced that the next step was to get top management at ABC and WNET/13 involved in the discussions. (I should point out that I did not own the rights to *An American Family*; I was functioning as a salaried staff producer. I had been given permission to look for money, but any deal had to be signed by Mr. Iselin and his lawyers.) Shanks said he would call me in a couple of days to let me know how negotiations were progressing.

He was as good as his word. But when he called me, the news was bad. It seems that when he had contacted the proper executives at ABC to get them involved in the project, he was told that they were not interested. They gave him two reasons for this decision, and I set those reasons down here exactly as Shanks repeated them to me: (1) if the programs were successful, they (the executives) would be asked why they hadn't done them in the first place, and thereby been able to avoid having to buy them from public television; and (2) if the programs were successful, they would be asked to do more of the same, which they (the executives) agreed unanimously they did not want to do. In other words, from the executives' point of view, it was a no-win situation. It seemed to me then, and even more so now, that the reasons they gave are a pretty good indication of the kind of thinking that prevails in commercial television.

In addition to the dispute over the number of episodes, there were other disagreements with the management of WNET/13 during the editing period. Any fairly frequent viewer of public television cannot help but be aware of how often a host is used at the beginning of a program to tell you what you are about to see, and at the end of a program to tell you what you have just seen. One day I was called to a meeting in the office of Jay Iselin, president of WNET, to discuss the advisability of having such a host for *An American Family*. When I asked why such a person was needed, I was told it would help to set the programs "in context." At the time I honestly didn't have the slightest notion of what "in context" meant, and I objected to the idea strenuously. It was finally abandoned.

I have thought quite a lot about "in context" since then, and I think today I have a better idea of what it means. It is a euphemism for blunting whatever uncomfortable impact the program may have on the viewer; relieving viewers of the necessity to think for themselves about the contents of the program; and getting the station management off the hook if the program should turn out to be socially, politically, or historically unpopular.

Although I argued successfully against the use of a host on *An American Family*, I lost my battle to prevent an hour-long discussion by assorted "experts" from being aired immediately following the broadcast of the final episode. I watched this discussion at home and then had drinks with several of the participants. One of them, an anthropologist, asked whether I had heard his perceptive remark about the credits in the last episode. It seems that he alone had noticed that the credits seemed to be dissolving, a subtle and telling commentary on the breakup of the family. He congratulated me on this deft touch. When I told him this "deft touch" was wholly unintended, that it was simply the result of a technical problem called "tearing," he was taken aback for a minute and then quickly recovered, giving the opinion that, intended or not, the effect was the same. Until then I had never been overly fond of panel discussions by experts; at that point my opinion of those television mutations reached a new low.

Perhaps the most violent argument I had during the editing period with the men who ran WNET/13 was over the question of an Executive Producer credit for Curt Davis. When the credit list was submitted as a matter of course to the proper executive, the uproar was such that you would have thought I was suggesting the series acknowledge its indebtedness to Adolph Hitler and Joseph Stalin, with perhaps a bow in the direction of Jack the Ripper.

As I pointed out earlier in this account, *An American Family* would never have been made had it not been for Curt Davis. In addition to prodding me into coming up with the concept and having the faith to pursue the possibility of what, in the beginning, seemed to me like a pipe dream, Curt had been enormously supportive of the project through all the shooting and the early months of editing. At that point, as part of the phasing out of NET, he had been fired.

We had never discussed what his credit would be, but there never was any question in my mind that the one he deserved and the one he would get was Executive Producer. When I was told that this was out of the question, I exploded. There were extremely heated words, and at one point I said that if Curt's name did not appear as Executive Producer, I would destroy the series and the station would be left with the task of explaining why it did not appear on the air. The battle continued for over a week; in the end, Curt got his credit.

You may well be asking why the station had such strong feelings about what seemed, on the surface at least, to be such an insignificant issue. The answer, which has been confirmed many times since then, has to do with the politics of public television. By the time *An American Family* appeared on the air, NET, which had been responsible for the series, had disappeared without a trace. Its functions, on a national level, had been taken over by the Corporation for Public Broadcasting and, on a local level, by WNET/13. Jim Day, the president of NET, and Curt Davis, the head of the Cultural Affairs Department of NET, were no longer on the scene. A revisionist history of public television, in which the dirty word, NET, would never appear, was in the process of being written. Three years later, while I was sitting in the waiting room of the corporation in Washington before an appointment, I leafed through the coffee-table literature that told the history of public television and listed its triumphs. Nowhere was there any mention of NET or *An American Family*. Quite simply, the intensity of the fight over Curt's credit had to do with the issue of whether, for those who cared and remembered, there would be a lasting reminder that before the Corporation for Public Broadcasting, before PBS, and before WNET/13, there had been another organization which, for all its faults, had represented courage, freedom, and a tentative, but growing, integrity.

The actual ending of the series was a long and laborious process, but it went well except for a difficult problem which arose quite early in the process. That problem had to do with the inability of one of the editors, Eleanor Hamerow, to live with the editing guidelines I had tried to establish.

I liked Ellie very much; she was an interesting, intelligent, warm woman. From the very beginning we got along well together. For many years she had been employed as an editor on issue-oriented documentaries—what recently have come to be known as "investigative reports." These documentaries are put together by shooting as much material as possible on both sides of the issue being examined within the time allotted by the budget and then bringing the footage back to the cutting room where it is given its shape by the editor. In other words, Ellie had spent a great deal of time creating interest, tension, conflict, and drama from footage which, in its original state, was essentially devoid of these qualities. She was an expert at "making something" out of interviews, silent footage, stills, stock material, and other random film.

Her first assignment on the series was to cut episode 1. After a reasonable length of time, I asked her how it was going. She said she was having some trouble but thought she knew how to solve it. Days and weeks went by, but still there was no rough cut of the episode. I began to get frightened and went to the cutting room to talk to her. To my horror, she said she was having trouble "making something" out of the material. When I asked her what she meant, she explained that she was trying to make Pat Loud a little more acceptable as a human being. In the next few days we talked at length about the problem, and slowly but surely it became clear that Ellie not only didn't like Pat but that she didn't like the entire family and was trying to make them less objectionable through her editing. Finally, regrettably, I had to let Ellie go. It was difficult for both of us.

Ultimately, the series employed three editors: David Hanser, Pat Cook, and Ken Werner. A large part of whatever distinction the series has is due to their skill as editors and to their decency and compassion as human beings.

Notes

1   There were two departments at NET: the Cultural Affairs Department, headed by Curt Davis, which produced shows having to do with the arts, history, literature, music, etc.; and the Public Affairs Department, headed by Don Dixon, which produced shows on politics, social issues, and topical news subjects. *Priorities for Change* was to have been produced by the Public Affairs Department, which several months earlier had been responsible for an NET Journal called *Banks and the Poor* and an installment of *The Great American Dream Machine*, in which there was a segment on the FBI. Both these shows had brought the full fury of the Nixon administration down on NET. I have a hunch that one of the reasons, but certainly not the only one, that Jim Day had given the go-ahead to *An American Family* and that the Corporation for Public Broadcasting had agreed so rapidly was a desire to shy away from any programming that could in any way be considered controversial. I am sure no one expected any trouble from what promised to be an innocuous series about an American family.

2   In an article entitled "Spy Drama," an unnamed writer in the March 5, 1973, issue of *The Nation* had this to say: "Further, anthropologists have long known that even the most tactful and unobtrusive intervention in the life of a social microcosm significantly changes the phenomena under observation; so that if one wished to generalize from the behavior of the peculiarly uncritical Louds, it would be necessary to ask first how natural was the presence of Gilbert, his camera crew, microphones, lights, reflectors and yards of black cable curling sinuously through the living quarters?"

3   For those whose ideas of how a *cinéma vérité* team works have been formed by movies and television, it should be noted that the new 16 mm technology has eliminated the old slate/clapsticks method of identifying the shot and providing a sync mark for the editor. To start shooting, the sound person simply flashes a light, which is recorded as a beep when the tape is rolling; the cameraperson photographs this light and continues shooting. All the editor has to do is line up the beep on the sound

tape with the light on the film and he is "in sync." This effectively eliminates the necessity of an assistant's standing up in front of the camera with a small blackboard and announcing, "*An American Family*, scene 10, take 1," and then clapping the sticks; it can be done so unobtrusively that it is sometimes hard to tell when shooting is actually taking place.

4   In a memo dated June 10, 1972, to a WNET/13 executive, which accompanied our list of episodes, I wrote ". . . this does not mean, by any stretch of the imagination, that this is the correct structure or the proper breakdown of the material. All it represents is our best guess as to how to solve the problem. I know that you are aware of this, but I am still reacting to the knowledge that—for a long time around here—guesses tended, in a remarkably short time, to be regarded as positive statements of opinion. . . . The only positive statements I or anyone else will be able to make about the structure will come out of working with the material in the cutting room."

5   In an article which appeared in the *New York Times* on January 22, 1973, John J. O'Connor, the television critic, succinctly explained the background and nature of the problem:

> *An American Family* began as a project of NET. Curtis W. Davis, no longer with public television, receives credit as executive producer. Last year, however, the New York operation was given a new executive regime headed by John Jay Iselin, now acting president of WNET/13, and Robert Kotlowitz, senior executive editor.
>
> As the programming focus switched from national to local levels, the nationally oriented NET was absorbed into WNET. Mr. Iselin and Mr. Kotlowitz were then faced with a decision on what to do about the 300 hours of material already filmed but not yet edited for *An American Family*. At one point it was thought 8 hours might be enough. Mr. Gilbert objected strongly, and the 12-hour format was accepted by all parties.
>
> Now Mr. Gilbert says that as the editing evolved, it became apparent that 12 hours would be inadequate for his creative purposes. Under the old NET regime, in which the film maker frequently prevailed, the producer may have had his way. But the current WNET management, acutely more concerned about costs and limited funds, insists it is not about to be swayed.
>
> The result is a classic illustration of the broadcaster versus the film maker, the editor versus the creator.

6   The first half of episode 1 covered New Year's Eve at the Louds' house at 35 Woodale Lane. The kids are having a party and at one point Lance calls from New York to wish his brothers and sister Happy New Year. We hear his voice but don't see him. We briefly see Bill, who has been living in a motel for three months. Halfway through episode 1 (as the kids and their guest are singing "Auld Lang Syne" to Pat) there is a slow dissolve to the entire family having breakfast seven months earlier. The narration says, "Our story begins on a bright spring day in late May."

From that point on we planned to move chronologically from the end of May to New Year's Eve again. The New Year's Eve footage in the final episode would have been some of the same that was used in episode 1. But there would have been new footage of how Lance spent his New Year's Eve in New York, including the circumstances under which he made the call to his family. And although there was a little footage in episode 1 of how Bill was spending his New Year's Eve, there would have been a lot more in the final episode, including a phone call which he received from Lance while having drinks at the home of the boutique manager.

23

American High: Documentary as Episodic Television

Ben Levin

Introduction

In August of 2000 a new program premiered on the Fox Network in the United States. It was a thirteen-week episodic series about a group of high school students navigating through their senior year. After just two weeks Fox canceled *American High*, but the program eventually found a home with PBS in 2001 where it achieved great success. It also spawned R. J. Cutler's Actual Reality Pictures, a company destined to become a key player in nonfiction programming for television in the future.

R. J. Cutler, the creator of *American High*, had been responsible for two previous major documentary productions, *The War Room* (1993) co-produced with Wendy Ettinger, and *A Perfect Candidate* (1996), which he co-directed with David Van Taylor. Both works dealt with political campaigns, Clinton's run for the presidency in 1992 and Oliver North's bid for the governorship of Virginia in 1994. They were feature length and *The War Room*, directed by D. A. Pennebaker and Chris Hegedus, garnered numerous honors including an Academy Award nomination.[1] Cutler learned much from his collaborators, benefiting from their wealth of experience with the genre, and his own appreciation for the history of the form. Assuming the additional role of co-director on *The Perfect Candidate* proved to be a rich experience, one that encouraged him to pursue new projects that would bring real life events to the screen. For *A Perfect Candidate* Cutler was joined by Dan Partland and Ted Skillman who, along with Jonathan Mednick, were to become key participants in the production of *American High*.

The Subject

Documentary filmmakers have been attracted to American high schools as subjects for many years. Perhaps a precursor to this interest was Arthur Barron's *Sixteen in Webster Groves* (1966) produced for CBS Reports. Charles

Karault was the field reporter and the film explored the lives of high school aged students in an upper middle-class St Louis suburb. While most of the footage was shot outside the school itself, it did raise issues about community values and student points of view. Frederick Wiseman's *High School* (1967), shot in northeast Philadelphia, examined the institution and its methods, with no footage shot at the students' homes and no participation by parents unless they were visiting the school. Shot in typical Wiseman style, with no narration, no interviews and no subject–camera interaction, it caused controversy, and was not officially screened within thirty miles of the school's location for nearly fifteen years. The film was interpreted by many as being intensely critical of the methods and ideologies applied in the day-to-day workings of the institution. In this case, the "fly on the wall" style of the film allowed for an array of interpretations, depending on one's perspective and point of view. Few disagreed about the events and interactions displayed in the film; it was the interpretation of the material, by attribution, that complicated matters the most.

In 1981 Jeff Kreines and Joel Demott's *Seventeen* (1982) shot at a high school in Muncie, Indiana, became the most discussed film in *Middletown*, a six-part series produced for PBS. This was in spite of the fact that it was not aired with the other five documentaries. In this case the controversy arose prior to the first official showing of the film. When the film was previewed for parents and members of the school board a month before the scheduled airdate, strong objections were made. Foul language, interracial dating, under-age drinking and the use of drugs in the film were a concern, along with a general complaint by many that the high school that was chosen did not represent the majority in terms of community values and standards (Hoover 1987: 63–4). Much of the footage is observational in character, but the students also interact with the camera to some degree in a manner that implies the filmmakers are their friends, or at least understand their predicaments and concerns. The filmmakers released the film separately, holding screenings in theaters, festivals and other events. Eventually it was reunited with the other five films for distribution to educational markets.

In 1985 Keva Rosenfeld made a film called *All American High*, which was shot at high school in southern California, and focused on the experiences of a student from Finland who was attending the institution. Finally, in 1994 Fred Wiseman released his *High School II*, a film about a progressive alternative institution in New York's Spanish Harlem that used teaching methods that were innovative and sensitive to individual student needs. There was no controversy surrounding this film, as it was a positive piece about an educational process that appeared to be successful at accomplishing its educational goals, while respecting the individuality of the students.

The above films were all made possible by the development of portable synchronous 16 mm technology in the early 1960s. Options for the documentary were further extended with the introduction of half-inch "portapak" video equipment in the 1970s, and the appearance of Hi-8 video cameras in the early 1990s. With the arrival of mini-DV technology in the late 1990s, a new revolution ensued, one based on the affordability of broadcast quality (or near broadcast quality) cameras and less expensive digital non-linear editing systems. For some this meant a shift in strategies toward the use of multiple cameras on location, in a few cases placed in the hands of the subjects. It also meant that there would be new possibilities in terms of the amount of footage that could be shot and controlled efficiently with digital editing. This created a new potential for an extended series on the same institution or group of people, while also altering the way documentaries typically had been produced in the past.

Several documentary projects that were to benefit most from the new technologies were *Senior Year* (2001), a thirteen-week series for PBS, *Chain Camera* (2001), a feature-length documentary produced for the Cinemax cable channel, and the *American High* series. All were completed at the beginning of the new century, all focused on the lives of high school students, and all made ample use of the new technologies by placing cameras in the hands of students. In the case of *Senior Year*, the students were recent graduates or current college film school students, and with *Chain Camera*, the equipment was passed from one group of students to another several times during the course of production. The press releases claimed that there were "no lights, no crews, no rules." *American High* was the most ambitious of the three and involved a multi-level use of material shot by professional video crews, a still photographer and the students themselves.

Production History

R. J. Cutler believed that a nonfiction television series could be created that would be as "dramatic and engaging as the fiction shows" if funding and a viable outlet were available. For Cutler "the next step was to shoot even more footage than previous projects, to emulate a continuing series, with each episode self-contained, but with characters and story developed over time" (Levin 2003a). In short, they were striving to replicate the approach traditionally used by network television for its dramatic series. As Dan Partland, supervising producer of the series stated:

> We felt like we were fighting to prove the viability of such a show, to prove that real people's real issues were every bit as compelling (and perhaps more so) than larger than life fictional narratives. With *American High* we thought we had our shot for all of our colleagues who have believed this since the very first *vérité* films of the sixties. (Levin 2003b)

The circumstances were similar to those faced by Robert Drew in the early 1960s with his *Living Camera* series produced for Time-Life Broadcasting, and Craig Gilbert, the producer of *An American Family* in 1973 for PBS. Most film-makers would agree that creative vision is essential, but sufficient funding and a firm distribution outlet are crucial. Ideas must be pitched and television executives must make a commitment to the project. Cutler and his associates were faced with a difficult challenge, but several developments would contribute to a renewed interest in this kind of programming.

Beginning in the mid-1990s British television producers had garnered great success with low budget, nonfiction television programming often labeled "docusoaps." Popular subjects in these series included *Airport*, behind the scenes at London's Heathrow, *Hotel*, documenting activities at the famous Aldelphi Hotel in Liverpool and *Driving School*, which followed several people of various ages who were trying to pass their driving test. These series, usually six to eight half-hour shows, were aired in prime time and received very strong ratings. The success of these low-cost shows, and series like *Cops* and *Real World* in the US no doubt created a more positive environment for a series like *American High*.

During the summer of 1999 two other circumstances contributed to the further potential for alternative programming. The US networks were losing audiences to the major cable channels, who were premiering their new series while the networks were still airing reruns of their primetime shows. The threat of a strike by the Screen Actors Guild and the Writers' Guild, however, turned out to be the deciding factor. If the strike occurred, the networks would need a significant amount of programming that did not require writers or actors. Because of this, they were open to considering alternative program-ming concepts of all kinds, and the timing for pitching a project like *American High* could not have been better.

Cutler developed a concept for a thirteen-week series that would follow stu-dents through their senior year in high school. He had just turned thirty-seven and it was getting close to his twentieth year high school reunion. "I felt alien-ated from the current generation of high school students coming of age at the turn of the century, and felt that this would be one way of reconnecting" (Levin 2003a). They pitched the idea to executives at Fox, the network that produced the popular nonfiction series *Cops* that had been running since 1989. No doubt Fox found the *American High* concept particularly attractive as it required no actors, no writers and no sets: potential insurance against the impending strike. Fox's reaction to the pitch: "Let's do it" (Levin 2003a).

Cutler and the Fox studio had agreed that they would look for a school in an upper middle-class suburban community. After visiting several possible locations, Highland Park High, a school in a suburb north of Chicago, was selected. It was similar to the kind of high school Cutler had attended on Long

Island, and students, parents, faculty and administrators appeared to understand the value that such a project might have for all concerned. Cutler related, "The producers had sought a community where people would appreciate the nature of the project and be willing to work as active partners as well" (White 2000: 8). Once the school was selected, Fox gave the series its final approval. Four months of difficult contract negotiations ensued between those in Highland Park, the filmmakers and ultimately the Fox studio executives until all involved were satisfied that the project could move forward successfully.[2]

While *American High* was supported with funding that probably seemed like a bargain for a major US television network, it was meaningful financial support for a nonfiction series. The filmmakers were able to spend the entire 1999–2000 school year there, with two crews shooting three weeks a month, and additional personnel added for the major school events. Using multiple postproduction teams, they started editing in Los Angeles while shooting was still in progress. Fox set an airdate of August 2, 2000 to premiere the series.[3]

The network made the decision to show two half-hour series segments on the same evening once a week. When the show aired it received very positive critical reaction in the vast majority of reviews, several of which appeared in national news magazines and major newspapers. Despite the accolades from numerous sources, the show had an audience range "only" 3.5 to 5 million viewers. This was not enough for the Fox network and they canceled the series after just two weeks (four episodes). The situation was not helped by the fact that the two episodes were aired opposite CBS's *Big Brother*, a reality series that was benefiting from a lead-in by the ratings champion that summer, *Survivor*. It is possible that by being placed in this time slot, *American High* was doomed from the outset.[4] Needless to say, the producers were disappointed, but felt that the series, which was still being edited, would find a home somewhere. Ironically, the series won a coveted Emmy award for best television reality series for the year 2000, after its demise.

Immediately following the cancellation, Cutler placed a call to Pat Mitchell, the new head of PBS, who had recently moved there from her previous role as president of CNN productions. Before he could tell her the show was canceled she proceeded to praise the series, stating that it was exactly the kind of observational program that she wanted to do on PBS, particularly in her quest for younger audiences. PBS had been successful reaching pre-school and elementary school demographics, but not high school age students. "I said, Good news. It's yours if you want it," Cutler recalled (Bauder 2001). It took three to four months for people at the Fox studio to work things out, but they remained supportive of the completion of the project. As a part of this unique agreement, Fox's production affiliate allowed Cutler to finish the series and the Coca-Cola Company contributed funding for acquisition and promotion.[5]

The series had its PBS premiere in April 2001 and went on to become one of the most successful ventures in PBS history. Some local markets ran the series multiple times and it continued to have a healthy life well into 2003. For the first time PBS was attracting an audience that it had not reached before, and the ratings for high school age people rose far beyond anything in the past. Pat Mitchell stated:

> It's worked out well for us. We are offering something relevant to teens that they have never seen in prime time in this way . . . It indicates what happens if you put something of quality on the air that teenagers recognize as real. It's not the baloney stuff that they think is programmed for them. And they are really responding to it. The parents are coming with them. (Bird 2001)

A very effective website accompanied the series, allowing for reaction to the programs, interaction among viewers, and access to footage not included in episodes that were aired. An educational guide dealing with family relationships further enhanced the process. Through an extraordinary set of circumstances *American High* not only survived cancellation, but also thrived in its new home.

Content

During the course of the series, themes common to high school juniors and seniors are developed, including friendships, dating and family. One of the more interesting friendships is the one shared by Brad, the only openly gay cast member, and his friend Abby. They appear to be as close, if not more intimate, than one or two of the straight relationships depicted. The pressures of high school, both social and academic, are obvious themes as well. Particularly with college on the horizon for the seniors, issues of placement scores and grades intensify as the year goes on. Relationships with parents are integral as well and three of the major characters in the series live with a divorced or separated parent. Issues of divorce and the effects they have on children psychologically are explored, as well as positive and negative interactions with estranged parents. Overly protective parents, especially where young women are concerned, are also part of the mix. Finally, issues surrounding the use of drugs and alcohol are explored, culminating with the inevitable party that gets out of control.

Key school events play a role as well, and this no doubt helped the filmmakers in scheduling and anticipating production priorities. Adjusting to the beginning of the school year, the big football game, the annual student dance show, the winter formal dance, auditions for all-state music groups, spring break high school style, the band's trip to China, the senior prom and graduation all become vehicles for the exploration of the key themes of the series.

They also serve as mileposts of sorts, so that the ongoing exploration of main themes can be anchored by events that supply a structure based on the school calendar. While there is nothing out of the ordinary about the issues, as they are common to the high school experience in the US, the manner in which they are developed is. There is no narration, but the themes arise from interactions and events depicted on the screen, further supported by the voice-overs from students and parents. They emerge from the material, rather than from an expository, narrated structure. Even the titles that were used by the production staff to identify the thematic emphasis of each episode were eliminated for broadcast. They simply were not necessary. What is even more effective is that the themes are ongoing through the series and often overlap in an interesting, complex way. This is one of the positive attributes of the approach—it respects the audience and it is true to the students, their points of view and concerns.

Character Development

While a total of twenty students were selected to take the class and participate in the series, not all of them appeared in the completed production with the same frequency. Several characters stood out as major players as the series developed. Morgan (otherwise known as the "Ritalin Kid,") was the most "in your face" person, who had regular confrontations with his family and persisted in his unwillingness to accept authority and the usual school customs. Brad was an openly gay student, an artist and dancer, who planned to move to New York upon graduation. Allie was the emotionally distraught daughter of a recently divorced couple, living with her mother in a situation of tension and anger, having serious problems with her classes as well. Pablo was a precocious, wisecracking, and at times very funny guy, who was the most uncertain about his future. He lived with his mother, who had been married three times. Kaytee was a junior and a singer/songwriter, who had a pleasingly cynical way of absorbing the events going on around her, using them as inspiration for her songs. Her parents were estranged as well.

Robbie and Sarah served as the main "couple" in the series and both utilized the camera diaries effectively. Anna was the attractive daughter of a very protective father. Kiwi was the star kicker on the football team who was looking forward to that role in college. Brad's close friend Abby and Morgan's girlfriend Salima also had a fair amount of screen time. There were other less conspicuous cast members, including Tiffany, the only African-American in the main group of students. There were many other minor characters as well who moved in and out of the episodes as they had interactions with the major cast members.

With this number of characters, it was a challenge to develop them carefully, and gradually, so that the viewer could stay involved and not be confused.

For example, Morgan is a prominent character from the start, while Pablo becomes more important during the last few episodes, and Kaytee is featured sporadically throughout, offering a less serious counterpoint to the other occurrences. From these characters come the main thematic threads of *American High*, along with dramatic tension, humor, irony, frustration and joy—all the elements of good drama and storytelling. Through the well-defined personalities of these characters we experience a sense of what it is like (or was like) to be a seventeen-year-old.

Key Elements

Much of the footage in *American High* is observational in nature, with the employment of the traditional "fly on the wall" method. The professional crews using high-end DV cameras shot this material, typically including students interacting with each other and observational footage of them attending school, socializing with friends, and spending time with their parents.[6] There are also more formal interviews with the students, often with the kind of lighting one would expect in a standard television interview format, and some include the addition of a backlight and do not take place in a discernible location. These are used sparingly, but have a very different tone to them. Informal interviews are used as well, although at times it is unclear whether a question has been asked or whether the students have simply decided to talk to the crew. A still photographer was brought on board to work with the students, and these images are used throughout the series to define the main characters visually and to serve as transitions. There is also footage shot by the students as they observe and/or interact with friends and family. Most important, however, were the video diaries made by the students themselves, to be discussed in more detail later.

The sheer volume of material (2,200 hours of field footage, 800 hours of diary footage) would have been unthinkable in the pre-digital era, but again the producers took full advantage of the technology available to them. The postproduction unit in Los Angeles worked with eight Avid systems networked together. Like the rest of the project, the editing process was collaborative. Editors initially worked with individual characters and then this footage was circulated for use in stringouts of individual episodes. According to Jonathan Mednick, it wasn't until the first episode was locked in that the basic form for the remainder of the series became clear (Levin and Watkins 2003: 162).

Music is used consistently during the series, both as interludes and as background. Some of it is original, like the opening title sequence, but much of it is music from other sources. Student Kaytee also performs her work at various times during the series. Much of the music from other sources functions as a comment on the action or storyline through lyrics and/or mood. It is clear that the multi-million dollar budget for the series helped support the volume of music that had to be cleared for use. There is no narrator except for the brief comment "previously on *American High*," spoken by a cast member at the beginning of the show. Much of the sound is synchronous, although there is extensive use of meticulously edited voice-over provided by students and parents throughout the series.

In many ways the style of *American High* resembles that of MTV's highly successful series *The Real World*, which premiered in 1992 and was still running in 2003, with no end in sight. The audience range is similar and the stylistic model for *American High* is clearly based to some extent on that format. The big difference here, of course, is that the cast members of *American High* are living in their real world, not one created by the producers. Slick looking crane shots and aerial shots are used a few times during most episodes, typically near or above the school and other relevant locations. These often serve as transitions and are in strange contrast to the informal hand-held shooting and the fragmented editing style. They are the kinds of shots usually reserved for dramatic films, commercials and music videos.

The standard frame is altered for the diary segments, the formal interviews and for some of the still photographs. The closing credits include black and white clips of the students, often reflecting on something that had occurred in the episode, and black and white was also used when a student's father interviews her from behind the camera. Occasionally the speed of the images is modified as well.

The editing pace is generally quite rapid, with much intercutting between the story elements of each episode. At certain points, particularly during the diaries, students are allowed to quietly express themselves, sometimes with very personal comments; these are allowed to play longer, often with striking effect and an increase in emotional tension. In a sense, these reflective moments represent an escape from the more hectic pace of school activities and social life. Scenes utilizing all of the shooting elements discussed earlier are energetically intercut to drive the storyline and plot development of each episode. In many ways the style of the series, one could argue, reflects the complexities of life for sixteen and seventeen-year-olds. For the most part this seems to have been a valid decision, given the intended audience, and it clearly separates *American High* stylistically from the earlier films by Wiseman (*High School*) and Demott/Kreines (*Seventeen*) with their slower pace and more "studied" approach. In short, the makers of *American High* are not stylistic purists. The viewer is provided with an interesting mixture of shooting and editing strategies, from the traditional to the unconventional, and one element in particular was to form the core of the series.

Video Diaries

It was during the location scouting process that one school administrator asked Cutler "what's in it for the kids?" In response to this, the producers decided that they would teach the students filmmaking, and that their work would be included in the series (Levin 2003a). Students participating in the series were each given a camera and enrolled in a class at the school taught by one of the series' producers, Jonathan Mednick.[7]

In earlier film examples where participants were taught to use equipment, the cost and complexities of shooting and editing 16 mm film restricted the process. A noteworthy experiment in this area was the *Through Navajo Eyes* series (1966), during which Native Americans were taught to use 16 mm cameras and editing equipment to make films about their own culture. During the late 1960s George Stoney's work with the Challenge for Change program at the National Film Board of Canada was produced, in part, with new half-inch portable video equipment, often placed in the hands of community members.[8]

The introduction of Hi-8 technology resulted in new efforts in this area during the 1990s. Near-broadcast quality images could be produced using low-cost equipment, thus increasing options in access, content and style. One television company took advantage of this potential by training journalists to operate these cameras for use in gathering footage while covering stories for print media. With the introduction of the mini-DV format in the late 1990s new possibilities emerged, and the producers of *American High* took full advantage of the new format.

The students learned basic shooting techniques and regularly critiqued their footage in class. Dan Partland related:

> Seeing each other's work and having it discussed, created a group environment that was supportive and encouraging, and one in which the students ended up pushing each other to new innovations and higher levels of artistic expression. (Levin 2003b)

Instead of being limited to producer/defined spaces, they could take the camera wherever they wanted to do their work. Their control over this aspect of the filmmaking no doubt gave them a sense of being an important link in the process. This was very different from the video diary concept utilized in *Real World*, where a camera is set up in a space, and cast members have little or no control over its operation.

Initially the *American High* diary segments involved comments on topics defined by the producers, things like "Fear," "Kissing," etc. They wanted students to discuss personal feelings and thoughts, providing a window into their world not otherwise possible (Cutler 2001a: 2). In most cases students gradually found a way to use the camera that suited themselves and their personalities, with much of the diary footage being shot in their own spaces at home. They were urged to use the camera expressively, rather than shooting scenes in the conventional sense. They were asked to interview someone close to them, and to capture conversations that could not be recorded by the professional crews (Cutler 2001a: 3). The students were also encouraged to shoot other footage in their home environments, resulting in some extraordinary on-camera interactions, particularly between Morgan and his family. At the request of the students the producers also set up an "Always Room" at the school so that the students could have access to a camera for spontaneous diary segments when necessary during the school day.

As time went on the students began lobbying for shooting other aspects of their lives—to shoot interactions with their parents and to take cameras outside their home environments. The students also wanted to "experiment," probably due, in part, to the concepts that drove the design of the class. They took the camera with them in the car, for example, and improvised an interaction regarding events in their lives and concerns they had about the future. In one exceptional case, a father interviews his daughter from behind the camera to try to get her to talk about some issues they were having difficulty resolving under normal circumstances.

As the diary footage began to arrive, it was apparent that the strategy had great value, even beyond what was expected. As R. J. Cutler stated: "The stuff we started to get was remarkable, and it became clear to us that this was going to form the heart and soul of our show" (Cutler 2001b: 2).

PBS Version

The original Fox series included commercials, so that the actual footage needed for each episode was about twenty-two minutes. Typically the segments opened with a tease, brief clips from previous episodes and the opening title sequence, the three main segments separated by commercials and a close. This meant that for the PBS version something had to fill the four to five minutes of time that remained, so the producers decided to do a "making of" segment after each episode, calling them "Scenes from the Field."

This turned out to be a brilliant move, as it enabled the producers to enrich the viewing experience and to reflect on the process from their perspective. The segments dealt with production matters, such as the casting of the series, the logistics of the video class, how the diary process evolved, the inclusion of the work of a still photographer and the decision to include parents and teachers.

One of these segments, "Recording Kaytee," dealt with footage of her CD recording session, which had been organized by Cutler. Her (estranged) parents were there, and it was clear that they had no idea how talented their daughter really was and the footage of their reaction as the recording took place is some of the most powerful in the PBS version of the series. The point here is that this material would not have been seen otherwise, partly because Cutler's comments here are crucial to understanding the significance of their reaction. It is a revelation for the viewer as well, since only bits of her performances are shown during the series, mostly when she is practicing or fooling around or performing informally at a coffeehouse, and not at her polished best.

"Also Starring" dealt with footage the producers really liked, but could not include for various reasons. The segment featured diaries by students who took the class but were not among the fourteen that ultimately ended up being featured. The clips were very strong and remind us that so much interesting material is left out of most documentaries due to limitations on length, key story themes and other factors. For example, there is a wonderful scene in which a young woman sets up a camera on a Lake Michigan beach and records a lengthy diary segment during which she discusses current concerns about relationships, the prospect of college and life in general. The footage works well as a self-contained piece, but did not fit into the series as it was structured. The excerpt included here suggested that her footage provided a unique way of revealing the thought process of a teenager with concerns shared by so many of her contemporaries.

A segment called "Romances" provided the producers with an opportunity to introduce aspects of romantic relationships that were not apparent in the series, either because they did not have the footage, or were restricted by access or logistics at some point. Two of the students have moving revelations after viewing footage of them together before they broke up, realizing what they might have had if the relationship had continued. As the producers, in fact, invited them to look at this material, one senses that the filmmakers and the students had an ongoing dialogue regarding the process.

In fact, the filmmakers regularly provided the students with an opportunity to view footage shot by the professional crews and some edited material as well. Jonathan Mednick expressed his concern for the delicate nature of the editing process and the typical manipulations that occur during editing, particularly when you have an "open" relationship with your subjects:

> I can think of situations we had in *American High* that were tricky in terms of moving things around. We often had to do this in order to tell a coherent story. However, it makes you nervous. Sometimes it doesn't matter to the telling of the story, but it hurts your credibility with the people who served as your documentary subjects. They see the finished version and can tell if you have moved things around in time, if you used an actor to speak a line that someone had actually said but your recording was too low. They see your chicanery. And this can undermine you as a producer. You have to be very careful. (Levin and Watkins 2003: 160)

The most extraordinary bit of footage in these "Scenes from the Field" came as a result of a tape received from Allie, the adopted daughter of a divorced couple who is featured prominently in the series, sometimes in very difficult situations. The field production team was in Chicago, while the postproduction teams were in Los Angeles. The students knew the team members that were with them, but found the editing process taking place out in Los Angeles something of a mystery, and the cause of some anxiety. In one of Allie's diary tapes she speaks to the editors in California regarding her concerns as to how audiences will perceive her and the other students. She expresses her feelings of vulnerability and her hope that the editing teams will be sensitive to the reality of the emotions she and the others are experiencing. After the producers saw the tape, they asked all of the students to make a statement to the viewer in their diary footage as to how they hoped the material would be watched by the audience. In all likelihood this footage would never have found its way into the Fox series, but provided another level of understanding regarding the students' perception of potential ramifications of their filmed behavior.

The final segment was called "Where Are We Now" and was shot nine months to a year after the series was completed. Several of the major characters talk about their lives at college or in their senior year in high school. These scenes are intercut with brief clips of them as they appeared in the series, providing some interesting revelations regarding the passage of time and life in a new environment. For example, Morgan is in college, but living at home, and his life seems to have changed the least since graduation.

What these short "Scenes from the Field" segments provide is a doorway into the nature of the process of how documentaries get made. The producers have a chance to talk about their sense of the procedure, supplying reflective insights not otherwise available to the viewer. This is very different from the fluff piece that is often done to promote the release of a new commercial theatrical film. The one flaw here may be that the producers appear to be interviewing themselves, in a sense, and at times their comments might be a bit glib or pseudo-scripted. Nevertheless, the information is there and it adds another level of understanding to the process.

Conclusion

The willingness of the producers to alter their initial strategies, based on the reality of the production environment, was one of the hallmarks of the series. From including two junior students, because they added a creative/intellectual dimension to the cast, to allowing students to expand the video diary concept, to setting up the "Always Room" at the school, there was an openness here that is often lacking where so much documentary making for television is concerned. More often it is about "setting things up" and stimulating the behavior of cast members by doing things *to* them rather than engaging in a dialog *with* them.

It has always been the case with the documentary process that there must be funding, talent, vision, technology and distribution. When dealing with network television in the United States, it is clear that the first and last of these are perhaps their principal methods of control. In the case of R. J. Cutler's *American High* a project initially designed for commercial network television eventually found a more appropriate home. It established new connections with audiences via flexible programming and use of the website to further engage the viewers in a dialog with the subject matter, the cast, the producers and each other. Allowing audiences to interact with programming clearly increases its value, long after the work has been aired, and this may be an area where public television has the potential to play a more significant role in the future.

It is clear that a major challenge for documentary filmmakers who care about the human condition will be to maintain areas of quality in an environment that is encouraging themes involving dishonesty, greed and the bizarre. What the ultimate success of *American High* illustrates is that intelligently produced work drawing upon past traditions, combined with a sense of innovation and imagination, can find its audience and achieve a positive impact on viewers and their society.[9]

Notes

1   R. J. Cutler attended the University of Southern California School of Cinema and Television for a time, and prior to embarking on the production of *The War Room* he screened *Crisis: Behind a Presidential Commitment* (Drew Associates 1963) on which D. A. Pennebaker was one of the filmmakers. See Mendoza 2003.

2   In fact, an actual contract was negotiated during this stage of the process. See Moses 2001 for further discussion of this process.

3   Figures on the exact amount spent on the series are not available, but the amount was probably in the three to four million dollar range.

4   Reality series that involve placing people outside their normal environments (*Survivor, Big Brother, Fear Factor*, etc.) will not be discussed at length, although their success no doubt contributed to a more positive attitude toward reality programs of all kinds.

5   It is possible that Coca-Cola's involvement may have, in part, been stimulated by negative publicity the company had received for what some viewed as an overly aggressive marketing campaign in schools.

6   The professional shooters included Joan Churchill and Nick Doob, both of whom had considerable experience shooting this kind of footage. In fact, Joan did some shooting on the seminal *An American Family* series.

7   The students used Sony TRV 900 mini-DV palmcorders. See Moses 2001 for more discussion about equipment used on the series.

8 George Stoney continued this work with the Alternate Media Center at New York University. They set up storefront video stations for use by members of the community, where residents could obtain cameras to shoot their own documentary material.

9 Actual Reality Pictures' new series *Freshman Diaries* premiered on the Showtime cable network in August 2003. It deals with a year in the life of a group of new students at the University of Texas in Austin. *Residents* will air on the Discovery Health cable channel beginning in October 2003. *The Real Roseanne Show*, behind the scenes with Roseanne Barr, premiered on NBC in August of 2003, but was canceled after a two-week run.

References

Bauder, David (2001, April 29) "American High finds an audience on PBS." New York: Associated Press. Source: www.canoe.ca/TelevisionShows/americanhigh.htm (accessed August 30, 2002).

Bird, Rick (2001, May 9) "American High is PBS's gain." *Cincinnati Post.* Source: www.cincypost.com/2001/may/09.pbs050901.html (accessed December 5, 2001).

Cutler, R. J. (2001a) "Dear Diary," *Scenes from the Field*, 2.

Cutler, R. J. (2001b) "Kids with Cameras," *Scenes from the Field*, 3.

Hoover, D. (1987) "The Middletown film project: history and reflections." *Journal of Film and Video* 19 (Spring): 52–65.

Levin, Ben (2003a) "Phone interview with R. J. Cutler in Los Angeles."

Levin, Ben (2003b) "E-mail interview with Dan Partland in Los Angeles."

Levin, C. M. and Watkins, F. (2003) *Post: The Theory and Technique of Nonlinear Motion Picture Editing.* Boston: Allyn and Bacon.

Mendoza, Manny (2003, August 31) "Making it real," *Dallas Morning News*, Aug. 31, 1G, 6G.

Moses, Jesse (2001) "R. J. Cutler's American High vérité factory." *indieWire.* www.indiewire.com/people/int_Cutler_RJ_0140404.html (accessed June 21, 2003).

White, T. (2000) "Be true to your school: R. J. Cutler and David Zeiger bring cameras into the classroom." *International Documentary* 19: 7, 6–9.

24

Documentary and Truth on Television: The Crisis of 1999

John Ellis

Documentary is a slippery genre to define; classifications can be out of date before the printers' ink has dried. Acceptable documentary practice depends on a subtle three-sided process of negotiation. On one side are the habits and beliefs of audiences, what viewers will put up with or believe in. On another are the demands of cinema and television as media, how the film or programme will fit with current practices and expectations. On the third are the aspirations of filmmakers and participants, cynical or idealistic, motivated to show, but also to hide.

Every genre is constructed and renewed through such a tripartite negotiation.[1] But it is more fraught and fast-moving for documentary because the genre is based on a logical impossibility. Documentaries are constructs, yet they seek to reveal the real without mediation. Watching a documentary involves holding these two contrary beliefs at once, a process of disavowal[2] which is not terribly unusual in human behaviour, but is inherently unstable.[3] The documentary genre bases its claims on showing reality (rather than fiction), truth (rather than artifice), authenticity (rather than pretence). So the activity of both making and watching a documentary involves reaching beyond the necessary fictionality and artifice that is any mediatised representation, as well as reaching beyond the 'performance of self' in the artificial activity of filming to find the authentic self beyond. No wonder documentary constantly reinvents itself, both in its technologies (always striving to get 'closer to the real') and in its forms (always looking for the fresh way of doing things). So there is a constant renegotiation of the generic relationship. Filmmakers and institutions alike have to get people to believe enough in what documentaries are doing for the whole thing to work. All that matters is that belief is sufficient rather than absolute; indeed the process of disavowal makes that inevitable. For a documentary to work and to be worthwhile it is enough that its viewers can make sense of it as reality rather than as representation.

It is scarcely surprising that the whole thing sometimes goes wrong. So it was with British TV documentary in the early months of 1999. The mid-market tabloid newspaper the *Daily Mail* filled its front page on 5 February 1999 with the question 'Can We Believe Anything We See On TV?' It was remarkable enough that a popular paper should pose a philosophical, indeed epistemological, question in its main headline. It was even more remarkable that it should, in common with other media, return to the question in subsequent weeks. It is equally remarkable that the whole affair was hardly remembered a few months later. Clearly this is a story of a crisis in the documentary genre which was subsequently repaired.

A clear light is often thrown onto obscure workings when something suddenly goes wrong. Taken for granted beliefs are revealed and re-examined. Such moments occur because many different factors come together in a moment of overdetermination which brings together factors of different duration, profundity and importance. Hence it is important, before telling the story of the crisis of 1999, to understand the many factors that played into it.

The Gathering Crisis

In mid-1980s, documentary was seen as 'an endangered species' on British TV. As Winston says 'no documentary of any kind . . . made it into the top 100 programmes of 1993'.[4] A rapid change in the nature and status of the genre took place from that low point. This change has been examined variously by Stella Bruzzi, John Dovey and Brian Winston, and is often encapsulated as 'the rise of the docu-soap'.[5] Winston dates this from the popularity of the BBC's *Vets' School* in autumn 1996 and of *Driving School* in summer 1997.[6] The first signs of a new popular factual programming, different in form and content from the earlier reality TV shows, such as the BBC's *999* (BBC 1992–) can be seen in the unexpected success of *Animal Hospital* week in August 1994.[7] By 31 January 1998 the *Radio Times* front cover featured three stars of the docu-soap. 'Jeremy from *Airport*' in a dinner jacket next to 'Maureen from *Driving School*' and 'Trude from *Vets in Practice*' in sparkling evening gowns, all posed in a dramatic 'dance finale' gesture over a large gold caption 'Fame!' and sub-caption 'It happened to them. Could you be TV's next docu-soap star?'[8]

The new docusoaps were distinguished both from conventional documentary subjects and forms and from the 'emergency services' shows of the early 1990s by their extensive coverage of relatively mundane lives. Their subjects were newly-trained vets, people taking their driving tests, traffic wardens, hotel workers: ordinary people, often service industry workers, faced with particular challenges. Documentary seemed to have finally abandoned its practice of casting people as social problems, discovering instead the puzzling and conflict-ridden nature of everyday life. The replacement of the issue-driven with the slice-of-life documentary quickly brought accusations of 'dumbing down', especially when some of these featured individuals became stars for a time, with spin-off programmes of their own.[9] An alternative line of critique was that of 'exploitation' of the subjects of documentary, who, it was argued, were not prepared for the kind of exposure that these early evening series would give them.[10] Documentary had found a new popularity by exploring the mundane, and this was one point of tension that fed into the crisis of 1999.

This tension was intensified by the simultaneous development of a daytime television which validated ordinary people and their discourses in relatively non-hierarchical ways.[11] British-produced shows like *Kilroy* and *Vanessa* played alongside imported series like *Oprah*, *Rikki* and, most controversially at the end of the last century, *Jerry Springer*. Television seemed to many more traditional commentators to have become both more raucous and more voyeuristically invasive, and indeed these daytime talk series would be caught up in the crisis which engulfed the docusoap in 1999.

The crisis of documentary would not have been possible if docusoaps had only dealt in new subjects. Another point of tension was the novel form of these programmes. Docusoaps were usually series in a thirty minute slot, rather than single documentaries. They were constructed with a strong narrative drive with cliff-hanger endings. Sometimes other explicit entertainment elements were introduced, including music to underline comic moments. The narration was explicit and jokey, often spoken by a comedian or a star from a soap opera and tended to anticipate and so define the meaning and tone of the activities shown. Docusoaps virtually dispensed with the formal interview, replacing it with an informal chat between director and subject whilst the subject was doing something else. Typically this would involve the subject driving a car whilst questions were asked, guaranteeing informality and increasing the chances of the subject letting slip a momentary revelation because their attention was divided. Series would seem to have caught almost every relevant moment of the subject's life, since in production terms the pre-arranged shoot day with a substantial crew had been replaced by the lone documentary-maker available 'whenever something happens'. Stella Bruzzi has perceptively defined this new aesthetic of 'contemporary observational films':

> [They] assume, in their very fabric, that a reality unaffected by the filming process is an impossibility, concluding that what they are able to achieve is the negotiation of a different understanding of truth—one that accepts the film-making process and one that acknowledges the essential artificiality of any filming set-up.[12]

The change was remarkable, but it had precedents.[13]

Technological factors made a crucial contribution in enabling a more intimate style and longer shooting schedules but at no additional cost. In 1995–97 both lightweight DV cameras and fast non-linear editing were introduced. During the period I was producing a series on Hong Kong following around a dozen residents through the period leading up to the handover to Chinese rule.[14] Shooting had begun in 1995 using analogue Hi-8 cameras. Sony announced the first DV camera as a consumer format, and it was available in London (though not in Hong Kong) at the end of 1995. With a modification to enable the use of radio microphones, I sent the first camera to Hong Kong in February 1996. The resultant footage was far superior to analogue Hi-8, but as yet no easy editing route existed. By the end of 1996, it became possible to feed the digital footage directly into an AVID with sufficient memory to produce an hour-long programme. Off-line non-linear editing provided a relatively inexpensive route to a far faster cutting rate and, crucially, more flexibility with sound editing than video had hitherto provided to TV documentary producers. Other London-based producers like Colin Luke at Mosaic Films were following the same route, as were BBC producers from Education and the Community Programmes Unit. The technology made possible the spread from experimental production areas of the techniques of long and casual observational shooting, leading to successful series like *Driving School* in the summer of 1997.

The docusoap emerged as a new mainstream form and was an unexpected success. BBC Education had intended that *Driving School* should concentrate not on the pupils but the instructors.[15] The producers found that the pupils provided the greater interest and shifted the focus of the series during production. It can also be argued that another experiment in extended coverage, *The House* (shot on film) was a precursor of the sudden development of the popular docusoap. This series, made for BBC2 by an independent company, followed the tumultuous regime of Jeremy Isaacs at the Royal Opera House, using a mixture of observation and often devastating interviews. Each programme told a parallel and sometimes interlocking story: the chaos and backstabbing of the administrative operation and the comparative discipline and restraint of the artists (this seems to have been one of the implications of the rhetorical structure adopted).[16] There are, however, significant differences. *The House* was made for BBC2 and shot on film over a long period and the notoriety of some of its incidents seems to have taken the makers by surprise. *Driving School* was a peak time BBC1 series, made to follow up on the unexpected success of *Animal Hospital*. The term 'docusoap' began to emerge around this time to describe this new phenomenon and was retrospectively applied by some critics to *The House*. What had once been a rarity, difficult to achieve and fraught with unresolved problems, suddenly became a feature of early evening television entertainment.

This shift in TV documentary was the result of a confluence of factors. Budget and scheduling issues played a crucial role, with a cash-strapped BBC embracing the new form as a low-cost ratings winner. Long-form news bulletins were experimenting with the inclusion of short documentary items of seven to ten minutes, reducing the need for issue-led documentaries. Other staple genres of low-cost early evening entertainment like gameshows and chatshows had suffered from generic overexposure in previous years. Soap operas seemed to hold their audience in a period of declining numbers for the mass channels, but required large resources and long-term planning. The BBC in particular needed a more immediate solution and found it in the docusoap.

Docusoaps represented a development of documentary practice on several fronts at once. They offered new subjects, new relationships with those subjects, a new visual system (both framing and editing), new forms of narrative construction and a novel place in the schedules. It is not surprising, then, that the nature of factual television was suddenly thrown into question, especially as it happened alongside other developments like the enfranchisement of everyday argument and opinionated speech in daytime talkshows.[17] The questioning became a crisis because of the particular relationship that exists between popular TV programming and the national press in Britain. This relationship is the final element in the overdetermined documentary crisis of 1999.

How the Story Developed

Scattered news stories had appeared through 1997 and 1998 about the issue of 'fakery' in the new breed of documentaries. In February 1998, it was a Channel 4 film *Rogue Males*, where rogue builders messing up jobs proved to be out of work actors;[18] and in May 1998 it was *Clampers* where an over-enthusiastic traffic warden was revealed to be an administrator for the service who returned to the streets for his moment of televisual fame.[19] These isolated incidents were the precursors of the crisis of 1998–99. The crisis was ignited, initially, by a piece of investigative journalism by the liberal broadsheet *Guardian* newspaper, which examined a traditional current affairs documentary. Over three days (5–7 May 1998), long reports examined *The Connection*, an hour-long documentary made for the ITV Network First slot,[20] which won eight awards and was subsequently sold to fourteen countries. The film claimed to show every stage in a new drug route bringing cocaine from Colombia to Britain. For the first two days, the story was the paper's front page lead, and on the third the second lead story.[21] The *Guardian* concluded that the programme was 'an elaborate fake', detailing how an interview with a drugs baron in a secret location was actually with a retired minor bureaucrat in the director's hotel room; how a sequence showing a 'mule' swallowing condoms filled with heroin and successfully bringing them into the UK was faked in separate stages. In the eventual inquiry, it was found that sixteen different deceptions were involved in the film.[22] These deceptions could not be brushed aside as journalists wilfully misunderstanding documentary practice, or as isolated lapses by errant filmmakers. An inquiry was mounted by Carlton TV at the insistence of the regulatory body, the Independent Television Commission.

With the inquiry hanging over the television industry, the press kept the issue warm. On 9 August 1998, the *Sunday Times* revealed that: 'the makers of one of British television's most prestigious natural history series have admitted to the routine use of captive animals to simulate scenes shot in the wild'.[23] The next day the *Independent* amplified the story in an interview with Hugh Miles, one of the most respected camera people in the business.[24] On 2 September 1998 appeared a different angle to the issue of documentary truth. Most newspapers carried the account of Stuart Smith and Victoria Greetham who had hoodwinked producers working on a Channel 4 commission. It was only when trailers for the hour-long film *Daddy's Girl* were shown that it emerged that Smith was not Greetham's snobbish father who disapproved of his daughter's partner, as he claimed to be in the film. Greetham's real father contacted Channel 4 to reveal that Smith himself was the partner . . . of whom he profoundly disapproved. Here was a human interest story to complement the intricate recital of facts provided by *The Connection* story.[25] Taking the two stories together, it appeared that something was wrong with the documentary system itself. Filmmakers could fool the public, but so could members of the public fool filmmakers. The *Daily Mail* carried a follow-up feature on 3 September about gullible programme makers, and this is probably the point at which informal popular discourse began to establish the view that 'documentaries are full of made-up stuff'. Then on 5 December the Carlton internal inquiry admitted that the *Guardian's* accusations were true in almost every particular. The ITC announced that Carlton was to be fined £2 million, to be pocketed by the Treasury. Perhaps the television industry hoped that a December settlement of *The Connection* issue would mean that public cynicism about truth and documentary would ebb over the Christmas holidays, but this was not to be.

On Friday 5 February, the *Guardian* reported on page 7 that 'another documentary fake rocks C4'. Firm action had been taken:

> Channel 4 yesterday slapped an indefinite ban on a programme-maker after the station admitted that a documentary purporting to expose the life of rent boys in Glasgow had included faked scenes.

The *Daily Mail*, however, made the story the front page lead. 'Can We Believe Anything We See on Television?' asked most of the front page, 'as another Channel 4 fake is exposed'. The collusive nature of the address in this headline is highly significant, and the article concludes with a catalogue of instances:

> Last autumn a £100,000 documentary, *Daddy's Girl*, was pulled from the channel's schedules a day before transmission when it emerged that the film-

makers had been duped by a couple who posed as father and daughter but were in fact boyfriend and girlfriend.

The biggest scandal was *The Connection* . . . which purported to penetrate the Colombian Cali drugs cartel's new heroin route to London.

In fact large parts of it were complete fabrication . . .

Last year the BBC admitted that some of the antics of learner driver Maureen Rees were faked for the hit fly-on-the-wall series *Driving School*.

Historical documentary makers have also been caught out. Last year . . . [etc.]

Then the following Friday came the second lead on the *Mail* front page. Under the strapline 'Can we Believe Anything We See on TV (Part Two)' a story about the real people appearing, not on a documentary, but in a daytime talk show: 'Vanessa and the fake chat show guests, full story pages 8 and 9'. On the same day the *Daily Mirror*'s whole front page (and pages 2–6 for that matter) were devoted to 'Trisha Is Fake Too'. The reference in the strapline 'We expose another TV show scandal' is unclear. It might refer to the *Daily Mail* or to previous 'scandals'. The Vanessa and Trisha stories combined the themes of duplicitous programme-makers and deceitful guests. The *Mail*:

> All daytime chat shows on the BBC are to be investigated for hiring fake guests following the suspension yesterday of three staff on Vanessa . . .
>
> Two producers and a researcher have been sent home as a BBC spokesman admitted that agencies had been used to book guests since Vanessa arrived from ITV last month. It discovered that four items on the show were certainly affected.[26]

The *Mirror* revealed 'ITV's flagship daytime show Trisha has also been duped by fake guests' with details on subsequent pages of cases such as Eddie Wheeler who 'was a womaniser, a stalking victim and a sex-addict father in 3 separate shows'. He was quoted as saying 'I can't believe no-one checked me out.'[27] The Mirror's editorial summed up the issue making clear that the status of factual TV as a whole was at stake:

> When you watch a film, play or soap on TV, you know it is not real. But factual programmes are supposed to be what their name says—fact, not fiction . . . Newspapers are accused of many evils and we sometimes get things wrong. But it is rare for a newspaper to lie. Certainly the *Mirror* never would. Factual television needs to adopt those standards. To respect truth and present facts and people as they are. If it does not, there will be only one possible result. Viewers will switch off in ever greater numbers.[28]

This was the high point of the crisis and heads rolled as a result, not necessarily those of any guilty party.[29] The aftershock stories continued for some time: on 19 February the *Daily Mail* revealed 'Countdown Fakes' (question-rigging in the venerable Channel 4 quiz show) and 1 March 'Is there life after docusoap?' (sad lives after 'their 15 minutes of fame is over');[30] the *Independent* on 24 March 'Channel 4 gun-running film was faked'; and the *Sunday People* 4 July 'BBC Killed My Babies' (vengeful father dupes documentary makers). The characteristic journalistic mode of attack in reporting each incident is to recite a catalogue of previous infractions, creating the impression of an institutional crisis rather than isolated infractions of established norms.[31]

The Role of the Press

Newspaper coverage was a crucial factor in the crisis, and provides a convenient record of it. But it was not, as we shall see, the only factor. Britain's press is different from that of the USA, for example. It is highly concentrated as a national press and has high per capita sales. Its titles are highly stratified (redtop tabloid; mid-market tabloid; broadsheet) and the comparative 'brands' have near-universal recognition for their distinctive approaches. Such a press is able to create a national discourse in the near 55 million population of Britain. Its obsessions and points of reference become common currency in a way that is the exclusive prerogative of television in other cultures. In Britain the news agenda is set by television and the press mutually and in tension. The editorial agenda of all national titles is clear and tendentious. The *Daily Mail* follows an anxious right-wing agenda, deploring each fragment of evidence of moral decline. The *Guardian* pursues a liberal republican policy, trying to locate itself as an unwished-for sympathetic critic of Labour governments. Newspaper coverage also plays a crucial role in creating 'event TV' by its large-scale coverage of series such as *Big Brother* and *Pop Idol*. This is a form of cross-promotion which nevertheless does not involve any cross-ownership other than that between News International and BSkyB.[32] It is based on mutual interest in pursuing the current and the popular rather than in maximising profits from popular brands. It therefore takes place in a climate of rather lopsided editorial independence.[33]

Study of the popular press reveals a surprisingly large number of stories that dominate one edition and then disappear almost immediately. It is almost as though newspapers try out stories and issues to see which will 'run'. The early examples of documentary 'fakes' seem to have fallen into this category. Yet the *Daily Mail* returned to its theme over almost a month from the banner headline of 5 February 1999. Clearly something had brought the story into public concern, and that something was radio, transforming print and TV broadcast into chat and community.

How the Crisis Spread

The 1998–99 crisis in documentary is by no means a matter of newspapers alone. The press is certainly a major factor in the crisis, and, for this study at least, provides the only remaining consistent base of evidence. The issue became a popular cultural phenomenon because the press stories were able to prompt and foster informal discourse, both within and beyond the media. Newspaper stories have, in Britain at least, a wide readership. They provide a convenient source of topics for media chat, which is an ephemeral activity that has scarcely been studied, to my knowledge. It is the reason for the apparently fickle attitude of British national newspapers with a popular address. Issues appear and disappear with no logic that can be determined from textual analysis. Newspapers float many stories, but continue only with those that enter into general circulation as part of the immediate ephemeral moment. The 1998–99 documentary crisis entered into such a general circulation. The remarks of DJs and the interventions of phone-in callers became part of an even more informal and unrecorded set of exchanges: everyday speech.

Morning drivetime radio DJs will make topical jokes based on the day's newspaper stories, or indulge in rants about particular items. Daytime talk radio phone-ins offer a large number of themes to their listeners, many of which derive from newspaper stories. Researchers for daytime TV shows (and documentaries) use newspapers as information bases, contacting writers and the subjects of stories with requests to appear. The pressure to be entirely contemporaneous and of the moment is particularly strong for radio. Radio presenters attempt to become part of the ordinary conversations of the moment through which their audiences constitute themselves as a group with a transient but real social identity. But these presenters are isolated in soundproof studios with, at best, small support teams. Phone calls and phone-ins have long been used to overcome this isolation. Now, the internet is becoming the major influence on radio talk, through the scanning of chatrooms and the use of listeners' emails to the producers.

In this way, a topic can develop 'a life of its own' by appearing in many forms of speech at once.[34] It then becomes part of the small change of social intercourse, a theme on which an average citizen is likely to have something to say. So people who lived through the period of the 1998–99 documentary crisis are apt to remember, when prompted, 'something about' this moment. They can recall the moment when 'everybody' distrusted documentaries, when scepticism became a general attitude and individual instances of documentary material seen on TV were picked over to see if 'we could catch them out'.

More direct and, as it were, textual evidence of this necessarily ephemeral speech has ceased to exist, as has almost all of the radio material as well.[35] Some evidence remains in the tenor of TV current affairs like Channel 4's attempted counter-attack against the *Guardian* on *The Connection* issue,[36] and may exist in daytime talk material as well. Other evidence of the public and general nature of the discourse can be deduced from the letters published by newspapers or the rhetorical nature of the *Daily Mail*'s front page question.

But the moment has passed, and the only consistent source for a narrative of the kind I have offered is one of its principal protagonists, the newspaper industry, tested against individual recollections and deductions about the subsequent response of programme-makers and the television industry. Yet the existence of such lost thought and speech can still be posited as a vital component of a particular historic event: the documentary crisis of 1998–99.

Fact and Fiction as Genres

The crisis was a crisis in genre relations. Genre is a set of practical (as opposed to theorised or even formalised) meanings and understandings that circulate between audience, makers and institution. Documentary depends on a constantly renegotiated understanding of the status of its footage as evidence, based as it is on an impossible but necessary project: that of aligning recording with reality, image with incident. This is what is happening in all the welter of accusations, suspicions and speculations in the early months of 1999.

Broadcast television is particularly sensitive to the practical renegotiations of documentary. Broadcasting has a particular relationship with the everyday world of its viewers. Through its co-presence, the liveness inherent in the fact of transmitting scheduled material, the currency of its habitual use of direct address formats as opposed to the historicity of cinema, broadcasting works through a society's collective concerns about 'our world', how we perceive it, how we are in it.[37] This renders it ephemeral yet central: important enough to figure on the front pages of mass newspapers and in the deliberation of governments. The status of its images matters because it connects with the everyday sense of reality, of human fact and potential, which contemporary citizens inhabit.

Documentary is the neuralgic point in establishing factuality in broadcasting. Broadcast television mixes 'the factual' and 'the fictional' and attempts to establish a boundary between them. The boundary is a soft one, pushed at from both sides: not only by programme-makers but also by 'members of the public', or the 'subjects of documentary'. The documentary crisis of 1998–99 demonstrates both kinds of pressure on that boundary. It embraces examples of people pretending to be what they are not in order to deceive factual programme-makers; and programme-makers pretending that their footage can claim a factual status.

The boundary may be soft, but it is essential. It defines two distinct regimes of attention, two distinct regimes of response: those of the factual, 'our world', and those of fiction 'a parallel world'. Different attentions are invited, sought and offered by each. Documentary invites a viewing activity of inspection and criticism. Fiction involves a 'suspension of disbelief' and empathy. Factuality involves a foregrounding of indexicality, of the specifics of each image. From a subject/performer's point of view, acting is appropriate to both, but different acting. Acting 'yourself' is appropriate to the factual. 'Hamming it up' being 'shifty' or 'reticent' are fine in modern factual programmes, so long as what is presented is a version of 'yourself'. Fictional acting involves convincing pretence, in a calculated and intentional emotional range appropriate to the particular generic register operationalised by the fiction (melodrama, naturalism etc). Those who take fiction as fact are viewed as rather simple, if not socially dysfunctional. Examples include the aliens in the film *Galaxy Quest*[38] who take a Star-Trek-like TV series to be 'historical documents'; or the obsessives who conflate soap opera actors and the roles they play.

Fiction can adopt the stylistic traits of factual filmmaking without problems. Fiction can adopt the visual and narrational styles of factual programmes to produce drama-documentary, and can exploit documentary conventions in sitcoms like *The Royle Family* and *The Office*.[39] Once fiction is passed off as fact, the situation becomes more complicated. Documentary tends to trade across the boundary between fact and fiction on an everyday basis, adopting, tactically, some of the habits of fiction in order to bring structure to the sometimes intractable indexicality of its imagery, and to complexify its portrayal of a multi-faceted reality. Problems occur when material proposed as fact involves more fictional elements than the current generic understandings would allow.

The renegotiation of the generic relations of documentary concern the nature of documentary's trading across the boundary between fiction and fact. Once documentary is in doubt, then the factuality of factual material (news included) is in doubt. This point is often misunderstood by industry practitioners. Shaun Williams, then Chief Executive of the producers' association PACT tried to claim that

> One of the problems here has been a blurring of a number of quite separate issues. There's a big difference between hoaxers unknowingly used, reconstructions and blatant deceptions and fakery.[40]

Such a separation cannot be maintained in the face of popular generic discourses and beliefs about the status of factual television. The regime of factuality is threatened equally by all of these practices, and their combination at the end of the 1990s ensured that a crisis of belief in television's regime of factuality was likely to happen.

The Issue of Trust

The crisis centred around two questions: whether undue artifice had entered into the construction of programmes, and whether the people appearing in documentary and factual programmes were assuming identities that were not their own. In both cases, at stake was not so much truth in general as trust and its betrayal. Implied in the criticisms is an understanding of trust:

> Here we are engaged in a chain of trust, from the director of programmes right through to producers, directors, editors and researchers to the viewer. If we claim something is astonishingly good, bad, surprising or in some way exceptional, it damn well should be. No poetic licence here.[41]

As a BBC spokesperson told the *Daily Mail*: 'The BBC has a contract of trust with audiences and they must be able to believe in the integrity of pro-grammes.'[42] An ITC spokesperson later told them: 'Viewers have a right to expect that anything they see on a factual programme has been properly vetted. We take this seriously.'[43] This is clear proof of the idea that generic values are based upon assumptions shared between audience, filmmakers and institution. This chain of trust was breached by programme-makers (*The Connection, Chickens*) and by those appearing on the programmes (*Daddy's Girl*) and in some cases both at different times on the same series (*Trisha, Vanessa*).

The crisis began to deepen when questions of artifice in construction gave way to questions of artifice in identity. The existence of a relationship of trust within the genre normally ensures that instances of reconstruction, elision and even (as in the sub-genre of history programming) straightforward staging of events are all taking place within the normally accepted trade across the boundary with fiction. Artifice in personal identity is quite another matter. The documentary genre, and the factual programmes that draw their values from it, involve a precisely defined set of values around identity.[44]

Graef's 'chain of trust' exists to guarantee authenticity. Authenticity has its levels, and the position of readership offered to the factual programme viewer is one which invites critical comment and analysis of the behaviour and motives of the factual subjects. Just because a subject bursts into tears, it is not necessary to assume that their tears are produced by their ostensible emotional state. It might all be a calculation; it might be crocodile tears. Making such deductions from the demeanour of documentary subjects is part of the con-temporary viewing pleasure of such programmes. But to discern levels of authenticity, concealment and calculation depends on an ultimate level of authenticity, a selfhood behind the veils. The fictional mode of performance, deliberately adopting an identity which is other than the self, undermines this relationship. And the fictional mode of performance was adopted alike by those who hoodwinked honest programme-makers and honest artists who were commissioned by programme-makers to perform identities not their own.

'Why didn't they check?' is the basic question asked even by the hoaxers themselves.[45] Within this generic relationship, viewers trust the authority and reliability of the television institution to police itself. Producer guidelines exist, training exists, professional discourses and practices exist and, in the last analysis, the regulators' sanctions exist to give institutional guarantees that this trust is justified. Yet this television institution was, at the time, working under the strains of a downward pressure on costs and an increasing 'just-in-time' production in both documentary and factual talkshows. Both of these pressures reduced the ability and even the possibility of checking the identities of documentary and factual participants. This does not, however, as many in the industry think it does, explain the whole of the situation. Nor does it account for the speed and efficiency with which documentary production moved to re-establish a working generic relationship. Trust had to be re-established between audiences, institutions and filmmakers. Documentary programme-makers had re-established a prominent position in the schedules by making a startling series of innovations at many different levels within the genre. These innovations may have caused the crisis of 1999, but they also provided its solution.

How Things Changed as a Result of the Crisis

Television adopted two solutions to the crisis. The first was a short-term damage limitation exercise, which ensured that newspapers would lose interest, and that the issue would fall out of everyday currency. The appropriate people and companies were punished; internal guidelines and practices were tightened up; and the BBC quietly retired the *Vanessa* show soon after. This was the organised institutional reaction. Amongst programme-makers, commissioners and senior executives, a shift in approach to documentary production can, with hindsight, be discerned. The view that the docusoap boom was over began to take hold, and the search was on for replacement formats. This period sees the criticism of *Lakesiders*[46] as a weak example of the format, together with the move towards 'lifestyle' programming like *Ground Force* and *Changing Rooms* in the slots occupied by docusoaps. Programme-makers already in production began to edit their material to take account of the general climate of scepticism about their work. Programme-makers about to enter production were more than usually wary of being duped by hoaxers. Out of these various reactions emerged a general trend, one which, surprisingly perhaps, sought to guarantee authenticity by increasing the level of explicit artifice.

Within the texture of programmes, this meant introducing or increasing the marks of intentionality and making explicit the constructed nature of the programme. Documentaries would include the marks of the unexpected and the unplanned, where the filmmaker was taken by surprise. These are intimate details of the camera or the microphone not quite catching something, the hasty zoom, the hurried reframing, the stumbled line, the bleeped expletive, or where the director asks a particularly stupid or inappropriate question. Such elements would previously have been eliminated; now they were prized. Such footage vaunts the honesty of filmmakers because it makes explicit some of the work of construction involved. This reaction was a reply to the accusations of excessive fakery in documentary construction. It also responds to the developing popular connoisseurship of the camcorder generation, an increasing awareness of 'how did they do that' which is demonstrated in phenomena like the examination of special effects as well as an ability to spot 'faked' footage.

At a more managerial level, the problem was one of responding to the faltering quality of documentary raw material. The solution developed was the development of formats which used explicitly manufactured rather than found situations. Some were well-established already. BBC2's *Back to the Floor*[47] was originated at roughly the same time as *Driving School*, but as a response to a different set of problems for documentary: the lack of companies willing to allow observational documentary filmmakers into their operations.[48] Confronted by public relations departments who made the simple deduction that documentary meant unnecessary problems, *Back to the Floor* artfully combined flattery with a situation that could allow a degree of control by PR departments. Senior or chief executives were invited to take on, for a week, the humblest job in their organisation and then take back to the boardroom the lessons learned. A certain latitude in observational rules could be accomodated.[49] The transparently constructed nature of the situation, a challenge to the documentary subject, rebalanced the documentary relationship, enabling a new take on documentary's challenge to the viewer: spot the authentic person behind the performance of self. From another direction (and broadcasting environment, the Netherlands) came a more audacious combination of the gameshow challenge and the observational documentary: *Big Brother*. This phenomenon takes the technological and aesthetic advances of docusoap, with its extended coverage and its use of ordinary people doing mundane things. It combines this with the most explicitly constructed of all situations, enabling an unhindered pursuit for the viewer of the game of spotting the truth of personality behind the affectations and postures of the performance of self. The performers know they are being watched. One of the few things they have to talk about is the fact of being watched and their motivations for being involved. *Big Brother* employs an extreme artifice in its format in order to access the truth of personality. In the success of *Big Brother* as a feature of Britain's summers from 2000 to at least 2005, we see the final closure of the crisis of 1998–99 in a reassertion of the impossible but necessary quest for truth through factual programme-making. It has changed, probably for ever, the relationship between documentary makers, their subjects and their audiences.[50]

Conclusion

From the perspective of the present, the most striking aspect of the crisis of 1999 is that it is now almost forgotten. The moment was ephemeral, but that is not to imply that it was unimportant. An enduring crisis in the generic relations of factuality in television would be insupportable within the fabric of contemporary society. So in this case an amended set of beliefs and behaviours was quickly elaborated and these continue to evolve. The remaining problem is an analytic one: how to grasp the complexities of those ephemeral moments which together organise the fundamental and enduring structures of genre.

Notes

1   See Steve Neale, *Genre and Hollywood*, Routledge, London 2000, especially pp. 7–47. Neale however totally omits the category of documentary from his exploration of genre, limiting himself to fiction only. The omission of documentary as a genre, logically distinct from all of fiction (rather than from particular genres of fiction) would disturb his basic categorisations. I have explored this question in John Ellis, 'A Minister is About to Resign: On the Interpretation of Television Footage', in ed. Anne Jerslev, *Realism and Reality in Film and Media*, Museum Tusculanum Press, Copenhagen 2002.

2   Disavowal commonly means 'to deny knowledge of'. Freud points out that to deny knowledge of something is simultaneously to articulate the possibility (if not the fact) of its existence. See for instance his 'On Negation' (Standard Edition of the *Complete Psychological Works* vol. XIX, Hogarth Press 1963, pp. 236–40). The term therefore becomes useful for describing the process of understanding the 'factuality' of documentary which we know not to be true even as we enjoy it as true.

3   This instability is easy to see in arguments about the status of documentary footage, which can provoke reactions such as 'they must have faked that scene', 'nobody would possibly allow themselves to be shown like that', 'I've been there and it's nothing like that'.

4   Brian Winston, *Lies, Damn Lies and Documentaries*, BFI, London 2000, p. 54.

5   Stella Bruzzi, *New Documentary: a Critical Introduction*, Routledge, London 2000. John Dovey, *Freakshow: First Person Media and Factual Television*, Pluto Press, 2000.

6   Winston, *Lies*, p. 54.

7   For a fuller account of the role of this series, see John Ellis, *Seeing Things: Television in the Age of Uncertainty*, I. B. Tauris, London 2000, p. 141.

8   *Radio Times* for week 31 January–6 February 1998.

9   This is particularly true of Jeremy Spake who originally appeared in *Airport* and has developed a career as a presenter, and Jane McDonald, for whom a role in *The Cruise* led to the success of her career as a singing star that had hitherto eluded her.

10   Winston, *Lies*, pp. 143–56 provides a catalogue of cases of exploitation from the history of documentary.

11   See for instance Joan Shattuck '"Go Ricci": Politics, Perversion and Pleasure in
     the 1990s,' in ed. Geraghty and Lusted, *The Television Studies Book*, Edward Arnold
     1998; and 'Empowering women? The Oprah Winfrey Show,' in ed. D'Acci and
     Spigel, *Feminist Television Criticism: A Reader*, Oxford University Press 1997.

12   Bruzzi, *New Documentary*, p. 98.

13   The change was remarkable, but it had precedents in Paul Watson's series *The
     Family*, a BBC1 series of twelve half-hour episodes running from 3 April 1974
     to 26 June 1974 showing the daily life of the Wilkins family in Reading. It had
     used many of the techniques, but was shot on film long before professional light-
     weight video was available. Watson's commentary, which he delivers, is remark-
     ably similar to those of the recent docusoaps. His concentration on the everyday
     life of one family brings forward the events of everyday, just as docusoaps do. But
     he is also justified in his assertion that he is not the father of the docusoap since
     his series was developed in the context of observational documentary, and cru-
     cially avoids any interviews with the participants, let alone the informal ones
     developed during the 1990s. *The Family* was a bold experiment, representing the
     limits of what documentary could attempt and involving a high level of invest-
     ment. Each programme was shot on 16mm film and edited for transmission a
     week after the events had been shot. Debate centred on the 'feedback' effect on the
     family of the intense public scrutiny of their affairs whilst they were still being
     filmed, together with their 'acting up' for the camera and their decision to bring
     forward their daughter's wedding date so that it could be filmed for TV. The dom-
     inating Mrs Wilkins had a subsequent brief career as a columnist in the *London
     Evening Standard*. 'The Family: Ten Years After' was shown on BBC2 on 10 Decem-
     ber 1983.

14   *Riding the Tiger*, produced and directed by Po Chih Leong and Sze Wing Leong,
     Channel 4 June 1997, 4 × 52 mins.

15   *Driving School*, six thirty-minute episodes, BBC1 10 June 1997 to 15 July 1997,
     8pm, repeated on BBC1 from 24 July 1998 at 8.30pm.

16   *The House*, six fifty-minute episodes, BBC2 9.30pm from 16 January 1996. For a
     detailed account see Bruzzi, *New Documentary*, pp. 83–5.

17   As two producers who found themselves caught up in the ensuing crisis put it:
     'The ratings success of documentary soaps, daytime chatshows and "reality-
     based" magazine shows have rendered "real life" as simply another one of televi-
     sion's generic labels—rather than as a distinctive guarantee of truth.' Adam
     Barker, Edmund Coulthard, *Guardian* 21 September 1998 (on the *Daddy's Girl*
     hoax).

18   Channel 4, 17 February 1998, 9.30pm, a documentary in the hour-long *Cutting
     Edge* slot.

19   *Clampers*, a six-part BBC1 series from 11 May 1998 at 9.30pm; followed by a single
     Christmas show *Clampers* BBC1, 21 December 1998 at 9.30pm.

20   A high-budget current affairs slot shown at 10.30, after *News at Ten*. *The Connec-
     tion* was shown on 15 October 1998 at 10.40pm.

21   As the hapless executive producer, Roger James, put it: 'to find oneself on the front
     page of the *Guardian*, competing with world news, not just for one day but for three
     days, I have to say was pretty shocking, and seemed out of all proportion to the

story if I'm honest' (interviewed on Channel 4, *Hard News Special*, 28 November 1998). James was well-regarded in the industry and was seen by most as the victim of a producer, Marc de Beaufort, who exploited his trust. But it should be said that James's editorial style fitted much better within Central Television than it did in the company that had taken it over, Carlton TV. James seems not to have adapted well to the Carlton environment where an ever-greater number of scoops, exclusives and headline-grabbing programmes were demanded from factual staff. De Beaufort must have seemed a very welcome provider of such material.

22   See for instance the *Guardian* Saturday 5 December 1998, pp. 4–5 and Winston, *Lies*, pp. 13–23 for exact details and discussion of the nature of its transgressions.

23   *Sunday Times*, 9 August 1998, p. 1.

24   *Independent*, 10 August 1998, p. 6.

25   The trailed programme *Daddy's Girl* was pulled from the schedules by Channel 4. However, a programme exploring the issue, *Who's Been Framed?*, was shown in the *Cutting Edge* series on 26 February 1999, right in the middle of the most intensive period of the crisis. This programme revealed that Smith and Greetham had been recruited late in the production's development to replace a couple who changed their mind about participating.

26   *Daily Mail*, 12 February 1999, p. 8.

27   *Mirror*, 12 February 1999, p. 3.

28   *Mirror*, 12 February 1999, p. 6.

29   The *Daily Mail* alleged that *Vanessa* researcher Debbie Price paid individuals from a modelling agency to play roles on the show. She subsequently received an out-of-court settlement from the paper as the claims were untrue.

30   1 March 1999, pp. 34–5.

31   So a story in the *Sun*, 21 March 2002, headed 'Fake TV Scandal' about how 'a TV producer aged 30 conned a school by posing as a spotty teenager to make a Channel 4 documentary' carried a sidebar reiterating the *Connection/Chickens/ Daddy's Girl/Vanessa* saga: www.thesun.co.uk/0,,20021 3075,00.html.

32   Some newspaper groups, particularly News International, effectively controlled by Rupert Murdoch, would prefer a greater degree of cross-ownership than legislation allows. Their editorial stance is indicated by the amount of cross-promotion with their own BSkyB channels, and their attempts to kindle the story (a notably thin *Sunday Times* front page story, see note 23), and to keep the story alive (a *Sun* follow-up over three years later see note 31). Thus the Broadcasting Act 2003 still prevents an 'excessive' degree of newspaper/broadcasting cross-ownership whilst permitting foreign ownership of core broadcast channels. Such is the perceived importance of the particular interrelation between newspapers and broadcasting to British political discourse and public sphere more generally.

33   In political terms, there are more national papers following a moralistic right-wing or conservative agenda than there are titles which lean towards the left or liberalism.

34   Marketeers know this process as 'viral marketing'.

35   Annette Hill lead a research project at the University of Westminster which interviewed a large sample in the period just subsequent to the one under discussion

here. Different issues arise, but the complexity of views and practical engagement with the ethical and philosophical underpinnings of documentary are very evident. Annette Hill, *Reality TV*, Routledge, 2004.

36 Channel 4, *Hard News Special*, 28 November 1998.

37 For a further exploration of these issues, see John Ellis, *Seeing Things: Television in the Age of Uncertainty*, I. B. Tauris, 2000.

38 *Galaxy Quest*, dir. Dean Parisot, 1999.

39 *The Royle Family*: three series of six thirty-minute episodes BBC2. Series 1: BBC2 from 19 October 1998 at 10pm repeated BBC1 from 5 July 1999, 10pm. Series 2: BBC2 from 23 September 1999 at 10.30pm, repeated BBC1 1 June 2000 at 9.30pm. Series 3, BBC1 from 16 October 2000 at 9.30pm. *The Office*: six-part series BBC2 from 9 July 2001 at 9.30pm, repeated BBC2 from 14 January 2002 at 10.30pm.

40 *Broadcast*, 9 April 1999.

41 Roger Graef, *Broadcast*, 9 April 1999.

42 *Daily Mail*, 12 February 1999.

43 *Daily Mail* February 1999 quoting a spokesperson of the Independent Television Commission.

44 This issue is explored in more detail by Dovey, *Freakshow*, 2000, especially pp. 103–53. However Dovey is concerned with 'the limitations of the docu-soap in which the form itself has the sense of flattening out difference leaving the viewer little or no room for understanding or empathy with any of the characters' p. 172), rather than, as I am here, with the tensions within the institutions of understanding of factual material which can bring viewer scepticism and even distrust and disbelief to the fore. The experience of contemporary factual programming seems to me to depend on engaging the viewer's critical assessment of programme subjects, their demeanour and their behaviour.

45 *Daily Mirror*, 12 February 1999, quotes Sharon Wolfers: 'I was astonished how easy it all was. They didn't even carry out any checks. Even when they were filming I thought "I can't believe we are getting away with this."' Noel Antony, who acted as her husband, is quoted: 'They didn't ask any questions to verify who we were. I got the impression they just wanted a good show.' The report further quotes Eddie Wheeler, who made three fake appearances in eighteen months, 'I can't believe no-one checked me out. The programme was going to be dealing with sex problems and as a dare to myself I rang up the night before and asked if I could appear. They agreed. Once I was on, inventing the story was easy. The girlfriend I spoke about didn't exist. It was all rubbish . . . I found it absolutely staggering. The fact that people like me can appear on these shows and tell a different story each time makes an utter mockery of daytime television.'

46 See Bruzzi, *New Documentary*, pp. 86, 92–3.

47 *Back to the Floor* began as a six-part series on BBC2 from 28 October 1997 at 9.50pm, and so would have been in production at the same time as *Driving School*. Series 2 ran from 10 November 1998; Series 3 from 28 October 1999 (an eight-part series repeated in August 2000) and Series 4, also eight parts, from 1 November 2000, all on BBC2.

48 As Roger Graef was able to do in *The Space Between Words* and *State of the Nation*, and most famously, in *Police* in the 1970s. See Brian Winston, *Claiming the Real: The Documentary Film Revisited*, BFI London 1995, pp. 207–10.

49 In the episode of 18 November 1999 at 9pm, for example, David Ford, chief executive of the catering company Gardner Merchant, does not carry a radio microphone, so chance remarks and asides, the meat and drink of the docusoap, are not captured.

50 'I've noticed a marked difference over the last seven or eight years in people's attitude towards being on television', says Rob Cary, executive producer for factual entertainment at indie Menthorn. 'I used to work on the first generation of reality shows like *The Real Holiday Show*, and they are far more media-savvy these days. One thing we found with *Britain's Worst Drivers* (C5) is how the drama and vocabulary of *Big Brother* has just seeped into the public psyche. So when we were doing challenges in cars with contributors they would refer to them as "tasks" and when we shoot the interviews with them on DV they would call that the "diary room" (*Broadcast*, 25 July 2003, p. 14).

Part V

Versions of History

25

History on the Public Screen, I

Donald Watt

A certain experience of going to conferences where historians and profession-als of the media—film and television—congregate has taught me that there are a number of fundamental "false problems" that have to be cleared out of the way before any intelligent discussion, let alone cooperation, is possible.

That this process should be undertaken is, I think, self-evident. For, at least on television, history has become big business. The Thames Television series *The World at War* was an enormous success, both commercially and in its public reception. The BBC series *The Mighty Continent*, though received with mixed feelings by television critics (of whom more anon) and professional historians, was also a considerable success. The degree of success of these two series can be measured in the immense sales enjoyed in each case by the book of the series. On the other hand one has such monstrosities as the BBC's series on the British Empire, which was even denounced on the floor of the House of Lords, or its equally appalling *Churchill's People*, a series of historical playlets sup-posedly based on Winston Churchill's *History of the English-speaking Peoples*, in which central episodes of English history are reenacted as seen through the eyes of the "common people."

The first of these false problems (indeed the first two) can best be expressed in opposed propositions, as follows: the historian's main concern is accuracy; the producer of film and television is concerned with entertainment. The unspoken premise of the first proposition is that to be accurate is to be dull. The unspoken premise of the opposed proposition is that to be entertaining, it is necessary to distort or misrepresent. A good lie, so it is maintained, is always more entertaining than a dull truth.

The second set of propositions, in some sense, complements the first. They may be stated as follows: The historian (or more properly, the academic histo-rian) is concerned only with words. Given his preferences he will lecture, and all the audience will see is a "talking head," that bogey of producers. The pro-ducer, by contrast, is really interested only in what appears on the screen, the visual impact of the medium. Given half a chance he will go after anything—provided that it is "good vision" (or good television)—irrespective of its relevance to the chosen topic. He will always prefer *art nouveau* "wallpaper" to the plausible, credible narrative.

To call these "false problems" is not to deny that they can exist. There are always unimaginative historians, just as there are always irresponsible ratings-bound producers. Indeed, when collaboration between historians and makers of documentary films for educational or television purposes began, one could collect encyclopedias of horror stories wherever proponents of either camp could be found in Britain. But in the last decade there has grown up, as a result of mutual experience and a sequence of conferences, a convergence of minds and a mutual comprehension of the technical problems, at least at the level of the producer and the historian. The problems the historian faces with the media at the time of writing are usually created by the administrators and policy makers, not by the producers and the cameramen.

The subject of this essay, then, is the problems the historian faces with the media in the making of historical films of a nonfictional kind. This, of necessity, excludes all film but the purely educational, much of which is made for sale to public service or educational television anyway. Examples will be drawn mainly from the author's own experiences, insofar as these can be discussed without risking action for libel. But, like most if not all of the other contributors to this book,[1] the author feels that it is intensely important that the new media should be made use of and understood in all their aspects.

It is, of course, self-evident that the making of a nonfiction film or television program on a historical theme is as much an exercise in historiography as is the composition of a learned monograph, the editing of a collection of historical source materials, the writing of a historical best-seller, or the composition of an article for an illustrated part-work designed for a mass audience. All of these present their own problems of composition and presentation, from the precise form a learned footnote or the citation of a source should take, in the first, to the problem of how much of, for example, the first Moroccan crisis one can compress into two thousand words, in the last example.

It is equally self-evident that a historical statement made audiovisually is different from one made in writing. The tempo is different, there can be no recall, no flipping back of the page, no elaboration of parallel themes by footnotes or parentheses. Then too, there is infinitely more written evidence than visual material. Paradoxically, this is least true of ancient and medieval history, where the paucity of written material must be made up by the wealth of artifacts and archeologically obtained materials. A series such as the BBC's recent *The Roman Way* illustrates how effectively this material can be used to enlighten and entertain (the use of Hollywood silent film of classical epics was a barely pardonable gimmick which neither added very much to nor subtracted very much from the total impact of the series). It is, however, characteristic of the problems presented by the visual evidence even here that it is at its richest for social history, and at its weakest on the political side. But the impact of certain film can be out of all proportion to its factual value. I know of few more effective ways of communicating the losses suffered by the frontline combatants in World War I than the panning shots of the military cemeteries employed, for example, in the much-criticized BBC series "The Mighty Continent." The real difficulty arises always in audiovisual historiography when the attempt is made to make a statement for which no visual material is available. This is a problem all historians and producers must face repeatedly and for which there is no universal solution.

The problems the historian faces with the media may best be described under the heading of curses. *Curse No. 1* arises because the media are administered by men of considerable sophistication, often highly educated, but of an education that in contemporary and recent history is usually a combination of out-of-date views and prejudices. It is embodied in the phenomenon of the amateur historian whose views were formed by the Left Book Club, an animal not tolerated for a moment in professional circles, who is rendered doubly intolerable by his monopoly access to the viewing audience conferred by the limited choice of television programs. One of the hardy perennials resulting is Paul Rotha's *Life and Times of Adolf Hitler*; another, equally objectionable, was the series on the Third Reich, *The Rise and Fall of the Third Reich*, made on the basis of William Shirer's best-seller on the same theme, a book severely criticized for its restatement of old myths by every professional historian who reviewed it. I have written elsewhere of the combination of tendentious statement with verifiable inaccuracies exemplified by these two series and do not need to repeat myself here.[2] The BBC's action in rescreening the Rotha series showed a remarkable insensibility to criticism. Rotha's reputation as a maker of documentaries was, and is, considerable; but this should not be adequate excuse for reshowing, without comment, a documentary film of a historical rather than a contemporary nature, the only valuable historical contribution in it being the reproduction of Rotha's viewpoint, one forever imprisoned in the populist prejudices and half-truths of the British filmmakers' popular front.

Curse No. 2 arises from the element of finance. The budgets for the great historical television series such as ITV's *The World at War* and the BBC's *The Great War* and *The Mighty Continent* run of necessity into hundreds of thousands of pounds. The BBC has attempted to deal with this by dividing the cost with foreign agencies such as West German Television or the Time-Life agency. This in itself already arouses problems of audience, since there is little experience or knowledge that a producer can assume to be common to British, American, and West German audiences. But the anxieties of the financial authorities can lead to other difficulties, such as, for example, the setting of a time limit for the making of the series that makes originality of thought or approach simply impossible. Four months was all that was given in one celebrated series for the unit responsible to produce the first program. A solution to the time-limit question recently produced is to engage a multiplicity of producers and writers, giving each a random allocation of programs from the whole—as it might be, programs one, five, eleven, and sixteen, irrespective of their having anything to do with each other—so instead of a single conception designing and unifying the various programs in the series, the series degenerates into a succession of individual programs united only by a title or possibly an outlook.

A third set of problems the heavy cost of historical series creates is the dissipation of know-how. The standard unit responsible for a historical film or television series consists of producer(s), writer(s), editors, musical contributors, cameramen, etc. It may or may not include a historical adviser. But much of the most essential work, the actual discovery of visual material, is the task of the lowly and underpaid researchers, often—too often—bright graduates fresh from university with degree qualifications only vaguely relevant to the subject of the series and only the remotest of indications as to where to go for material. By the time they have finished the series they probably have amassed between them a very considerable body of knowledge of the available material. But with the end of the project the team is broken up and its members scattered to the four winds. So when, four or five years later, a Granada mogul, or a BBC deputy director, or whatever, strikes the desk with his open hand and says it is time for another historical epic, the whole process has to be begun again with a new team which has to learn the business from the beginning. The temptation, the necessity almost, of using again the same familiar material is obvious, Only the expertise, acquired on a shoestring, of the professional film archivists (which must include the invaluable catalogue of the Slade Film History Register), with their international connections, can save them from banal repetition or, most heinous of all faults, the misuse of material to illustrate something which it does not in fact depict.

Curse No. 3 of the media is the battle for ratings and the competition between the channels. The BBC is particularly open to accusation here. One remembers the deliberate placing of its highly publicized exercise in voyeurism, *The Family* (a slavish copy of an American original), so that it conflicted with the last five or so programs of Thames Television's *World at War* series; the reshowing of *The Great War* on a Sunday afternoon; the preemption of the normal time slot of the Tuesday documentary for *The Mighty Continent*, which gave gratuitous offense to the fairly sizable audience of autodidacts and "concerned" who regularly watched the displaced program.

Curse No. 4 is the straitjacket of time. If a multiple-program series is envisaged, then it must for program-planning purposes consist of six, seven, nineteen, or twenty-six programs, since program planners always work on three months at a time, or rather on quarter-years of thirteen weeks each. Within this, each program has a fixed running time, usually of forty-five to fifty minutes or so (shortened on commercial television by the necessity of allowing for the insertion or addition of advertising material). This is not always too serious a problem for the producer, though it may offer a temptation to visual padding and it certainly sets problems of balance over the series as a whole. The worst sufferer is the Open University, whose time slot is severely limited to twenty-four minutes, far too short to deal adequately with the chosen subjects. Anyone who has participated in making films on historical subjects for the Open University will remember the agonies of cutting what seems an excellently balanced forty minutes or so down by half its length.

The worst curse of the media, however, is the contempt shown by the top brass for the taste and judgment of their audience. Despite the abundant evidence of their own statistics that there exists an enormous television audience for mildly educational material, especially on subjects connected with recent and contemporary history, war history in particular, they are petrified by the fear that if anything intellectually above the children's history book market is shown on their screens there will be a mass rush of viewers into alternative channels. The success of highly specialized general-knowledge programs such as *University Challenge* or *Mastermind* ought to have persuaded them that the large lay audience which they know to exist for films and series on historical subjects is intelligent enough to deserve respect. But the fear remains, to be expressed in such gimmicks as the introduction into serious historical programs of showbiz personalities carefully talking down to the audiences,[3] or the metamorphosis of a collective historical view into that of a single personality, as in Alistair Cooke's *America*, itself a gorgeously produced exercise in amateur and myopic pontification by a writer-journalist whose ideological view of Anglo-America is one to which few professional historians would subscribe today.

This perhaps is the point to bring in another curse with which historians and media men alike have to contend: the absence of any serious and well-informed criticism of historical films and television programs. Television criticism itself is confined to the dailies, the Sundays, and the occasional weekly. Each paper or magazine usually employs only one critic, who is expected to cover everything from documentaries to drama, from *University Challenge* to *Top of the Pops*, from *Yesterday's Men* to *Tomorrow's World*. What respectable journal would expect one book reviewer to cover everything from *Winnie the Pooh* to Winston Churchill's *War Memoirs*? Yet this is what the television critic is supposed to do. Only one critic, Philip Purser of the *Sunday Telegraph*, has to the author's knowledge displayed any interest in the debate between producer and historian.[4] Alone among the weeklies, *New Society* has employed a leading professional historian, Douglas Johnson, to review series such as *The World at War* and *The Mighty Continent* on the basis of having seen more than two random selections from the entire series at a preview. It is the lack of a solid body of informed criticism that is most felt by the practitioners in the field of historical documentary. The *Journal of the Society of Film and Television Arts* is too much of a trade journal to supply this lack.[5] Nationally, perhaps, there is too small an audience or readership to keep a journal devoted to this field alive, but room might be found for something on an international scale if funds were forthcoming. At the moment, those who choose to use film or television for the making of historiographical statements have only the praise or censure of the ignorant or the appraisal of audience research as a guide to their success or failure. The first is only of use or disadvantage when they are seeking to convince the bureaucracy of the feasibility or desirability of their tackling another historical theme. The second may be in addition a gratifying reward for the effort spent and the tension generated by the making of the program. But in answer to their questions it tells them little or nothing in detail as to variation in style and technique. With a multi-producer series like *The World at War* such mass approval is of little help to the individual producer.

In this it is easy to be cynical about the lot of the historical adviser. In many series he simply acts as a consultant: that is to say, he is consulted by the program researchers or the producer whenever they feel the need to do so but takes no responsibility for the final product. The historian who is inveigled into such a relationship is well advised to insist that his name be left off the credits or he may find himself held responsible by his professional colleagues for all the points on which be ought to have been consulted and was not. In some cases he simply functions as a means of internal persuasion. He will be asked to write a paper or a historical memorandum on suggested approaches or treatments, with which an ambitious aide may convince a reluctant department director to embark on a new enterprise or entrust it to him. He will often be lured, if unwary, into giving much unrewarded time and effort to the guidance of the plausible and ambitious, only to find in the end that the finished product incorporates all the received historical error against which he has given so careful a warning. He may find, too, that his name in the credits is being employed as a kind of British Standards Kitemark [mark of quality], a guarantee of the historical acceptability of the view to which the series or program on which he is advising is dedicated.

It is to this latter case that the remainder of this essay must be directed. The historian's criteria for judging a program from a professional viewpoint are three in number. First, the subject must be completely covered, within the limits set by the length of the program and the material. Second, the view presented of the subject must be objective within the acceptable definition of that term as understood by professional historians. It must not be *parti pris*. It must not be anachronistic, ascribing to the actors sentiments alien to the time and culture or condemning them for not recognizing values dear to the producer. It must not be ideological or slanted for purposes of propaganda. There must be no recognizable and obvious bias. It must seem to understand rather than to condemn. Third, the events described, the "facts" outlined, must be accurate, that is, in accordance with the present state of historical knowledge. Hypothesis, reconstruction, inference, are all legitimate, but only if they are presented under their own colors.

To ensure this, the historian rash enough to take on the post of historical adviser must insist on the right to vet the finished article in adequate time for alterations to be incorporated and distortions of statement or balance removed before showing. He must vet scripts before the film is dubbed. It would be advisable for him to be familiar with the shooting script and the producer's proposed manner of treatment. It is his job to be the conscience of the unit, to keep an eye on continuity and coverage, to stand back from the myriad and one day-to-day problems of TV shooting on location or of putting the film together in workshop and studio. He will find he has to be diplomat as well as heavy gun, the producer's ally in dealing with intervention from above. He must, if possible, deter the producer from using modern film to illustrate the past or film from fictional reconstruction as if it were actuality. He must have an accurate ear and memory for the kind of misstatement that creeps in through a commentator's ad-libbing. Lastly, he has to realize that it is an adviser's job to advise and that final responsibility lies with the producer. If he does not establish as early as possible where final responsibility lies, he is in for trouble later. (He would be well advised to keep a diary of his actions toward and arguments with the producer.) In the end he will still be regarded by those who notice his name among the credits as responsible for all with which they disagree. And he will long for a chance to make his own film to show how it should be done.

This is perhaps where another false problem arises: who should be dominant, historian or producer? Those who despair of ever getting the media to treat history responsibly tend to gravitate toward the British Inter-University History Film Consortium, an enterprise which conjoins the subscriptions of a number of university history departments so as to enable one of their number every so often to make its own film on a historical subject. Inevitably there is an element of home movie about the final product, even where it has been made in conjunction with a university department of film. The historian as amateur producer is no more satisfactory than the producer as amateur historian. And the pressures of academic life do not normally allow those who have made one film to make another within the time span in which they might learn from their own mistakes.

The producer-dominated series, on the other hand, leads directly to disasters such as that of the BBC's *British Empire* series, with its glaring omissions of central facts, its facile anti-imperialist prejudice, its reconstructions of the siege of Cawnpore and the demise of Ned Kelly on the cheap, its distraction by the contemporary televisual, and its general catalog of "awful warnings" for the future. The true relationship between historian and producer must be a kind of partnership, shading into symbiosis, where each understands, even if he cannot practice, the craft of the other. Audiovisual historiography is a bimedial art, like ballet or opera.

This ideal state has been most closely approximated by the producers of the Open University, whose profession it is to work with historians who cooperate by writing the script and selecting the material they wish to see incorporated into the film. This body of expertise is now being dissipated in turn, since the Open University's budget will not allow new series to be made: the constriction of the very limited time slot allotted by BBC-2's program planners is a source of constant frustration. Even here, the producers have to unlearn their BBC-instilled terror of the switch-off or switch-over. Early programs wasted valuable minutes establishing a locale—cameras panning around an archaeological site, for example.

With that the historian and producer still face the abiding problems of audiovisual historiography. What material is available? Is it to be used to illustrate a lecture, or should it be made into a silent film with a voice-over commentary, talking head, or mobile wallpaper? How do you make an essential point where no material exists? Do you use interviews with eyewitnesses or participants in the events you are describing? There was an excellent two-part series on Austria in World War II shown on West German television, made up almost entirely of selected eyewitnesses telling their story cut cleverly into each other so as to preserve the proper chronology. Can you avoid "bang-bang film" of the kind that might have been shot anywhere from Brest to Brest-Litovsk? Can you spot faked-up film (as the BBC documentary on the General Strike of 1926 most notoriously did not)?[6]

Each set of problems can only be resolved on the job itself, usually on the floor of the cutting room. There are enough and to spare without having to cope with the biggest problem of them all, the state of mind of those who direct the media, who cannot believe that waiting in front of their sets there is an educated, interested, mass audience, people unsure of their knowledge and avid for more, particularly if it will help them understand their own lives and lifetimes, and for whom there is no conflict between learning and entertainment, only between bad and good, pretentious and honest, programs. It is this amorphous and not easily defined lump of bureaucracy in the media that has created the present unsatisfactory state of audiovisual historiography in Britain, with its three equally, if differently, unsatisfactory types of material:

the media epics, mutilated before birth by the top brass; the home movies of the British Inter-University History Film Consortium; or the straitjacketed expertise of the Open University, forever trapped in its twenty-four-minute time slots and starved of money to develop from its present level of expertise.

Notes

1   This essay was originally published in *The Historian and Film*, ed. Paul Smith (Cambridge: Cambridge University Press).
2   In *History* 55 (1970): 214–16; 58 (1973): 399–400.
3   For example, see *The Times* television critic's reaction to Mr. Benny Green's pictorial history of London, a two-part series made for Thames Television under the title *London: The Making of a City*: "Looked splendid . . . a script which, when it did not drown every fact in cliché, was plain straightforward vulgar . . . an opportunity not lost but determinedly rejected by the producer who was his own writer; a deliberate and coldly calculated decision to ruin a good idea by trying to slice it so as to serve everyone" (*The Times*, Feb. 12, 1975).
4   See his entertaining account of a *rencontre* at Cumberland Lodge in the *Sunday Telegraph*, April 28, 1974.
5   See, for example, vol. 2, nos. 9–10 (1974), on *The World at War*. *History* carries reviews of films but does not seem to be read at all in television circles.
6   See the letters of Frank Hardie and Paul Rotha in *The Times*, April 22, 1974, and the reply of Elizabeth Sussex, ibid., May 3, 1974.

26

History on the Public Screen, II

Jerry Kuehl

Relations between academic historians and producers of television documentaries have always been uneasy. Historians are maybe offended by the superficiality and incompleteness of programs made without their active collaboration, while producers resent efforts by academics to impose their standards and concerns in a field which may, they think, lie outside their area of competence. What lies behind this mutual unease is, I think, a serious failure in communication between the two professions. Each misapprehends the job of the other, makes wrong assumptions about what the other can or should do, and as a result is unable to appreciate fully either the other's achievements or his limitations. In the previous chapter Donald Watt examined this problem from the standpoint of the professional historian; I write as a producer of historical documentaries for mass audiences.

Let me say right at the beginning that what seems to me to be at the heart of the matter is the question of the commentary, which is an integral part of every documentary: who should write it, how should it relate to the film, to whom should it be addressed, and above all, what should it contain?

Most television documentaries are fifty minutes long. So let us consider just how much can be said in fifty minutes. BBC newsreaders, who are professionally trained to speak rapidly and comprehensibly, talk at about 160 words a minute; this means that by talking *nonstop* they could deliver, in fifty minutes, a text not twice as long as this chapter. But in fact, as a rule of thumb, competent documentary producers begin to worry when a commentary takes up more than about a quarter of a program's length. In other words, a commentary of between one thousand and fifteen hundred words is quite long enough—any more, and the film is liable to become a kind of illustrated radio program. It will appear to viewers as dense, overstuffed. They will be repelled, not informed. The consequence of this may be quite sobering to an academician: that is, whatever the writer wishes to say ought to be said in the equivalent of a single-page *New Statesman* article or a *fifteen-minute* lecture. There is no way around this. If he tries to say more, his audiences will understand less. They will, in time, simply switch off—figuratively or literally.

Once this point is taken, it is easy to see how inappropriate much academic criticism is. Consider for a moment the persistent academic complaint that historical documentaries invariably omit significant details or even major themes of matters which they touch. To take a particular instance, Thames Television's *World at War* series' introductory program, which dealt with domestic events in Germany from 1933 to 1939, was reproached, both in public and in private, for not dealing with events in Germany from 1918 to 1933. It was also reproached for not dealing with international affairs from 1933 to 1939, for not dealing with British domestic affairs from 1933 to 1939, and even, by one earnest correspondent, for not having examined the United States government's 1938 contingency plans for the mobilization of American industrial production in the event of war breaking out in Europe. All this in a program lasting fifty minutes.

The historian who wonders tartly why we omitted Stanley Baldwin from our account of prewar Germany should pause to consider what he would have included, and left out, in his own fifteen-hundred-word comprehensive account of the Third Reich (even if he were not limited by the necessity to confine his exposition to subjects about which film was available). That is, by misunderstanding the nature of the activity, the academic may find himself applying to it assumptions and expectations which have no hope of being fulfilled. Small wonder that professional television producers, for their part, so often think of academic historians as behaving like small children, helpfully offering their services as referees or peacemakers to Mommy and Daddy because they have not quite grasped that their parents are not really *wrestling.*

What I should like to do here is, first, elaborate on what I think conscientious producers of historical documentaries do or try to do; second, discuss how and why academic historians are liable to misunderstand both their intentions and their achievements, and what the consequences of their misunderstanding may be; and third, offer a suggestion about what academic historians and documentary producers in fact should be able to offer each other.

First, what is it that television producers try to do? The first thing the good ones learn is that what they make are television programs, that is to say, works which should follow the rules of *television*—which are not at all the same as those which govern the production of learned articles or, indeed, purely literary works of any sort. The second thing they learn is that their audience is a mass audience—never fewer than several hundreds of thousands of viewers, and sometimes more than twenty million. Now, these two points—that television is television and not something else, and that television is a mass medium—may seem self-evident, but their implications are often misunderstood even by many who earn their living in television. It is hardly surprising that academics may fail to appreciate them.

One characteristic of television as a communication medium is that it offers its audience virtually no time for reflection. It is a sequential medium, so to say, in which episode follows on episode, without respite. This clearly means that the medium is ideally suited to telling stories and anecdotes, creating atmosphere and mood, giving diffuse impressions. It does not lend itself easily to the detailed analysis of complex events; it is difficult to use it to relate coherently complicated narrative histories, and it is quite hopeless at portraying abstract ideas.

The reason is simply because there is no stopping en route, no feedback between audience and program maker, which means that the viewer's interest in any program is no more than the curiosity any audience has in the performance of a storyteller, who invites his listeners to attend to what he says and tries to hold their attention by all manner of devices, but does not invite, or even tolerate, interruptions. It is, of course, true that there is no opportunity for feedback in literary works, either; but it is possible to stop midway, to reread, to reflect at leisure. It is also true that much effort has gone into trying to minimize or overcome television's defective feedback mechanisms, but none of the attempts made by such admirable agencies as the Open University are very relevant to the problems of program making for general audiences.

It is not the fact that the skills the historians prize most are precisely those which television can use least that is surprising, so much as the idea that anyone should ever have thought otherwise—although it does become less puzzling as soon as one takes into account the intensely literary and verbal background of so many people who commission, produce, and publicly evaluate historical documentaries.

A second point about the uniqueness of television as a medium relates to commentary writing, and I have already touched on it. Commentaries are intimately related to the images which they accompany, point up, explain, call attention to, make sense of. Because of their brevity, they cannot be in any real sense exhaustive or comprehensive. They need not even be coherent, in the sense that they need not unambiguously argue that one thing or another is the case. They do not lay down the line: they evoke. The one thing they cannot do with any hope of success is to use as their models such literary forms as the learned article, the public lecture, or even the popular journalistic review. They are not an independent literary form.

Moreover, since a great many significant events, processes, decisions, were never, could never, be filmed, the gaps in commentary may be dictated not by the writer's conscious decision—as would be the case if he or she were writing a brief article for a part-work—but by what is or is not available on film. An example again: relations between church and state were very important to the leaders of the Third Reich and, it goes without saying, to ordinary Germans too. But very little film was ever made which even showed National Socialist leaders and churchmen together, let alone doing anything significant. So considerations of church and state were virtually omitted from our films on Nazi Germany—and from our commentary.

A third point focuses on commentary as well, but really involves the totality of the program: how much should it try to say, or at least mention? How much dare it leave out?

Historical documentaries do not exist in a vacuum. Nearly forty years after regular broadcasting began in this country, and with three channels transmitting over a hundred hours of programs a week, it is highly unlikely that a subject will be done for the first or last time ever. Yet just this kind of awesome prospect seems to brood over the producer and academic critic alike as they approach major undertakings. No one would seriously reproach Hugh Trevor-Roper for not including in his book *The Last Days of Hitler* a comprehensive account of the organization of the NSBO or of the Reichswehr (though if he were thought to be particularly knowledgeable about those topics, his admirers might well be disappointed if he never turned his attention to them). Yet this kind of reproach is regularly directed against documentary series, and even single programs, and it is more than just a quarrel with the producer about the relative importance of various elements in a story. From the producer's point of view the fear is that *this* is the only chance there will ever be to do something—so everything possible must be done. It is this desperate last chance to catch the moving train attitude that accounts for the presence of a great deal of bewilderingly superficial elements, as for instance the brief mention of the Polish question in episode 25 of *The World at War*—not long enough to be informative, yet long enough to be controversial and, almost certainly, offensive to those with knowledge of the matter, and there simply because it seemed inconceivable that a twenty-six-part series should totally omit any mention of Poland once it had been conquered by the Germans in the first reel of the second program.

Turning now to the second general consideration, that of television as a *mass* medium, a number of other special characteristics are apparent. The very numbers involved in programming for mass audiences are daunting. Any competent university lecturer alters the style and the content of his presentations, depending on whether he is dealing with a class of 150 first-year undergraduates, 25 third-year specialists, or a postgraduate seminar. And he also shapes his manner and matter depending on whether his post is a permanent one, totally free of student pressures, or whether he is teaching in an institution where student assessment of his performance has a bearing on whether he continues in employment. Academics assume, and rightly, a high degree of professional motivation on the part of their students: they are articulate and sociable; they expect to work in a systematic and sustained fashion, guided, if not positively directed, by their instructor or supervisor; they are verbally relatively skilled; they are young.

The audience to which a television producer addresses himself is not like that at all. A television producer has no students. The proportion of viewers who watch television as a part of their work is statistically trivial; the rest watch it to relax, to entertain themselves, only sometimes consciously to inform themselves. They are under no obligation to watch; they are not a captive audience in the sense that a university class or seminar is. They are unlikely to be highly educated—most of them in fact have had no more schooling than is required by law. Some are young, some middle-aged, some are old-age pensioners. Many are not articulate, they are all individuals, and there are at least twenty-four million of them.

It is insulting and wrong to think of this mass audience as uniform, homogeneous, ignorant; but it is equally unrealistic to think that its members will be or ought to be interested in a program intended to entertain or instruct a highly literate, highly educated minority. A producer making a documentary for such an audience could legitimately make assumptions about its cultural furniture which would leave a popular audience utterly bewildered. (Producers know that it is as dangerous to overestimate a mass audience's knowledge as it is to underestimate its intelligence.) To take a homely illustration: any serious account of the early years of National Socialist Germany must deal with the Roehm purge. To understand this, it is obviously necessary to describe the internal organization of the SA, its relations with Hitler, and its relations with the army. This background is not difficult to acquire from a handful of appropriate scholarly works. But it is quite unrealistic to expect that a working-class school-leaver, now working on a building site, would have an intimate knowledge of the intricacies of National Socialist infighting in the years before Hitler's accession to power. I cannot pretend that any of the films in our *World at War* series made luminously clear what the *Sturmabteilung* represented to the life of Germans living in the Weimar Republic, still less the transformation it underwent when the government fell into the hands of the National Socialists, but I suspect that had we been better at our jobs, we could have made such things clearer—and, moreover, that it was our job to make such things clear. Now, admittedly, there is an element of running with the hare and hunting with the hounds in what I am saying: claiming on the one hand that it is beyond the capacity of mass television to explain intricate relations between events and institutions, and on the other hand reproaching myself and my colleagues for being unable to do it *better*. So perhaps it would be more accurate to say that television's capacity to portray abstract notions is strictly limited and depends on striking a series of very fine balances between simplicity and precision. Believing that, I have little patience for producers whose film may have failed to impress viewers because they assumed that their audiences would be so intimately familiar with the persons and events that they need no more than say "SA" or "SS," and their entire audience would instantly grasp who they were and what their significance was.

There is a vulgar way of putting this: it is that a television producer has one bite at the cherry of audience interest. If he fails, then he loses his viewers, and that is the end of the song. The academic has repeated chomps at the fruit. If his audience fails to follow him, that is its own hard luck. If it does not understand, *it* is deemed to have failed, not the "producer": professors do not get fired when attendances at their lectures start to fall off. So the obligation that a responsible television producer has is to make his thought comprehensible to an audience about which he can assume nothing, so far as its degree of specialized knowledge is concerned. What he can rely on—and it is a pity that more producers do not take advantage of the fact—is a high degree of shrewdness, worldliness, and common sense. To put it in a slightly different way, to make a program for a mass audience is to make a program for an audience whose ordinary mode of apprehension is not literary. People who watch a great deal of television do not as a rule read many books; viewing and reading are for them mutually exclusive, not complementary, activities.

That means that for most of the audience *The World at War* was not a complement to the memoirs of Albert Speer, the learned volumes of Captain Liddell Hart, or the speculations of Mr. A. J. P. Taylor; it was *all they had*. Many of my colleagues are inclined to dismiss or simply not understand those whose education does not equip them for the task, or the pleasure, of translating Alan Taylor's flights of fancy into sober assessments. They, I believe, fail utterly to understand what their own job should be. It is not to furnish pictorial counterparts to the knowledge that their audience has acquired through its reading; it is to tell, and show—in a word, to *do* history for—people who do not, as a rule, read very much.

I confess that this understanding came late for me. An American exserviceman in his fifties told me after a projection of one of our programs how, through it, he had come to understand how his own job as a stoker on an American troop transport in the South Pacific helped shorten the war and so helped save Dutch Jews from extermination. My initial harsh reaction was to think, aghast, that if he had bothered to *read* even one popular account of the war in the past thirty years he would not have needed the film to reveal that to him. But a moment's reflection showed how wrong I was to think that way. The point was precisely that here was a man who did *not* enjoy reading books for pleasure or instruction, but who was pleased to use his eyes and his ears instead. No book about the war had struck his fancy—our films did. And our films were not made for book lovers who wanted more, they were made for film lovers who had little else.

If I am right about this characterization, then a great deal about the soured relations between academics and producers becomes clearer. Academics often think that their talents are ignored or misused because they have such a lot of knowledge at their fingertips (or in their file cards) which television producers perversely refuse either to acknowledge or to make use of. An academic views a documentary and asks its producer, "Who was your historical adviser?" The answer "I was myself" he finds an insult and an outrage. Yet, I would argue, there is no reason why it should be felt as such. No one forces producers to deal with historical subjects. If they do choose to make films about the past, it is because they want to, and the idea that historical studies are in such a state of anarchy and confusion that none except a professional historian has the qualifications necessary to thread his way through conflicting accounts of, or make public judgments about, the past seems to me to be arrogant and wrong. And even it were true, it would not change matters at all. Because, as a matter of logic, a producer incapable of making sound judgments about historical events because of his own inherent defects must also be incompetent to judge between the claims of rival historical advisers—unless of course the competitors were to speak with one voice, in which case there would be no problem in the first place. And the producer who knows enough to decide which of two or more competing advisers he is to trust clearly knows enough to form his own judgments without the supervision of any advisers at all.

What he does is turn to the same sources academic historians turn to: standard historical works, conversations with knowledgeable friends, learned articles, his own researches. Where the professional academic goes wrong is to think that the point of the producer's labor is to produce a work that will win the esteem of fellow historians: if it does not break new ground, if it does not contain new insights, then it is not worth doing. But this is simply not the case. Because it is the popular history that it is, television history is unlikely to be innovative. Let me give examples, once again, from our own series on World War II. I cannot think of a single program which contained doctrines unfamiliar to any competent practicing historian, though a great deal of what individual writers said and producers endorsed was novel, and offensive as well, to large sections of the viewing public. I do not simply mean—though it is true—that numbers of young people were surprised to learn that the Soviet Union fought on the side of the Allies during the last four years of the war, or that Britons of all ages were surprised to learn that Japanese troops had to acclimatize themselves to fight in the Burmese jungles, just as British troops did. What must have been incredible, judging from the correspondence generated by the programs, were, among others:

1. Our remarks about the contribution the Luftwaffe made to its own defeat in the Battle of Britain. Popular belief in this country has always been that

the RAF defeated the Luftwaffe against all hope and expectation—not that
the Luftwaffe's attempt to secure air supremacy over southern England
was a desperate gamble, almost inevitably doomed to failure from the start.
2.   Our judgment about the magnitude of the Soviet contribution to Allied
     victory. Few viewers knew that at least twenty million Russians died, or
     that the bulk of Germany's forces fought on the eastern, not the western,
     front. Still less did they know that the Soviet Union was probably capable
     of defeating the Germans single-handed.
3.   The idea that Hitler was a social reformer, whose destruction of the politi-
     cal power of the Prussian aristocracy and the military establishment
     made possible the emergence of a stable parliamentary democracy in
     postwar West Germany.

Now, none of these notions is incontrovertible, but no one could claim that
any would outrage the sensibilities of conscientious professionals. They are the
commonplaces of routine contemporary historical exposition; it hardly takes
any special expertise to be able to grasp them or their significance. The expertise, it seems to me, comes in making them understandable to the mass audience. And that is not a historian's expertise.

There is another, less obvious, point. Historians see one of their principal
tasks as that of conveying information (those with literary skill, of course,
delight in conveying information pleasurably). But producers of programs for
mass audiences—and in this they do differ from producers for adult education
programs or for schools—must be more concerned to convey their own *enthu-
siasms*. The form that their best efforts take is not "Here are some things you
all ought to know about the Battle of Stalingrad" but rather "We are passionately concerned about the Battle of Stalingrad. If you will watch our program,
we will try to share with you some of our passion and some of our concern."
This is not a sentiment which, in my experience, informs the pages of the
English Historical Review.

I have not said anything so far about the producer's use of historical evidence, a matter of evergreen concern to academics. This is because I think it
is of only peripheral interest. If producers were making films for an audience
of professional historians, they would work in quite different ways. But their
films are not densely packed arguments, and they neither need nor use the kind
of *apparatus criticus* obligatory in scholarly articles or even textbooks. If there
is a literary analogy, it is not the doctoral dissertation but the reflective essay
in which nothing is said recklessly but in which the flow of the text is not
burdened with a scholarly apparatus either.

It ought to be self-evident that competent producers are scrupulous in their
use of film. They do not try to pass off feature films as newsreels or an interview made in 1960 as a faithful representation of the interviewee's views in

1970, but that is not because either the film or the interview is "evidence." "Evidence" is something used in arguing a case. If all films argued a case, then the elements incorporated into them could properly be called evidence. But many documentaries do not argue a case—they explore possibilities, or they present alternatives, or they tell true stories. To misuse film in such contexts is not to fudge the evidence; it is simply to use film and interview less than honestly.

So far, I have been muddling prescriptive accounts with descriptive accounts—talking as if all producers were good and all good producers behaved the way I said they did, and as if all historians were on another side of a sharp dividing line. But perhaps this is the wrong kind of distinction to make. Some producers do make films (indeed, whole series) that are based on literary models, deploy arguments as if they were trying to convince a skeptical donnish audience, and introduce indifferently selected and irrelevantly deployed visual material. And, equally, some academics do exhibit a lively awareness of the limitations and resources of the television documentary, are careful not to confuse genres, and are capable of communicating with large audiences. In other words, the distinction is not between dons and academics on the one hand and professional producers on the other, but between those who are sensitive to the points I have raised about the world of the past and those who are not.

A final point. That there is academic discontent with the state of historical documentary seems to me to be obvious, and I have tried to account for some of its causes and consequences. What seems to be unfortunate is one form in which academic discontent has crystallized. Dissatisfied with what they take to be the superficiality, triviality, and incompleteness of popular accounts, concerned historians have begun to produce their own works. They have done so under difficult conditions with the help of devoted collaborators and on very small budgets. Their enterprise, and their ingenuity, deserve praise, but I fear that they have mistaken a profound characteristic of the medium for a simple defect in execution on the part of existing practitioners. So their work, far from breaking new ground, has only reproduced the worst faults of the kind of documentaries it has sought to replace. Films need a high ratio of visual material to commentary, and a low ratio of information to noise. In other words, trying to say too much is a recipe for not being understood at all, whether the subject is the Potsdam conference or the Spanish civil war. But this should not be construed to be a claim that there is no place for historical documentaries made by academics for academic audiences. What it does mean is that very careful thought ought to be given to what those documentaries ought to be like. Academic filmmakers ought to think not twice but three times before embarking on expositions of diplomatic encounters, analysis of abstract concepts, or complex narrative histories. I hope I have shown why. What they might consider instead is the production of films about historical topics which do not have wide popular appeal and of which no nonpartisan accounts yet exist: the internment of aliens in the United Kingdom during World War II, for example, or the persistence of British working-class hostility to Winston Churchill.

But in any event, I think that the universities would never wish to become major centers of documentary film production. Their efforts would be more valuable if directed to making filmed records of persons or events which would otherwise go unrecorded and, above all, to doing the sorts of thing they do best, traditionally. Rather than despising and dismissing popular television for being what it is, still less trying to replace the mass television history of our day with their own mandarin versions, they should concentrate on doing their jobs as historians as well as they can, so that the history they write will be as good as it can be, so that the popular accounts which we provide will be as true as they can be.

27

Historical Analysis, Stage One: Content, Production, and Reception

John O'Connor

This essay is taken from John O'Connor's edited collection Image as Artifact. *For coherence of argument, we have left in the references to the video compilation that accompanied the collection.*

Historians characteristically ask three basic types of questions of any document or artifact before them, questions about its content, production, and reception. The very same questions can be asked of moving image documents:

a. Questions about its content—what information can be gleaned from the document itself (from a close study of what appears on the screen), either through direct or indirect analysis? How is this information determined by the visual and aural texture of the film? What is the connection between the medium and the message?

b. Questions about its production—what influences were at work in shaping the document and, perhaps served to limit or bias the information it conveys? Beyond the images themselves, how might the background (personal, political, professional, etc.) of the producer, director, actors, etc., have influenced their performances? How might the institutional conventions and the larger purpose of the sponsoring agency (a Hollywood studio, an industrial organisation, or a Washington lobbying group) have coloured the message of the production?

c. Questions about its reception—regardless of the nuances of meaning we can derive from an analysis of the document today (comparing it with other contemporaneous materials or judging it in the knowledge of what subsequently took place), what effect if any did the document have on the pace or direction of events at the time it was made? Who saw the film and how might it have influenced them?

By taking this approach to film and television documents, historians can make significant contributions to the evolving methodology of film studies research. At the same time they further sensitise themselves and their students to the skills of visual analysis. It is important that none of these three areas of inquiry be considered in a vacuum. Factors of production often dictate both content and reception, as factors of reception define the content as perceived by the audience. When dealing with the analysis of a specific moving image document, it makes sense to preserve a chronological approach by looking at the production history first. But let us address them here in the order set out above.

Questions about Content

Focusing on the content of a moving image document can be more difficult than with a verbal document. In part this is due to the breadth of individual interpretation that the viewer brings to the experience (more on this later in this section and in the section on reception). All critical viewers must bring some elementary information into the screening room. For example, unless an early silent film has been "step printed" to compensate for the change from an 18 to the more modern 24 frame per second standard, we often see such film projected at one and one half times the normal speed. In this and in other more subtle ways the historian's use of ordinary analytical tools sometimes proves inadequate when applied to moving images.

Early filmmakers realised that film allowed them the ability to play with time and space. Edwin S. Porter, D. W. Griffith, and others pioneered in the use of editing to collapse and to expand time (drawing out a chase for dramatic effect, for example) and to cut from one location to another as an enhancement to dramatic tension (as in intercutting between chaser and chased). In the process they challenged the audiences' expectations and, over time, taught them to understand film (and conceivably other arts and forms of communication) differently.[1] Editing can transform an ordinary series of images into an extraordinary one. An interesting historical example is the famous footage of Hitler's jig after stepping from the railway car in which he had accepted the surrender of France in 1940. It never really happened. With the help of a laboratory device called an optical printer, a team of patriotic British film editors was able to take an otherwise benign image of Hitler raising his leg and turn it into a diabolical little dance. Shown on the newsreel screens of all the allied nations at this psychological low point in the struggle against Nazism, the footage became powerful propaganda, a force for rededicating opposition against the heartless Führer. Filmmakers may not set out to misrepresent, but the creative tools that they use nevertheless reshape and manipulate reality. It should be clear that, to the extent that questions of time, and place, and what really happened, are of concern to historians and history teachers, they must become fluent in the rhetoric of images.

To comprehend more than the surface content of a moving image document, therefore, one must develop at least a basic knowledge of visual language—the elements of a shot (duration, field size, camera angle, camera movement, lighting, colour, depth of field, lens characteristics, etc.) and the editing techniques (cuts of various kinds, dissolves, fades, and washes) with which filmmakers communicate their ideas. It would be foolish indeed to try to study the "Declaration of the Rights of Man and the Citizen" in the original text with students who cannot read French, yet we regularly show them moving image documents without addressing the language of images. This adds complications because unlike the frustrated readers who don't know French, passive viewers unconsciously assume that they have in fact fully comprehended the visual document. (Our clichés are instructive: "Seeing is believing," "Pictures don't lie," "I saw it with my own two eyes.") Untrained viewers may indeed have taken in the message that the filmmaker meant them to (manipulated them to?), but this is never enough. Realising that surface comprehension represents only the most rudimentary level of meaning, historians would never be completely satisfied with that level of analysis of a written document. We must learn to demand the same depth of analysis in regard to moving images as well.

The first step is to look closely at the image. For a moving image, close viewing requires repeated viewing, an awareness of the technical tools developed by specialists in cinema studies, and the ability to apply them where appropriate. A moving image document communicates through visual signs and symbols; and through the mixing of those visual elements with the dialogue and music on the sound track. Their meaning may seem self-evident, but it always depends on an interaction or negotiation between the viewer or spectator and the moving image being viewed. The only time that it is correct to think of film as a static object is when it is rolled up in its can on the shelf. Any effort to elucidate meaning from it demands a consideration of the spectator (for the historian this often means a spectator from some past time, but more on this under reception). To a large degree, therefore, studying the content of a film involves the identification of the signs it presents and the consideration of how they work together and with the mind of the audience.

People make meaning from images (or signs) by relating them to a series of codes, among them cultural codes, shared artistic codes, and cinematic codes. Consider, for example, some of the images from *The Plow That Broke the Plains* (1936).

There are some images that derive their meaning from cultural experience or tradition, such as the planting of a settler's stake in the virgin soil of the frontier. A European, less sensitive to a historical tradition based on the gradual opening up of the West, might not get the message as quickly. Other images make sense in terms of codes drawn from the other arts. A good example is the body language of the depressed and psychologically defeated farmers pictured in a migrant camp in the closing scenes of the film as they sit dejectedly and whittle while the women do the work of unloading the trucks and trailers. A painter might use the same imagery or an actor might assume the same expressive stance in a stage play to depict victims overwhelmed by their situation and unable to help themselves. Finally, there are cinematic codes, patterns of meaning which derive from the unique elements of film and television in comparison to the other arts. One good example from *The Plow* is the shot which closes the sequence on the establishment of productive farms on the Great Plains with the image of a puffing locomotive which traverses the entire screen from left to right. Besides ending the sequence cinematically by "wiping" the screen clean for the next scene, the train shot suggests the logical end result of the successful farming of grain—the transportation of the product to Eastern markets (screen movement from left to right is usually interpreted as west to east).

By definition, the subject in front of the camera lens must always be something specific, yet filmmakers often intend a shot to lend itself to abstract generalisation. The train referred to above was meant to be seen not as a specific train, but as representing the thousands of trains that carried grain to midwestern and coastal cities. Scholars versed in cinema theory might describe the image of the train as a sign (or signifier) and the business in grain it represented as the signified.[2] In his *Signs and Meaning in the Cinema* (Bloomington, Indiana, 1972) Peter Wollen suggests three ways in which cinematic signs can work. They may be (1) *iconic*, referring simply and directly to what they represent; (2) *indexical*, referring to a larger subject of which the specific image is a part or a measure; or (3) *symbolic*, when the only connection between the object and the meaning is an arbitrary intellectual or cultural convention. Early in *The Plow*, the images of huge mule-drawn combines can be understood as iconic—they seem to refer primarily to themselves. Later in the film, when we see rows of tractors breaking the delicate surface of the plains to meet the needs for food in war-torn Europe, the message is more clearly indexical—these specific tractors refer to the thousands of others at work on the plains and suggest (especially in comparison with the flanks of tanks intercut with them) a measure of the damage they are doing to the delicate ecology. Other images from *The Plow* that lend themselves to indexical reading include overflowing bags of grain and harvesters working at night, both measures of the great productivity of the soil—at least until the drought came.

Symbolic images are often the most difficult to interpret because the connection between signifier and signified is completely arbitrary. The infant pictured in the film next to an idle plough on an apparently dry and dusty landscape is clearly not meant as an icon (we have no idea of who this specific child is and we have no earlier images of this child or any other children to compare with this one). Neither does the meaning seem to be indexical (there

is no reason why we should be led to identify this child with a larger population of children). But there are potential symbolic readings—several of them—
based on the basic incongruity of a tiny infant pictured next to a grown man's
tool. One might get the message that the farmers of the plains were as powerless as infants in the face of their environment, or the quite different message
that they were as innocent as babes, blameless for the plight that had befallen
them.

Other symbols, though just as arbitrary, may be more or less explicit to an
audience, depending on the clarity with which they relate to some cultural,
shared artistic or cinematic code. In the montage that closes *The Plow*'s fifth
major sequence, shots of belching smokestacks and hoppers overflowing with
grain are intercut with images of a stock ticker that goes wild and begins to
dance around on its pedestal and other shots of a black jazz drummer. In
designing the sequence the filmmaker brought together indexical images of
productivity (belching smokestacks and overflowing grain hoppers) with the
symbolic images of the musician and the stock ticker to create a visual message
about the misplaced optimism of the 1920s. The connection between these
things is completely arbitrary. They can only convey their intended meaning
to audiences familiar with the cinematic coding device of montage (an intercutting of a series of otherwise unrelated shots, often with a repetition of some
of them, in a way that creates new meaning), and with a cultural code that
presumes a recognition of the "jazz age" and other indicators of the carefree
1920s—a period which ended, as the sequence does, with the stock ticker
"crashing" to the floor. The "crash" seems funny in the film because the symbolic reference to 1929 is so obvious.

Another approach to the study of signs concerns whether they derive their
meaning syntagmatically or paradigmatically. *Syntagmatic* meaning is that
which is drawn primarily from the relation of the image or sign in question
with the other images surrounding it in the film. *Paradigmatic* meaning is less
dependent on the context of surrounding images and keyed more to a broader
identification of the thing represented with other alternative representations.
Thus the shot in the midst of *The Plow*'s sequence on the dust bowl which
shows a dog lying on the ground apparently panting for breath, derives some
of its meaning paradigmatically (this dog does not look like the dogs we usually
see or might expect to see) and some of its meaning syntagmatically (the dog's
problems seem to come from having breathed in the blowing dust pictured in
the shots immediately preceding and following it). The belching smokestacks
mentioned above derive their meaning syntagmatically (the context of the
surrounding images of productivity is essential; without them the image
might more easily represent pollution than prosperity). The stock ticker which
crashes requires little contextualisation; its meaning is paradigmatic.

We have said nothing yet about the element of sound in film and television.

The dialogue, music, or sound effects that accompany an image can dramatically influence its meaning. Tony Schwartz, well-known media consultant and producer of hundreds of award-winning radio and television commercials, argues that sound is more important than sight. He suggests, to prove his point, that people look at almost any television commercial with the sound turned off. One might try this experiment with Tony Schwartz's own famous "daisy spot" from the 1964 Lyndon Johnson presidential campaign, included in the video compilation. Even in such a carefully structured sixty-second production it is usually impossible to get a clear idea of what's going on without the sound component. In contrast, we usually can get the point by listening to the sound without the pictures—much of the power of *The Plow That Broke the Plains* comes from the authoritative voice of the narrator—and the use of music in the film is crucial to its overall impact.[3]

Beyond the close attention to images and sounds, the analytical process should involve the conscious breaking down of the structure of the document (parsing it as one would a sentence) to perceive patterns in it which also communicate meaning, but which might not be apparent at first viewing. Film scholars often turn to models for structural analysis proposed by Russian folklorist Vladimir Propp in his *Morphology of The Folktale* (1928) or by anthropologist Claude Lévi-Strauss in his *Structural Anthropology* (1972). It is helpful to outline the basic sequences of a film, dissecting it into its constituent parts, or trying to reconstitute the kinds of "story boards" the filmmakers may have used in trying to design and order the images they put into the film in the first place.

Understanding the dramatic structure of Pare Lorentz's second film, *The River*, for example, is crucial to understanding its effectiveness in communicating its points about the need for erosion control and the potential for projects like the then infant Tennesee Valley Authority. The film is in a distinctly nonnarrative style, avoiding chronology for the most part and using the device of narrative and visual repetition to reinforce its arguments. The film takes viewers on two trips down the Mississippi, first as it was when virgin forests covered much of the northern United States, and again after many of the forests had been denuded, industrial cities had been built in the place of small river trading towns, and over-intensive agriculture had stripped the fertile soil from much of the South. By the end of the second trip, the unfortunate results of irresponsible environmental policy and unplanned economic development are evident in the terrible flood conditions that Lorentz photographed.[4]

Most films adopt a more traditional narrative structure, but there are always distinctive elements that help to define the film's content and message. From whose point of view is the story being told? If the story unfolds through the eyes of one character, to what extent are viewers restricted to only that person's experience—is the audience privileged with some information while certain other information is kept from them? How might the structure of a scene prejudice an audience to respond in one way or another to a forthcoming event? For example, consider a sequence from Vincent Minelli's *Lust for Life* (MGM, 1956). This Hollywood biography of Vincent Van Gogh shows him early in life going off as a missionary to a desperately poor mining area of Belgium and winning the respect of a people who regard him at first with disdain. The sequence shows us numerous shots of his interaction with the people there, going down into the mines with them, giving them his food and clothing, even his bedding, and ministering to their sick. He becomes as poor and as dirty as the people are in order to be accepted by them. Then an inspection team from the Church comes and, appalled at the conditions in which he is living, criticises him for undermining the image of the clergy. There is no question that the conditions are appalling, but this sequence has been carefully structured so that we tend to side with Vincent against his critics. Had the sequence included earlier shots showing the ecclesiastical administrators worried about ministers in the field getting too close to the people and not living in a properly dignified way, then viewers might read the confrontation with Vincent differently.

Theorists are sometimes faulted for taking their analyses too far. A thoroughgoing semiotician, for example, concentrating on the identification and decoding of every sign, might fail to appreciate the aesthetic qualities of a film. More to the point of this study, too rigorous an attention to such internal analysis of a moving image production might lead scholars to undervalue—or even ignore—historical context. Robert Sklar and Janet Staiger, both distinguished cinema scholars, demonstrate the value of theory, not as an end in itself, but as a means to historical understanding. Both of them also stress the integration of theoretical film analysis with the study of more traditional forms of historical evidence. Historians concerned with the moving image cannot afford to simply turn their backs on film theory. The specific structural models put forth by Propp, Lévi-Strauss, and others are complex and controversial, but there are situations in which individual historians can make use of such preconceived systems for analysis.

It is important to recognise that differences do exist in analysing the content of images in film and in television. There are characteristic differences in the form and structure of television programmes, often driven by institutional and economic pressures and by developing styles in shooting and editing. And the media often influence one another. The standard conventions for the editing of the interview, developed in TV newsrooms in the first decade of television, have become a staple of documentary film producers as well.[5]

To summarise then, although close study of content is the approach a historian would normally take to any document, a moving image document may require resort to different kinds of tools. Historians must consider the nature of visual communication, learning at least some of the technical terminology used to characterise the elements of a motion picture shot and the types of editing devices available to the filmmaker. In addition, we cannot ignore film theory. To the extent that anyone who sits down to study a film has at least an unconscious assumption of what a film is and how it communicates its message, each of us brings some concept of theory to the task of analysis.

Questions about Production

Whereas the content questions deal with what's on the screen, production questions deal with the background elements: how and why things got on the screen. In studying a letter or a diary entry as a piece of evidence, historians seek to put themselves in the place of the author, trying to understand the conditions under which the document was written and how those conditions may have influenced its content. To some extent, therefore, the analysis of a moving image document requires that we learn something about how it was produced.[6]

Manuscripts or printed documents are often the product of one person, but such individual authorship is rare in moving image documents. Despite the tendency of some critics to credit one *auteur* with the style and creativity of a production, most film and television scholars now recognise that productions are the result of complex collaborative efforts in which scores of people (producers, directors, screenwriters, cinematographers, editors, actors, publicists, etc.) contribute creative ideas at various stages in the process.[7] To some extent our understanding of this collaborative process has been demonstrated most clearly by historians who have concentrated on digging in the recently opened archives of the Hollywood studios in search of a "paper trail" to document the production process.[8]

The production of *The Plow That Broke the Plains* was, more than most films, the work of an individual artist. Pare Lorentz had been a film critic and an outspoken booster of the Roosevelt administration before he won the approval of the Resettlement Administration, one of the myriad new alphabet agencies set up in the early days of the New Deal, to make his first film. The Resettlement Administration wanted a movie that could be used to train its many new employees and introduce them to the agency's goals, which were to provide rehabilitation loans to farm families and to facilitate the resettlement of people from depressed areas of the country to places where there were better opportunities for employment. The Great Plains, a depressed area that was suffering from environmental as well as economic woes, held special interest for Lorentz. In addition, the Resettlement Administration was impressed by Lorentz's insistence that such a film could be made with production values advanced enough to allow commercial release as well. The agency had drawn sharp criticism from those opposed to Roosevelt's policies, because it represented the increasing role of government in social planning, and it saw the film as a much desired opportunity to explain and defend its programmes. Moreover, Lorentz wanted to utilise the dramatic power of the medium to convince audiences to accept his film's important social and political messages.

If we took the analysis of the production process this far and no further we would have access to a much more informed comprehension of the film. Any document means more to a scholar who understands the reasons for which it was written. The production of commercial entertainment films and television programmes must always be understood as profit-driven, but many other types of productions should be understood in the context of the political or other ideologies which they were meant to represent and foster. It seems unfair to compare *The Plow* to such blatant propaganda as *Für Uns* (1937), a Nazi party film reproduced in its entirety in the video compilation.[9] Yet both were driven by political ideologies and both were intended to influence the public perception of public issues. The informed scholar should understand in detail what these intentions were, whether or not they were fulfilled (or even comprehended) by audiences all the time. Among other types of production related papers, the study guide to the video compilation includes excerpts from the successful grant applications that led to the production of *Molders of Troy* (1979) and *Women of Summer* (1986). How better to begin to judge the success of a film than to consider it in light of the specific goals set down by the producers in the planning of the project?

Studying the production background of a film or television programme must include a consideration of the background and experience of the people involved. As noted above, Lorentz had an abiding identification with both the Great Plains and with the Roosevelt administration; he knew about film as a critic, but he had never made a film before. The crew he pulled together to work on the project were extremely talented men who went on to famous and creative careers as filmmakers and photographers in their own right, but they had serious differences with Lorentz. This is important information for anyone who wants to understand this film as a historical document.

The study guide to the video compilation details the intriguing production history of *The Birth of a Race* (1918). Originally conceived as black America's response to *The Birth of a Nation* (1915), much of the money for the project came from a fundraising campaign among black leaders and their liberal white supporters. Before the production was complete, however, the project had changed hands, and the script of the film was transformed to accommodate several new agendas. By the time the movie appeared, neither the originators of the film nor its financial backers could identify the elements of the film they had planned. In the case of this film, as with many others, the full analysis of it as a historical document demands a very close study of the production process and a careful consideration of alternative ways that it might have developed. The real value of *The Birth of a Race* as a historical document lies as much if not more in an understanding of the forces at work in its production than what viewers can see on the screen.

Besides the intended purposes of a project, the orientation/background of the people involved, and the unexpected experiences faced in the production process, there are always other limitations to be considered. For example, what were the technological limitations of the medium at the time a film or TV programme was produced? What went into the decision to make *On The Waterfront* (1954) in black and white even though most other films of the period were in colour? Live television drama is usually thought of as one of the special aspects of the golden age of television because the limitations involved forced the actors and directors to innovate, but how might these limitations have also influenced the types of historical dramas attempted and the ways in which they had to be presented?[10] Pare Lorentz's major limitation in making *The Plow* was his very meagre budget, but other filmmakers have spent monstrous amounts of money in making films of meagre interest.

The social and political influences at work in the production process may be more or less explicit, but they must be taken into account for a complete analysis of the document. Jack Warner's support for Franklin D. Roosevelt and his involvement in the writing of the National Recovery Administration (NRA) code for the motion picture industry clearly influenced the pro-New Deal films made by his studio in the early 1930s. To view these films without such knowledge clearly limits the insights that can be drawn from them. Any attempt at analysis of such a social problem film as Warner Brothers' *Wild Boys of the Road* (1934) without a realisation that by that time the form had become a genre in its own right, would surely invite a misreading.

Questions about Reception

Questions about reception and spectatorship have been most troublesome for film scholars and historians alike. Many assertions have been made regarding direct impact of film and television upon society. The *Payne Fund Studies* of the 1930s associated movie watching with juvenile delinquency and a perceived general decline of morals in America at the time. More recently, television viewing has been tried as a defence in the courtroom, with a defendant's attorney claiming that, brainwashed by the violence on TV, his client was unable to distinguish right from wrong. Neither of these efforts offered convincing proof. How can one go about evaluating the impact a film or a television programme has on its audience? Published reviews are available, but they represent only individual points of view. Studio commercial records (where available) and trade newspapers such as *Variety* provide some data on the financial success of many productions. Yet, no certain way exists to measure the impact of even the most popular film on the people who saw it.

Much of the current work in cinema studies involves what is termed "reception analysis." If a film is seen as communicating through visual symbols which derive their meaning at least partly from the viewer's cultural values or from other films the viewer has seen, then the viewer must be involved in the construction of that meaning. An older "illusionist" position argued that films created the illusion of reality, an illusion which spectators simply absorbed as passive receptacles. Today this is generally replaced by a much more complex understanding of reception in which the viewer is an active agent in the making of meaning from a film. In *The Classical Hollywood Cinema*, David Bordwell borrows from art historian E. M. Gombrich in suggesting that film-makers build upon traditional formal patterns for the ways of presenting things, "schemata" he calls them, which have been normalised over years of studio production. After looking at scores of films, the viewers have become experienced at interpreting these schemata and have developed a series of "mental sets," through which they process the images presented to them. The viewing of a film, then, is not a passive experience. Rather the audience member tests each twist in the plot, each cinematic event, against the relevant mental set. If subsequent shots do not obey the schemata, the viewer turns to the next most likely alternative. Piecing together the meaning of a film represents a complex negotiation between producers and viewers.[11]

Another problem relates to the varying experiences and frames of mind that any audience brings to a moving image experience. Different cultural experiences, different racial or class associations, different sexual or political predispositions—all these influence the ways in which people carry on this negotiation. To some extent, therefore, every viewer, or at least every group of viewers distinguished by differences of class, race, or gender, sees a unique version of a film. Feminist film criticism, for example, concentrates on studying the ways in which films make meaning for women.

Reception characteristics change over time as well. A 1980s audience is very different from a 1930s audience in terms of its experience with interpreting images as well as in the expectations it would apply to social or cultural situations portrayed on the screen. *The Plow That Broke the Plains* was well received by the critics when it was originally released, but viewers responded differently depending on their political orientation and the part of the country they were from. Audiences watching the film today have a very different experience from people who saw it in 1936 with the experience of the depression and the political issues of the period fresh in their minds and, conceivably, with the taste of dust in their mouths. Besides being distanced from the issues, audiences today may be influenced by their wider experience with the media. Familiarity with the fast-paced editing of television may make the pacing of *The Plow* seem too slow.

Certain moving images can be so closely tied to the cultural situation of their times that their point is lost on audiences of a later day. The chief key to the effectiveness of the commercials Tony Schwartz makes is the research he puts into targeting the audience and trying to understand their state of mind. When students today see the "daisy spot," many of them miss the point entirely. Some even confuse the voice intoning the countdown with President Johnson's and think that the commercial is saying that he will use the bomb. Those viewers who cannot remember the state of mind of America in 1964 can get confused about this commercial because it relies so much on that state of mind to communicate its message. The point of the piece, as Schwartz has explained, was less to give people information than it was to stimulate them to take information (or impressions) that they already had and draw a conclusion based upon them. Although the commercial is clearly meant to focus people's attention on Barry Goldwater's statements regarding the use of the atomic bomb, it does not mention his name. It didn't have to, because everyone who saw it in 1964 understood exactly the point that was being made.

The historian can learn much about our understanding of the past from studying the reception of historical films over time. Consider, for example, Alain Resnais's documentary *Night and Fog*, which combines black and white archival footage of the concentration camps with colour images taken at the time of production in 1955. When first released, the film was praised as a comment on the inhumanity of nazism, but perhaps due to the proximity of the war, it was not seen as a "historical film." Since that time, of course, it has become standard fare for many teachers struggling for ways to introduce their students to the plight of the Jews in Nazi-dominated Europe and the horrors of the Holocaust. In this context, however, the film has come in for criticism it had not received before. It has recently been argued that the film presents a biased interpretation in that it does not acknowledge the Jewishness of the victims (in fact the narrator mentions the word Jew only once, and the word does not appear at all in the English subtitles). To bring the history of the film full circle, when Resnais was recently asked how he might explain this apparent bias, he explained that it had never been his central purpose to comment on the Jews and their Holocaust in the first place. He reminded the historian asking the question of him that it had been 1955, a time when France was critically embroiled in Algeria, and he explained that his main interest in making the film had been to warn Frenchmen against the dangers of falling into patterns of inhumanity themselves.[12] Resnais's observations allow us to see the film much more clearly as a document of 1955, but the film should also be interesting to us because of the ways that it has influenced (however unintentionally) the historical perception of thousands of history classes since then.

The reception experience with television is very different from that with the big screen. Whatever illusion of reality there may be in the darkened theatre is broken in the context of the living room. The viewing experience must be understood in the context of the "flow" of programming (from a news broadcast to a quiz show to a baseball game, for example), all punctuated by commercial interruptions. Watching TV with other people is characterised by very different patterns of personal courtesy: people are much more willing to carry on a conversation over a TV programme in their living room (or to put up with one going on around them) than they would be in a movie theatre. Although we may not watch the TV screen as attentively as we do the movie screen, we tend to watch it more frequently, and therefore the repetition of TV messages (whether the generalised messages of violence in police drama, or the repetition of specific commercial messages) may have more cumulative impact. Finally, the fact that the same electronic box on which so many rely as their prime source for news information also provides so much of everyday entertainment, must necessarily influence the ways in which people "make meaning" about the world around them.

There are cases linking the reception of a moving image document and the progress of historical events. The history of television and of recent American politics offers such interesting examples as the impact of Walter Cronkite's February 1968 special report from Vietnam on Lyndon Johnson's decision not to run for a second complete term, and the role of Roger Mudd's special interview with Edward Kennedy in defeating his bid for the 1980 presidential nomination. Edward R. Murrow's March 1954 "See It Now: Report on Senator McCarthy" has often been credited with beginning to turn the public mind against the senator, but there had been many print and at least a few radio journalists who had already taken that stand. Certainly the credibility which Murrow had with the American public must be considered as a factor in the reception of the broadcast, and the tens of thousands letters and telegrams CBS received (90 percent of them agreeing with the programme) cannot be discounted. But absolute proof is elusive. The televised Army McCarthy hearings which began only a few weeks later have also been credited with deflating McCarthy, but Daniel Leab has elsewhere pointed out that only a few stations carried those hearings from gavel to gavel. Whenever thoughtful scholars have addressed the problem of audience impact, they have noted the complexity of the connection.[13] Still, imprecise as such connections must be, there is a growing literature on the intersection of media reception and culture. Most impressive is the National Institute of Mental Health's summary of research on the impact of television on American society, *Television and Behavior: Ten Years of Scientific Progress and Implications for the Eighties* (Volume I, Summary Report, Washington D.C., 1983), which does make categorical statements (on the relation of TV violence and attitudes among youth, for example).[14]

Popular writers have been quicker to suggest how changes in social values can be credited to popular films—styles in the wearing (or not wearing) of men's undershirts, for example, are traced to the barechested appearance of Clark Gable in *It Happened One Night* (1932). More important examples centre on the changing roles of women and of racial minorities, but they are still impressionistic and substantially undocumented. The patterns of reflection and refraction which form the connection between screen images and social values are wonderfully complex.

Once the content, production background, and reception history of a moving image document have been closely studied, the field is open for a stage two analysis in which one or more of the four frameworks for inquiry are brought into play. In the combination of the two stages of analysis we have a comprehensive adaptation of the traditional tools of historical methodology to the critical study of film and television.

Notes

1 For a dramatic example see the excerpt from *The Life of an American Fireman* in the video compilation. It is shown in two versions, one edited the way the film was originally made in 1902 and the other the way it made sense to viewers of a more modern time.

2 These terms and many others in the discussion of the theory of semiology have their roots in the work of linguist Ferdinand de Saussure and have come to film study through the related field of literary theory. For a helpful survey see Terry Eagleton, *Literary Theory: An Introduction* (Minneapolis, 1983).

3 For more on sound in general, and in *The Plow* in particular, see the other chapters in *Image as Artifact*.

4 David Bordwell and Kristin Thompson, *Film Art: An Introduction*, 2nd edition (New York, 1986), pp. 55–62.

5 See, for example, the selection from *Women of Summer* in the video compilation and study the ways in which the editing is used to weave together various elements of interview and commentary. There is also a selection in the compilation that deconstructs the production of an interview filmed especially for this project. It is a very effective way to demonstrate to students the use of the cutaway in film and video editing.

6 An interesting short survey can be found in the opening chapter of Bordwell and Thompson's *Film Art: An Introduction*. For a fuller introduction to some of the important aspects of production in a historical context see: Tino Balio, ed., *The American Film Industry*, revised edition (Madison, Wisconsin, 1985), and Douglas Gomery, *The Hollywood Studio System* (New York, 1986). Several of the less technical and more intelligent handbooks for film and video production can also

be helpful for the scholar trying to comprehend the production process. See, for example, Jay Kaufman and Laurence Goldstein, *Into Film* (N.Y., 1976), and Brian Winston and Julia Keydel, *Working With Video: A Comprehensive Guide to the World of Video Production* (London, 1986).

7   See, for example, Donald Chase, ed., *Filmmaking: The Collaborative Art* (Boston, 1975).

8   There are now several edited volumes of production related papers that can be instructive to someone new to the field. Several deal with the making of specific important films such as Robert Carringer's *The Making of Citizen Kane* (Berkeley, 1986), and John Sayles, *Thinking in Pictures: The Making of Matewan* (Boston, 1987). The more general collections of papers include: Gerald Mast, ed., *The Movies in Our Midst: Documents in the Cultural History of Film in America* (Chicago, 1982); Rudy Behlmer, ed., *Memo From David O. Selznick* (New York, 1972); Behlmer, ed., *Inside Warner Brothers, 1935–1951* (New York, 1985); and Richard Taylor and Ian Christie, eds, *The Film Factory: Russian and Soviet Cinema in Documents, 1896–1939* (Cambridge, Mass., 1988).

9   The comparison may seem less unfair when, after reading the case history, the reader realises that Lorentz was proud to have the film screened on a bill with German and Russian propaganda films, and when one realises that, as originally released, the film had a quite didactic (propagandistic?) ending which was removed in response to opposition.

10   There has been no comprehensive study of early television historical drama, but some interesting work has been done on the form of televised live drama. See for example, Kenneth Hey, "*Marty*: Aesthetics vs. Medium in Early Television Drama," in John O'Connor, ed., *American History/American Television: Interpreting the Video Past* (New York, 1983), pp. 95–133.

11   David Bordwell, Janet Staiger, and Kristin Thompson, *The Classical Hollywood Cinema: Film Style and Mode of Production to 1960* (New York: Columbia University Press, 1985), pp. 7–9.

12   Charles Krantz, "Alan Resnais' *Night and Fog*," *Film and History* 15, no.1 (February, 1985), pp. 2–15.

13   See, for example, Gregory W. Bush, "Edward Kennedy and the Televised Personality in the 1980 Presidential Campaign," in John O'Connor, ed., *American History/American Television*. David Culbert has written on LBJ and the Cronkite broadcast in his "Johnson and the Media," in Robert A. Devine, ed., *Exploring the Johnson Years* (Austin, Texas, 1981).

14   See also Joshua Meyrowitz, *No Sense of Place: The Impact of Electronic Media on Social Behavior* (New York: Oxford University Press, 1985).

28

Narration, Invention, and History

Jeffrey Youdelman

In recent years, a significant body of social and historical documentary films has been created by politically conscious filmmakers using oral history interview techniques. These films capture for the first time the voice of people who have shared in the making of working-class history and culture. A common characteristic of this genre of documentary is its avoidance of voice-over and other forms of narration associated with the older tradition of documentary filmmaking. Such unanimity of purpose among contemporary filmmakers indicates the emergence of an esthetic operating from within a defined political trend.

At a workshop on the historical documentary held during the 1979 U.S. Conference for an Alternative Cinema at Bard College, filmmakers discussed their reactions to the voice-over narrator when asked by a history teacher if some form of voice-over commentary might serve as a useful means of supplementing the viewpoints of those interviewed. The suggestion was generally rejected as the filmmakers present summoned up their impressions of narration in older documentaries. The old films had that "detached, authoritarian male voice," said one filmmaker, "Yes, like the voice of *The March of Time*," added another. A third cited the narrator in the cold war TV program *I Led Three Lives*.

Progressive filmmakers have just reason to reject these particular models, but they neither exhaust the vast possibilities for narration today nor represent the sum total of the past. Materially limited by the relatively primitive state of recording technology, the old documentary films rarely showed people talking. Yet the "substituted" soundtrack voices were not all like "*The March of Time*. Many of the filmmakers assembled at Bard, particularly those under thirty, had seen or read little of the documentary art of the thirties and forties. When Leo Hurwitz's *Strange Victory* (1948) was screened later in the conference, the audience was mesmerized by a style of filmmaking most had not seen before: a film composed by the now rejected method of montage, full of varied sequences, mixing newsreel and acted episodes. The film is held together by a narrative voice that assumes many styles and personas and by an overall structure that the writer Warren Miller described as "so complex it would require diagrams to explain it"—a structure that "gives the film the density of a poem."

The documentary voices of the thirties and forties that sought to identify with people's struggles were often strong, haunting, and lyrical. A rich cross-fertilization existed between literature and the visual arts, with close collaborations between writers, filmmakers, and photographers. Drawing on these talents, but exercising centralized artistic control, classical documentary directors like Joris Ivens could fashion fully composed films from outlines and scenarios. Spoken narrations were part of an orchestrated totality. "In filmmaking," Ivens wrote, "the writing, the words, are part of an interplay with pictures, sound, music, brought together in an editing that changes the quality of every component."

The texts of many writer-photographer collaborations of the thirties and forties spoke in a documentary voice that was rarely dull or detached. The writer often aspired to a collective voice—something not heard anymore, something that might sound "corny." Richard Wright's blues-based text for *12 Million Black Voices* (1941), describing Afro-American migration, evokes the tone of soundtrack narrations of the period:

> "Don't do this!" we cry.
> "Nigger, shut your damn mouth," they say.
> "Don't lynch us," we plead.
> "You're not white," they say.
> "Why don't somebody say something," we ask.
> "We told you to shut your damn mouth."
> We listen for somebody to say something, and we still travel, leaving the South.
> Our eyes are open, our ears listening for words to point the way.
> From 1890 to 1920, more than two million of us left the land.

Something in the current sensibility prevents filmmakers from turning to poetic forms. The old documentaries experimented with such things as rhythmic synchronization between the words, music, and images. In one segment of Willard Van Dyke and Ralph Steiner's *The City* (1939), the speeded-up montage of city bustle is matched by the increased tempo of Aaron Copland's music and Lewis Mumford's commentary. In Basil Wright and Harry Watt's *Night Mail* (1936), W. H. Auden's verse narration draws its rhythm from the momentum of the train wheels.

Joris Ivens, who began in the cine-poem tradition, saw the documentary as the "poetic pull" of film. *New Earth* (1934) examines the effects of a land reclamation project in Ivens's native Holland. After finally completing the arduous

reclamation, the workers learn that "the grain is not for food, but for speculation," that "there is too much grain and not enough work." Ivens chooses the
form of a satirical ballad to close the film:

> I would like to be in a country where
> the wind from the sea ripples over the wheat.
> In this land of fertile promise they ask for
> workmen to throw the wheat into the sea.
> There is too much grain in the fields.
> Bread seems to be a gift of the devil.
> One bagful brings too small a price.
> Throw half the harvest into the water.
> Throw it in, my boy.
> What a winter it will be.

The irony was not lost on a French censor who forbade a showing in a working-
class suburb of Paris, reasoning that "many poor people live in these districts.
After seeing this film, they would get ideas and march on City Hall and ask
for bread."

Not all artists exhibited Ivens's closeness to or identification with the
working class. Much of the documentary impulse of the thirties and forties is
pervaded by a political liberalism which, while breathing verve, interest, and
compassion into the art, does operate from a distance. Other artists attempted
to use the folksy and lyrical "we the people" voices popularized by poets like
Stephen Vincent Benet and Carl Sandburg. They looked back on Walt
Whitman as the archetypal "democratic" American poet—the documentarist
who cataloged the country, its cities, rivers, and mountains, celebrating the
common people building America. This is the voice echoed throughout the
narration of Pare Lorentz's *The River* (1937) as he takes us down the Platte,
the Skunk, the Salt, the Black, the Minnesota, to where poor people, ruined by
the Depression, try to make do with poor land. For Lorentz, the solution to their
poverty lies in the coming of the Tennessee Valley Authority alone and not in
any form of collective action by the valley's people, who are only fleetingly
depicted in the film.

The Whitmanesque lines represent not just a literary form but a view of
America. A more radical version of "we the people" is articulated by those
artists who attempted to blend Marxism and populism by portraying the
Depression years as the triumph of monopoly and privilege over a prior
form of people's democracy. Probably no film of this period more clearly
embodies the strengths and weaknesses of this radical populist voice than
Native Land (1941), made by Paul Strand, Leo Hurwitz, and the Frontier Films
collective.

Native Land began as an attempt to dramatize the revelations of the 1937
LaFollette hearings on the use of Pinkerton operatives and "labor spies" to

smash the growing movement for industrial unionism—a story detailed in Leo
Huberman's book *Labor Spy Racket*. Frontier Films eventually broadened its
concept to include the wide-ranged assault on the masses of people. One powerful, early sequence culminates with Arkansas sheriffs gunning down a black
and a white sharecropper who have just left an organizing meeting. The narration for the film is delivered in the rich and beautifully booming voice of Paul
Robeson. Despite these progressive, antiracist aspects, despite the virtuosity
and power of so much of the film, there is something disingenuous about significant parts of the narration Robeson delivers, a narration couched in an
indiscriminate "we." It is by no means a classless "we." It is "we the people,"
but an identity shorn of contradictions and historical differences.

There is something of a lie in an Afro-American announcing that "we came
to Jamestown . . . in search of freedom" without mentioning who came as
freemen and who as servants; that "we established a Bill of Rights" without
mentioning that the rich white men who wrote in this universal language dis-
enfranchised the propertyless, women, and slaves; or that "led by Lincoln we
fought a Civil War to extend these rights to the whole people" without scruti-
nizing Lincoln's differences with the abolitionists over the centrality of the
slavery issue or his hesitancy about issuing the Emancipation Proclamation.

When I saw *Native Land* at the Pacific Film Archive in 1970, almost all of
the younger members of the audience laughed at much of the narration and
at the political assumptions and ideas behind it. One could say we were a bunch
of hippies showing no respect for those who preceded us in the struggle; who
were we to laugh at Leo Hurwitz, Paul Strand, and Paul Robeson? But I must
defend the critical kernel within that ridicule, for many of the people sitting in
that audience, whose consciousness was so much determined by the summers
of urban uprising in America and by the anti-imperialist upsurge throughout
the world, could see the thematic flaws. They could see that, ultimately, *Native
Land* misinterpreted the struggles of its own time. While it provided populist
gloom and populist hope, it rests on a false premise.

The overall theme of *Native Land* is that the Bill of Rights, the cornerstone
of people's democracy, was being taken away by the forces of reaction. There
is little hint of the capitalist state and its development. Like Walt Whitman, the
filmmakers saw Democracy as the name of the social system, rather than as a
particular, and always changing, form of bourgeois rule. They provide no real
analysis of the precise relationship between class and national (racial) oppression in this empire/nation. In fact, they never considered America as an
empire, which it was even in the late thirties. It is in an empire that the very
notion of "we the people" most needs to be scrutinized. The attempt to sani-
tize Marxism ultimately gutted its message. *Native Land* calls not for decisive
revolutionary change, but for a return to some period when the Bill of Rights
worked—a time that never existed in our history. By 1968, a political genera-

tion had come into being which, despite all its theoretical weaknesses, knew the bankruptcy of Communist party chairman Earl Browder's assertion that "communism is twentieth-century Americanism."

The earlier generation of filmmakers believed in commentary, intervention, and invention. They believed in taking responsibility for the statement the film was making. The *cinéma vérité* critique of this style of filmmaking faults the filmmakers for not capturing actuality. Weighed down by bulky, immobile equipment, scenes often had to be carefully set up and "staged." Moreover, they have been criticized for presenting preconceived ideas and committing the terrible sin of lecturing. ("My main feeling about film," Richard Leacock said in 1960, "is that film should not lecture, and it's a terrible temptation to lecture. You have all that dark room before you, there is no other place where the eyes of the audience can go, so they have to keep watching.")

In the mid-sixties, Ivens was often asked what he thought about *cinéma vérité* vis-à-vis the old-style documentaries, particularly whether the new mode and style ruled out written commentary. Ivens's response was measured. "Cinéma direct," he told a 1965 interviewer, "is both indispensable and insufficient." The new technology gave "material authenticity" to certain parts of the film, for "it gives us the chance to hear the people in the film speak for themselves, and adds another dimension of physical reality. Even if it is a foreign language, the voices bring the film's subject closer, and give more evidence to judge what sort of man or woman is speaking." Yet overall, direct cinema was "insufficient because only commentary can express the complete, responsible, personal action—the involvement of the author, director or commentator." Ivens concluded that "in *vérité* people talk too much and the director too little."

In the old documentaries, the author's recourse to invention sometimes took the form of reenactment. Initially rooted in technological limitations, reenactment also rested on principle. It didn't occur to the old documentarists that such activities on their part were "manipulative." In fact, reenactment often proceeded with great care, and in some cases filmmakers lived for many months with the people they were filming. They learned about their subjects and created episodes meant to capture the essence of the situations and personalities. Reenactment usually involved the difficult task of directing non-professional actors, but the belief in the legitimacy of reenactment also extended to fictionalizing and using trained professional actors. Dramatic episodes were often interwoven with newsreel and other material. The key segment of *Native Land*, for example, involves the activities of a company "snitch." As played by Howard Da Silva, this character is presented in a realistically complex manner. The old documentarists did not have to search for the perfect *vérité* situation and did not limit themselves to a single technique. Filmmakers across the ideological spectrum could concur with the liberal

British documentarist Paul Rotha in asserting that every known technical device could be used, because "to the documentary director, the appearance of things and people is only superficial. It is the meaning behind the thing and the significance underlying the person that occupy his attention."

George Stoney's *How the Myth Was Made* (1979) points up some of the differences between the old and new documentaries. The film was motivated, Stoney relates, by his observation, while teaching at NYU, "that most of my students—all children of the sixties and *cinéma vérité*—are so dominated by that genre of filmmaking that they find it hard to open their minds to any other approach." As a result, "they miss the power and poetry of the earlier films while they fret about the veracity of details." *How the Myth Was Made* chronicles Stoney's return to his father's birthplace—the Aran Islands—to study how Robert Flaherty "staged reality" in *Man of Aran* (1934).

Flaherty is a well-chosen subject, because he embodies the seemingly contradictory aspects of the problem. He was able to make clear, well-crafted films using real people because he believed beyond question that artists choose and mold material according to their viewpoints. Having a viewpoint needn't preclude further investigations into the particulars of reality, or refinement, or changes in viewpoint. Flaherty's point of view, his thematic purpose, was literally a backward one—one seeking preindustrial man battling to survive against the natural elements: Nanook in the North, and the fishermen and community of the Aran Islands. So he ultimately sought to impose a mythic reality on the world before his eyes. He had to manipulate his "real people" to get them to do things they wouldn't ordinarily do.

Interviewing Aran Islanders who played in the film, as well as film people who worked with Flaherty, Stoney reconstructs how Flaherty went about creating many of the film's famous scenes. In illustrating the methodology of the classical documentarists, Stoney does not ignore the problem of manipulation. He shows how Flaherty created the climactic fishing in the storm scene by persuading the men to go out in a storm they would never normally fish in, and to use fishing implements which their grandfathers had used but which they themselves had long ago abandoned. To create his backward-looking view, Flaherty subjected the fishermen to great risk.

The desire not to manipulate, coupled with the avoidance of the older forms of artistic invention (including montage), has created a host of esthetic problems for contemporary filmmakers. The most important and most dramatic moments do not always take place spontaneously when the camera is ready to roll. A friend, on location doing a documentary portrait of two fourteen-year-old girls, wrote, "We've gotten a lot of nice things on film so far—but not the conflicts. The frustrating thing is that the problems are *there*—and not hidden either. It's just that we don't have them on film. So as the weeks pass, we are beginning to get extremely nervous."

Recourse to invention, filmmakers fear, might upset the hard-won trust they have been given by their subjects. My friend prefaced the difficulty about getting things one wants on film by describing how well integrated into the community the filmmakers had become, overcoming the initial reaction of being seen as social workers. The strength of many contemporary political filmmakers lies precisely in their ability to integrate themselves into the lives of people, and both the promise and difficulties are similar to other forms of political work and expression. The filmmaker, like the organizer, approaches a new situation with prior suppositions, a stance, and a theoretical orientation. This needn't be a form of closed-mindedness or dogma, for theory should be a guide to understanding the complexities of reality. It is not "manipulation" to say something "more" than the interviewees are saying. Such a belief, however, requires some form of narration or other device for supplying a fuller point of view.

Filmmakers today admit to giving little preparatory attention to such possibilities. The closeness they feel toward their subjects informs the composing and editing process. In editing, they first look to the words in the interviews, hoping to find key phrases which will articulate the viewpoint they want or the one closest to it. The desire for any narration usually comes when they find that the assembled footage doesn't quite say enough, that "facts and figures" are needed or that "transition" is lacking.

In the interest of nonmanipulation, the decision is sometimes made to use no off-screen narration at all, to let the story speak for itself without making its potential themes explicit. *Taylor Chain* (1980), the Kartemquin Collective's depiction of a seven-week strike at a small Indiana factory, combines scenes of worker camaraderie on the strike line and at a clubhouse with a series of union meetings at which the rank and file, the local leadership, and the international representative are at odds over the issues, strategy, and tactics.

A carefully constructed narrative, *Taylor Chain* does not hide behind *vérité* theory, but its makers clearly don't want to manipulate anyone—not even the audience—by drawing conclusions. Unlike such films as *Harlan County, U.S.A.* and *The Wobblies*, which seek commercial distribution, *Taylor Chain* is a "discussion film" aimed primarily at union audiences. According to a catalog description (which Kartemquin may or may not have written), it is hoped that "both membership and leadership will see some of their own dilemmas and frustrations as the story unfolds" and that "there are no heroes or villains." The film pretends not to interpret reality but only to present it for analysis, risking all on the quality and consciousness of post-screening discussion groups.

An audience which includes politically progressive union activists would most likely be able to subject the incidents in the film to critical analysis. They might criticize the international representative when, at a key moment and faced with rank and file objections, he proclaims, "I don't care whether you vote the contract up or down, I get paid by the union." They may well notice the ways the international rep tries to contain the strike within known and "legal" limits, playing by the rules, getting outfoxed by management moves, and always being surprised by the outcome: "I've never known a company to drop insurance before," he says when they do just that. More important, they might be able to put the story in the context of larger issues. They might know enough about labor history, of how the industrial unions, once all "illegal," were formed and of their subsequent development, to be able to fruitfully discuss what people involved in the union can do to change things.

Yet an audience could just as well not see or know these things. People might simply react by thinking that the union is hopeless and that it's a waste of time to be involved. When I saw the film at a Labor Film Conference for union people, audience response ranged from confusion over the film's purpose to the disgust of one union rep, who said, "I'd never show this." Kartemquin's leave-interpretation-to-the-audience strategy is an interesting attempt at minimalism—a long way from the fully composed, inventive, and explicitly thematic documentaries of the past. It raises the possibility that the reaction against voice-over narration could result in an abnegation of the role of the political documentarist.

Films that include other materials beyond the interviews and simple storyline take a step toward achieving a more explicit point of view. Connie Field's *The Life and Times of Rosie the Riveter* (1980), for example, attains a certain level of historical and cultural commentary by ironically juxtaposing the remembrances of its multiple narrators—five women who worked in factories during World War II—with rose-colored visions of the period presented in *March of Time* pieces. Another recent film, Deborah Shaffer and Stewart Bird's *The Wobblies* (1979), is technically the most cinematic of the historical documentaries. Built around a core of oral history interviews, it employs a wide variety of other materials: paintings, archival photos and films, old union songs, and a chorus of fifteen voices reading from working-class and ruling-class documents ("I can hire one half of the working class to kill the other," boasts Jay Gould). Many aspects of the organizing done by the Industrial Workers of the World (IWW) are covered, and many of the segments and episodes hold together quite well. Yet the overall thematic view is not all that clear, and at moments where more precise political analysis seems needed the film is somewhat evasive.

In an illuminating interview with Dan Georgakas (*Cineaste*, Spring 1980), Shaffer and Bird touch on some of the links between political analysis and the use of narration. Georgakas suggests that the reaction among progressive filmmakers against the "voice of God" narration has gone so far that filmmakers resort to some very awkward devices to avoid using a narrator. Shaffer and Bird explain that they hadn't realized they might need a narrator until the advanced stages of editing. Ultimately they chose one of the oral history informants—Roger Baldwin, a somewhat tangential and nonrevolutionary ally of the Wobblies—to also serve as the main narrator of the film. The film-makers also state that they were unable to present such issues as the impact of the Russian Revolution, the demise of the IWW, and the ideological differences between the Socialist party, the IWW, and the Communist party as fully as they would have liked because the people interviewed were either reluctant to talk or incapable of substantive analysis.

Could these constraints have been overcome? In a section of the film exploring the effects of the Russian Revolution on the split in the IWW, the film-makers interview Tom Scrivener who, as a Wobblie lumberjack, was present in the camps where the issue of "political action" was debated. According to Scrivener, one side would say, "Hell, the damned Ruskies beat us to it and had their revolution. We better study and learn from that," while the anarcho-syndicalists complained that the Bolsheviks were "just another bunch of damn politicians." The film then cuts to the anti-Bolshevik Roger Baldwin—the targeted "narrator" of the film—for his commentary on the ensuing raids and criminal prosecution of the Wobblies. The impression left by the entire section is that practically the sole influence of the Russian Revolution was to bring down repression on the IWW via the "Red scare" and cause its demise.

Do we owe this viewpoint to Scrivener's reluctance to get further into the issue or his failure to make critical distinctions? The best argument against this supposition lies in the existence of a mimeographed book Scrivener has written on his sixty years in radical movements, in which he uses the same words to describe the opposing IWW factions but carries the story forward by pointing out that "the great works of Lenin were to come in a short time into general circulation, which would soon change the picture." The changed picture included Scrivener's own progress from the IWW to the communist-led Trade Union Unity League and eventually into the Communist party, joining such former IWW leaders as Big Bill Haywood and Elizabeth Gurley Flynn. Unlike many of the veterans appearing in recent historical documentaries, Scrivener today remains a Marxist-Leninist—one who eventually left the Communist party to build a new "nonrevisionist" Marxist-Leninist party.

Cutting out Scrivener's communist background is, in fact, typical of the methodology of many recent films. Ex-Communist party members, and occasionally present members, pop up in a great many films. Politically and historically knowledgeable members of the audience can spot them, but their identity is hidden from the general audience. Such is the case with *Union Maids* (1976), a film by Julia Reichert, James Klein, and Miles Mogulescu featuring three wonderfully vibrant and enthusiastic women, two white and one black, who were active in the organizing drives of the thirties and are still politically aware and active today, and who collectively tell their story with conviction and humor.

Although they do offer important descriptions of the activities and feeling of radical organizers in the union struggles of the thirties, nowhere does the film explicitly probe any of their individual political affiliations. Is it the unwillingness of the women to talk? Such an explanation seems to be contradicted by an oral history anthology, Staughton and Alice Lynd's *Rank and File*, which includes an interview with Stella Nowicki, one of the women in the film. In the book, she talks openly about her work in a Young Communist League/ Communist party unit, about writing articles on Marxism for the party's mass paper for the stockyard and packing-house workers in Chicago, and a little about the party's factions inside mass organizations where strategy for the organizing drives was discussed.

The exclusion of this sort of material from the film denies its audience a knowledge of the historical role played by communists in the labor movement. The film audience, including those already interested in socialism, is kept from knowing exactly what socialism meant to people like Stella, how they organized around it and explained it, and how they viewed the relationship between militant trade unionism and revolutionary socialism. Any such information would be helpful in understanding and evaluating that work and historical period. The Lynds, at least, are more honest by pointing out, when introducing their subjects, that "most were some kind of socialist, many belonging at some point in their lives to an organized radical group. . . . Most of the organizers who were active in the 1930s were connected to the Communist Party." They were also honest enough to remind their readers that the people interviewed were "not selected at random."

Socialism in many of these historical documentaries is, therefore, often utopian and rarely "scientific." The IWW and the Communist party are nostalgically viewed as associations of heroic men and women. The filmmakers seem to feel that, in these times, it's enough for people to know that a past tradition of struggle, of people fighting against capitalist oppression, exists. The homages to the warriors of the past are loving, and love is important to the revolutionary process, but the films are rarely critical in any analytical ways. There is little attempt to sort out political and ideological tendencies, to show what exactly we should learn from the past. One gets the feeling that filmmakers share an embarrassment about the more recent historical past, the sixties and early seventies. With few exceptions—like Barry Brown and Glenn Silber's *The War at Home* (1980) and Joanne Grant's *Fundi: The Story of Ella Baker* (1981)—that period is rarely examined. Filmmakers seem to think that the upsurge of the sixties and seventies was a failure and that most answers lie farther in the past, in simply recapturing a sense of the militance, camaraderie, and "closeness" to the working class.

The importance of having a clear view of the past is, of course, to know how to interpret the present, act upon it, and thereby influence the future. If we fail to be discriminating about what we think happened in the past, we're likely to be equally imprecise about the present. If we can't discriminate among politically conscious veterans, it will be harder to make sense of the beliefs of contemporary rank and file community people. In his review of Richard Boardman's *Mission Hill and the Miracle of Boston* (1979)—a film about the effect of land development and housing master-plans on a particular community—historian David Paskin finds that "ironically the very genuineness of the film is part of the problem." Although the filmmakers have gotten close to the people—living in the community, being wary of manipulation, and being able to capture real moments on film—they fail to take a critical enough stance. The filmmakers fail to draw a distinction "between the historical description and analysis of working-class beliefs and the critical judgment one places on those beliefs." While *Mission Hill* "succeeds wonderfully as a description of ethnic working class life," Paskin maintains it is foggy "as a political statement meant as a practical guide to action in Mission Hill and other urban communities" because it fails "to unravel the political implications of the internal beliefs of the community." Oral history doesn't quite speak for itself.

Current filmmakers, most of whom were politically nurtured in the sixties and seventies, seem both close to their subjects and unwilling to become spokespeople themselves. They have made it a principle to distrust all "outside" points of view—including their own. At the Bard workshop on historical documentary, one of the makers of a well-known film explained, "At first, we studied the various aspects of the issues, developing our own viewpoint. But we abandoned that. We didn't want to preach." The decision to shun narration and commentary is ultimately an ideological one. "Preaching" is considered by many to be authoritarian by nature, elitist and paternalistic. The fear of "preaching" stems from a rejection of what many filmmakers call "vanguard politics," particularly the Leninist notion that the working class needs to have political knowledge brought to it from outside. This attitude among filmmakers distorts the dialectic between politically conscious artists and the masses of people. The hundreds of radical filmmakers, as well as the thousands of Marxist academics, have done important work documenting our political past and present, unearthing working-class culture, and showing the links between daily life and politics. They all were created, in a sense, by the popular uprisings of the preceding period. Marxists are in the academy, for example, because those uprisings smashed at its walls. Swept forward by this wave, activists and artists are left to continue their work. It is fitting that they first go back to the people—to find out what is happening in people's lives, to find out the historical roots, the traditions and culture, to hear and record the veterans and the young. After taking from the people, however, after recording and transcribing, conscious political artists owe something more. What they owe is some leadership.

29

Against the Ivory Tower: An Apologia for "Popular" Historical Documentaries

Dirk Eitzen

What makes a documentary good? What makes one bad? These two little questions account for probably eighty-five percent of the ink that has flowed in discussion of documentaries in general and historical documentaries in particular—both in academic circles and in the popular press. These questions continue to provoke strong disagreements. It is a safe bet that they are in no danger of a speedy resolution. Nonetheless, when it comes to the practical matter of doing things with historical documentaries—using them in the classroom, at conferences, in our writing—they are questions that insist upon answers. I do not have any all-purpose answers. I would like to make a case, however, concerning how we ought to approach the questions.

I recently completed a lengthy study of the public response to popular historical documentaries: reviews, letters to producers, public debates, and interviews with filmmakers. The purpose of this study was to discover how people generally make sense of historical documentaries—that is, what people suppose to be the purpose of doing history, what they expect of documentaries, what constitutes "evidence" in the minds of viewers, how they evaluate[1] depictions of the past, and so on.

The public response to historical documentaries turns out to be rather complex and, predictably, to vary considerably depending upon individual viewers' interest in and previous "knowledge" about historical events depicted in a film. It has also varied quite a lot historically, just as the form of historical documentaries has. Nevertheless, there is one striking constant that cuts across all of the variables. Namely, non-academics tend to discuss historical documentaries in very different terms than academics do. The evidence of this is so strong that one might with reason suppose that the two groups even see historical documentaries differently. To state the difference simply (indeed, over-simply), non-academics are overwhelmingly concerned with the emotional "pull" of documentaries about the past, while scholars prefer to adopt a more critical, self-conscious stance. Historians and film scholars are no doubt well aware of the strengths of their scholarly approach to movies about history. The question I wish to ponder here (as an academic writing to other academics) is, What is wrong with the other way, the "popular" way, of watching, thinking about, and discussing documentaries about the past? Indeed, what is wrong with historical documentaries that deliberately appeal to this "popular" mode of reception?

Historians and film scholars have an admirable if somewhat impractical tendency to talk to each other about how filmmakers ought to make films. My ambition here is somewhat more modest. I wish to discuss only how historians and film scholars ought to talk about films. This discussion is aimed not at people who make historical documentaries, but at people who write about them and use them in their classes. It is not about what historical documentaries ought to do. It is about what scholars ought to do with historical documentaries. Rather than making specifications for historical documentaries that may be made in the future, it speaks to the problem of what to do with those that are already history, so to speak.

Academic historians naturally tend to evaluate historical documentaries according to how well they do what academic historians are supposed to do. Their verdict, when analysing extant historical documentaries, is almost always that they do not do that very well. This is not just a matter of factual inaccuracies; in fact, it has to do more with the kinds of questions that historical documentaries pose and answer. It has to do with how they function as *discourses* about the past.

This view is reflected in the numerous essays by historians in a special issue of *American Historical Review* on "The Filmmaker as Historian." As Robert Brent Toplin writes in the introductory essay,

> By presenting subjects in a conclusive manner, films imply that the study of history is a tidy operation, that it involves little more than laying out a chronology and "getting the story straight." Films rarely give audiences a sense of the challenges in historical interpretation. They address subjects authoritatively, suggesting that the investigator works with an orderly universe of evidence. They fail to show that a filmmaker must give shape and meaning to the sources. In short, films rarely point out that the facts do not speak for themselves and that the filmmaker must speak for them.[2]

Toplin goes on to discuss numerous exceptions to this rule. Still, the general consensus among historians is that documentaries about history, particularly popular ones, are simply not sufficiently scholarly.

This may be true. I certainly do not wish to argue otherwise. Nevertheless, it must be said that there is something a bit perverse about these arguments. They are analogous to a James Michener fan complaining of a scholarly history that it is insufficiently entertaining. It seems more appropriate to judge something in terms of what it is *supposed* to be than for what it is not.

Historians seem to assume that historical documentaries are supposed to be akin to scholarly history—that is, historians assume that popular or "ordinary" audiences tend to draw the same kind of conclusions from historical documentaries that scholars draw when they do or read academic history. Toplin's essay and others suggest that what modern historians are most interested in is the complexity or multidimensionality of the past. They regard the past as something to be considered from a number of angles. Another common view among historians, traditionally, is that the past is something to be explained.

It seems clear from the public reception of historical documentaries like Claude Lanzmann's documentary about the Holocaust, *Shoah*, and Ken Burns' acclaimed series for American public television, *The Civil War*, that popular audiences of historical documentaries are not particularly interested either in the complexity of the past or in explaining it. What they want more than anything (and what they generally find, if a historical documentary is at all "successful") is a powerful emotional "experience." This can be a vicarious experience or an aesthetic experience or an experience of belonging to a special group. In many cases, it is all of these. These considerations, in turn, appear to be rather remote from the concerns of academic historians. In other words, it appears that what academic historians "get out of" their studies of the past and what popular audiences mainly "get out of" historical documentaries are two completely different things, judged according to completely different standards.

Of course, in having an "experience" of the past, popular audiences may also jump to improper conclusions. They might conclude, for example, that having seen the ugly, seamy side of former U.S. President Lyndon Johnson "exposed" in a documentary, they now know all there is to know about the man. Or they might conclude that having "relived" the experience of the gas chambers through *Shoah*, they have now seen the Holocaust as it really was— "*wie es eigentlich gewesen*." This kind of false or improper generalisation from the "experience" of a movie is the danger that concerns historians.

Typical viewers of historical documentaries know that movies are not "real life." They are also surely aware that "real life" is not all there is to history and that having had the sense of "experiencing" an event in the past does not mean knowing everything there is to know about it. Viewers of historical documentaries probably also have a decent intuitive grasp of the differences between academic and popular history. They are clearly pretty adept at distinguishing "fact" from "fiction." Still, knowing all of these things does not prevent viewers from jumping to false or improper conclusions. Even professional historians sometimes jump to wrong conclusions. More importantly, knowing all of the things I outlined above does not necessarily instil the kind of sceptical stance that modern historians espouse: a stance that is always looking for other angles on the past, that is always doubtful of conclusions, that is never so caught up in an emotional "experience" that it fails to think critically about the past. This sceptical stance is one that popular historical documentaries, with their traditional emphasis on "facts" and "feelings," do little to encourage. That is the main reason that historians tend to be somewhat leery of them.

Still, it needs to be said that historical documentaries are generally not supposed to instil a sceptical stance on the past, which is to say that audiences neither want nor expect them to do so. Historical documentaries, by and large, are supposed to be popular. This supposition entails a different set of standards—a set of standards that historians tend to dismiss because, as scholars in the academy, they are primarily engaged in a very different kind of discourse. What are we to make of these popular standards? Are they at all good? Or do they *deserve* to be dismissed?

On questions of good and bad or right and wrong we are all forced, in the end, to base our answers upon opinions. My opinion is that to simply dismiss popular standards, as historians tend to do, is both too pat and too simple. If people say, as many have, that watching *Shoah* helped them grow, or brought them closer to other people, or did something else that they regard to be beneficial to themselves, who am I—who is *anyone*—to discount or disparage their claims?

Critic Loudon Wainwright wondered why people bothered to attend *Shoah* at all, since the movie is so long, so painful, and dwells on so terrible a topic. When he asked, he found that the reasons people gave are varied and complex. Some were simply curious. Others felt somewhat guilty at having escaped the experience by accidents of birth or geography. Others had actually lived through the experience. But the one reason that people gave most often, Wainwright found, is that the film "keeps the memory alive." The viewers he questioned all seemed to regard this to be a powerful *good* of the film.[3]

To the extent that people regard such things as good, I think we need to simply accept them as good. That does not mean that is all we need to do. Historians can teach another way of looking at *Shoah* that is not completely compatible with the way popular audiences tend to look at the film and one that accomplishes different sorts of objective. But they can do this in a way that holds out the possibility of alternative "readings" and enhances the *total* experience of the movie, without disparaging or diminishing popular readings.

Modern historians value having access to a variety of vantage points on the past. In the same way, I advocate having access to a number of vantage points on movies about the past. In other words, I advocate seeing movies as complicated *discourses*. Movies are not constrained to do just one thing or another. As texts, they are free to move among a variety of discursive contexts, affording a variety of possible benefits (and, of course, representing a variety of possible dangers).

The Atomic Cafe, by Kevin Rafferty, Jayne Loader, and Pierce Rafferty—an ironic compilation of "instructional" films about the atomic bomb from the fifties and sixties—is a film that some historians have suggested is particularly dangerous to use in history classrooms because it encourages a kind of smugness toward which college students are already somewhat too prone.[4] Their solution is simply not to show the film in order to steer clear of the possibility of smugness altogether. I suggest that it might be better to deliberately show the film in order to address, head on, the possibility of adopting a smug attitude toward the past. Such smugness has real dangers that college history students would do well to recognise. And what better way is there to teach them this than by showing and discussing with them something that is often construed (even by reviewers in the popular press) as an example of this tendency?

It is also valuable to recognise that even such "smugness" may have its benefits. Permit me to offer my own experience here, as an example. I took part in anti-nuclear marches in the early eighties. Although I might not do the same today, participating in those marches was an experience I still cherish. I think it did *me* good, even if it had no political impact whatsoever. I remember how, when I saw *The Atomic Cafe* at the time, it motivated and inspired me and made me feel like I was one of an important group of concerned people. Even in retrospect, I think that was good. *The Atomic Cafe* may be awful as history. But it is not *just* history, it is also a movie. As a movie, it has (or had for me) certain benefits quite apart from its possible uses as history. Historical documentaries are complicated discourses about the past, with certain typical limitations and dangers, but many possible benefits, besides. Scholarly history, too, has dangers, lest we forget—the danger of the "ivory tower," to name just one.

Like historians, film scholars have also had a tendency to dismiss ordinary viewers' responses to documentaries—especially emotional responses. Film scholars' reasons are somewhat different than historians', however. Film scholars are generally not so concerned about the particular wrong or improper conclusions that viewers may draw from a documentary. In a sense, they seem to have by and large accepted the inevitability that people will jump to false—or at least unwarranted—conclusions while watching movies. Indeed, people always generalise from their experience. This is as true of their "real life" experience as it is of their experience of movies. People's specific generalisations might be said to be a product of the interpretive "frame" that they bring to their experience. This "frame" is in turn in large part the product of culture—which is to say, it is steeped in ideologies of various kinds. That, too, is unavoidable.

What troubles film scholars is a particular kind of "frame" that traditional documentaries—including most documentaries about history—seem to encourage. As Toplin points out, documentaries tend to make representations in a conclusive fashion and to address subjects authoritatively. They often seem to imply that there is but one correct view of reality to which they have privileged access. Even a relatively "open" and apparently non- or anti-authoritarian documentary, like Fred Wiseman's "*cinéma vérité*" documentary, *High School*, may seem to suggest that, because it shows "just the facts," its implicit conclusions are incontrovertible. What *High School* actually represents is not Northeast High at all but Wiseman's *High School*, a highly selective, ordered, and judgmental "take" on reality—a "reality fiction," as Wiseman puts it, not the "truth." But because the film creates this "reality fiction" out of snippets of actual film footage of Northeast High—a real place inhabited by real people—it may mislead viewers into believing otherwise. In other words, documentaries—even relatively "open" documentaries like *High School*—can encourage people to think, "*Now* I see things as they really are (or were)." The "frame" that documentaries invite might be called a "know-it-all" frame. Again, the reception of *The Atomic Cafe* makes this particularly apparent.

There is some question about just how susceptible typical viewers of historical documentaries actually are to a "know-it-all" frame. For instance, reviews of *The Civil War* and letters to the producer make it quite apparent that in the minds of many viewers, that series is a highly constructed account of the American Civil War—a work of "art" or "rhetoric"—not a God's-eye view of history. Even viewers who are quite taken with the series do not seem to suppose that it "knows it all" or that, after seeing it, they "know it all." Still, it appears that viewers of *The Civil War* who are most taken with the series are also somewhat prone to be "taken in" by it, at least to the extent that they do not notice the ways in which ideology is working through the discourse. The possibility of being "taken in" in this fashion is the danger that tends to be of most concern to film scholars.

The danger here is not in being taken in *per se*. It is not that viewers do not *really* know it all, or even that they may think they do. Such "delusions," if you will, are an ordinary part of our day-to-day existence and, ordinarily, quite helpful. (To see a wall or a precipice in ambiguous or less than positive terms, or to spend minutes or hours pondering possible alternative meanings of "Please pass the salt" would ordinarily be extremely counterproductive.) The problem that film scholars perceive is that documentaries *lay claim* to *special power* or *privilege* on the basis of a supposed relationship to reality. It is this exercise of power that is the real danger.

Most if not all discourse involves some exercise of power. But to the extent that documentaries invite the "know-it-all" frame I described earlier, they may be especially prone to a particular kind of abuse of power. When we bring a "know-it-all" frame to our interactions with other people, it can have serious and grave social and political consequences. In other words, people are liable to get hurt by documentaries in ways that they rarely are by fiction films.

Scholars of documentary have responded to this danger by dwelling on the ways in which documentaries do not truly represent reality. They have tended to devote their energies to showing how documentaries are constructed or artificial or "fictive." For example, in the introduction to his new anthology, *Theorizing Documentary*, Michael Renov argues (quoting Hayden White) that, "all discourse *constitutes* the objects which it pretends only to describe realistically and analyse objectively" and (summarising filmmaker Trinh Minh-ha's essay in the same anthology), "documentary film [is] an historically privileged domain of truth . . . whose claims for authority demand to be rigorously questioned on political and philosophical grounds."[5] An extreme example is another recent book by William Guynn, *A Cinema of Nonfiction*, which develops a case that documentaries merely *purport* to reproduce the real by disguising their relationships to fiction films.[6] Documentary theorist Bill Nichols and others have retreated from such extreme claims, recognising the extent to which non-fictional discourses can have real, instrumental consequences. Still, much if not most of Nichols' recent book on documentary, *Representing Reality*, is also devoted to exploring the ramifications of what he terms the "incommensurateness between representation and historical reality."[7]

I do not wish to dispute any of these claims. My question concerns their social consequences. The question is, How should we treat the responses of "ordinary" viewers of historical documentaries, which tend to be predicated upon the notion that documentaries can somehow put us in touch with reality? For example, what are we to respond to the claims of people who feel that *Shoah* somehow truly reflects the "reality" of the Holocaust and truly keeps it "alive" in memory? Are these viewers being deceived? Are they wrong? In a strict sense, yes, they are deceived and wrong, since both the text and the memories it supposedly keeps alive are merely compelling constructs— creations, representations, "fictions." Still, it is my opinion that this answer is, again, both too pat and too simple.

Philosophically speaking, reality and our representations of it are truly "incommensurate." Practically speaking, however (and *practically* is the way viewers of documentaries ordinarily speak about the films), documentaries have the power to really put us in touch with reality—just as "really," that is, as our senses put us in touch with reality. We can never know reality, it is true, but we can very definitely know certain things about it. Evolution has guaranteed this. Philosopher William James put the same idea very nicely nearly a century ago, in describing what he called his pragmatic method:

> Where direct acquaintance is lacking, "knowledge about" is the next best thing, and an acquaintance with what actually lies about the object, and is most closely related to it, puts such knowledge within our grasp. [Light waves] and your anger, for example, are things in which my thoughts will never *perceptually* terminate,

but my concepts of them lead me to their very brink, to the chromatic fringes and to the hurtful words and deeds which are their really next effects.[8]

Shoah does succeed in giving viewers some acquaintance with what actually lies about and is most closely related to the actual, historic event of the Holocaust. I think that, as a practical matter, film scholars are wrong to ignore or minimise the extent to which this is so. I am impressed, again, by how well William James articulated the potential value of the kind of "knowing" that documentaries can provide—a value that historians and film scholars alike, in their eagerness to point out the legitimate dangers of documentaries, have tended to either ignore or dismiss.

> The towering importance for human life of this kind of knowing lies in the fact that an experience that knows another can figure as its *representative*, not in any quasi-miraculous "epistemological" sense, but in the definite practical sense of being its *substitute* in various operations, sometimes physical and sometimes mental, which lead us to its associates and results. By experimenting on our ideas of reality, we may save ourselves the trouble of experimenting on the real experiences which they severally mean.[9]

Where we have no direct access to the real experience, as in seeking to comprehend the past, this kind of knowing is not only useful, it is indispensable. My conclusion, then, is that we would all do well to devote more attention to what *viewers perceive popular historical documentaries to do* (like "bringing the past to life") even if this means paying somewhat less attention to what historical documentaries do *not* do (like affording a scholarly view of the past) or that viewers do not *perceive* them to do (like advancing ideologies). It is in what people perceive in historical documentaries that one finds the most (perhaps the *only*) significant potential for good in them. It is also in what viewers perceive in historical documentaries that one finds the most immediate and consequential possibilities of harm.

Discourses are (whatever else they may be) eminently *pragmatic* affairs: practical, instrumental, ends-oriented, "useful," "down-to-earth," governed by participants' perceptions and expectations, driven by participants' aims and desires. If we wish to understand historical documentaries as actual forms of discourse, we need not only to acknowledge this, we need to study the ways it is so.

Historian Michael Frisch, one of the most astute commentators upon and critics of public history, has written that the chief problem and concern of public historians, at least in the U.S., ought to be the extent to which the relationship between history and memory is fractured in contemporary life, the extent to which our public culture is disconnected from the past.[10] What we need to overcome this problem, he suggests, is more history like Marcel Ophuls' documentary, *The Memory of Justice*—a documentary dealing with the Nuremberg trials that is actually less about history than about how people remember it and relate it (or try not to relate it) to their own lives and to events of the present. *The Memory of Justice* is not an especially scholarly film, nor does it go out of its way to expose its own ideological operations. Nonetheless, Frisch says, it is an unusually "intelligent" film, not for what it knows or says, but on account of the "the care, depth, insight, and sensitivity with which it reflects on and explores a profound problem."[11]

"The Ophuls film," Frisch writes, "helps to focus on what I think must lie at the heart of [the role of memory] in a public history that will matter—a fundamental commitment to the importance of that verb at the heart of memory, making it something *alive and active* as we confront our own world." "We need projects that will involve people in exploring what it means to remember, and what to do with memories to make them active and alive, as opposed to mere objects of collection."[12]

If Frisch is correct in these claims, then surely the perception of many viewers that *Shoah* "keeps a memory alive" and that *The Civil War* and other popular historical documentaries "bring the past to life" is not something to be scoffed at or dismissed. I must agree with Frisch, in the end, that, to the extent historical documentaries even appear to put us in touch with a real "living" past, they are "seizing an opportunity not nearly so accessible to conventional academic historical scholarship, whatever its virtues: the opportunity to help liberate for that active remembering all the intelligence [in the way Frisch defines the word] of a people long kept separated from the sense of their own past."[13] That opportunity can no doubt be exploited for good or for ill, but it is an opportunity nonetheless. And it is an opportunity that scholars will realise only to the extent they engage with documentaries as complex discourses about the past, rather than merely as more-or-less academic representations of the past or as more-or-less illusory fabrications.

Notes

1   *"Bringing the Past to Life": The Reception and Rhetoric of Historical Documentaries*, Dissertation, University of Iowa, 1994. I gratefully acknowledge the support of a Dissertation Grant from the National Endowment for the Humanities in performing and writing this study.

2   "AHR Forum: The Filmmaker as Historian," *American Historical Review*, No. 93 (December 1988): 1216–17.

3   "A Movie Made for Remembrance," *Life*, No. 8 (Dec. 1985): 7.

4   I am referring to a recent discussion on the history and film list on Internet, H-Film (H-Film@uicvm.uic.edu), among I. C. Jarvie, Peter Rollins, myself, and others.

5   "Introduction: The Truth About Non-Fiction," *Theorizing Documentary*. New York: Routledge, 1993, p. 7.

6   *A Cinema of Nonfiction*. Rutherford, NJ: Fairleigh Dickinson University Press, 1990, p. 241.

7   *Representing Reality: Issues and Concepts in Documentary*. Bloomington: Indiana University Press, 1991.

8   "A World of Pure Experience" [1904], *The Writings of William James: A Comprehensive Edition*, ed., John J. McDermott, New York: The Modern Library, 1968, p. 207. James actually wrote "etherwaves" instead of "lightwaves," a scientific "error" that does not detract from his argument but that I nonetheless expunged here in order to avoid distraction.

9   Ibid., p. 203.

10 "The Memory of History," in *A Shared Authority: Essays on the Craft and Meaning of Oral and Public History*. Albany: State University of New York Press, 1990.

11 Ibid., p. 26.

12 Ibid., pp. 25 and 27; my emphasis.

13 Ibid., p. 27.

30

The Event:
Archive and Imagination

Stella Bruzzi

Documentary is persistently treated as a representational mode of film-making, although at its core is the notion of film as record. In its examination of documentary's purported struggle for objectivity, this chapter will be concerned with the relationship between film as record and as representation, centred on the idea—or ideal—of an original unadulterated truth . . . The material to be considered here will be the Zapruder footage of the assassination of Kennedy.

The crux of the problem when considering the potential differences between film as record and as representation, is the relationship between the human and the mechanical eye. Dziga Vertov posited a relationship between the eye and the kino-eye (the latter he referred to as the 'factory of facts' [Michelson 1984: 59]), espousing the idea that cinema's primary function was to show what the human eye could see but not record:

> In fact, the film is only the sum of the facts recorded on film, or if you like, not merely the sum, but the product, a 'higher mathematics' of facts. Each item of each factor is a separate little document, the documents have been joined with one another so that, on the one hand, the film would consist only of those linkages between signifying pieces that coincide with the visual linkages and so that, on the other hand, these linkages would not require intertitles; the final sum of all these linkages represents, therefore, an organic whole. (Michelson 1984: 84)

For a compiler of images and a recorder of life, such as Vertov, the recording procedure is always subservient to the facts being committed to film; the mechanical eye is simply capable of showing and clarifying for its audience that which initially stands before the naked eye. The act of filming concretises rather than distorts and is in itself a way of comprehending the world. Later the French documentarist and theorist Jean-Louis Comolli returns to the relationship between the human eye and its mechanical counterpart, but reaches very different conclusions, believing that, through the advent of photography:

the human eye loses its immemorial privilege; the mechanical eye of the photographic machine now sees *in its place*, and in certain aspects with more success.
The photograph stands as at once the triumph and the grave of the eye. (Comolli
1980: 122–3)

Comolli, from a perspective that acknowledges the ambivalence of the mechanical eye, argues that Bazin, for one, is naïve to think that, because the camera
records a real event, 'it provides us with an objective and impartial image of
that reality', as 'The *represented* is seen via a *representation* which, necessarily,
transforms it' (p. 135).

The underpinning issue is whether or not the intervention of the filmmaker
and, therefore, the human eye renders irretrievable the original meaning of
the events being recorded. Linda Williams, like many others currently writing
on documentary, detects a loss of faith 'in the ability of the camera to reflect
objective truths of some fundamental social referent', a loss which she goes on
to say 'seems to point, nihilistically . . . to the brute and cynical disregard of
ultimate truths' (Williams 1993: 10 [reprinted as Chapter 4 of this collec-
tion]). Later Williams comments that 'It has become an axiom of the new documentary that films cannot reveal the truth of events, but only the ideologies
and consciousness that construct competing truths—the fictional master narratives by which we make sense of events' (p. 13), so doubting entirely that the
image-document itself can mean anything without accompanying narrivati-
sation and contextualisation. The problem with Williams' analysis is that it
expediently singles out examples (such as *The Thin Blue Line* and *Shoah*) rooted
in memory and eye-witness testimony, films that intentionally lack or exclude
images of the events under scrutiny, thus making a plausible case for a 'final
truth' (p. 15) to be dislodged in favour of a series of subjective truths.

Whilst not advocating the collapse of reality and representation, what I will
attempt is an analysis of film as record from an alternative perspective to
the one implicitly proposed here by Williams [or elsewhere by Renov, Winston
and Barnouw], namely that documentary has always implicitly acknowledged
that the 'document' at its heart is open to reassessment, reappropriation and
even manipulation without these processes necessarily obscuring or rendering
irretrievable the document's original meaning, context or content. The fundamental issue of documentary film is the way in which we are invited to
access the 'document' or 'record' through representation or interpretation, to
the extent that a piece of archive material becomes a mutable rather than a
fixed point of reference. This is not, however, to imply that a filmmaker such as
de Antonio disregards the documentary source of his films, or that his films are
mere formalist exercises that tread the post-modern path of disputing the distinction between the historical/factual and the 'fake' or the fictive. Rather his
films and those, such as *The Atomic Cafe*, which have been overtly influenced by

his 'collage junk' method, play on the complexity of the relationship between historical referent and interpretation: they enact a fundamental doubt concerning the purity of their original source material and its ability to reveal a truth that is valid, lasting and cogent. De Antonio's films do not simply deny or suppress the existence of an independent truth contained within the raw footage they re-edit and comment upon, and it is perhaps this sort of equivocation that problematises the perception of archive's role in documentary.

Film as Accidental Record: 'The Zapruder Film'

To test some of the assumptions about film as record and its transmutation into archive it seems appropriate to turn to the most notorious piece of accidental footage: Abraham Zapruder's 22 seconds of 8 mm film showing the assassination of President Kennedy, 22 November 1963, in Dallas, Texas. Several factors make 'the Zapruder film', as it is commonly known, an interesting example. The film is the work of a very amateur cameraman, a classic piece of home movie footage that Zapruder simply intended as a family record of the President's visit. The discrepancy between quality and magnitude of content and the Zapruder film's accidental nature make it particularly compelling. The home movie fragment almost did not happen as Abraham Zapruder, a local women's clothing manufacturer, had left his Bell and Howell camera at home on the morning of 22 November because of the rain, but had been persuaded by his secretary to go back and fetch it; it also almost looked quite different, as Zapruder found his position on the concrete block just in front of the 'Grassy Knoll'[1] at the last minute. Additionally, as illustrated in the film itself, it is evident that this position gave Zapruder a view of the motorcade that was partially obscured by a large road sign, tantalisingly blotting out certain details of the assassination. In keeping with this accidental quality is Zapruder's own tentativeness when discussing the film before the Warren Commission, commenting humbly, 'I knew I had something, I figured it might be of some help—I didn't know what' (quoted in Wasson 1995: 7). Similarly important is Zapruder's lack of expertise as a camera operator. The silent film jolts in response to the shots and Zapruder finds it difficult to keep Kennedy centre frame: at the crucial moment when the fatal head shot hits him, the President has been allowed to almost slide out of view, leaving the most famous frames of amateur film dominated, almost engulfed, by the lush green grass on the other side of Elm Street. 'Zapruder' became shorthand in American film schools in the years following the assassination for a piece of film of extremely low technical quality whose content was nevertheless of the utmost significance.[2] For Bazin, the apotheosis of the photograph is the similarly artless family snapshot whose documentary equivalent would be the home movie. So it was that students and others sought to emulate the style of the Zapruder footage; as Patricia Zimmerman comments with reference to home movies, 'the American avant-garde has appropriated home-movie style as a formal manifestation of a spontaneous, untampered form of filmmaking' (Zimmerman 1995: 146). The home movie is, virtually by definition, the documentation of the trivial, the personal and the inconsequential, events of interest only to the family group involved. What makes Zapruder's home movie exceptional is that it happens to capture an event that is not private and trivial but public and of huge importance. Footage that by accident rather than design captures material this monumental transgresses the boundaries between the official and unofficial uses of broadcast film, offering an alternative point of view, a perspective that is partly predicated upon the absenting of the film *auteur*, the conscious creator of the images. Zapruder's accidental home movie, like George Holliday's similarly spontaneous video recording of the beating of Rodney King by members of the LAPD in March 1991, became the official text of the events it recorded.

Why is this combination of the accidental, the amateur and the historically significant event so engaging? If one were to devise a method for classifying archive material in accordance with its purity or level of distortion, the Zapruder film would be at the top of the scale. Paul Arthur comments on the 'mutual agreement' between film theorists such as Siegfried Kracauer and Bela Balazs that 'newsreels and documentary reportage in general are "innocent" or "artless" due to their lack of aesthetic reconstruction' (Arthur 1997: 2). Arthur goes on to quote Kracauer when positing that 'it is precisely the snapshot quality of the pictures that makes them appear as authentic documents' (p. 3), concluding that 'the absence of "beauty" yields a greater quotient of "truth"' (p. 3), thereby establishing an inverse ratio between documentary purity and aesthetic value. The Zapruder film, by these criteria, is exemplary in its rawness, innocence and credibility as a piece of non-fiction evidence or documentation. Zapruder, unlike those who copied him, is not consciously manipulating his amateur status, and it is this naiveté that audiences still find compelling, as exemplified by the preponderance of the 'accidental video witnessing of spectacular events' (Ouellette 1995: 41) that dominates the American series *I Witness Video*. Andrew Britton mentions, as if it is a foregone conclusion, that 'there can be no such thing as a representation of the world which does not embody a set of values', so ensuring that the documentary's 'greatest strength is its availability for the purpose of analysis and ideological critique' (Britton 1992: 28). There is no space in this claim for non-fiction images such as the Zapruder film, accidental footage that is not filmed with a conscious or unconscious set of determining values—'value', in Britton's estimation, being automatically attached to the author/filmmaker as opposed to a film's content. Yet historical documentaries are made up of such non-critical fragments as the Zapruder footage. Within such a context, the film's 'value' is presumed to be that, because of the singular lack of premeditation, intention and authorship, it is able unproblematically to yield the truth contained within its blurry, hurried images; but therein lies its problem and the factual film's burden of proof.

The Zapruder footage very quickly became an object of fetishistic fascination. As film that shows the moments of Kennedy's death, its 'imagery operating as the equivalent of the snuff film', the Zapruder frames bear uneasy comparison with the pornographic ideal of 'going all the way' to the moment of death (Simon 1996: 67). However, the fact that for twelve years the images were only known as single frames published in the Warren Commission Report[3] into the assassination or in *Life* magazine (which secured the rights to the Zapruder film on the night of the assassination for $150,000) inevitably rendered them mysterious. By 1975, when the film was first broadcast, the rights had been returned to the Zapruder family, although the original footage now belongs to the US government, which paid the heirs of Abraham Zapruder £10 million to keep it in the national archives (a deal that was agreed on the day John Kennedy Jr died in a plane crash). In the immediate aftermath of the assassination, the Zapruder film was thus not available as film, although the surrounding events were: the arrival of the motorcade at Parkland Memorial Hospital, Jackie Kennedy accompanying her husband's coffin on Air Force One's flight back to Washington, the funeral, the arrest and subsequent murder live on television of Lee Harvey Oswald. The absence of the key assassination images was exacerbated by the presence of these surrounding pieces of tape and film and by the knowledge that the Zapruder film was all the time being examined, re-examined and re-enacted by the Warren Commission. Such absence or lack was especially marked when considering the fatal shot to Kennedy's head, as these frames (Nos. 313–15) were deemed too traumatic to show (*Life* omitting them from early publications of the images), or, as occurred in the published Warren Commission Report, were distorted, as two frames (313 and 315) were 'accidentally' reversed, which gave the impression that Kennedy's head was thrust forward by the impact of the bullet, thus supporting their lone gunman theory. When these frames did become readily accessible, the 'involuntary spasm' shown as the bullet hits Kennedy itself 'became the site of an investigatory fetish' (Simon 1996: 68), the Zapruder film's most over-scrutinised images.

Although the Warren Commission said that 'Of all the witnesses to the tragedy, the only unimpeachable one is the *camera* of Abraham Zapruder' (my italics; *Life* magazine, 25 November 1966, quoted in Simon 1996: 41), its status as evidence is ambiguous: it can show that President Kennedy was assassinated but is unable to show how or by whom, because Zapruder's camera (and it is revealing that the apparatus is singled out for unimpeachability and not the man) is effectively facing the wrong way—at the President

and not at who shot him. Other photographic material, taken from the opposite side of Elm Street, which could potentially reveal more about the
position of the assassins—such as Orvill Nix's film and Mary Moorman's
photograph—has been allegedly subjected to greater Security Services intervention and violation,[4] although the Warren Commission did omit Zapruder
frames 208–11 from its final report, despite the assertion that the first bullet
struck Kennedy at frame 210 (Simon 1996: 40).

If documentary putatively aspires to discover the least distortive means of
representing reality, then is not footage such as the Zapruder film exemplary
of its aim? It is devoid of imposed narrative, authorial intervention, editing and
discernible bias and yet its contents are of such momentous significance that
it remains arguably the most important piece of raw footage ever shot. The
Zapruder film as a piece of historical evidence has severe limitations. Despite
its value as explicit raw footage, the truth that its frames can reveal is restricted
to verisimilitude of image to subject; the non-fictional image's mimetic power
cannot stretch to offering a context or an explanation for the crude events on
the screen, thus proposing two levels of truth: the factual images we see and
the truth to be extrapolated from them. Or is that 'truths'? One of the consistently complicating aspects of the Zapruder film is that it has been both 'unimpeachable' and 'constantly open to multiple interpretations' (Simon 1996:
43), an open series of images that can be used to 'prove' a multitude of conflicting or divergent theories about the assassination. This is the footage's
burden of proof: that, as an authentic record, it functions as incontrovertible
'evidence', whilst as a text incapable of revealing conclusively who killed
President Kennedy it functions as an inconclusive representation. What the
Zapruder film demonstrates is an irresistible desire (on the part of theorists and
probably practitioners as well) for manipulation, narrativisation or conscious
intervention, despite the avowed detestation of such intrusions upon the
factual image. The Zapruder footage has, for example, led Haidee Wasson to
speculate wildly that the footage 'becomes the threshold to an imaginary and
real space where seemingly contradictory rituals are re-enacted' (Wasson
1995: 10). Exemplifying this duality, the Zapruder footage's continuous
paradox is that it promises to reveal what will always remain beyond it: the
motivation and the cause of the actions it depicts. This has, in turn, led consistently to two impulses, the first being to focus obsessively on the source
material itself, to analyse, re-analyse, enhance, digitally re-master Zapruder's
original in the vain hope that these images will finally reveal the truth of who
killed Kennedy, the second being to use the same sequence of images as the
basis for an interpretation of the assassination that invariably requires and
incorporates additional, substantiating material, usually drawing from an
ever-dwindling number of eye-witnesses and an ever-increasing pool of conspiracy theorists. Although Zapruder's footage is an archetypal example of

accidental, reactive and objective film, it has rarely been permitted to exist as such because, as Bill Nichols comments, 'To re-present the event is clearly *not* to explain it' (Nichols 1994: 121).

It is this central inadequacy that has led to a peculiar canonisation of certain emotionally charged pieces of film and video, images that could be termed 'iconic'. Recently the transmutation occurred with the endlessly repeated and equally endlessly inconclusive shots of the mutilated car in which Princess Diana and others were killed in a Paris underpass on 31 August 1997. Although these images could really only tell us that Diana, Dodi Fayed and Henri Paul had died, they were, alongside the hastily edited compilation documentaries that started running on the afternoon of the crash, played again and again, as if, miraculously, they would suddenly prove less inconclusive, or indeed that looking at them hard enough would enable us to reverse the events they confirmed. The iconic status afforded the Diana and Zapruder footage, is the result of other factors; imbuing the images with significance beyond their importance as mere film or video, they function as the point where diverse and often conflicting mythologising tendencies, emotions and fantasies collide. A comparably hyperbolic and intense language was adopted to describe both deaths—'the day the dream died', 'the end of Camelot'—and the mass outpouring of grief that followed them more than adequately repressed the shortcomings and failings of the individuals struck down. The Zapruder film has become the dominant assassination text, onto which is poured all the subsidiary grief, anger, belief in conspiracy and corruption surrounding the unresolved events it depicts. The text is simple, its meaning is not; as Roland Barthes observes, 'Myth is not defined by the object of its message, but by the way in which it utters this message: there are formal limits to myth, there are no "substantial" ones' (Barthes 1957: 117).

With each repeated viewing of the Zapruder film, do we still simply see it for what it is, see the death? This question might seem needlessly obfuscating, but at issue is how we look at any image that is so familiar that we already know it intimately before we begin the process of re-viewing. Iconic documentary material such as this is, in part, forever severed from its historical and narrative contextualisation. The killing of President Kennedy is perpetually reworked in the present; each theory about who killed Kennedy and why urges us to impose a closure in these malleable images, adopting the language of certainty ('who killed Kennedy will be shown here for the first time')[5] whilst knowing presumably that they will be superseded in due course by a new theory, a new set of certainties. The Zapruder film remains the core text of the Kennedy assassination, 'invisibly back-projected on all the other film evidence' (Simon 1996: 47), and our obsession with it is in no small part due to ambivalent desire to have it both reveal and keep hidden the truth behind the 'world's greatest murder mystery'.[6] Its iconic and fetishistic status is due to its familiarity and its instability as evidence; Zapruder captures a public death and presents us with a personal viewing experience (a home movie)—as Errol Morris comments, 'we're there ... it's happening before our eyes.'[7] If a piece of archive footage becomes so familiar that a mere allusion to one detail or one frame triggers off a recollection of the whole, then the experience of watching that film is not simply that of observing the representation of an actual event. The Zapruder film has significance beyond the sum of its parts; despite its subject matter, it begins to function like a melodrama, to comfort the viewer almost with its known-ness, its familiarity. Knowing the end ironically frees us to speculate upon alternatives ('what if?', 'if only'), to reconstruct the sequence just as we see it relentlessly repeating the very events we are trying to suppress. This is particularly the case when it comes to the frames immediately prior to the shot hitting Kennedy's head; the pause (even at real speed) between gun shots always seems implausibly long, Kennedy is slumping into his wife's arms and Zapruder has almost lost him from view when suddenly the right side of his head explodes. In that hiatus between points of intense violence, the impulse is to re-imagine history.

The Zapruder film shows us everything and it shows us nothing; it is explicit but cannot conclusively confirm or deny any version of the assassination. Perhaps, cynically, one could proffer this as the reason for its enduring mystique, that because it will never solve the murder mystery it is a perfect fantasy text. Too often the indissoluble ambivalence of the Zapruder film is forgotten in favour of an 'anything goes' approach to it as an historical document that has no meaning until it has been interpreted or given a story, an attitude that Wasson succumbs to when treating the footage as just another cultural artefact, suggesting that 'the film *qua* film quickly dissolves, becoming intimately linked to the cultural phenomena which infuse it' (Wasson 1995: 10). This conclusion resembles the inflexible formalism of Hayden White (1987: 76) as he says that 'any historical object can sustain a number of equally plausible descriptions or narratives.' The essential ambiguity surrounding Zapruder's images hinges on the awareness that their narrativisability does not engulf or entirely obscure their veracity. Nichols is thereby wrong to believe that inconclusive pieces of film record such as Zapruder's leave the event 'up for grabs' (Nichols 1994: 121–2); what is 'up for grabs' is the interpretation of that event. If the footage's realness is merely to be fused with its imaginative potential, then why is the actual Zapruder film so different from and more affecting than its imitators, all of which effectively represent the same event? There have been countless reconstructions of the home movie fragment, from a dream sequence in John Waters' *Eat Your Makeup* (1966) in which Divine parodies Jackie Kennedy reliving the day of the assassination, to the countless more earnest versions made for quasi-factual biopics, to the documentary restagings of the events undertaken (from the Warren Commission onwards) to attempt to establish the facts. One anomaly is that the closer or more faithful the imitation is to the Zapruder original, the more it emphasises its difference from it. An interesting example of a Zapruder re-enactment is the accurate reconstruction undertaken for *The Trial of Lee Harvey Oswald* (David Greene, 1976), a film made before copies of the Zapruder film were widely available. The Zapruder simulation is repeatedly used during the hypothetical trial of the film's title, and those in the courtroom are shocked by what they see. But whilst Oliver Stone's *JFK*, in a comparable courtroom situation, uses the real Zapruder footage digitally enhanced, enlarged and slowed down (thus compelling the cinema spectator to identify directly with the diegetic audience's horror), the reconstruction for *The Trial of Lee Harvey Oswald* differs from its prototype in one crucial respect: it omits the blood and gore of the fatal shot to Kennedy's head. This is citation, not replication—a mythologised rendering of the original, brutal snuff movie.

The ultimate, uncomfortable paradox of the Zapruder film as raw evidence is that the more it is exposed to scrutiny, with frames singled out and details digitally enhanced, the more unstable and inconclusive the images become. The industry of what Don DeLillo has termed 'blur analysis'[8] has always flourished, but the results are confusing and frequently fanciful, despite Simon's assertion that:

> The film must be slowed down to be legible; its twenty-two seconds go by too fast for its vital content to be adequately studied. As a result, it speaks its own impossibility as film . . . Its status as evidence relies simultaneously on duration and its arrest, film and still frame. (Simon 1996: 48)

Run at proper speed, the Zapruder footage is brief and incomplete; the action starts and stops convulsively, in mid-action. This indeterminacy is the overriding characteristic of accidental footage, its jolting, fragmentary quality not only producing an unfinished narrative, but also preserving a conscious viewpoint from being imposed on the images by either the person filming or the audience. The speed with which the assassination occurs is thereby a crucial factor, as Noël Carroll (1996: 228), intimates: 'Unexpected events can intrude into the viewfinder—e.g., Lee Harvey Oswald's assassination—before there is time for a personal viewpoint to crystallize.'

The paradox remains, however, that it is only when viewed at proper speed that the true impact of Kennedy's death becomes apparent. In his analysis of the trial of the LAPD officers accused of beating Rodney King in March 1991, Bill Nichols suggests that, far from being an elucidating technique, the slowing down of the original George Holliday video tape could be used to distort the facts. The LAPD defence team demonstrated this with their assiduous dissection of the same footage that the prosecution alleged proved the case for police brutality to corroborate their case for acquittal. The defence argument:

appeared to fly in the face of common sense. But it took the *form* of a positivist, scientific interpretation. It did what any good examination of evidence should do: it scrutinised it with care and drew from it (apparent) substantiation for an interpretation that best accounted for what really happened. (Nichols 1994: 30)

Similar distortions have occurred around the Kennedy assassination. Two examples are the magnifications of a piece of film and a portion of a photograph—Robert Hughes's film showing the Texas School Book Depository and Mary Moorman's photograph showing the Grassy Knoll. Both have been digitally enhanced to the point of allegedly revealing shady figures at a window or crouched behind a picket fence. The evidence, in the enhanced versions, might be convincing, but played at real speed or unmagnified these two records of the assassination day appear inconclusive, the results of a desperate desire to find something plausibly human amidst the play on light and shade. One person's figure is another person's shadow.

The Zapruder film (and Holliday's video of Rodney King) make us perhaps question 'the truth-bearing capacities of film' (Simon 1996: 48). This returns us to the notion that Abraham Zapruder's camera, though able to produce an unfailingly authentic record of the Kennedy assassination, is pointing the wrong way, that the film may just be one of many texts that can be used to explain the assassination, not the only one. Still one of the most compelling investigative films made about the assassination and its aftermath is Emile de Antonio's *Rush to Judgement* (1966) on which he collaborated with lawyer Mark Lane. Lane had written a book of the same name, published on 15 August 1966, that took issue with key areas of the Warren Commission Report, made public on 27 September 1964. Neither the book nor the film attempts to solve the 'murder mystery' of the assassination, but merely to insinuate that the Warren Commission's conclusions are unconvincing and that there are grounds for arguing that there had been a conspiracy to kill Kennedy; hence the adoption in both of an examination/cross-examination structure. As Lane stipulates in the documentary's first piece to camera, the film will be making 'the case for the defence'. More tantalising than the inconclusiveness of the Zapruder footage is the lack of testimony from Lee Oswald, Oswald having been shot in the basement of the Dallas police headquarters by Jack Ruby on 24 November as he was being escorted to the County Jail. *Rush to Judgement* is the first of several television and film attempts to give Oswald's defence a 'voice'.[9] The majority of the film's interviewees support the theory that Kennedy was shot at least once from the front as seems logical from the movement backwards of the President's head in the Zapruder footage; it is ironic and apposite, therefore, that the majority of de Antonio's witnesses are facing the Grassy Knoll, and so literally looking the other way from Zapruder. With the absence of any archive material of the assassination itself, *Rush to*

Judgement is reliant on memory presented, within its prosecutional framework, as testimony. The difference between the Zapruder film and *Rush to Judgement* is the difference between the event and memory, between a filmed representation of a specific truth and the articulation of a set of related, contingent versions. In a film such as *Rush to Judgement* the human eye replaces the mechanical eye as the instrument of accurate or convincing memory; as the photographic evidence yields fewer rather than more certainties, the eyewitnesses interviewed by de Antonio and others usurp its position. The obvious problem with the growing dependency (from the 1960s onwards) on interviews as evidence not (supposedly) manipulated by the *auteur*-director, is that what can too easily be revealed is a series of truths (or what individuals take to be truths) not a single, underpinning truth. Just as the Zapruder film remains an inconclusive text, so *Rush to Judgement* ensures that the assassination inquiries are not closed by the appearance of one hastily complied report, having one interviewee, Penn Jones, state directly to camera at the end of the film:

> I would love to see a computer, faced with the problem of probabilities of the assassination taking place the way it did, with all these strange incidents which took place before and are continuing to take place after the assassination.[10] I think all of us who love our country should be alerted that something is wrong in the land.

The fundamental discrepancy between 'raw' archive material as exemplified by the Zapruder film and a memory/interview-based documentary such as *Rush to Judgement* highlights the source for the growing disillusionment with the notion of image as document. If pieces of unpremeditated archive as ostensibly uncontaminated and artless as Zapruder's or Holliday's home movies can produce contradictory but credible interpretations, then the idea of the 'pure' documentary which theorists have tacitly invoked is itself vulnerable. In *Il Giorno della Civetta* the Sicilian writer Leonardo Sciascia adopts the artichoke as a metaphor for describing the authorities' pursuit of the Mafia: that no matter how many leaves the police or the judiciary tear away, they never reach its heart, or if they do, its heart proves to be a strangely inconclusive place. Likewise the hounding of the 'pure' documentary; for is it not the case (as with gruesome and ubiquitous reality television or the stop-frame 'blur-analysis' to which the Zapruder and Holliday films have both been subjected), that the closer one gets to the document itself, the more aware one becomes of the artifice and the impossibility of a satisfactory relationship between the image and the real? Not that reality television should be doubted and immediately classified as manipulative fiction, but even the least adulterated image can only reveal so much. The very 'unimpeachability' or stability of the original documents that form the basis for archival non-fiction films is brought into question: the document—though showing a concluded, historical event—is not fixed, but is infinitely accessible through interpretation and recontextualisation, and thus becomes a mutable, not a constant, point of reference. A necessary dialectic is involved between the factual source and its representation that acknowledges the limitations as well as the credibility of the document itself. The Zapruder film is factually accurate, it is not a fake, but it cannot reveal the motive or cause for the action it shows. The document, though real, is incomplete.

Notes

The original text from which this is an extract moves on to consider further issues and examples.

1   The Grassy Knoll is on Elm Street just to the right of the presidential limousine as Kennedy was shot.

2   'The Zapruder Footage', *The Late Show* (BBC2, 22.11.1993).

3   The Warren Commission (so called because its president was Justice Earl Warren) was set up 29 November 1963 by President Johnson to investigate the assassination of John Kennedy. Its findings were that Lee Harvey Oswald alone killed Kennedy from the sixth floor of the Texas School Book Depository, a building behind and to the right of the President's car. In order to prove their findings (and thus to refute all claims of a conspiracy) the Warren Commission had to prove that the shots could have all been fired by one person which necessitated what became known as the 'magic bullet theory': the theory that one bullet could have entered Kennedy's neck from the back, exited, changed direction in the air, hit Governor Connally (also in the car) twice before emerging from his body unscathed. The Warren Commission's report omitted certain key frames from the Zapruder film (Nos. 208–11), despite asserting that the first bullet struck Kennedy at frame 210, claiming this was an oversight. Very quickly the report's use of the Zapruder film to substantiate its claims became the focus of conspiracy theorists who believed the Commission deliberately obscured the truth of Kennedy's assassination. In May 1964 the Commission conducted a re-enactment of the assassination based on the Zapruder footage. As Simon comments, 'The re-enactment's production as representation thus came to substitute for the real event but was used in a process that rewrote the event' (Simon 1996: 39).

4   Certain frames from Nix's film disappeared, conspiracy theorists assume because they would have contradicted the Warren Commission Report's findings. Also, in *The Men Who Killed President Kennedy* (Central Television, 1988), Beverly, one of Jack Ruby's ex-employees, maintains that the home movie she shot from just behind Morland was handed over to the FBI but subsequently disappeared.

5   From the introductory commentary of *The Men Who Killed President Kennedy* (Central Television, 1988).

6   *The Men Who Killed President Kennedy.*

7   *The Late Show* (BBC2, 22.11.93).

8   *Don DeLillo: The Word, the Image and the Gun* (Omnibus, BBC1, 27.9.91).

9   Cf. *The Trial of Lee Harvey Oswald* (David Greene, 1976) and *The Trial of Lee Harvey Oswald* (London Weekend Television, 1986). The former dramatisation of Oswald's hypothetical trial presumes that Ruby did not kill Oswald so the latter was able to stand trial but ends just before the verdict is announced, thereby circumventing the problem of establishing his guilt or innocence. The latter was part of an occasional LWT series in which individuals were put on trial in a studio but using real lawyers, witnesses and jury members; the verdict in this instance was that Oswald acted alone in the murder of President Kennedy. (The other people put on trial in the series were Richard III, Roger Hollis and—using a slightly different format whereby her policies are tried as opposed to her—Margaret Thatcher.)

10   Just such an example of the 'strange incidents' impinges directly on *Rush to Judgement* as one of the eye-witnesses, railway worker Lee Bowers, is killed in a car accident three months after giving the interview. De Antonio does not explicitly make the connection between Bowers' interview (in which he talks of seeing three cars apparently casing the car park behind the Grassy Knoll in the run up to the assassination) and his death, but coupled with Jones' powerful words the implication is obvious.

References

Arthur, Paul (1997) 'On the virtues and limitations of collage', *Documentary Box*, 11 (October): 1–7.

Barthes, Roland (1957) *Mythologies*, London: Paladin [1973].

Britton, Andrew (1992) 'Invisible eye', *Sight and Sound*, 1 (10; February): 27–9.

Carroll, Noël (1996) *Theorising the Moving Image*, Cambridge: Cambridge University Press.

Comolli, Jean-Louis (1980) 'Machines of the visible', in Teresa de Lauretis and Stephen Heath (eds) *The Cinematic Apparatus*, London: Macmillan.

Michelson, Annette (ed.) (1984) *Kino-eye: The Writings of Dziga Vertov* (transl. Kevin O'Brien), Berkeley and Los Angeles: University of California Press.

Nichols, Bill (1994) *Blurred Boundaries: Questions of Meaning in Contemporary Culture*, Bloomington and Indianapolis: Indiana University Press.

Ouellette, Laurie (1995) 'Camcorder dos and don'ts: popular discourses on amateur video and participatory television', *Velvet Light Trap*, 36 (Autumn): 33–44.

Simon, Art (1996) *Dangerous Knowledge: The JFK Assassination in Art and Film*, Philadelphia: Temple University Press.

Wasson, Haidee (1995) 'Assassinating an image: the strange life of Kennedy's death', *CineAction!*, 38 (September): 5–11.

White, Hayden (1987) *The Content of the Form: Narrative, Discourse and Historical Representation*, Baltimore and London: Johns Hopkins University Press.

Williams, Linda (1993) 'Mirrors without memories: truth, history and the new documentary', *Film Quarterly*, 46 (3; Spring): 9–21.

Zimmerman, Patricia (1995) *Reel Families: A Social History of Amateur Film*, Bloomington and Indianapolis: Indiana University Press.

Part VI

Docudrama: Border Disputes

31

Dramadoc/Docudrama: The Law and Regulation

Derek Paget

'Legalling'

My argument here will be that the law has become ever more important to the dramadoc/docudrama, partly because of the ambiguity of dramatic realism as practised in film. Responsibility for the documentary element has increasingly devolved on to legal teams partly as a result of changes in the television institution and partly because of the shifts in form.

The legal and regulatory frameworks that have grown up around dramadoc/docudrama are more significant than for any other category of television programme, which is strange given that dramadoc/docudrama is an occasional rather than a regular part of scheduling. 'Legalling' is the term that has come to designate the process of legal checking of programmes before and during their making. Although the ultimate responsibility rests with the owners or governors, programme makers have to accept that they are the ones who may be asked, in court, to justify their decisions and to demonstrate that the factual basis for their programme is legally sound. Legalling provides a kind of anticipatory defence for the media institution—one that is designed to avoid the courts and the costs of a successful suit. Some claim that this can act as a brake on creativity, amounting to censorship, and can lead to a 'writing by committee' . . . Drama that is 'based on fact' is something of a legal minefield precisely because it relies so much on information both in and at the edges of the public domain. Even where events are a matter of record, the extent of the understanding of those records can be an Achilles' heel. Facts can easily be contested by those who claim to know more or to know other facts or who assert that certain facts have been misunderstood. The investigative thrust of research can lead the drama into difficulty. It is easy too for similarities to exist in work in different media based on the same facts and for accusations of research plagiarism to arise. Mixed forms are more in danger of breaching copyright laws than freely imagined fictional forms.

In 1996 several writers accused Granada of using their work without acknowledgement in the factual drama series *In Suspicious Circumstances*. This popular programme presents crime costume dramas in which historical cases are re-enacted and is in many ways the direct descendent of the illustrated newspapers of the nineteenth century and of the 'True Crime' type of periodical of today. Although the series has the obvious advantage over dramadoc of telling stories from the past, so that protagonists are beyond suing the producers, its reliance on research means that overlaps with the work of other researchers have occurred.

One such writer, Andrew Rose, felt things had gone beyond overlap; he believed that his book *Scandal at the Savoy* had been plagiarised for an episode of *In Suspicious Circumstances* ('*Crime passionnel*'). While Granada openly acknowledged that the book was known to their researchers, their defence was that the episode and the book happened to be based on the same material, which was in the public domain. Ian McBride said in the *Observer*: 'I don't think some writers appreciate how much research we do from a wide variety of sources, such as the Public Record Office, Crown Prosecution Service and newspapers' (27 October 1996).

The level and quality of the research in the dramadoc/docudrama are not only what set it apart from other television drama, they are what enable lawyers to defend producers and television companies against such charges of plagiarism. When the case against Granada came to court, of twenty-one claims made for infringement of copyright, four were upheld and the others dismissed. Being challenged on authenticity of research is, in terms of the response, perhaps rather like being in a traffic accident—you should never admit liability but you have to be aware that blame could eventually be apportioned according to the law of the land.

The territory of the dramadoc/docudrama, however, is living individuals and the organisations they work for. The principal worry here is that persons who have become unwilling dramatic protagonists will claim they have been 'defamed' by the programme (in other words, had their reputation damaged in the eyes of the world). If they think they can show that the programme's view is inaccurate or unfair according to the facts, they may seek damages by becoming the plaintiff in a court case. Similarly, if an institution thinks it has been defamed, it can have recourse to the law. Institutions and their representatives can command large resources and are often very jealous of their public image.

Geoffrey Robertson and Andrew Nicol, in their standard British work on the subject, note that media law is 'lucrative . . . high in profile . . . and in a state of exponential growth' (1992: xvi). Costs are increased in a controversial programme category like dramadoc/docudrama, and in co-production further costs are incurred because legalling must also be done by lawyers from the coproducing nation or nations. Although the two legal systems in Britain and America have many common points of reference, there are key differences. In any event, the legalling process is a necessary and unavoidable one, which takes account of both the legal responsibilities of broadcasters and the requirements of the law. I shall first summarise the latter.

Defamation

Defamation in legal terms is the publication or broadcast of false information that causes damage to the plaintiff's reputation. It is understood as either libel (the written form of defamation—hence 'publication') or slander (the spoken form—or 'broadcast' in its most general sense). In terms of these definitions, a television programme can be regarded as both publication and broadcast. Although dramadoc/docudrama is especially vulnerable to charges of defamation, court cases are relatively rare. This is partly because of the expense and uncertainty associated with litigation, partly because the research element can be mobilised to justify what has been published and/or broadcast to the satisfaction of the law, and partly because the law on both sides of Atlantic is still amenable to the notion that 'fair comment' on a public subject, made in an informed manner, is justified in the wider public interest.

Fundamentally, media lawyers assess risk by applying 'a working test of "potential actionability" to the material contained in programmes they legal' (Robertson and Nicol, 1992: xvii). They must be satisfied that the possibilities are low to non-existent before they can perform their most significant pre-transmission task—the signing of the insurance certificate that protects the television company and its employees from legal action by third parties. 'We cannot start shooting', Sita Williams told me, 'until Goodman Derrick [Granada's London-based legal representatives] underwrite the script.' Having sought reassurance that that programme defames neither persons nor organisations, the lawyers' opinion persuades insurers to give 'E & O' (errors and omissions) cover to the programme maker. In the event of action this insurance will pay for a defence (and any costs incurred should the case go against the defendants).

[However] a good deal of legal comment on the form occurs at the margins of the law. The notion of dramadoc/docudrama as a 'media event' is useful here, as it points up the fact that debate in a society continues around and beyond a transmission, especially if it is controversial. There are similarities with the 'moral panic' of sociology (or the flurry of discussion that can occur around some contentious social problem or event). The agenda for wider public debate is at least partly set by the media, and in particular cases politicians and even governments join the fray. This occurred, for example, in the case of the 1980 Associated Television (ATV) dramadoc *Death of a Princess*, which famously occasioned a Middle Eastern nation, Saudi Arabia, to break off diplomatic relations with Britain. It is not unusual for the opening exchanges in the public argument to be evident in pre-publicity and at press previews. When controversy is generated by the contesting of the programme's view of the facts, the news media tend to become very active, as the 1992 Granada/HBO production *Hostages* demonstrated (a dramadoc about western captives in Beirut).[1]

At such times the air can become thick with the threat of legal action. Solicitors, especially those retained by wealthy individuals, are particularly fond of the 'letter before action' as a ploy to try to prevent publication or transmission. The letter characteristically warns an organisation or individual that action may be taken against them. The request for withdrawal and/or emendation of the offending material is then made overtly or tacitly. The print media are willing enough on such occasions to follow up on the implication of such manoeuvres: that there may be some kind of inaccuracy in a planned programme. Casting doubt on factual provenance [as a letter from the Beirut hostages did on the morning of *Hostages'* transmission in Britain] can be a problem at the point of reception.

With drama-documentary, the Granada executive Ian McBride remarks, 'there's always somebody who doesn't want it made.' Both *Hostages* and *Fighting for Gemma* [about a child leukaemia victim who lived near the nuclear plant at Sellafield in Cumbria] were opposed, the former by the hostages themselves, the latter by a powerful commercial organisation, British Nuclear Fuels Limited (BNFL). In neither case did opposition result in legal action, but lawyers' letters are nonetheless routine elements in the making of a dramadoc/docudrama. Hostage John McCarthy's literary agent Mark Lucas was particularly active in this regard before the transmission of *Hostages* and, although he was unable to prevent the broadcast, he may have helped to reduce the audience for the programme.

The Lawyer's Work

During the production process legalling involves regular, even daily, consultation between producers and lawyers. At Granada complete scripts are sent, and alterations to scripts faxed, to Goodman Derrick. As scripts are honed and refined, so the assembly of documentary material authenticating the script also proceeds and lawyers cross-check the factual basis for particular lines and whole speeches with the producers and/or researchers. Of course, all television drama is checked for potential legal problems, and to some extent dramadoc inherits the potential for controversy possessed by the factual, documentary side of its provenance. But it is a form that needs even more careful vetting because of the sensitive nature of the material that often dramatises the lives of living people and active contemporary institutions. In practice, this means that lawyers must see all scripts at all stages of their production—from treatment to post-production—for them to be able to advise and comment.

The producer's marginal comments in working scripts of *Fighting for Gemma* demonstrate the close interface between the creative and legal teams. Although aesthetic questions are sometimes raised, the bulk of marginal comments refer to legal matters and the programme makers' fear of running foul of a large institution like BNFL. On Sita Williams' 'Principal Working Script' of *Fighting for Gemma* such marginal comments as 'Q RP', 'Send to RP' and 'RP' are by far the most frequent ('RP' is the lawyer Robin Perrot of Goodman Derrick). Next in frequency is the comment 'Check', which refers to the research base within the Granada organisation itself. In practice, this usually means files that are compiled and held by producers themselves. The present costs of making television programmes tend to preclude the option of the writer-researcher, so the responsibility for the factual base lies very much with the producer, aided by the lawyer.

There are many places in the script of *Fighting for Gemma* where 'input' was very direct and a speech or section of dialogue was cut or amended as a result of legalling. In general, this produces a circumspection that is the antithesis of plain speaking. A line spoken by the mother: 'Sellafield caused her [her daughter Gemma] to have leukaemia' was changed as a result of Robin Perrot's view that such a statement might be taken as defamation by BNFL. It became a more circumspect but less passionate interrogative: 'Are you saying Sellafield didn't cause her leukaemia?' Lawyers find such a phrase altogether easier to defend. On page 75, a line of the Mother's was again altered for similar reasons: 'That place caused Gemma to have leukaemia!' became 'Gemma's got leukaemia.'

The effect of the linguistic shift is inevitably to diminish the real mother's 'fight' somewhat. The contrast with the language the real mother, Susan D'Arcy, tended to use during her traumatic suffering could not be more stark. When she was interviewed by the *Today* newspaper's reporter Penny Wark (10 November 1993) she described how she refused to allow her husband, a contract-worker at Sellafield, to blame himself for their daughter's illness: 'I said, "That's not true. It's Sellafield done it to you without you knowing." ' The article's headline is even stronger, paraphrasing Susan D'Arcy in a way that would certainly have caused problems in a dramadoc: 'I want them to admit they [Sellafield] killed my girl.' In law, Susan D'Arcy (the character in a filmed drama) does not have the same rights of free speech as Susan D'Arcy (the real-world individual).

Because the lawyers work a good deal with the media, their sensitivity to legal requirements is tempered by their recognition of the values and aspirations of the programme makers. They become quasi-media professionals as a result of collaboration. In Alasdair Palmer's words, a lawyer 'has this very difficult job—not wanting to destroy the film, but wanting to protect us legally'.[2] Robin Perrot and Patrick Swaffer of Goodman Derrick have often been involved with Granada dramadocs (Perrot legalled *Hostages* and *Fighting for Gemma*, Swaffer *Goodbye My Love*, and Oliver R. Goodenough of New York's Kay, Collyer and Boose and Harvard Law School has legalled extensively for HBO, including *Hostages* in the USA). As lawyers particularly experienced in entertainment law in general, and dramadoc and docudrama in particular, their work is a little-understood but vital part of the process. The success of the collaboration can be measured in one sense by the infrequency of court action.[3]

Regulatory Bodies and Frameworks

Programme makers are constrained not only by the law but also by the various regulatory frameworks that exist in Britain and the USA. In recent years these have developed rapidly, especially in relation to factual broadcasting. So, for example, the members of the Granada team interviewed for this work were bound by the ITC *Programme Code* and the ITV Network Centre's *Statement of Best Practice*. They had also to be wary of offending the Broadcasting Standards Council (BSC) and the Broadcasting Complaints Commission (BCC). In 1996 these two organisations became one.

The BCC is of course bound by its Charter and has broadly similar internal publications to those of ITV (its *Producers' Guidelines*, for example). Patrick Swaffer observes that broadcasters in general tend to find this panoply of regulation 'onerous and burdensome', but makers of documentary and documentary derivatives find it especially so, particularly when they look in the direction of theatre and film, and even journalism. They feel people are, relatively, freer from restriction in these industries.

The ITC *Programme Code* is a representative example of the assumptions, language and declared intentions of such regulatory instruments. Its Section 3 deals with the question of impartiality and gives the Independent Television Commission's (ITC) response to the 1990 Broadcasting Act's strictures on the preservation of 'due impartiality . . . as respects matters of political or industrial controversy or relating to current public policy'. 'Due' is here defined as 'adequate or appropriate to the nature of the subject and the type of programme'. Paragraph 3.7 of this section deals especially with drama and drama-documentary. It recommends that 'plays based on current or very recent events be carefully labelled' and asserts that dramadoc (it does not use the term docudrama) 'is bound by the same standards of fairness and impartiality as those that apply to factual programmes in general'. In a crucial sentence it also recommends: 'The evidence on which dramatic reconstruction is

based should be tested with the same rigour required of a factual programme.'
The *Statement of Best Practice: Factual Drama on Television*, published by the
Independent Television Network Centre in 1994, underscores these regulatory
requirements. Its 'Guidelines for drama-documentary' contains almost identical statements (see Corner and Harvey, 1996: 253–4). The BBC's *Producers'
Guidelines 1993*, meanwhile, talk similarly of the 'obligation to be accurate'
(see Kilborn and Izod, 1997: 153).

Additionally to the requirements in other kinds of factual programming,
the ITC *Programme Code* document recognises that: 'Impartiality may need
to be reinforced by providing an opportunity for opposing viewpoints to be
expressed.' The dramadoc, which is bound in part by the constraints of what
are called 'fictional elements', becomes something of a special case, and the
regulations specifically recommend 'a studio discussion following the drama
itself, or a separate programme providing a right of reply within a reasonable
period' to ensure impartiality. An example of the dramadoc-followed-by-
discussion format was BBC2's *The Late Show* of 21 September 1992, when one
item was a follow-up discussion of *Hostages*.

The ITC *Programme Code* acknowledges cultural anxiety about the form by
providing this self-reflexive scheduling. Acknowledging that 'the boundaries
between what is fact and what is fiction may become blurred', it attempts to
legislate by stating: 'a clear distinction should be drawn between plays based
on fact and dramatised documentaries which seek to reconstruct actual
events'. Its answer, in many ways the 'custom and practice' answer of the
Granada dramadoc tradition itself, is that anything which attempts reconstruction should be 'clearly labelled as such, so that the fictional elements are
not misleadingly presented as fact'.

Because dramadocs often address issues of public policy, there are always
likely to be vested interests contesting the view taken by the programme. The
form's claim to be a vital part of the democratic process in Britain and America
rest partly on this factor. Todd Gitlin quotes Barbara Hering, an NBC lawyer:
'If justified by the facts, [docudrama] performs a public service, but if the facts
are not as portrayed, the possible undermining of the public's faith in their
institutions would not only be unfair but a real disservice to our audience'
(1994: 173). This distinction is crucial, and the public's faith in the main
source of its day-to-day information—the television—is at issue here.

In the USA there is a central regulatory agency, the Federal Communications Commission (FCC) which was developed from the earlier Federal Radio
Commission in 1934. This body is currently extending its control of modern
media to include the new technologies of cable television and the Internet.
Historically, it has been concerned primarily with such matters as the allocation of frequency bands for transmission and the limitation of monopoly in
broadcasting. It has had some influence over the content of commercials and

programmes, but is often seen by media commentators as a somewhat craven servant of the commercial interests that have always dominated American broadcasting. First Amendment guarantees of free speech have ensured a rather looser monitoring of US docudrama. At times, monitoring can come down to State, rather than Federal, legal precedent.

Before a docudrama can be transmitted by an American network, the script must pass through three layers of scrutiny: by the network's own legal, 'errors and omissions', and 'broadcast standards and practices' departments. All networks have guidelines, just as the BBC and ITV do. Guidelines offered by the NBC (see Rosenthal, 1995: 248–50) do not refer specifically to docudrama but to 'fact-based movies and mini-series'. This is a much broader swathe of fact/fiction drama, which is to be expected in view of the less substantial cultural commitment to the investigative dramadoc tradition in the USA.

If the reasons for this looser definition are historical and cultural, the demands made are very similar to those in the ITC *Programme Code*. NBC requires the producer to provide 'substantial backup, including multiple sources', and to 'send one copy of the annotated script to the NBC Program Standards Department and a second copy to the NBC Law Department'. The NBC *Annotation Guide* offers detailed instructions on this aspect of the script preparation. Finally, NBC draws the attention of producers to various independent research agencies whose assistance they recommend; specifically, they mention Fact or Fiction, an organisation formed expressly to deal with the fact-based movie and the mini-series. Granada, of course, still has its own research department to assist its producers.

'Release forms', which are used extensively in documentary proper, are recommended for use in docudramas too. A release form, signed by the real protagonists in a true story, will ensure that they cannot take action after they have been portrayed in a drama. As Robertson and Nicol put it, 'Consent to publication is a complete defence' (1992: 94). Rhona Baker reproduces a dummy release for would-be producers to copy (1995: 258–9) and Alan Rosenthal gives advice on waivers (1995: 212). Granada dramadocs have yet to go down this road; they are still governed by the rights of the investigative journalist to comment on matters in the public domain. This resistance to allowing a power of veto to protagonists has advantages, and not just financial ones. The British tradition has, perhaps, more room for manoeuvre. Oliver Goodenough remarked in his 1996 conference paper that in the USA 'the legal end [was] more advanced', but described British dramadoc as 'creatively stronger'.

In and Out of Court

Goodenough observes that 'the [US] courts have worked out a First Amendment analysis that permits [docudrama] to be made with relative safety from legal challenge'. He stresses, however, that 'staying in this area of safety . . . depends on the producer acting responsibly'. The case which helped to establish this situation legally was that of Davis *versus* Costa-Graves (1987), in which the latter film director's depiction of historical events in his 1982 *Missing* was challenged. His opponent in court represented a US State Department unhappy with the way American involvement in the Chilean Army coup of 1973 had been portrayed in the film. Goodenough quotes the final view of Judge Milton Pollack:

> Self-evidently a docudrama partakes of author's license—it is a creative interpretation of reality—and if alterations of fact in scenes portrayed are not made with serious doubts of truth of essence of the telescoped composites, such scenes do not ground a charge of actual malice. (Goodenough, 1989: 29)[4]

What should be especially interesting to the student of the media here is the judge's apparent invocation (and misquotation) of the celebrated definition of documentary given by John Grierson in the 1930s (the 'creative treatment of actuality'). As is often the case, Grierson's 'treatment' is rendered as 'interpretation', and his 'actuality' becomes 'reality'. Such semantic shifts bear out a widely held critical view that documentary's aesthetic power of 'creative interpretation' has been at least as important as its claim to represent the actual/real. The slippage between 'real' and 'true' has a long history. It would be a mistake to expect the law to have anything other than a pragmatic view on this; as Goodenough said in his conference paper, 'the law is a working-through at a societal level of ethics and morality'. The status of documentary as a mode of communication is routinely collapsed into its status as a mode of social exploration. But problems multiply as soon as drama is introduced into the equation. It is no wonder that cultures that have developed a 'documentary perception' struggle with forms that merge aesthetic and informational functions.

At the legal level, however, producers on both sides of the Atlantic are channelled towards a notion of 'due impartiality' by both legal and regulatory frameworks. The balance in both legal systems is in favour of the 'responsible producer', and it is this that ensures that programmes continue to be made. What can happen if the process goes wrong, however, was illustrated all too clearly in the case of a 1989 BBC television play *Here is the News*, written by G. F. Newman, in which a character called David Dunhill was so closely modelled on a real journalist—Duncan Campbell—that he was able to sue the BBC (and win) in 1990.

Deploying his own investigative skills to devastating effect, Campbell demonstrated just how much detail of his own life had gone into Newman's Dunhill, proving that a change of name is not a sufficient tactic to avoid the charge of defamation. Goodenough says on this point: 'Merely changing names, events, locations or physical features will not in itself prevent recovery by someone who claims to be recognisably portrayed.' He cites a 1983 case in America that was similar but racier: an actual 'Miss Wyoming' 'was able to win the issue of identity against *Penthouse* magazine when it ran a story about a fictional Miss Wyoming of a different name, who twirled batons and levitated men through oral sex' (Goodenough, 1989: 5).

In the UK particularly there is a further, unfortunate dimension: the law-suit has become the privilege of the rich and litigious. Robertson and Nicol remark: 'Libel actions launched by wealthy and determined individuals can be enormously expensive to combat' (1992: 43). The notion that you have to be rich to get justice is not a happy one for the British legal profession: 'Massive libel awards to unprepossessing plaintiffs contrast too starkly with the inability of the average citizen to obtain a right of reply or to be protected against media intrusion into private joys and griefs' (Robertson and Nicol, 1992: xviii).

Although Granada's programme makers have become inured to the occa-sional 'furore' and to the solicitor's 'letter before action', they did face legal action on the 1990 film *Why Lockerbie?* (called *The Tragedy of Flight 103: The Inside Story* in the USA). This had just concluded when I interviewed Alasdair Palmer in 1994. According to him, the problem with *Why Lockerbie?* was that it was 'critical of a large American company which hadn't yet gone bankrupt'. On this occasion, Palmer had to go beyond the normal legalling procedures and provide lawyers with a 'script in which each line had a number which referred to a document attached to it'. The case was eventually settled out of court.[5]

Nor is reference to the regulatory body for independent television an unheard of event. The ITC censured Carlton for its film *Beyond Reason* (a 1996 film based on a sensational 1991 murder case in which an army officer's wife was murdered by his lover). By contrast, in 1997 it upheld as valid the treat-ment of the subject of child abuse in the Meridian Television dramadoc, *No Child of Mine*, against a series of complaints. The censure followed complaints by the murdered woman's parents. Doubts about the facts in the second example were dispelled by the programme's use of confidential files made avail-able by a real-life victim. Oliver Goodenough believes that more developed American precedents on the matter of privacy will soon become part of British law too and that the days of reliance on regulatory checks and balances are as good as over.[6]

The BBC's problems with fact/fiction mixes in recent years have made the organisation more cautious. In addition to *Here is the News*, two other films caused controversy: the Charles Wood tele-play *Tumbledown* and Alan Bleasdale's *The Monocled Mutineer*. *Tumbledown* told the story of Robert Lawrence, a Guards officer who was badly wounded in the 1982 Falklands War. Necessarily, it depicted in a way that might be seen as controversial not only a number of Lawrence's actual colleagues, but also the institution of the British army itself, and it was due for transmission on the eve of a General Election. Alterations were made to the film and transmission was delayed until 1987. Ian Curteis' *The Falklands Play*, meanwhile, caused almost as much of a problem even though it was not transmitted at all. I have argued elsewhere that this particular controversy over representations of the Falklands War betrayed a society deeply troubled by, and unable to resolve, antithetical views—unable any longer to smoothe them into the kind of consensus that was evident in, say, 1950s films representing the Second World War.[7]

In 1988 *The Monocled Mutineer* was shown as a four-part dramatisation based on a book by William Allison and John Fairley. It told the story of a First World War deserter from the British army, Percy Topliss. The film was heavily attacked for allegedly taking liberties with the truth. The *Daily Mail* was prominent in claiming errors and several newspapers ran editorials on the subject. In the context of a decade in which the government in power was prone to regard the BBC as a left-inclining, hostile institution it was perhaps not altogether surprising that the BBC lost its appetite for factually based drama for a while after these problems. The institutional aim of Charter renewal left the BBC vulnerable at this point in its history—the last thing it needed was controversies over fact-based drama.

The end result of a combination of regulation, increased legal activity and general cultural suspicion of the form has been a defensive-mindedness on the part of broadcasters. They are after all likely to be under simultaneous attack (in the worst scenario) from several quarters: persons or institutions depicted in a dramadoc (and unhappy with their depiction); the legal representatives of such persons or institutions; regulatory bodies; their own employers; and a wary public. Granada's Ian McBride takes the view: 'Because you know this kind of thing will happen, the demands on you are so much higher. We do quite a lot of work in pre-production in trying to construct what kind of attacks are likely to be launched against us.'

Nevertheless, there is a tendency towards strategies that avoid risk, which is to some extent reinforced by the training and institutional practices of lawyers themselves. Robertson and Nicol make the point that lawyers are 'inevitably more repressive' than the law itself:

> because they will generally prefer to err on the safe side, where they cannot be proved wrong. The lawyers' advice provides a broad penumbra of restraint, confining the investigative journalist not merely to the letter of the law but to an outer rim bounded by the mere possibility of legal action. (1992: xvi–xvii)

Libel actions are customarily fought on a combined defence of 'justification' in terms of available facts and 'fair comment' following from this, and Patrick Swaffer notes that 'a jury finds this difficult'. With courts finding it more difficult to attribute meaning than any student of literary theory, it is no wonder he admits that 'lawyers are cautious about meaning'.

International co-production makes the process of legalling still more diffi-cult and the likelihood of cautious solutions more probable, because of inher-ent differences not just between two legal systems, but also between two cultures of broadcasting. In Britain and the USA the test of potential action-ability takes slightly different forms. For Americans, as I have noted, the First Amendment to the Constitution grants a right of free speech to citizens. Britain currently lacks a constitutional guarantee of this right. In the USA the prin-ciple has also been established, through precedent, that 'recovery [for public individuals] is only possible if it can be shown that the publisher of the false libel acted with actual malice'; for private individuals, 'a showing of negligence in the publication of the defamatory falsehood' is required (see Goodenough, 1989: 5). In Alasdair Palmer's words, 'the burden of proof is not on you as the film maker [as it is in the UK], it's on the plaintiff to prove that you're wrong.'

There is no doubt that US broadcasters have benefited from First Amend-ment-protected precedental cases such as the *New York Times versus* Sullivan case of 1964 (in which the US Supreme Court ruled that a newspaper has a right to make allegations against a public figure provided these could be proved 'honestly and diligently made'). As Robertson and Nicol remark, this judge-ment paved the way for such historic exposés as Watergate and Irangate; in the UK this kind of investigative journalism tends to attract a debilitating barrage of writs (1992: 103). As a result, caution is the watchword in Britain. Although Robertson and Nicol define journalism as 'not just a profession [but] the exercise by occupation of the right to free expression available to every citizen', they acknowledge that, historically, Britain has hedged around this right with 'special rules' developed by Parliament and the courts. In the absence of any legislation on freedom of information, a largely precedent-led tradition of free speech has grown up (1992: xv–xvi).

Significantly, in offering advice to would-be programme makers, Patrick Swaffer notes three principal legal 'worries' for any British lawyer dealing with dramadoc:

1. Defamation: Is anybody identified in the programme whose reputation is likely to be reduced as a result of the programme?
2. Confidentiality: Is any material used in the programme that is confiden-tial or was obtained in confidence?
3. Regulatory framework [Swaffer lists some examples of this].

So Swaffer's training causes him to take the position of the defendant having to prove a case against a plaintiff.

In contrast, Goodenough lists four areas of potential difficulty in relation to media depictions of [real people]:

- Libel and slander
- Privacy
- Publicity
- Trade name
  (Goodenough, 1989: 5)

The shift from defendant to complainant, and the more commercial awareness inherent in 'Trade name', clearly marks out a difference in the American legal view (as does the apparent absence of worry about regulation). But the absence of a strict liability, which in the UK puts the burden of proof on the defendant, is the most notably different feature.

Differences in State and Federal legislation do make for some potential confusion in the USA. With 'privacy and publicity', for example, 'each of the 50 states has its own laws' (Goodenough, 1989: 5). It is true, also, that the American system is prone to entrepreneurial activity as a result of the 'contingency fee system' (a kind of 'no result—no payment' arrangement which actually encourages litigation). The real difference in the two systems, however, remains in the positioning of the burden of proof: in the British system it is necessary to prove that everything that is claimed is true; in the American the plaintiff must demonstrate malice and negligence. Goodenough summarised it in his 1996 conference paper: 'in the UK, the question is, is it the truth? In the USA, the question is, did they do their homework?'

Regulating, Legislating or Censoring?

If the basic structures of criminal law, civil law and legally mandated regulatory bodies are broadly shared by both British and American broadcasting, UK media agencies have been hedged around historically by the kind of informal, gentlemanly (and I use the word deliberately) lobbying and state-sponsored benign repression that have resulted from a self-protecting culture of caution in public matters. But the USA is not necessarily any better. The pre-eminence of the commercial interest has made things simultaneously freer in terms of the legal framework and more restricted in terms of the kinds of programme it is possible to make. Because advertisers want above all programmes that will draw popular audiences, US television has a tendency to take fewer risks with the formats of programmes—and its docudrama tradition is not as 'fact-rich', to use Goodenough's phrase, as the comparable British dramadoc tradition.

In recent years, however, the two cultures and their media institutions have been moving closer together under global market pressures. Robertson and Nicol comment: 'The recent history of moral and political censorship in Britain has been characterised by a move from criminal law to statutory regulation' (1992: 594). As the amount of regulation has increased, so the degree of freedom in Britain has reduced; and as the commercial competition in the USA has become hotter, so the capacity to be innovative and daring (and to be free in that sense) has equally reduced. The co-production dramadoc/docudrama provides a site for the analysis of these cultural pressure-points . . .

[The whole history and structure of British broadcasting, in particular its relationship to regulation and to political, including governmental, controversy] affects British drama-documentary in as much as it is documentary; the rigour expected of a purely factual programme is the base from which the programme must be made. The main laws that must be acknowledged by the makers of dramadoc/docudrama are, therefore, the criminal laws of contempt of court, official secrecy, sedition and obscenity, and the civil laws of libel and breaches of copyright and of confidence. These are reinforced by the various regulatory bodies on both sides of the Atlantic, behind whose rhetoric lurk the twin concepts of 'due impartiality' and 'good taste'. These rough rules of thumb can seem as if they are intended mainly to dissuade programme makers and broadcasters from taking risks, but they can also be seen as a permitted freedom-within-boundaries rather than a free-for-all.

For Granada, the requirements of the ITC *Programme Code* govern all practical decisions, anchoring the drama-documentary to rules of 'due impartiality' inherited directly from the news and current affairs programme. Film, of course, is similarly subject to the law and to censorship, but Ian McBride, for one, believes there is effectively no comparison between the two media:

> The requirement of due impartiality is actually a duty; no feature film maker has that responsibility. Cinema is not regulated like that because it's not seen as carrying a public information role. It's not current affairs, it's essentially seen in an entertainment role, in which the audience elects to go along and watch.

His view as a programme maker is that 'the reasons for the television regulations are actually sound given the more random way television is watched.' Of all the laws likely to impede the making of a dramadoc/docudrama, libel laws are now foremost in the minds of media lawyers, especially as the form focuses more and more on the 'personal story'. British dramadoc producers like Alasdair Palmer look at the US system with something approaching envy: 'I have to think the American system is best because they actually do believe in the freedom of the press—it's constitutionally protected.' He feels that the US system is more enabling in matters of genuine public interest. On the other hand, he is also in favour of the kind of *sub-judice* procedure that obtains in the UK and that prevents the pre-judging of trials, or 'trial by media'. The events surrounding the O. J. Simpson trial of 1995 would seem to bear out this view; an in-built disadvantage of the First Amendment, perhaps, is that it virtually guarantees the trial-by-television that the UK Contempt of Court Act of 1981 prevents.

Robertson and Nicol, however, sound a note of caution: although 'the British media enjoy relative freedom from censorship by comparison with most Third World countries', the situation in America, Canada, France, Scandinavia and Australia is much better from the point of view of freedom of expression. These countries use Article 19 of the Universal Declaration of Human Rights of 1975 as their definition of that freedom. The Declaration reads, in part: 'Everyone has the right to freedom of opinion and expression: this right includes the freedom to hold opinions without interference and to seek, receive and impart information and ideas through any media and regardless of frontiers' (1992: 35). According to international studies quoted by the same authors, the UK was 'sixteenth in the league table of countries that most enjoy freedom to publish'; and this was before the changes in Eastern Europe in 1989 occasioned further slippage. There can be no doubt that the rhetoric of democracy in the UK is beginning to look decidedly windy and that the controversial drama-documentary is at a point at which the culture is very clearly at odds with itself. Brian Winston suggests that 'for non-commercial, state-funded broadcasting not inevitably to mean state control requires, as a first essential, that freedom of expression be constitutionally guaranteed' (Hood, 1994: 39).[8]

Legal Advice

In spite of all the difficulties, broadcasters can and do get programmes on matters of public interest on to a television screen in Britain and America—a part result of the complex but not ineffective history of tradition, case law and precedent. A decreasing consensus on the degree of openness in public information has generated an increasing public distrust of information agencies. As a result, the running check that is legalling has acquired more and more importance since dramadoc first became controversial in the 1960s. The legal contribution to the process is now so direct that it can be easily read as a kind of censorship, and many writers now fight shy of working in a field that is overdetermined by legal and regulatory constraints: no wonder Rob Ritchie (writer of Granada's *Who Bombed Birmingham?*) warns: 'It is a hard and exacting task to write dramadoc.'[9]

It is against this background that we must view the making of drama-documentaries in the British tradition, which is to say programmes that attempt to provide public information on issues of collective importance by means of dramatisations that are firmly backed by research and documentation. It is, however, unsettling to note the sober advice offered by the two media lawyers most closely associated with the programmes discussed.

Oliver Goodenough lists the following 'Suggested Procedures':

- Select a Topic and Characters of Legitimate Public Interest.
- Get Releases.

- Do Voluminous Research.
- Have a Factual Basis for Every Aspect of the Script.
- Stay as Close to Factual Truth as Possible.
- Respect Chronology.
- Do Not Use Composites for Major Characters.
- Depict Dead People [death wipes out rights of libel, slander and privacy].
- Take Particular Care With Certain Topics [gloss: especially 'sex and nudity'].
- Have a Legal Review of the Script and Film.
- Use Disclaimers.
  (1989: 29)

Patrick Swaffer lists four 'Golden Rules' for dramadoc. These are briefer, but not dissimilar:

1. Firstly, fairness and accuracy.
2. Detailed and good-quality research must underpin your description of any events.
3. Work with the evidence you have got, rather than [the evidence] you wished you had: don't listen to rumour and gossip.
4. Best of all make a programme about historic events where the participants are dead and therefore can't sue.

The example (given earlier) of *In Suspicious Circumstances* demonstrates that dead protagonists of course only protect programme makers from the most directly obvious litigants.

While Oliver Goodenough, like many Americans, admires the 'fact-rich and fact-rooted' British tradition, the increasing tendency in dramadoc/docudrama is to focus on specific stories—often of private individuals projected by some experience or other into the public domain—and to steer clear of politically dangerous topics. US networks, like tabloid newspapers, actively seek and often pay for personal stories of unusual (and frequently salacious) experience. Co-production and shared culture have ensured that this tendency is gaining ground in the UK.

Patrick Swaffer notes that in dramadoc there 'is always the risk that, in the most extreme cases, the dramatisation of the story will overwhelm or remove the documentary element of the programme'. This is a tendency that he sees as increasing: 'More recently, this problem has become more acute with the development of drama/ documentaries [*sic*] dealing with personal life stories.' The filmic emphasis on personal detail, buttressed by naturalistic acting techniques, here shifts the ground on which the dramadoc stands somewhat dangerously. Even with a subject of proven public interest, such as euthanasia, there is now a real possibility that the documentary element may be implicit rather than explicit and that legal cases will increase. As Swaffer remarks, more acute problems come with drama/documentaries of personal stories where events have often taken place both in public and in private and there may be entirely conflicting viewpoints on individuals' motives and, indeed, the actual events.

His view appears here to bear out Julian Petley's conclusion that the debate about dramadoc/docudrama 'has become far less politicised in the 1990s' (1996: 24).

'Again and again,' Swaffer says, 'you review with the [creative] team the meaning of the film.' The lawyer must therefore be 'part of a team to assist you with identifying and reducing, or removing risks'. As a result, the lawyer will have 'a good deal of input into the meaning of the programme'. This is seen as a mixed blessing. Programme makers, as we have seen with Palmer and Williams, will often praise the sensitivity of their lawyers on this issue, but the creative shoe undoubtedly pinches at times. At a public debate in 1997 the Channel 4 executive David Aukin called the control exerted by lawyers 'a terrible compromise'—to general acclaim from an audience principally composed of film makers and writers. Charles McDougall, director of Granada's 1996 *Hillsborough*, offered this stoical view: '[lawyers] are there right through to post-production and you have to put up with them.'[10]

I have characterised the new-style programmes more as American docudrama than British dramadoc. They are more fraught with danger than ever before because they aim to be more filmic and less logocentric. Kilborn and Izod note that they claim to offer 'a different level of understanding' (of the documentary) and 'a qualitatively different level of viewer involvement' (as far as the drama is concerned); but perhaps the latter begins to obtrude on the former (1997: 143).

It may be tempting for programme makers to see lawyers as people who pick away at lines of dialogue, whereas artists work beyond words, trying to capture a visual and aural *Zeitgeist*. It is perhaps better to see modern media lawyers having a cultural as well as a legal role. In these times of uncertainty about, and increasing challenges to, facts and information they have become a kind of arbiter of meaning-in-the-text for the industry and within the culture. As well as trying to fix meaning, they have come to represent a figure past whom it is necessary to smuggle other meanings. The job of 'meaning-making', theorised almost out of existence in the modern academy, has devolved on to the lawyer. Patrick Swaffer observed to me caustically that theoretical finessing of the concept of meaning would not get far in a court of law.

Notes

1 In fact, objections to *Hostages* began to be voiced in the press at the beginning of 1992, eight months before transmission.
2 I interviewed Alasdair Palmer in London on 7 October 1994.

3   Both Patrick Swaffer and Oliver Goodenough spoke at the 'Reality Time' conference in Birmingham in 1996; both allowed me to read and make notes on their papers.
4   See also Horenstein et al. (1994: 380–1).
5   The company he was referring to was the airline Pan Am, whose jumbo jet had gone down over Lockerbie. Patrick Swaffer, however, was the lawyer involved in the case, and he pointed out to me (letters of 14 March 1997 and 11 September 1997) that Air Malta was the company which actually sued Granada and Pan Am was 'not involved in any legal challenge to the programme'.
6   In Britain in June 1997 there was a renewal of serious debate about press intrusion into private life following the 'James Cameron Memorial Lecture' given by the *Guardian*'s editor Alan Rushbridger. The so-called 'sex/money debate' is about whether industry self-regulation is sufficient to curb tabloid interest in the sexual peccadilloes of the rich and famous, and whether legislation is required to facilitate more serious investigations of financial malpractice. The death of Diana, Princess of Wales, on 31 August 1997, fanned the flames further and new guidelines from the Press Complaints Commission were issued in September 1997.
7   See Paget (1992: 154–79).
8   Following the 1997 general election, the situation was set to change. The British Labour government pledged to investigate freedom of information legislation and to sign the European Convention on Human Rights.
9   Rob Ritchie was speaking at the 'Reality Time' conference (April 1996).
10 These remarks were made at a British Academy of Film and Television Arts (BAFTA) debate, 'True to the facts', held in London on 3 March 1997.

References

Baker, R. (1995), *Media Law: A User's Guide for Film and Programme Makers*, London, Blueprint.

Corner, J. and S. Harvey (eds) (1996), *Television Times: A Reader*, London and New York, Arnold.

Gitlin, T. (1994), *Inside Prime Time*, London, Routledge.

Goodenough, O. (1989), 'Avoiding legal trouble in preparing docudramas', *New York Law Journal*, 24 November, 5 and 29.

Hood, S. (ed.) (1994), *Behind the Screens: The Sructure of British Television in the 90's*, London, Laurence and Wishart.

Horenstein, M. A., B. Rigby, M. Flory and V. Gershwin (1994), *Reel Life Real Life*, New Jersey, Fourth Write Press.

Kilborn, R. and J. Izod (1997), *An Introduction to Television Documentary: Confronting Reality*, Manchester, Manchester University Press.

Paget, D. (1992), 'Oh what a lovely post-modern war: drama and the Falklands', in Holderness, G. (ed.), *The Politics of Theatre and Drama*, London, Macmillan.

Petley, J. (1996), 'Fact plus fiction equals friction', *Media, Culture and Society*, 18:1, 11–25.

Robertson, G. and A. Nicol (1992), *Media Law*, London, Penguin.

Rosenthal, A. (1995), *Writing Docudrama: Dramatizing Reality for Film and TV*, Boston and Oxford, Focal Press.

32

US Docudrama
and "Movie of the Week"

Steve Lipkin

Film and television docudrama have become attractive, significant means of representing both past and current actualities because they fuse narrative and documentary modes of representation. That same fusion makes docudrama particularly well suited to launch persuasive argument, when its narrative structure warrants the claims developing from documentary "data." The issues of historical validity and ethical commitment entailed in the proximity of a work to the actuality it references become particularly relevant to movie-of-the-week (MOW) docudramas, since these works depend upon being recognized by their audience as topical and current.

This inquiry into MOW docudrama begins, accordingly, by asking why these works have been important, particularly in broadcast and cable programming from the late 1980s through the mid-to-late 1990s. When I asked that question to network executives, producers, and writers, it led to responses so similar it was comparable to listening to the reciting of a mantra: docudrama offers effective television programming material because it is "rootable," "relatable," and "promotable."

The MOW Mantra

Since the 1980s cable outlets have steadily taken audiences away from the three original broadcast networks. Concurrent with audience crossover, MOW docudrama has become a significant part of network and cable programming. While long form television docudrama production may have peaked in the early 1990s, it still provides a substantial portion of program material.

The production of docudrama movies, particularly by ABC, CBS, and NBC, has been a response to the loss of network audience to cable. What television executives, producers, and writers term the "rootable," "relatable," and "promotable" qualities of docudrama properties have made docudrama production an important, logical strategy for attracting audience, and for the networks, recapturing lost demographics. Due to its "rootable" material—the current and often notorious nature of its actual subject matter—docudrama can be convenient to promote. The desire for "relatable" material has led to narrower choices of subject matter. The preference for stories "based on" or "inspired by" actual events with female central characters reflects directly the ongoing effort by both network and cable to win, recapture, and maintain what they define as the core of their target audience, women between the ages of eighteen and forty-nine. The desire for rootable, promotable, relatable material has also resulted in new means of commodifying sources of story product, has fostered a "headline" concept (comparable to "high concept") approach to production and promotion, and has increased the importance of the writer as an intermediary between story subject and producer. The decrease of "torn from the headlines," "true crime" MOW production beginning in the mid-1990s, however, suggests a saturation of the market, the need for alternative strategies and further shifts in the types of docudrama produced.

The Presence of Docudrama: Shifts in Audience

What started in the 1970s with *Brian's Song* and longer form programming such as *Roots* resulted in "true story" material by the late 1980s becoming a major staple of television film fare (Gomery 1987: 203–7). One NBC vice-president estimated that in 1987 docudrama amounted to 75 per cent of both his and other networks' production of made-for-TV movies.[1] That amount remained at around 50 per cent through the early 1990s.[2] It was also during the early and mid-1980s that cable outlets began to attract the audience for network broadcasting (Carter 1994: D1). The erosion of the network audience has continued steadily since then (Mifflin 1995: C13). The dependence on sweeps periods has only intensified the competition for viewers between cable outlets and the original networks. During the February 1997 sweeps, for example, Fox made its strongest showing, historically, earning second place in the number of adult viewers between the ages of eighteen and forty-nine. Fox was the only network of the Big Four to increase its total number of viewers during this period (Rice 1997: 5). This performance added substantially to the pressure the major networks were already under to regain viewers. According to a former network development executive the sweeps only fuel network efforts to get programming material on the air quickly.[3]

Since the late 1980s docudrama MOWs have been a logical form of programming for the networks to turn to in an effort to compete more effectively for audiences. TV movies based on actual subjects are potent weapons in the ratings battles for three reasons. First, docudramas can exploit story subjects that are highly recognizable for their audience. Second, docudramas offer easy and efficient promotion possibilities. Third, docudramas have come to target directly the very audience the networks are attempting to win back.

Rootability

"Rootability" in the MOW mantra means simply that story subject matter has emerged from current events. A story's origins and possible recognizability as "news" confirms its reality status. The unlikely gains plausibility. When a life story becomes entertainment, no matter how bizarre or unlikely the events it will tell about may be, it is a "true" story, rooted in real, established occurrences.[4]

The "roots" of docudrama plots run to varying depths, depending upon how close they are to actual events, actions and people. To codify the issue of proximity, the industry recognizes two basic categories of material: docudramas "based on" their referents, and those "inspired by" actual people and occurrences. Stories "based on" true events have the closer proximity to their subjects and are governed by stricter legal guidelines than stories that are "inspired by" their sources. Generally, it will cost producers more to develop a property that is "based on" true events, not only for the life rights they acquire from the principals, but also to adhere to the criteria enforced by network Broadcast Standards departments. "Based on" scripts require extensive annotation documenting line-by-line dialogue, and character and scene descriptions.[5] "Inspired by" properties offer the attractions of lower cost and greater freedom for artistic interpretation of the original events.

The need for rootability has spawned a sub-industry, dedicated to databasing potentially exploitable news stories and so linking the worlds of journalism and entertainment. The purpose of this service business is to ensure that networks and producers have quick access to likely material, including not only true stories for movies, but also for news magazine shows or talk shows. A major provider of this kind of database subscription service has been Industry R&D (research and development) founded in the early 1990s by Tom Colbert. Over five years Colbert created a network of 550 newspaper and television reporters to feed stories to the IRD database. IRD categorizes and cross-references the stories it brokers by topic.

Dave Caldwell, former IRD story coordinator, explains why the service has been so effective:

> IRD has been able to find and develop over 4,000 stories in five years. [T]hey've had 30 stories optioned for movies, 15 of which have been made. That's remarkable in five years . . . to have that many stories made into movies. Because of that the industry has recognized that IRD is a valuable resource. They've got one

exclusive deal with NBC for movies. If [they] found a story that was of movie calibre [they] would contact NBC immediately. [NBC] would have 24 hours.[6]

The desire for rootable story properties, then, has not only resulted in the further commodification of recycled news, but has also helped codify the classifications of story material. These classifications then become creative constraints that affect the choice and development of possible projects.

Promotability

The very currency of docudrama story properties also ensures their promotability, since news media have already placed these people and events on the public agenda. Thanks to news exposure, audiences probably will "know" something about the figure(s) in a story. Media promotion has only to sell the rest of the equation, the promise that now we'll find out what "really happened."

Docudramas, like other MOWs, must be promoted differently from series programs. A dramatic series with a continuing story line faces promotion constraints that do not limit docudramas. Series can be promoted only during limited periods. The promotion campaign requires extensive advance planning. Multiple episodes are necessary in order to determine if there is an audience for the offering.

A television movie, on the other hand, may only have one crack at an audience, but offers the flexibility of appearing whenever the schedule might accommodate it. The recognizability of docudrama subjects has allowed them to fit well within the demands of television scheduling. Comparable to "high concept" feature film marketing, these stories come pre-equipped with headline concepts that foreground encapsulated explanations of their subject matter. Victoria Sterling, a story editor and former development executive for NBC and CBS, confirms that:

> Docudramas are a lot easier for networks to sell to a movie audience. Their notoriety is one source of how we perceive them. TV movies . . . can be promoted based on what time of year they're airing. During sweeps they're going to be promoted much more. Out of sweeps, it could just be a week prior. You have to be able to get the promos on the air, get the TV guide out, get all your press materials out, and have people very quickly grasp what they'll be watching. They want to get them as quickly as they can, and to get them in numbers. Docudramas have really proliferated because they fit this very well.[7]

Promotability, like rootability, has also shaped the very nature of the docudrama form. Sterling adds that 'as a result of [promotion], I think there's been a retreat from trying things that are going to be riskier, more character-driven, anything that would require more difficulty on the part of the audience'.

Relatability: Narrowing of the Typology

"Relatability" of a story property in the docudrama MOW mantra means that a viewer perceives a character to be "just like me" in circumstances "that could happen to me."[8]

One effect of this has been, as Victoria Sterling's observation (above) suggests, that over the last decade the search for "relatable" properties has progressively limited the range of docudrama story types. Another, less observable, implication of "relatability" has been that the role of the script writer has acquired the additional weight of acting as liaison and even as advocate for story principals.

Relatability will be a function of how a network tries to target what it perceives as its strength in addressing the basic television audience of women between the ages of eighteen and forty-nine. Sterling describes how efforts to link audience and story operated in her work in network story departments:

> The networks always hope for a core of relatability to the main characters in a movie. This was primarily more laid out at CBS when I was there than at ABC, when I was there. At ABC we had a lot more diversity in the movies because it was a different kind of audience. They also were oriented more to family. They would cast movies with both male and female leads. This allowed them to have movies centered more on family stories. Stories at that time would fill family objectives. There was always woman in jeopardy, family in jeopardy, child in jeopardy. You had your basic thriller, your character piece, and your prestige piece. At that time [late 1980s] the leads were also much older: Joanna Kern, Jaclyn Smith, Tyne Daley—the women in those roles were in their thirties, if not close to forty. They were programming primarily for women, for mothers, housewives, women not working outside the home, and most of the dramas had a domestic orientation. The stories were primarily domestic settings. Things that would take place in a suburban community. Suburban Chicago, Atlanta, Detroit.[9]

A corollary of the suburban setting has been to cast characters as white and middle-class, regardless of their actual race and social status, as a way of maximizing property "relatability."

The narrowing of story types has in part been as a result of changes in network management. In 1994–95 CBS attempted to recuperate audience it was losing to NBC by redefining its niche of the target audience. In the early 1990s the CBS audience included rural and older viewers. With a drastic turnover in management in 1994, CBS attempted unsuccessfully to mimic its competition:

> There was a big mandate because they were starting to lose audience, and NBC was competing very strongly. In a very rash and brash move [CBS execs] decided they were going to go all young. Go for a young audience. In order to go young they decided they were going to utilize younger actors, mimicking what NBC was doing. NBC started it, and they started beating out CBS for the movie ratings.[10]

The shift to stories targeting younger, rather than older audiences (and requiring a commensurate shift from casting older to younger actors) has also been
accompanied by a stricter focus on female-centered stories. Through the mid-
and late 1980s docudrama stories were more diverse and inclusive. Dennis
Nemec, whose docudrama screenwriting credits begin in the early 1980s, has
seen this change in relation to his own work:

> TV docudramas have become . . . female oriented. If you look at [my] other docu-
> dramas, in *A Long Way Home* (1981), a family is broken up and tries to get itself
> together, but it's a boy's story about how he can find his brother and sister.
> *Murder in Coweta County* (1983) was a crime drama, your basic good guy, black
> hat vs. white hat, and a period piece. *The Ray Mancini Story* (1985) was a boxer
> story. *A Case of Deadly Force* (1986) was an attorney story. *Held Hostage* was a
> political story in some ways, but with a female lead. The whole demographics of
> it, in my experience of it, began to shift toward the female lead.[11]

In light of the mission to produce a "relatable" product the script writer's role
assumes the functions of an intermediary. The writer represents the interests
of the story principals in the production process, as well as in the completed
script. The added responsibility potentially makes the docudrama screenwriter
increasingly vulnerable to ethical dilemmas. Authenticity of the script necessarily begins with the writer–subject relationship. "Authenticity" cuts both
ways for the writer, who is faced with, on the one hand, the need to present
the substance of the real-life principal, and, on the other hand, to shape creatively a believable, "relatable" character in a fiction narrative.

Typically in a docudrama project it is the producer who initiates the production process by negotiating with the principal(s) for their life rights. The
producer then enters into reporting relationships with the network development executive and, indirectly, the vice-president who ultimately greenlights
the production, all based upon a satisfactory script.[12]

It falls upon the writer to work most directly and extensively with the real-
life principals of the story, not only in gathering the material that will become
the script, but also in explaining to that person what happens to the stuff of
their life once it becomes part of a film.

Writer Bruce Miller (*The Stranger Beside Me*, ABC, 1995) believes it is necessary to exclude the real-life principals from the script-writing process once
he has finished his research with them. He describes the closeness he reaches
with his subjects during the research phase as "gut-wrenching." However, as
he begins to shape a script he tells his principals that "they are dealing with
other priorities than the truth" in the need to present a dramatically effective,
engaging story.[13]

While this approach relieves the pressure of responding to the concerns of
story sources, it limits the potential of their further collaboration, as well as

leaving them susceptible to exploitation. Writer Tom Cook (*Tuskegee Airmen*, HBO, 1995; *Forgotten Evil*, ABC, 1996) argues that the ties he develops in working with real-life principals become the basis for protecting their interests:

> One of the things that really drives us crazy, that really hurts us emotionally, is that we develop relationships with the sources. We're the ones that go out and spend days and weeks in the homes of the people who have been killed or lost a child, or having had something awful happen to them, and we develop the friend-ships with those people. Friendships that are not often respected by the director and the producers that come after us. And more times than I can count, I've been sitting in a story meeting, and having the producer or the network people, for whom this is just one of a dozen things they're dealing with, say, well, why can't we have this guy die a little earlier? And I'm thinking back to the people, that I sat in their living room and wept with over this event that happened. It's hap-pened more than once. I've just lost it. We'll just be holding hands and crying over this horrible event. Now these people, for their reasons which make sense to them, want to change this and move it around and manipulate it. What am I going to go back and tell these people? That this is what's going to happen to their story? Sometimes I can protect them. Sometimes I just won't do it. But I've had the experience where people will look and me and say, why did this thing happen here? That never happened. We never told you that. And I have to try to explain to them what our needs are, what the network's needs are, and that's very difficult.[14]

Dennis Nemec believes that part of his work is to prepare his story subjects for the transformations their material must undergo when he scripts it:

> I have found, without exception, that if you explain to people why you're doing what you're doing, they understand it. If you treat them like they're idiots, like, hey you don't know about the TV business, so I don't want to be bothered by you. I once had a producer say, let them see it when it comes out. I find if you tell them why they understand it. Little by little, scene by scene you prepare them for what's coming. They understand. If I say, look, the network wants this to happen. We know that you know the guy was a bad guy from day one. But that doesn't give the network the suspense it needs. So we're going to play it that you weren't quite sure. They understand. And as long as they see that you're on their side, and it helps me, because I need them for those details. Those wonderful details really give the piece an authenticity that may take the place of some of the accu-racy that's missing. So that it has a tonal authenticity, even if detail and fact may have been bent to accommodate 95 pages.
>
> So I feel good about that in terms of my moral compass, but I let them know what's going to happen.[15]

Tristine Rainer, a docudrama producer/writer who has also published *Your Life As Story* (1997), agrees that the script writer must not only enlist the collaboration of the subject if the script is to be authentic, but that even more, it is the writer's responsibility to foreground the essential uniqueness of that person's story:

> I feel everybody has a completely unique life story and so that, in fact, I hold this idea of story, of personal mythology as something sacred. Each person has a main core story, and that is their contribution. To me, it is a profound concept. My principal allegiance and bond in working with true stories, and in the ones where I have worked with people's stories is to that person.[16]

The practical constraints the docudrama script writer faces in creating "relatable" characters and plot structure then lead logically to ethical considerations. The writer must balance the need to respect the "truth" of a principal's life story with the need to shape a dramatically compelling character. Ultimately the value of the story as history will stem not only from from its proximity to actuality, but also from the extent to which an audience will find what it has to say about that actuality at all compelling.

Further Shifts: Current/Future Trends

Docudrama movies of the week have been a central strategy in the efforts by networks and cable outlets to capture and maintain television audience. The same economic constraints that have led to the production of rootable, relatable, promotable TV movies through the mid-1990s also determine the subsequent direction of docudrama. This is evident in the decreasing amount of docudrama currently on the air, and the concurrent shift in story types from "true crime" to more character-driven, more "inspired by" and more fully fictionalized pieces.

Through 1995 and 1996, approximately 11 per cent of all movies available on broadcast and cable television fit into some form of docudrama.[17] In 1998 an NBC executive estimated that while CBS probably would base onefourth of its movie production on true stories, NBC had dropped from 40 per cent in 1995 to 10 to 15 per cent in 1997, and reduced 1998 docudrama MOW production to 10 per cent of its output. ABC "is somewhere in between, but also dropping fast."[18] The reductions were due to the market reaching its saturation point in 1995.

A number of writers and producers believe that the "true story" market has changed to support less crime-oriented, more inspirational stories. The turn away from "true crime," "ripped from the headlines" story types is due to increasing scrutiny of network and cable outlets through the rating system initiated in early 1997, and continuing pressure from special interest groups to tone down violent programming. In this view the market favors looser, more fictionalized stories because of the lower cost (fewer rights to acquire) and less rigorous legal demands of "inspired by true event" material. Whether such a modified strategy gratifies the needs of TV program providers to win elusive demographics, or the needs of the audience to be told compelling explanations of events and phenomena of their daily lives, or both, remains to be seen.

Notes

1   Charles Freericks, Vice-President of Movies and Miniseries, NBC. Correspondence with the author, April 29, 1997.
2   Alan Rosenthal confirms that in 1991, 43 out of 115 TV movies were docudramas. Rosenthal *Writing Docudrama*, p. 9 (Boston: Focal Press, 1995). See also Steven N. Lipkin, *Real Emotional Logic* (Carbondale: SIUP, 2002), p. 143, for the percentages of docudramas shown during primetime between 1994 and 1997.
3   Victoria Sterling, interview with the author, March 1997.
4   There are literally hundreds of examples of these films with warranted credibility because they are based on events rooted in the news; my personal favorite remains *The Positively True Adventures of the Alleged Texas Cheerleader Murdering Mom* (1993), in which, as described by my local cable guide, "A Texas mother hires a killer to kill off her daughter's rival."
5   In an annotated script page from *Princess in Love*, "BBC" refers to a transcript of an interview with Princess Diana that aired on the BBC in the UK, and "Dimbleby" is the author of a book on Prince Charles referenced in a key to the script. Numbers noted on the page refer to a bibliography of newspaper and magazine articles. See Steven N. Lipkin, *Real Emotional Logic*, p. 145.
6   Dave Caldwell, interview with the author, March 1997.
7   Sterling interview.
8   One writer explained it this way:

> You want to know what the archetypal TV movie is, particularly the NBC movie? We describe it as, "She was just like us, until . . ." You plug in what was unusual about her life. There's several things implicit in the first part of that. The first word, "she," means that most of the focus of these TV movies is about women and women's issues. And most of the network's divisions are run by women. The consensus is that that's the segment of the population that's watching them. They're programming to half the planet, basically. Ever wonder why men don't watch? The second part of it, "she was just like us," who's "us"? "Us" is upper-middle-class white women, living in the suburbs of the cities. It's not rural, full of black folks. So we have a distinct filter, here, on the American experience. (Interview with Tom Cook, March 1997)

9   Sterling interview.
10 Ibid.
11 Dennis Nemec, interview with the author, March 1997.
12 The network vice-president (of movies and mini-series) in turn reports to the vice-president of programming.
13 Bruce Miller, interview with the author, March 1997.

14   Tom Cook, interview with the author, March 1997.
15   Nemec interview.
16   Tristine Rainer, interview with the author, March 1997.
17   See Lipkin, Appendix 1 (143) for the statistics for the Kalamazoo, Michigan area
     cable market for this period.
18   Charles Freericks, correspondence with the author, April 29, 1997.

Bibliography

Caldwell, Dave. Personal interview. March 1997.

Caldwell, John T. *Televisuality: Style, Crisis and Authority in American Television*. New Brunswick, N.J.: Rutgers University Press, 1995.

Carter, Bill. "Rebound for Broadcast TV." *New York Times*, 20 Apr. 1994: D1.

Cook, Tom. Personal interview. March 1997.

Edgerton, Gary. "High Concept Small Screen." *The Journal of Popular Film and Television* 19:3 (1991): 114–27.

Feuer, Jane. *Seeing Through the Eighties: Television and Reaganism*. Durham: Duke University Press, 1995.

Freericks, Charles, Vice-President of Movies and Miniseries, NBC. Letter to the author. 29 Apr. 1997.

Gitlin Todd, *Inside Prime Time*. New York: Pantheon Books, 1983.

Gomery, Douglas. "Brian's Song: Television, Hollywood, and the Evolution of the Movie Made For Television." *Television: The Critical View*, (ed.) Horace Newcomb. 4th ed. New York: Oxford University Press, 1987: 197–220.

Hoffer, Tom W. and Richard Alan Nelson. "Docudrama on American Television." In Rosenthal, *Why Docudrama?* pp. 64–77.

Lipkin, Steven N. *Real Emotional Logic: Film and Television Docudrama as Persuasive Practice*. Carbondale: Southern Illinois University Press, 2002.

Mifflin, Lawrie. "Cable TV Continues Its Steady Drain of Network Viewers." *New York Times*, 25 Oct. 1995: C13.

Miller, Bruce. Personal interview. March 1997.

Nemec, Dennis. Personal interview. March 1997.

Rainer, Tristine. Personal interview. March 1997.

Rapping, Elayne. *The Movie of the Week*. Minneapolis: University of Minnesota Press, 1990.

Rice, Lynette. "NBC Wins; Fox Grows." *Broadcasting and Cable*, 3 Mar. 1997: 5.

Rosenthal, Alan. *Why Docudrama?* Carbondale: Southern Illinois Press, 1999.

Rosenthal, Alan. *Writing Docudrama*. Boston: Focal Press, 1995.

Sohmer, Steve. Personal interview. March 1997.

Sterling, Victoria. Personal interview. March 1997.

Tetenbaum, Abby. Personal interview. March 1997.

Yonover, Neal S. "Ripped From the Headlines! The Absolutely True Story About Writing True Stories as Told by Actual WGA Members!" *The Journal of the Writers Guild of America, West*. August 1995, pp. 14–18.

33

Death of a Princess:
The Politics of Passion, an Interview
with Antony Thomas

Alan Rosenthal

Antony Thomas's *Death of a Princess* reconstructs a journalist's investigation into the death of a young Arab girl. Though its first broadcast generated what is possibly the biggest row ever in the history of British television, the original incident had passed almost unnoticed by the world.

On 15 July 1977, a royal princess and her lover were publicly executed in Saudi Arabia. It took six months for a British newspaper to identify the victims and their crime as adultery. Later a British carpenter, who'd been working in the Gulf, claimed he'd photographed the double execution. Soon another witness entered the scene, a German nanny who claimed to have been a family friend and known the princess well.

As more and more conflicting stories appeared in the press, a major debate opened up in the British Parliament. When the debate and criticism threatened a major diplomatic confrontation with the Saudis, the British foreign secretary apologised to them for his former condemnation of the execution.

At the time of the debate, Antony Thomas was regarded as one of the most noted and probing documentary directors working in England. In 1977 his three-part series on South Africa had won him the highest British television award of the year. More important, in 1974 Thomas had also made three films exploring the Arab world, so that the story of the princess was to fall on fertile ground. *Death of a Princess* is, in fact, based on Thomas's own six-month trail through four countries, as he tried to explore and understand what happened to the Arabian girl and why.

It took some while to settle on the form of the film. Doing a standard documentary was ruled out because of fears expressed by various interviewees. The originally scheduled writer favoured a straight drama. Executive Producer David Fanning, from coproducing station WGBH Boston, argued for a documentary drama because "it combines a rigorous concern for facts, that characterizes the best of journalism, with the narrative thrust and dramatic strength of a screenplay." Docudrama won.

In the film, Antony Thomas becomes the journalist, Chris Ryder (played by Paul Freeman). The story begins at a London dinner party where the question of the princess's fate and what it represents is raised. The action then moves through different locations as the quest for truth goes on. The carpenter recalls the Saudi execution (actually staged in Cairo) in grim detail. The nanny Elsa Gruber (played by Judy Parfit) tells us about the private life of the princess. We visit the school she was supposed to have attended in Beirut. We see the civil war in Lebanon and visit clubs where Arab oil millionaires dance. An elderly Arab princess describes how rich Arab women go looking for sexual outlets by trailing men in their chauffeur-driven Mercedes. Someone else accuses the Saudi government of having taken fifty rebel air force officers up in a government plane and then throwing them to their deaths.

All of this is woven in and around the princess's story. The complete truth about her is never learned. It appears that she bungled her escape plans and was killed on the orders of her grandfather, but much remains unclear. The story of the princess is almost incidental to Thomas's plan. What he is really attempting to do is investigate the social pressures, ideals, and strains of a modern Arab society. It is a society whose inner workings (at least in the late seventies) were mostly hidden from Western eyes.

The central theme of the film and the dilemma of the Arabs is laid down in one of the first scenes, when an Arab professor asks, "How much of our past must be abandoned and how much of your (Western) present is worth imitating?" The issues then discussed include the force of Islam and its relationship to a royal house described by one character as "an autocratic regime having nothing to do with Islamic thought"; the general behaviour of women and their place in Arab society; the civil war in Lebanon; the Palestinian morass; and the question of honour in society and family relationships.

Thomas covers a vast canvas, and his projections have a *Rashomon* quality. Was the princess merely a party lover, or was she a rebel who absorbed the passions of the Palestinian freedom fighters? Was she content with the veil or fighting for a new pure Islam? In the end, it doesn't matter because it is the deeper issue of cultural conflict that stays with us.

When *Princess* was finally transmitted in England by ATV Television on 9 April 1980, all hell broke loose. The Islamic Council of Europe attacked the film, saying, "It has angered the entire Moslem community in the United Kingdom . . . and the British Government cannot escape its responsibility for its ugly conspiracy to discredit the Royal family." When the Saudi Arabian ambassador protested the film, the British foreign secretary sent a personal message of regret to King Khaled. This in turn caused various British members of Parliament to attack the apology. As Labour MP David Winnick remarked, "It is undignified to see the Foreign Secretary apologise to a reactionary State." The furore deepened when Penelope Mortimer, Thomas's first script colleague, wrote a letter to the *New Statesman* magazine on 18 April. Mortimer claimed a deep involvement with the film (denied by Thomas) and damagingly stated that, "with the exception of three people and a family, every interview and every character in the film is fabricated." She also added that no real effort was made "to check information about the domestic life of the Princess, and the man hunting." What the charges implied, in short, was that *Princess* was a work of fiction masquerading as documentary truth.

David Fanning answered the charge a week later, and Thomas discusses this at length in my interview with him. However, controversy over the film increased when it was scheduled for American broadcast by PBS. Five stations belonging to South Carolina public television, as well as stations in Houston and Los Angeles, refused to show it. The Saudi Arabian ambassador protested to the US State Department about the pending broadcast. Representative Clement Zablocki of Wisconsin said the decision to show the film was ill advised. Mobil Oil, which funds much of PBS, called the film "A New Fairy Tale." It also ran huge newspaper advertisements, which quoted Mortimer's "fabrication story" and urged PBS "to exercise responsible judgement in the light of what is in the best interests of the United States." The ads did not mention Mobil's economic interests in Saudi Arabia. In spite of the pressures, Lawrence Grossman, then president of PBS, decided to go ahead with the broadcast.

After the Mobil ads appeared, Mortimer herself seems to have had second thoughts. Thus she wrote to the *New Statesman*, "By fabrication I meant manufacture or construction. If I had meant invented or forged I would have said so." Fanning and Thomas had won a victory but at tremendous personal cost. Apart from the political hullabaloo and the question of documentary truth, there was also considerable personal fallout from the film. Following the broadcast, a number of Egyptian actors were placed on a veritable Arab "black list" and had their films boycotted in Saudi Arabia, Iraq, Sudan, Abu Dhabi, and Oman.

Most of the issues raised by *Princess* are still very much with us today. Of these the most important is freedom of speech. In 1998, freedom of speech and freedom of subject choice in broadcasting are still under fire in too many places. Here I include the Western world, not just the Middle East. One wonders whether *Princess* could be made today. I have my doubts. Thomas managed to say what he wanted and go on living a normal life. Salman Rushdie has not been so lucky. The situation is not good, but with awareness and action there is hope.

Since finishing *Death of a Princess*, Antony Thomas has made *The Most Dangerous Man in the World* (1982) and two programmes on the Christian Right in the United States, *Thy Kingdom Come* and *Thy Will Be Done* (both in 1987). In 1992 and 1993, he also made two films for HBO on the quest for eternal youth and group prejudices in America. In 1996 he published a biography of Cecil Rhodes, the South African entrepreneur and statesman, and also wrote a nine-part TV series on Rhodes, which was broadcast by the BBC in the autumn of that year.

This interview was done with Antony Thomas in Jerusalem in 1993 and marked the beginning of a wonderful friendship.

Rosenthal: Death of a Princess *tells a specific story but also describes the problems within a culture. How did you get involved?*

Thomas: The newspaper reaction to the original story was sensational but didn't really affect me. It was a tragic story, and I didn't want anything to do with it. Then in London I met a very highly placed Saudi gentleman and was given an extraordinary version of the girl's death. It was a version that beautifully expressed the Arab dilemma and had a great deal to say about the democratic nature of our justice. It was a fine, wonderful, classic romantic story. I believed what I heard, and I knew enough about the Arab world that the story connected. And I thought I could tell that story as a drama. I had a lot of leads from that first meeting. I was told that the princess had been to school at the Arab University of Beirut, and I was determined to put flesh on the story, travel through the Middle East and find out as much as I could about her. And I would do a drama, a rather conventional drama on the life and death of an Arab princess, because I felt I had an awful lot to say on that particular story.

Who backed you, and how did you put substance on your research leads?

I presented the idea to ATV, a member of the British Independent Television Network. They were interested in it and off I went, only to discover the research was utterly baffling. I discovered very early on that many of the elements of the story I'd been told were simply not true. The most solid lead I had been given was that the princess was supposed to have met her lover at the Arab University of Beirut. So I felt I should begin there, in Lebanon, and find people who had known her, who had taught her, and her classmates. I also had a lead outside Saudi Arabia, a German woman who had been governess in the household of the princess's grandfather and who knew her personally. However, she was very complicated and legalistic, and it was going to take weeks before we had an agreement and would talk to me. So I thought I would go to Lebanon first and check everything out there. I also thought I should talk to some Arab women about some of the finer details of life in Islamic society, what it means to be a woman in an Islamic society. Then came the shock. After two days in Lebanon, I discovered part of this wonderful dramatic story was nonsense. The girl had never been to the Arab University of Beirut.

However I soon discovered something else very interesting: that the girl had become some kind of mythological figure in the Arab world. Everybody talked very passionately about her, even people who had never known her. She had become both a personal symbol and also a political symbol, and everyone was adopting her to their cause. Thus for a Palestinian family that talked to me about her, she had become a freedom fighter. This ability in the Arab world to deal in myth, hearsay, and legend found strong material in the story of the princess. I was slow to realise this but after a while began to see the importance of all these elements in the story.

How far did you let people know what you were doing? And were you sure from the start it would be a docudrama or were you thinking of a more conventional form?

I think *Princess* would have made a marvellous documentary film based on a journey to discover the truth, where everyone has their own version of who this girl was, depending on who they were themselves. However, when I then started recontacting my interviewees and said, "I'm thinking of a documentary and want you to repeat what you said to me," almost without exception they said, "Are you mad? We are never going to appear on film making these statements about Arab society and womanhood in Saudi Arabia. It's impossible!"

Then I moved to a second stage, which was to say, "Well, what if I dramatise this journey?" I questioned everyone I had interviewed and asked them whether if I used their exact words, they would trust me to create a character who is completely different from themselves, exists in a different context, yet speaks those exact words? The permissions were given, and they formed the basis for the film. I took the interviews, I cut some of them down, but I was very careful to retain their essential sense as in the original.

You were doing your research in Beirut in the middle of a civil war. You must have had many conflicting feelings.

To be in Lebanon at the time of the war was very difficult. And I felt very uncomfortable sitting in this hotel and pursuing some personal obsession while a war was going on. I remember looking out of my bedroom window and across the street onto an apartment block. There was an old man sitting on a balcony lit just by oil lamps, and we made eye contact. And on his face there was such a mark of suffering and tragedy. I felt very uncomfortable. What the hell right did I have going there doing what I was doing? But in a way, it's a little experience like that which is argument for dramatised documentary. We can show those little subtle moments and observations that we remember that don't have a place in normal documentary. It's these very small, subtle moments that one can go back and re-create.

In Lebanon I had a feeling of intrusion, but Saudi Arabia was different. The subject was enormously sensitive, and there was no way I could interview someone and just say, "I am here to ask you about the death of this princess."

Unless I knew the interviewee personally, I would always talk about the general political situation in Saudi [Arabia] and about Islamic law and so on. And then, in the most offhanded way possible, I would say something like, "And what about the story of the princess?" "What story?" And I'd say, "You know, the one that was executed." I would make it seem a little parenthetical thing that I was adding as an afterthought at the end of the interview. I had to go through that charade every time.

Script to Film

Rosenthal: *Was it difficult translating your research into a script?*

Thomas: It was the easiest script that I ever had to write because it simply followed the progress of my journey, and it wasn't necessary to reorder the time sequence. I transcribed all the interviews, and then the only creative thing I did was to say, "Well X is a housewife, I'll make her a journalist. Y is a journalist, I'll make her a teacher." After that it was just a matter of making sure I'd created the right recognisable context for the person.

The first draft I did contained everything. Then David Fanning and I would read the lines and try to feel the point where the attention dragged or the argument stopped being clear. So we were continually cutting and trying to get down to the essence of the drama. It wasn't like the normal way you handle a dramatic script. We weren't changing structure or adding new scenes for old. It was very different.

I understand ATV didn't cover all the budget. How did you raise the rest? And, to deal with what seems the basic problem, how did you find an Arab location for such a potentially controversial film?

It had a ludicrous budget by modern standards, £250,000 sterling. That was ten years ago, and we had to make a drama with forty-five speaking characters in three countries: England, Lebanon, and finally Egypt, where we did the major part of our shooting. ATV gave me half the money, and I raised the other half in two days in MIFED, the international film market, where everybody buys and sells TV ideas.

The big problem of course was finding an Arab country that would let me film the script. That was really tough. I tried everybody; I tried everyone from the Iraqis to the Tunisians to the Algerians. All these countries have got censorship departments, and I had to be very up-front with them. They were all very polite. The Algerians even told me that they applauded the sentiments of the film, but no one wanted to get into a political hassle just to help Mr. Thomas make his film. Finally the Egyptians agreed to let me do the main filming in their country. I guess the deciding factor was their anger at the Saudi rejection of their stand in the '78 Camp David talks with Israel. Lebanon was no problem. It was a country without a government, and you just went in and filmed. As for Saudi Arabia, I had some establishing material that I had shot there previously. Not executions but long shots and general street scenes and atmosphere.

How difficult was it casting your Arab characters?

There's no structure in the Arab world. There's no simple casting book like Spotlight. In fact, a good Lebanese friend of mine said, "You are about to do the most foolish thing in your life. You want to make a realistic film, and you are using Arab actors? You don't understand just how far that is from Arab acting tradition. You'll become a laughing-stock. You are going to produce something so unreal that it will be the end of your career. You'll never get a job again."

Nine weeks before we were supposed to start shooting, I was introduced to this man who was supposed to be the biggest casting director in Egypt. We spent hours talking about every character. He took notes, supposedly knew exactly what I wanted, and we agreed I would come back two weeks before shooting to make my final selection. Well, eventually we came back to this famous casting director, and what did he have? Three Polaroids of his sister, her friend, and somebody else. That was all—and we had to cast forty parts.

So David Fanning and I did everything. We had all sorts of dinners with radio people and film directors. I described every character, and they gave me names. It was frantic. Every day people came pouring into our rooms for preliminary casting. Some thought it was some big Hollywood-type film, and my room was crowded with flowers from actresses who'd sent a bouquet ahead for these parts and sent a bouquet ahead for Mr. Thomas. Then lots of people sent me these sepia photographs. I'd see a handsome man with a Ronald Colman moustache looking about thirty, and then a man of eighty would arrive. It was an absolute scramble, and we were still casting during filming. In fact, when we started we only had half our cast.

How did you feel about doing drama since all your previous experience was in documentary?

Actually it was incredibly easy. I was trying to get as close to reality as possible, and it is simply the story of a man travelling through the Arab world meeting and interviewing people. Now, one of the things that breaks reality is too much choreography within the space, which comes from the tradition of theatre. My rule was that nobody moved unless there was a dramatic reason to do so, because when you interview people you sit side by side, except for when you answer the phone or make coffee. You don't conduct interviews in a highly choreographed way.

My guiding principle was not technique in a theatrical sense but reality, and directing actors toward that end was terribly exciting. It meant draining away all preconceptions and histrionic qualities and bringing it all down to real speech and a truthful reality. Many of the actors, particularly the Arab actors, told me how exciting this was. It was the first time they had been given a chance to attempt realism, and they did it very well because they were talking about things they felt and which concerned them. Their training made them act way over the top, and my purpose was to drain that out of them and recapture a truthful quality and a certain stillness.

As for Paul Freeman, who plays the journalist, he had maybe the hardest job, and he did it marvellously. All he does is say "yes" or "no" and ask the occasional question, yet he brings life to it. The idea was that this traveller should have no context. We wouldn't know whether he was married or single. He's almost a half shadow, and that's not a pleasant demand to place on an actor.

Tell me more about how the actors' roles would sometimes reflect their lives.

In the film, a girl who is supposed to be a teacher represents radical Islam. Now, the film was made before the Khomeini revolution. So it was possible to be very idealistic about what Khomeini stood for, because nothing had been seen in practice. And the girl herself really believed in all those future possibilities. She read the script, became tremendously excited, and the words really became her words.

It's very hard for anyone coming from England or America to imagine the hassles of working in Egypt. I would imagine the difficulty with casting was just the beginning.

You're right. We faced enormous problems of organisation. The telephones didn't work. To call actors, you had to send runners off across the city and all that kind of difficulty. We were often working inside, and because of the lights and lack of air-conditioning the heat was unbelievable. And because the government had the script, we were always frightened that pressure from the Islamic fundamentalists would start to build, and we would be thrown out of the country without completing the film. We were really terrified of that since there had been a number of hostile articles in the Islamic press as to what we were doing, or what they feared we were doing. So we lived on our nerves. At any moment something could explode.

The most difficult day was the day we shot the execution. The budget was tight. We had to shoot a complex scene, and we had 250 extras that we could only afford for one day. We were working under incredible pressure in the fierce heat, and the crowd was starting to get very tense and uncomfortable. The princess was going to be shot and her lover executed with a sword. The scene was very disturbing to the Egyptians, and on the first few takes there were lots of gasps and exclamations of shock. Then we set up for the final shots where the square empties after the execution. Of course, once a square drains, it's a hell of a business to get everyone back in position. We did the shot, the square drained, and just before we wanted to cut, a lad comes in in motorbike gear and leather jacket, stands in front of the camera, and waves. I said, "For Christ's sake, you killed the shot." The crowd was upset, didn't quite know what was wrong, and before I knew what had happened had turned around and had started to lynch this man for destroying the shot. I tried to separate them, and finally a very bloodied motorcyclist hobbled out of that square.

You mentioned there was one scene where the censor interfered.

The censor was present during most of the shooting, and I couldn't persuade her to pass some of the lines in the first or second scene where we hear the princess's side of the story. She was adamant that the lines couldn't be filmed, and we argued and argued. The lines were essential for understanding the story, and without them the scene at the dinner party wouldn't play. The way I eventually got these lines was by taking advantage of the fact that the censor had tummy troubles that day and was a frequent visitor to the lavatory. So while she was out, we shot the vital lines.

Reactions and Anger

Rosenthal: *The film is superb in its depiction of the life of the princess, Arab society, and the conflicts in the Arab world. However, the film itself seems to have been overtaken by all the governmental and political furor around it. Did you have any sense that the film would engender such an uproar?*

Thomas: When the film was cut and had a rough premix, I wanted to show it to one of the senior men who had originally given me permission to shoot and make sure he was satisfied. I also wanted to show it to the cast in case any of them wanted to remove their credits or felt nervous about being associated with the film. But I had no idea what the reaction would be when they saw the whole film. In the end the cast were wonderful and said the most flattering things about what the film represented. Then I showed it to the senior man who had given me the first permission. He was very flattering and said he only wished that an Arab director had had the courage to make it. I then asked him if he was concerned about possible Saudi reaction, and he said, "Mr. Thomas, they are far too sophisticated to publicise your film by creating a fuss." So I went back to London very relaxed and wrote a memo to Lord Windlesham, who was the chairman of ATV, and for whom I had created problems in the past. This time, I told him, we could relax. And then the storm broke.

The prepublicity had unfortunately been rather sensational and had alerted the Saudis, who were trying to stop the transmission. But it went ahead. The following day, I expected the reviews to be on page thirteen or whatever, but they were front-page. Most were marvellous, but there were a few which were very disturbing. The reactions from some papers, like the *Daily Express*, were frankly racist. There was a vicious cartoon about Arabs tempting to stifle us British. "This is a democracy," the papers said, "and didn't the WOGS know that we had the right to show what we wanted to show."[1] I was very offended by that line and knew it was going to lead to serious trouble, but for the moment I could cope with the reactions. Then two things happened that made everything much worse. To explain that I need to backtrack a bit.

When I thought that this film was going to be a Joan-of-Arc drama, I'd approached novelist Penelope Mortimer to write the script. Penelope came with me on the research but was very resistant to the way I saw the story in the form of a journey. She thought it should be pure drama, and the direction I was going was doing her out of a job. Then she compromised and agreed to write the first draft, but it really wasn't terribly suitable. I thought we had an amicable understanding. I apologised for changing direction, for bringing it back into documentary, which wasn't her area, and we parted as friends.

Then I got a warning signal a week after the film was shown, when she wrote critically about the film in an English paper. I was confused because she had congratulated me so warmly during the previews, saying how right I was and how wonderful the film was. When I phoned her she apologised but a week later wrote her famous letter to the *New Statesman*. The first thing the letter did was more or less reveal who one of our characters was, which was extremely unfair because it caused that person a lot of problems. She also claimed that the film and the interviews were a fabrication. That was all that was needed. It gave ammunition to all the enemies of the film. The letter was used by the Saudis. It was also material for the politicians who were against the film, because now the issue was fabrication, instead of the democratic right to show the film, come what may. When I came back on the attack, Penelope recanted, but by then the beast was out of the stable, and I had to defend myself all over the place.

Two weeks after the transmission of the film, the Saudis broke diplomatic relations with Britain and our ambassador was expelled. I knew the consequences would be terrible, and then the heat was really turned on. One reviewer who had written a most complimentary review suddenly recanted. The foreign minister got in there and fought really dirty. The government's view, as put by the Foreign Office, was that the film must never be shown again under any circumstances. It must be buried and forgotten. With Miss Mortimer's help, they were now attacking on this moral front. When the British Film Academy wanted to show the film, they were subject to unbelievable pressure to abandon the screening. When it was invited to the Edinburgh Television Festival, again there was this pressure, and armed guards arrived at the viewing, which made everyone nervous and uncomfortable. They were there "in case there was a riot", because feelings were said to be so strong. Of course, there was no riot. It was all nonsense. People just came to watch the film.

Then the whole issue came up [over] the showing of the film in the US. On this matter, the Carter government behaved extremely responsibly, not like the British government, which got down on its knees and used every dirty trick to stop the screenings. The US government said to the Saudis, "If there are things in this film that are inaccurate, then you must send us a list of these inaccuracies and we can make a judgement." The final list that the Saudis sent was crazy. It contained complaints that the robes the Arabs were wearing in the crowd scene were too dirty, and so on. There wasn't a single point of substance. Then the government said, "You are welcome to sue the people, and you've got all those channels, but this is a democracy." And because the Americans behaved so calmly and responsibly the film was shown.

Meanwhile, David Fanning and I were doing various radio and television interviews, and on one of them we faced Congressman Zablocki. He was going on about this ghastly film and what a disgrace it was, and what an insult to Islam and the Saudis. After a commercial break, David said in a very polite way, "Congressman Zablocki, can I just establish one thing? This awful, dreadful film that shouldn't have been made, have you actually seen it?" There was a long pause, and then Zablocki said, "No, but a friend of mine in Milwaukee has." And I felt that that really was an extraordinary comment on the level of some of the other stuff.

Problems of Dramadocumentary

Rosenthal: *Many people dislike dramadocumentary. They feel, amongst other things, it plays fast and loose with truth. In your film, you make certain strong accusations or assertions. One concerns the way the Saudi princesses conduct their sex lives. Another accusation concerns the way the CIA acted in Arabia and the way Arab air force officers were thrown out of planes. Are there any major points or incidents in your film that were not based on fact?*

Thomas: All those scenes you mentioned were reported to us as factually true, either by people who claimed they had directly witnessed them or claimed a close relationship with somebody who had. None of our statements stood without a hell of a lot of cross-reference. The film was about people's distortion of the truth, so we weren't going to accept as fact merely what one person told us. Nothing appeared in the film without the kind of meticulous cross-referencing such as one does in a documentary investigation. Of course all the hostile newspapers all seemed to concentrate on the business of "the sexual pickup road." Well, there *was* a pickup road, and the cars cruised it, and the women went looking for men. Now, one particular paper said that the road scene was unprovable and appalling, and so on. Yet, six months later, the same newspaper published its "exclusive revelations" about the pickups. Evidently *Princess* had been conveniently forgotten.

There have been a number of articles in recent years that have talked about Arab stereotyping in the media. Have you been attacked at all on these grounds?

No, and I would have been very hurt if anyone had done that. The people we see in the film are based on my friends and contacts in the Arab world. They are the foreground characters while the princess is really background. The people are highly informed. They speak English. Obviously, it was a journey through the Arab middle class, but none were stereotypes. Perhaps it could be regretted [that,] because I don't speak Arabic, I couldn't conduct my investigations in the back streets and meet peasants and ordinary people. It was a very upper-middle-class view of the Arab world. Again, I think it could be fairly said that I chose a sensational event, a public execution in a town square, which is untypical of the Arab world.

How do you feel looking back on the film after ten years and in a post-Khomeini era? Did it have a radical effect on your career?

As far as the political message of the film [goes], it strongly endorsed a radical Islam that went back to the teaching of the Koran and had nothing to do with the Saudi royal family. In that structure, Khomeini was regarded as a revolutionary figure who was going to clean up the regime. I guess what has happened subsequently has made that aspect of the film seem rather foolish. On the other question, I thought I would be labelled "too hot to handle," but that didn't happen. I didn't know the US well then, but I soon discovered that a controversy like that gives you a cachet. I didn't suffer professionally, but I did suffer personally. I was very battered by the sheer strength of the assault after the showing. It took a long time for me to calm down and get into another subject.

Note

1   The crude and derogatory term WOG is an abbreviation of a British army expression for an Arab, literally "Wily Oriental Gentleman."

34

Dramatised Documentary

Leslie Woodhead

Leslie Woodhead has long been regarded as one of Britain's most noted documen-
tarists with work ranging from films on Ethiopia in the Disappearing World *series*
to acting as Executive Producer on a history of British television. He is also seen as
one of the founding fathers of the modern British TV docudrama and in the mid sev-
enties set up the docudrama department of Granada TV. What appears below is the
text of a public lecture sponsored by the Guardian *newspaper and given at the British*
Film Institute, May 1981.

First, the bad news: "The so-called dramatisation or fictionalisation of alleged
history is extremely dangerous and misleading, and is something to which the
broadcasting authorities must give close attention." That alarm was sounded
by the Lord Privy Seal Sir Ian Gilmour in the House of Commons on 24 April
1980. And the spring of 1980 was a rough season for drama-dockers across
the land. The hunt was roused, you'll recall, by the uproar surrounding the
transmission of *Death of a Princess* in early April; and within days, Dutch
Muslim activists, Australian diplomats, and American State Department officials had joined British politicians and the furious Saudi government to generate what was arguably the biggest single row in television history. The
curious fact was that, under all the immediate rumpus about whether
princesses really hunted for boyfriends in black Mercedes and the wider
concern for the effect on our future oil supplies, the row was really about the
legitimacy of a television form.

Now you'd be understandably amused to find the aesthetics of the sitcom
or the creative hazards of discontinuous recording in the single play surfacing
for debate on the Commons order paper. But the central thrust of the *Death
of a Princess* affair was made quite explicit by Lord Carrington speaking in
the House of Lords. Responding to a question about "the tendency of some
television companies to present programmes deliberately designed to give the
impression of documentary based on fact," Lord Carrington said: "It might be

as well for those who are producing these programmes to have a good look at the consequences of what they are doing." Well, as one of those practitioners of dramadocumentary squarely in the Foreign Secretary's sights, I'm grateful to the BFI for giving me the opportunity of this *Guardian* lecture to prepare my defences.

Actually it's not quite like that. At the risk of sounding perverse, I should say at the outset that I find myself in some sympathy with the minister and his parliamentary colleagues about some aspects of the current dramadocumentary boom. And I certainly share his conviction that it's an area where debate and self-examination are imperative. I also have a hunch that over and above the specifics of the dramadocumentary debate, the public unease has to do with the wider concerns of television's accountability and the contract with the audience. But I should add that I imagine I part company with the Foreign Secretary in believing that properly deployed dramatised documentary is a valuable television form. But more of that in a moment.

To be sure, there do seem to be an awful lot of the things about these days. Bewilderingly labelled as *dramatised documentary, documentary drama, docudrama, dramatic reconstruction, documentary re-creation,* and even, in a highly coloured American variant, as *faction,* an example crops up somewhere most weeks. A vigorous academic tradition is already established, pursuing dramadocumentary fossils in Shakespeare, in Greek tragedy, and even in prehistoric cave paintings.

But however distinguished the claims for its pedigree, there is no doubt that the television dramatised documentary is a troublesome beast. For programme makers, it's hard to get right and involves the wedding of some disciplines that are, on occasion, difficult to reconcile; for companies, it's uniquely time-consuming and alarmingly expensive; and for broadcasting authorities and now, it seems, governments, it inevitably raises questions about the blurring of fact and invention, the erosion of journalistic disciplines, and the confusion of the viewing public. Only the other day, the director of the BFI suggested to me, with some kindness, that we dramadocumentarians were saddling ourselves with an impossible burden, charged as we were with responsibility for the resolution of fundamental debates about historical accuracy, imaginative truth, and journalistic credibility. It all seemed likely, he implied sadly, to end in tears. So why do it? Why unleash such an unruly beast at all?

Here I must at last declare a massive interest. As full-time keeper of the bothersome creature with a unit at Granada specifically set up to make dramatised documentaries, I believe that it is worth all the aggravation. It seems to me quite simply that the dramatised documentary does allow us to do some things on television we couldn't do any other way and to articulate some important and difficult themes and ideas with a vividness and clarity that couldn't be achieved by any other means.] That's the commercial—the realities are, as usual, somewhat messier.

There is, of course, a basic and I think insoluble problem with definition. Dramadocumentary makers swap labels like cigarette cards, but the resultant sets are hopelessly ill matched. One of my colleagues has identified three major strands to the form, while another has isolated six varieties. Yet another has produced an intriguing analysis based on mathematical parameters of drama and accuracy. For my money, there are about as many valid definitions as there are dramadocumentaries. At the end of last year, I found myself on the British Academy of Film and Television Arts platform for yet another dramadoc tussle with no fewer than seven distinguished programme makers, all of whom could be considered employers of the form. You won't be surprised to hear that not one of us could agree on what it is. I find it much more useful to think of the form as a spectrum that runs from journalistic reconstruction to relevant drama with infinite gradations along the way. In its various mutations, it's employed by investigative journalists, documentary feature makers, and imaginative dramatists. So we shouldn't perhaps be surprised when programmes as various as *Culloden* and *Oppenheimer*, or *The Naked Civil Servant*, *Suez*, and *State of the Nation*'s cabinet reconstructions refuse tidy and comprehensive definition. To a degree, I go with Jerry Kuehl, who said at the Edinburgh Television Festival during another hunt for the dramadoc: "The terminological confusion and the lack of common agreement about what a dramadocumentary is, is a sign of vitality." Since then of course we've also discovered that it can mean trouble. It's my feeling that much of that trouble grows out of those confusions about form and intention both in the audience and in the programme makers.

For the moment, rather than make theological points around the formal issues raised by a comparison of, say, *Edward and Mrs Simpson* with *Three Days in Szczecin*, I fancy it might be more useful to try to locate the impulse behind the dramadocumentary form.

My own motive for taking up the dramadocumentary trade was simple, pragmatic, and, I suspect, to some degree representative. As a television journalist working on *World in Action*, I came across an important story I wanted to tell but found there was no other way to tell it. The story was about a Soviet dissident imprisoned in a mental hospital. By its very nature it was totally inaccessible by conventional documentary methods. But the dissident General, Petro Grigorenko, had managed to smuggle out of the mental prison a detailed diary of his experiences. As a result, it was possible to produce a valid dramatic reconstruction of what happened to Grigorenko and tell that important story. That pattern of motives and intentions seems to me to summarise why many dramadocumentaries get made—and also to indicate why they raise understandable doubts and reservations. The basic impulse behind the drama-documentary form is, I suggest, simply to tell to a mass audience a real and relevant story involving real people. The basic problem is how to get it right after the event.

My own priorities have remained obstinately journalistic, with a fundamental emphasis on detailed research, often extending to years of cross-checking and amplification, and on high-grade source material, such as tape recordings and transcripts. A preoccupation with accuracy of design and the employment of camera crews schooled in documentary rather than drama have sought to give our reconstructions a definition apart from that of established television drama.

At the same time, I'm conscious that I used the word *story* in talking a moment ago about the Grigorenko reconstruction. While it's an established journalistic shorthand, it's perhaps revealing about the dilemmas inherent in the narrative formulation of historical events. There is at the moment a revival of enthusiasm for the narrative mode in historical writing with historians like Emmanuel Le Roy Ladurie in books like *Montaillou*. The gains in vividness over more austere and analytical methods is apparent, but it's clear that the form is better at answering "what" and "how" questions than it is at responding to "why" questions. Drama, of course, adds to the confusion.

From the fundamental requirement to re-create as accurately as possible using the techniques, forms, and values of imaginative drama comes the unease that many people feel for the dramadocumentary form. How are we to respond to this television mongrel—crossbred from the techniques of fiction and the factual claims of journalism and documentary? What level of authenticity is being offered, and how sceptical should we be about claims of accuracy? Does the blurring of documentary and dramatic values imply a dilution we should worry about? Is our audience confused?

Well, there is clearly potential cause for concern here, and not just to Foreign Secretaries. The modish boom in dramadocs over the last few years, fuelled on occasion perhaps by fashion and a sense of where the big budgets may be buried as much as by a real concern with content, has led to some understandable unease. But I think that there's a lot that's positive on the dramadoc balance sheet, and I suggest that the debate over the form could prompt some long overdue scrutiny of factual television in general and as a result, I believe, some refreshment of the contract with the audience. But for the moment some history.

Dramadocumentaries have been made for British television since the early 1950s. From the start, practitioners have not lacked confidence in the originality and worth of what they were doing. Setting aside the fine tradition of film documentaries stretching back through Humphrey Jennings to Georges Melies at the end of last century, one of the earliest TV dramadocumentary makers, Caryl Doncaster, claimed in 1951: "The dramatised story documentary is one of the few art forms pioneered by Television." It seems likely, however, that the initial motivation for that pioneering was in part sheer necessity.

At a time when television was almost exclusively studio-bound and film was anyway limited to four-minute magazines on heavy 35mm cameras with optical sound, one of the most effective ways of bringing documentary preoccupations to the screen was to offer them in a dramatised form, using an acted script based on thorough research. The same technique was used in the 1950s by Duncan Ross in his courtroom series *The Course of Justice* and by Colin Morris in carefully researched documentary plays about delinquent children, unmarried mothers, and strikes. But on the whole, in the apolitical doldrums of the late '50s, television was slow to follow up on the welding of documentary and drama achieved in wartime films like *Target for Tonight* and *Fires Were Started*. It's worth recalling that both *Coronation Street* and *Emergency Ward 10* were described as dramadocumentaries when they arrived in the early '60s. About the same time, Tim Hewat and his *World in Action* team enlisted the aid of actors to re-create incidents in journalistic documentaries like *The Great Train Robbery* and the Portland spy case. But for the most part, television journalists were preoccupied with the liberation offered by the new lightweight film equipment for observational documentary.

The frustration with existing forms was at that moment more apparent amongst people making television drama. And the conviction that there was a valuable tool for the expression of relevant concerns in the fusion of documentary techniques and imaginative drama was left to a new generation of programme makers in the television drama of the mid '60s.

That fusion really came of age with *Cathy Come Home* in 1966. I would draw a distinction between the issues raised by documented drama like *Cathy* and the documentary that dramatises real events. But the excitement and controversy surrounding *Cathy* uncovered many of the worries that have troubled critics of dramatised documentary. The programme came from the drama department; and it's undeniable that until recently most of the heat in the debate about confusion of categories has been centred around work with dramatic priorities rather than programmes at the documentary end of the spectrum. Whether that is because drama people make better plays or documentarians do better research is an open question.

Cathy Come Home was certainly a powerful piece of television, but as well as widespread reservations about the glamorisation of the central characters, serious doubts were also raised by many people professionally concerned with social welfare about the programme's accuracy. On its second showing, most of the documentary captions giving relevant statistics were omitted because of doubts about accuracy. Yet despite these reservations, *Cathy* was effective enough for its writer, Jeremy Sandford, to be able to claim that "as a result of the film and certain meetings we held afterwards, Birmingham and certain other towns ceased their practice of separating 3 or 4 hundred husbands per year from their wives and children." The underlying assumption that television drama should seek not only to reflect but also to change society has informed much of the most interesting work in the field of documented drama over the past decade, from *The Lump* to *Law and Order* and *The Spongers*.

It seems to me it's that assumption in the work of people like Tony Garnett, Ken Loach, and Jim Allen that has really caused discomfort rather than formal worries about the confusion of categories, which their programmes often arouse. The implied worry, it seems, is that the forms and credibilities of documentary and news are being recruited to smuggle a political message. But it seems also that the worry is somewhat selective. As Ken Loach pointed out, "Criticisms about confusing fact with fiction are reserved by certain papers for political films, but ignored when Edward VII or Churchill's mother are romanticised and glorified."

There was one programme of the late '60s that did, however, isolate the issue of confusing categories. *Some Women*, produced by Tony Garnett and directed by Roy Battersby, was a play by Tony Parker about women in prison. Parker had interviewed several women who had recently been in prison. Five actresses read and absorbed the original transcripts and, without a script, reenacted the interviews on location. Although intended as a *Wednesday Play*, transmission of the resulting film was held up for two years because it "blurred" the border between fact and fiction. It was eventually transmitted, without the Wednesday Play identification but with an explanatory introduction by Tony Parker, to enthusiastic reviews. In particular, Maurice Wiggin of the *Sunday Times*, while insisting that he was "always concerned about the tendency to smudge the distinction between fact and fiction," called the film "reporting raised to the level of art." He also warned would-be imitators to "ponder the indispensable integrity of the pioneer."

From the late '60s, programme makers from the documentary side of the fence became increasingly interested in the possibilities of dramatisation. There was, I think, at once some exhaustion with the conventions of current-affairs documentary, a frustration about access to a range of important stories, and a sense of the increasing complexity of relevant issues.

It is with the proliferation from the late '60s of dramatised documentaries impersonating real people in real events authenticated by journalistic sources, such as transcripts, tape recordings, and eyewitnesses, that the debate about categories and credibility really begins to bite. Some early examples established the guidelines.

In his reconstruction of the *Chicago Conspiracy Trial*, Christopher Burstall compiled his script exclusively from official court transcripts. Having spent a couple of weeks sitting in the Chicago courtroom for a *World in Action* documentary, I know how accurate Burstall's dramatisation was, down to details of setting and wardrobe. For Granada in 1969, Mike Murphy made *The Pueblo Affair*, calling it "a compilation" in which every speech or statement was a verbatim transcript of an actual source. My own dramatised documentaries, like the film on General Grigorenko and others on a Red Guard trial during China's Cultural Revolution, the Szczecin dock strike, an investigation of the worst midair crash in history, and an account of the Soviet invasion of Czechoslovakia, have similarly been anchored in transcripts, tape recordings, and eyewitness records. I would argue that dramatised documentary of this kind, pursued for a specific journalistic purpose and maintaining journalistic priorities even at the risk of inadequate drama, does have a particular status. I would accept that, because of its special claims to accuracy, it also has particular obligations.

I'll return to those obligations in a moment. For now, a preposterously small footnote about an ultimate theme—Absolute Truth. The debate about absolute truth versus mere accuracy is of course a favourite dramadoc pastime. I have a favourite Ernest Hemingway quote to contribute.

> A writer's job is to tell the truth. His standard of fidelity to the truth must be so high that his invention out of his experience should produce a truer account than anything factual can be. For facts can be observed badly, but when a good writer is creating something, he has time and scope to make it an absolute truth.

In fact, the Americans, who seem to have an enviable appetite for big questions, appear particularly exercised on this issue. I was reading the other day the transcript of a rather bizarre "docudrama symposium," where fifty Americans in the expanding docudrama business met for a truth-telling session in California. In a stylish keynote speech, that improbable dramadocker Gore Vidal observed: "We don't go to Shakespeare for history. He is never true, but he is always truthful."

Well, the superiority of absolute truth over mere accuracy doesn't need my recommendation. But that's surely more valuable as a corrective against arrogance than as a prescription invalidating notions of journalistic accuracy. "Getting it right" does have validity in journalistic terms, not against the standards of an elusive absolute "truth" but against standards of evidence as they might be understood in a court of law.

But this is of course where we came in. By its very nature, dramatised documentary makes special claims to accuracy, and such claims are often heightened by the deliberate deployment of techniques and mannerisms derived from factual documentary. And the context of television inevitably sets these programmes in the territory of news and current affairs, creating an expectation of authenticity.

In his Edinburgh article, Jerry Kuehl argued, "There is a complicity between

producer and audience which involves using dramatic criteria to judge truth
or falsity." He further argued that no amount of underpinning by documentation, tape recordings, or eyewitness evidence can resolve the dilemma that
dramatic artifice and selection employed by the producer crucially condition
the material. As a result, no dramadocumentary can possibly live up to claims
of accuracy, or rather, and more worryingly, the audience cannot tell at what
level of credibility to accept any particular sequence.

It's at this point that it seems to me that the thrust of objections to the dramadocumentary form cut deepest and pass on to embrace a debate about the
nature and credibility of the whole range of factual television. It's also, I would
argue, where dramadocumentary, properly pursued and signposted, can
refresh that debate in an important way. For, if we accept that dramatised
documentary can only be a subjective construct, we must allow that the same
is inevitably true to some degree of current-affairs documentary and of news
itself. Reading Tony McGrath's piece in the *Observer* about the dramatic contrivances of news crews in Belfast, and recalling an earlier piece about similar
staging by American crews in El Salvador is merely a nasty illustration of what
can happen when subjectivity goes sour.

It's of course inescapably true that, even after four years' research, *Three
Days in Szczecin* remains a network of editorial judgements, ranging from
where to select from nine hours of tape recordings to where to put the camera.
But it's a defining strength of the form that it allows me to tell the audience
about these conventions. When I make an observational documentary with
many of the same editorial interventions, it's much more difficult for the audience to locate the subjective content and for me to find a way to tell them
about it.

To a degree, the demythologising of factual television is already well established. The delusion of absolute objectivity is almost laid to rest, and television
itself has in a small way begun the job of owning up about documentary and
news to point out the inescapable subjective content in every camera movement and edit. The contrivances of the documentary maker have been
rumbled, and there's a growing public awareness that the manipulative
presence of the director is as significant in *Johnny Go Home* as it was in *Cathy
Come Home*.

I'm not myself convinced that the viewer is as bemused by the professional
capers of news editors and documentary makers as television academies
would sometimes claim.

Our audience in 1981 is, I fancy, a good deal more sophisticated and suspicious than either broadcasters or authorities often allow. Few viewers of even
the most convincingly mounted dramatisation will mistake it for actual documentary or imagine that they have somehow been provided with a clear
window on recent history. An audience will be aware that they are watching

the producer's best approximation of what happened. But only last week I was reminded during a talk by Peter Fiddick of Huw Weldon's observation to programme makers: "Never underestimate an audience's intelligence—or its lack of information."

I am myself convinced that makers of dramatised documentary do have a special obligation to let the audience know what they're up to—what's been called by one American critic "the right not to be deliberately misled." In any one programme, it's likely that the material being dramatised will be derived from a variety of sources of varying status. It seems to me vital to signpost material to avoid as far as possible a confusion in the audience about levels of credibility. For *Three Days in Szczecin*, the central source was a smuggled tape recording of the crucial meeting, but alongside this, the writer Boleslaw Sulik also had scenes developed as a result of debriefing witnesses, involving the imaginative recreation of dialogue. We felt it necessary to indicate to the audience the differing status of this material.

And if I were making that film today, I would make even greater efforts to signpost those differences on a continuing basis throughout the film. I'm now involved in developing a dramadocumentary investigation of the birth of Solidarity in the Gdansk shipyards in the summer of 1980; and before moving from research to scripting, we're exploring ways of building into the form strategies to permit the continuous clarification of sources and status—in effect to try to evolve a kind of "television footnotes."

During that American "docudrama symposium" I was talking about earlier, one contributor described the good writer of "dramatised documentary" as "a playwright on oath." But American critics have come to regard the docudrama form with intense suspicion, levelling charges of gross inaccuracy, wilful distortion, and the reckless rewriting of history under the guise of authenticity.

Docudrama has even been branded unpatriotic. Given the glamorisations and confusions of television, like *Washington: Behind Closed Doors, Roots*, and *The Trial of Lee Harvey Oswald*, the mistrust is hardly surprising. Here, despite the recent claims of politicians, the form has had a less tarnished career. For me it will remain a form of last resort, a way of doing things when conventional documentary can't cope. But rigorously pursued and properly signposted, I contend that far from muddying the television pond, while allowing us to explore some important and difficult themes, dramatised documentary can also provide a valuable opportunity to share with the audience a debate about some of the practices of factual television.

That said, it's worth remembering that the one British dramadocumentary almost exclusively concerned with exploring the idea of alternate realities, the power of myth, and the elusiveness of objective truth was a target for parliamentary abuse and diplomatic uproar. *Death of a Princess* vividly demonstrates what a hazardous and vulnerable form dramadocumentary is, even when pursued with such skill and intelligence. For me it also reinforces the crucial importance of fastidious labelling and signposting.

Anthony Smith's warning about the daunting precedents for the drama-documentary debate was well taken. It is of course hardly likely that a handful of television makers will resolve the dilemmas that have plagued writers and historians over the last two thousand years. I keep on my office wall a quotation from Henry James that in times of confusion does at least serve as some kind of consolation. "The historian," James said, "essentially wants more documents than he can really use. The dramatist only wants more liberties than he can really take." I'm not quite sure where that leaves the worthy drama documentarian, but it's nice to know we're in good company.

35

Where Are We Going, and How and Why?

Ian McBride

This chapter first appeared as a paper delivered at a conference on docudrama in March 1996 organised by the Department of Drama of Birmingham University, U.K.

For many in England, the late seventies and mid-eighties were seen, and are seen, as the golden age of dramadocumentary. And in this marriage of the fact and the drama, the reign of fact was absolute. In *Invasion*, for example, the Czech and Soviet Politburos are portrayed in all their pomp and glory, and it is clear that authenticity is the threshold, not the ambition. So every medal, every button, every military insignia is spot-on. Admittedly they were all facts that were relatively accessible, but the ring of authenticity was absolute. Alexander Dubček years later gave it unique validation. When he was interviewed for *World in Action*, he watched the scene with incredulity, and said: "Yes, it was just like that."

Was it really a golden age? If so, have we lost it? Where have we come to, and where are we going? And more importantly, like the questions posed in such films, how and why?

Those are the sort of questions I'm going to try to stimulate you with. First of all, can I thank David Edgar for inviting me and thank you all for turning out? A session labelled "dramadoc theory" sounds very cerebral for 9:30 on a Saturday morning, and I'm flattered—and unnerved—at seeing so many people here. But, a bit like the meeting before the first-draft script is commissioned, this session was hatched over a table in an Italian restaurant, and David's real brief followed that of any dramadocumentary filmmaker—"Be authoritative, but be a bit provocative."

When you're sitting in the cutting room watching the rough cut of a dramadocumentary, the first thing that usually comes on the screen is a black frame with one word in small white letters: "disclaimer." It's usually referred to by the production team with typical irreverence as the health warning. It's written largely by the lawyer to the everlasting pain and disgust of the writer and director, and it's cared for and kept alive only by the executive producer, who as we all know has one eye on the film and one on the company and needs to prevent one frightening the other with the prospect of a clutch of writs. It is of course the paragraph that finally says that composite characters are portrayed and dialogue has been created, that the chronology has been changed—but that it's a true story.

Well, I'll give you my own disclaimer on this session now. After years in television, I probably am a composite character, and I may play fast and loose with the chronology. I'm distorting David's brief a little by seeking to be a little more provocative than authoritative. There are sometimes sessions at the Edinburgh Television Festival in which a captain of the industry gives what's called "a view from the bridge." Well, this is more informal and best regarded as "a view from the engine room." The thing that is good about engine rooms is that you hear at one remove what's going on up on the bridge, but you have a damned good idea of your own of what the ship is really doing.

I need to start with some delineations. Whenever you put the toilers in the dramadocumentary vineyard together, you seem to have almost as many definitions as individuals. I'm head of factual drama at Granada Television, custodian of the true story dramatised on-screen, and it's a broad slate. *Suspicious Circumstances* revisits an atmospheric past as Edward Woodward intrigues the viewer by walking through period sets and examining the unknown quirks of a crime gone by; *Fighting for Gemma* confronts the present in full-blooded dramadocumentary to examine whether childhood leukaemia can be shown to be linked to the nuclear industry; *The Trial of Lord Lucan* visits a "what if" future by pretending that Lucan is alive and well and available to the constabulary and putting him on trial, with the real evidence and a real jury.

The television spectrum is so wide. Much contemporary drama is as heavily rooted in fact as ever—whether it is implicit, as in *The Bill*, or explicit, it's worth recalling that both *Coronation Street* and *Emergency Ward 10* were described as dramadocumentary when they were born thirty-odd years ago. Many of you will notice that Kay Mellor's *Band of Gold* carries an acknowledgement to the working women of Bradford for the real firsthand research that has been carried out among the prostitutes of the north to deliver that authenticity and insight.

But when one moves into the "true story" the definitions are necessary. Derek Paget has written about "the promise of fact" and points out that a prior assurance of truth provides a cultural passport to credibility. When the filmmakers tell us "this really happened," they seize our attention and invite us to suspend more easily our disbelief in the performances that follow.

So let's mark out some territory. I believe there are two kinds of production currently paying occasional visits to our television screens that are sometimes loosely lumped together as dramadocumentary, and I'll return to that lumping together later and what I see as its dangers. There is dramadocumentary, and there is the dramatisation based on a true story.

One of the early proponents of dramadocumentary, Caryl Doncaster, said in 1951: "The dramatised story documentary is one of the few art forms pioneered by television." Personally, I think it more likely that necessity, not creativity, was the mother of invention. Television was largely studio-bound; film was limited to bulky 35 mm cameras with optical sound and four-minute magazines. To research a documentary subject thoroughly and to take it to the screen through an acted script was a very effective technique.

British television of the fifties showed little appetite for capitalising on the potential of fusing the imperatives and techniques of documentary and drama, which had been achieved so well in wartime films like *Fires Were Started* and *Target for Tonight*. Again out of necessity, in the sixties the journalists occasionally picked up the tools—Tim Hewat and *World in Action* recruited actors to recreate incidents in documentaries on the Portland spy case and *The Great Train Robbery*. But documentary makers were by then largely enthused by new lightweight film equipment, which they wanted to use in observational films. It was a new generation of television dramatists who succeeded in fusing drama and documentary techniques in the mid-1960s, and we all know that a real television force arrived with the production of *Cathy Come Home*.

Cathy Come Home was of course a documented drama, created by dramatists, not a reenactment of real events—a powerful technique, which was to be followed honourably, for instance, in G. F. Newman's *Law and Order* or much later in *Tumbledown*. Most can be accurately described as dramatisations based on true stories: the emphasis on the dramatic priority and the stir that this drama provokes have long sat at the heart of the everlasting debate about whether the viewer is confused.

It came back to the documentary makers, the journalists, to develop the dramadocumentary in its very British form, the reenactment of events—the true, true story. Again I believe it was necessity, rather than free-flown creativity, that at least acted as midwife. (No doubt the form was alluring—how do you make a compelling documentary about homelessness to follow *Cathy Come Home?*—but as my colleague Alasdair Palmer, no stranger to dramadocumentary, wrote in *The Spectator* in 1995, truth may be stranger than fiction, but it also takes much longer and is far more complicated)!

The documentary makers' forays into dramatisation were born as much of a need to gain access as a wish to experiment: a frustration with the limitations on their trade was as powerful as a wish to explore new forms. Lightweight equipment and the jet age had brought them access to stories and issues all over the world, it seemed. An audience less blasé and less well-informed than that of today would receive quite well documentaries and current-affairs films on issues in places they'd never been and were unlikely to be able to visit. And the filmmakers became adept at unravelling the issues of the modern world by focusing on the microcosm, especially by visiting the United States: an open society, few inhibitions about television and the camera, and people who talked well without need of subtitles. But the filmmakers were aware that this was an oversimplification of the world. Stories and issues were increasingly complex, and access to the really important stories was often totally denied to television, or at least denied in a form that was watchable and attractive to the viewer.

This was of course at its most acute in the closed countries of the world—behind the Iron Curtain, say, or in China. People like Leslie Woodhead became ever more frustrated at an impotence in treating issues as huge as the fate of dissidents in Soviet Russia while making films about the plight of tenants in squalid tenements in New York.

So for Woodhead and those who followed, the dramatised documentary was taken up in the fashion it has subsequently been described as—the journalism of last resort. There was no way *World in Action* could go to Soviet Russia and film the trial and imprisonment of a notable Soviet dissident; no way in which the audience could get an insight into the manipulation and denial of human rights embedded in the society of a superpower. But when General Petro Grigorenko's diaries were smuggled out of the Soviet Union and were painstakingly corroborated and double-checked, there was a way—reenact the events that have been documented; what David Edgar has eloquently described as joining up the dots in history.

Dramatised documentary in this form, anchored in transcript, tape recording, and eyewitness testimony, was aimed at delivering the audience a picture of the unglimpsed—philosophical and political issues as big as totalitarian oppression—with all the hallmarks of authority and credibility. The objective was clear: take the camera where the camera couldn't go, loosen wooden tongues, rehearse the evidence when the witnesses were all dead or too dutifully mute to testify. The risk of inadequate drama was traded for the particular status earned by those special claims to accuracy. I rather liked Ian Curteis's reference to Madame Tussaud's wax museum figures.

It's only right in that context to recall the restraints those programme makers were working under, aside from their self-imposed austerity. Anyone who's been to a Chinese restaurant with Leslie Woodhead knows. For five years or so after he made a dramadocumentary on a Red Guard trial during China's Cultural Revolution, the routine was the same: introductions all round, to everyone in the restaurant. Mr. Woodhead was the director of the film in which the beaming waiter had starred, puzzled diners would be told. The desperate balancing act between the budget and the need for scores of extras meant

Leslie had recruited every Chinese waiter within about seventy-five miles of Manchester.

But what probably brought the journalists and the dramatists together, whether in *Cathy Come Home* or *The Man Who Wouldn't Keep Quiet*, was the thought that television could not only reflect on the world but could perhaps change it. I believe that it is that feeling, of a potential for energising change if only by informing the audience well about something others would prefer they remain in ignorance of, that has led or driven many of those in the field.

The other factor that unites dramatist and journalist is conflict, but in different places and on different levels. The dramatist needs conflict within a production; the journalist wants conflict to be created outside and by it.

The truth is that joining up the dots of history might have delivered varying doses of conflict within the drama, but too rarely did it provoke conflict outside. Dramadocumentary was fine, laudable even, when the location was the shipyards of Gdansk or when Soviet tanks were rumbling through a Czechoslovakia simulated in Salford. It wasn't sort of subversive; the audience wasn't confused; no one was misled. I'm sure that it would be too simplistic to suggest that those in power have no problem with the dramatist or the journalist when they're trying to tell the truth about a regime or a political system that our establishment opposes. It's when the truth sits uncomfortably close to home, or to the perceived national interest, that the dramadocumentary begins to bite and the conflict really starts.

So to April 1980 and *Death of a Princess*. Within days of transmission, American State Department officials, Dutch Muslim activists, and Australian diplomats joined British politicians and an enraged Saudi government in denunciation. The row was ostensibly about accuracy—did princesses really hunt for boyfriends in black Mercedes?—but was of course really about oil supplies, arms deals, and lucrative trade customers. Sir Ian Gilmour, then Lord Privy Seal, voiced the concern in the House of Commons: "The so-called dramatisation or fictionalisation of alleged history is extremely dangerous and misleading, and is something to which the broadcasting authorities must give close attention."

So this was where the lode seam was. This was what energised this form. Take something really sensitive, something they didn't want you to know a lot about. Dig and dig and dig. Loosen those wooden tongues, liberate those mute witnesses. Join up the dots, but maybe in one of the darker corners of recent, very recent history. Keep it very close to home. Use the skills of some of our best dramatists. Transmit, and retire to a safe distance.

That was the spirit that brought us Michael Eaton's *Shoot to Kill* and Rob Ritchie's *Who Bombed Birmingham?* The investigative journalist had grabbed hold of the form without apology and harnessed real dramatic talent to tell untold stories, to reveal. Why should only the devil have the best tunes, after all?

And the rows of course followed on cue: Margaret Thatcher told us after *Who Bombed Birmingham?* that WE—presumably as in grandmother—do not believe in "trial by television." At least one newspaper was moved to comment that television was the only place the Birmingham Six were likely to receive a fair trial. The chief constable of the West Midlands took the "princesses in black Mercedes" line and denounced the film as "shot through with half truths," an attack launched on the basis of the decor and layout of a room and the format of a meeting held therein to have been inaccurate. The rows did serve a constructive purpose—more than ten million people watched *Who Bombed Birmingham?*, nearly twice as many as had watched documentary after documentary I'd produced on the injustice. People knew much more of the whole picture; the issue then never moved off the national agenda, and the rest is real history.

And the rows didn't leave any of us squirming. The public service imperative—the journalistic validity—of these enterprises meant that no one felt uncomfortable in the arguments.

In the meantime, one of those other little accidents had happened. In a hotel room in the United States, on one of those empty evenings between business meetings, a woman channel-hopped to PBS and landed on something strange. It was *Invasion*. The woman was English but had lived and worked in America for a long time. And she'd never seen anything like this on television. When the credits rolled, she made a couple of notes and picked up the phone.

The woman was Bridget Potter, then an executive vice-president responsible for original programming with HBO Showcase. What followed was an alliance not only of function but of form. With Granada, and subsequently with the BBC, HBO set about eradicating the austerity of the programmes and making them into full-blown dramatic films. In came the search for dramatic strength, if not perfection, in the script; the incidental music; the marquee names; the name talent and investment behind the camera; the filmic alongside the journalistic. There followed *Coded Hostile, Why Lockerbie?, Hostages, Valdez*: some of the best marriages we've seen between the journalist and the filmmaker.

A conference speaker mentioned talking with friends—viewers, punters!—about why they watched factual drama, and they said because it was important. I believe that some of the films I've just mentioned have delivered in that contract with the viewer. The transformation from the austere or puritanical to the relatively lavish television event has been made without breaching the fundamental contract to inform properly, to entertain, and not to mislead.

Which takes us to the two key issues raised by David Edgar—the intention of the programme maker and the reaction of the audience. I believe that both have changed and continue changing, but I would differ with David on the significance of the points. I believe the biggest single factor in determining the current and future shape of dramadocumentary in British television is now the intention and agenda of the programme *commissioners*, and the biggest single factor in *their judgements* is in their perception, or guess, at the audience's expectation.

The biggest shift in television—regardless of genre—has been from the power of the producer to the demand of the broadcaster. When Woodhead started work on *Invasion*, he did so because senior people at Granada were intrigued and arrested by guessing at events surrounding the Soviets' forced entry. "Make the film," they said, knowing that they would command its slot on ITV. They paid, and had to pay, only scant regard for the demands of their audience—if three million people watched it, three million people watched it. The contract with the audience was honoured by quality—integrity—not quantity.

Today in ITV that commissioning power is held not by producers but by broadcasters. And their preoccupations are with the size and shape of the audience: how many people are going to watch; what are their demographics?

That shift is mirrored in the preoccupations and standards of today's journalism. Inasmuch as I have approached my analysis from a journalistic standpoint, it's always worth keeping one eye on the mirror, to see where modern journalism is heading. Through history and across the range, to the heaviest of broadsheets, it has moved from the abstract and the philosophical to the human interest—the "people" story, long favoured by television as the journalism of first resort. So we cover the war in Bosnia with stories about neighbours at war or the snatched meetings of separated families.

And so it now is with factual drama—the small people in the front of the frame play to illuminate the big issue at the back. In drama it was ever thus, and I don't have a problem with that. Sean Deveraux is murdered in the upfront story, and we gain an insight into the price of the arms trade; Gemma D'Arcy fights for life in the memorable scenes, and we grapple with issues of nuclear power, children, and leukemia. It may be condemned as "cultural tourism" and questioned as exploitative or manipulative, but the programme maker has strong public service clothes to his or her arguments.

Without those clothes, the human interest story is naked when picked up by dramadockers, even when the journalists are among the most accomplished and the dramatist honourable. It is no coincidence that *Beyond Reason*, having been born at the *Daily Mail*, the slickest exponents of tabloid journalism, wandered through the marshes around the ocean of chequebook journalism, traduced some of the facts, intruded on the privacy and sensitivity of some of those portrayed, had no public service clothes, and was brought to the screen by one of the most commercially conscious of today's broadcasters; no coincidence that it led to a debate in the House of Commons, for the worst of reasons, to a thousand column inches condemning the form, to multiple complaints to the regulators, and to a reinforcing battery of new rules and restrictions on all of us.

As one very senior ITV executive told me recently: "We simply should never have made it."

We can still be in the golden age. That's up to us. What we really have to guard against is the journalist's imperative and the dramatist's vision being thrown by either the journalist's or the broadcaster's guess at what the audience wants and allowing that to become our sole determinant.

A cultural "market force," if you like, is capable of pushing a perceived appetite for human interest over the edge, shoving dramadocumentary out of any golden age into a rapid dishonourable discharge.

Index

Lightning Source UK Ltd.
Milton Keynes UK
11 February 2010

149865UK00002B/14/P